HOOKED

Also by Pauline Kael

|||||||||||||||||||||||||||||||||||||||||||||||||||||||||

I Lost it at the Movies   (1965)
Kiss Kiss Bang Bang   (1968)
Going Steady   (1970)
The Citizen Kane Book   (1971)
Deeper into Movies   (1973)
Reeling   (1976)
When the Lights Go Down   (1980)
5001 Nights at the Movies   (1982)
Taking It All In   (1984)
State of the Art   (1985)

Pauline Kael
HOOKED

A William Abrahams Book

E. P. DUTTON | NEW YORK

*Published in the United States by E. P. Dutton,
a division of Penguin Books USA Inc.,
2 Park Avenue, New York, N.Y. 10016.*

*Published simultaneously in Canada
by Fitzhenry and Whiteside, Limited, Toronto.*

Library of Congress Cataloging-in-Publication Data

*Kael, Pauline.
Hooked / Pauline Kael. — 1st ed.
    p.   cm.
Articles originally appearing in the New Yorker.
"A William Abrahams book."
Includes index.
ISBN 0-525-24705-X. ISBN 0-525-48429-9 (pbk.)
1. Motion pictures—Reviews.   I. Title.
PN1995.K235 1989
791.43'75—dc 19*   *88-10328
                                                      CIP*

Designed by Steven N. Stathakis

Index prepared by Trent Duffy

10 9 8 7 6 5 4 3

All material in this book originally appeared in The New Yorker.

CONTENTS

||||||||||||||||||||||||||||||||||||||||||||||||||||||||||||||||||||||||||||||||||||||||||||||||||||||||||||||||||||||||||||||||

AUTHOR'S NOTE

||||||||||||||||||||||||||||||||||||||||||||||||||||||||||||||||||||||||||||||||||||||||||||||||||||||||||||||||||||||||||||||||||||||||

Readers of *The New Yorker*, where my reviews have appeared for the past twenty years, frequently ask if I don't sometimes just go to the movies for pleasure. My answer is that I always do. I got hooked on movies at an early age (around four or five, when I saw them while sitting on my parents' laps), and I am still a child before a moving image. I want to watch it; I want to see what comes next. This desire to be caught up—to be entranced—doesn't interfere with my critical faculties. If anything, it sharpens them. My high hopes make my disappointments all the keener; my high hopes make the pleasures keener, too.

Movies seem to me the most mysteriously great of all art forms. A movie like *Blue Velvet* or *The Unbearable Lightness of Being* has the richness of a fairy tale for adults. We can respond to it at so many levels that it's a thrilling, open experience.

No other art is as inclusive or expansive or diverse; no other art has such sensual fullness. And so movies are for everybody—except people with arctic temperaments. You can't be prim and enjoy pictures such as *Law of Desire, Down and Out in Beverly Hills*, and *My Beautiful Laundrette*. And if, as I suggested in one of these reviews, the only really fresh element in American movies of the eighties may be what Steve Martin, Bill Murray, Bette Midler, Richard Pryor, Robin Williams, and other comedians have brought to them, you'd better enjoy impudence.

The period covered in this book—from late 1985 to mid-1988—begins rather lamely, and then suddenly there's one marvellous movie after another. The Hollywood studios have abandoned any idea of art, yet so many millions of people love this art form that it's constantly renewed—sometimes, it seems, from out of nowhere. Pictures like *Dreamchild* and *Eat the Peach* and *The Hour of the Star* arrive here without fanfare, and Americans come up with surprises like *The Stepfather*, or John Huston's last, magnificent *The Dead*.

I want to thank John Bennet, my editor at *The New Yorker*, for doubling up at even the smallest of my jokes, and I thank the checkers, for not doubling up when they spot a goof. And once again, I must express my gratitude to William Shawn, who gave me my chance at *The New Yorker*, and to William Abrahams, who has been the editor of all of the books I've published. (This is the eleventh.) I thank my daughter Gina for her patience when I'm distracted thinking about movies, and I thank her son William for being hooked.

HOOKED

ARF

||||||||||||||||||||||||||||||||||||||||||||||||||||||||||||||||||||||||||||||||||||||||||||||||||||||||||||||||||||||||||||||||||||||||||||||||||||||||

Robert Altman has more sheer stubborn effrontery than any other great American director, as he proved in the string of recklessly original movies he made in the first half of the seventies: *M*A*S*H* (1970), *McCabe & Mrs. Miller* (1971), *The Long Goodbye* (1973), *Thieves Like Us* (1974), *California Split* (1974), *Nashville* (1975). He has always been erratic, and he has an equally long list of bummers and valiant efforts that failed, but when he's working in top form there's nobody who can touch him. They can't even get near him. And in the eighties, working on a smaller scale, mostly with backing from cable television, he's still a terror. In 1982, he turned the most unlikely material—the sappy theatre piece *Come Back to the 5 & Dime Jimmy Dean, Jimmy Dean*—into an ethereal, balletic film that's unlike anything else he has ever done. (In lyricism, it rivals *McCabe* and *Thieves Like Us*.) His version of *Streamers* in 1983 was all rant, and despite the visual beauty he lavished on Marsha Norman's hour-long *The Laundromat*, which was shown on HBO in April, the awful play defeated him and the hardworking performers Amy Madigan and Carol Burnett. But the Altman film that has already played in much of the country and has only now opened in New York City, his 1984 version of *Secret Honor*—a one-character, one-room-set play—is a small, weird triumph. Robert Altman, the master of large ensembles, loose action, and overlapping voices, demonstrates that with the help of a hot cinematographer (Pierre Mignot, the Canadian who shot *Jimmy Dean, Jimmy Dean*) he can make film fireworks out of next to nothing. *Secret Honor* was filmed, with student assistants, in a residence hall at the University of Michigan, where Altman, who financed it himself, has been a visiting professor.

The actor is Philip Baker Hall, playing Richard Milhous Nixon, and the room is Nixon's wood-panelled study, where for ninety minutes Hall's Nixon paces the floor and raves and reminisces, like a caged Richard III.

1

The play—a one-man docudrama by Donald Freed and Arnold M. Stone—is this semi-fictional Nixon's wild rumination on his life. It's a last testament, a mixture of confession and self-exoneration, delivered to a tape recorder by a man who toys with the idea of ending his life—he takes a revolver out of a fine case and puts it on top of his desk. Hall's Nixon speaks rapidly, and more and more incoherently. Words spew out of him, he stammers, sentences aren't finished, digressions interrupt digressions, and, as he becomes more and more self-justifying, conflicting half thoughts fight with each other in the air. And, constantly dissatisfied with his errant remarks, he keeps instructing his secretary to erase "all this crap." The material, much of it familiar from various memoirs, from journalists' accounts, and the Watergate tapes and transcripts, is like a nightmare mythology. He rails against Kissinger and Ike and the Kennedys, against Hiss and against Castro, against the Eastern Establishment, and, most of all, against the Committee of 100—the powerful men who, in this film's view, were his bosses. And he swigs down Chivas Regal. The movie has a heightened quality, as if all the tumult of Nixon's last year in the White House, his resignation and his pardon—all the news that we devoured from magazines and the papers and TV, and the constant stream of revelations—were compacted into this frazzled monologue. It's a seizure, a crackup, and the near-pornographic excess of the display is transfixing.

While Hall's Nixon flings himself about the room, glaring at the portraits on the walls—George Washington over the fireplace, Woodrow Wilson, Lincoln, the stern, baleful Kissinger—and howling out his resentments, Altman keeps the camera dancing. The visual pyrotechnics and the cutting have a basic purpose: to sustain the illusion of an unbroken harangue by a distraught—and gradually drunken—man. A few shifts and edits break the flow, but Altman picks it up so fast that they barely have time to register; the hypnotic spell isn't broken. And, of course, Altman's visual sleight of hand does more for *Secret Honor* than just make it appear seamless. He holds Nixon's unfinished thoughts and their overtones and associations in suspension. This film is as layered as any of Altman's seventies movies, but what he did with voices in *California Split* and with characters and plot threads in *Nashville* he's doing with elements that you don't see or hear, that you can only intuit. He's juggling with thistledown; we don't know how he does it, and neither does he. (If he did, he wouldn't have so many flops.)

A bank of four TV security monitors gives us a roomful of Nixons, and the movie is always in motion; it's recording the turmoil inside this man, whose post-Watergate plight is obscenely tragic, and obscenely

2

funny, too, because he blames it all on the big guys, who made him feel that he was playing out of his league. His self-pitying bitterness, his feeling of being used, and the anger that's right under the surface are grotesquely vivid; they're a hyperbolic form of emotions that seem common among struggling, defeated lower-middle-class men, and they bring him pitiably, repellently close. He's a lot like John Schuck's Chicamaw in *Thieves Like Us*—the robber whose attitude toward the world was screw or be screwed, and who wound up alone on a country road, yelling. Nixon poses in front of the four TV screens and addresses them as if he were speaking to a court of world opinion. He waves the gun about, then gets out his family Bible and rages at Kissinger for revealing that he knelt and prayed on the rug that was a present from the Shah. He clutches his sainted mother's photograph and barks "arf" for her, calling himself her little dog. He preens, holding his arms up in front of a glass-panelled window, and his reflection is divided into sections; he's splintering right before our eyes. We watch Nixon rehearsing to play Nixon; he's his own creation, and he despises it and despises the world that he believes forced him into being what he is. He keeps looking for himself in the TV screens—framing himself—until at the end there's nothing to frame.

It's an acting feat by a man who probably isn't a great actor. I'm not sure what is missing, but there's a grayness about Hall, a lack of personality; he isn't enough of a force on his own—he isn't enough of a star—to replace Nixon in the mind's eye. The smooth-voiced Hall, who originated the role on the stage, doesn't create the character; he steps into Nixon's skin—there's an element of impersonation in the performance. At times, his face and hunched shoulders suggest Ed Sullivan, and he suggests other people, too (José Ferrer, Sinatra); he's slightly anonymous. Yet it's partly Hall's not being a great actor that makes the performance work so brilliantly. Hall draws on his lack of a star presence and on an actor's fears of his own mediocrity in a way that seems to parallel Nixon's feelings. Though he doesn't closely resemble Nixon, he's got the Nixon twitches down pat, and he gets inside him with so much historical accuracy that it's as if we were watching the actual Nixon in the wildest scenes that others wrote about, and as if we were seeing the man we heard on the tapes. At the same time, there's enough of a stunt about the performance to distance us, so that we can respond more freely than we could if footage of the actual Nixon were cut to make him look rabid or viper-eyed.

The least convincing part of the material is Freed and Stone's notion of having their Nixon plead that he has "secret honor"—that is, that he deliberately "orchestrated" the Watergate mess rather than give in to the Committee of 100, who offered him a third term if he'd prolong the war in Vietnam (so the huge kickbacks on American aid to Vietnam would keep coming). But so much of the craziness of what the film's Nixon says rings little bells in the memory that this leap in the conspiratorial dark doesn't do much damage. It may even add a hallucinatory streak to the burlesque: Nixon's big revelation is a phony. It certainly doesn't hurt Hall's performance, or Altman's, either. He directs like a man on a roll, who can do no wrong.

There's a virtuoso naughtiness about the sureness of Altman's touch here. Morally, there's probably no way to justify this movie. Unlike Richard III, Richard Milhous Nixon hasn't been dead for centuries. And I think our knowledge that he's still around—that he was the President just a few years ago, and that Ronald Reagan is actually the President now—is part of what gives the movie its kick. I feel a temptation to try to justify it—and it would be possible to say that it isn't an act of political revenge, that its portrait of Nixon transcends revenge by making him creepily sympathetic. But it's only if you accept Freed and Stone's view that he was just the hireling and stooge of the Committee (which means accepting the playwrights' whole paranoid outlook on American capitalism as a monolithic, controlled system, and on the Presidency as a post for an indentured servant) that the character we see is a victim, an Every-man, and sympathetic. The film's Nixon is practically a werewolf; he's horrifying—an intellectual slob. And that, I'll admit, is what held me. The movie has the power of the most raucous, mean, and dirty caricatures of our thirty-seventh President, and those caricatures are alive here. Maybe it's because Nixon in office began to look—to some of us—like some crazy Kabuki figure that no exaggeration seems too vile.

It's only dramatically (and aesthetically) that I can justify this gonzo psychodocudrama. It has a grandeur to it because the trapped, rancorous man it shows us made a raw spectacle of his Presidency.

■

Movies that are consciously life-affirming are to be consciously avoided, and the warning signs are easy to spot in the ads for *Cocoon*. Look at the quotes: "The biggest hug of the summer," and "Offers something for everyone who's perennially young at heart," and "You'd have to be a Scrooge to resist it." You'd have to be a damn fool not to heed all that. *Cocoon* is sunny, freckled, and flatulent—a science-fantasy sitcom. In Victorian fairy tales, children who died were lifted up to Heaven; in *Cocoon*, it's the oldsters who go to Heaven. These oldsters—a lovable, crotchety breed, familiar to us from TV—are like sagging teen-agers. And dolphins, who now seem to be the officially designated ambassadors for the beyond, fill the function of the loons in *On Golden Pond*.

The plot is less than ingenious. Disguised as earthlings, several aliens from the planet Antares arrive in St. Petersburg, Florida, where their leader (Brian Dennehy, all six feet five of him, and with his fathoms-deep voice) calls himself Walter. He's as bland as a baby-food salesman, and that's not part of a disguise. Walter rents an estate with an indoor swimming pool; then he charters a fishing boat, and he and his three helpers proceed to dive into the Gulf for twenty big, heavy clamshell-like cocoons, covered with barnacles and algae, which they move, a few at a time, to the pool. Three old men from a nearby retirement community have been sneaking in for a daily swim in this pool; with the first batch of cocoons in it, the water has a rejuvenating quality, and the men—played by Wilford Brimley, Don Ameche, and Hume Cronyn—frisk in it happily, and emerge cured of afflictions and eager for sex. But if we assume that the cocoons are responsible for their renewed vitality, we're wrong—as we discover when a whole batch of the oldsters rush into the pool (which now has all twenty cocoons). It turns out that the Antareans have been pumping some sort of life force into the water (though we never see them do it). Their purpose is to energize the members of the ground crew left behind from an expedition ten thousand years earlier, who have been in the cocoons all this time, and the oldsters by draining out the life force are killing them. This demoralizes Walter, who turns weepy, and the movie creaks to a temporary halt. It never recovers from this messy explanation scene and from the fact that the superior being Walter gives up too easily; it's left to roly-poly Brimley and the other oldsters to save the day. Or sort of save it. When the best that Walter and the Antareans and earthlings working together can do for the cocoons is throw them back in the Gulf, nobody involved in the movie seems very resourceful.

The script, by Tom Benedek, based on a novel by David Saperstein, has no internal logic, and plot devices keep popping up and shutting down. The worst comes at the end, with a trumped-up final crisis: Should a little boy (Barret Oliver) go off to the Shangri-La in space with his grandparents (Brimley and Maureen Stapleton) or stay behind with his mother

(Linda Harrison)? This is a way of getting into a big-chase finish, with the faces of the old people irradiated by the light of the alien craft that's picking them up, while cars and helicopters and a Coast Guard cutter are speeding after them. The sequence isn't helped by the fact that the tired wizards of Industrial Light & Magic, who did the spacecraft effects, have once again come up with warmed-over versions of the basic imagery of *Close Encounters of the Third Kind*.

If audiences are responding to *Cocoon* and turning it into a huge success, it's largely because of the elderly actors and the affection that the young director, Ron Howard (whose last picture was *Splash*), shows for them. Brimley, with his walrus mustache and his friendly belly, brings an ornery impudence to his role. I particularly liked the way he moves in the early scene (before the revitalization) when, having failed the eye examination for renewal of his driver's license, he covers his car with a white tarpaulin that billows in the wind with the finality of a shroud. Brimley is good and gruff until he has to begin showing what a decent, sage fellow he is. And Don Ameche, who holds his head back with his chin thrust forward, plays a vain, natty old sheik, and he's amusingly light on his feet when he's dancing with his womanfriend (Gwen Verdon). Ameche gives an entertainingly stylized performance that's marred by the crude joke of his doing a breakdance—with the obvious help of a double. And Cronyn has a tough, buzzardy quality after the water has cured his cancer. The actresses—Stapleton, Verdon, Jessica Tandy— bring the film the bearing of major performers, but they aren't as lucky. They're playing such warm, loving helpmates that even rejuvenation doesn't change them much.

Ron Howard is an infectiously good-humored comedy director, but he overworks his "heart" and his ecumenical niceness—his attempt to provide something for all age groups and all faiths. In addition to the grandparents and the little boy with divided loyalties, the film features Steve Guttenberg, who's wet-eyed and overenthusiastic as the skipper of the fishing boat; this overgrown puppy develops a crush on the one Antarean girl, played by the spectacularly pretty Tahnee Welch—daughter of Raquel, though she looks more like Ali MacGraw. (One of the other young aliens, who are background characters, is played by the fourth-generation actor Tyrone Power, Jr., who, like Tahnee Welch, is so pretty he looks unreal.) The way the performers are directed, it's as if the little runaway boy and the group in their twenties and the retired folks all represented different stages of the same waxworks figures.

Ron Howard keeps trying to extract tender emotions from scenes that could get by only as slapstick, and from scenes that can't get by as anything. Since the retirement community has just one Jewish couple, Bernie and Rose (Jack Gilford and Herta Ware), and one black man (Charles Lampkin), they could be taken satirically, as the community's tokens of integration. But Howard treats them so gently and seriously that they become the *film's* tokens of integration. Bernie is also the film's token spoilsport; at times I could practically hear Shirley Temple's piping little voice demanding to know why he was such a worrywart and grumpy grouch. That's the level on which he's conceived. Bernie is the scaredy-cat who doesn't believe in miracles. He won't go into the water, and he won't let his Rose, whose mind is failing, go in, either. He adores her, though, and when she dies he carries her in his arms to the estate and takes her into the pool—but it's too late, the water has been drained of its magic. This cloying scene suggests that Ron Howard doesn't know how thin the material is—that he thinks he's making a drama, and, perhaps, a religious allegory. Bernie stays behind when the other members of the community leave for the promise of eternal life in the hereafter; he isn't saved.

Bernie could be the lucky one: when the equable Walter (whose followers are serene, obedient space cadets) assures Brimley and the other recruits for eternity on Antares that "you will all lead productive lives," the remark has sobering undertones of "Better Red than dead." *Cocoon* seems to have been made by people who were suffering from a slight malfunction of the noggin.

July 15, 1985

LIVING OUT A SONG

||||||||||||||||||||||||||||||||||||||||||||||||||||||||||||||||||||||||||||||||||||||||||||||||||||||||||||||||||||||||||||||||||||||||||||||||

The least publicized of the American movies that have just opened in New York, *Songwriter* is the freest and funniest of the bunch—the most sophisticated, too. It's about the devious and sometimes felonious tricks that Doc Jenkins (Willie Nelson), a country-and-Western composer, uses to extricate himself from his legal entanglement with a Nashville

7

gangster entrepreneur, who takes all the profits from his songs. Fed up with life on a tour bus—with the camaraderie, the partying, and the confusion—and unable to make any money from recordings of his music, Doc has turned to what his ex-wife, Honey (Melinda Dillon), calls "mogulling." He has been managing the career of his old singing partner Blackie Buck (Kris Kristofferson), the roué of the road, who loves the cash and the near-anonymous sex. And in the course of the movie Doc takes on another client, a woman singer—Gilda (Lesley Ann Warren), a sweet, insecure, boozing hysteric—who provides the leverage that Doc needs to outwit the gangster.

Songwriter is a satirical comedy about an artist trying to break free of the crooks who are binding him, but it never loses its sense of perspective on what a wily, frisky old pirate Doc himself is. With the stud in his ear, and his headband and long hair and graying reddish beard, Willie Nelson's Doc Jenkins is like a country-music version of Alec Guinness's scalawag painter Gulley Jimson in *The Horse's Mouth*. The theme, which comes through explicitly in the songs that Nelson and Kristofferson wrote for the movie, is that artists are driven to become con artists in order to survive. And since the material is loosely based on Willie Nelson's own life and legend and financial misadventures (it's said that the song "Night Life," which he sold in 1961 for a hundred and fifty dollars, went on to be recorded by over seventy performers and sold more than thirty million copies), Nelson plays his role with considerable bite. Doc is tough and determined—he's trying to save his life, and get back to Honey and sanity. He needs some solid ground under his feet, and he needs to make music on his own terms.

The script, by Bud Shrake, provides Nelson and Kristofferson with a steady flow of sharp lines, and though the picture starts off at full tilt and it's cut fast, leaving you to fill in for yourself, the director, Alan Rudolph, has a freewheeling responsiveness to the performers, and he allows room for the two stars' amiability and their ad libs. You can feel how much they enjoy singing together and drinking and hanging out together. Their mellowness is the essence of their "outlaw" country music, and it's right there on the screen; they harmonize even when they're not singing. Kristofferson, who's usually so detached that he seems camera shy, looks completely happy when he's just up on a stage performing in front of a crowd. Playing a vain, laid-back sensualist, the silver-bearded Kristofferson has a smiling glow; he has never been more at ease or a more chesty cavalier, or carried a larger sign that says, "I'm a good guy, but I don't want to be bothered."

8

Working with Shrake's material, which is much less high-toned and art-conscious than his own (his last picture was *Choose Me*), Rudolph is able to bring out the scrounginess and ribaldry of the down-home music scene. Whenever the mellowness threatens to get too warm and friendly, Rip Torn comes on and sideswipes the action. As a crumbum promoter who specializes in ripoffs—he draws audiences by advertising stars that he hasn't booked—Torn is the picture's insurance against gentility. Everything he says sounds mean and dirty, and even when you can't understand his snarled-out words he makes you laugh. (He's like W. C. Fields letting out his broadsides, but he's much speedier.) This grumbler feels he isn't getting his due—his whole being shouts it. And the moviemakers were smart enough to realize that Doc and Blackie would be as smitten by his cocky pride as we are. He becomes their pal, and soon three sets of beer-soaked whiskers are lined up at a honky-tonk bar.

The picture offers a wide range of rowdy slapstick, and some that's fairly highbrow and still rowdy. The performers seem up for everything that's handed to them. A girl who works for Doc at his headquarters in Austin, Texas, after he pulls up stakes in Nashville is played by a blond newcomer, Rhonda Dotson. She resembles the appealingly mysterious Marina Vlady of *Two or Three Things I Know About Her* and has something of Teri Garr's manic alertness and dippiness, too, but in a softer form. She's a romantic comedienne with awesome poise—she manages to be a lovely, still presence among the frantic people she shepherds. And, as the gangster whom Doc fears, Richard C. Sarafian (the director of *Vanishing Point*) is big, and has a whomping comic menace; this gangster has the deadpan, self-righteous conviction that he's fully justified in screwing Doc—that that's business. The way Sarafian plays him, he's so totally, aberrantly self-centered that you get to like the slob. (His smile recalls the lopsided idiot's grin on Peter Sellers' face in *Being There*.) Melinda Dillon has a special gift: as Honey, she blends right in with the gags. She doesn't have nearly enough screen time, but she gives a gentle, very pleasing performance. And you develop respect for the director's craftsmanship when you see how gracefully he plays down the idyllic scene in which Doc comes to see Honey and the kids, and sits right down to play guitar with his little girl, who shows him what she has learned.

Lesley Ann Warren's Gilda is a showier part, and the performance is spectacular. When we first see Gilda, she's a singer with no belief in herself and no class; she's an incredibly beautiful girl in a red dress bumping and grinding like a dumb floozy's idea of a hot mama. She's touchingly gawky, as if not sure how to move her long-limbed body, but

9

her red lips and the excitement in her eyes are dazzling. And the cinematographer, Matthew Leonetti, knows that you don't get a camera subject like Lesley Ann Warren very often. Gilda winds up her rendition of "Great Balls of Fire" with a couple of pelvic twitches, and you're conscious of the intersection where her abdomen disappears into her thighs, and conscious that the men around her must want to dive into it. You can't say much more about her singing at this point than that it's loud, but Doc sees the possibilities in the total package. When he grooms her to go out as the opening act for Blackie, she begins to learn something about taste and musicianship, and her voice flowers. Besides being one of the great beauties of the screen, Warren can sing.

Plainness, naturalness, that's Willie Nelson's style, and he's a master at it—not just in his singing but in his acting, too. About the only thing that was lacking in his performances in *Honeysuckle Rose* and *Barbarosa* was an actor's tension—what Rip Torn has with such pungency that the atmosphere around him seems to reek. Nelson keeps (and polishes) his plainness here—it's his glory. And as Doc he's intense and almost Zen-like in his moment-to-moment decisiveness. Maybe because he respects the hipness of Shrake's dialogue, the suggestion of a few grains of sand in his throat—the grittiness that keeps his singing voice from being too sweet—works in his line readings. His jazz-inspired musical phrasing carries over, too. Nelson delivers a line so fast that he seems to be brushing it off, but though his lines have the casualness of throwaways, they're like the exit lines of a matinée idol—they linger in the air. For the first time onscreen, he's consciously using himself as an icon, and Kristofferson is doing it, too. They're looking at themselves in the mirror and they're also seeing each other as mirror images. You can sense the canniness that it took both of them to become stars. That's what the interplay between them comes out of, and they both recognize it and are undercutting each other in the friendliest possible manner. They're living out a song.

In the movie, Doc finds a way to outwit the Nashville operators. But Nelson and Kristofferson haven't found a way to outwit Tri-Star. The newest of the major production companies, Tri-Star is flush with the success of *Rambo*, and in only the third year of its existence it is trashing movies as buoyant and entertaining as *Songwriter*—not giving this one even a token New York campaign or so much as a press screening. (The music was one of only three song scores nominated for an Academy Award earlier this year, but there's no space in the minuscule newspaper listing to say so.) *Songwriter* opened in New York at a tiny theatre—Film Forum 2, on Watts Street; if the movie has disappeared, there's some consolation in its being available on video cassette. But that doesn't make up for the fact that Lesley Ann Warren can give a performance as stunning as the one she gives here and not have it recognized. *Songwriter* is so good-natured it's like a fairy-tale satire. Is it possible that the gents at Tri-Star saw themselves in the caricatured Nashville thugs, and took revenge by deciding that there would be no audience for the picture?

■

*B*ack to the Future is a piece of Pop Art Americana, featuring Christopher Lloyd as a small-town crackpot inventor who putters in his garage and builds a nuclear-powered Rube Goldberg time machine on the chassis of a gull-winged DeLorean. It's a clever, generally likable screwball comedy, with, basically, a very small cast. The inventor has only two friends: a big, floppy dog named Einstein and Marty McFly (Michael J. Fox), a seventeen-year-old high-school senior who visits him to escape his drab family life with a complaining, uptight mother (she belts down her liquor), a couple of loser siblings, and a whipped father who's a failure in just about every department. (The man is such a forlorn creep that he laughs in sync with the TV laughtrack.) Almost everything that happens in the first part, set in Hill Valley, in Northern California, in 1985, is preparation for gags and plot devices that pay off when Marty escapes from a team of terrorists (whose plutonium the inventor has stolen to power the DeLorean) by jumping into the machine, which hurtles him to Hill Valley, 1955.

There Marty meets his parents as seventeen-year-olds going to the same massive, ugly high school he has been attending. It's a different era, though; it's the period when large numbers of teen-agers first began to have money to spend on clothes and records, and became a targeted consumer group, and when they also began to have access to cars, which meant freedom, and maybe even sex—or, at least, necking. Lorraine (Lea Thompson), Marty's mother-to-be, is a moony kid who lives in a state of dazed aphrodisia—her hormones seem to have blurred her expression—while George McFly (Crispin Glover), his father-to-be, is a tall, skinny, pathetic wimp who secretly writes sci-fi stories. Marty's arrival balls things up. Lorraine thinks he's a dreamboat, and develops a lascivious crush on him. Marty is panicked: How is he going to get her

11

to switch her fixation from him to George, so he can eventually be born? The fun in the time-travel genre is, of course, in the hero's interfering with the course of history; specifically, Marty has to change the weakling George McFly—has to stop him from cringing, and make him stand up for himself, so he can win Lorraine. And while Marty's doing that the audience has the incidental fun of catching the comparative pop-culture references of the eighties/fifties time warp.

Directed by Robert Zemeckis, from a script he wrote with his regular teammate, Bob Gale, *Back to the Future* is ingenious; it has the structure of a comedy classic, and it's consistently engaging. If I can't work up much enthusiasm for it, it's because I'm not crazy about movies with kids as the heroes—especially bland, clean-cut, nice kids like Marty. In this role, Michael J. Fox (he's one of the stars of the NBC series *Family Ties*) approaches acting as a form of aerobics—he's primed, he's nimble and proficient, and he delivers a processed, TV actor's charm. Everything he does is on the surface. Talking to George, he's like a feisty football coach trying to psych up a sad-sack player. And he's exactly, I think, what the moviemakers wanted. Steven Spielberg, under whose aegis the picture was made, says, *"Back to the Future* is the greatest *Leave It to Beaver* episode ever produced."* That's what's the matter with it. I don't watch *Leave It to Beaver* reruns, and when I go to the movies I don't want to see a glorified *Leave It to Beaver.*

Actually, this movie, with its high-school-age hero and the dream that he fulfills—the dream of being part of a deluxe happy family, like the ones in TV commercials—represents a culmination of the fifties' appeal to the youth market. Teen-age tastes now dominate mainstream moviemaking, and that's where Zemeckis and Gale are working. (The movie is their fantasy about becoming mediocre—i.e., successful.) Marty doesn't have the consciousness of an adult hero, and he doesn't have a child's imagination, either; he's a hero for the young audience—a teen idol. And the picture doesn't have anything like the rambunctiousness or the maniacal edge of Zemeckis and Gale's wonderful 1980 film *Used Cars* (which was also made under Spielberg's aegis, but before he became a youth-market czar, and which failed at the box office). Zemeckis knows how to set up a gag, and how to set his players on collision courses; his films—including *Romancing the Stone* (which he and Gale didn't write)— have comic drive. But scenes here, such as the ones in which George is bullied by a big jock, are laid on too thick and then repeated; at times, *Back to the Future* makes you feel you're at a kiddies' matinée. (Maybe it's too bad that this movie is as satisfying as it is: a few more pictures like *The Goonies*, and even kiddies may be bored watching kiddies.)

What keeps *Back to the Future* from being a comedy classic is that its eye is on the market. Despite Zemeckis and Gale's wit in devising intricate structures that keep blowing fuses, the thinking here is cramped and conventional. I wish that moviemakers and their designers would stop using old *Life* magazines for their images of the American past. Hill Valley in 1955 has no pop glint, no vitality; the town is embalmed—it's printed on glossy paper. And the film's idea of happiness in the eighties—with one of Marty's siblings turned into a Yuppie and the other into a deb, and his parents strolling like lovers amid the pastel sofas in a living room that looks like a commercial for a furniture-warehouse sale—should be a satirical joke but isn't.

Christopher Lloyd is a blissful silly, though. His wild-eyed glare doesn't seem to be directed toward anything in front of him—he's glaring backward into his own knotted-up mental processes. He makes you feel that the wires in his head are crossed; he's missing connections. And his thoughts seem to work independently of his gestures: his long arms swing about helplessly. He's like Frankenstein's monster as a sweetheart. And Lea Thompson is a gifted mime. Her woozy-faced young Lorraine has a sly lustiness that's entrancing. Crispin Glover's George McFly, with his cowering posture and his tortured mouth, is almost too painful a caricature. He has more force than anyone else in the movie—possibly because he's the only character that Zemeckis and Gale push to the limit. (In addition to the other horrors piled on him, he's a teen-age Peeping Tom.) I'm not sure what to make of the performance, but the movie would be considerably more innocuous without it.

■

Midway through Lawrence Kasdan's *Silverado*, from a script he wrote with his brother Mark, I began to be reminded of another roguish, mechanically plotted movie, *The Sting*, which had also left me cold. *The Sting* had Marvin Hamlisch's arrangements of Scott Joplin's piano rags to give it some push. The orchestral score of *Silverado* is a mistake: it pounds you on the head trying to inflate the emotions that the movie intended to arouse, and so it makes you more aware of the hollowness of what you're experiencing. These movies aren't about anything but pinning index cards to a wall.

Lawrence Kasdan is an impersonal craftsman, hip in a postmodern way that's devoid of personality. He uses accomplished actors: the four heroes journeying west to Silverado in the eighteen-eighties are played by Kevin Kline, Scott Glenn, Kevin Costner, and Danny Glover, and they're variously involved with Linda Hunt, Rosanna Arquette, Brian Dennehy, John Cleese, and Jeff Goldblum. But these actors don't seem sure what their characters are meant to be, and though I kept waiting for the four men's stories to converge and the villains to turn out to be linked, as far as I could see, this didn't happen. Probably, to enjoy the movie you'd have to watch it as a cool, Western equivalent of TV's *Miami Vice*, and accept the fights and shoot-outs as decorative, as part of the scenery. In this arch, uninvolving atmosphere, every time the director shows his good intentions—as he does in his treatment of the black hero's family, and in his concern for the terror experienced by a little boy—the film gets groggy. (Outraged by the news of some chicanery, the black cowboy uses his deepest chest tones on "That ain't right. I've had enough of what ain't right.")

July 29, 1985

POP MYSTICS

Iiiiiiiiiiiiiiiiiiiiiiiiiiiiiiiiiiiiiiiiiiiiiiiiiiiiiiiiiiiiiiiiiiiiiiiiiiiiiiiiiiiiiiiiiiiiiiiiiiiiiiiiiiiiiiiiiiii

In an interview published in *American Film* last year, Pete Hamill asked Sergio Leone, who had cast Clint Eastwood in the spaghetti Westerns that made him an international star, just what Leone had seen in Eastwood that no one in America had spotted. Leone said, "When Michelangelo was asked what he had seen in the one particular block of marble which he chose among hundreds of others, he replied that he saw Moses. I would offer the same answer to your question—only backwards. . . . What I saw [in Eastwood], simply, was a block of marble." When Leone was asked how he would compare an actor like Eastwood with someone like Robert De Niro (whom he had just directed), he said,

14

"They don't even belong to the same profession. Robert De Niro throws himself into this or that role, putting on a personality the way someone else might put on his coat, naturally and with elegance, while Clint Eastwood throws himself into a suit of armor and lowers the visor with a rusty clang. It's exactly that lowered visor which composes his character. And that creaky clang it makes as it snaps down, dry as a Martini in Harry's Bar in Venice, is also his character. Look at him carefully. Eastwood moves like a sleepwalker between explosions and hails of bullets, and he is always the same—a block of marble. Bobby, first of all, is an actor. Clint, first of all, is a star. Bobby suffers, Clint yawns."

That just about sums up Eastwood: he was a world-class yawner. But in recent years he has been too self-conscious to yawn, and in his new Western he seems eager for the world's good opinion. *Pale Rider*, which he produced and directed, from a script he commissioned from Michael Butler and Dennis Shryack, lifts its general outlines from *Shane* and its specifics from Leone, but it's an art Western, shot in art color— shades of dirt, with gray, brown, and black trimmings, and interiors so dark you can barely see who's onscreen in the middle of the day. Eastwood himself, a ghost who materializes as the answer to a fourteen-year-old girl's prayer for a miracle, seems to be playing some spectral combination of Death, Jesus, Billy Jack, and the Terminator. This tall, gaunt-faced Stranger sometimes wears clerical garb and is addressed as Preacher. When he takes off his shirt, his back has shapely bullet holes, like stigmata, and when he opens his mouth sententious words of wisdom fall out of it—gems like "There's plain few problems can't be solved with a little sweat and some hard work." If this is how people beyond the grave talk, I'd just as soon they didn't come back to visit.

The story centers on the battle between the good people, gold miners called tin pans (because of their principal tool), and LaHood, a land baron who uses hydraulic strip-mining methods that scar the earth. The movie is set in the California Sierras during the gold-rush era before the Civil War, but the twenty tin pans' claims seem to be clustered in an area smaller than a city block; they work a few feet apart, panning the little stream that runs through their campsite, and talking to each other while they work. Yet, in the midst of thousands of acres of unexplored wilderness, LaHood is determined to drive them out and grab this itty-bitty piece of land; he sends his workers on raids to destroy the defenseless miners' sluice gates and tents and shacks and livestock. When the Stranger helps the pans stand their ground, LaHood hires a band of seven mercenaries to kill him and finish driving the others off.

15

Pale Rider has the kind of Western situations that were parodied years ago by Harvey Korman on *The Carol Burnett Show*. Once again, a harmless, likable old duffer is tormented by gunmen who force him to dance by shooting at his feet. And the movie actually establishes how bad the bad guys are by having them kill the little girl's puppydog. (Weeping shiny glycerin tears, she picks up an obviously stuffed toy animal, and buries it; it's on this hallowed spot that she prays and is heard.) Eastwood has been getting a lot of mileage out of dogs lately, and out of little girls, too—in *Tightrope* he had his own daughter threatened with rape by his doppelgänger—and this dogless little girl tells him she loves him and wants him to teach her how to make love. (I know that Clint Eastwood is a big star—some say the biggest in the world. Still, isn't it a bit unseemly for this man—he's fifty-five now—to have a scene in his own production in which a fourteen-year-old girl wants to have sex with him?) When he declines, she rightly detects that he's more taken with her mother (Carrie Snodgress), though it beats me how anybody could detect his feelings. (There don't seem to be many disadvantages to being dead: this resurrected preacher-gunslinger is sexually potent and gets to spend a night with the mother.) Soon the little girl can't think of anything better to do with herself than borrow a horse and ride into LaHood's base of operations, so she can be molested by the whole evil pack, which—for a touch of the outré—includes the gigantic Richard (Jaws) Kiel, slavering with desire. The Stranger rescues her, of course, and takes her home. (Neither of them remembers to take along the borrowed horse.)

Actors love to play these misterioso bozos. Eastwood makes his entrance riding down from distant cloud-covered peaks in images that are superimposed on the maiden at her prayers; that must have been enough right there to delight him with the Butler-Shryack script. And he gets to do a lot of impassive staring, clenching his teeth and twisting his tight mouth just the teeniest bit to show anger. (He never laughs.) Eastwood (or a double) gets to twirl an axe handle so it sparkles in the sun, like John Wayne's rifle in *True Grit*. Eventually, he reënacts Gary Cooper's *High Noon* walk to the final confrontation, and his spurs jingle-jangle. The movie is full of recycled mythmaking, but Eastwood goes through his motions like someone exhumed, and as a director he numbs out what he borrows.

There isn't a gleam of good sense anywhere in this picture. When the tin pans talk about not wanting to leave, because they've put down roots here, and say that they came to this site to raise children and that

16

they have family graves here, you think, They've been working these dinky claims for generations? They must be crazy. But the music track is reverential, as is to be expected when people talk of family values. Eastwood came up with the idea for this movie himself, but could Butler and Shryack have started out with a script about homesteaders, decided to make it look a little different from *Shane* by changing them to gold miners, and failed to make the necessary readjustments? (This may be an ecologically minded Western, but it's strip-mining *Shane*.) Plot details are slovenly. It's explained that Carrie Snodgress's husband simply took off, but his still being around somewhere doesn't seem to bother Michael Moriarty, the leader of the pans, who keeps asking her to marry him. And Moriarty has a baffling sequence of riding into town for supplies, passing over patches of snow (the shots don't match), and then arriving at the store and talking cheerily about putting in provisions before the cold weather comes, as if it were weeks in the future.

Horses are supremely photogenic, so a Western always has something going for it. But *Pale Rider*, with its attempt at a folkloric hero, doesn't provide what Eastwood's public can usually count on in his tough-cop pictures: the tension that makes him dangerous. When Eastwood's cop, baiting a bad guy, says, "Make my day," it's a laugh line, because he's acknowledging what the audience already knows—that he's holding back, that he *wants* to shoot. The climactic gunfight in *Pale Rider* is a bust, because although Eastwood as Avenging Angel gets to knock off all seven mercenaries, he isn't revved up. Is it the art bug that got into him? He kills them methodically. It's like target practice, and the audience doesn't get the charge it gets from his chief emotion when he's Dirty Harry—his feeling angry so deep down that he's almost trembling, he's on the verge of exploding. (What's disgusting about the Dirty Harry movies is that Eastwood plays this angry tension as righteous indignation. He never seems to examine the insides of the character.)

As an actor, Eastwood never lets down his guard. His idea of being a real man is that it's something you have to pretend to be—as Sergio Leone put it, he's wearing a suit of armor. This actor has made a career out of his terror of expressiveness. Now here he is playing a stiff, a ghost. It's perfect casting, but he doesn't have the daring to let go and have fun with it. Even as a ghost, he's armored.

■

17

John Boorman is drawn to subjects on which he can project his obsessive theme: that civilized man, having lost tribal man's magic unity with nature, is spreading his brutal, nature-destroying sickness. His latest film, *The Emerald Forest*, is set in Brazil, where Tommy, the seven-year-old son of an American engineer (played by Powers Boothe), wanders off during a family picnic at the edge of the Amazon rain forest and is abducted by the members of a tribe called the Invisible People. The Invisibles take little blond Tommy to save him. The child, seeing their shaman-chief (Rui Polonah), smiles at him, and the chief, perceiving that the child is still in innocent harmony with nature, doesn't have the heart to let him go back to The Dead World of the Termite People. The chief raises Tommy as his son, teaching him jungle lore, the mysteries of earth and air, and such useful arts as out-of-body travel. For ten years, the engineer searches for the boy during whatever time he can take off from the job of clearing the rain forest to build a giant dam (which fosters the rise of a city). When, at last, the father locates the seventeen-year-old Tommy (played by the director's son, Charley Boorman), he realizes that Tommy's consciousness surpasses his own and that the boy's life is superior to anything civilization has to offer, and he returns to the city alone. Some large-scale melodramatic incidents follow, but this variation on John Ford's *The Searchers* is the core of the first half of the movie. It reëstablishes the myth of the noble savage by imbuing it with modern hallucinogenic romanticism. Tommy has trance visions and can call up his familiar—an eagle—when he needs to travel. In the father's brief stay with the Invisibles, he, too, has visions, and learns that his own familiar is a jaguar.

John Boorman isn't anything as simple as a sentimentalist or a fraud; he's a Jungian. In the actual kidnapping—of a Peruvian child—that the story is based on, the Indians were a warlike tribe who carried out raids, and they attacked the Peruvian family's campsite at the time that they made off with the child. But all that is really beside the point. Boorman makes his aims clear in his book *The Emerald Forest Diary* (Farrar, Straus & Giroux): "We were all tribal a couple of thousand years ago. It has been forgotten too fast. We have to acknowledge what is still tribal in us. That was my aim in *Excalibur*—to touch the mythic, archetypal sources that begat us. So my aim here is mythic, not naturalistic. I am not going to film a real tribe. I am going to invent tribes." And he explains his grand ecological framework: "The destruction of the Rain Forest is expressed by the vast clearing of the area to be flooded by the construction of the dam. The dam itself stops the flow of a river. It is a perfect symbol of man's determination to harness, tame, control, destroy nature. It forces two Indian tribes away from their lands and into conflict with each other. The father who builds the dam is unwittingly the cause of the tragedies that befall his son's tribe." He goes on to say, "The relationship between our modern, acquisitive, greedily all-consuming society and the balanced tribal life proceeding in harmony with nature is perfectly dramatized in the persons of the father and son divided by these extraordinary circumstances."

The film touches on all sorts of major themes, especially the fate of the rain forests. But what we actually see is puerile, because, ready as viewers may be to agree with Boorman's denunciation of our society, his plan requires him to show us this "balanced tribal life proceeding in harmony with nature." And when he does, only the swooniest, most impressionable softies could fall for it, or maybe people so suggestible that they find the father-son idea profoundly affecting even though it isn't carried out affectingly. The faults that have plagued Boorman's films— his lack of interest in character, his rather lordly failure to dramatize the issues that excite him the most, his wacko ear for dialogue—really pile up this time. The storytelling is slack. On the engineer's last trip into the jungle, he's accompanied by a glib, cynical European journalist (Eduardo Conde), and we wait to see where the friction between them will lead; it leads nowhere. Boorman invites us into complicity with his wishful thinking (*The Emerald Forest* and *Greystoke* form the Lush Vegetation Diptych), but he doesn't seem to be able to get any kind of seductive flow going. His great gift for ecstatic, enraptured imagery barely comes into play, because he's working in staggeringly difficult conditions: filming in what he himself describes as the "clammy confines" of the rain forest (while trying to present it as a lost paradise); training mostly inexperienced actors and actresses to be Invisibles and run around innocently naked; and coping with all the financial, logistical, health, and morale problems involved in shooting in faraway locations.

The overriding fault is that there's no pleasure to be had from the performances. The principal actors can't carry us past the foolish seriousness, because Boorman doesn't want Tommy or his father to be strong characters; he wants them to be symbolic representatives of normal types. The dialogue (the script is by Rospo Pallenberg) has no texture, no layers. Charley Boorman, whose blue eyes are psychedelically clear, is passable as Tommy—he looks like a stoned seraph—but there's nobody who would

19

be right for the role. It's just a dreamy notion—a sweet, docile child-man brought up by loving tribal methods. (As far as we can tell, he's not much different from his docile sister, who has been raised in a city apartment.) And although Powers Boothe—who's thinner than usual here, with a comic-strip hero's clean jawline from ear to chin—can usually take the camera with a sullen aplomb that's pretty funny (singlehandedly, he makes the Philip Marlowe series on HBO semi-watchable), his role is crushingly undeveloped. We don't feel that the father is deeply shaken when he realizes that the dam he has supervised is destroying Tommy's tribe. Even his out-of-body travel as a jaguar—which is a bit of a kick for the viewer—doesn't seem to give him any special lift. Powers Boothe looks as if he were cast for his I-rape-rain-forests macho, and when the child first disappears he's furiously upset; hacking his way into the jungle, he has the face of a Kabuki demon. But he's used as an ordinary nice-guy jaguar-man who just hasn't given much thought to what this dam he's in charge of is doing to the environment.

It's facinating to read Boorman's *Emerald Forest Diary* after seeing the picture, because you begin to understand moviemaking as a species of self-delusion. Boorman writes of the necessity of conning the money men, but he's conning himself most of the time. He thinks he's getting all sorts of marvellous things on film; he rides on a tide of enthusiasm, and that's what keeps him going—that and his will. Even when he looks at the footage he has just shot and admits that "the actuality is never quite as good as the film in my head," he doesn't seem to register basic things, such as how florid and musty the dialogue of the Invisible People is. And, from the look of Tommy's courtship scenes, Boorman must have wanted them to be completely "natural." The result is that they're completely bland and unsexual. When Kachiri (Dira Paes), the girl Tommy loves, explains to him how boys and girls in the tribe will pair off, it's as if we'd entered a new kind of theme park.

The film has a cuckoo climax—a mixture of Ayn Rand's *The Fountainhead* and Peter Weir's *The Last Wave*. The engineer, bearing the guilt of all those who have destroyed nature, goes to redeem himself by blowing up the dam. At the same time, Tommy and his tribe are performing rain rituals—calling forth Tommy's eagle, who calls forth the frogs—and whipping up a torrential downpour to surge over the dam and smash it. So when it goes, we can't tell: was it the engineer or was it the frogs?

The picture leaves us with a message about the tribes of the Amazon;

we're told that "they still know what we have forgotten." (The samples we're given—such as the shaman's warning "When the toucan cries, danger is not far"—aren't too inspiring.) A friend of mine who works in a Santa Monica bookstore says that some of his customers are hooked on Lynn V. Andrews, a writer in the Carlos Castaneda pastures, who has brought out *Medicine Woman* and *Flight of the Seventh Moon.* Her next book, *Jaguar Woman,* has been announced, and customers are coming in and asking, "Does she give workshops?" After *The Emerald Forest* and its apocalyptic deluge, that's what John Boorman ought to do: offer workshops, with out-of-body travel, economy flight. Maybe if he got his fill of communing with a past that never was he could move on to making movies.

■

When a new, inexperienced administration at United Artists gave the go-ahead to Michael Cimino's Western *Heaven's Gate,* the project, which had been turned down by executives at other studios (and by at least one of the previous administrations at United Artists), was clearly booby-trapped. The new management team, put in position by the officers of U.A.'s conglomerate parent, Transamerica, were aware of the risks, but their predecessors, who had left, en bloc, to form Orion Pictures, jeered at them in the press, and they were overeager to establish themselves by coming up with a slate of films that would confer prestige on them. Proposed at seven and a half million dollars, eventually budgeted at roughly eleven and a half million, and written off finally at forty-four million, *Heaven's Gate* brought nothing but torment to the executives of United Artists, which is now virtually defunct. (Transamerica, humiliated by the publicity, sold the company to Kirk Kerkorian's M-G-M, which wanted it because of its distribution apparatus, and dismantled the production side.) About the only good that has ever come from the movie is the new book *Final Cut: Dreams and Disaster in the Making of "Heaven's Gate"* (Morrow), by Steven Bach—perhaps the best account we have of American moviemaking in the age of conglomerate control of the studios, and (though this isn't made explicit) in the druggy age.

Steven Bach was part of the new U.A. team, and was head of production when *Heaven's Gate* was premièred, late in 1980—the book might be called *Apologia pro Fiasco Suo*. It's that, but it's considerably more than that. There are a lot of emotions bumping into each other under the surface of Bach's precise, thoughtful, sometimes hilarious and macabre story. He begins by describing the formation of United Artists, in 1919, by Charlie Chaplin, Douglas Fairbanks, Mary Pickford, and D. W. Griffith; outlines the steps that led the company to become a subsidiary of Transamerica in 1967; and then gets into the whole *Heaven's Gate* debacle. That picture is only a part of what is going on at the studio, though—it's one debacle among many. (There are also imagined future triumphs, but the regime and the company didn't last long enough.) Bach is particularly good in his observation of how the marketing and distribution people start taking over the decision-making process about what films should be given the go-ahead—a power grab that's also taking place at other studios and helps to explain why we've been getting so many teen pix in the last few years. And the choices that were made by the U.A. team are covered in an interlocking series of fine, juicy anecdotes indicating why U.A. turned down what it did and financed what it did, and why it lost projects it wanted and had to settle for others.

The book is a short course in the realpolitik of how projects come to be accepted; it's set in a cutthroat business, where betrayal is the rule, not the exception. It takes Bach a while to grasp that, and his loyalty and affection go to the man who doesn't fit the pattern. The hero of Bach's story isn't Bach. It's shy Andy Albeck, the new president of United Artists—not because he was the right man for the job (he wasn't) but because he treated his staff and the people he dealt with fairly and considerately. Bach's greatest contribution may be his recognition that even in the movie business there are decencies that transcend success or failure. (Neither he nor Albeck is still in the business.) That's what gives the book its distinction: it has the touching, melancholic quality of a story told by someone who knew he was on a sinking ship but felt honor-bound not to try to save himself.

As I see it, Bach—intelligent and knowing as he is—wasn't the right man for his job, either. From his own description of the day-to-day workings of United Artists, it appears that there was a vacuum of leadership even before the decision was taken to make *Heaven's Gate*, and that he was part of that vacuum. In all probability, Michael Cimino could read Steven Bach a lot better than Bach could read Cimino. And if Cimino could, others could, too. The new management team looking for projects that would redound to U.A.'s glory and keep Transamerica proud and happy were perfect patsies. The movie business attracts flimflam artists, megalomaniacs, and pathological liars from all over the world; the essential part of the head of production's job is having the instincts and the experience to know what and whom to say yes to. And in a period when—because of the widespread consumption of pills, cocaine, and God knows what—stars' and directors' track records may not be a valid guide to how they will perform next time, the executive needs genius instincts. And he has to exercise them before a picture begins rolling, because once it starts he has about as much control over the director as a hospital administrator has over a doctor during surgery.

When Cimino's picture is out of control and is costing the company a million dollars a week, Bach is in a terrible bind. His account of the steps he takes—talking to an eminent director about possibly replacing Cimino, asking advice from an eminent producer, and so on—makes for good reading. But what he's doing is remarkably tepid and ineffective. Obviously, if he fires Cimino, whose last picture, *The Deer Hunter*, has just won five Academy Awards, including Best Picture and Best Director, he and the other officers of U.A. will be vilified in the press and go down in history as hatchet men and philistines. But he doesn't seem to be doing anything but wasting time giving people in the Hollywood community the chance to sympathize with him. When you get down to it, Bach conveys an impression of connoisseurship, erudition, and understanding while misunderstanding the problem: he's the problem. He doesn't do much except wring his hands until the last weeks of filming, when it finally registers on him that he has to show some force. By then, Cimino, who's utterly dedicated to his amorphous vision, has shot over two hundred hours of film.

Bach looks back to a golden age in the fifties when the heads of United Artists "were able to draw upon a pool of thoroughly trained, knowledgeable professionals to whom independence was not synonymous with indulgence, self- or otherwise." He looks back to the time "before poetic license had become the intellectual justification for all manner of creative licentiousness." This hokey nostalgia isn't worthy of him. When he complains about "licentiousness" and lack of discipline, he's really saying that he couldn't handle Michael Cimino. Maybe nobody could have, but the members of the U.A. team were the ones who said yes to him, because they thought they could. I admire the sensitivity and taste that Steven Bach shows in this book, but these are not the qualities that make a studio head. Whether artists have self-discipline or not, executives are supposed to be disciplined people with the strength and the smarts to impose discipline on others when it's needed. That's what they draw astronomic salaries for.

August 12, 1985

TANGLED WEBS

||||||||||||||||||||||||||||||||||||||||||||||||||||||||||||||||||||||||||||||||||||||||||||||||||||||||||||||||||||||||||||||||||||||||||||||||||||||||||||||

Kiss of the Spider Woman is an ambitious yet slack piece of moviemaking, but, with its two heroes who share a prison cell in a nameless South American country—men who have nothing except each other— it can work on audiences in the way that *Midnight Cowboy* did back in 1969. And, the times having changed, it can make explicit what was potential in that earlier relationship. In schematic terms, the movie is about a homosexual and a revolutionary locked up together by a repressive society. Molina—"a silly old queen," he calls himself—is played by William Hurt; he is a window dresser in his late thirties who has been given an eight-year sentence for "corrupting a minor." Valentín, played by Raul Julia, is a pompous doctrinaire Marxist from an upper-middle-class background; he is being held for his political activities and has been tortured by the police, who want the names of his confederates. A puritan about pleasure, the radical Valentín treats Molina as a disgusting inferior, a degenerate. But Molina has beautiful, generous instincts: he shares his food with Valentín and nurses him when he's sick, tenderly cleaning him up when he's incontinent. Molina tries to comfort Valentín and help him forget his pain and misery by telling him the stories of old movies—one, in particular, he embellishes by evoking the luxury of the atmosphere and the elegance of the heroine's hairstyles, her gowns, her gestures. And Valentín, who at first is openly contemptuous of Molina's queenly affectations and his identification with movie goddesses, gradually comes to admit that he likes the storytelling, the movie lullabies.

The famous 1976 novel by Manuel Puig on which the film is based is more than a defense of escapism—it's an homage to escapism. The glory of the book is that the reader feels the power of fantasy. Puig, who grew up in a remote small town in Argentina, has said that in his childhood

24

the movies were his only escape from drabness. In a recent interview in *The New York Times*, he explained, "It doesn't matter that the way of life shown by Hollywood was phony. It helped you hope." Yet Puig isn't a sentimentalist. Most of the novel is in the form of a dialogue between the two cellmates, so there is no authorial voice as such, and the motives behind what the men say are elusive. But there are undertones—subversive hints that the two men are using each other—which may or may not be picked up by a reader. They have definitely not been picked up by the movie, directed by Hector Babenco, from a screenplay by Leonard Schrader, with, reportedly, some assistance from Puig. The movie is essentially about two men who give to each other and learn from each other. (This is the first film that Babenco, the director of *Pixote*, has made in English; the production is Brazilian, though, and it was shot in São Paulo.)

The story that the movie tells is of how the narrow-minded political martyr Valentín learns humility and becomes more of a man through his close friendship with the sweetly maternal Molina. And Molina, who says that he "takes it like a woman," and that he's incapable of falling in love with another homosexual—Molina, who dreams the impossible dream of being loved by a heterosexual man, has that dream fulfilled when the eminently heterosexual Valentín has sex with him, and even grants him his request for a kiss. The movie is primarily the story of Molina's transfiguration through the power of love and happiness and a new self-respect—that is, his shedding of his effeminate mannerisms.

William Hurt, whose performance took the first prize at Cannes this year, is just about the only thing to look at. As Molina, he has a henna rinse that gives his hair a peculiar, slightly rancid coloring, and he first appears wrapping a red towel around his head as a turban—a Scheherazade flourish—and wearing the thick, coquettish makeup of an aging vamp. Each time he picks up the plot threads of the Nazi-made spy romance that he narrates, he inhales mightily before every line he delivers. It has been said that Hurt sometimes seems to move in slow motion. Here his voice goes into slow motion: he stretches out his words, lingering over them, and he springs each new detail for its maximum effect. His prancing mannerisms give the opening sequences some kick, and there's the promise of fun in the interpolated snippets of the film he's describing— *Her Real Glory*, Puig's invented superproduction. Babenco stages it with the Brazilian actress Sonia Braga as dark-eyed, dark-haired Léni Lamaison, the "foremost diva of French song" and a woman of true nobility. Léni falls in love with a high-ranking blond, blue-eyed Nazi (played by

Herson Capri), but doesn't allow herself to show it until after he opens her eyes to the vile schemes of the Jews in the Resistance; then she realizes that the Nazis aren't her enemies—they're saving mankind. The snippets are entertaining, but they're overdeliberate, studied.

Hurt's performance as Molina gives the movie its only liveliness, and liveliness doesn't come easy to William Hurt. He's very likable in the scenes where Molina reveals his tenderness and warmth and humor. But as an actor Hurt holds back; he has a knotted, bunched-up presence. Part of the acclaim for his work here must be because he's so wrong for the role that you're aware of what a showy feat his performance is. He gives the role an honorable shot, but he's miscast physically (he seems to be a North American who wandered into the South American setting—you don't know what that big cross is doing around his neck), and, worse, he's miscast spiritually. As a transsexual friend of mine put it, "Hurt as Molina is like having a basset hound playing a Chihuahua." Hurt doesn't fall into any of the obvious traps. He isn't condescending, and he handles Molina's adoring talk about his mother, and his saying that he has loved only two people—his mother and Valentín—in a straightforward, unembarrassed way. But Hurt's virtues are mainly negative, and his carefully constructed performance is all from the outside. There's nothing lyrical or iridescent about his Molina. Glamour doesn't hit a responsive chord in this guy's soul; his soul doesn't even vibrate sympathetically with the movie-goddess pictures on the wall of his cell. The role of Molina needs someone who can get lost in himself, in the bedazzled, imploding way that some homosexuals do when they talk about the movies they love. As Hurt plays the part (and as Babenco directs him), there's no humor in Molina's transformation when his feelings for Valentín deepen, and he stops using the epicene makeup and his face begins to shine with an inner glow and a purity that are worthy of Léni herself.

This is where the movie subtly departs from the novel: I don't believe that Puig saw any need for Molina to be redeemed. In the book, when Molina takes a self-sacrificing risk for the sake of his beloved's political ideals, and behaves like the valiant, noble movie heroines he identifies with, there's a strong possibility that Valentín, in giving him the kiss he asked for, has consciously manipulated him into risking his neck—has exploited his homosexuality. But the movie deeply—and deliberately, I think—sentimentalizes the novel, in order to make the material more touching, more urgent. From the way Babenco directs, his whole being seems to be charged with good intentions and the desire to be a firebrand. He pushes for a basic, "universal" meaning; he pushes for audiences to respond to Molina's humanity. The film's Molina is a wonderful person in every way—practical, earthy, and warm, and, finally, because of his contact with Valentín, selfless. This redemption drama is as phony as the forties screen romances that Molina is infatuated with.

That is to say, it moves an audience at the obvious points. Of course, it also holds your interest the way those forties movies did; you want to know how the picture is going to turn out. (There are a fair number of surprises, even if in discussing the film here I have to give away some of the plot.) But those are the only terms in which it works. Homosexual groups may think the film is politically correct, but its squareness is a betrayal of something in movie-loving gays: their carrying a personal theatre of romantic fantasy inside themselves. Molina is the moviegoer as *auteur*, and we should all feel as if some inner space had been opened in us when we see the clips of Léni's romance with her golden-haired Nazi, Werner (he's like an ersatz Conrad Veidt, with a suggestion of Helmut Berger). This glossy old movie in pseudo black-and-white—it's in desaturated, monochromatic color that looks faintly metallic—should make our heads spin. Some of the casting, such as that of Denise Dummont as the naïve, round-faced girl in the Resistance, has a witty accuracy, even if it recalls Hollywood films rather than Nazi films. And the footage adds a modernist flavor to the framing movie. But it doesn't do anything more—it never pulls you out of the framing movie and carries you away, though you keep expecting it to. It has no whirl, and Léni has no erotic undercurrents—just her brave, saccharine, masochistic surface. Léni's waxenness and lack of vivacity seem to go back to the novel. It may be that the playful, sly Puig was deliberately giving Molina a window dresser's version of old movies (Molina is very precise in his description of fabrics), and that Babenco, putting the material on the screen, stayed with this skewed perspective. Léni is like a mannequin—a South American Joan Crawford on Quaaludes. And, partly because the movie clips are flat, Puig's celebration of the positive side of movie escapism—the way movies can become jewelled by imagination—doesn't really come across. There's hardly even a shift in tone between the clips and the rather garish prison squalor and the scenes from their pasts which Molina and Valentín remember. (Some of the memory scenes are staged like movie pastiches, but you can't tell why. An example: the one with the woman Valentín loves telling him, "If you leave, don't come back.")

The film is also marred by a hopelessly awkward sequence in which Molina, out of prison and trying to make contact with the members of Valentín's group, tells them on the phone that he'll be wearing a red scarf, and sets off to meet them. On the way to the meeting place, he sees that the police have him under surveillance, and we wait—and wait—for him to take off the red scarf. Inexplicably, he doesn't (perhaps his scarf is meant to be a flourish from the soul, like Cyrano's white plume), and the movie, making no sense, falls to tatters. It doesn't recover when the action returns to Valentín in prison, freshly bruised and tortured.

Raul Julia isn't broad and loud in this role, as he sometimes is on the stage; once Valentín stops being crudely contemptuous of Molina, Julia settles into an inoffensive, rather colorless, lightweight performance. (When in doubt, he stares straight ahead.) Valentín isn't the great role that Molina could be, but a little more might have been done with it if the sexual relationship between the two men had been ongoing (as it is in the book), and not just the one-night affair of the movie. Puig didn't have much affection for this Marxist prig, though, and the movie can't work up much of a charge for him, either. If he were really transformed, we'd feel that some dam in him had burst—that he was flooded with feeling. But in his physical embrace of Molina he's polite rather than passionate, and he never develops a real craving for the movie stories. And so Molina's legacy to him doesn't have the bittersweet ambiguity it should.

After Molina finishes telling the Nazi movie, he begins another story—this one about a shipwrecked man who lands on a tropical island, where a woman takes care of him (as Molina has been taking care of Valentín). This woman (also played by Braga) is caught in a spiderweb that grows out of her own body. Valentín visualizes her as the woman he still loves, but Molina, who always identifies with the heroine, thinks that he is this spider woman. And, of course, he is. Molina the entrancer, the spellbinder, has used his recollections of old movies to spin a web and draw Valentín into it. Valentín has drawn him into a web, too: they're both the spider woman. Alone, and suffering horribly from wounds inflicted by the police, Valentín at least knows the blessings of fantasy. Given morphine by an interne in the prison hospital, he's able to tell himself a movie story—he drifts back to the tropical island, where he's happy with the mysterious woman. Molina has restored him to his early dreams of a perfect love.

Somehow, this final tribute to the seductive, consoling power of movies doesn't click; its meaning doesn't register. I think this is because the picture has a conflicting impulse that's stronger. Babenco is reaching for something larger, something tragic and aggressively moral. The picture makes a show of its commitment to the highest human values. Puig's novel is saying that queens may be useless, silly window dressing, on the order of movie romances, but that can be lovely fun, can't it? It enhances life, makes it more rapturously giddy. Gay groups may consider this politically incorrect (right now, anyway), but it's what the book is about; Puig's plea for the indulgence of romance is much like that of Tennessee Williams, and the novel speaks to that part of us which wants more than is strictly essential—wants the delirium of excess. Babenco, in all his earnestness, is out to prove that silly old queens are useful, upstanding citizens, and he has steamrollered the romance and absurdity out of the material. His *Kiss of the Spider Woman* is a more exotic *Guess Who's Coming to Dinner*. And it pours on pathos. The last words that the infinitely kind and good Molina hears before the police throw his body on a pile of garbage in an empty lot are "You fucking fag." Old Hollywood never topped that.

■

A few months ago, an English critic, expressing the widespread English enthusiasm for *Dance with a Stranger*, which features Miranda Richardson as Ruth Ellis, the last woman in England to be sent to the gallows, wrote that it "cuts like a comet across the winter sky." The comet must have fizzled out over the Atlantic. What it looks like here is an assaultingly cramped and monotonous movie about obsessive love. Fatalistic in a Q.E.D. sort of way, *Dance with a Stranger* might be described as kitchen-sink film noir. The audience I saw it with applauded heartily when Ruth finally put a few slugs in her weakling young lover (Rupert Everett), the upper-class amateur racing-car driver she can't live with and can't live without. He regularly gets drunk and slaps her around, but the applause—as far as I could judge—wasn't because the audience felt particularly antagonistic toward him. It was thank-God-somebody-made-a-decision applause.

Set in London in 1954 and 1955, *Dance with a Stranger* seems to be saying that Ruth Ellis was a victim of the class system—a tormented masochist who never had a chance at a decent life. When we first meet her, she's working as the hostess-manager of a tiny Mayfair private club; she lives (with her small son) on the floor above, and just above her is the brothel that's attached to the night club. We are given to understand that Ruth has graduated from prostitution but still takes care of a few

29

customers—regulars—and accepts the devotion of a grubby businessman (played by Ian Holm in an odious little mustache) who's as obsessive about her as she is about her spoiled playboy. This is an *Of Human Bondage* triangle.

Working from a no-nonsense script by Shelagh Delaney, the director, Mike Newell, doesn't give you a minute's relief. He's obviously biting off a serious theme—he might be chewing on tinfoil. Ruth isn't allowed any charm or levity or hopefulness even at the start of her affair with the upper-class wastrel. Platinum blond, with cherry lips and mascaraed dead eyes under black brows, she has a tight, pale face, and her cosmetics are applied incredibly neatly—they look etched on. Ruth's manner is precise and quick and snippy, and her banter is sharp—it's on the bitter side. I guess we're supposed to find her independence sexually taunting; she's so hard-edged that you can certainly understand her drunken young lover's wanting to hit her. (Apparently, he's far from the first to beat up on her.)

Newell seems mortally afraid of light. He shoots in dim, smoky interiors, in a color range from olive drab to gray. The picture is all style—style used to pin the characters down in their environment, style used to show us the shabbiness of their lives and how everybody is trapped, doing what's inevitable. I think it's a hideously misconceived movie. When you combine kitchen-sink realism with all this film-noir design, you get a deterministic view of people that closes them off from the audience. They're denied any responsibility for what they do, and there's nothing for us to respond to in them. All that's left is the film's hardboiled chic.

Miranda Richardson's much admired performance took a lot of technique, and you see it all. She points up everything she says, in an actressy way. When her lover says, "I shan't have any peace until we're married," she whips out, "I've *never* had any peace," and it has the tone of cosmic accusation. (We're supposed to accept it as self-knowledge and truth, and maybe see her as a Sylvia Plath, a Zelda, a sexual woman being driven mad.) Ruth's voice gets more and more shrill and screechy as the movie goes on; this awful sound is deliberate, of course, like her loud laugh, but it makes you cower in your seat, because it's so obvious and overdone. Richardson acts as if every cell in her body were overstimulated; she can't stop acting, even when a viewer is begging her to, hoping for a glimpse of something besides all this white-knuckled control. In a few scenes, she's posed to recall Marilyn Monroe, but she has none of that wet-lipped, tarty looseness that suggests the appeal of the forbidden. In the one photograph I've seen of the actual Ruth Ellis, she has it, all right.

It's easy to see what attracted men: she's a girl who's out for a good time. Her eyes may be a little blank, but she has a whory, libidinous smile, and there's a sparkle and a poignancy about her. This film is trying so hard for an unsentimental look at England's cold hypocrisy about class and sex that it leaves out the fun a good-time girl chases after. It's like a High Anglican *I Want to Live!*

August 26, 1985

THE GREAT WHITE HOPE

||||||||||||||||||||||||||||||||||||||||||||||||||||||||||||||||||||||||||||||||||||||||||||||||||||||||||||||||||||||||||||||||||||||||||||

Stan White (Mickey Rourke), who served in Vietnam at least as heroically as Rambo and has more decorations for bravery than any other cop in the history of the New York City Police Department, is the demigod of the new Michael Cimino picture, *Year of the Dragon*. A police captain from Brooklyn who calls himself a proud Polack (though he shortened his unwieldy last name), Stan is assigned to put a damper on the murderous youth gangs who are disrupting the placid surface of life in Chinatown and hurting tourism. He's told to leave the businessmen alone. But he knows that the traditional calm was corruption with a lid on it—that the city officials have been accepting bribes and looking the other way for years while the entrenched businessmen of the major crime families, the Chinese Triads (a criminal organization that predates even the Mafia), imported heroin and controlled gambling, prostitution, and extortion rackets. Stan White can't live with compromise any more than saintly Dirty Harry Callahan could. This may be the Chinatown precinct of New York City, but his conception of himself is clear: "There's a new marshal in town—me." And he doesn't have to conquer his own indecisiveness, the way Kris Kristofferson's marshal-hero did in Cimino's last picture, *Heaven's Gate*. He immediately starts to create chaos in the community and make enough fuss to get media attention so that he can—in some unexplained way—tear out the roots of crime. In the thinking of Oliver Stone and Cimino, who collaborated on the script, this can somehow be accomplished by crude insults and by locking up hookers,

31

pushers, and small-time racketeers. And they must have thought it would help if Mickey Rourke played his Rambo–Dirty Harry synthesis with stubble on his sweaty face, a bloody bruise on the bridge of his nose, and what the young Los Angeles critic Elvis Mitchell called "mood hair"—it keeps shifting tones from prematurely white to prematurely gray.

Trying to embody the macho mystique that's necessary for the role of the passionate, cursing saint Stan White, Mickey Rourke, who has a purring-pussycat voice and a shy, baby-face smile, pushes himself hard. He shouts and fulminates; he tries to act crazy and exciting. He takes over the tricks of the actors in thirties cops-and-robbers movies, where gimmicks such as the cops wearing their hats down low, just over their eyes, worked as colorful bits of characterization. But when Rourke tries them he's like a kid in adults' clothes and mannerisms. It's as if he didn't believe in himself as Stan: he's game, but he has no gift for playing a fanatic bully, and he has a lost, defeated quality. The performance never really works, except maybe in the scenes at Stan's wife's funeral, where Rourke can forget about the romanticized potency he's supposed to have. I don't know if any actor could fill up the role, because Stan White, who is supposed to be accepted as the hero the minute he appears, has no core—he's all blowhard pose. He's Cimino's dream of the grungy splendor of a nakedly honest tough guy. And when Stan's superior officer accuses him of having "delusions of grandeur" it's clear that he's standing in for Cimino. De Niro's compulsive, perfectionist hero stood in for him in *The Deer Hunter*—he was even called Michael—but De Niro didn't have to carry the load of anger and resentment that Stan White carries. On some obscure principle, Stan is rude to *everybody*.

When the Chinese Mafia bigwigs put pressure on the politicians because Stan is interfering with business, and he's ordered to lay off, he flatly refuses. According to Stan, "If I give up, the system gives up." He says that "this is Vietnam all over again"—that "nobody wants to win." Stan White is continuing the Vietnam War in Chinatown; the issues are simple—it's a war between good and evil. Stone and Cimino don't bother their heads with distinctions among Asian peoples or their beliefs. To hear Stan White tell it, New York's Chinatown is the hub of international evil. And he's the one man tough enough to fight it. When his superior officers inform him that he has been reassigned (he's to go back to Brooklyn), and one of them explains the transfer by saying, "You care too much, Stanley," it's unmistakable that this raw extravaganza is shaped as a vindication of Cimino the misunderstood artist. "How can anybody care too much?" Stan asks wonderingly. He's musing. Cimino wants us to ponder the question of how it is that a man as honest and dedicated as Stan is (and as Cimino is) goes among us unappreciated. *Year of the Dragon* has a galloping case of movie-director megalomania. A key passage in the movie is Stan's inspirational talk to the officers under him when he enunciates his credo. "I give a shit," he says, "and I'm going to make you people give a shit." (We in the audience are the "people" Stan is addressing.) When his men, who are being sent out on raids, express their concern about violations of civil rights, he has a ready answer: "Fuck their civil rights."

The picture isn't voluptuous, like *The Deer Hunter*, or eerily dissociated, like *Heaven's Gate*. It's hysterical, rabble-rousing pulp, the kind that generally goes over with subliterate audiences—people who can be suckered into believing that the movie is giving them the lowdown dirty truth about power. Yet it isn't involving. It doesn't have the crude propulsion of good pulp storytelling, and although it's full of catastrophic acting—especially by the grating-voiced Ariane, a model, of Dutch and Japanese parentage, who plays Tracy Tzu, the TV-newscaster heroine, and is officious and nostrilly, like an Oriental Ali MacGraw—it's directed too listlessly to be enjoyably bad. When Cimino can't think of any way to cram in more beatings or shootings—when he just has two or three people in a room—he sets them to arguing. To cover the void, he has them raise their voices, and their hollering at each other is so obnoxious that when they die gruesomely you don't care. The picture seems to be going on without you, anyway. Tracy is subjected to a gang-bang rape, just as the heroine of *Heaven's Gate* was. And when she and Stan meet for dinner at the Shanghai Palace Restaurant and a pair of masked gunmen break in and start mowing the guests down, the scene is like a replay of the disco-restaurant carnage in De Palma's *Scarface* (which was also written by Oliver Stone). In some ways, the movie is like an extension of what goes wrong in *Scarface*. It's sunk in torpor.

Parts of Chinatown's Mott Street—storefronts with pagodas and lanterns, plenty of neon, and blood-red façades—were re-created in Dino De Laurentiis' new studios in Wilmington, North Carolina. There's at least one marvellous, atmospheric set—a basement soybean factory with walls so wet it's like a series of mist-filled caves in a mountain. And the film has its full quota of parades with banners and fireworks and a huge paper dragon, and funeral processions with a marching band. It has a heroin transaction in the Golden Triangle; it has a severed head. It even has a shoot-out on a railway bridge (with the built-in irony that the Chinese were brought to this country as coolies to lay track). But viewers are distanced from what they're looking at by one of the tawdriest and stupidest scripts that can ever have been put into production as a major film. The script is loosely derived from a novel by Robert Daley, but its mixture of maladroitness, sleaze, and ignorance might have been devised by some little (white) schoolboys on a very hot day. It suggests a twelve-year-old's idea of hipsterism. The characters share a flat, stunted vocabulary—about twenty-five words, most of them the basic four-letter expletives. And the plot devices have some of the canned, echo-chamber effect that the later scenes in *Scarface* had. Tracy isn't just a celebrity newscaster who lives in a lavish Manhattan loft with a magisterial view (one that you actually have to go to Brooklyn for), she's also an "aristocrat"—her family has moola. Stan forces himself on her, in a hostile, roughneck way (she seems to represent the Vietnamese to him, plus people who have had it too easy), and, as in so many he-man fantasies enshrined in the movies, his aggression makes her fall in love with him. Later, when she's raped (by three of the Chinese youth-gang thugs), Stan flails his arms to show he's upset by this latest villainy instigated by the criminal kingpin. Corpses have been strewn all over the screen, Stan's own wife has had her throat slit, but after the rape he announces, "He went too far this time."

The only performance that has any true intensity is the quiet one given by John Lone (the star of last year's *Iceman*) as the power-grabbing, ruthless Joey Tai, the sneaky new, young Godfather. Joey Tai is written as the treacherous, unfeeling Oriental—he's Cimino's Heart of Darkness and Yellow Peril, too—but Lone, fine-drawn and elegant, just about turns the movie upside down. He's sleek, like Nils Asther as the sexy Chinese warlord in Frank Capra's *The Bitter Tea of General Yen*. And his stoic, malevolent Joey Tai is the only character who seems to have any brains or any emotional life: you feel his seething hatred of the boorish Stan White. Lone has such a strong, graceful presence that he survives even the crummy dialogue he has to deliver. He cuts off Tracy's line of questioning about the Chinese Mafia's involvement in the heroin trade with these words: "Why do you media people insist on emphasizing this sinister Charlie Chan image? Why don't you talk about the chair in Chinese history our association has endowed at Yale University, our twelve-million-dollar loan fund for our ten thousand members, our free meals for the aged and unemployed, free burial, things like that—positive things?" You'd think that someone on the set would have pointed out to Cimino that Charlie Chan wasn't sinister; he was a wise, roly-poly daddy-o. (Oliver Stone and/or Cimino must have got him confused with Fu Manchu.) And, howl-

34

ers apart, this is miserable verbiage; it has no eloquence, no respect for phrasing—it's an insult to a daring actor. Another character delivers that old hoot about how the Chinese had a civilization—and a shipping trade— a thousand years ago, when you uncouth white men were living in caves. (This speech—or variants of it—was a staple of the Charlie Chan pictures, and Boris Karloff's Fu Manchu may have lisped it out in 1932 while folding his arms and tucking his long fingernails into his embroidered satin sleeves.)

Year of the Dragon isn't much more xenophobic than *The Deer Hunter* was, but it's a lot flabbier; the scenes have no tautness, no definition, and so you're more likely to be conscious of the bigotry. And as a sexist Cimino is incredibly inept. He can't even think up a plot subterfuge for the nude footage of Ariane he includes, and it's so "artistic" you want to laugh. In terms of any kind of controlling moral intelligence, Oliver Stone and Michael Cimino are still living in a cave. Stone, whose credibility as a writer is based on his having taken an Academy Award (for *Midnight Express!*), and Cimino, whose first movie credit was for the script that John Milius and he wrote for *Magnum Force*, the seamiest of the Dirty Harry movies, are evenly matched. *Year of the Dragon* suffers from a form of redundancy. One brazen vulgarian working on a movie might enliven it, but two—and both xenophobic—bring out the worst in each other. They're bouncing their ideas off a mirror, so neither one knows when he has become a public embarrassment.

The torpor goes deeper than the stupidity of the script. In a sense, the Chinese don't come off worse than the Caucasians, and the women don't come off worse than the men. (The men in the Police Department roll over for the incorruptible Stan White the same way his wife and Tracy do.) As I see it, Michael Cimino doesn't think in terms of dramatic values: he doesn't know how to develop characters, or how to get any interaction among them. He transposes an art-school student's approach from paintings to movies, and makes visual choices: this is a New York movie, so he wants a lot of blue and harsh light and a realistic surface. He works completely derivatively, from earlier movies, and his only idea of how to dramatize things is to churn up this surface and get it roiling. The whole thing is just material for Cimino the visual artist to impose his personality on. He doesn't actually dramatize himself—it isn't as if he tore his psyche apart and animated the pieces of it (the way a Griffith or a Peckinpah did). He doesn't animate anything. That's why, despite all the action, the movie seems so apathetic. If he "cares too much," it's not about how to tell a story by images—it's about his own "creativity." He's aiming for a lurid high art. He's trying to arrange the roiling so it's

35

just right: he drags in big ideas like Vietnam for depth and tone; he uses cruel, villainous Asians to inflame emotions and a naked girl for a turn-on; and he works to make it all appear impassioned. He gets an imitation of movie realism and an imitation of passion. Members of the audience can be hoodwinked because what they see has so many associations with the powerful images and themes that have moved them in the past. But Cimino doesn't really draw the audience into the movie, except in the way this fantasist makes himself—the artist-hero—the issue. In *Year of the Dragon*, Stan White–Michael Cimino tries to impose his masculine will on everybody. Cimino demands to be taken seriously; he double-dares you not to take him seriously. The only thing that's clear at the end of the movie is how Cimino wants to be taken—as bloody proud, as possessed and smoking hot.

■

In a movie era like this one, you become grateful for small pleasures, such as the fresh dialogue rhythms in *Compromising Positions*. The screenplay, adapted by Susan Isaacs from her likably crafted 1978 detective novel, set on Long Island, provides a batch of actresses with a chance to show some comic verve. Susan Sarandon's smile has never been more incredibly lush, and she does some inspired double takes—just letting her beautiful dark eyes pop. She's the heroine, whose unquenchable curiosity saves her from the doldrums of affluence in the suburbs with a good-provider lawyer husband, played by Edward Herrmann (who has become the closest thing the movies have to a walking doldrum). When her lecherous dentist (Joe Mantegna) is murdered in his snazzy office, she can't resist poking into the case, because it reveals so much about what has been going on around her which she has been unaware of. She's an innocent, deeply conventional woman who loves being rudely awakened.

Her best friend and opposite number—a frisky cynic who seems to have been wised up from birth—is played for a slightly brassy sanity by the bright-blue-eyed Judith Ivey. The screen hasn't done her justice before: being allowed to show some experience of men does wonders for her. (Using a Texas twang helps, too.) Deborah Rush is startlingly poignant as the sad little horror that the dentist's fat, bald brother-in-law is married to; this tarty, uneducated blonde, with scars on her tummy, frightened eyes, and several tics, suggests a lifetime of trying to please men, of being pawed and bawled out. Mary Beth Hurt, in a boyish haircut, is oddly piquant as the woman who lives across the street from the heroine. Anne De Salvo, who manages to be consistently good, no matter what the part, is the fishy-eyed widow, whose uppity, tragic demeanor suggests a Long Island Jewish princess and Lady Macbeth in full regal mourning, at the same time. They're quite a crew, and Raul Julia shows another side as the male romantic lead, the Hispanic police lieutenant from Homicide who's investigating the murder. The lieutenant isn't really sure of himself; he seems capable of disappointment, and this makes him appealing, almost plaintive in the early, better-written scenes. (When he becomes enamored of the heroine and their dark eyes bulge at each other, you may worry that if they got together they'd produce pollywogs.)

The director, Frank Perry, does some good work modulating the performances. Most of the film's weaknesses, such as his rushing over the solution of the crime—so that we barely get a chance to sort out who actually did it—are minor. And there are quibbles one could raise that are really compliments: I wanted more of Joe Mantegna's smiley-eyed lecher, and was rather hoping for a flashback or two. (His liquid dark eyes are photographed very amusingly. I don't know why there's so much emphasis on dark eyes, though; Judith Ivey may be the only blue-eyed member of the cast.) Visually, this fairly pleasant, light entertainment has an eccentricity: in scene after scene in the various characters' homes, the camera is angled upward and the ceilings are used to give the compositions geometric lines and patterns. This isn't offensive, but it's a little distracting; I don't think I've ever seen so many shots of actors framed against ceilings. The movie has just one real mistake, but it's a whopper. After all those years of the Pandora legend, it's fun to have a movie about a woman whose curiosity is her salvation. And Sarandon's spontaneous, impetuous fixation on the murder is charmingly irrational: we can feel that something is bubbling up from way down inside her. But, in guiding Susan Isaacs on the adaptation, Frank Perry has tried to give the film a serious theme: the heroine's need to prove that she's something besides a wife and mother, her need to find meaning in her life. And so poor Ed Herrmann, who starts out as a lively, friendly fellow, is turned into an oppressor, telling his wife that he needs peace at home, and that her days as an investigative reporter (which, she has reminded him, she used to be) are over. Their scenes together become a series of domestic squalls. When Sarandon has to assert her personhood and Herrmann has to bend with the times, the movie is depressingly off base. These squalls kill the finish, because after you've been watching this woman, who has been a delight with everyone except her stick of a husband, you don't want her to be left with him while he tries to change. That's not a happy prospect; it's grisly.

September 9, 1985

AIRHEAD'S DELIGHT

|||||||||||||||||||||||||||||||||||||||||||||||||||||||||||||||||||||||||||||||||||||||||||||||||||||||||||||||||||||||||||||||||||||||||||||||||||||||||||||||||||||||

Martin Scorsese directed *After Hours* confidently, with a knowing air, as if he were making a hip and witty movie. His laughter is built right into the film's tone, and in the early scenes I felt eager to laugh along with him. The crack timing of the titles put me in an expectant frame of mind, and it was a relief to see that Scorsese is no longer using the frozen setups of his last picture, *The King of Comedy*. His work here is livelier and more companionable than it has been in recent years; the camera scoots around, making jokes—or, at least, near-jokes. But the movie keeps telling you to laugh, even though these near-jokes are about all you get. Soon it becomes clear that the episodes aren't going anywhere—that what you're seeing is a random series of events in a picture that just aspires to be an entertaining trifle and doesn't make it. It sags.

Joseph Minion wrote the script as an assignment when he was a graduate student in the Columbia University Film School, and it's a film student's knickknack, reminiscent of the experimental short films made by avant-gardists in the twenties. The central character is Paul (Griffin Dunne), a young word-processor operator in midtown New York, who goes down to SoHo for a date and finds himself trapped in a nightmare world. He loses his money and his shirt and is buffeted about in a pouring rain, contending with one flaky, threatening woman after another and being betrayed by each person he trusts. It's a paranoid fantasy, but of a skittish variety. The episodes don't have any particular ties to what's going on in Paul's life or his psyche; they're devised strictly to extend the movie. In the opening scene, Paul is instructing an office worker, played by Bronson Pinchot, in the use of a word processor, and while

Pinchot speaks of what he'd rather be doing Paul's eyes wander around the vast office. Seizing the opportunity for a little jokey camera movement here, the jittery Scorsese puts us on the wrong track—we're led to think that Paul has other things on his mind. If he does, we never find out what they are. And if all the emotionally hungry bohemian women who surround him—Rosanna Arquette, Linda Fiorentino, Teri Garr, Catherine O'Hara, Verna Bloom—represent anything more than a twenty-six-year-old screenwriter's sexual fears we're not briefed on it. *After Hours* is an external film on an internal subject, and though there are recurrent motifs—keys, burns, death's-head emblems, Paul's lost twenty-dollar bill, allusions to *The Wizard of Oz*—they don't come together. They're just free-floating trimmings.

The small, dark Griffin Dunne is onscreen almost all the time. Anxious and exhausted, he keeps looking in the mirrors of freaky women's bathrooms, brushing his hair back with both hands. Is Paul meant to be the norm, an Everyman bewildered by the treacherous, demanding occupants of this SoHo Oz? I guess so—we see everything through his eyes. But the writer hasn't come up with ways for Paul to discover more about himself and become more inventive; he just rushes around in a panic. So Dunne (who was wryly amusing as the hero's werewolf chum in *An American Werewolf in London*) has nothing to work with but whatever charm and ingenuity he can summon up. He becomes repetitive very fast. Whirling about impishly, he may remind you now and then of Dudley Moore, but it's Dudley Moore without his resourcefulness, and without the special quality that's linked to it—the feeling you get that the child is still alive inside the man. As Paul, Dunne makes you think he's got a gopher inside him.

Most of the performers in smaller parts come off much better. As a cocktail waitress with a blond beehive, who does sketches of her sixties idols, Teri Garr has a glittering eccentricity; she plays this kind of role better than anyone else ever has—she makes the waitress's nuthead scariness pretty damn scary. In her apartment, this woman has a top shelf covered with cans of hair spray: she must be hoarding them for the post-nuclear age. (Too bad Scorsese doesn't give the joke a bit of a spin by having Paul spot them.) The tall, low-voiced Linda Fiorentino—a relative newcomer to films—is enjoyable as a lusty sculptor who works in papier-mâché. (Dunne's most convincing scene is the one where his conversation puts her to sleep.) As for Rosanna Arquette, who plays Paul's date: at movie after movie I've been waiting for her to reveal more of the zonked sensual mystery she had in the TV film *The Executioner's*

39

Song. This picture—in which she plays a girl who keeps switching gears and changing her mind—doesn't offer her much of a chance. Still, she acts like somebody in a high-school play. In the cafeteria scene where she meets Paul, he's reading *Tropic of Cancer* and she introduces herself by reciting a passage in a quaint rush of words. (What is she doing? What does Scorsese think she's doing?) It's no compliment to her to say that she may be perfect for the picture. The standout performance is given by John Heard, who plays a bartender. He fills the role, and then some; he gives the movie its only rooted moments. His scene behind the bar— he answers the phone and is told that the girl he loves has just killed herself—takes the movie to a different plane. When he's onscreen, it's possible to envision what the picture might have been like if Heard had played the normal man Paul. Something might have seemed to be at stake. (The slender material might have played best with a young Bob Newhart type—a decent but completely unimaginative fellow, the kind who gets a joke too late.)

After Hours has obvious similarities to that other SoHo screwball fantasy, Susan Seidelman's *Desperately Seeking Susan* (which was actually shot several months later). Scorsese's movie isn't in the ditsy sentimental-romantic mode, though; he's too savvy for that. This isn't necessarily an advantage: audiences may get more to respond to from Seidelman's think-pink fairy tale of life among the punks than from Scorsese's cooler, more controlled approach. (And her picture isn't motiveless, like this one.) What's surprising about *After Hours* is that, given the opportunity to show downtown funkiness from the inside, and to show us how the square Paul recoils, Scorsese adopts the square point of view. (The artists are all crackpots.) Scorsese doesn't identify with the downtown existence; he doesn't satirize it with any strong feelings, either. It's nothing he cares about. We don't get any impression of SoHo life in this movie: the streets are bare, the cafeteria is empty, and the subway station Paul goes into is deserted. The picture was shot on city locations, and Scorsese catches architectural details and the thickly layered paint on a fire escape, but it's a vacant-looking city, with everything primed for the camera.

Since there's nothing in the script to express, the cinematography, by the gifted Michael Ballhaus, isn't expressive. It's elegant, crisp, and flashy. Scorsese has made a classroom exercise, with perky zooms and cute little dissolves. The scene of Linda Fiorentino tossing her keys down to Paul, so he can enter her building, is shot so that we get the visual sensation of the keys coming right smack at our faces—the sensation

40

Paul gets. It's almost like 3-D, and it's certainly a speedball effect. Its only purpose is to give us a little visual zinger in a movie where, after a while, that's all we can hope for.

Produced independently by Dunne, Amy Robinson, and Robert F. Colesberry, with a bank loan arranged on the basis of a pickup and release by the Geffen Company and Warner Brothers, *After Hours* is a low-budget film (about four million dollars), but it's as airheaded as the current Hollywood package jobs, and almost as impersonal. Some of Scorsese's camera tricks and teases are like a master professor's gags, and there are also his recognizable characteristics: his short attention span, and the way he gets a sudden fix on something and the camera bears down on it but you don't know why and neither does the character who's doing the looking. Scorsese slips in a few self-referential bits: at one point, Rosanna Arquette says something that sounds like a reprise of a line Sandra Bernhard delivered in *The King of Comedy*; and the director who had the sociopath of *Taxi Driver* wearing a Mohawk haircut for a ritual killing now has Paul trying to keep his head from being shaved when he goes into a club on Mohawk Night. (It's such a mild joke it verges on self-parody.) Scorsese slips himself in, too: he's in the club, whipping around a big spotlight. But he's using his skills (and even his personality) like a hired hand, making a vacuous, polished piece of consumer goods—all surface. This flyspeck of a movie represents a new kind of precious, craftsmanlike emptiness. It's a technique-conscious movie that may seem sparkling and wondrous to technique-crazy moviegoers.

September 23, 1985

DEAD ON ARRIVAL

||||||||||||||||||||||||||||||||||||||||||||||||||||||||||||||||||||||||||||||||||||||||||||||||||||||||||||||||||||||||||||||||||||||||||

*P*lenty, David Hare's sick-soul-of-England play, which he adapted for the screen and Fred Schepisi directed, features an all-inclusive malaise: hypocrisy, purposelessness, emotional atrophy. Meryl Streep's Susan Traherne lives as aimless an existence as Jeanne Moreau did back in Antonioni's *La Notte*, but she's a whole lot more vocal about it. In the

41

Second World War, Susan, who is still in her teens, serves heroically as a British courier for the French Resistance, but her youthful idealism about the future is shattered by the ignoble decline of Britain, and within a few years she's speaking her mind and blistering just about everyone she comes in contact with. David Hare had a bright (sneaky) idea when he wrote this play: he uses Susan Traherne to voice his own judgments of what has gone rancid in England since the war. That is, he has turned his own preachiness into the courage and intellectual clarity of an abrasive woman. Disillusioned with England's materialistic values, Susan Traherne doesn't lie to herself, and she can't keep what she thinks to herself, either. She's always telling people off, and her outspokenness turns her into a scourge, and eventually into a basket case. The social changes from the mid-forties into the sixties, and especially the shock of the messy Suez crisis, are reflected in her life story. She lands in one dead-end job after another, but it's the postwar boom and each one is better-paying; she asks a Cockney hipster (Sting) to impregnate her but can't conceive, cracks up, and then marries a stuffy, self-effacing diplomat (Charles Dance), who takes care of her in exchange for her wrecking his career and making his life hell. The only way he can find a little peace is by keeping her doped up. We're given to understand that there's no place in the society for her ruthless, embittered honesty; her mind will have to be dulled, she will have to be treated as an invalid or, worse, a lunatic.

Hare asks us to swallow rather too much. It's impossible to believe that Susan's astringent nastiness and the scenes she makes in front of her husband's associates and guests are directly connected with the dismantling of the Empire and the frustration of her hopes of changing the world. Leaving aside the young Susan's naïveté about the splendid, high-principled future, there's a peculiarity in the grownup Susan's view of the moral ugliness around her: she reacts as if she personally were being betrayed, and as if she alone, in her natural superiority, spoke for the honorable way to formulate public policy. As Hare lays it out, Susan never does a single useful thing after the war, and she isn't politically active or even cogent. All she does is exercise her gift for cultured, sardonic invective. During the film, I kept asking myself why it was that Jimmy Porter's raging outbursts in John Osborne's *Look Back in Anger* carried the day and hers don't. Jimmy Porter was no more effective in action than Susan Traherne, and he was almost as self-destructive. Yet there was gumption and grandeur in his rant; he just let the wild words rip. His excessiveness fed on itself and drove him on to greater excesses, and the sheer tumult of his emotions stirred the audience, made us feel

42

as if Osborne had given us an infusion of his own blood. Osborne gives over; Hare withholds, and Susan's rant has a horrible, self-righteous precision. If we enjoy her speeches, it's for their snide wit. I think that David Hare misunderstands his own theatrical gift, which is for devastating, rude putdowns, for whiplash lines and irascible exchanges, not (as he appears to believe) for inspiring audiences to revolutionary action. Hare's means in this movie are every bit as constricted as what he's attacking. Angry Young Manhood has become mannerism.

Schepisi and his fellow-Australians—the cinematographer Ian Baker and the composer Bruce Smeaton—have worked together on all his pictures, and they give *Plenty* a lustrous, sensuous texture. The locales— a French town during the Occupation; the handsomely appointed British Embassy amid the devastation of Brussels; the drizzly London streets, the docks and embankments; the British Ambassador's residence, with its archways, in the Jordanian desert—are full of unexpected bonuses. With the help of the justly celebrated production designer Richard MacDonald, Schepisi and his team have made a film that, shot by shot, is distinctively smooth and burnished. Their superb craftsmanship and their small shafts of humor held me, but it takes more than that to win one's emotional assent. Possibly Hare and maybe Schepisi, too, would say that they don't want that kind of assent, that they're trying to reach a thinking audience. Certainly the film's time-jumping transitions seem designed to keep you alert. The action moves forward in an abrupt, jagged way, without providing easy signposts, and, yes, this does keep you alert, but you're distracted from what's going on by niggling questions about how much time has elapsed and where, exactly, Susan has got herself to. The we-won't-help-you editing technique is willfully highbrow—a small aesthetic sin of pride. (The audience has to look to Meryl Streep's ever-changing hairstyles for basic information.)

The role of the martyred independent-minded woman is bound to magnetize actresses, but Hare's putting his denunciation of the stultifying affluent society into Susan's mouth and having her go over the edge from the strain of carrying around so much truth is a *bad* bright idea. The center of the material is nothing but showoffy verbiage—Susan Traherne is a walking harangue. An actress with a vivid presence might give the role something of her own substance—as Vanessa Redgrave does in Hare's *Wetherby* (reviewed below)—but Meryl Streep isn't that kind of actress. She's strictly an interpreter, and her interpretive skills don't help her here. I can't point to any scenes where she falters, except in the opening and closing moments, in which she's the teen-age Susan. In the first, she seems coated with makeup, as if youth were a matter of a perfect wax job, and she overdoes her openmouthed fear; she's brittle and eccentric. In the last (a flashback), she's fake naïve, and the material defeats her: it reëmphasizes the irony of Susan's blasted hopes which we've already gnawed on for two hours. For the rest, she's proficient, yet vocally bland and totally lacking in the neurotic strength that might lend the role a semblance of believability. As she plays the part, there's no imploded energy in Susan's rudeness and no force in the film. She just isn't there.

John Gielgud gives the film's jazziest performance. As a dignified, arrogant senior official at the Foreign Office, who lives by the rules he was trained in and quits at the time of Suez because he is lied to by his superiors, Gielgud delights the audience with the sporty perfection of his craft. He can make you laugh by an almost imperceptible straightening of his head and neck; his calibrations must be the teeniest any clown has ever mastered. There was an audible happy stir each time he appeared. (When he makes an exit speech, you pity the actors who are left behind, because the energy goes with him.) Tracey Ullman, the broad-faced young pop singer and comedienne, who plays Alice, Susan's roommate, is cheery and dimpled in her first scenes, and she generates happy feelings, too. Since Alice is working-class, Hare allows her to be good-hearted and spontaneous; during the forties she dresses and acts like a premature hippie, and she's independent without having to be sterile and fragile and distraught. I think it's almost inevitable that moviegoers will ask themselves why the picture couldn't be about likable, rowdy Alice rather than about the fine-boned Susan. But, of course, it's obvious that Hare isn't out to entertain us with lively characters, and as the film progresses Alice is relegated to the post of Susan's lifelong confidante and comes on mostly to cluck over Susan's troubles. Among the men who figure in Susan's life, Sam Neill, as the Resistance fighter with whom she has a couple of brief sexual flings (they grapple fully clothed, like Moreau and Mastroianni in *La Notte*), underplays agreeably—particularly in his sheepishness at the end. Schepisi varies the men's performances skillfully, with one exception: Susan's verbal duel with her husband's boss—the head of personnel at the Foreign Office, played by Ian McKellen—is shot close in on his face, as if to make us register that every pore is cruel and malicious. He's a hypnotic caricature of frostbitten bureaucratic villainy. The scene is an extreme version of what's wrong with the whole picture: everything is too explicit and ultimately too conventional in its nostalgia for England's "finest hour" and the old-fashioned moral principles.

Plenty seems meant to be the cinema of ideas, but it's the cinema

44

of stale ideas. Dumping on England has become the tradition of quality there. A couple of decades after Joseph Losey, working with scripts by Harold Pinter, made his spiritual-wasteland pictures (*The Servant, Accident, The Go-Between*), and John Schlesinger and Frederic Raphael chimed in with *Darling*, the Brits are at it again, with *Dance with a Stranger* and the David Hare double-header, *Plenty* and *Wetherby*. They keep flogging themselves for being repressed, as if they'd get over it that way—and as if emotional ventilation were necessarily the key to spiritual health. (Seeing through your stale ideas might do more for you.) Hare's exercises in flagellation are infinitely knowing about how uptight his countrymen are and how hopeless it all is. If Hare had written *E.T.*, the little goblin playmate would arrive on Earth and be dead.

According to Hare, *Plenty* is "a film about the cost of spending your whole life in dissent. When you disagree with the way that the society you live in is run, then you pay a very high price for detaching yourself from that society. And Susan is prepared to pay that high price." But that's not what the film is about. Susan isn't prepared to pay anything; she doesn't make choices—she's driven. And she isn't a dissenter in any recognizable sense. She's the mouthpiece of an upper-crust leftist playwright expressing his contempt for his class as if that were a revolutionary act. Hare has nothing to offer us except the condemnation of materialism and duplicity which we've heard over and over for decades. He doesn't actually believe in a revolutionary course of action for England; if he did, Susan—or somebody else in the movie—would be out working for that goal. The big difference between Susan Traherne and David Hare is that she's being given dope to shut her up and he's been honored and encouraged for his overarticulate, preening despair. That may tell us something more about Anglo-American culture than he gets at in this movie.

■

Without Vanessa Redgrave, Hare's *Wetherby*, which he wrote for the screen and also directed, is just about inconceivable. As Jean, a secondary-school English teacher in the Yorkshire village of Wetherby, she's that cliché the spinster teacher who never married because her lover was killed. (I think I heard variants of that story about every attractive unmarried woman teacher I ever had.) In Jean's case, her lover went off in the R.A.F. thirty years ago and was murdered in Malaya.

After that loss, Jean became fearful of emotional involvement—fearful of experiencing pain. As Redgrave plays the role, Jean has so much ease and command that her shy, solitary quality—her repression—is the underside of her character. Jean is good-humored by nature, but has a simplicity and a stillness about her. Popular with her students, she strides into the classroom, happy to be there, keyed up for the give-and-take. She's radiant: there's nothing she'd rather be doing. And, as the movie comes across, it's her radiance, with the loneliness piercing through—her tragic ambience—that makes her a target. (The other characters in the movie don't give off light or warmth; they have nothing to be destroyed.) John Morgan (Tim McInnerny), the university graduate student who shatters Jean's precarious calm, suggests an updating of the gorilla-suited David Warner character who won Vanessa Redgrave in the 1966 *Morgan!* He is a stranger who comes, apparently, to shake the people of Wetherby out of their complacency; he has the same function that Susan Traherne has in *Plenty*, but he's not onscreen for as long. Morgan's dead eyes are tucked under the overhang of his forehead; he's sallow and cadaverous. When he looks at Redgrave—at her lavender-blue eyes, her light, bright hair, her blooming, ever-changing skin tones—she must seem to him as colorful as an English garden. (There has never been a more colorful major screen actress. Garbo we saw only in black-and-white, and the actresses of the color era, such as Jane Fonda, Diane Keaton, and Debra Winger, don't have Redgrave's heroic physical dimensions. As canvases, they can't match her. Even when Hare subjects her to ravaging closeups, she's still a work of art.)

The movie, with its trumped-up enigma—why does John Morgan crash a dinner party at Jean's house, and why does he blow out his brains the next day right in front of her, in her kitchen?—seems meant to have some sort of universal resonance. The question being asked is: Who is to blame? Morgan the zombie and another student, Karen (Suzanna Hamilton), who turns up on Jean's doorstep after Morgan's funeral, moves into her cottage, and gives off spooky vibes, represent Dispirited Youth—a generation whose souls are bombed out. And Hare can't resist scene after scene showing us the spiritual desiccation of the members of Jean's generation. Her friends, who come in pairs, snipe at their mates, don't even try to communicate with the sullen, graceless young, and are disgruntled in a way that's familiar from earlier tradition-of-quality films. Jean says that a librarian (Judi Dench) is her best friend, but it's actually the librarian's husband that she's close to. He's a solicitor (played, inevitably, by Ian Holm), and he sums up the frigid misery of the middle-class English and their inability to express emotion when he says to Jean, "If you're frightened of loneliness, never get married." The police inspector (Stuart Wilson) who comes to investigate the suicide is gloomy and depressed, especially after his silent young girlfriend leaves him. The whole atmosphere exudes defeat. Hare is out to show a society where nobody connects with anybody—a national nervous breakdown.

Wetherby does have the advantage of having been conceived for the screen. The puzzle structure that Hare devised and all the interlocking flashbacks he toys with are ingeniously worked out. If you look for any depth in the why-did-Morgan-do-it detective story, you won't find it, but the movie sustains an atmosphere of mystery gamesmanship. This is the first movie that Hare has directed, but he's an experienced director in the theatre and in television, and he's assured enough to use a fragmented narrative. He assembles slices of the present, of the recent past (just before Morgan appeared at the dinner party), of events during the party, and of the distant past (Jean's love affair, in the fifties). Hare plays with the possibilities of the film medium, using forced associations: for example, he cuts from Jean's seeing Morgan kill himself to her memory of having sex with her lover thirty years ago. (The young Jean is played by Redgrave's tall, blue-eyed daughter, Joely Richardson, whose soft, natural manner matches up well with Redgrave's performance. The young Jean's gentle, tentative voice rhythms fit the sound of the later Jean in a way that would seem uncanny if the two actresses were not related.) Hare's fractured assemblage gives us some very chic psychological connections. There's a danger in this kind of editing: it can make the moviegoer overconscious of the mechanical nature of the medium. But Hare's material is essentially so shallow that it can only gain from trickery. When he gets to the nugget—the supposed revelation of what provoked Morgan's action—it's so paltry that moviegoers might mutter "Cheat!" if it weren't for all the psychological heightening and gimcrackery that carry them past it.

The only real mystery is the starshine that Vanessa Redgrave gives off. Probably Hare meant Jean to be nothing more than an emotionally stifled, ineffective woman of good will, less damaged than her friends yet just another paralyzed member of her generation. As a teacher, she has only feeble answers to the key questions her students ask. But Redgrave, through her own artistry, irradiates Jean, and saves the movie from being a totally arid puzzle. Here, too, quick bouts of fully clothed sex are central to the story. Hare must be telling us something about love in our time. I have a strong feeling we've heard it before.

October 7, 1985

HEROINES

||||||||||||||||||||||||||||||||||||||||||||||||||||||||||||||||||||||||||||||||||||||||||||||||||||||||||||||||||||||||||||||||||||||||||||||||

In *Sweet Dreams*, Jessica Lange plays the pop-and-country singer Patsy Cline with a raw physicality that's challenging and heroic. "Patsy didn't hold anything back," Lange has been quoted as saying. "Patsy had a way of hitting life head-on." That's exactly how Lange plays her. It took courage for Lange to abandon her blond silkiness and appear as a raw, small-town Southern girl with bushy dark hair who dresses in outfits that her mother makes for her. (Patsy's mother seems to have cornered the market in shrill-blue fabrics.) And it took intelligence not to tone up the story with genteel movie-star conceits. Lange's interpretation of Patsy Cline's character is based on the best possible source—her singing—and she creates a hot, woman-of-the-people heroine with a great melodic gift. Almost insistently clumsy and completely unpretentious, her Patsy is like an American backcountry version of the young Anna Magnani. The singing voice that comes out of her is from the vocal tracks of recordings that Patsy Cline made between 1960 and 1963. (In some cases, new instrumental tracks with new background singers have been laid on.) It takes a few songs before you get used to Lange's body with Patsy Cline's voice, but as Lange's Patsy rises to stardom, bouncing and dancing as she sings, you feel the unity: Patsy's voice is generating Lange's performance.

Patsy Cline was one of the rare full-throated belters with the ability and stamina to belt musically, exultantly, and Jessica Lange's body lives up to the sound. So does her speaking voice, which she modulates so that it's in the same range as Patsy's singing. Growing as confident as the singing voice coming out of her, Lange even puts a raucous growl on a line of dialogue to match Patsy's growl. Lange and Patsy Cline's voice energize the picture, give it a vigor that women have rarely had a chance to show in starring roles. *Sweet Dreams*, which was directed by Karel

48

Reisz (*Saturday Night and Sunday Morning, Morgan!, Isadora, The Gambler, Who'll Stop the Rain, The French Lieutenant's Woman*), is a woman's picture of a new kind—a feminist picture not because of any political attitudes but because its strong-willed heroine is a husky, physically happy woman who wants pleasure out of life. Lange's Patsy Cline doesn't have to talk about her art: we can see that she's happiest and rowdiest and most fully alive when she sings, and when she's rolling in the hay. What the movie makes you feel is her lust for living. And what makes the movie different from the women's pictures of the past is that there's no call for the heroine to be punished, and no suggestion that she shouldn't want *more*. *Sweet Dreams* doesn't step back from her; she's taken on her own terms.

The big weakness in this kind of bio-pic is that once it's on the rails (*Sweet Dreams* starts in 1956) you can see where it's heading: Patsy is going to marry Charlie Dick (Ed Harris) and be battered on the climb to stardom, and she's going to die in a plane crash in 1963, at the age of thirty. And you recognize the signposts: honky-tonks, the Grand Ole Opry, top of the charts. So in basic story terms it's almost inevitably going to seem banal. *Sweet Dreams* doesn't transcend this limitation, but the fighting and boozing are kept to a minimum, and, scene by scene, the script, by Robert Getchell (who wrote *Alice Doesn't Live Here Anymore*), has a funny, edgy spontaneity, a tang. Getchell cuts through the familiarity of the material by providing mean, lowdown banter for Patsy and Charlie, with innuendos right out on top. And he writes scenes between Patsy and her mother (the soft-faced Ann Wedgeworth, a marvellous comedienne) that have a lovely, tickling humor. Patsy's mother was married at sixteen and raised three children by herself—by her sewing. She has never had anything to her name. Yet she's imbued with middle-class moral niceties, and she giggles shyly, as if she were the fluttering essence of gentility. She's disturbed and titillated—in about equal parts—by Patsy's swinging hips and uncouth language. So, of course, Patsy delights in shocking her. These scenes have a real mother-daughter rapport; they stir so much recognition that they're small comedy classics. (Wedgeworth plays prudishness as a sly form of flirtation.) Almost every scene in the movie comes up with something that nips at you and makes you laugh or takes you by surprise. And you like the people more when you hear them taunting and kidding each other. Patsy gives a delayed party to celebrate her younger sister's graduation from high school; she explains the delay to the guests (she didn't have the money earlier), and then she explains why the event called for a major celebration: her sister is the

49

first person in the family to graduate from high school. And with that wry, proud announcement a whole raft of details you've been noticing fall into place.

Patsy and Charlie are passionately in love but have never learned to control their tempers or their impatience. They flare up at each other, and Patsy the smartmouth gives as good as she gets; they keep destroying their own happiness. But they keep experiencing it, too. After Charlie has been drafted, Patsy goes to see him at Fort Bragg and they go to a motel; she makes a very simple postcoital speech—she tells him, "You can't go to your grave sayin' you weren't ever loved"—and it has a resonance that carries through the movie. Ed Harris brings out Charlie's tragic, pitiable sweetness. This husband, who's in awe of his wife's talent, wants a stable marriage more than he wants anything else in the world, yet he has never known how to live on an even keel. Charlie comes on at first bristling with sexual confidence, but the essence of Harris's acting style is the intensity he brings to quietness. Gradually, Charlie loses his bravado, and becomes quieter, more bewildered, and his big scene—a jailhouse monologue about the death of his father—is perhaps the most hushed, most introspective moment he has.

When Charlie and Patsy dance (to music such as Sam Cooke's "You Send Me," on a car radio), it's just about their only tranquil time together. They weave and sway rhythmically; they barely move their feet. The stillness is hypnotic, and it's the only time when Charlie seems at peace and in control of things. Harris has done this erotic swaying in other movies recently—with Amy Madigan in *Places in the Heart* and *Alamo Bay*—but it's effective here, too. When Patsy, dressed in a cowgirl outfit, appears on the Arthur Godfrey show, Charlie watches her at home on TV, and he dances alone to the rhythm of her singing. It's sexy, but it's also desolate. When he and Patsy dance together, it points up the marriage of opposites: the mysteriously quiet man who's suspended in the middle of nowhere, who never finds himself, and the woman who has it all, who knows her gift almost from childhood. It's Patsy's singing—the sureness of it—that attracts him. As Charlie is presented, he's sure he knows how to have a good time, and he's sure of his sexual prowess, but of not much else.

Sweet Dreams should look better than it does: the sets and costumes are fine, but the cinematography is very ordinary, especially in the interiors, and a few sequences are almost ostentatiously dark. There are also a couple of scenes that raise issues without any follow-up, leaving gaps in the continuity. Reisz's staging isn't inspired, either, though he comes through now and then. But Reisz, a Czech-born Englishman, brings the American humor out of the script, and he does beautiful work with Ann Wedgeworth and with Ed Harris. He doesn't interrupt Patsy Cline's songs, and he stays out of Jessica Lange's way. She doesn't have the opportunities for brilliant nuances that she had in the dud movie *Frances*, and her performance may not have the suggestion of worldly ripeness or the affecting qualities that Beverly D'Angelo brought to her few scenes as Patsy Cline in *Coal Miner's Daughter*, but when Lange's Patsy slings her strong young body around she gives off a charge. Lange has real authority here, and the performance holds you emotionally. This is one of the few times I've seen people cry at a movie that wasn't sentimental— it's an honest tearjerker. People can cry without feeling they've been had.

■

The English film *Dreamchild* is about a moment of epiphany. Just before her eightieth birthday, in 1932, Mrs. Alice Hargreaves (Coral Browne) sails to New York to speak at the Lewis Carroll centenary celebration at Columbia University. The voyage is disorienting, and her mind goes back to her childhood days, and to the lazy boating party of July 4, 1862, when the young Reverend Charles Dodgson, Lecturer in Mathematics at Christ Church, Oxford, where her father was the Dean, had attempted to entertain her and her sisters by spinning the nonsense tale that grew to be *Alice's Adventures in Wonderland*. Later, during the ceremonies at Columbia, when a men's choir sings the Mock Turtle's song, "Will you, wo'n't you, will you, wo'n't you, wo'n't you join the dance?," she remembers the Reverend Mr. Dodgson's shyness on another summer day. There were adolescent boys on the excursion, along with the grownups, and she was self-conscious in their presence. When Mr. Dodgson, feeling her rejection of him, tried to recite, he stuttered. She had giggled in embarrassment; her giggles had set off giggles from one of her sisters, and that had got *her* going again. The humiliated, pink-faced little Dodgson had stuttered so much he had to break off in the middle of the "Will you, wo'n't you." Apologetic when she saw how hurt he was, the young Alice had gone over to him, kissed him gently on the cheek, and embraced him. It's only now, at this commemoration and with her own death close at hand, that the elderly Alice, remembering how

51

he shrank back from her touch, grasps how deeply tormented he was, and that he loved her. The full force of the revelation shakes her while she speaks at Columbia. She recognizes that she knew it then, yet didn't quite know it. And she almost loses control. It's a fine, affecting scene: Coral Browne suggests the shock to the wide-eyed little girl who is alive in her still, and it's clear that that girl—Dodgson's dreamchild—has learned enough in her eighty years to value his love now for what it was.

Nothing I've seen Coral Browne do onscreen had prepared me for this performance. In the past, this Australia-born actress (who's in her early seventies) seemed too bullying a presence; she was too stiffly theatrical for the camera, and her voice was a blaster. Here, as Mrs. Hargreaves, she has the capacity for wonder of the Alice of the stories, and when she's overtaken by frailty her voice is querulous and fading. Through most of the film, her decisive tones suggest the practical-mindedness and vanity that link her with the bright, poised, subtly flirty Alice at ten (played by Amelia Shankley), whose conversations with her sisters have an angelic precision. The sound of these imperious little-princess voices blended in idle chitchat is plangent, evocative. It makes you happy and makes you respond to the happiness of the Reverend Mr. Dodgson as he loiters outside the little girls' windows, eavesdropping.

Ian Holm, who plays Dodgson, has to achieve almost all his effects passively, by registering the man's acute and agonizing self-consciousness and his furtive reactions to what goes on around him. As Holm interprets Dodgson's stifled emotional life, pleasure and terror are just a hairbreadth apart. The freedom of imagination that Dodgson shows in the poems and stories he writes for little girls (there were many of them—generations of them—after Alice) disappears in his dealings with the adult Oxford world. Dodgson the Don is a priss—a scholarly celibate who is obsessive about purity of thought. The movie, which was directed by Gavin Millar, from a screenplay by Dennis Potter, doesn't have to formulate most of this; it's all there in Holm's performance. It's all there in the single shot of Dodgson feeling so gratified by Alice's pecking at his cheek that he must retreat from her, squirming in his oversize stiff collar. (His clothes make him look like a wizened naughty little schoolboy, a close relative of his dressed-up brainchildren in Tenniel's illustrations.) It's a wonderful performance—sneaky-dirty in its recessiveness, funny and painful at the same moments.

The picture is a curio; it's anomalous in the way the projects that Dennis Potter (*Pennies from Heaven, Brimstone and Treacle*) instigates often are, and its structure and techniques suggest a literate TV show rather than a movie. Despite the collaboration of Jim Henson's Creature Shop, *Dreamchild* is not a movie for a wide audience; it simply isn't conceived in the broad, narrative patterns that please most moviegoers. Yet it's very enjoyable; it has a twinkling subtext, and in some scenes it achieves levels of feeling that the new mainstream films don't get near. It's about how children can hurt us, and it's about how a man who forbids himself any transgressions against propriety—a man who looks to be dying inside—can split his life between writing "nonsense" and writing mathematical treatises and never, ever crack. I wish that we could have seen other areas of Dodgson's life. How did this prodigy comport himself when he was around the artists he knew, such as Ruskin, Millais, Ellen Terry, Tennyson, and the Rossettis? Did he allow something of the sweet, fey fellow who amuses Alice to come through? And was it creepy for Alice when she passed beyond his favored age range and saw him transfer his devotion to her successors—other bright little Victorian girls?

But Dennis Potter has his own obsessions, and American pop entertainment of the thirties is one of them. The movie is plotted around the impoverished Mrs. Hargreaves' trip to New York, in the company of an adolescent girl (Nicola Cowper) whom she has taken from an orphanage to serve as her nurse-companion. This girl also serves as the film's ingénue. Potter has devised a ramshackle romance between her and a young American (Peter Gallagher), a brash reporter who, having been fired from his job, becomes Mrs. Hargreaves' agent and sets her to delivering product endorsements on the radio and in the press. This aspect of the movie is like a parody tribute to Hollywood's newspaper comedy-romances (such as *Love Is News*), with Gallagher, who is all curly lips and dimples and black eyebrows, doing the Irish charm and blarney that the young Tyrone Power was a wizard at. The romance allows for some pleasant enough musical numbers. ("I Only Have Eyes for You" is sung at a tea dance at the Waldorf-Astoria, and Mrs. Hargreaves has a scene at a radio station that serves no great purpose except to allow us to hear a crooner's gloriously nasal rendition of "I'm Confessing That I Love You.") But Millar, the director, who has a lovely touch with Dodgson and the Dean's little daughters, doesn't seem to know what to make of Potter's quirky affection for Hollywood's exhausted conventions, and Mrs. Hargreaves' Potteresque adventures in the Art Deco New York wonderland have wobbly tonalities. (I began to visualize an old-fashioned Hollywood story conference, with Potter trying to explain his ideas to a studio head like Louis B. Mayer or Harry Cohn.)

The conception is pure fluke, but it almost works. The picture is magically smooth, and it's full of felicities, such as Nicola Cowper's unsentimental ingénue (this orphan is a fast learner) and Peter Gallagher's playing the high-pressure charmer in a loose, affable style. Billy Williams' cinematography has a glowing dreaminess; his lighting helps us over the transitions between 1932 and 1862, and into the glimpses of the world inhabited by the eerie Lewis Carroll–Tenniel–Jim Henson creatures. There are six of them here, complexly detailed creations, and rather malign—as they are in the book. (They're almost too fascinating for the brief appearances they make.) The Gryphon and the sorrowful Mock Turtle live among ledges of rock on a darkling seashore with rippling plastic waves—a Fellini-like night world of the imagination that the aged Mrs. Hargreaves visits. The March Hare has broken, yellowish-gray teeth and soiled-looking whiskers, and he seems to be chewing even while he's speaking. He, the Mad Hatter, and the Dormouse, and the Caterpillar, too, converse in the same matter-of-fact, egalitarian manner that the visiting little Alice does. They—and little Alice herself—rattle around in Mrs. Hargreaves' mind as she experiences a second childhood in the cocky splendors of New York. She knows that her flashing back is a sign of senility, but her new experiences are jogging her out of her confining Victorian primness, and when she flashes back she sees the riches that she has cut herself off from for seventy years.

■

*M*arie stars Sissy Spacek as Marie Ragghianti, who, in 1976, became the first woman to head Tennessee's Board of Pardons and Paroles, and discovered that she was expected to rubber-stamp the deals of the state officials who were selling pardons, commutations, and orders of executive clemency. The movie, which is based on Peter Maas's *Marie: A True Story*, shows us that the politicos erred in taking her for a yes woman. Directed by Roger Donaldson (*Smash Palace, The Bounty*), who is working here with the cinematographer Chris Menges, the film tells Marie's story cleanly and briskly; the structure that the screenwriter John Briley (*Gandhi*) has provided is somewhat like that of the tense Costa-Gavras political thriller *Z*, but Donaldson's pace isn't rat-a-tat—his style is more fluid, less emphatic. *Marie* is a highly accomplished piece of work. It moves, it looks professional, and it's well acted: by Spacek, who conveys the idea of an inner-directed person; by Jeff Daniels, who, as the governor's legal counsel and toady, suggests the dark side of Southern chivalry—he's Marie's protector for only as long as she does just what he tells her to; by Fred Thompson, the lawyer who figured in the Watergate case and also represented Marie Ragghianti in court, playing himself; and by just about everybody else in the cast. Yet the picture is weightless.

It may be that the moviemakers, faced with the inspiring story of a modern heroine who fights the corrupt system and proves that the individual can make a difference, were a little wary, and played it down. Or it may simply be that John Briley thought the facts of Marie Ragghianti's life would be more effective without much dramatization. We see Marie in 1968, when she leaves Georgia and the husband who's brutalizing her, and, with her three small children, goes to live with her invalid mother in Nashville; she supports her kids and herself by working as a cocktail waitress while she attends Vanderbilt University. She graduates, at thirty-two, in 1974, and goes to work for the government, in a series of jobs that culminate two years later in the chairmanship of the parole board. It all zips by quickly—her chronically ill child, crisis after crisis— and the events don't seem to be of interest in themselves. They're preparation for the courtroom proceedings at the end, after she has refused to go along with the orders she is given. Governor Ray Blanton charges her with irregularities in her expense accounts and fires her publicly, on television; she sues him for unlawful dismissal, and creates a political scandal. The implicit question is what formed Marie's character. How did she develop the moral resources to fight the state machine? But all we get is the hardships she goes through—not how she is strengthened by dealing with them. Things never seem to register on her fully or sink in; nothing even leaves a residue—Marie seems untouched.

Fine, magnetic actress though she is, Sissy Spacek doesn't appear to have any way of communicating experience, maturity, womanhood. (This weakened the second half of *Coal Miner's Daughter*.) It isn't her tininess that limits her; it's the girlish, small-voiced acting style that she developed because of it. In *Marie*, she's playing a woman in high position who is involved in making life-and-death decisions, but she moves and talks like a private, unobtrusive person; at parole hearings, her words have a tinkling unimportance. Spacek's manner might have been used to dramatic effect if the officials who put Marie in office were counting on her to be as docile and slight as she looked and then she surprised them. But Briley's script doesn't take account of her gossamer quality, and we never see her turn the tables and show some shrewdness, some aware-

55

ness. The story the movie tells doesn't add up right: What did she think she was getting into when she took the job? Could she have been as naïve as the movie presents her as being and still function? This Marie may be an exact replica of the real Marie Ragghianti, but she has no existence as a character; she's too good—and too dinky—to be believable.

October 21, 1985

KNIFE, BIKE, AND BOOK

The thriller *Jagged Edge* doesn't offer the pleasures of style; it's a remarkably unimaginative piece of moviemaking, considering that it does the job. It catches you in a vise—it's scary, and when it's over you feel a little shaken. The title refers to the serrated hunting knife used in the murder of a wealthy San Francisco woman—she owns the city's leading newspaper—and her maid. The title has a possible wider meaning, too: the border between morality and immorality is very rough in the prosecution of the rich woman's husband (Jeff Bridges) by a less than scrupulous district attorney (Peter Coyote), and in the defense by a woman attorney (Glenn Close) who used to be an assistant to the D.A. and knows his predatory tricks. The script that Joe Eszterhas wrote for this courtroom suspense movie is smart, pared down, efficient—a no-frills script, except for Robert Loggia's role as the profane, hard-drinking private investigator who tracks down witnesses for the defense. The few puckish curlicues granted to Loggia are about the only nonessentials that the director, Richard Marquand, permits himself, but the characters are distinctively pungent, the way they sometimes were in the thrillers of the forties.

As the lawyer, who falls in love with the man she's defending, Glenn Close is the star, and her strong face makes the movie seem more substantial than the high-tech mechanics of the script might suggest. This lawyer—a radiantly blond divorcée with two children—isn't just another imperilled woman. She has an aura of intelligence and moral convictions—she stands for something. Disgusted by the scumminess she encountered

56

in the D.A.'s office, she has been living as if being unsullied in her profession were the highest goal in life. Now, tired of her own cautiousness, she's eager to believe in her client—her new lover. This smart, likable woman isn't timid. She has scheming bright-blue eyes. She likes the tense cat-and-mouse games she plays in the courtroom, and we feel an immediate, empathic connection with her excitement, her point-by-point victories. Good thrillers have an electric current running through them; here it runs through Glenn Close's performance, and then charges the film's last section.

Jeff Bridges and Peter Coyote do their jobs, too. There's no trace of the affable, bearlike Bridges this time. As the astute publisher and editor of his murdered wife's newspaper, he's quick-witted and attractive, a sportsman and sexual athlete—yet there's something off. His physical movements have nothing instinctive about them; they suggest a monitoring system—a regulator in the conscious mind. He's controlled, hooded. He tilts his head so that his eyes are hidden, and when he makes love to his sexy lawyer we don't have a clue to his emotions. He passes a polygraph test, but he's never at ease, never quite trustworthy. Bridges is a different man here; this is some of the best work he has done. And, as the ruthless D.A., Peter Coyote has a tight, slightly twisted mouth. This D.A. once suppressed evidence in a case that his blond assistant was prosecuting, and an innocent man went to prison. She quit working for him because of it; she knows he plays dirty, and that he has every reason to be vindictive toward the publisher, whose paper has opposed his political ambitions. Coyote gives us the suggestion of something rancid about this handsome D.A.; his scorn for people starts with himself. There is also a series of sharp smaller performances. Among those called to testify, Leigh Taylor-Young is especially entertaining as a shallow, debauched rich bitch—the murdered wife's best friend—who gets caught in a stupid lie.

Jagged Edge has its negligent side: the lighting in the homes and in the courtroom is mediocre, and, despite a well-planned wardrobe for Glenn Close, she wears one disastrous too tight beige dress that emphasizes her tummy and makes her look broad-hipped. But the film moves along, setting up the situations and delivering the payoffs, and it would be a good scary, trashy thriller that you could have fun chewing over with friends if it weren't for the quiet, creepy way the murderer's sawtooth mutilation of his victims is described in evocative clinical detail by a final, surprise witness (Karen Austin), who survived an attack the year before. In a movie like this, which is all shrewd manipulation, with virtually every component calculated to draw you into the mystery, quicken your pulse, and give you a kick, it seems too cheap and easy to jack up the horror in this suddenly serious way. The scene is intense—it works—but it has a porno queasiness about it. I was grateful that Loggia, who walks off with his scenes, turned up again at the end; his four-letter words sounded sweet and sane.

■

Pee-wee Herman wakes in the morning in a bedroom full of candy-colored toys and knickknacks. Model airplanes hang from the ceiling, along with balloons, birds, and marionettes, and trucks and plastic dinosaurs line the shelves—the room is like a set for a children's ballet. Pee-wee starts the day fully dressed in his crisp gray polyester suit that's short in the sleeves and skintight in the legs. He betrays no recognition that he has outgrown it; he feels dapper in his wrinkle-free suit and in the red bow tie and gleaming-white shoes that are color coördinates of his lipsticked mouth and smooth, pale (though rouged) face. Pleased with himself and all the possessions in his Hansel-and-Gretel cottage, he coos and squeals and laughs with a bark, and he's always grimacing—twisting his bright-red mouth in a half leer or sticking his tongue out. When he tries to discourage his girl friend Dottie (Elizabeth Daily) from making advances to him, his voice is a nasal whine—he doesn't like that lovey-dovey stuff. Perky and squeaky-clean, he stands before us: the grownup male as prepubescent. He may sound off-putting, but *Pee-wee's Big Adventure* has been playing for a couple of months now, and it isn't hard to see why: it's funny. Directed by the twenty-six-year-old Tim Burton, who was already a veteran of the animation department at Disney, this slapstick fantasy has the bouncing-along inventiveness of a good cartoon. It seems to be taking place in an alternate world—L.A. as a playground. And it's set in a period of its own—a fifties-eighties Twilight Zone, where you might not be surprised to bump into Harry (the baby) Langdon or Steve Martin as the Jerk.

The love of Pee-wee's life is his red-and-white bicycle—a custom-designed two-wheeler that's as covered with ornaments and accessories as his home. But Pee-wee has a rival—Francis (Mark Holton), a fat, rich braggart who bathes like a Roman emperor and suggests an overgrown version of the stinky nasties in the *Our Gang* comedies. Francis is as infantile as Pee-wee (they seem to be on the same wavelength), and knows how much that bike means to him. Out of sheer malice, Francis masterminds its theft. The story—a debased variant of *The Bicycle Thief*—is about Pee-wee's search for his stolen treasure, which takes him all the way to Texas, to the Alamo, and back. He hitches rides, and encounters a series of American-movie archetypes: an escaped convict, a waitress out of *The Petrified Forest* who dreams of going to Paris, hoboes, rodeo riders, and a mean, wild motorcycle gang—Satan's Helpers. It's when Pee-wee gets on the road that Tim Burton shows his flair for the silly-surreal. The L.A. sets are a little fussy and confining, but there's an untrammelled giddiness about the incidents in Texas and along the way.

The people Pee-wee meets are all much nuttier than he is, and the men are such big, slobby, hairy brutes that you can see why the waitress, who longs for a little refinement, takes a shine to him. The movie is full of scroungy bearded giants—they make you think of Paul Bunyan or Bluto—and you see them from Pee-wee's point of view. He looks at the dirty, uncouth, threatening men and would rather remain a ten-year-old. Pee-wee is polite and neat and varnished; dirt couldn't stick to him. In the single sequence that has any sexual overtones, Pee-wee saves the escaped convict (big, deep-voiced Judd Omen) from the police by pretending to be his girl; when the police are gone, the convict looks at him appreciatively—and speculatively.

Some of the best moments involve cartoon-style tricks: a woman trucker, Large Marge (Alice Nunn, who suggests Beatrice Arthur carried to the ultimate), goes through a physical transformation, with Pee-wee watching; Pee-wee is in a car that flies off a road at night, and we see nothing but his spooked eyes travelling across the black screen; he snaps on a light in the darkness of the desert and sees that he is surrounded by wild animals. The film has its limp moments, especially toward the end, and it has an excruciatingly fancy dream sequence featuring clowns (always a mistake). But each time you think it's running out of steam it comes up with something new and totally out of nowhere. Jan Hooks has a juicy comedy routine as a smiling, cheerfully officious tour guide at the Alamo, who won't let Pee-wee interrupt her spiel. (It's a bit like some of the all-American-girl scenes in Michael Ritchie's *Smile*.) Pee-wee triumphs in the gag involving a chorus of Texans clapping when he sings "Deep in the Heart of Texas" and in the funky scene at the Apache Bar, the hangout of Satan's Helpers, where he climbs on the bar top and performs a dance to "Tequila." He's wearing huge high-heeled cowboy boots, and he dances on the toes. He has a commanding intensity in this scene; he has to distract the bikers, who mean to kill him, or, at least, beat him up, and he puts all his instinct for self-preservation into the number. If the movie audience hadn't been won over to him long before, this spaz dance would do it.

Pee-wee Herman shares the writing credit (with Phil Hartman and Michael Varhol) under his own name, Paul Reubens. He's a thirty-two-year-old actor who began as a kid in summer stock, and later worked with the L.A. improv troupe the Groundlings, where he first tried out the bratty Pee-wee character; he developed it in rock clubs and TV appearances. He prefers to stay in the character in his public appearances now, and in the movie he never relents: he's never not Pee-wee. He never tips us to what he would like us to see in the character, either. But as the movie goes on there's something touching in his petulant weirdness, and sometimes, when his makeup isn't quite as thick and stylized as usual, you may feel that you can perceive a sensitivity, a gentleness, in him.

As a character, Pee-wee Herman doesn't fit any pattern of behavior, yet the actor has the sureness of touch to make you accept the contradictory things he does—the infantile ones and the sophisticated ones—and see them all as facets of Pee-wee. It could be said that he appeals to young audiences because he represents the confusion of a boy who refuses to grow up—that he's a Peter Pan of the shopping-mall era or a male equivalent of the young ballerinas who ward off physical maturity by becoming anorexic. But there's another element in the character: like a lot of teen-age consumers, he's hooked on American kitsch. And, with its peppermint-stripe storefronts and polka-dot décor, the movie is somewhere between a parody of kitsch and a celebration of it. Pee-wee himself plays to the audience like a cartoon version of the host of a kiddie show (the character he worked out in his club shows), and he's as manically good-natured as a TV pitchman.

Pee-wee's Big Adventure seems no more than a slapstick novelty, but Pee-wee is part of a—perhaps warped—tradition. The heavily lip-sticked, masklike face recalls the god-awful stage makeup on the silent-screen comics of the twenties and also evokes Marcel Marceau in all his preciousness. Pee-wee is like a dangling marionette, with just his tippy-toes touching the floor. Whether he's twirling in pleasure because some new toy or gizmo has come into his life, or his face is lighting up because an idea just hit him, his whole body is involved. He moves with the precision and imagination of a gifted mime. (At one point, he makes a glorious dive onto a freight train.) What saves him from being cloying is that he uses his skills without trying to tell us that he's an artist. He gives everything he's got to gags such as the one in which he breaks into a pet shop that's on fire and rescues each species—wanting to pass over the snakes, but finally, his face turned away in revulsion, carrying them out on his arms. I liked the movie's unimportance. It isn't *saying* anything.

■

Reading Paul Coates' essays on movies, *The Story of the Lost Reflection* (Verso/Schocken Books), I envied him the freedom he seizes to range over the films of such directors as Truffaut, Altman, Godard, Buñuel, Coppola, Bertolucci, Antonioni, Rosi, Tarkovsky, and Herzog, offering perceptions, summary judgments, poetic flashes, leap-in-the-dark insights. Coates doesn't go through the chore of explaining what's in the films he writes about; he assumes that his readers will be familiar with at least a fair number of the key works of these directors—enough of them to respond to the speculative, visionary connections he makes. I think he's right: there is by now a body of modern work in movies which literate people can be assumed to share, even if in fact they don't. Coates recognizes that the film critic "cannot rely on his readership having seen the films he needs to quote in order to convey his argument," but he goes ahead anyway. And I admire the audacity that this young Englishman shows. He leaves the dross out of criticism and goes right for the gold: the intellectual ecstasy (and sheer fun) of participating in the creative process, taking it further.

The kind of criticism that Coates practices wasn't possible until the sixties, when social changes spurred public acceptance of new kinds of moviemaking, and the films themselves became more ambiguous, disconnected, and puzzling. As he puts it, "Whereas the masterpieces of the past are more or less 'readable,' being evidently inscribed within a certain realist or nonrealist tradition, those of the present tend to be only semireadable." And to Coates, who was born in 1953, these films of the sixties and seventies are basic texts, comparable to the works of fiction he writes about. Movies are only one of his fields. In his book *The Realist Fantasy*, published in 1983, he ranges over fiction—Kafka, Proust, Dickens, Poe, Hawthorne, Henry James, Goethe, Musil, Pynchon, D. H. Lawrence, Büchner, Richardson—and he has a book called *Words After Speech: A Comparative Study of Romanticism and Symbolism* coming out early next year. There's no doubt that his interests cross-pollinate each other, and he must be maddening to academic grinds, because he's so quick. In the film essays, he heads into the major theoretical issues, says what he has to say in a few glittering paragraphs, and moves on to the next thing that interests him—the differences between American and European films, the breakdown of film narrative, the comparative possibilities of opera and movies as total art works, and so on. In passing, he may tweak the grinds in the blandest of deadpan statements, such as "The recent efflorescence of theory is a reflex of the academic institutionalization of film studies. A knowledge of film theories can be imparted to students who have as yet seen too few films to be able to practise criticism."

Coates' applications of Freud and Marx sometimes suggest the eager graduate student, and a few of his sociological observations are rigid and lifeless. And novelists or scriptwriters who read him will be dismayed that he doesn't treat the films' source materials; after acknowledging the difficulty of ascribing credit, he sticks to the finished films. But he's as clear and straight an analytic thinker as anyone I've ever read on movies, and, perhaps because he takes up many of the liveliest issues and the liveliest directors, he's one of the most pleasurable theoretician-critics to read. There's none of the kind of inflation that's common in film books now; he doesn't enshrine the artists, making a fetish of everything they've done. It's elegant, pithy writing. I regret a certain highbrowism in his tone (and in his interests, too), and the title essay (the title is from E.T.A. Hoffmann) is a touch too labyrinthine for my taste. (Coates spins theories so ingeniously that he may get caught in them—become their prisoner.) But if you start by reading about the directors you're particularly interested in you're very likely to be held by the way Coates' mind works. The best thing about him is that his poetic shimmers aren't soft or ornamental; they're not like the mannered flourishes of Frenchy critics— they come out of some close reasoning. At a certain point, he simply takes flight, and everything he has been getting at zooms up in an image.

Here are some of his throwaways and observations:

The first silent films gravitated so readily towards expressionism because the silence of beings so akin to ourselves is absurd and frightening.

Antonioni's characters move like the drowned under water.

One reason why Godard enjoys such critical favour is because his films are machines for transforming viewers into critics.

Where the American star is a mover of the world, the European is the still point round which it turns.

Surrealism sought to dissolve the Victorian antithesis between the higher and the lower animal functions. Nevertheless, there was in Buñuel a pornographic delight in the juxtaposition of the two that stemmed from seeing the two areas as genuinely separate, and that linked him in his prurience with provincial Spanish matrons and with the Victorians themselves.

It was perhaps the very virtues of [Truffaut's] first films—their desperate and incandescent gentleness—that rendered inevitable the end of his revolt.

When identifying the *auteur*, the critic's task should . . . be to distinguish him or her from a mendacious double: Fellini from "Fellini," *Nights of Cabiria* from *Orchestra Rehearsal*.

The depressive indifferentism of [Fassbinder's] films renders them virtually impossible to sit through. . . . The mute unprotesting audience does not feel it deserves any better.

Colour images lack the ghostly poignancy of black-and-white. The monochrome film spontaneously peels off interesting images from the world: it sees things we do not see, and thus insists on the existence of a phantom presence within reality, a world we cannot perceive.

The Cohen songs in *McCabe & Mrs. Miller* come from the inner voice to which the characters alone attend: even on the frontier, people walked around with headphones on.

Julie Christie lights her opium pipe in the golden undersea cave of her brothel room whilst Warren Beatty, nervously extrovert, struggles with roles like a man trying to hold a map straight in the wind. The fragile romance parodies our expectations and underlines with casual irony—so casual as to be melancholy to the point of blankness—the fact that not even the strongest power on earth (the mutual magnetism of Hollywood stars) can subvert isolation.

Cinema is the dream of an after-life from which to comprehend this one.

November 4, 1985

STRAITJACKETS

||||||||||||||||||||||||||||||||||||||||||||||||||||||||||||||||||||||||||||||||||||||||||||||||||||||||||||||||||||||||||||||||||||||||||||||||||

Αt thirty-seven, the Mikhail Baryshnikov of *White Nights* isn't the lighthearted seducer that he played in his only other movie, *The Turning Point*, in 1977. He has a tragic, melancholy dimension now, and more depth. If he can be said to embody the aesthetic of classical dance, he has also reached the point where he's fighting that aesthetic—fighting his body. You can't see the fighting in the dance sequences of *White Nights*; at least, I couldn't detect it—he leaps and soars as if it were effortless. But you know that it's happening, just as you know that it's not happening to the tap dancer Gregory Hines—his co-star here—who, belonging to a different tradition of dance, may be able to go on just about forever. You can sense it in the perfection of Baryshnikov's face: he's not boyish anymore. His face is drawn now and as expressively modelled as his muscular body—he has a man's awareness. Baryshnikov is magnificent in *White Nights*. He might have been created for the movie camera, and he shames the movie he's in.

In *White Nights*, a great star of the ballet world who defected from the Soviet Union in the seventies and became an American citizen is on his way to dance in Tokyo when his plane crash-lands in Siberia. The Soviet authorities apprehend him and put him in the care of a black American tap dancer, who defected from the United States during the Vietnam War, and the tap dancer's Russian wife. This may have seemed like a sharp idea—a gimmick with a built-in dialectic—but it's transparently opportunistic. The tap dancer is conceived as an embittered man who deserted from the U.S. Army because of American racism and the folly and horror of Vietnam. Except for the happiness he has found with his wife, he's miserable, yet he can't admit to himself that he's allowed to dance (in a moth-eaten provincial theatre in Siberia) only if he toadies to the bureaucrats and accepts humiliating tasks. And now a K.G.B. colonel tells him that he must persuade the ballet star to renounce the

U.S. and perform in just a few days at a Kirov gala at the company's base in Leningrad's old Maryinsky Theatre. His own future depends on it: if he fails, he'll be sent to work in the mines.

This cheap plot is like a straitjacket that the director, Taylor Hackford, got into voluntarily and can't wriggle out of. The film opens with the credits on one side of the screen and Baryshnikov's face on the other side—he appears to be lying back on his bed and smoking a cigarette contemplatively; then he leaps up and dances in a garretlike studio, where he's joined by a ballerina. It's a minute or two before we recognize that they're performing Roland Petit's *Le Jeune Homme et la Mort*, and that the garret is in fact the stage of a huge theatre crowded with people, who break into applause. This sequence is superb. It has us watching a ballet before we know we are; even the closeup of Baryshnikov's face is part of the dance. Lighted by the cinematographer David Watkin, this ballet has an entrancing naturalistic formality. But once the plot begins, the dance numbers—solos by Baryshnikov and Hines, and a duet choreographed by Twyla Tharp to the fast rock rhythms of David Pack's "Prove Me Wrong"—aren't as exhilarating as we want them to be, because they're followed by so many scenes of the trapped Baryshnikov trying to figure out what to do and of Hines sitting around morosely.

White Nights is meant to be about freedom of movement—about two dancers who, each in his own way, have fled their countries in quest of it. But what we get is a movie about dancers in a funk. They go from the cramped quarters in the Siberian playhouse to the ballet star's luxurious old apartment in Leningrad and the rehearsal studios at the Kirov; the tap dancer is glum just about every step of the way, and the picture itself is stagnant. The script, credited to James Goldman and Eric Hughes, keeps going back over the same muddy ground, and when heroic climaxes are wanted it insults the dancers (and our intelligence) by relying on stunt work—on doubles climbing out windows and swinging from ropes. With its solemnly melodramatic mixed-twins premise, the picture certainly can't be accused of excessive artistic integrity, yet it doesn't gratify the audience by letting the performers do what the audience wants them to do. Baryshnikov, a *danseur noble* if ever there was one, is given no love partner; the movie does its best to unsex him. Hines, whose loose, casual style of tap suggests breezy comedy and joyous goofing around, is even more crushed and abject here than he was in *The Cotton Club*. Instead of playing a dapper, debonair fellow who has an underlayer of suffering, he puts the suffering on top. And he's at a particular disadvantage because he doesn't have a dramatic presence as a dancer, while Baryshnikov's

65

dance movements are large and spectacular. As Hines' Russian wife, Isabella Rossellini—the great beauty brought forth by Roberto Rossellini and Ingrid Bergman—evokes her mother around the time of *Casablanca,* and her voice is low, like her mother's, but gentler, more caressing. She appears here in shabby clothes and a mousy schoolgirl haircut, and has almost nothing to do except act meek and soothe her husband's raw nerves. Hackford and David Watkin manage to enrich some of the compositions by working her profile in, and there's a lovely closeup of her at the end, but she's never allowed to blossom. (If Hackford directed "Cinderella," the poor girl would never get to go to the ball.)

Admittedly, Baryshnikov isn't easy to cast except as a great Russian ballet dancer who defects to the West. He could play other roles; though he's an erratic actor, his confident, quick inflections give his lines a comic snap. But, of course, we want to see him dance. The screenwriters' answer here—adding another defector—compounds the problem. The Cold War dialogue scenes, designed to advance the pesky plot, are never convincing. Even the supporting players are all working to push the unwieldy mechanism along. The Polish expatriate director Jerzy Skolimowski plays the K.G.B. colonel as a jokey turn; he acts with the smirk and relish of a cartoon predator. He has a sly, bemused nastiness (and a teasing resemblance to Zbigniew Brzezinski), but he stays in one key, and he may be entertaining himself more than he entertains the audience. Geraldine Page's role as the ballet dancer's manager is purely functional, and so is Helen Mirren's as the lover he left behind when he defected—she has become the director of the Kirov. Mirren makes her impact, though; probably no other actress can let you know as fast and economically as she can that she's playing a distinguished and important woman. The only supporting actor who offers much surprise is John Glover, in the tiny role of Wynn Scott, an official from the American Embassy; Glover has an off-center style—even when he plays a good guy, as he does here, he gives it an extra squirt of energy, a kinky originality. The film's title—but nothing else—is lifted from Dostoyevski. The action is set during the "white nights" phenomenon, yet that doesn't seem to serve a story point, and if it's a metaphor it passed me by. Maybe it merely served the purposes of the moviemakers: city streets could be photographed in daylight (the exteriors were mostly shot in Finland) without the expense of traffic or extras, because the scenes are said to be taking place in the middle of the night.

Unsatisfying as the movie is, you keep pulling for it. You want it to be good for Baryshnikov's sake. I remember feeling this same way at some of Garbo's feebler pictures, yet people still watch those pictures that didn't rise to the occasion of her presence. There's enough footage of Baryshnikov here to carry you past the embarrassments of the tacky script. And there are scenes where Hackford shows an instinct for what he should be doing. When the ballet dancer says goodbye to the director of the Kirov in her apartment at the theatre, she flips on her video machine to a tape of him twenty years earlier, and as the scene ends he sees himself as a youth leaping and suspended in the air. The blurred video image has a ghostly magic. The scene that follows—his farewell to the empty old Maryinsky—is trite, but it's almost as affecting as it's meant to be, because the theatre that is used (the Teatro de São Carlos, in Lisbon) is glorious: a theatre that lives up to a performer's dreams of appearing before princes and gods. The best reason to see *White Nights* is that Baryshnikov demonstrates that he found the freedom of movement he defected for.

■

Re-Animator makes good on its title. At first, it just makes you smile or giggle, but pretty soon you laugh out loud, and as the ghoulish jokes escalate you feel revivified—light-headed and happy, the way people do after an evening at Charles Ludlam's Ridiculous Theatrical Company. The picture is close to being a silly ghoulie classic—the bloodier it gets, the funnier it is. This is the same blood that flows through the Hammer horror movies; it's theatre-of-the-absurd blood, slapstick blood. *Re-Animator* is the first film directed by Stuart Gordon, who was one of the founders of the Organic Theatre, in Chicago, in 1969; the screenplay, which Gordon wrote along with a couple of the Organic's playwrights— Dennis Paoli and William J. Norris—was adapted from a series of six stories that H. P. Lovecraft published in 1922. The movie features a bunch of relative newcomers who have had their training in regional theatres, and they perform with a straight-faced, hip aplomb. (They need it.)

Nothing fazes Herbert West, the medical student who comes to Misketonic University in (the apocryphal) Arkham, Massachusetts, from Zurich, bearing an unbreakable bottle full of a fluorescent greenish-yellow serum. He injects it in any corpse that's handy, restoring the dead to hideous, unpredictable activity. The pale, imperturbable Herbert, with his grave manner and his forced little smile, is played by Jeffrey Combs with pursed lips and a clammy-prissy set of the jaw. Herbert, the re-animator, is like a crawly little slug, and he has something of the obsessiveness of Dwight Frye as Dracula's spider-eating assistant. (He laughs only in hysteria.) Herbert's moment of greatest triumph is the resuscitation of the medical school's treacherous, hypocritical chief neurosurgeon (David Gale) after he has been decapitated. This fellow spends the rest of the movie literally holding his head in his hands, but being in two parts doesn't seem to slow him down much; he continues with his vile scheming. Resuscitation has done something to him, though: his libido appears to have been liberated. The severed head is soon busily engaged in making love to the Dean's beautiful blond daughter. David Gale has a long-jawed, sorrowful look—he suggests Boris Karloff—and his eyes roll in lascivious delight as he licks the soft flesh of the helpless, spread-eagled blonde (Barbara Crampton) who has been trussed to a table in the morgue.

These scenes are like pop Buñuel; they're explosively batty, yet the actors manage to keep their professional dignity. Barbara Crampton, who's creamy pink all over, is at her loveliest when she's being defiled; lying there in the morgue with the head moving around on her, she's like a nude by Fragonard or Boucher floating on a ceiling. Skinny-faced Bruce Abbott, who plays her adoring fiancé—he goes in and out of a state of shock—and Robert Sampson (a familiar face from TV), who plays the Dean, her adoring father, round out the key members of the cast. Sampson has what is perhaps my favorite scene. Tied in a straitjacket and locked inside a cubicle, the Dean can't see out, but his daughter and the surgeon (still in one piece at this point), who are in the next room, can see him through one-way glass. In torment, the Dean bangs against the glass, and the vicious surgeon, who is courting the daughter with expressions of concern for her father's mental health, slams back at him furtively with his elbow. The maddened Dean butts his head against the glass, banging at the surgeon. The hatred in this exchange—the pure aggressive meanness in it—is just about peerless, though no doubt some will prefer the wilder moment that comes late in the movie when Herbert decides to try yet another experiment with his greenish-yellow guck, and gives the surgeon's trunk a mighty overdose. The body parts spin off in a scene that recalls the Schwarzenegger robot being dismantled while the machine keeps going in *The Terminator* (which recalled the relentless Yul Brynner robot of *Westworld*), but that joke is topped here when the surgeon's intestines fly out and coil around Herbert like a boa constrictor. (This is an Organic Theatre movie.)

68

It's monkeyshines like these that raise this horror-genre parody to the top of its class. *Re-Animator* doesn't give you a lot of time to think. The score, by Richard Band, has a whoopiness about it, like Bernard Herrmann with hiccups, and Gordon brings the movie in at an hour and twenty-five minutes. Early scenes featuring a re-animated cat named Rufus, who has the scream of a banshee, seem the climax of decades of cat jokes. These jokes hit you in a subterranean comic zone that the surrealists' pranks sometimes reached, but without the surrealists' self-consciousness (and art-consciousness). This is indigenous American junkiness, like the Mel Brooks–Gene Wilder *Young Frankenstein*, but looser and more lowdown. The dialogue isn't particularly polished—the comedy isn't so much in what the characters say as in what they do. There's a suggestion of *The Beast with Five Fingers*, and there's a sequence that recalls Romero's *Night of the Living Dead*, but this is a much rowdier movie—it's not out to scare you, it's out to make you laugh at what other movies have scared you with, and at what they'd have scared you with if they hadn't pulled back. (*Re-Animator* wasn't submitted to the Ratings Board.)

Stuart Gordon's début film carries something intangible from live theatre. The mockery here is the kind that needs a crowd to complete it; ideally, you ought to see it with a gang of friends.

November 18, 1985

HUGGING

||||||||||||||||||||||||||||||||||||||||||||||||||||||||||||||||||||||||||||||||||||||||||||||||||||||||||||||||||||||||||||||||||||||||||

In the three-part TV presentation of *Thérèse Raquin*, in 1981, Kate Nelligan had a marvellous sexual vibrancy that kept getting harsher, more animal. The 1981 movie *Eye of the Needle* might be a standard genre piece if it weren't for Nelligan as the lonely wife. The way she plays the part, all the woman's accumulated spiritual and sexual longings come pouring out; when a big emotion goes through her, it's like the wind snapping a sheet. Nelligan doesn't editorialize on the emotions that her characters are gripped by; she cauterizes those emotions—burns away everything easy or too girlishly appealing. She can do that and still be lyrical, as she demonstrated on the stage in New York in 1984, in her performance as O'Neill's virginal Irish-American farm girl in *A Moon for the Misbegotten*. And in New York early this year she gave one of the least heralded great performances I've ever seen, in Edna O'Brien's *Virginia*. Speaking Virginia Woolf's own words, in a play that is constructed almost as a monologue, she did an ecstatic, transcendent piece of acting, bringing out the beauty of Woolf's language without ever losing the tough complexity of mind that went into it. At the end, when she released her concentration, I looked down at my clasped hands, and the knuckles were white. There is something immaculate about Nelligan's sustained intensity—you never feel she's protecting herself. But her clean acting style is all wrong for the mythmaking propensities of *Eleni*.

This epic-scaled film, directed by Peter Yates, was adapted from Nicholas Gage's book about the execution of his mother—a peasant in a remote mountain village in Greece—in 1948, during the Greek Civil War. The able-bodied men had fled as the Communist guerrilla army approached. The guerrillas, who claimed to be liberating the village, confiscated food supplies and forcibly conscripted girls over fifteen—they took one of Eleni's daughters. Then they ordered the women to turn over their (by now hungry) younger children, who were to be sent to Communist countries (Albania and Czechoslovakia), where they could be fed and, presumably, trained as young Communists. Instead, Eleni packed off her three other girls and her nine-year-old son, Nikola, at night, arranging for them to join their father, who was in America. That, embroidered with other charges, was the crime for which she was condemned and lined up with a group of men in front of a firing squad. The movie tells the story of how, thirty-odd years later, the son, Nick (played by John Malkovich), who by then was a celebrated journalist working for *The New York Times*, went back to Greece determined to track down those responsible for her death.

The job of writing the script was entrusted to the Yugoslavian-born Steve Tesich, who showed a lot of cocky humor in *Breaking Away* but has since brought a delirious, flag-waving Americanism and/or a clanging anti-Communism to such projects as *Eyewitness*, *Four Friends*, and *American Flyers*. His contribution here is as disastrous as it was to those movies. He turns the story into a glorification of a mother's sacrifice— it's her triumph, since Eleni, who lives only for her children, dies knowing they are safe. (She dies with her fists flung up high as she cries out in exaltation, "My children!") Tesich doesn't have much instinct for the specifics of dramatic construction. Eleni's last request is to see the conscripted daughter; we expect her to brief the girl on how to hook up with the other kids and get to America, but it turns out that what she wants is to tell the girl about the joy of motherhood that the girl will someday experience. Eleni is motherhood incarnate. She's above doubts, conflicts, fears—she's even above torture. (Tied up, she's subjected to *falanga*—hideous blows to the stretched feet. It's surprising to see her a day or two later walking to the firing squad.) Motherhood functions as an ideology in this movie—the script is a piece of anti-Communist, pro-motherhood poster art. Eleni is the answer to the Reds.

At the film's opening-night party, a writer for the *Village Voice* asked Christopher Reeve how he liked the picture, and reported that Reeve's answer was "I fell to pieces at least half a dozen times. It makes you want to hug your children or somebody else's if you don't have any." And that may be the effect the movie has on very impressionable people. It can be experienced as a scare picture with a message: the family is all.

Tesich has been quoted as saying, "Eleni's love for her children was something I knew and understood. It was a familiar part of life in that part of the world, where mothers were totally loving and nourishing." This is a case of you can take the boy out of the Yugoslavian village but you can't take the Yugoslavian village out of the boy. American movies finally abandoned that primordial movie subject the sacrificing mother because, as Americans became better educated and more knowledgeable, they realized that those noble women exacted a toll on their children, and that maybe having a mother with nothing in her life but kids wasn't such a blessing.

Kate Nelligan is a scrupulous actress trying to play a believable heroic woman when the Red-baiting script calls for a shameless humbug—a lusty, defiant young Katina Paxinou. The picture would be much worse that way, but more colorfully bad. (Imagine the heartfelt histrionics that Paxinou would have provided for the Easter scene when Eleni and a friend—played by Linda Hunt—walk around greeting the other women with "Christ is risen.") As Nelligan plays the role, she's never embarrassing, but quiet dignity isn't enough to make us warm to a character, and the performance doesn't take off. Even her big effects aren't piercing—there's nothing memorable in them. But the role as written is virtually unplayable, anyway. Tesich may think he knows Eleni, but the dialogue he has given her doesn't indicate anything but raw and largely undifferentiated primitive emotion. And Yates, a cool, detached director—comedy comes more naturally to him—doesn't give Nelligan any

71

kind of backup. Eleni is introduced to us by images showing her in the terraced mountain fields herding the family's goats, and her lines are variations on "My children, I bless you all." I'd love to see Yates and Tesich herding goats. Then they could take turns delivering the joyful vision of maternal bliss that the condemned Eleni speaks to her conscripted daughter.

Emotionally, *Eleni* is as slobby and retro as a Stallone cartoon, yet it makes some claim to authenticity and literacy. The storytelling device— the constant cutting between what happened in the forties and what happens in the eighties as the grownup Nikola gradually puts the facts together—is meant to build suspense. But it does just the opposite: it dissipates whatever momentum develops, and as most of it develops in the forties we come to find each return to John Malkovich an interruption. (We miss out on learning how the children's escape was arranged and how the girl soldier got together with them.) It's Malkovich's first starring screen role, and you might expect to see a hip new actor playing a dedicated investigative reporter who uses the skills he developed when he wrote about the Mafia to track down war criminals. You might expect this reporter to draw you into the case. But what you get is a hesitant, dulled-out obsessive whose mouth hangs open. As Nick, Malkovich is one of the most joyless actors I've ever seen. He's like a wraith wandering through the picture; he speaks in a nervous light, high voice, and he sounds as if he had no energy in reserve—as if he were depleted. So he can't give his scenes any drive. It's the kind of risky, oddball interpretation that has to be brilliant to work at all, and it isn't brilliant.

Malkovich makes the character so sickly and unappealing that you don't know what you're meant to feel about Nick and his mission; the film seems devoid of any point except to bring on an orgy of baby hugging. And if you think over Nick's limp, indecisive lines you may wonder whether Malkovich's role is playable, either. When Nick encounters one of his old playmates—the man is now a baker—he fails to ask the question that comes to a viewer's mind: what happened to him and the other children when they were taken to Communist countries? (You have to go back to Gage's book to learn that although the Civil War ended in 1949, in some cases it was as much as six years before the children could return.) And after an audience has waited two hours for the climactic moment when Nick will confront his mother's murderer, it's a real letdown for him to look at the killer and say (weakly), "Why are you still alive? How can you live knowing what you've done?" (I get stronger verbal assaults than that from readers who just disagree with me about a movie.)

The two English actors who play the Red villains give off the only energy. As the young guerrilla leader who orders Eleni's death, dark-eyed Oliver Cotton has a handsome, hatchet-faced mercilessness; he's unshaven, with bluish shadows on his cheeks and chin, and he has a loud, abrasive voice and a frightening hollowness and flash. He's a bit diabolic. As the village Communist schoolteacher (and officer in the guerrilla forces), Ronald Pickup is a mangy, treacherous ingrate; Eleni has protected him from the monarchist soldiers, but he won't do anything to save her from his comrades. Even when he begins to have qualms about the leader's decisions, he likes his new position of power too much to jeopardize it. Actors ought to have a little prayer thanking God for skunks and vipers.

■

Gene Hackman can give gloriously jaunty, unpredictable per-formances—two of the least seen are in *Under Fire* (1983) and the comedy *All Night Long* (1981). He can be the best we've got. But he can also do the kind of "seemingly effortless," manly, squared-off acting that's said to have truth in it because it's fundamentally unexciting. He's a "dependable" actor, a latter-day Spencer Tracy, in two new pictures—*Target* and *Twice in a Lifetime*. He works like a saint in these pictures, and he gives them a rootedness that they don't deserve. He's also a teensy bit boring.

Arthur Penn's *Target* is an action movie, full of spies and chases and booby traps. Hackman plays a quiet, cautious fellow who owns and manages a lumberyard in Dallas and likes to go fishing. His son (Matt Dillon) wants some thrills in his life; he thinks the old man is a plodder—a fud who never had the nerve to go anywhere or do anything. And the over-protective father worries about the boy, who has dropped out of college and is mucking around with stock-car racing. They just don't get along, and the last thing that Hackman's wife (Gayle Hunnicutt) says to him as she leaves for a Paris vacation is "Would you do me a favor—break through to the kid, huh?" A few days later, Hackman gets word that she has disappeared from her group tour, and he and the boy fly to Paris to find her. As soon as they land, the shooting begins, and the kid discovers that his old-fogy father is a whirlwind—a tough former C.I.A. agent who speaks French and German, knows his way around guns, fast cars, and women, and is a demolitions expert, too. Naturally, father and son get closer to each other—the boy grows up fast—and after they've found

73

and freed Hunnicutt, the father embraces his wife and his son, and the restored family is photographed having one big hug.

Target is Arthur Penn trying to make a hit action film that is also a personal statement; he says that the film is about the "father-son relationship" and "the family." According to Penn, "all successful pictures, *E.T.* or *Back to the Future* or whatever, have a tender, personal core." Well, what he's got here is as impersonal as any of the other movies with stupidly spectacular car chases. The ordinary-family stuff is nothing more than a hook to involve us in the action—the same kind of hook that TV cop shows keep sticking into viewers, and a clumsy one, at that. The father-son tensions are laid out like a lesson in exposition for fourth graders, and the gradual rapprochement has the same awkward pointedness. And, what with all the dashing around and the corpses that accumulate, the action seems overscaled for the theme: it takes a lot of killing to make Matt understand and love his dad.

Penn has trouble getting a conversational rhythm going. When the father explains to the boy that he had to change his identity and be relocated in order to protect the family, the boy's reactions are noisy and inappropriate—he seems like a callow loudmouth. Penn simply goes off-key here; he does it frequently—it's as if he had lapses of attention— and Matt Dillon is the principal victim. (He must have been directed to speak louder than anyone else.) For a second or two near the start, he's reminiscent of the young Montgomery Clift, but it's no more than an optical illusion. This is the most self-conscious and generally confused performance Dillon has given. Gayle Hunnicutt's face matches his well enough for them to be a convincing mother and son, but her scenes (at both the beginning and the end) are so maladroitly staged that you find yourself staring at them blankly. Some of the other performers fare considerably better. The young West German television cutie Ilona Grubel plays a seductive backpacker who attaches herself to the boy, and the Russian actress Victoria Fyodorova, whose autobiography, *The Admiral's Daughter*, told the story of how she came to this country, has her glamorous moments as Hackman's former lover. "You were my love story," she tells him, and Penn ladles on the soulful rue. There's also a tiny role, as the proprietress of a *pension*, in which Jany Holt smiles the sad smile she had as the prostitute in Renoir's *The Lower Depths* almost a half century ago. As one of many agents rushing about, Ulrich Haupt has a scene of slapstick desperation in which he grabs a violin and plays it. And Guy Boyd shines as the slightly stupid blond assistant to the head of C.I.A. operations in Paris; he's the designated red herring—he's so crude and inept that the father dislikes him and suspects him of villainy.

Target has some strong similarities to last year's moderately pleasant comedy thriller *Cloak & Dagger*, directed by Richard Franklin, in which a little boy (Henry Thomas) has an imaginary friend—his father (Dabney Coleman) as an international superspy. *Target* isn't nearly as well worked out. Penn's attempt to create a realistic family situation makes the action scenes—especially the long one with Hunnicutt immobilized and all wired up to detonate—look nutty. *Target* seems to be saying that the only way the twenty-year-old son can respect his father is to find out he's a movie hero.

■

Bud Yorkin's *Twice in a Lifetime*, from a script by Colin (*Chariots of Fire*) Welland, is a miracle of psychobanality. It presents the basic story of the long-married middle-aged man (Hackman) who experiences a renewal of vitality when he has an affair with a younger woman (Ann-Margret), but the story is now so dressed up in the language of self-help books that the man is a life-affirming force—and not only for himself but also for his wife of thirty years (Ellen Burstyn), whom he leaves. The movie could be every errant husband's self-justifying fantasy. The shrewdest touch in it is that the husband isn't some soft, middle-class wimp in L.A. or New York—he's a blue-collar man in Seattle, a straight and honest steelworker, the kind of man who built the country. He's a vigorous fifty-year-old, and the woman he falls for (a widow) is as fine and wise and loving as he is. The dishwater-dull wife wears an apron and watches game shows; her expressions of love for her husband are of the pathetic, lip-gnawing variety. So he has to be strong enough for the two of them when he leaves. The film goes on demeaning her. She keeps saying, "I didn't deserve this," as if she thought that life works in terms of whether you deserve things. And when she wins at bingo she carries on like a ninny. A series of scenes record her bitterness, her moping, and then her gradual awakening, which is possibly even more offensive. The signposts on her road to mental health include getting her hair dyed and going to a male-strip disco, where her eyes glisten and she giggles in shocked pleasure as the strippers taunt and tease the feminine clientele. At the end, she's preparing to "take some classes." (The husband doesn't need reëducation.)

75

Hackman's broad, average-guy face is the center of consciousness in this movie: it registers the other characters' emotions and suffers for their suffering. This actor functions as a human seismograph; he even improves on what he's reacting to—especially in his scenes with Burstyn. She plays her clichés to the hilt, and with the metallic ring of her voice she demands a hundred per cent of your attention. It's deathbed acting: she plays each scene as if there were no tomorrow. As her older, married daughter, Amy Madigan manages to bring a spark to her material: she's supposed to be distressed and angry, and she has to come on hard, screaming at her father, but she has an original fierceness about her, and a comic flair. (It comes out especially in a scene at the supermarket where she gets sore at her little girl.)

The subject of this movie has been treated lightly and farcically and even tragically for centuries; it took Yorkin and Welland (and perhaps a divorced, twice-married President) to give it a new aura of wholesomeness. If there's any one factor that can account for the crowds at the theatre, it's the film's upbeat tone. And that must be the explanation for the enthusiasm of many reviewers. ("To enjoy this film, one needs only to feel." "The first four star movie of 1985." "One of those once-in-a-lifetime experiences." "*Kramer vs. Kramer, Ordinary People, Terms of Endearment,* if there's one a year we're lucky. The luck of this year lies in *Twice in a Lifetime.*") The picture is all about healing and renewal. It doesn't have a freshly imagined character in it, and it has no life as a piece of moviemaking, but it has all this positive thinking. It's like a sermon on the therapeutic value of adultery, divorce, and remarriage, given by a minister who learned all he knows from watching TV.

December 2, 1985

SACRED MONSTERS

*O*ut of Africa dribbles on—adult, diligently cryptic, unsatisfying. This is a movie with a highborn heroine (played by Meryl Streep) who fights off a marauding lion with a whip, and somehow the scene isn't tempestuous—it doesn't give you a quiver. Possibly the director, Sydney Pollack, and his screenwriter, Kurt Luedtke, started out to tell a straightforward, reasonably accurate romantic adventure story and then became so ambivalent about their heroine, the Danish Karen Dinesen, and her big-game-hunter lover, Denys Finch Hatton (played by Robert Redford), who was the younger son of an earl, that they were no longer sure how to shape the footage. As the film presents her life, Karen, who is spurned by the cousin she loves, impulsively settles for his twin brother, Baron Bror von Blixen-Finecke; she sails to British East Africa in December, 1913, where she marries him. Although they had arranged to buy a dairy farm on the money her family provided, he has switched plans without consulting her, and they go off to start a coffee plantation. The Baron (played entertainingly by the sly-eyed Klaus Maria Brandauer) is a playboy and a rake; he leaves his bride to run the place, and infects her with syphilis besides. But the grandeur of Africa enraptures her; so do the twelve hundred Kikuyu and Somali who are her servants and field hands, and after her husband moves out, her lover uses her house as his home base between safaris. The movie telescopes the events of Karen Blixen's eighteen years in Africa to roughly a decade, and tells us at the close that when she lost the farm she returned to Denmark and, using the pen name Isak Dinesen, wrote the works that made her famous (*Seven Gothic Tales*, published in 1934, and *Out of Africa*, in 1937).

The year just ending is the centenary of Dinesen's birth, and you might expect the film's theme to be what Africa meant to this woman and how it changed her into the author we know. But each time a situation calls for a dramatic clarification Pollack waffles and sidesteps. The movie doesn't point up the fact that the Baron's putting his bride's money into the farm was a fatal mistake—that she labored all those years to make a go of coffee in a region where it couldn't be grown successfully. Issues much larger—central issues about the character of the principal figures—don't fully emerge. As the movie has it, Karen virtually buys the Baron: she points out to him that he has run through his money and needs the bourgeois fortune she can bring him. And she's indecently eager to call herself Baroness—she uses the title even before the marriage. Pollack appears to want us to see her as a bit goofy and pretentious but a strong-minded, wonderful woman. He hedges on what kind of woman she was. In her writing, she said of her Somali majordomo, the Muslim Farah (Malick Bowens), "The servant may be the more fascinating of the two, still it holds true of him as of his master that his play of colours would fade and his timbre abate, were he to stand alone. He needs a master in

77

order to be himself." Pollack doesn't sort out his feelings about this woman who wrote that "Farah was my servant by the grace of God." He doesn't include the high-strung, hysterical side of her character that some of her contemporaries described, and her love affair with Finch Hatton, which was possibly platonic, is presented as physical. But it's apparent that the young Baroness finds fulfillment in the role of patrician. She plays white goddess, and Denys is in the ivory trade; even the Baron is a hunter and safari leader. The movie wriggles around trying to make these people morally acceptable to a modern audience. (An example: when Karen and Denys are on safari together, they don't shoot the two lions they see until the beasts spring at them.)

Part of the problem that Pollack has in showing us how Africa formed Karen Blixen as a writer is the kind of writer she became. Her baroque stories are lacquered words and phrases and no insides. Some seem meant to be morality tales, but you never get the moral. And the supernatural effects in them aren't connected to any spirituality—they're a display of literary armature, of skill. As author, she's the teller of the tale; nothing is presented more passionately than anything else—she seems to refuse to draw from her own experience. (And you end up with a Meryl Streep.) In the movie, after leisurely dinners Denys starts the Baroness on a story by giving her a first sentence, and she takes off from it, charming him and his affable, gregarious business partner, Berkeley (Michael Kitchen), by spinning her fantasy through the indolent night and into the dawn. It's a mandarin form of Trivial Pursuit. And, like these spun-out stories, her *Seven Gothic Tales* are a form of distraction; they read as if she had devised them in the fevered atmosphere of all-night debauches (although actually she'd been working on them since her girlhood, and a bit of mold clung to them). It's awkward when Redford as Denys gives Karen a pen and tells her to write down her stories; his gesture and his words stick out—you can feel that the movie is reaching for a theme and trying to give him a function in making her a writer. (Actually, Karen Dinesen had published stories, in Danish, as early as 1907.) Onscreen (as in fact), the stories Karen confects to please him are told in her delicately accented English, and Isak Dinesen wrote her *Gothic Tales* in English. This may have been a way of keeping Denys and the long nights of storytelling alive in her memory; it had a practical purpose, too, for a woman who hoped to earn a living.

Out of Africa was also written in English, but she was no longer playing Scheherazade. A memoir of her years in Kenya, of the tribesmen and the farming, the book has a sovereign plainness; it's lordly, but it's magnificent, too. Nothing in the movie suggests the directness and power of Dinesen's writing in *Out of Africa*. I wish that the anecdotes in the book didn't so often exalt her; I wish that she weren't so determined to be her own heroine. But she is a real writer, and though her love for the Africans appears to be inextricably tied to her seeing herself as the master, the love rings true.

Meryl Streep has used too many foreign accents on us, and this new one gives her utterances an archness, a formality—it puts quotation marks around everything she says. Still, she's animated in the early scenes; she's amusing when she acts ditsy, and she has some oddly affecting moments. Her character doesn't deepen, though, or come to mean more to us, and Redford doesn't give out with anything for her to play against. So she pulls back—the energy goes out of her performance— and they both spend a lot of time displaying their profiles. Redford carries his sunny aura from picture to picture; when he first shows up, you look for his baseball bat. The two best-known things about the dashing aristocrat Denys Finch Hatton are that he was British and that he was bald. (He wore a wide array of hats.) Redford is as American as ever, and his fluffy hair is a golden dream. He speaks his lines crisply, but he seems adrift, lost in another movie, and Pollack treats him with unseemly reverence. His role is a series of grand entrances and lingering exits. Pollack must be trying to set up a glorious doomed romance in an exotic setting, but when Streep and Redford are on safari, drinking wine out of crystal goblets and dancing on the earth between two campfires, or when they're in the wilds and he's shampooing her hair, or even when they head for a jungle tent and everything is primed for passion, they seem too absorbed in themselves to notice each other. At times, Streep looks waxy and abstracted in the manner of forties movie stars—it's as if she were wearing a facial mask—and Redford, playing another of his elusive, detached heroes, looks as if he'd been blow-dried away. When Karen suddenly becomes demanding and explodes at Denys—she wants him to marry her—it's as if a couple of pages from a bad novel about a possessive woman had been pasted into the middle of a *National Geographic* photo essay.

This is "classical" big-star narrative moviemaking, but without the logic, the easy-to-read surface, and the sureness that contribute to the pleasure of that kind of picture. A scene during the First World War in which Karen is told that the women and children can't be protected on the farms and must move into town has no follow-through. And when the Baron, who's fighting with the British forces, sends a message to his wife to arrange for supplies to be delivered to them, and she takes them herself, leading an oxen-drawn transport across a sizable chunk of Africa, we aren't cued to know why she has done it, or whether, after she arrives and the Army men stare at her, her husband is proud or aghast. The movie hums a little when Brandauer or Michael Kitchen or Suzanna Hamilton (as the young equestrienne Felicity) is on the screen; they're recognizably human. And several of the black performers are great subjects for David Watkin's camera—Malick Bowens, with his faraway eyes, in particular. There's the occasional stunning moment, such as the night scene of the victorious troops returning from the war, the proud black soldiers holding up torches as they march. Sydney Pollack packed the picture with historical verisimilitude, but it seems to be about something nebulous; he failed to give the two main characters and the story an independent existence. I think he picked the wrong woman writer to make a movie about; he must have been haunted by the familiar image of the aged Isak Dinesen—the bony, syphilitic high priestess who looked as if she were holding out a vial of poison. His work here exudes uncertainty.

■

During the making of *The Color Purple*, Steven Spielberg's version of the Alice Walker novel about black women's lives in the South in the first half of the century, the advance publicity suggested that he was attempting something "serious." But when you see the movie you realize that he was probably attracted by Walker's childlike heroine, Celie, and the book's lyrical presentation of the healing power of love. He may not have understood this, because he approaches the material with undue timidity. It's no wonder the novel was popular. On the first page, the fourteen-year-old black drudge Celie is raped by the man she believes to be her father. She gives birth to two children by this brute; he takes the babies away, and she has no idea what he has done with them. Tired of her, he forces her to marry another brute—a widowed farmer who needs her to take care of his children. This man uses her sexually and beats her. When her younger sister, Nettie—the only person who cares for her and doesn't think she's ugly—runs away from the raping father and comes to stay with her, her husband makes advances to Nettie and, when Nettie fights him, throws her off the property. Poor Celie toils on, with never a kind word coming her way, until her husband brings home Shug Avery, a honky-tonk singer—his true love and sometime mistress—who is sick and needs care. Celie falls in love with the raucous, gutsy Shug (short for "sugar"), and Shug, seeing Celie's true worth, makes love to her. It's the turning point of Celie's life: after experiencing sexual pleasure, she becomes confident of her self-worth, goes out into the world, and returns to make a success of herself running a small business.

But *The Color Purple* isn't just the story of Celie; it's an extended-family saga spanning generations and two continents. (The cast-out Nettie has gone to Africa, with a missionary couple.) The novel is about the bonding of the generous, artistically gifted, understanding black women (no matter how worn down they are, they never speak a harsh word to a child). It's also about the insensitivity, cowardice, and meanness of the black men (Nettie is able to brief us on how the men oppress the women in Africa, too). The glue that holds it all together is a pop-folk religiosity that also serves to keep the book's anti-male attitudes in check. Walker allows some of the lazy, lecherous oppressors to redeem themselves by accepting their inferiority to their wives and developing their aptitudes for cooking and sewing. So the many characters all come together for a series of reconciliation scenes.

Probably Alice Walker gets by with so much rampant female chauvinism because it's put in the mouth of her battered fourteen-year-old heroine. The book—or, rather, the best part of it, roughly the first third—is made up of Celie's letters to God, which are written in a raw, cadenced dialect, an artful version of a rural near-illiterate's black English. The book has a joyous emotional swing to it, and this swing can carry a reader right through inspirational passages such as the one where Shug teaches Celie that God is inside her and inside everybody else, that everything wants to be loved and "it pisses God off if you walk by the color purple in a field somewhere and don't notice it."

Spielberg has been quoted in *The New York Times* as being worried about "doing a movie about *people* for the first time in my career," and fearing that he'll be "accused of not having the sensibility to do character studies." But the Walker material has about as much to do with character studies as Disney's *Song of the South* did. Spielberg's *The Color Purple* is probably the least authentic in feeling of any of his full-length films; the people on the screen are like characters operated by Frank Oz. But

81

they're not much phonier than the people in the book: Spielberg's problem is that he can't give the material the emotional push of that earthy folk style of Walker's. He just doesn't have the conviction that she has.

Spielberg's version comes from a man who filters everything through movies. He sees Georgia in 1909 the way a European director might; visually, the picture suggests *Song of the South* remade by Visconti. When Celie (played in the early scenes by Desreta Jackson and then by Whoopi Goldberg) and Nettie (Akosua Busia) do their jive talk—clapping their hands in fast, intricate rhythms as they chant—it seems to be going on in a faraway, magical kingdom, in a field of pink flowers from the florists who supplied the daffodils for David Lean's *Doctor Zhivago*. Spielberg has all this facile, pretty camera technique, but he can't find an appropriate tone, and so the incidents don't click into place. The movie is muffled, bombed out, and a gooey score by Quincy Jones calls attention to the emotional void—Jones seems to have been waiting all his life to metamorphose into Max Steiner.

Spielberg soft-pedals the lesbian side of the Celie and Shug romance, and the men may be more buffoonish than they are in the book and so less threatening, but he has tried to be faithful to Walker. This doesn't do the movie a lot of good. Working from a script (by Menno Meyjes) that hasn't reshaped the novel into a dramatic structure, Spielberg has trouble getting about two dozen characters in and out of the action, which spans some thirty years. (Performances, such as Rae Dawn Chong's as Squeak—Celie's stepson's mistress, who wants to be a singer—have obviously been truncated.) A scene of several women standing on Celie's porch is the worst piece of staging this director ever dreamed up. It tops even the crowd scene where the people singing outside a church converge with the people singing inside—a jubilee that reminds you of fire drills in junior high. And this is the only film that Spielberg has ever made where the editing looks to be from desperation. The crosscutting between Nettie's experiences in Africa and Celie's life back home is staggeringly ineffective. In one sequence, we hop back and forth between Celie, who has just learned of her husband's full treachery to her and picks up a straight razor to shave him, and Shug, who is at a distance and starts running to the house because she intuits that Celie is about to cut his throat, and Nettie in Africa dashing to a ritual of initiation where children are to have their faces incised. The passage rivals the famous parody of editing in *The Apprenticeship of Duddy Kravitz*, where Denholm Elliott played a drunken filmmaker who, having been hired by a father to record his son's bar mitzvah, got carried away with his art and intercut the gathering with bloody primitive rites. (Spielberg's African ritual may even be a first on film: a coed tribal initiation.)

Except for the dimpled Oprah Winfrey as the powerhouse Sofia, whose mighty punch at a white man lands her in jail for twelve years, the performers don't make a very strong impression. Whoopi Goldberg's Celie may be a little less "real" than the title character in *E.T.*, but, given the conception of Celie—who has to be meek and then discover her power—she does a respectable job. (If we feel a letdown when she takes over from Desreta Jackson's teen-age Celie, it's because Jackson is warmer and more open to the camera.) Willard Pugh is likable and peppy as Celie's stepson, who keeps falling through roofs, and Danny Glover, in the difficult role of the husband who slaps her around, probably does as well as anybody could with material such as the stupid comedy routine where he proves the ineptness of men by trying to prepare a meal for the bedridden Shug and burning everything. (It's the kind of humil-iation that Katharine Hepburn went through long ago in *Woman of the Year*; it's no less offensive when the sexual tables are turned.) As Shug, Margaret Avery is in a tough spot, because of all the press attention to Tina Turner's being offered the role and turning it down. (You can't help imagining how Turner might have played it.) Margaret Avery makes a terrific entrance, grinning, with a jagged front tooth sticking out, and she looks great singing in a glittering red dress in a juke joint. (She's dubbed by Tata Vega.) But then an awful thing happens, which has to be at least partly the director's fault: she plays the rest of her scenes in a refined, contemporary manner that dulls out all interest in Shug. If you're among the millions of people who have read the book, you probably expect the actors to be more important than they turn out to be. The movie is amorphous; it's a pastoral about the triumph of the human spirit, and it blurs on you.

■

Probably everyone will agree that the subject of a movie should not place it beyond criticism. Still, Claude Lanzmann's nine-hour-and-twenty-three-minute documentary epic, *Shoah*, which is made up of in-terviews with people who have knowledge of the Nazi extermination centers—whether as slave laborers, railroad workers, technicians, bu-reaucrats, or just onlookers—may seem a special case. I ask the forbearance of readers for a dissenting view of a film that is widely regarded as a masterpiece. I found *Shoah* logy and exhausting right from the start, and when it had been going on for an hour or longer I was squirming restlessly, my attention slackening. Then Filip Müller, a survivor of the Auschwitz "special detail," began to talk. A sturdy Czech in a white shirt, he has a simple, unforced dramatic power as he describes how in 1942, as a boy of twenty, he was sent, along with a group of other Jewish prisoners, to work in the incineration chamber of the crematorium in Camp 1 at Auschwitz. His job was to undress the corpses, then to feed the ovens and stir the bodies. Müller speaks with urgency in a beautiful, light voice; he's a fluent storyteller, who sets his own rhythms and brings out the progression of his experiences. But when Lanzmann, who does all the questioning himself, moves on, the film once again becomes discursive; we watch him putting pressure on people—pouncing on a detail here or there—and we register the silences, the hesitancies, the breakdowns. Despite the fine, painful moments, such as Müller's testimony, in Part I (four hours and thirty-three minutes), and the account of starvation in the Warsaw ghetto given by Jan Karski, who was a courier for the Polish government-in-exile, in Part II (four hours and fifty minutes), sitting in a theatre seat for a film as full of dead spaces as this one seems to me a form of self-punishment. A large proportion of the audience may agree: Part I plays in a crowded theatre; only a handful of people attend Part II.

The focus of Lanzmann's inquiry isn't the concentration camps; it's the death factories, which were set up in rural areas of Poland (sometimes in conjunction with work camps). Lanzmann speaks French, German, and English, but he doesn't speak Polish, and so for much of the time he asks questions in French and a woman translator puts them into Polish; the subject replies in Polish and the translator puts the answers into French for Lanzmann while we read the English subtitles. (A translator is also required when those interviewed speak Hebrew or Yiddish.) This method of questioning inflates the scale of the film. The theme is, of course, infinitely large, but Lanzmann's method gives the filmmaking itself a deadening weight and solemnity. *Shoah*—the word is Hebrew for "annihilation"—is oral history treated on a grand scale as an elegy or meditation. Lanzmann has taken the Holocaust as his art work, and he aestheticizes everything for us. The text of the film—*"Shoah": An Oral History of the Holocaust*, published by Pantheon Books—runs less than two hundred pages. He slows down this material, stretching it almost languorously. While the subjects speak, the camera stays on them for very long takes; at first, the faces may be fascinating, but then nothing more is revealed to us and the camera is still on them. Eventually, it moves, and during the questions and answers it scans the peaceful, vernal countryside where the ovens used to belch smoke in Chelmno, Treblinka, Auschwitz, Belzec, and other places. The landscapes are used as a poetic visual accompaniment to the spoken words, and the camera keeps circling back to the railroad tracks and ramps and platforms that marked the end of the line—the arrival at the camps. The long camera movements are repeated ritualistically. We hear the rolling of heavily loaded boxcars, and, with the camera mounted on the front of the train, we're in the position of someone entering the death compounds, over and over.

Shoah presents itself as art, and Lanzmann, who demands that it be considered as such, has said that it contains not one unnecessary frame, yet there's also an element of moral blackmail in his approach. It's as if he were saying, "I spent eleven years of my life scrounging for money and hunting down survivors in fourteen countries. I shot three hundred and fifty hours of footage on the subject of genocide, and you can't curb your impatience for a few hours?" But, to put it plainly, not everyone who has the dedication to make a film on a great theme is a great moviemaker. Lanzmann's techniques are often crude: when he wants us to know that the authority he's talking to—the American historian Raul Hilberg, author of *The Destruction of the European Jews*—is saying something especially cogent, he moves the camera in and shows us Hilberg's eyes, nose, and mouth in giant closeup. In Part II, Hilberg, who talks in slow, imposing rhythms, quotes a small joke that the Warsaw diarist Adam Czerniakow wrote down, and Lanzmann has him explain it and explain it again. Lanzmann's closeups can be tyrannically close— invasions of a face—and they're frequently followed by wandering long-shots. The camera sweeps around the interior of a booming German café, and an elderly (rather macabre) couple dance endlessly. The scene serves only a moralizing purpose: Think what this prosperity is built on! In Part II, when the landscapes of Part I are replaced by visual tours of New York City, Washington, D.C., and the Ruhr, the message appears to be: See, all this goes on as if nothing happened! And there are times when Lanzmann loiters over scenes that have practically no content: at one point, he drives through city streets in his red-and-white van, and we have to watch him park, jockeying into the space. When the film cuts to the video equipment inside the van, we spend time looking at the broad back of one of his assistants. The film lags: it's as if there were white space between the frames—you feel as if someone had thrown a big carpet

85

over you. As it happens, the assistant in the van is watching a video monitor while Lanzmann conducts a surreptitiously photographed interview—one of his more compelling interviews, a talk with a former S.S. man, who delivers a precise, detailed report on how Treblinka operated at full capacity when the Warsaw ghetto was being emptied. But in general Lanzmann is not a stirring interviewer. You don't feel the play of a wide-ranging intelligence in his questioning, and when he prods the Jewish survivors into talking about things they don't want to talk about, you don't have the feeling that he's getting fresh perceptions from them.

A journalist, Lanzmann, who was born in Paris in 1925 and began working at *Les Temps Modernes*, with Sartre and de Beauvoir, in 1952, has made one other film, *Why Israel?*—a documentary completed in 1972. Though he took a doctor's degree in philosophy, he works like a detective (and sometimes a prosecutor) rather than a philosopher. *Shoah* has nothing resembling the moral questions raised in Marcel Ophuls' *The Sorrow and the Pity* (which is about the reactions of the French to the Nazi Occupation). Lanzmann sets out to document how the virtual annihilation of European Jewry was accomplished: he goes after the minutiae of the railway schedules, the exact number of people who died of thirst and disease on the trips in the sealed cars, the details of how they were stripped, the types of gas used, the capacity of the centers (how many people could be processed), just how long it took from the time the people arrived on the trains to the disposal of their ashes in the nearest river (best time: two hours), and so on. *Shoah* is certainly a vivid presentation of the nuts and bolts—and the hideousness—of genocide. But many questions that come to a viewer's mind are left unanswered. We spend a long time with the Jewish survivors whose youth was spent working in and around the ovens, yet the interviews are conducted in impersonal settings, so we don't find out what sort of lives these men managed to make for themselves afterward. And although Jan Karski—tense, tortured by his memories—explains that the Jewish leaders asked him to take their plans of how the slaughter could be stopped to officials of the Allied governments, we don't learn how far he got or what the responses were.

The film's slackness isn't the only reason you may feel restless; there's a deeper reason. When you come out of *The Sorrow and the Pity*, there has been so much packed into its four hours and twenty minutes—so many widely differing instances of collaboration and resistance, and such a steady accumulation of perspectives—that your mind is buzzing. All the circuits are busy—something that rarely happens at a movie. It's a genuinely challenging experience, a tonic. *Shoah* doesn't set you to thinking. When you come out, you're likely to feel dazed, and confirmed in all your worst fears. It's not just the exact procedures used in the extermination process that Lanzmann is hunting down. He's after the Gentiles' attitudes toward the process. *Shoah* presents a world in which a Gentile rarely shows any human feeling toward a Jew. The Polish peasants who saw Jewish children being thrown into vans by their feet don't seem to have been upset, or even touched. The former S.S. officer describes the operation of the ovens in terms of the efficiency and the technical accomplishments of the S.S. A German woman, the wife of a Nazi schoolteacher in Chelmno, where four hundred thousand Jews were killed (and two survived), talks about the frightful screams—how depressing they were, day after day—while we look at her pinched face. (She's like an elderly woman in an Edvard Munch painting.) I think we're meant to feel her dissociation from the people screaming, feel the indifference behind her calling it "sad, sad, sad." When she rattles on about how primitive the town's toilet facilities used to be, she shows more involvement, and that has to be the reason this chatter of hers is included.

Lanzmann succeeds in making the past and the present seem one, and this appears to be an aesthetic victory—the result of that circling camera, and of the death-factory survivors, with their memories. It has another aspect, though: implicitly, the film says that the past and the present *are* one—that this horror could happen again. See, the Polish peasants are still talking about how the Jews killed Christ and hoarded gold. They saw the smoke from the ovens—the death centers were in fields adjoining their farms—and they think the Jews deserved to burn.

The way the evidence is presented in this movie, you can't keep from passing judgment, and it's almost always facile judgment against the Gentiles—even those who were powerless. The survivors of the extermination centers explain that most of the work—cutting off the victims' hair, cleaning the gas chambers, stoking the furnaces—was done by Jews assigned to "special details" and then killed. (The Nazis didn't want to leave any witnesses.) The few Jewish workers who survived did so through rare, unpredictable circumstances, such as recovering after being shot in the head. Suppose these workers had been Gentile slave laborers, and as bewildered and terrified as the Jews. Would Lanzmann have treated survivors among them with the loving respect he shows the Jewish survivors? Or would he have been eager to seize on signs of ignorance and prejudice among them—as eager as he is with the other Gentiles here?

The film is diffuse, but Lanzmann is blunt-minded: he's out to indict the callous. If you were to set him loose, he could probably find anti-

Semitism anywhere. Maybe any of us could if we looked for it, but he looked in special places, and it's shocking to see the unself-conscious forms of it that he turned up among people who lived close enough to the death centers to smell the stench. Of course, he's not very fussy about his subjects: in some passages he seems to be conducting his interviews at Woody Allen's convention of village idiots. But even if you accept his examples as valid and representative, what doesn't seem valid is the significance that the film confers on them. Lanzmann's dominant visual metaphor—putting you on the trains that keep rumbling toward the extermination factories—isn't just saying "Never forget!" The heart of his obsession appears to be to show you that the Gentiles will do it to the Jews again if they get a chance.

Shoah is a long moan. It's saying, "We've always been oppressed, and we'll be oppressed again." This is implicit in the mood of the film—in the claustrophobic inevitability of the trains moving toward the ovens. Lanzmann explained to *The New York Times*, "It is all on the theme of anti-Semitism, but each time it is picked up at another level," and the whole film can be seen as a Jew's pointing a finger at the Gentile world and crying, "You lowlifes—you want to kill us!" This is not necessarily an aberrant or irrational notion, and a moan is not an inappropriate response to the history of the Jews. But the lack of moral complexity in Lanzmann's approach keeps the film from being a great moan. When you're watching the Ophuls picture, your perspective expands: you keep changing your mind, and you can see that he's changing his, too. You don't just become self-righteous about gloating, mean-spirited peasants and unfeeling Nazi bureaucrats.

Shoah accumulates data compulsively; you learn more and more about the railway schedules, but your vision becomes narrower. The film is exhausting to watch because it closes your mind.

December 30, 1985

MACRO, MICRO, STINKO

Kurosawa has said of his epic spectacle *Ran* that it is "human deeds as viewed from heaven," and the film gives you the feeling that you're looking down from a great height. Even its fiercest battles are serene, as if preordained. In the publicity, the Japanese word "ran" is defined as "chaos," but that's a loose translation. "Riot" or "war" or "uprising" would be more like it, and in terms of the film's emotional tone this fighting is seen from a detached point of view. Kurosawa says that his primary influence in the work (which he had been planning—and trying to finance—for nearly ten years) was the legend of a sixteenth-century warlord who retired to live in peace after dividing his lands among his three devoted sons. Kurosawa turned the legend upside down to demonstrate that a lord who achieved his wealth by brutalizing everyone who stood in his path couldn't retire and have a tranquil old age—that at the first sign of weakness he'd be a target. Then Kurosawa thought of *King Lear*, and it's clear that he drew from Shakespeare's characters and plot. But without Shakespeare's language this warlord Lear isn't a towering figure with raging emotions. Viewed from heaven, he's just a speck, like everyone else. As Kurosawa presents him, this lord has no psychological interior; he's a symbolic figure—almost a puppet. And this Lear, the seventy-year-old Lord Hidetora Ichimonji (Tatsuya Nakadai), has earned every bit of his punishment. *Ran* is like *Lear* as a silent film unfolding inexorably. In a massacre at a fortress on the slopes of Mt. Fuji, where Hidetora sees his retinue and his concubines butchered by his own sons' troops, Kurosawa cuts off the noise of the flaming arrows and the cries of the warriors and their victims; the carnage is a horror show, an elegiac ballet with no sound but Toru Takemitsu's harshly poignant music. The imagery here is suddenly fluid, with warriors running this way and that in flattened perspective—they're like a winding river on a Japanese screen.

In 1954, when Kurosawa made *The Seven Samurai*, he was perhaps the most dynamic (and Shakespearean) of all moviemakers. *The Seven Samurai* is an action film; its spirit is unruly—it's about what can't be tamed. But now he shows no interest in dynamics. (People go on writing that he's the most Western of Japanese directors, but that hasn't been the case for a long time.) *Ran* is *about* action—action viewed pictorially from a godlike distance—and for its first forty minutes or so the picture seems dead. It still has two hours to go, though, and I found myself becoming attuned to its magisterial style, and the measured preparation for the choreographed scenes, with their color-coded troops. Yellow banners designate the soldiers of Hidetora's eldest son, Taro; red banners are for the middle son, Jiro; and blue for the loyal, if brusque and tactless, Cordelia figure—the youngest son, Saburo. The film is a totally conceptualized work—perhaps the biggest piece of conceptual art ever made. Kurosawa doesn't want to drag us into the muck of battle; he's absorbed in logistics—in the conceiving of the shots. The brilliant colors on the performers and the clarity of these tones against enormous landscapes make the figures look helpless, miniaturized. They're easy targets for each other; you might say that they dress as targets—certainly the soldiers do.

Kurosawa's approach has its flaws and its peculiarities. That long opening that makes you drowsy is a heavy dose of preparation, and there are too many sequences where you wait for the point—such as the scenes with Jiro's wife, Lady Sué, a peaceful Buddhist in pastels and floral prints, and those with her blind, flute-playing brother. And Hidetora's honest and loving Fool, Kyoami—played by a glamorous transvestite pop singer, who is known in Japan simply as Peter—wears a version of motley that suggests pajamies, and prances about in a way that is probably supposed to indicate freedom but comes across as wholesome and self-conscious. Kyoami is like a well-heeled, serious-minded college girl dressed as a clown for a charity benefit, and the sexual ambiguity is puzzling, especially since no one on the screen appears to notice it. (This Fool and this Lear just don't go together, though we get the idea that Kurosawa, at seventy-five, may see himself as half one, half the other.) In the early scenes, at a boar hunt where Hidetora announces the decision to divide his property he is painted to resemble a demon, and later, when he has gone mad and the violent acts he committed come back to haunt him, his scraggly white hair and red-rimmed eyes suggest a sorrowful scarecrow. Hidetora's painted, masklike appearance (with its evocation of Noh drama) might be affecting in its own terms if the externals of the Lear story didn't set up expectations—for Western audiences, at least—of Lear's depth of suffering and Shakespeare's burst of passion. As the role is played, Hidetora is rash but so paper-thin that he doesn't seem capable of the blood lust he must have had when he struck down whole families and gouged out a child's eyes. (It was he who blinded Lady Sué's brother.) Tatsuya Nakadai's Hidetora doesn't suggest the ferocious past ascribed to him, and he doesn't move like an old man, either—he's a painted actor impersonating a stylized figure of tottering old age.

Shakespeare's *Lear* is about primary emotions. Lear is attacked by those he never harmed; he stands for every undeservedly abused parent figure who believed in his children's show of love for him. Hidetora is the victim of his own misdeeds. He and his dynastic plans for the House of Ichimonji are undone by a vengeance planned by his son Taro's wife, Lady Kaede (Mieko Harada), whose family Hidetora wiped out. Essentially, *Ran* is about color and pattern, the formality and pageantry of warfare, and the fun of melodrama. Very still and seemingly passive, her eyes modestly averted, Lady Kaede is a demon whose every breath is devoted to the destruction of the Ichimonji. And though this plot element diminishes the meaning of the Lear story as we know it, it has a pragmatic appeal (Kurosawa is saying, "Hey, a big lord like that didn't get where he is without stepping on toes"), and it gives the movie some nasty, sexual peppiness.

With the director's having planned virtually every shot in advance, the actors don't have much room for creative participation. (That's part of what makes the early section seem dead.) But Mieko Harada, performing in the stylized manner of Isuzu Yamada's Lady Macbeth in *Throne of Blood* and Machiko Kyo in *Rashomon*, has the chance to play a perfectly behaved wife who hides her feelings under a demure expression. She's the only character who gets to pull us in, and there's some theatrical charge and comedy in seeing that what's inside her is pure hatred. She draws blood and kicks the plot forward. (Women viewers may be more likely than men to register that Lady Kaede can hold to her plan of vengeance against the Ichimonji clan because she has no children.) The actress's finest moment is also a triumph of the sound engineer: having become Taro's widow, Lady Kaede glides across the floor on her knees, her silks rustling and hissing, as she moves to seduce Jiro.

At the climax, when four color-coded armies, with their plumes and armor and insignia, are poised on the landscape, you're *seeing* the conception. The whole movie has been pointing to this setup. And the fastidiousness and the monumental scale of what Kurosawa has undertaken can flood you with admiration. The conception is not one that lends itself to the movies, but he's carried it out anyway. He has done what he couldn't quite do in his last film, *Kagemusha*, in 1980. He has made all the preparation pay off. One army advances, and another, which has taken cover in a woodland, fires at the exposed men; the orange-red flashes that come from among the trees are extravagantly beautiful, and the use of timpani in the score helps to create a neo-barbaric mood. And Kurosawa has marshalled the heavens to his purposes: the changes in the light, the war clouds, the wind, the sun are all part of his absorption in logistics. Hidetora has no psychology; but we enter into his temperament in a different way. When he wanders over a windswept volcanic crater and the clouds churn, the convulsive natural world is his interior landscape—his own brutal psyche is taking revenge on him. This epic is static, but it deepens, and it has its own ornery splendor. Kurosawa's pride in his command of the medium is indistinguishable from his command of the elements.

■

The Trip to Bountiful is the kind of small picture that actors revere, because what you see on the screen is nothing but actors acting. *Bountiful* has a director, Peter Masterson, in what is referred to as his first film, but he hasn't made his first film yet. What he has done here is put the cameras at a discreet distance from the actors and stand back. (The material is still so nakedly a play that if two characters are on the set and one leaves, a third has to come rushing on.) The dialogue, which Horton Foote adapted from his 1953 teleplay, is stage dialogue, devised to carry the play and set its rhythms, and it has an archaic, overcalculated ring to it. This play was always thin and musty—Foote himself must have sensed that back in 1953, when he set it in 1947. Actors lust for character-sketch roles like the ones here, but they don't really flower in them; they look as if they were giving well-prepared, slightly ponderous demonstrations in front of an acting class. In the central role (the part played by Lillian Gish on *The Goodyear Television Playhouse* in 1953, and on Broadway later that year), Geraldine Page gives the sort of controlled all-out performance that makes actors in the audience say, "Isn't she great? Isn't it wonderful to see her in a part she can sink her teeth into?" The answers are "Yes, but not here" and "No." People love to see the triumph of the human spirit in an actress playing a baggy-housedress role, and Page's old-age pensioner Carrie Watts wears some fine seat-sprung specimens, but the camera here is meant to be the mirror of Carrie's soul, and we look in that mirror for so long that finally all we see is Geraldine Page acting.

Carrie Watts lives in a small Houston apartment with her sad, defeated, middle-aged son (John Heard) and his shrill, indolent wife (Carlin Glynn), who is constantly at her—picking on her in humiliating ways. The son is caught between his affection for his mother and his wife, who have their petty clashes over and over. The wife's worst complaint is that Carrie sings hymns as she goes about the cooking and tidying. (Shall we have a moment's silence in recognition of this sterling bit of dramaturgy?) The movie is about Carrie Watts' longing to escape and return to Bountiful, the Gulf Coast town where she grew up; she runs away, gets on a bus headed in the right direction, and lives out her dream. Along the way, she meets a soldier's young wife (Rebecca De Mornay) and a Texas sheriff (Richard Bradford), but the movie is underpopulated. Geraldine Page is the whole shebang, and she's fun to watch (at first): she lights up with girlish smiles; she lets her face sag and go mushy; she even displays a streak of old-lady flirtatiousness. But the effects lose their power when they're repeated.

Like *Tender Mercies*, which Horton Foote also wrote, *The Trip to Bountiful* is a "spiritual" picture. It's a tribute to the decency of the common people who just barely scrape by, who endure by doing the best they can. It's about how we should love the timid, the drab, the failures, even the bitchy (like the daughter-in-law). And it has the glow that movies get when they're about the need to have compassion. You see the glow in Carrie Watts' face, and, of course, it's there in her hymns. Foote wants *The Trip to Bountiful* to be a hymn; he's trying to make something poetic out of plain, everyday American life. And at one point, when Carrie talks to a small-town stationmaster and they both enjoy their ritual exchange of commonplace remarks, Foote does hit something nifty and comic. But he can't make poetry out of material as laundered and denatured as what he comes up with here. All he and Masterson can do is give some of the characters a limp, anesthetized grace.

■

Movies about the American War of Independence have traditionally been failures. Trying to find a style that seemed right for the period, the actors became stilted and cut themselves off from the audience. The opposite approach—playing the characters as if they were contemporaries—has its own perils. Hugh Hudson goes so far in this direction in *Revolution* that the picture is certifiably loony from its first minutes, when a crowd on Broadway in July of 1776 pulls down a gilded statue of George III on a horse. An equestrian statue of George III actually was pulled down in 1776. (It contained enough lead to make forty-two thousand bullets.) Yet the way Hudson, trying for an exciting mob, for hue and cry, for immediacy, has staged the scene, with several hundred extras milling around obligingly and a feeble hubbub on the soundtrack, it's like watching an opera chorus of peasants or gypsies. The rock star Annie Lennox, of the Eurythmics, turns up in a raffish, tight-fitting blouse as the spirit of liberty inciting the rabble to action. Nastassja Kinski, in a bonnet, hops out of a carriage—an instant, slogan-shouting convert to the cause of freedom. This introductory sequence is the American Revolution as you might expect to see it on MTV.

The picture's star, Al Pacino, appears in the harbor in a boat, as Tom Dobb, a Glasgow-born frontiersman who grew up in the Adirondack wilderness and has come downriver, with his young son, Ned, to trade pelts and hides for provisions. Tom's boat is confiscated by the revolutionaries, his son is hornswoggled into the militia, Tom himself joins up to protect the boy, and soon he's a tough guerrilla fighter, waving the flag. Kinski, who's his inspiration, is assisting at field amputations, and she's running supply wagons through enemy lines. As an eighteenth-century trapper, Pacino talks with a Scots accent but in the rhythms of the Bronx, and Kinski—Daisy McConnahay her name is here—has Joan Plowright for a mother. Daisy's father is a wealthy merchant who socializes with the British aristocracy, but Daisy is inflamed with rebelliousness—she seems hectic and feverish, and keeps oozing tears. When her mother insists that she attend a ball, she shows where her sympathies lie by taking a flag out of one of her Tory sisters' three-foot-high coiffures and jabbing it into a lord's groin. The lord calls her "a Yankee bitch whore," and her mother throws her out of the McConnahay house.

Hudson and the scriptwriter, Robert Dillon, present the War of Independence as a primal, Oedipal revolt of the Colonies against the parent country, and the relationships of Ned and Tom, Daisy and her mother, and several other sets of characters are meant to be variations on the larger revolutionary pattern. Hudson dabbles in both Freud and

Marx. When Plowright's Mrs. McConnahay is miffed at Daisy, she takes out her pettish rage by whacking a slave girl in the face with a bunch of flowers. The redcoat officers are sadistic swine. The officers of the militia are bums and bullies—when they're on horseback, they routinely whack the foot soldiers with their riding crops.

Revolution goes from 1776 to the end of combat, in 1783, plunging us into gritty, muddy restagings of famous campaigns, but we don't find out what's going on in these campaigns, or what their importance is in the course of the war. When Hudson wants to involve us, he stages his centerpieces—two torture orgies. In the first, redcoat officers and dissolute, effete English aristocrats have a full-dress fox hunt, with packs of hounds, and Tom Dobb and another Colonist as the foxes. In the second, little Ned Dobb is carried off by a redcoat sergeant major to be a drummer-boy-in-training—i.e., a catamite. Chosen for the night by a general, Ned bites his hand, and the sergeant major (Donald Sutherland, with a big, black, hairy mole on his jowl), a rabid disciplinarian and sexual psychopath, has him strapped to a cannon and proceeds to whip him on the soles of his feet, and whip him and whip him. Hudson can't seem to get enough of the scene, which is followed by the longest, most outré emotional display in the movie. Tom rescues Ned, darting off with the boy in his arms. Then, in a cavern, he holds the boy tight against his chest while he whispers and murmurs comforting words: his life story— how he was orphaned on the streets of Glasgow as a child and shipped to the Colonies, and how they're going to make a better world for themselves. He keeps talking while kindly Indians apply poultices to the boy's raw flesh, and cauterize the wounds, burning him and burning him. The film comes to a standstill for this anguished monologue in closeup accompanied by Ned's screams. It's the movie's big number—it's when Tom finally understands what he has been fighting for.

Hudson has Pacino, in eighteenth-century homespun, spouting lines such as "My mouth belongs anywhere I put it" while people in the audience stare at each other, as if to say, "Did you hear that?" Everything in the movie seems dissociated: a rabbi addressing a rebel soldier, "Go back to your guns—shalom, Israel Davis"; the Indians, with their folk medicine; the grownup Ned marrying a Jewish girl named Bella; a line on the soundtrack to inform us that the blacks are still in bondage. The ads for *Revolution* show Pacino and the American flag; he isn't wrapped up in it, like Stallone in the ads for *Rocky IV*, but the association with Stallone is established, and it's established within the film, too. Just after the victory has been won, Tom, the loudmouth who's going to have his say, delivers a speech in the spirit of *Rambo*—it's about the country's failure to appreciate those who fought in the war. Searching the wharves, looking for Daisy, he also passes a visual reminder of Stallone—a boxing ring with black and white contestants. When Tom finds his Daisy among the people celebrating peace, what is the angelic freedom fighter doing? She's kissing children—a random bunch of little tots. She sees Tom and runs into his arms, and we hear a reprise of his monologue to Ned—his words about making "a place where our babies can sleep safe through the night." *Revolution* is so bad it puts you in a state of shock. The credits include one for "keening" (by Catherine Kenny), and that's about all you can do for this movie.

January 13, 1986

LASSO AND PEASHOOTER

||||||||||||||||||||||||||||||||||||||||||||||||||||||||||||||||||||||||||||||||||||||||||||||||||||||||||||||||||||||||||||||||||||||||||

Nobody could have predicted that Robert Altman, who from 1970 to 1975 moved toward a looseness and openness of form and took talking pictures as far from theatre as any American director ever had, would be filming plays in the eighties. And I doubt if anybody could have predicted that the Altman who brought off the almost insuperably difficult transferral of play to film in 1982 with *Come Back to the 5 & Dime Jimmy Dean, Jimmy Dean* and again, in 1984, with *Secret Honor* would come a cropper with Sam Shepard's *Fool for Love*. On the face of it, Altman and Shepard seem an ideal matchup. The herky-jerky instability of Shepard's plays wouldn't faze Altman—it would delight him. You'd think that if anybody could film *Fool for Love* and keep it metaphorical and rowdy and sexually charged it would be the intuitive Altman. His collaboration with Shepard represents one of the rare opportunities that moviemakers and playwrights have had to work together freely, and its failure can't be blamed on any commercial calculations, or on anyone's not doing his damnedest. You can see an immense amount of effort in the film—perhaps too much. The material seems to congeal on the screen, and congealed rambunctiousness is not a pretty sight.

96

In the theatre, *Fool for Love* works somewhat like a Pinter play. From start to finish, everything is unresolved but suggestive. Actors delivering fragments of dialogue hold the stage space by creating tensions out of inexplicable transformations and quick changes of mood—aggressions, murder threats, temper tantrums, sudden laughter, pangs of guilt and fear. But Shepard, always manic, loves flamboyant, dreamlike stage images, and he whips up more of a free-for-all ruckus than Pinter does. The high that audiences can get from his plays comes out of his fermented mixture of junk culture, hard-nosed poetic language, and counterculture macho (circa *Easy Rider*) gone mythic. To keep a play cooking, he'll throw anything into the stew—animal, vegetable, or mineral. In *Fool for Love*, it's an automobile graveyard, horses, spurs and lassos, a mad countess in a Mercedes, gunshots, and fire—a whole conflagration.

During production, Altman said, "The content is done. I'm not going to alter the content. . . . I've concerned myself more with the arena, the environment that the play takes place in—in other words, in the stage, the stage that I'm making." That has more or less been his approach to all his filmed plays (including David Rabe's *Streamers* and Marsha Norman's *The Laundromat*). Altman didn't come from the theatre, and he wasn't rebelling against it in his seventies pictures; in the early eighties, when he was stymied as a moviemaker and began to direct plays, it was as if he'd just discovered the theatre, and he approaches a playwright's text with a respect that's at the opposite pole from his treatment of a screenwriter's work. If *Fool for Love* seems thickened on the screen—seems like an anchor-weighted hulk—it may be precisely because he regarded the content as "done" and unalterable. In his finest work, Altman feels his way along. Here he sets about providing a visual frame for Shepard's finished play—a carnal (and existential) screwball comedy, with absurdist suffering and a Dionysian fizz. (If there's any pain in Shepard's work it's like what a happy drunk might feel if he stubbed his toe: it's no big deal—just another sensation.)

The 1983 play is about the no-exit, tormented sex relationship between Eddie, a broken-down rodeo cowboy (Shepard), and his half sister, May (Kim Basinger), who lives in a cheap motel "on the edge of the Mojave Desert." Eddie and May have been lovers erratically for fifteen years; they get together, he walks out on her, then he wants her again—as he does now. She wants him, too, but she can't take being hurt anymore, and she fights him off. These two had the same father (Harry Dean Stanton), who sits on the stage, looks on, and occasionally speaks, but, as the author puts it, "exists only in the minds of May and Eddie." There's too much fizz for the lovers' torment to be strong drink; it's Pepsi-generation existentialism—it's for young audiences taking a deep swig of the dark side of things. But Altman directs this material almost reverently, as a series of near-static pictures. The wide screen—fine for the outdoor shots—is murderous indoors. The dialogue, set off by the compositions, has the sound of theatuh, and, of course, with that phantom father poking around the junk heap outside May's room and making mournful sounds on his harmonica, the movie has the devices of theatre.

Sitting there, you think this stuff isn't much but maybe it could get by as a slapstick dance-of-death entertainment if it were just faster and more kinetic, if there were less mood and atmosphere, and Eddie and May were ferociously passionate and excitable, and we felt the connection between them—felt that they were dangerously alike. But the twists and turns, and the ominous passage when May's gentleman caller, Martin (Randy Quaid), arrives to take her to the movies and Eddie taunts him, are all fixed in place. What happens is not unlike what happened in the film versions of Pinter's plays—Clive Donner's *The Caretaker*, in 1964, Friedkin's *The Birthday Party*, in 1968, and Peter Hall's *The Homecoming*, in 1973. The stage tensions disappear when the camera rules the space. About the only play I can think of that has walled-in emotional violence like that of *Fool for Love* and was successfully transferred to film is Cocteau's 1949 *Les Parents Terribles*, where he used the camera to emphasize the claustrophobic family-apartment setting, and to put us right in there. (The characters batted around like moths in a lampshade.)

Shepard calls his adaptation "an exploded play," but to a viewer it looks like the usual "opening out the play"—he lets the two lovers out of their cage. (It's a fatal mistake.) And he includes a sticky lament for lost innocence: a lonely golden-haired little girl at the motel represents May as a child, and this ties in with a scene of May regressing—expressing her vulnerability by lying down in a sandbox. The film also brings on Eddie and May and the Old Man in flashbacks to earlier points in their lives, adds characters who are merely referred to in the play, and expands the setting to the whole motel complex and the highway. Some of the casting—such as that of the teen-age May (Sura Cox) and of May's mother (Martha Crawford)—is remarkably convincing, and Altman gives an affecting, ambiguous lyricism to the bright, sunshiny flashbacks. But they dissipate the energy of the primal, raw love tangle.

Sam Shepard looked terrific in *Days of Heaven* and *The Right Stuff*; he had the rugged handsomeness and skinny haunches of an American archetype, and not much acting was required of him—or, at least, not much survived the final cuts. He's a feeble presence here, and since he plays Eddie as worn out and withdrawn (and maybe weak), he doesn't go in for any glamourizing makeup or lighting; he looks haggard, and puffy under the eyes. He may believe that the lines he wrote are strong enough to carry the character, and that all he need do is speak them. If so, he's wrong. His plays are written for an actors' theatre; when he delivers the dialogue, it has no visceral force, and most of Eddie's macho antics with his lasso just seem tiresomely symbolic. Altman gives us too many shots of Kim Basinger with tendrils of her burnished-gold hair tumbling down. She's likable, though, and she works hard—you can plainly see her stretching to be up to her role. With Pierre Mignot as the cinematographer, she's lighted so that her gray-blue eyes look lovely, and she has a flushed, smeary-faced, wounded quality. (I think she's meant to be so sultry she's shimmering with heat.) But she has no spirit. If she were fortyish, she wouldn't look out of place on *Dynasty*. Randy Quaid's performance as Martin—a yokel variation of his Mitch in the 1984 TV production of *Streetcar*—is a relief, because Martin is just what he appears to be, and Quaid gives him a solid, hick doggedness. He makes Martin a definitive square, and Shepard does his best acting in his hipster-outlaw gamesmanship with Quaid. (Though Martin is harmless and nothing is at stake, Shepard is more alive doing this version of Bob Dylan's snide put-ons than he is as a raging, ambivalent lover.) As the half-seen Old Man, a presence rather than a character, and perhaps the dreamer of the dream we're watching, Harry Dean Stanton has the right tequila-swigging grunginess (except for his sparkling-white teeth), and he can pass for Shepard's father, but he seems as lost here as he does playing an angel in *One Magic Christmas*. (I have no idea why the Old Man smiles in apparent pleasure at the desperate brawling of his children and grins happily when Eddie does dumb stunts with his rope.)

What you're likely to experience at the movie is a numbing discomfort—the result of the conflict between Shepard's flinging-things-together method and the flossy high-art embalming he and Altman give the play. There's all this crazy stuff going on. Eddie and May flip out with no visible provocation—they're shouting at each other and suddenly he's tender, or she's clutching him and, presto, she knees him in the groin—and their tussling is pumped up with dead air and country-song interludes, as if this were an American classic about rootlessness (which I guess some people think it is).

Trying to be faithful to Shepard's stylization, Altman makes a big number of its being sunset in the first sequence, and then calls our attention to each change of the light. He may be assigning himself a modest role as the interpreter of Shepard's work, but his own artistry is ever present—we have nothing to react to but his brushstrokes. And the impresario director never leaves you alone with the characters; you feel him controlling everything, and it can drive you a little nuts. So can the Greek-tragedy aspect of the material: Eddie and May as the incestuous lovers who can't stay apart—who are fated to love each other and suffer for it. Altman and Shepard push fate over the top when the Old Man goes inside the burning wreckage of the motel and stands amidst the flames playing his harmonica.

■

There's a coziness about the familiar murk and gloom of Victorian London, around 1870, in Barry Levinson's *Young Sherlock Holmes*. Hansom cabs rattle over the cobblestones, stuffy rooms are crammed with bric-a-brac, and plump men in their winter woollens proudly display their bushy mustachios and muttonchop whiskers. The schoolboy Holmes— Nicholas Rowe, a gracefully gawky six-foot-four adolescent, stick-thin, with a slender, ascetic face—has a gentle, sweet precociousness. (He suggests a schoolboy Jonathan Miller.) Holmes' sidekick, the good-hearted Watson, is a country bumpkin who has just transferred to boarding school in the city and hero-worships the older boy. As this stocky, loyal chum— a junior version of an old duffer—little Alan Cox has to keep stumbling and sprawling, and he takes his falls like a pro. The movie has devised a way to bring out the malign potential in Victoriana. The fiendish killer that Holmes goes after is armed with an Egyptian blowgun (which is basically a peashooter). This fiend, hidden in cloak and hood, and as faceless as Death or the bogeyman, blows poisoned thorns into a series of elderly men, who then have such terrifying hallucinations of being attacked by the objects they're surrounded by—the carved snakes and griffins on their hatracks and bureaus, the saintly knight in a stained-glass window, the gargoyles that are everywhere—that they destroy themselves. This sounds like a funnier, zestier picture than it turns out to be.

Young Sherlock Holmes is handsomely lighted (by Stephen Goldblatt), and it has some diversions, such as Holmes' old teacher, the smiling, dotty Professor Waxflatter (Nigel Stock). Waxflatter's niece Elizabeth, played by the lovely Sophie Ward, could have used some of her uncle's eccentricity; she's too sugary a heroine. As Dudley, the rotter and school snob, Earl Rhodes makes his blondness seem slimy, and, as the fencing master, Anthony Higgins recalls Armand Assante's smoothies. Young Watson, who can't resist the dessert tray, has a hallucinatory moment of comic terror when a small army of squishy cream-and-custard pastries attacks him. And it's charming to see this normally slow-witted fellow come through in a crisis: torn between the plight of Holmes, who's trapped in a building and about to be consumed by flames, and the plight of Elizabeth, who's being kidnapped outside, Watson looks helpless, as if paralyzed and unable to help either one, then comes up with a single trick that saves them both. As long as the movie stays within the conceits of the Holmesian legends, it's mildly, blandly amusing. But when one of the imperilled old men gives an elaborate account of the background of the villainy (an archeological dig in Egypt, the burning of a village, the activities of a religious sect, and on and on) your mind drifts and you lose the plot threads. And when the picture forsakes fog and coziness and the keenness of Holmes' intellect—when it starts turning him into a dashing action-adventure hero—the jig is up. This boy actor (with his eyes that don't quite take the light, and his pensive manner) doesn't have the exuberance to give the fighting scenes a comic bounce; if he did, he'd be wrong to play Holmes.

The movie lets you down with a thump when Holmes and his companions enter a wooden pyramid-temple hidden under the London streets, where members of the sect chant and offer up human sacrifices (beautiful girls are wrapped like mummies and covered in molten wax). Couldn't Levinson and the twenty-seven-year-old screenwriter, Chris Columbus, have waited a decent interval before ripping off Spielberg's *Indiana Jones and the Temple of Doom*? You don't need much in the way of worldly experience to write an entertaining Sherlock Holmes pastiche, but you ought to at least have a little pride. These two don't even cover their tracks. What it comes down to is: they didn't have enough faith in the young-Sherlock Holmes idea.

It used to be that when a director's hits were copied he was far from happy about it; he understood that his pictures were being devalued—cheapened. But Steven Spielberg "presents" *Young Sherlock Holmes*, just as he presented *Gremlins* and *The Goonies* (both also written by Columbus). Spielberg has said that he had "virtually nothing to do" with this movie except to offer some advice on the special effects, and there's no reason to doubt that. But didn't he even look at the script? Chris

Columbus writes passable smooth dialogue, and he ties things together squarely and neatly, as if he were a machine designed to churn out material for what booksellers call "young adults." But there's a resounding hollowness at the center of this picture—Levinson's temple of doom, with its solemnly chanting choir. (The pomposity of this music is lethal; it's like a High Mass for a dead mouse.)

Would the picture be more popular if it were faithful to its premise and if Levinson knew what sort of tone he was after? I doubt it. But it would certainly be more satisfying to those of us who went to see it. And we'd think better of those who made it. (Levinson's comedy sense seems to desert him just when he's got legions of bald men with pigtails running around waving scimitars.) The picture still wouldn't be more than marginally entertaining, though. The movies of the sixties and seventies made so many leaps in perception and style that you feel a time warp when you watch the fare of the mid-eighties: pictures made by directors who were only looking for a good commercial project—pictures that don't seem to have any reason to exist. It would take a deliriously gifted director—a real hellcat—to wire up *Young Sherlock Holmes.*

January 27, 1986

WHITE AND GRAY

||||||||||||||||||||||||||||||||||||||||||||||||||||||||||||||||||||||||||||||||||||||||||||||||||||||||||||||||||||||||||||||||||||||

Set in a pastel consumers' paradise, Paul Mazursky's new comedy, *Down and Out in Beverly Hills,* is almost immorally luscious. The cinematographer, Don McAlpine, gives you a vision of the sensuousness of money wrapped in sunshine, and Mazursky introduces you to a race of anxious people who feel "unfulfilled." Driving downtown in his Rolls-Royce with the top down, a self-made millionaire—a manufacturer of wire hangers—listens to Dr. Toni Grant's psychological advice on the radio. You're often at a loss to know why you're laughing, but jokes you can't explain may be the best kind, and Mazursky is a master of them. When he gets rolling, you're not responding to single jokes—it's the whole gestalt of the movie that's funny.

Down and Out takes off from the play, by René Fauchois, that served as the basis for Renoir's 1931 film *Boudu Saved from Drowning* (which was first released in the United States in 1967). A bum (Michel Simon in the Renoir film) is rescued from drowning by a middle-class man, who tries to turn him into a responsible citizen like himself. In the new version, Nick Nolte is the shaggy, smelly drifter; left with nothing when his scroungy dog, Kerouac, deserts him, he stuffs his pockets with ornamental stones from the grounds of a Beverly Hills mansion and walks into the clear blue swimming pool. Though slightly built, Dave Whiteman (Richard Dreyfuss), the wire-hanger magnate who owns the house, struggles manfully to pull him out and then gives him artificial respiration while Mrs. Whiteman (Bette Midler) and the servants look on in horror. The bum's filthiness is a moral affront to them.

A creamy-skinned, pampered Beverly Hills matron, Barb Whiteman can't believe what's happening when her husband insists on taking the ungrateful, foul-tempered fellow—Jerry—to the guest cabaña. Like Boudu, Jerry isn't one of the "deserving poor"; he's a dropout who wants to be left alone, and his eyes don't communicate—they don't tell you a thing. But he settles in fast, and in the next few weeks he ingratiates himself with the lady Barb, with the Whitemans' hot live-in maid Carmen (Elizabeth Peña), with their cool daughter Jenny (Tracy Nelson), and everybody else he encounters. Matisse, the family dog, who growls and yaps at Dave, does tricks for big, lazy Jerry, decked out now in silk lounging robes.

Like Mazursky's last picture *Moscow on the Hudson*, *Down and Out in Beverly Hills* is what a friend of mine calls "cultural comment without a hair shirt." This movie is silky in every department—the clothes, the bedding, Dave's white Rolls, which is the twin of his record-producer neighbor's white Rolls. I don't think conspicuous consumption has ever been made so integral to a way of life; it *is* the way of life here. Trying to persuade Jerry to rejoin the world and go to work, Dave takes him to his hair salon for some grooming, buys him expensive clothes, and drives him down to the plant where the hangers are made; a paternalistic employer, he's proud of the health care he provides the workers, proud of the business he built up. But Jerry is way past wanting a job. He's lord of the sunshine manor. One day, he persuades Dave to take him to the beach and meet his bummy old pals, and at sundown graying Dave and big, muscular Jerry talk together silhouetted against the opalescent water and the pale distant mountains. The beauty of this Southern California world plays off our sense of reality, even though it's as real as can be.

All through the picture, Mazursky uses the deluxe settings and the natural splendor as comic counterpoint to the dialogue. Beverly Hills is presented as a bastion of the new rich, where nobody feels fully accepted. The record-producer neighbor (Little Richard) shouts in protest that the police department comes out in greater force for Whiteman's (accidental) burglar alarms than it does for his own (accidental) alarms, because he's black; he claims that Whiteman rates a police helicopter and he doesn't. An unspeakably rich Iranian neighbor is offended because the Whitemans don't think to invite him to their New Year's party. Dave's father always worries that he won't have enough of the white meat of the turkey.

Mazursky and his co-scriptwriter, Leon Capetanos, aren't afraid to plant the beginnings of their gags and then have them pay off an hour later; the movie keeps erupting as gags reach maturity and crisscross each other. And it's full of the kind of social detail that makes Beverly Hills different from communities of the old rich. (Seeing Whiteman looking harried, the Japanese gardener suggests a vacation and offers him the use of the place he has bought in Hawaii.) As an actor, Little Richard uses the maniacal energy that went into his singing: the millionaire record producer's denunciation of the police department is a virtuoso piece of rant, with just a hint of a whine in its singsong, gospel rhythms. He stands outside in his silk dressing gown, singsonging furiously, and when he says the name "Whiteman" he gives it a twist. The whole movie spins off that name.

Bette Midler has never before been this seductive on the screen. This is only the fourth picture she has starred in, and you see a softer, less funky Midler; she's playing the role of a bored, dissatisfied housewife who has something extra—a warped charm rather like that of Teri Garr, but riper, juicier. Barb looks as if she might be listening to angels tinkling coins; money has beatified her, and so have a succession of gurus and yogis. Whether Barb Whiteman is reclining in the enormous peach-colored bedroom she shares with Dave (it's blissfully harmonious, like a motel in Nirvana) or sitting cross-legged before the statue of an Oriental idol or trotting through the halls jiggling in her frilly dresses and making tippy-taps with her high heels, her eyes are pixillated. She's ready for anything. (I think I'd be happy to watch an evening of Midler just doing her bobble-jiggle walks.)

Richard Dreyfuss's Dave Whiteman is devoted to his cool, slender, above-it-all daughter, irritated by his confused, semi-androgynous son (Evan Richards), and wild about Carmen, whose bed he pads off to as soon as Barb closes her eyes. Dave plays straight man to everybody in the movie; he even plays straight man to the little black-and-white Border collie Matisse, who gets laughs by chasing him around. Lean now, Dreyfuss is more precise and agile than he used to be, and he uses his slightness for comic effects vis-à-vis Nolte. When Dave is trying to hold the unconscious man's head above the water, he looks as if he were being overpowered by Jerry's bulk (and the stones). And when Jerry, shaven and groomed, walks down the street with Dave he towers over the blithe little guy. Dreyfuss isn't acting up a storm; he just slips into the character of Dave the patsy and stays with it. He hasn't been on the screen for a few years, so we get to rediscover what an enjoyable actor he can be. His Dave is the traditional henpecked husband brought up to date: Dave is henpecked upstairs by Barb and downstairs by the demanding Carmen. Elizabeth Peña plays Carmen as tantalizing and sulky; she has a bedroom mouth, and when it says no to Dave the rejection is brutal, because that mouth looks as if it were made to say nothing but yes.

Nick Nolte looks great as Jerry; his high cheekbones and strong physique and fair hair—the abundance of it—suggest a Nordic seafarer but one with the sneaky, foxy eyes of a con artist. He looks a bit like Kris Kristofferson here but much more powerful. And he has that deep rumble of a voice which seems to come from under the ocean floor. Jerry never tips his hand; he's as much of a mystery at the end as he was at the beginning, and that seems right, because explaining his background would diminish the movie—would suggest that it's about clearing up the mystery of who and what Jerry used to be. But the Beverly Hills we see is about the wonders of rootlessness; a shrewd bum *should* rule the roost. Taxpaying residents may panic when stray leaves fall on their plush greensward; it takes a bum like Jerry to be lordly enough to pee on the plants.

The film has some minor flaws. In the opening scenes, Jerry, looking for his mutt Kerouac, abandons the shopping cart with his pack rat's hoard of possessions, and he never goes to reclaim it. (Perhaps the cart-pushing fellow we see under the end titles is meant to have taken it.) And the advice that Jerry gives the Whitemans' son is no different from what a radio psychologist might give him. So when it backfires you expect Mazursky to come up with a snapper of some sort. (The boy is made too poignant anyway; Mazursky treats his sexual-identity problems in the constrained way he treated the heroine's rising consciousness in *An Unmarried Woman*.) And the film makes the mistake of leading you to expect a resolution that it can't provide. But these are nits. The picture is peppy and pleasurable in the way that *Moscow on the Hudson* is, and with a modulated visual texture that makes it one of the most sheerly beautiful comedies ever shot. Mazursky, who appears in a small part, as Dave's accountant, wears the wild curly wig of a bandit. He isn't afraid of uproarious silliness. I haven't laughed at cuts to a dog reacting since *Used Cars*, but Matisse provides the capper to some dizzying slapstick numbers. The dog's startled response to Barb's orgasmic vocalizing is stupendous. And there's a wonderful feeling of a warrior at his rest when Nolte relaxes sleepily in the peach bedroom with Matisse snuggling on his hip.

■

The title of Terry Gilliam's *Brazil* is used nostalgically in a semi-jokey, ironic way. It refers to the 1939 pop song, sung here by Geoff Muldaur, about the romance of a Brazil "where hearts were entertained in June." The lyrics end with "Return, I will, To old Brazil." Heard as a refrain in the background of the movie, the music is meant to evoke the pop escapism of the past. Old Brazil is what you want life to be, and what can only be dreamed about in the squalor and sporadic terrorist violence of an Anglo-American police state "somewhere in the twentieth century"—which means the next fifteen years. Gilliam's vision comes across as a stoned, slapstick *1984*, but it's not a political cautionary tale, like Orwell's novel—it's a melancholy, joke-ridden view of the horribleness of where we are now and the worse horribleness of where we're heading. It's an anarchistic attack on all present and future states—an attack on reality itself. And it dissolves the boundaries between fantasy and reality.

An American, born in 1940, who moved to London in the late sixties, Gilliam—and five Englishmen—formed the troupe Monty Python's Flying Circus, and he first became known for the animated segments he did to fill the gaps in the group's TV shows. When the group started making movies, he got the chance, in 1974, to co-direct *Monty Python and the Holy Grail*, and then, in 1977, he directed *Jabberwocky*; he wanted to make *Brazil* next but couldn't get it financed, and it wasn't until after he'd made the hit film *Time Bandits*, in 1981, that he got the go-ahead. The movie that he mulled over for years is clearly the work of an image-maker. Gilliam says he's never read the Orwell book, and that isn't hard to believe, because *Brazil* is like the impression you might get of *1984* if you'd just heard about it over the years and it had seeped into your visual imagination.

The characters that Gilliam devised (with his co-screenwriters, Tom Stoppard and Charles McKeown) have something of the comic-strip quality of Godard's characters in *Alphaville*, but Godard's dehumanized metropolis was made up of the sleekest parts of Paris; Gilliam's dehumanized metropolis is made up of the most medieval-looking structures in and around London, with a few picked up in other parts of England and in Marne-la-Vallée, France, and some designed and built. Visually, *Brazil* is an original, bravura piece of moviemaking; I assume that it was storyboarded, because the shots keep taking us from high up in towers (which have a perverse grandeur) to way down at street level and up again. The buildings are cold and dour—oppressive stone structures with ramshackle interiors. Inside, they look as if they had been blitzed in the Second World War and never repaired, and the offices and apartments are so high-ceilinged and cavernous that every room seems to be an atrium. The picture has a weirdly ingenious vertical quality: the camera always seems to be moving up and down, rarely across, and this seems like a violation of nature. You get the feeling that people live and work squashed at the bottom of hollow towers, and that everything has been grayed out: the bureaucrats wear suits that are as alike as prison uniforms, and the wide-brimmed fedoras worn straight across their heads are as gray and drab as stone. The women's freakish clothes, like the furnishings and the ancient TV sets and assorted gadgetry, suggest that nothing has been made or manufactured since the forties. It's a thrift-shop world of the future.

The central character, Sam Lowry (Jonathan Pryce), is a lowly functionary, a drone, but a dreamer—a Winston Smith–Walter Mitty. He's a clerk in the Ministry of Information (MOI) who lives in his fantasies of himself as a knight in silver armor with great, Icarus-like feather wings. Soaring way up high amongst the clouds, he encounters a beautiful blond maiden. The story line is very simple. Sam glimpses the girl of his dream flights when he goes to deliver a check—a "refund"—to a woman whose husband has been "deleted" by bureaucratic error. A bug that was swatted fell into a computer, causing the name Tuttle to be changed to Buttle. And so the state's Security Forces—i.e., official murderers—killed innocent Buttle, and the freedom fighter Tuttle is still at large. On a realistic level, what happens to Sam is simply that in pursuit of his dream blonde, Jill (Kim Greist), he forgets his usual caution and runs afoul of the state apparatus. There's also a superrealistic inevitability about this—a fatalism that is tied to fantasy.

107

If you don't respond to Sam Lowry's plight, the picture has no core, but it's hard to worry about whether somebody will get killed if he doesn't seem alive to start with. Jonathan Pryce's Sam is pale and dead-eyed; he looks like a taller version of the young Alec Guinness, but Guinness's anonymous men let you in on their furtive sparks of nonconformity, and they had some charm. Pryce plays Sam too straight and too wistfully. It's a real crapehanger's performance. The marginal characters—especially Katherine Helmond as Sam's nut-brain mother and Robert De Niro as Tuttle—are far more entertaining. (I hate to think what the movie would be like without them.) Helmond, the American actress who appeared as Mrs. Ogre in *Time Bandits*, is the rich, powerful widow of a government minister here, and she delivers an elegant, broad caricature of a woman obsessed with plastic surgery, who keeps looking younger and younger. It's not a big role, but she gets to wear one awe-inspiring dingbat ensemble: a form-fitting leopard jacket with a matching leopard shoe—an outsize one—worn upside down as a hat. De Niro's role is even smaller—no more than a cameo—but, all revved up and chomping on a cigar, he's a prankster-daredevil, a comic-strip hero, high-spirited and the life of the party. He even has a healthy color. Tuttle repairs heating systems illicitly (he doesn't have a license), and when he's in danger of being caught he slides down a rope as if he were jet-propelled, dropping from the top of an astoundingly tall skyscraper to street level in the blink of an eye. (Tuttle must be the first kinetic Underground Man in the movies.)

Brazil is more antic than comic. It's full of jokes—some of them very clever—but most of them don't quite make you laugh. I'm not sure Gilliam wants you to. His intention seems to be to create a new movie genre of nightmare comedy in which the comedy is just an aspect of the nightmarishness. He presents a retro-futurist fantasy (like *A Clockwork Orange* or *Blade Runner*) and keeps it perking by cartoon techniques and black humor. The jokes may be something he does compulsively, because that's how he works—without worrying about whether they're set up to get a laugh. He uses pop-surreal effects the same way: the heating ducts in Sam's apartment are like huge intestines stuffed in the walls; when they're pulled out, they fill the place. But Gilliam never prepares the instant when these gross tubes and cords will invade your consciousness and make you break up. And that's even more true of the enormous Rube Goldberg–like truck that Jill drives—a mass of cylindrical shapes that you can't imagine the purpose of. I waited for the joke, expecting Sam to discover what the truck was for, or to ask about it and be rebuffed, but it just goes clanging along. The chase sequence, with Jill and Sam in this monster truck and the authorities in pursuit, is, I think, a crucial mistake. It's pointless: you know that it wouldn't be necessary if Sam just asked Jill a simple question and she gave him a straight answer. Instead, they go smashing through barricades, getting themselves into more and more trouble. Any developing interest in them collapses, and you begin to think the picture is too long. (It's two hours and eleven minutes, Gilliam having cut it a little in order to appease Universal.)

It's fascinating at *Brazil* not having a clue to what's coming next, but the things that do show up run together and blur in your mind, because the episodes lack dramatic definition, just as the gags do. Gilliam's gags don't have that wonderful zing you experience when the timing itself is a thing of beauty. Asked by Owen Gleiberman, of the Boston *Phoenix*, if his imagination was always working, Gilliam said, "Yeah, and I don't try to control it. I do everything in my power to keep things from falling into neat little slots." Does that mean that his timing has to be lousy? Maybe it does. Maybe it means that his work has to be both torpid and frantic. (Gilliam distrusts the conscious mind as if it would destroy his creativity—though it's probably the only means of bringing his creativity to fulfillment.)

Brazil is the kind of ornery, intellectually fuzzy labor of love that is bound to strike some people as just about "the worst thing I've ever seen," and perhaps it will affect others as a picture they want for their VCRs, so they can look at it over and over. What Gilliam presents is a vision of the future as the decayed past, and this vision is an organic thing on the screen—which is a considerable accomplishment. I was held by the vertical, anti-human look of things and the sometimes mysteriously eccentric images. When Sam is transferred to Information Retrieval—a place with corridors that go off to infinity—he is shown to a tiny, cell-like office with a half a desk; the other half is on the other side of the wall, where another clerk tries to pull it his way. Sam has to hold on to his half and put all his weight on it to keep it from disappearing through the wall. (It's a neat, Kafka-esque variation on a very old gag.) A torture chamber at the bottom of an empty, vast domed structure suggests a twenties Expressionist set for a trial, or perhaps a giant amphitheatre for surgeons to display their art. (This movie certainly takes the romance out of high ceilings.) The hugeness of the space in the amphitheatre plays off our awareness that Sam is strapped down and can't move, but the space also represents his unbounded imagination. One of the "surgeons" (Michael Palin) wears a mask that looks like the face of an evil Oriental

109

doll-child. It's in hyperbolic images like these that Gilliam's not letting things fall into "neat little slots" seems the right—possibly the only—way for him to work. Yet I must admit to a feeling of relief when the film was over. What Gilliam appears to be saying is that reality is so intrinsically awful that fantasy will always be needed. But fantasy itself, in Gilliam's hands, seems something you want to escape from. This image-maker leaves you with nothing but images; they're like shards or scraps. *Brazil* makes you feel that no rational understanding of the world is possible—that all we have is what T. S. Eliot called "a heap of broken images."

February 10, 1986

COUPLES

"A soufflé flipped like a Frisbee"—that's how Ron Shelton describes *The Best of Times*, which he wrote and Roger Spottiswoode directed. The description also fits other small-town comedies where the whole population is caught up in some glorious foolishness, such as Preston Sturges's *Hail the Conquering Hero* and *The Miracle of Morgan's Creek*, and Jonathan Demme's *Citizens Band*. The town in *The Best of Times* is Taft, California (population roughly five thousand), where every smart aleck has been ribbing Jack Dundee (Robin Williams) for thirteen years—ever since he fumbled the beautiful touchdown pass that the high school's star quarterback, Reno (Kurt Russell), threw to him at the end of the Big Game with Bakersfield (population roughly a hundred thousand). That game in 1972 was Taft's only chance to beat Bakersfield in sixty years of competition, and it doesn't look as if the townspeople will ever stop taking out their sour feelings on butterfingered Jack, who's vice-president of the local branch bank. (His father-in-law is the president, in Bakersfield.) Dressed in a three-piece suit, and with his hair parted low on the side and plastered across his forehead as if it had crawled that far and died, Jack is the image of a smarmy, self-satisfied tightwad. Underneath, he's ticked off, and cantankerous voices rasp out of him—manic takeoffs of the kidders who infuriate him. One afternoon, during Jack's weekly visit to a hooker (she was an attendant in the home-coming queen's court), when he's complaining, as usual, about the never-ending shame of having dropped the ball, she suggests that he should replay the game, and he fastens on this addlepated notion and won't let go of it.

Reno, whose bright future as an athlete was cooked when he threw that pass and half the Bakersfield team jumped on top of him and wrecked his knee, now runs a garage that specializes in repairing vans. (He also paints reproductions of masterpieces on them.) Reno is more tolerant of Jack than other people are, but he refuses to get involved in the idea of a rematch; he doesn't need to redo the past to make himself a hero—he *was* a hero. At this point, Jack's gimmicky, manipulative brain goes to work: he tricks the people of Taft into thinking that Bakersfield has insulted them, rounds up the former players and starts them working out to lose their beer bellies, and sees to it that Reno is riled up and ready to train by gulling him into believing that the wife whom he adores (for good reason) has been humiliated by Bakersfield bullies.

The town of Taft comes to life; it's charged with a new do-or-die spirit. But not Jack's wife, or Reno's wife, either—they don't go for this football enthusiasm, and what makes the movie more than a football fantasy is how the rematch affects the marriages. This movie does one of the best jobs of putting couples together that I've ever seen. As the two pairs of high-school sweethearts who are now married lovers, Robin Williams and Holly Palance and Kurt Russell and Pamela Reed are as close to comic perfection as we're likely to get. When Jack's tall, lanky father-in-law (Donald Moffat) drops in on him at the bank, his hooting contempt for his squatty, ball-fumbling son-in-law is unconcealed. But when Jack and his tall, lithe wife embrace, her arms wrap around his shoulders and her thighs wrap around the rest of him. When he dances with her, it's as if he's enveloped in woman. Nobody has done a better job of demonstrating why a short man would dream of a tall wife than Holly Palance does here; she's cool and smart and funny. And Pamela Reed may be the only major young American actress who has the comedy flair to sing a song—as she does in her job at the local night spot, the Safari Room—while keeping her mouth in a Kewpie pout. Reed recalls the Claudette Colbert of *It Happened One Night*, but with an eighties independence. Her big-eyed doll face is so pretty here that you have to grin when you look at her; after thirteen years of marriage, Kurt Russell still melts and goes weak in his bad knee whenever she's around. This movie gives marriage a good name, in the way that *The Thin Man* pictures did, but with a more farcical (and open) sexiness.

Jack's standing date with the hooker doesn't reflect any dissatisfaction with his marriage; on the contrary, he's so happy at home he wants even more. He's a horny little Caspar Milquetoast. Robin Williams' Jack is a cartoon figure playing off the film's skewed naturalism, yet, even with uncontrollable, vicious mimicry breaking out of him, he never loses the character of Jack. He goes through the whole movie with this crazed multiple personality inside the runty bank official. He's like a Preston Sturges–Eddie Bracken hero with a murderous alien inside him, and Spottiswoode keeps the other performers reacting to him as if he were simply smiling Jack, the guy who always louses things up. In a dinner-party scene, where the two men are trying to pacify their touchy wives, the wine and the careful talk are having their effect and the wives are softening until Jack thinks he can get by with surreptitiously watching Monday Night Football on TV, and everything goes to hell. What's weirdest about Robin Williams' performance here is that his character is always at maximum awareness: Jack's loony psyche operates at full tilt. And he'll get his way. If one ploy doesn't succeed, his teeming noggin is ready with others and others and others. He's so nervous he's unstoppable. The mellow Russell is a great straight man to him: the way Russell plays Reno, you see his transparent normality in every curve of his face. His Reno has the sexual presence of a jock, but he's not a boor; his love for his wife has gentled him.

Maybe you have to know Bakersfield to appreciate the joke when the people of Taft refer to it as the big city, but we've all known people who screwed up when they had their one big chance—or, at least, people who claim they did. The movie has a good comic premise and, since eccentricity blossoms in small towns, some fine, knobby marginal characters, such as Margaret Whitton's Darla the hooker. In the scenes at the men's club, the Caribou Lodge (which were shot at the Moose Lodge in Glendale), M. Emmet Walsh is the head Caribou, and if he puts a motion before the house Dub Taylor, with the alacrity of a born lickspittle, chimes in to second it. Eager to improve Taft's morale, the Caribous get behind the game in a big way, and attend it wearing their antlers. *The Best of Times* is a movie of absolutely no importance, but it's an enjoyable soft-shoe farce. Spottiswoode and Shelton are the team who worked on *Under Fire*, and they think out their material—they don't put the stresses in the same old places. The rematch at the climax is satisfyingly wacko, but the two couples are the movie's real creations. Robin Williams is prodigious: Jack is the kind of aggressive schemer who threatens to call in the mortgage on his friend Reno's garage if Reno won't play ball, yet you can't help being pleased when he's finally able to stand up to his father-in-law. You like the little swine.

■

Woody Allen's *Hannah and Her Sisters* is an agreeably skillful movie, a new canto in his ongoing poem to love and New York City which includes *Annie Hall* and *Manhattan*. The principal characters are members of a show-business family, with the stable, dependable Hannah (Mia Farrow), a successful actress who manages a career and children with equal serenity, as the pivotal figure. At the start, the whole clan gathers at her sprawling Upper West Side apartment for Thanksgiving dinner. It includes her two flailing-about sisters: the wildly insecure cocaine-nut Holly (Dianne Wiest), whose acting career has never taken off, and the unsure-of-herself Lee (Barbara Hershey), who goes to A.A. and turns to men she can look up to. It includes the three sisters' bickering show-business-veteran parents: their boozy, habitually flirtatious mother (Maureen O'Sullivan) and their affable, but underconfident father (Lloyd Nolan). And it includes Hannah's financial-consultant husband (Michael Caine), who is swooning with passion for Lee, and an assortment of friends and relatives. Not in attendance is Lee's artist lover (Max von Sydow), who has no patience for social chatter. The movie ends at another Thanksgiving celebration, two years later; by then, Holly has pulled herself together, Hannah's husband has had his fling with Lee, and Hannah's ex-husband, Mickey Sachs (Woody Allen), a TV writer-producer, has rejoined the clan. And things are rosier. Like Ingmar Bergman's *Fanny and Alexander*, which was also about a theatrical family, the film is full of cultured people, and it has a comfortable, positive tone. Bergman's central character, Alexander, was clearly based on Bergman as a child; Allen's heroine is clearly based on Mia Farrow. And, like Bergman, whose cast included old friends, an ex-wife, an ex-lover, and a few of his children, Allen uses several actors he has worked with before, has Mia Farrow's mother playing Hannah's mother, and uses Farrow's actual apartment and seven of her eight children.

113

Hannah is meant to be the still center of the film, but mute would be more like it. Casting Mia Farrow as an ideal creative, nurturing woman in demure, plain-Jane dresses, Allen turns her into an earth-mother symbol and disembodies her. Most of the time, Hannah the Madonna seems barely animate. Allen has got her so subdued and idealized that she seems to be floating passively in another world. Barbara Hershey has a luscious presence here. She has a sexual vibrancy about her, and she fits her role—it's easy to believe that her brother-in-law would become obsessed with her. But Allen hasn't written enough sides for her—or for anyone else—to play. Dianne Wiest does all she can with her role—she makes a style out of neurosis. Her Holly is so fouled up that she's always angry at herself and everybody else, too. Her nerves aquiver, she seems to be holding back either screams or tears; she lives in a tizzy. (And she's so completely lacking in confidence that she's bound to match up with the Woody Allen character.) But Allen's script, for all its shrewdness about sisterly relations and its considerable finesse, doesn't cut very deep. There's a basic, bland unadventurousness about the picture: it never makes us wonder about anything. Hangups are there to be got through; the characters are like patients in the hands of a benevolent, godlike therapist.

Hannah and Her Sisters would be lifeless without Woody Allen's presence as Mickey Sachs, who is convinced he has a fatal disease. It needs his mopey personality, and it needs his jokes, even though they're throwbacks to earlier gags. It's a funny thing about Woody Allen: the characters he plays learn to accept life and get on with it, but then he starts a new picture and his character is back at square one. Mickey is a hypochondriac, terrified of dying and obsessed with the same old Woody Allen question: If there's no God and no afterlife, what's the point of living? Mickey takes a year off from his work in TV to ponder the meaninglessness of everything. He tries to find faith in Catholicism and then, for a moment, in Hare Krishna (because of the sect's belief in reincarnation); he attempts suicide. Then he sees the Marx Brothers in *Duck Soup*, and when they sing "Hail, Fredonia" he realizes that he wants to enjoy life for as long as he can. He'll settle for romantic love, for a "relationship." But we've been through all this with him before.

Still, the picture needs him desperately, because the other roles are so thin that there's nobody else to draw us into the story. Michael Caine flails around confusedly trying to bring something to a role that's out of bedroom farce but that he seems expected to give other dimensions to. At first, you attribute Caine's discomfort to the character's crush on Lee, but afterward he goes on being ill at ease. Maureen O'Sullivan (who was born in 1911) comes through with a ribald-old-trouper performance that's gutsier than anything she ever did in her M-G-M years. But it's a small role. So is that of Lloyd Nolan (born in 1902), who made his final appearance here; he brings to his part the dapper weariness of a vain man whose wife goads him unconscionably—he may suspect that tormenting him is what keeps her on her toes and beautiful. In a larger role, Max von Sydow has nothing to play but an aspect of the earlier Woody Allen characters: he's a rigid intellectual, a man so devoted to high culture that he's exasperated by other people's delight in pop. He's like the Woody Allen of *Stardust Memories,* and his determination to educate Lee recalls the Woody of *Annie Hall.*

This character's gloom and the way he cuts himself off from other people tell us that Woody Allen is saying here that the high arts are not everything—that we also need the ease and relaxation of pop culture, that superficiality isn't all bad. Allen's love for the romantic, "civilized" pop music of the past is expressed throughout the movie, which features Rodgers and Hart songs, a couple of Harry James recordings, and some Count Basie, as well as Gustav Leonhardt playing Bach. Allen draws the line at high-powered rock, though: part of Holly's coming to her senses is her graduating from the downtown life of CBGB to classical music. Woody Allen can't seem to get rid of a streak of draggy pedantry; he's still something of a cultural commissar. (I could have done without the quick tour of Manhattan's architectural marvels that's included in the movie.)

Like Bergman, Allen shows his intellectuality by dramatizing his quest for meaning and then shows his profundity by exposing the aridity of that quest. This celebration of family is essentially a celebration of sanity and of belonging to a group—of satisfying the need for human connections. It's a tribute to human resilience, a look-we-have-come-through movie, and the people who were deeply moved by *Manhattan* are likely to be still more deeply moved by *Hannah.* The infertile Mickey even becomes fertile; the picture goes the traditional life-affirming route. Yet what he has come through to is so lacking in resonance that it feels like nowhere. *Hannah* is very fluid in the way it weaves the characters in and out; Allen's modulated storytelling has a grace to it. The picture is certainly better than three-fourths of the ones that open, and it's likable, but you wish there were more to like. It has some lovely scenes—I was particularly taken with the one in which Holly and a good friend (played by Carrie Fisher) are out in a car with a man (Sam Waterston) whom they're both interested in, and at their last stop before calling it a night they discuss the logistics of which one he should drop off first. Yet, over all, the movie is a little stale, and it suggests the perils of inbreeding. It might be time for Woody Allen to make a film with a whole new set of friends, or, at least, to take a long break from his sentimentalization of New York City. Maybe he'd shed the element of cultural self-approval in the tone of this movie. There's almost a trace of smugness in its narrow concern for family and friends; it's as if the moviemaker has seen through the folly of any wider concern.

Woody Allen has joined a club that will have him, and that may help to explain the awesome advance praise for the film. Like the Robert Benton picture *Kramer vs. Kramer,* which also stirred up enormous enthusiasm in the press, *Hannah* evokes the "family/style" pages in *The New York Times* and all the books and editorials and "Hers" columns about people divorcing and remarrying and searching to find meaning in their lives. It's about people that members of the press can identify with; it's what they imagine themselves to be or would like to be. They're applauding their fantasy of themselves.

All the vital vulgarity of Woody Allen's early movies has been drained away here, as it was in *Interiors,* but this time he's made the picture halfway human. People can laugh and feel morally uplifted at the same time. The willed sterility of his style is terrifying to think about, though; the picture is all tasteful touches. He uses style to blot out the rest of New York City. It's a form of repression, and from the look of *Hannah and Her Sisters,* repression is what's romantic to him. That's what the press is applauding—the romance of gentrification.

■

Directed by Robert Mandel, from a script by Robert T. Megginson and Gregory Fleeman, *F/X* is an ingenious suspense film about a movie special-effects wizard (Bryan Brown), based in New York, who lets himself be bamboozled by a couple of men from the Justice Department's Witness Relocation Program. They hire him to stage the fake assassination of a Mafia boss (Jerry Orbach) in a crowded restaurant, so that this gangster can give evidence against his associates and be relocated without fear of reprisals. When things don't go according to what our wizard thought was the plan, he's in the position of the innocent heroes in such Hitchcock films as *The 39 Steps* and *North by Northwest*, except that he has all his special skill at creating illusions to aid him in staying alive. He also has the awareness that he has been played for a sap—that the government men flattered him into the trap. Bryan Brown underplays niftily, and Mandel keeps you inside the beleaguered man's consciousness; killers are out to get him, but he doesn't know why, or who they are. (The premise of *F/X* may seem farfetched, but there have been actual cases of special-effects men being asked to stage fake killings; whether any of them have risen to the bait isn't known.)

The film has a dark, rich glint to it; much of the action takes place with people charging through the streets at night, and the cinematographer, Miroslav Ondříček, gives the glassy surfaces of cars and buildings a loving sleekness. You can almost feel their texture; the city seems dangerously alive. Mandel's work is clean and brisk; the movie is gory—our wizard specializes in splatter films—but there's no real nastiness in it. It's not the kind of kicky thriller that leaves a viewer feeling debauched. Despite the high body count, you have a fast-moving hour and three-quarters and then it's over—no aftermath, no lingering, childlike dread of "evil." Horror fans may miss that after-fear, but *F/X*—the letters are the movie-industry shorthand for "special effects"—has a snappy professionalism that gives it a different kind of kick.

Bryan Brown is joined by a second hero—swaggering Brian Dennehy, built like a barn and sporting a big, messy mustache, as a rogue cop. They make a fine pair: Brown acts close to the vest, while Dennehy grabs the movie in his choppers and shakes it up. Diane Venora, who hasn't been seen much in movies, has a few good, showy moments as Brown's actress girlfriend—especially at the opening, when she's playing a blond tart in a cheapo-picture massacre scene (it appears to be a deliberate evocation of De Palma's *Scarface*). Joe Grifasi, as Dennehy's serious-minded, deadpan partner, has the best scene in the movie. He's in his squad car and he plows through a wholesale meat market, with the slabs of beef flying over the hood; it's mysteriously beautiful and funny. I thought that the film lost something—that it breached its rapport with the audience—when it took a turn toward an acceptance of corruption; but as a suspense fantasy it all holds together. Megginson and Fleeman give Dennehy some sharp tough-guy lines, and he sends them home like a master comedian. Dennehy is so enthusiastically overscaled that he fills the screen. He's the kind of actor John Wayne would have been if he'd been an actor.

February 24, 1986

YES, YES

‖‖

My Beautiful Laundrette is the unprepossessing title of a startlingly fresh movie from England. The director, Stephen Frears, threads his way through life in South London among the surly white street gangs who live on the dole with no hope of anything better and the Pakistani immigrants who are trying to make their way upward. The movie begins in a small apartment with a Pakistani father phoning his brother to arrange a summer job for his son, whom he expects to start college in the fall, and it gradually expands until you get the sense of the Pakistanis moving in everywhere, and forming a community inside a larger slum community. As the assorted skinheads, punkers, and thugs see it, the "Pakis" were allowed into England to do the dirty work, to be *under* them, yet are getting ahead of them; and these thugs, with their remnants of colonial, master-race attitudes, take out their frustrations on the unlucky Pakistanis who cross their path. That's the milieu of the movie; it's intrinsically fascinating, and you wouldn't normally see it. You're taken into it by guides who know their way around, and you're caught up in the texture and decay of modern big-city life. Though it's South London, you have the feeling that this is what's around you, too—that your blinders have been taken off. The movie defines a world and the people in it, and keeps redefining them. In the foreground is a homosexual romance between a dark-eyed, softly handsome, almost flowerlike Pakistani teenager, Omar (Gordon Warnecke), who grew up in this neighborhood, and a young dyed-blond-on-brunet street lout, Johnny (Daniel Day-Lewis). They chummed together years before, as schoolkids, and they become partners when Omar, having taken the summer job washing cars in his uncle's parking garage, persuades the uncle to let him have a ratty-looking failed laundrette.

118

Omar's mother couldn't take the cultural dislocation of the move to London and killed herself. Papa (Roshan Seth), a member of a distinguished family that was highly respected in Pakistan, was a left-wing intellectual journalist in Bombay, and he expects Omar to become an educated man and carry on the family traditions, though he himself is now a vodka-soaked dreamer, a near-invalid too sodden to get out of bed. There's not much left of Papa, except bright eyes and a tongue that's still quick. Omar's uncle (Saeed Jaffrey) has been amassing money; it's the only way he sees for a Pakistani to win respect in London. A plump sensualist, he's a slumlord and low-level capitalist entrepreneur, with a handful of enterprises, some of them shady. Saeed Jaffrey—he was Billy Fish, the interpreter, in *The Man Who Would Be King*—plays the uncle as a man who's a slave to his appetites; he loves his white-Londoner mistress (Shirley Anne Field), he loves his wife and daughters, he loves the sweet, docile Omar. He wants Omar to marry his playful, smart, uncontrollable daughter, Tania. He wants everybody to be happy, and he wants to be sated with sex and oiled and massaged like a pasha.

Omar, who's eager to learn and not afraid of hard work, is soon making pickups of dope and porno videos, and, as amoral as a puppy, he steals from a racketeer relative. That's how he and Johnny get the money to transform the run-down laundrette into a neon-decorated establishment that looks like the flashiest new disco in town. It's a slum dweller's dream of hot chic, and on the re-opening day Omar and Johnny are so exhausted and elated that they have to make love before letting the customers in. As Daniel Day-Lewis (son of the poet C. Day Lewis and grandson of Sir Michael Balcon, who was the head of Ealing Studios) plays Johnny, he's morally aware in ways that Omar isn't. He doesn't enjoy being a dull-eyed, semi-fascistic loafer; he hates the hanging around doing nothing that has been his life, and he has outgrown his old street gang—he's too intelligent to go on shouting insults at Pakis and threatening them. But he still feels a loyalty to his old pals—he knows how pathetic they are under their loudmouth jeering and Paki-bashing. When he's in a car with Omar, and the racketeer relative, who's driving, angrily runs down and cripples a gang member, an old friend of his, and then speeds off, Johnny is torn by conflicting loyalties. And Omar has his conflicts, too. He uses his come-hither eyes on Johnny, but he also plays boss to him—exacting revenge for all the times that Johnny and other street toughs insulted him. Race and sex, resentment and pride, and just plain ignorance are hopelessly (and comically) intertwined in this story.

The scriptwriter, Hanif Kureishi, who's not yet thirty, was born in

South London, to a Pakistani father and a white English mother. His first play was staged at the Royal Court Theatre when he was eighteen; it was about the immigrant experience, which he has kept at in all his work since. *My Beautiful Laundrette* was written for television, and Frears made it in 16-mm., on a budget of under $850,000. After it was shown at several European festivals and opened in English theatres, Frears was asked why he hadn't got together a bigger budget and shot it in 35-mm. He answered, "You couldn't seriously have gone out and said to a financier, 'I'm going to make a film about a gay Pakistani laundrette owner,' and confidently expected that there'd be an audience." As it turned out, the blowup to 35-mm. is near-miraculous; it's only in the first scene or two that a viewer is conscious that the definition is not as sharp as it might be. Frears has directed more than a dozen films for British TV since his first, in 1971 (the most famous is probably the 1979 *Bloody Kids*); he has also made a couple of theatrical films (*Gumshoe*, with Albert Finney, in 1971, and *The Hit*, with Terence Stamp and John Hurt, in 1984). What we see in *My Beautiful Laundrette*—the title grows on you—is a sensual, highly developed visual style. The 16-mm. may even contribute to the film's informal, dropped-in-on quality. Kureishi's script is filled to the rafters with characters and incidents, and the way Frears stages the various interactions it's almost as if they were simply going on in the environment and he and his cinematographer, Oliver Stapleton, just happened to pick up on them. This is particularly true for the women characters. With the exception of Shirley Anne Field's good-natured, aging bawd, the women's roles aren't as fully developed as the men's, but the women's visual presence is so strong that we get a sense of what their lives are—particularly that of the hit-and-run driver's wife (Souad Faress), who's always sticking her head out in hallways to see what's going on, and the unmanageable Tania (Rita Wolf), who becomes more attractive and impressive with each appearance. Even the loving relationship between Omar's Papa and uncle develops new meaning when we finally see the two together, and see how they accept each other's weaknesses.

Over the years, Frears has refined a magical instinct for just how long we want to see a face and just how long a scene needs to be. If he could bottle this instinct, it could be called "Essence of Moviemaking." His images here are quick and unexpected, and they feel exactly right. But Frears' editing rhythms that seem so right are actually very odd. *My Beautiful Laundrette* doesn't feel like any other movie; it's almost as if he's cutting to the rhythm of Pakistani-accented English—to what you can hear even in the quirky lilt of the title. The stew of interrelationships that Kureishi supplies seems appropriate to the Pakistanis' ornate ceremoniousness; it even suggests Islamic decorative art. The Pakistanis bring their tastes with them, but what comes through even more strongly is that Western capitalist culture appeals to their senses and blends with their traditions. Omar's eyes shine when he sees flashing lights; his relatives love their VCRs. Frears and Kureishi are unapologetic about showing Pakistanis as lowlifes or as possession-crazy, and they don't hem and haw about showing that Omar is a bit of a harem girl, slithering through various groups. He brings nothing into any environment; he just takes on protective coloration. You gradually get a sense of how he operates—he's a young man on the make. The people in this movie want something more than they have, and you feel the enticement of their goals: Omar wants flash. Tania wants independence. Johnny wants to get away from the street kids who feel that they're in a dead-end society, and so he joins up with the Pakistanis who know that this society is the best they can hope for, and try to wriggle through the cracks.

Frears is responsive to grubby desperation and to the uncouthness and energy in English life—he's responsive to what went into the punk-music scene and to what goes into teen-age-gang life. You could feel it in the way he released the energy of the young hood Myron, played by Tim Roth, in *The Hit*. That picture had something: a style, a tone, a streak of humor. But its flamboyant existentialism was spare and abstract; the picture was empty compared with this one—it was all craft and artifice. Here Johnny is more central to the action than Myron was, and Daniel Day-Lewis's performance gives the movie an imaginative, seductive spark. As the skinny-faced John Fryer in the 1984 *The Bounty*, Day-Lewis stuck out; he seemed like a bad actor. But if he can do only certain kinds of roles Johnny must be in his very best range. When Johnny refocusses his attention, it shows in his face, and when he looks at himself in the mirror to fluff his hair, his face is different from how it is when he looks at other people. This Johnny wants to make something of himself, and he'll go through more than his share of humiliation to do it. He also enjoys wooing the cuddly Omar. He can't resist touching Omar with his tongue when they're out on the street, right in front of the laundrette, with white-racist rowdies all around them. He can't resist being frisky, because it's dangerous, and that makes it more erotic. The movie captures some of the wonderful, devil-may-care giddiness that's part of the joyride of teen-age sex. Johnny and Omar behave as if they had invented the thrills of perilous public display; for all they know, they did. And the messy tensions of the multiracial South London community feed into the tenderness of their love affair.

It's an enormous pleasure to see a movie that's really about something, and that doesn't lay on any syrupy coating to make the subject go down easily. (It's down before you notice it.) Frears and Kureishi take a pile of risks in this movie, and take them in stride.

■

*K*aos, the latest film by Paolo and Vittorio Taviani, the brothers whose earlier work includes the 1977 *Padre Padrone* and the 1982 *The Night of the Shooting Stars*, is composed of adaptations of four Pirandello stories set in Sicily, plus a prologue and an epilogue, and it runs three hours and eight minutes. Partly financed by Italian television, it was intended to be shown on TV, in four installments, as well as in theatres, and when foreign distributors bought the rights to present it theatrically the Tavianis suggested that they should cut one story or another—the one least likely to appeal to their country's tastes. The American distributor, MGM/UA Classics, decided to run the film in toto. That might be called exemplary, but it's a mixed blessing. I'd have gone further than the Tavianis suggested: I'd have asked their permission to cut both the third and the fourth stories. What was left would have been, I think, a superb film, because *Kaos* has breathtaking moments, two marvellous stories, and a rapturous epilogue. But altogether, in its three-hour form, it's too much movie, and too much harsh beauty. The panoramic grandeur wears you down; you feel surfeited until you reach that revivifying epilogue, which is a full-fledged epiphany and sends you out dazed and happy.

The prologue is brief: A group of peasant men spot a male crow sitting on a nest; one of them holds him at arm's length and the others grab the eggs he was trying to hatch and throw them at him to see who will get to kill this disgrace to their sex. Then one fellow has a better idea: he ties a big bell around the crow's neck and sets him free to make music. As the bell-ringing bird flies high above, swooping and sailing across the skies, we get aerial shots of the jagged, parched terrain—the broken stones of ancient temples, the houses built into the steep mountains of rock, and a green valley way down below. The folkloric stories in this anthology film are linked by the crow's music and its flights over

122

the blighted area where the stories take place—the area where Pirandello was born, in a village near the forest called Càvusu, which he said was a corruption of the Greek word "kaos."

The first story, "The Other Son," stars Margarita Lozano. In *Shooting Stars*, she was the elderly woman who finally goes to bed with the man who has loved her for forty years. Here, she's a grieving, desolate peasant madwoman, at the turn of the century. Her two sons have gone off to America—to Santa Fe—and she hasn't heard from them in fourteen years. The core of the story is that she has a third son—younger than the two who left—who's always close by. He's devoted to her and tries to do everything he can for her, and she ignores him. She refuses to acknowledge his existence. She knows he is not to blame, but he was the result of rape by the man who killed her husband, and he looks the exact duplicate of his rapist father. This story has some of the crazy logic of a dream: the letters that the illiterate mother pays to have written and tries to send off to her missing sons are loose squiggles that don't resemble language; in a flashback to the time when Garibaldi opened the prisons, the rapist criminals who are freed cut off her husband's head, and she sees them using it as a boccie ball. But it's the mother's obduracy toward the despairing, cast-out son and her refusal to give up her illusion that the older two will come back and help her that's the material of folk myth. Margarita Lozano's unlined, broad, childlike face has something stony about it here; it's as bare as the countryside—she seems locked in her madness. She needs it in order to go on living. (This is the story that justifies the title *Kaos*.) When she throws a head-size squash at the adoring son, you can see that keeping her mind twisted and closed is her way to take revenge on life. As Lozano plays her, this woman suggests an Eleonora Duse whose soul has contracted. And the Tavianis, by setting the story on the road that the young men of the village take when they leave for America—a road with traffic going only one way—give the tale a pitiless, comic horror. I'd have a rough time accounting for it, but the sun-blistered soil, the weeds, and the rocks are somehow satirical—a joke that nature plays on people. Sicily seems to spawn people who leave or turn to stone.

The second story, "Moon Sickness" (or perhaps simply "Moonstruck"), is an account of a bridegroom (Claudio Bigagli) who can't control his violent animal impulses during the full moon; he tells his bride (Enrica Maria Modugno) to keep him locked out of their farmhouse. Visually, this werewolf story resembles a piece of naïve folk art, but it has a modern pungency. The Tavianis use effects that are reminiscent of the whisper-

123

ing-sacred-oak scenes in *Padre Padrone*: when the groom is alone outside and in pain, branches and leaves wave against the dark-blue night sky. And there are details to make you gasp: in the morning, the bride, trying to escape from the farm without being attacked by her husband's dog, tosses it her pet kitty. The tormented husband, with his mule, follows his wife to town, and watching him you may feel a swelling in the chest because of the primitive, passionate landscapes, and the emotional heightening provided by Nicola Piovani's musical score, and the Tavianis' storytelling, which seems so simple. When the husband arrives in the dusty town square, he doesn't knock on his wife's mother's door. In his misery, he stands outside in the hot, deserted piazza. Hours pass. All the doors of the houses are closed, and the windows are covered; the people are hidden inside. And then someone brings him a chair. At times like this, the Tavianis have you widening your eyes while you're grinning. The rest of the story isn't quite up to its first half, but it's still a triumph.

The first two stories are about fate; the next two are about trickery. The third, "The Jar," is the most familiar; a play version is sometimes staged in little theatres in this country. It's a piece of folk vaudeville, and the two main characters—the arrogant landowner whose huge jug, designed to hold the oil from his entire olive crop, splits in two, and the hunchbacked potter who comes to repair it—are played by the comedy team of tall Ciccio Ingrassia and hammy little Franco Franchi. "The Jar" represents the kind of hearty, laborious folk humor that usually gets me sprinting up the aisle, and though I stayed put, out of respect for the Tavianis, they didn't lighten things up. It's a stiff, and it seems to go on indefinitely, expanding to fit the monumental terrain. The fourth story, "Requiem," is an elaborate anecdote about a community of a hundred peasants who want their own cemetery and have to outwit the landowner—a city-dwelling baron—to get it. This is something of a shambles, and it's hardly worth sitting through, but it takes you to the epilogue.

The title of this passage is translated as "Conversing with Mother" (though perhaps "Talking to Mother" or "A Talk with Mother" would do the job). Omero Antonutti, who was the father in *Padre Padrone* and the peasant leader in *Shooting Stars*, plays the aging, world-famous Nobel Prize winner Pirandello, a dapper gentleman with a pointy little goatee, returning after many years to his family home. Getting off the train from Rome, he sees a couple of boys taking turns diving down a pile of sand, and the image stirs something in him. When he's in the house and has a vision of his dead mother, he asks her to tell him once again about an adventure she had as a child—a story he has never been able to put on paper—and we go back in time as she describes the day when her own mother took her brood of six children in a red-sailed fishing boat for the three-day trip to visit their father, a political exile, in Malta. On the way, the boat stopped at a volcanic island—a mountain of white pumice—and she and her brothers and sisters stripped to their underclothes, climbed up the slopes, and, flapping their arms, floated down the powdery white sand to bathe in the sea. As they slide into the turquoise water, the clouds of pumice drifting down with them merge with the skies and the foaming whitecaps of the Mediterranean. The children are flying through whiteness, and the music carries the sound of a bell, recalling the swooping, soaring crow. The Tavianis themselves are flying high here: the images seem to comprise all memories of childhood pleasure and all nostalgia. The music, the sights, the longings that the children have evoked all come together, and for a moment we're not sure how many of our senses are being affected. And, of course, we can see why the Tavianis have their Pirandello figure say that he could never find a way to tell this story: you need to be a moviemaker to fuse sensory impressions as the Tavianis have done here. For sheer transcendence, these moments are peerless; we're with the children, cascading through eternity.

March 10, 1986

TWITS, TURTLES, CREEPS

E. M. Forster began writing *A Room with a View* in 1902; he put it aside and wrote two other novels, then completed it and published it in 1908, when he was twenty-nine. It's a whimsical social comedy about a muddled young girl, Lucy Honeychurch, whose passionate nature is expressed only when she's at the piano playing Beethoven. She desires yet fears sexual love; she runs away from the man who stirs her emotions, and becomes engaged to a rich twit. Lucy Honeychurch suggests an English variation of Henry James' American girl Daisy Miller, but Forster's story, in its polite-pagan way, also anticipates some of D. H. Law-

125

rence's themes. Lucy needs a room *with a view*; she mustn't become a captive of the twit, who believes that the maiden he marries should look up to him as man the master. The story is about Lucy's need—everyone's need—to be freed from the "shamefaced world of precautions and barriers," and freed from terrors of the physical side of love. If the book—which has a lot of charm—slips out of your mind almost completely, it may be because it's an outline of passion, with no passion. (It's a bit too programmatic; so is the subtext: that the English have to go abroad to discover their own true sexual feelings.) The movie version, produced by Ismail Merchant and directed by James Ivory, is from an adaptation, by Ruth Prawer Jhabvala, that pares down the text skillfully and takes much of the dialogue directly from Forster. Lucy is played by the nineteen-year-old Helena Bonham Carter, who certainly fits the author's description: "a young lady with a quantity of dark hair and a very pretty, pale, undeveloped face." Bonham Carter fits it and then some. Under her masses of dark hair and thick eyebrows she has the face of a child—wide and soft, with no visible cheekbones. And she's top-heavy like a child. Her head seems very large for her tiny, voluptuous body, and she doesn't have the carriage of a trained actress—her head often juts forward, depriving her of a neck. Bonham Carter lacks the presence of an actress, too; she's recessive. She suggests the beauty of a girl in a painting or of an exotic night bloom rather than that of a sentient young woman. Her strange, droopy beauty and her ungainliness have a fascination, and when you get used to her she becomes fairly appealing. Still, when a radiant and apparently assured blonde (Isabella Celani) turns up as a coachman's girlfriend in the scenes set around Florence, I thought, Why didn't the moviemakers cast *her* as the passionate Lucy, and Bonham Carter as the driver's girl? Celani may not speak English, but she's *svelta*.

With the unradiant Bonham Carter at its center, the movie lacks centrifugal force. The Forster novel is slight, but it's about a girl who's teetering between expressing her emotions and stifling them. It isn't as trivial as the movie, which can make you feel that Lucy is simply taking too long figuring out which man she loves. The novel might be called a feminist cautionary comedy, and some of its underpinnings wouldn't go over too well now. The young Forster seems to have been steeped in a utopian form of humanism; he regards sexual love as holy and eternal, and he takes a romantic, mystical view of the equality of the sexes in marriage. When the moviemakers lift out the story and shake the philosophical mold (and meaning) off its roots, they have something light enough to serve as the book for a musical comedy. The movie is more

126

than a little precious, but its frivolousness is pleasant. Forster's dialogue is lively (and dizzy, too), and this is the best paced of the (many, many) James Ivory films that I've seen. It's *enjoyably* trivial—a piece of charming foolishness. The director might even have been having a good time on the set as he watched the ingenious, farcical plot take shape.

The film opens in Florence at the Pensione Bertolini, which caters to English tourists. It's there that Lucy, on holiday under the chaperonage of her spinster cousin Charlotte (Maggie Smith), first meets the boyish, fair-haired George Emerson (Julian Sands), who has been raised by his freethinking father to be unconstrained by "superstition and ignorance." George is Forster's idealized conception of what a "natural" young man should be. He's a silent, moody fellow and something of a sleeping beauty until the moment in the Piazza della Signoria when a young Italian is stabbed and falls bleeding at Lucy's feet. George catches her as she swoons, and carries her to the steps of the Loggia. Something in that moment—the sensual mixture of Italy, the dying man's blood, and holding Lucy in his arms—awakens him. (The moment has a comparable impact on Lucy, but she hides her feelings in order to be proper, to be nice.) Sands has been given nothing to play except Forster's flimsy—almost abstract—dream of a perfect uninhibited lover, and he's rather vague, but his watchful, half-smiling manner is likable enough. When George sees Lucy alone in a field of flowers, he moves swiftly and kisses her. He's like a woodland deity—possibly Forster's silliest creation, a satyr with nothing but goodness and honor in his soul, a handsome, forthright satyr.

This paragon's father is played by Denholm Elliott, and the role is like an early draft of the Mrs. Moore role, played by Peggy Ashcroft, in *A Passage to India*. Mr. Emerson is this story's resident saint. A man whose wholehearted kindness is misunderstood at the Pensione Bertolini, Elliott's Mr. Emerson is elderly and physically broken down, and he has the "anxious, aggressive voice" that Forster described; he doesn't talk, exactly—he expostulates. (His name is a nod to our Mr. Emerson, though his character appears to be drawn more from Samuel Butler.) This Mr. Emerson wants people to use good sense; he sees so much inhibition and pettiness in the behavior of his countrymen that he's always upset. It's a lovely cranky performance: Elliott is so thoroughly into his role that the outspoken Mr. Emerson is like a Dickensian portrait—no more than a sketch, yet complete.

Lucy's fiancé, the effete Cecil Vyse, is the essence of everything that makes Mr. Emerson despair. He's a priss and a poseur—a vise is what marriage to him would be. (But Lucy feels safe with him: he doesn't make her "nervous," the way George does.) As Forster wrote the character, and as Daniel Day-Lewis (of *My Beautiful Laundrette*) plays him, Cecil Vyse is an excruciatingly self-conscious young aesthete who sneers at people because he has no way to connect with them. He condescends to the world—that's his only relationship to it. Cecil holds his head up high and looks down his nose, as if he wanted to avoid the sights and smells of common people. He lives in a London flat with his mother and stays as far from "nature" or anything physical as he can get, even when he's visiting Lucy's home, in the Surrey hills. He thinks that refinement is everything, yet he's so supercilious that he grimaces contemptuously when he meets Lucy's mother's friends. Basically, the crime of Cecil the collector is that when he gazes at Lucy he doesn't see a woman; he sees a new acquisition, an objet d'art. (But, unfortunately, that's how she looks to us, too.) In some scenes I wished that the camera were at a more discreet distance from Day-Lewis, because you can see him acting and you're too conscious of his black hair and mustache—you suspect he's made up to be ascetic and all profile. And it's as if you were in the first row at a stage performance—you can feel the actor's animal energy, and sense the pressure he's under. This portrait is a caricature and perhaps overdone, but then, toward the last, when Cecil's view of himself has been shaken, his youth breaks through his masklike pallor, and he's suddenly human; he looks almost bereaved, and he's very touching. Day-Lewis brings it off with the sweet ease of a Gielgud.

The movie never loses its hold on a viewer's interest or affections, because it's so thoroughly *inhabited*. The actors who circulate around Lucy create a whirring atmosphere—a comic hum. Maggie Smith's Charlotte sees sins against propriety everywhere; they're a constant threat to her, and her face is pinched up in eternal vigilance. Yet she has a glimmer that she missed the boat. The role is somewhat too constricting, but Smith has one triumphant scene: Charlotte, who lives in straitened circumstances and envies the more fashionable existence of her Honeychurch relations, arrives for a visit and doesn't have the right change to pay the cabdriver. Lucy's younger brother, Freddy (Rupert Graves), quietly takes care of it, but then, in the presence of the Honeychurches' young friends who have assembled for tennis, Charlotte, who's intensely aware of her comparative poverty, insists on a "settling of accounts" and is caught in a confusion of various kids making change; it's like a Marx Brothers routine, with the glorious Smith fingers and wrists fumbling and flying in all directions. The cast is studded with performers who create a character in their first appearance and then make you grin a little each time they reappear: Simon Callow is the stout, cheerfully celibate Reverend Beebe; Rosemary Leach is Lucy's mother, who's outraged by Cecil's snobbishness; Judi Dench is Forster's detested "clever lady," Miss Lavish, who writes popular romances and is endowed with a surplus of vivacity. Even the Italian coachman (Lucca Rossi) is striking—he looks like an earthier De Niro.

Ivory doesn't build from scene to scene or use any directorial magic, or even much resourcefulness. He's essentially a director who assembles the actors, arranges the bric-a-brac, and calls for the camera. But the Forster-Jhabvala scenes are shapely, and Ivory holds to a light, ironic manner. The imagery isn't as static and pictorially composed as in some of his other films; the cinematography, by Tony Pierce-Roberts, flows along, and the movie is almost all of a piece. Ivory has a slight problem of tone in the scene where Freddy and George and the Reverend Beebe go skinny-dipping in a tiny pond in the woods. The three begin to splash each other, they hop out, chase each other around, jump back into the water, and so on. What's awkward about the scene, which is rather long (though not as protracted as it is in the book), is that we know it's supposed to demonstrate natural, unrepressed good fun, but frisking around with no clothes on can't feel natural to the actors when the camera is running. The scene is reminiscent of the nude wrestling in *Women in Love*, but that wasn't as awkward, because it had hostility in it; this is a brave attempt at innocence. Just as Freddy and George are at their most delirious, dashing across a path, Lucy, her mother, and Cecil come along, all buttoned up in their Edwardian finery; Lucy's amused giggle rescues the scene, gives it a point, and gets Ivory off the hook. (That giggle also makes us like her more.)

It's a novelty now to see a movie that's full of allusions to art and literature. The opening credits have the heraldic ornamentations of an illuminated manuscript, and they're used playfully, not pompously; they accompany Kiri Te Kanawa's rapturous version of a Puccini love aria (which is misleading: it's too richly emotional for the movie). And from there we go to talk of Giotto and Dante and so on. Made in England and Florence, on a budget of under three million dollars, *A Room with a View* flaunts its culture, acknowledging that it's not for everybody—which is just as well, because Ivory's films don't the energy to succeed with a mass audience (though this one could be modestly popular). At one point, the director appears to forget the appetite for high art that he has been whetting. When George and Mr. Emerson meet Cecil for the first time, it's in the National Gallery, right smack in front of the great Uccello *Battle of San Romano*. It's a very frustrating scene, because the men go on talking without moving. You want to call out, "Would you step aside, so we can see the Uccello?"

■

In John Irvin's low-key, fastidious film version of the Russell Hoban novel *Turtle Diary*, from Harold Pinter's script, Glenda Jackson and Ben Kingsley play the two Londoners who separately develop the fantasy of liberating the three giant turtles from the Aquarium at the London Zoo and taking them back to the sea. When these two strangers (who are psychically like twins) meet, they combine forces and, with the aid of the head keeper (Michael Gambon), carry out their mission. The book, published in 1975, was popular in a special way. One of the blurbs on the book jacket provides some clues: "Like other cult writers—Salinger, for instance, or Vonnegut—Hoban writes about ordinary people making life-affirming gestures in a world that threatens to dissolve in madness." It's rather late now for a counterculture fable about two people who turn into secret activists for a weekend, and maybe Hoban's material (like Vonnegut's) just doesn't touch susceptibilities in the same way when it's on the screen. The movie verges on the deliberately quaint, and the central metaphor turns into something like straight-faced parody, because the two reticent, self-deprecating loners, who can barely say a word without trying to retract it, are like turtles themselves. (I assume this is intended.) Their wary, awkward hesitancies—starting to say something, then pulling their heads back in and not venturing to finish—are comic routines about fear of making contact. Jackson's boyish haircut is almost cruelly severe; the terraced back of her head suggests the reptilian, and Kingsley has a darting, shiny-eyed furtiveness. The movie is like a *Brief Encounter* between turtles; the two strangers come out of their shells a bit, but not with each other.

Though the language is very close to what the characters say in the book, the terse dialogue sounds like quintessential Pinter. (The way his characters have snapped at each other, he might always have been writing for turtles.) Jackson and Kingsley give their lines an especially tight-lipped, staccato reading. Jackson holds her words back as if she were biting her tongue to shreds, and Kingsley clamps down on his words, smiling as if he had a secret wellspring of self-satisfaction. These two are so private and tense and minimalist that it's amusing to see them staying controlled every instant and yet varying their performances enough to keep going. They manage to give the middle of the movie—the weekend drive to the coast with the turtles—a balmy comic spirit of adventure. But their story has been given the same maudlin orchestration as in the novel—the same symbolism and angst. Kingsley's William, who left his wife, his two children, and the life of a businessman, and works as a clerk in a bookstore (where Pinter turns up in a bit as a customer), lives in a rooming house, with kitchen privileges, and we're given something like a cross-section of the lonely people there, preparing their solitary meals (in a closet-size upstairs kitchen) and longing for companionship. We get more of this when the young woman who works at the bookstore with William makes overtures to him, and still more at the apartment house where Jackson's Neaera, a well-known author of children's books about small, timid creatures, such as a vole, lives. We get a bellyful of sad and lonely people reaching out, or so locked in their shells that, like the rooming-house tenant played by Eleanor Bron, they can't give anyone a sign of their misery and quietly kill themselves. The awful artfulness of this stuff! Do Irvin and Pinter think that they're not doing what they're doing just because they're doing it with precision?

■

Joyce Chopra's *Smooth Talk* has lovely touches in its first half, when she shows us the lazing-in-the-sun sensuousness of adolescent girls during school vacation. Fifteen-year-old Connie (Laura Dern), blond, leggy, and narcissistic, is restless and bored at home, but she and her friends (Sarah Inglis and Margaret Welch) parade happily around the shopping plaza for hours and hours—testing their skills at attracting boys and bantering with them. Connie dresses and walks as seductively as she knows how; she teases boys her own age or a year or two older, because she doesn't know what else to do about the way she feels. She loves to neck with a boy in his car and get excited, but when she senses that things are getting out of control she slips away. This is the sort of material about young girls and their wanting to be touched but fearing to be penetrated that has been turning up in films in recent years, since women directors, such as Amy Jones (*Love Letters*), Amy Heckerling (*Fast Times*

131

at Ridgemont High), and Martha Coolidge (*Valley Girl*), started showing the other side of the boys' sexual-initiation problems, and comediennes, such as the team of Gail Matthius and Denny Dillon on *Saturday Night Live*, began to make plaintive sketches out of the conversation of teen-age girls looking for boys. Tom Cole, the short-story writer and playwright who did the script for *Smooth Talk*, adapting and expanding the brief Joyce Carol Oates story "Where Are You Going, Where Have You Been?" (first published in 1966), has a fine ear, and everything to do with Connie and her friends on the prowl raises the film above the ordinary. But the parts at Connie's home, where she and her mother (Mary Kay Place) bicker, are mostly very tired; the mother is given so many put-downs of Connie that she seems to be persecuting the kid. (One redeeming domestic scene: Levon Helm, as Connie's pleasant-goofball father, expressing how proud he is that he doesn't owe a penny and after a day at work he can sit on his porch in the evening smoking a cigarette.)

The movie's texture is thin from the start. Even so, there are confusions: Elizabeth Berridge, who plays Connie's sister June, looks as if she were her kid sister but is meant to be older, in her twenties. The second half isn't just stretched out—it's a little screwy. The Oates story is a teen-age girl's sex-and-horror fantasy that's harrowing for the reader; its pulp sensationalism is almost unbearable. Connie, in her strutting and teasing at the plaza, has attracted the attention of a sordid creep, an older man who hangs around the hamburger juke joint where high-school kids gather. He arrives at her house when she's alone, like the materialization of her ugliest fears, and tells her he is to be her lover. Helpless, afraid he'll do something violent, and in a state of hysteria, she is lured into his car. End of story and, the reader assumes, probably the end of poor Connie. Unaccountably, Chopra and Cole try to turn this material into a coming-of-age movie with a happy ending. As the creep, Treat Williams gives some sort of neo-Method performance that's all affectation; he dances around and waves his beckoning arms, as if he were doing an homage to the Brando of the fifties. A viewer isn't horrified, exactly— aghast is more like it. And a few hours after Connie has gone off she returns, and is now less selfish and more appreciative and understanding of her family; the breach with her mother is quickly healed. The end of the movie suggests that she has grown up—matured—via what amounts to terrorization and (possibly) rape. The experience seems to have made her a better person. I find the acclaim for this film almost as baffling as its final point of view. I expect that some people will think she got her punishment for not listening to her mother—for being a tease. Laura

Dern's Connie seems just right—shallow and tantalizingly lovely—but she's in every scene, and about a half hour before the end I felt she had nothing more to give. (Women may come out thinking what a shame it was that Connie didn't let the handsome young boy who stroked her hair in his car be the one to initiate her. Has there ever been a young boy so accomplished at foreplay?)

March 24, 1986

MARS

||||||||||||||||||||||||||||||||||||||||||||||||||||||||||||||||||||||||||||||||||||||||||||||||||||||||||||||||||||||||||||||||||||||||||||||||||||||

All that holds *Pretty in Pink* together is Molly Ringwald's charismatic normality. When the picture was shot, she hadn't yet turned eighteen, but she looks completely free of self-consciousness or affectation. The poise with which she plunks herself in front of the camera is uncanny. And this redhead goddess of the ordinary carries the movie, though she has nothing particularly arresting to do or to say. John Hughes, who wrote the script, uses the same basic plot that served him in *Sixteen Candles*: once again, Ringwald is caught between the boy of her dreams (this time, Andrew McCarthy in a BMW) and the smartmouth nerd who follows her around (this time, Jon Cryer on a bike). But Hughes hasn't bothered to provide the new Ringwald heroine—her name is Andie—with the teen-agers' slang that gave *Sixteen Candles* its wigginess and its snap. He and the first-time director, Howard Deutch, whose work he supervised, have fallen back on something much easier and more traditional.

Andie is an A student who wins a college scholarship, and she's blessed with quiet good taste, but she's a poor girl who lives in a dinky, rattletrap house on, yes, the wrong side of the tracks. And her dream boy is a richie who, like his friends, lives in a stately mansion, with neatly clipped grounds. In the movies of the twenties and thirties, it was common for heroines (and heroes) to be ashamed of their poverty and to feel a vast social gap between them and the secure rich. But in the years after the Second World War, as people moved up in the society, the movie

133

fantasy of marrying rich lost its romantic appeal. Has this fantasy been returning in eighties movies such as *Flashdance, An Officer and a Gentleman, Valley Girl,* and *Pretty in Pink* because the ostentatiously wealthy have become more brazen and lower-middle-income people feel more trapped? Whatever the reason, class consciousness has been making a comeback, but not in any kind of realistic or political context; what we're getting is strictly the fantasy theme of love bridging the gap.

The spoiled-rotten richies who go to high school with Andie are snobby hunks and painted sluts; they're mean to our heroine because she's poor. Even her shy rich prince, who invites her to the senior prom, is so spineless that he's intimidated by the threat that he'll be ostracized for dating her—that he won't have a friend left—and he reneges on the invitation. This movie's class consciousness is pushed to cartoon extremes of blandness. In its sociological details, *Pretty in Pink* might have been made by little guys from Mars. Andie works in a record shop after school; her wonderful, understanding dad (Harry Dean Stanton) is generally unemployed and alcoholic—he fell apart three years earlier when his wife walked out on both husband and daughter. Things are rough for these two. But when Andie is at home, in her colorfully cluttered room, and her dad comes in to talk to her there's a large floral arrangement in the background to brighten up the visuals of poverty. (It must have cost in the hundred-and-fifty-dollar range.)

Sporting a porcupine hairdo and then the world's tallest beehive (it just about doubles her height), Annie Potts plays Andie's co-worker at the record shop. This character comes out of nowhere, but Annie Potts brings it her own outré specificity; she makes piquant, ticky little routines out of everything she does—she may be the finest unsung comedienne in the business. Her winsomeness is given a hard edge here, while Ringwald is made up and photographed to be all fair, soft tones. (That makes sense, but it's confusing when we're told that Annie Potts' character is an older woman, twice Andie's age; this actress hasn't had a full youthful fling yet.) Jon Cryer's Duckie, the lonely, misfit clown who adores Andie and perceives her specialness, wears a hat on the back of his head (so as not to disturb his ducktail upsweep), and he has a rockabilly–Jerry Lewis look. He's given junior Pagliacci material—he lip-syncs Otis Redding's "Try a Little Tenderness," which doesn't do anything except make us uncomfortable. Cryer does have one good scene: he tries to talk his way past the guard to get inside a rock club that Andie is in. (He's still talking when she comes out.)

The movie is slight and vapid, with the consistency of watery Jell-O. Andie has a blobby brown dog with no personality—it goes with the rest of the picture. *Pretty in Pink* is nothing, but it moves along, with rock songs giving a little zip to the nothingness. When in doubt, Deutch (whose background is in music videos) goes for closeups—mostly of Ringwald. The title is from a 1981 disk by the Psychedelic Furs (whose music is heard, along with that of New Order and Orchestral Manoeuvres in the Dark), but it has a special application. Andie cuts up two pink dresses she has been given and redesigns them into a stunning gown for the prom. It's the kind of dress that billows like a sail in a light wind, and it isn't flattering to her, but it's great for a Cinderella entrance. The film is among the top box-office attractions in the country, and I've heard of one little girl, age eight, who went straight home from the theatre and started cutting up her clothes; I would bet that she has sisters in other cities across the land. That's the strongest reaction anybody is likely to have to *Pretty in Pink*. It's the essence of dreamy safeness—a romantic movie for kids that their parents can approve of. Parents can dream their anxieties away when they see Molly Ringwald enshrined here as a star: the teen-age ideal. The rich kids may get drunk and hot and loose, but Andie is the opposite of trashy. She's proudly conventional.

There's a trick to John Hughes' pictures—probably an unconscious, instinctive choice—that helps to explain what makes *Sixteen Candles*, *The Breakfast Club*, and *Pretty in Pink* so appealing and satisfying to young audiences: he never goes beyond a kid's point of view; even the supposedly adult characters are seen only in kids' terms. This was obvious in the presentation of the high-school dean in *The Breakfast Club*, and in the quick glimpses of the parents and in how the kids talked about them. And Andie's drunken father here is always clean, sweet Daddy. In Hughes' films, parents are either villains or, when they're good, inept and forgetful. (Andie has to take charge of her daddy—the way Shirley Temple used to—and talk him out of his self-pity.) There is never any suggestion of a world of possibilities and passions beyond the experiences of kids. And I mean *kids*: *Pretty in Pink* isn't actually about teen-agers—it's closer to being a pre-teen's idea of what it will be like to be a teen-ager.

■

135

Art-consciousness is an affliction that hits moviemakers in the legs as well as the head: when they have a bad case of it, their feet don't touch the ground. Sometimes their films' whirling-in-the-air lightness can be intoxicating, as it is in Jacques Demy's *Lola* and *Bay of the Angels*, and Beineix's *Diva*, or fluky and diverting, as in Alan Rudolph's *Choose Me*. More often, art-conscious projects crash, like Altman's *Three Women*, or never take off, like Coppola's *Rumble Fish* and Beineix's *The Moon in the Gutter*. Rudolph's new *Trouble in Mind* is of this latter, dismal group. It's a pile of poetic mush set in some doom-laden, vaguely universal city of the past and/or the future. (It was shot mostly in Seattle.) The hero, Hawk, played by Kris Kristofferson, wears a black hat and walks with a limp that suggests a metaphysical wound. He was a cop until he killed a man; released from prison, he returns to his old hangout—a diner called Wanda's Café, named for its proprietor (she's played by Geneviève Bujold), who used to be his lover. Wanda's is a gathering place for thieves and hijackers; it's where they plan their heists. Those who saw *Choose Me* (which Rudolph also wrote and directed) and were charmed by its flowing giddiness are likely to have a sinking sensation as they become aware that the situations are much the same in *Trouble in Mind* except they're not fun this time. The mixed-up lovers have been replaced by mixed-up gangsters, and what was comic and lyrical is now fatalistic.

Hawk is meant to be a gallant man of action whose protective impulses toward the weak force him to use his fists and his gun; he's supposed to be the Bogart hero living in an evil, semi-fascist era. What we're looking at, though, is Kris Kristofferson, a happy-go-lucky guy who's all glands. With his silver-striped beard and his black duds, he looks appropriately romantic, yet he doesn't seem very daring or bright. There's an essential mildness about him, and he can't give his scenes any excitement or momentum—he simply isn't a trained actor. Rudolph used him to fine comic effect in *Songwriter*—he was properly mellow as a cool country singer who liked the easy sex "on the road." But that picture wasn't Rudolph's baby: Bud Shrake, who revels in the rowdy "outlaw" country-music scene, wrote the script, and Rudolph regards himself as having been on hire when he directed it. He's a good professional director with an unusually sophisticated visual sense, but *Trouble in Mind*, which he regards as a "film" (rather than a "movie," like *Songwriter*), brings out his aspirations and very little of his skill. He's got the film-noir bug; you can tell that it's eating away his judgment when you hear Joe Morton, as a crook called Solo, reciting verses in a booth at Wanda's. This bitter, ironic black bard recalls *The Petrified Forest*; Morton combines the roles of Leslie Howard's

136

poet and Bogart's gangster, and he comes to an end so sadistically, penny-dreadful gaudy that you wonder if Rudolph did it on a dare. (What other excuse could he have?)

Moviemakers who work on their own material are likely to be wizards at self-delusion. (Take a look at Ingmar Bergman's *The Serpent's Egg*, if he hasn't buried it.) Rudolph probably aimed to create a glamorous, funky trance-world; I certainly don't think he set out to make his actors look ridiculous, but that's what he does. Keith Carradine, who in *Choose Me* seemed to have graduated forever from callow roles, plays the callowest role of his career. As Coop, an ignorant, greedy young hood, he appears in a series of ever more gross and gooey pompadours—punk-fop styles, with matching cosmetic jobs and earrings. His hair and makeup turn his appearances into a freak show; you want to look away from him. And the ravishing Lori Singer (she's like a teen-age Jessica Lange), who plays Coop's dewy-eyed country-girl lover and the mother of his infant son, is meant to be simple and uneducated but is made to be openmouthed, dropped-jaw dumb. The actor known as Divine, who made his reputation as a female impersonator, plays a semi-male role here—he's an epicene mobster named Hilly Blue who's made up to look like a plump plucked chicken. Lavishly rich, he lives in a neo-modern palace that's full of paintings and glass and Lucite objects. (It's actually the Seattle Art Museum.)

Rudolph's extravagances don't come together; each embarrassment just sits up there on the screen all by itself. And he has so many bad ideas squirrelling around that even the promising ones don't quite come off (though John Considine has a moment or two as a crook with a re-spectable façade, except for his addiction to role playing: the petite crea-ture whom he addresses as his innocent child bride is actually his brassy longtime mistress). In *Choose Me*, Rudolph seemed to be developing a control of rhythm and mood—a musical and choreographic way of story-telling. It made you pass over the flossy hipster-philosopher babble that he gave his actors to speak. But his control fails him here. The scenes often have a shimmer that makes you feel hopeful, but they become stagnant, and the people talk with an intellectual lisp. When he gets to his climactic shoot-out at Hilly Blue's party for *le tout* underworld, it's a horribly bungled piece of staging. It might be crude to suggest that Rudolph should come down to earth and look for a good script; there's always the chance that if he soars higher he'll reach something. But on the basis of *Trouble in Mind* I wouldn't bet on it.

April 7, 1986

137

LOST SOULS

‖‖‖

I would dearly love to see Federico Fellini work on material that doesn't come out of his world-weary loins. If he worked with a script that had a story and characters and some propulsion, and if its contours made it impossible for him to get a bellyful of decadence and soullessness or to display grotesques, hermaphrodites, or even transvestites, he might be renewed and show fresh aspects of his poetic imagination. He might once again show some joy in moviemaking.

His latest film, *Ginger and Fred*, has one big thing going for it: that yummy, alluring title. Those two names have a happy aura all over the world; they're probably part of every moviegoer's (and many a TV watcher's) pantheon. But the movie isn't about those tapping, twirling icons. It's about two mediocre dancers, Amelia (Giulietta Masina) and Pippo (Marcello Mastroianni); in the nineteen-forties, they entertained Italian vaudeville audiences by copying the ballroom numbers from the Astaire-Rogers movies, and were billed as Ginger and Fred. Lovers, they quarrelled and broke up in the mid-fifties; presumably they could flourish only as imitations, because their stage careers ended, and they haven't seen each other since. Now they are being brought to Rome and reunited for a nostalgic appearance on a Christmas TV Special. Essentially, the situation is that of Neil Simon's *The Sunshine Boys*, except for the crucial detail that those two men were once famous performers. These two were small-timers, curiosities. And the point is driven home by the assortment of other guests who have been rounded up for the three-hour show: celebrity look-alikes (Clark Gable, Ronald Reagan, Kafka, Proust, Kojak); a troupe of midgets who tango; an orchestra of centenarians; a housewife who (for pay) went through the torment of giving up TV for a month; a celebrated imprisoned Mafioso, with a police escort; a levitating monk; an ancient, decrepit war hero; a cow with eighteen teats. In other words, the movie is another Fellini circus and freak show. But this time it's TV that's to blame—TV which has taken over the society and is debasing and trivializing everything.

Arriving in Rome after an absence of many years, Amelia is in a city that looks like a combination of New York and Vegas. She becomes part of the flow of traffic in the railway station, which is dominated by huge, garish posters celebrating TV and such products as cat food and a dish of sausages and lentils; on the way to the hotel where the swarms of guests for the show are to be put up, she sees enormous billboards advertising TV programs. Wherever she turns in the hotel lobby and in her room, TV sets are spewing inanities. The functionaries for the Special who shepherd her around are impersonally efficient, like humanoids, and at the climax she's in the mazelike passageways and studios of Tele-City itself. It's a city within a city, like the Vatican, but this one is in the business of destroying men's souls and keeping its victims diverted so that they're not aware of their spiritual squalor.

The whole movie has been given the cosmetized look of TV; visually, it's muted—it's blah—and then it's overbright in Tele-City. The lighting is unimaginative, yet in some ways that's a relief: would anyone want more of the engorged surreal imagery of Fellini's *Satyricon*, or his *Roma* or *Casanova* or *City of Women*? The undistinguished cinematography here doesn't make you feel as if you were hung over from drinking sticky liqueurs. But Fellini has picked the wrong metaphor when he indicts TV for exhibiting people as freaks; he himself is too culpable on this score— freakdom has been his specialty. Besides, what's likable about Fellini's work is the feeling you get that he can laugh at his own vanity and conceits—that he sees himself as a bit of a freak. (It's something he has in common with Paul Mazursky.) Fellini's spoofs of TV programs and commercials go on throughout the movie; he "flashes" them as if they were obscene images, and he means them to be obscene. They're images of piggy abundance—big-breasted women, pasta with a thick sauce, olive oil being poured—and they're richer-looking than ordinary life. Oral and infantile, they have the glow of something lusted after. Fellini also uses Dante for a TV puppet show. This may have a point: it exposes the surface quality of TV entertainment and its tacky subversion of high culture. But Fellini himself has invoked Dante's Hell for surface effect a few too many times.

The film has a secondary theme, shadowing the attack on television: it's simply that Fellini hates getting old. At sixty-six, he's saying that he's not as graceful as he was—he's tired, he's winded, he stumbles. If you put this together with the primary theme, what you get is the complaint that he's not on top of things anymore; TV is. It's as if Fellini were condemning TV for being a green slime that's absorbing everything, and denouncing it, too, for passing him by.

In story terms, most of *Ginger and Fred* is simply the preparation for Amelia and Pippo to get together and do their number. After they broke up, Amelia married and raised a family; now widowed, she runs a small business in her home town, near Genoa, and has become a neatly dressed, contented grandmother. Masina still scrunches up her features when she shrugs, pulling her mouth down in a way that's familiar even if you haven't seen her for decades. She's still saucer-eyed and trim-figured, and when she clowns she still has that slightly pie-faced, Harry Langdon look; she has aged without really changing much. Yet when Amelia finds Pippo he looks at her—flabbergasted—and winces comically. He shakes his head in mock horror, as if she had become a fright and were barely recognizable. We're told that they were lovers for fifteen years and that he suffered when she left him, but there are no emotional depths in their encounter; it isn't even funny—it's just inert. The story of their romantic partnership seems no more than a pretext for Fellini to have a few whacks at TV.

Though Masina gives the only big performance in the film (most of the people we see are not professional actors, and don't need to be), and she plays the role with a pleasing modesty, the character is ultimately unsatisfying. Fellini and his writing cohorts (Tonino Guerra and Tullio Pinelli) present Amelia as a practical woman who accommodates herself to circumstances—a woman with some inner strength but no passion, no strong emotions of any kind. And though they seem to be trying to be fair to this unadventurous, proper little bourgeois their hearts aren't in it, and the film treats her with an element of condescension. (It's not unlike the way the mousy Juliet and her fantasies were treated in the 1965 *Juliet of the Spirits*.) Mastroianni's role is much sketchier. What's clear is that Pippo is Fellini as a bum. This drunken, heavyset wreck of a man, sweaty and slightly disoriented, is Fellini's view of himself as a sensualist who yields to temptations and has wound up like many a man who cons himself: selling encyclopedias. We're never brought close to Pippo; we don't feel we know him. Yet since he's not going anywhere but down, his silly dirty jokes, the half-formed leftish ideas he spouts, and his hopes of hustling a job as a TV host all seem messily human. Amelia's self-control makes her seem like a prosaic, well-behaved child—a neat little doll. Pippo is at least falling apart, and in a play or a movie the characters who are in chaos are almost guaranteed to be more magnetic

140

than the chaste, tidy Amelias. But Fellini may be too honest—or too indifferent—to pull the strings that would bring Pippo to some kind of endearing life. Pippo isn't even guilt-ridden or a great scalawag; he isn't much of anything. (He just plays at rebellion—the way Fellini just plays at satirizing TV, without getting involved.) I don't think Mastroianni has ever had less presence or less resonance; he has never worked with Masina before, and it may be that in trying to adapt to her matter-of-factness he wiped himself out.

The only suspense is: Will the two old imitation Americans make it through their act without disgracing themselves or without one of them keeling over dead? And Fellini squeezes a little tired drama into this: Pippo shows off at rehearsal by lifting Amelia so many times that he's near collapse, and then orders brandies for himself while he's backstage waiting to go on. We do develop a faint rooting interest in the two; we want them to get by with their terrible dancing and be applauded—if only to spare ourselves the mortification of hearing them laughed at. We don't want them to be destroyed by TV. And so the film is able to milk us. It makes us admire the trouper's spirit in Amelia's firmly controlled dancing posture and in Pippo's ability to lurch through the steps when he's sloshed and dazed. (That's the only positive aspect of the entire picture.)

Ginger and Fred isn't painful to watch, and Nicola Piovani's score has a lovely finesse—he brings stray undertones of melancholy to the gaiety of the songs from the Astaire-Rogers pictures. But the movie is imprecise in a way that produces discomfort. Fellini's parodies of TV lack the slaphappy knowingness that younger directors, who grew up with TV, have brought to movies such as the American comedy-revue *The Groove Tube* and the dadaist farce from Spain *What Have I Done to Deserve This!* Fellini has no zest to energize his skits. He's venting his disgust with the changes in the society, and he does it in a way that makes you feel he's out of it. There may be a sick joke about television that's waiting to be filmed: a satire that gets into the possibility that those who watch TV the most are the members of the underclass, who remain in the economic pits because they don't learn any skills while sitting at home. (It has been suggested that one of the reasons that recent Asian immigrants to this country have been moving up so fast is that initially they couldn't understand American TV—or were willing to forswear it—and so didn't waste their lives zonked out with the box.) But Fellini looks at TV with the offended eyes of a poet and aesthete, and he finds it vulgar—perhaps the easiest and least productive approach,

141

especially when it's taken (as it usually is) by those who aren't themselves TV watchers.

Fellini has got TV and its effects on the culture mixed together with the ugliness of old age and decay. He has always counted the old among his grotesques, and now, seeing himself as one of them, he doesn't like what he sees. Mastroianni exhibits a bald spot like the Maestro's, with skimpy, longish gray hair around the sides and back, and he wears outfits like those the Maestro is often photographed in. He's a crumbling tower of a man—but without the Maestro's fabled rascal's charm. *Ginger and Fred* is a wobbling, insecure movie. Maybe it seems to be pulling in different directions because Fellini knows that he, like his sodden surrogate, Pippo, would be an m.c. in Hell before he'd consider the quiet life up north with Amelia. You don't expect Fellini, of all people, to be pious about the craziness of junk culture. And you don't expect him to be so upset about aging. (It isn't as if he hadn't lived.) As Ovid said, time devours everything. So why be cranky about it? While time is devouring everything we have some good moments.

■

"**W**hich phenomenon is more depressing—John Hughes or Ron Howard?" That's the question a sharp, no-longer-young director threw at me on the phone the other day. Both Hughes and Howard showed promise just a couple of years ago, and both had hits and went flabby practically overnight. I was stumped. I couldn't choose between them, and proposed a compromise candidate: Walter Hill. He came to mind because I had sat down to review his *Crossroads* the day before and nodded off in the middle of a sentence. John Mortimer, in his autobiographical *Clinging to the Wreckage*, says, "The only rule I have found to have any validity in writing is not to bore yourself." I had violated that golden rule. And it wasn't even that *Crossroads* was totally awful—I've seen a lot worse of late. (Actually, parts of the film are mildly enjoyable, and though it would be easy to quarrel with Ry Cooder's blues numbers, they're dramatic—they have a twangy intensity.) It was that a person's mind needs more to chew on than the box-office calculations that shaped this movie and destroyed a great subject.

This is what I was writing: Walter Hill's *Crossroads* takes its title from the legend that the Mississippi Delta guitarist and singer Robert

Johnson—perhaps the finest bluesman who has ever lived—sold his eternal soul to the Devil at a lonely crossroads. What, exactly, he had to gain isn't clear: Johnson died, in 1938, at the age of twenty-six, and so it couldn't have been fame and fortune. Musical talent seems to be the answer. And, in the movie, that appears to be what sent Johnson's (fictional) friend, the harmonica player and singer Willie Brown, to the crossroads a few years later. The movie tells the story of a white teen-ager, Eugene (Ralph Macchio), a student at Juilliard, who locates the eighty-year-old Willie (Joe Seneca) in a prison nursing home in Harlem. Eugene, a guitar prodigy, is trying to track down a lost Robert Johnson song; he thinks that if he can record it it will be his ticket to glory. Willie, who wants to go back to Mississippi to undo his pact with the Devil, promises the kid the song if he'll help him escape and get home.

The first three-quarters of an hour—with the white-bearded old hipster Willie venting his sarcasm on the kid—is junkily entertaining. Willie snarls at Eugene's softness, his easy life on Long Island, his musical pretensions, his wanting to follow in the footsteps of other whites who have ripped off black music. And there's an extra layer of justice to Willie's remarks, because the toneless-voiced, emotionally flat Macchio is a totally unsurprising actor: the apotheosis of the term "adequate." When they're on the road in the South, though, Willie turns into a gruff, curmudgeonly guardian angel, and Eugene starts learning lessons about life. He begins to understand that you have to live the blues in order to play it, and the picture is contemptible, reaching its nadir in the sequences that introduce a teen-age girl hitchhiker (Jami Gertz, less than adequate) so Eugene can have his sexual initiation. The three of them learn from one another, while Hill—deliberately, perhaps—forgets just about everything he ever knew about moviemaking (which, as he demonstrated in such pictures as *The Warriors*, *The Long Riders*, *Southern Comfort*, and *48 Hrs.*, was considerable). What does Hill think, I wonder, when Willie, contemplating death, says, "The only thing I ever wanted anybody to say was 'He could really play. He was really good' "?

In *The Karate Kid*, Macchio was taught the martial arts by an elderly Japanese, and if *Crossroads* were a comparable financial success no doubt he'd go on mastering as many arts from as many cultures as the public would queue up for. As the Karate Kid, Macchio defeated opponents twice his size, and it's obvious that the producers hope they've got a junior Rocky. This film was shot in the interregnum between *The Karate Kid* and *The Karate Kid: Part II*, and it climaxes in a musical variant of a prizefight, with Eugene battling guitars with the Devil's top musician.

(The musical tastes of patrons in Hell dives run to heavy metal.) Taking the story of Robert Johnson and other bluesmen and trying to give it a teen hook, Hill and the young screenwriter John (one-piece-of-information-per-scene) Fusco have made a movie that isn't likely to please blues lovers or the young movie audience that it panders to, either. (And it's not likely to delight women: when Willie is explaining to the jilted Eugene that "the blues is nothin' but a man losin' a good woman and feelin' bad," didn't anybody on the set have a passin' thought for Bessie Smith?) The picture belongs to Joe Seneca, whose energy drives it along, especially in the scene where he sings "Willie Brown Blues" in a jam-packed juke joint that rocks with excitement. But the picture keeps being handed back to Macchio, as if the audience would naturally identify with this bland white kid. Compromises can lead a movie into real insanities: *Crossroads* begins by treating black country-blues musicians with love and awe, and ends with Eugene the Juilliard boy as the champion bluesman, who wins his match with the assistance of Mozart.

How many damn sweet-faced kids do we have to watch maturing . . . That's where I fell asleep.

April 21, 1986

MAN IN A BIND

||||||||||||||||||||||||||||||||||||||||||||||||||||||||||||||||||||||||||||||||||||||||||||||||||||||||||||||||||||||||||||||||||||||||||

Nothing wrecks a comedian's timing more than trying to be "nakedly" honest—trying to be himself. In the semi-autobiographical *Jo Jo Dancer, Your Life Is Calling*, which Richard Pryor produced and directed, and wrote together with Rocco Urbisci and Paul Mooney, the incidents are familiar, but they've lost their manic, raucous exuberance. The whole movie is an inadvertent tribute to Pryor's imaginative powers as a stand-up artist. When he works alone onstage, he creates a world of interacting people, animals, landscapes, objects. When he's making a movie with actual people and landscapes, he doesn't know how to animate them. As a stand-up entertainer, he sees the crazy side of his sorrows; he transforms pain and chaos into comedy. As a moviemaker, he's a novice

144

presenting us with clumps of unformed experience. It isn't even raw; the juice has been drained away. You sit there thinking, Doesn't he know that he has already done his autobiography? He drew on his life in his great 1979 one-man movie, *Richard Pryor Live in Concert,* and in the 1982 follow-up *Richard Pryor Live on the Sunset Strip,* on his L.P.s and in TV and club appearances. He was himself—demons, genius, and all— in those two movies (and perhaps also in the rarely shown 1973 film *Wattstax,* in which he's said to have been photographed spritzing in a ghetto bar). Now, trying to be sincere, he's less than himself.

In form, *Jo Jo Dancer* is like a less knowing *All That Jazz,* in which Bob Fosse took off from his heart attack. The Pryor film begins with Jo Jo the cokehead comedy star preparing to freebase and bursting into flame—the 1980 conflagration that was covered on the TV news, and also served as the climactic event in *Live on the Sunset Strip.* Then, as Jo Jo lies swathed in bandages in the burn ward, and no one knows if he'll live or die, he thinks back over how he got there. As he recalls his experiences in Morton, Ohio, first as an eight-year-old (played by E'lon Cox) whose grandmother (Carmen McRae) is the madam of a brothel where his luscious mother (Diahnne Abbott) works, the scenes don't have an independent life. They just keep reminding us of how funny and rowdy Pryor made them when he played all the parts. The incidents have even less life when Jo Jo gets a little older and Pryor takes over the role. Pryor has always had a boyish cunning, but here when he needs to be boyish he looks blank and anxious, with an almost tragic cast to his features— especially during Jo Jo's quarrels with his big, powerfully built father, played by Scoey Mitchlll. (For a while, after scrawny young Jo Jo leaves town, he goes to cities that seem to be populated with huge, threatening figures.) When people are kind to Jo Jo and he feels grateful, his eyes blur and his mouth is drawn in an expression of teary, Chaplinesque pathos.

Pryor plays Jo Jo's youth so charmlessly that the kid doesn't appear to have a speck of show business in him. And something is terribly off in Jo Jo's acts as a rookie night-club performer. Pryor seems to be using these acts merely as illustrations of the sort of thing he did when he started out; you don't feel a performer's energy in what Jo Jo is doing, and although he's seen convulsing the night-club patrons, his routines don't build—his timing is off, and they don't have any kick. When Jo Jo is at the Club Shalimar, a Mafia-run joint in Cleveland, where his friend Satin Doll (Paula Kelly) does a sumptuous striptease, he traipses onstage and does a soigné, ultra-chic impersonation of her. But he keeps his puckered-up, drop-dead manner for too long. He's too cool to be laughing-out-loud funny; Jo Jo isn't uncontrollably tickled at what he's doing, and so we're not, either. If I had never seen Richard Pryor before, I couldn't have guessed—on the basis of what Jo Jo does here—that he has an excitable greatness in him. Billy Eckstine, who plays the amiable m.c. at the Shalimar, offers Jo Jo some pills to relax—so he won't step on his own jokes. I guess we're meant to think he's been so jittery he's been going too fast, but he sounds recessive and slow.

Although you can see that Pryor is trying to be tough and not fall into the harmless-smiley-black-fella routines of many of his thirty-odd movies, he fudges on the central conflict in his career. In *Lady Sings the Blues*, Diana Ross's Billie Holiday was turned on to dope by a slimy blond dude. Here Jo Jo is corrupted by a rich white party-giver (big, blond Wings Hauser), who serves his guests cocaine as if it were a cream-cheese dip, and then lures them into group sex. This maneuver—presenting Jo Jo as an innocent who accepts nose candy from a (white) stranger—is too easy. It's on a par with a scene of the eight-year-old Jo Jo not being able to show his mother his good report card, because she's busy with a (white) customer. What Pryor never pokes into is the rela-tionship between getting high and the pressures of performing. He him-self expressed the conflict very clearly back in 1977, in his meeting with a team of TV comedy writers who were waiting for him when he returned home exhausted from a day of acting in a movie. A *Newsweek* reporter who was present set down his words. After a session of tossing around ideas for the première of the new variety series *The Richard Pryor Show*, Pryor said, "You know something? I don't *want* to be on TV. I'm in a trap. I can't do this—there ain't no art." Breaking into tears, he said, "I'd rather you people know it than 50 million people. I bit off more than I can chew. I was turning into a greedy person. They give you so much money you can't refuse." A black woman writer pleaded with him, "You've got the chance to do something different on television." "You want to see me with my brains blown out?" Pryor replied. "I'm gonna have to be ruthless here because of what it does to my life. I'm not stable enough. I don't want to drink and I don't want to snort and I can't do it no other way."

Earlier in the seventies, the explanation that was sometimes offered for Pryor's volatile, on-again, off-again career was that he was a junkie—i.e., on heroin. And then it was said that he, like a lot of other junkies, began taking cocaine to compensate for the down effect of heroin—that he used it as an antidote. Whatever the background to his use of cocaine, by the late seventies it was hardly a secret. And, as he acknowledged in the blurted-out statement that *Newsweek* printed, he felt he needed to be wired up to perform—needed the feelings of omnipotence that coke gave him. And who could dispute it? His isn't the classic comedy of control and polish. It's an edgy, overemotional, confessional comedy that works on a demonic level, on seeming not completely in control. But Pryor also knew that booze and coke turned him into a self-destructive megalomaniac. This conflict between the terror of staying straight and flopping and the terror of jolting himself so high he'd blow his brains would have explained the film's taking-off point—the exploding flames and the burn ward.

As it is, there's no accounting for why Jo Jo the Hollywood star is a violent-tempered, drunken wreck. Pryor simply skims the incidents of his life, skips around (the editing is sloppy), and presents a conventional show-biz bio, with a procession of disaffected wives. I liked the ghostly stretch limousine that transports Jo Jo as he travels back to his childhood, and there are fond touches, such as having Jo Jo the star present himself to the child Jo Jo and hug his beautiful, whorey young mother. There are also such infelicities as cracks about "Italians," as if the word were synonymous with "Mafiosi." (Are those the only Italians he met?) A larger infelicity: we don't get a sense of the ferment that this black underground man catapulted out of. The picture drops the name Angela Davis, and Jo Jo appears in a modified Afro and spouts a few four-letter words, and Pryor also makes some effort to show that Jo Jo stopped telling detachable jokes. This doesn't even begin to do the job. In 1982, Pryor was the No. 1 box-office star in America. How can a movie about his emergence in the sixties and his rise in the seventies not mention Lenny Bruce (who died in 1966)? In a way, it would have seemed berserk if *Jo Jo Dancer had* suggested that its hero was carrying through what Lenny Bruce started, because Jo Jo isn't. Jo Jo doesn't perceive the dirty joys of blasphemy and mean-spiritedness, the way Richard Pryor did. He doesn't have the self-mockery to give cowardice its due. He doesn't improvise with the whooping, screaming, ghetto-poolroom naughtiness of a Richard Pryor, whose upper tonal range would shame a banshee.

In all probability, Pryor simply didn't recognize that there was also an art to directing a movie. He doesn't know how to create the charged atmosphere that he was part of. He doesn't know how to tell a joke visually. A shot of Jo Jo soaked in rum and lighted up may be meant to show his death wish, or perhaps it's a gag—a spoof of Pryor's lawyer's attempt to conceal how he got burned. The awful thing is that Pryor got burned again when he decided to make a movie of his life. This Jo Jo isn't smart enough for us to accept him as Pryor. Pryor has a hellion's fear that drives him on. He's always testing the audience the way a kid tests his parents: How far dare he go? How far can he get on his cuteness and his nerve? It gives a tension to everything he does, and he's exhilarated, his beady, wary eyes darting about, checking on how he's doing. He knows and we know that he can't stop, that he has to go where his heated-up imagination takes him, and that he can't do it without audience feedback. What a great humorist does at his desk, Pryor does in front of an audience: he makes discoveries; he surprises himself. (That's what a real movie director does, too.) This dimension of Pryor—Pryor the artist—is lost in the movie.

■

*V*iolets Are Blue is a slim, undeveloped movie about Gussie and Henry, a pair of young lovers in the late sixties who plan to leave their home town—Ocean City, Maryland—and explore the great world. But, as it turns out, Gussie (Sissy Spacek) is more restless and confident than Henry (Kevin Kline). She goes away and becomes an airline stewardess and then—making good on her talent—a well-known photojournalist. He stays at home working on his father's newspaper, marries, takes pride in his wife (Bonnie Bedelia) and son, becomes editor of the paper and makes it a force in the community. (Henry, like every other good person in the movies now, fights to protect the environment.) The movie takes up what happens sixteen or seventeen years after Gussie left Ocean City, when she feels lonely and rootless, and returns to spend a vacation with her parents. The romance with Henry is rekindled, and she persuades him that it isn't too late for him to fulfill his high-school ambition of becoming a free-lance magazine writer. They make plans to go off together—to leave his wife and teen-age son (Jim Standiford) to lump it. The problem-play idea is fairly clear: Can the modern "career" woman who has given up the simpler, more basic satisfactions go back and retrieve the man she left behind? That is, can she have everything—the excitement of her work and the solidity of a Henry, too? And does the man who has been a useful, contented stick-in-the-mud for so long really want to ditch his responsibilities and become a risk-taker? Questions like these don't give the audience a stake in a movie unless the characters

148

get to us. But the characters here were devised so that the questions could be raised; Spacek and Kline are playing "concepts," and they don't scratch the abstract surface.

In earlier movie eras, Gussie would probably have been a villainous vamp, "the other woman," a deliberate home breaker—which might at least have been entertaining. Now she's just a vaporous figure standing in for all the women who got into what they once thought were the glamourous occupations and find themselves shading thirty-five or forty and alone. The movie, produced by Marykay Powell, from her idea, and from a screenplay that's credited to Naomi Foner (it probably started out as hers), tries for some complexity. It tells us that Gussie refuses to recognize that Henry made his choice through all the small, cumulative choices that kept him in Ocean City. What comes across is that there were reasons Henry stayed behind—reasons rooted in his character. And maybe Kevin Kline's doughiness in the movie—his total lack of magnetism—is the result of his effort to play Henry as a born husband. But that doesn't keep people in the audience from tittering at him, and they're right to titter; it's a fuddy performance—Kline gives you the feeling he's an actor with nothing inside. Spacek at least plugs away at her non-role, although, with tendrils of her long red-gold angel hair forever spilling over her face, you wonder how the hell she takes pictures. The director, Jack Fisk, has a feeling for naturalistic acting, and he modulates the dialogue so it has a gentle tone. He uses the oceanside-resort-town locale, with its sailboats and its amusement park, to get the love scenes between the two retro-adolescents moving, but he can't do anything like the flowing, expressive work he did in *Raggedy Man*. All he can accomplish is to keep the movie lightweight.

Even so, Bonnie Bedelia comes through. She gives the stay-at-home wife a flirtatious vibrancy that makes you want to forget about whether those two noodles Gussie and Henry are going to grow up or go on trying to flip back the calendar. Bedelia has the advantage of playing anger— which is the only strong emotion anybody in *Violets Are Blue* gets to express—and she makes her anger sexual and down to earth. The picture doesn't really get started—to the degree that it ever gets started—until she's around. When I last saw Bedelia, in the 1983 *Heart Like a Wheel*, she seemed to be trying too hard and she was tense, but she's relaxed here, and her prettiness, which was so broad-domed and childlike in the days of *They Shoot Horses, Don't They?* and *Lovers and Other Strangers*, has gained a new depth. You feel that this wife has lived a little and knows what's what. (The other two are like moderately intelligent dummies.) It's one of the mysteries and blessings of movies that something as inconsequential as *Violets Are Blue* can be fluttering by and suddenly a performer like Bonnie Bedelia lights up your consciousness.

■

Maybe it's a mercy to the audience that the elements of *Violets Are Blue* are left undeveloped. *Just Between Friends*—which is another homemaker/husband/career-woman triangle—spells everything out, according to accepted TV procedures. This ode to pseudo-liberation stars Mary Tyler Moore as the California homemaker and mother of two teenagers, with Ted Danson as her seismologist husband and Christine Lahti as her best friend, a TV newscaster. The writer-director, Allan Burns, has prepared a carefully constructed script about how the timid-mouse wife must grow and become self-reliant after her husband is killed in a car accident, and how the friendship between the two women is sustained after the wife learns that her friend was having an affair with her husband and is pregnant by him. But the two women meet at an exercise class, and the subtext, which is tied in to that exercise class, dominates the movie.

For two hours, we're invited to admire what terrific shape Mary Tyler Moore is in. There are so many shots of her tight, trim rear end in leotards as she gyrates for the camera that the film begins to seem a vanity production. On television in the sixties and seventies, Mary Tyler Moore's girlish personality made her America's sweetheart, but now she looks agonizingly ill at ease about her age, and this exhibition of her beautiful state of preservation makes her seem much older than she is. (She's around fifty.) Her self-consciousness was always part of her comedy style. Now she's still playing that kind of hesitancy; she has scenes just like the ones she used to play as Mary Richards—scenes where she wishes she weren't so conventional, and wishes she could use the "f" word as casually as her friend does, and so on. But what she's really self-conscious about is at war with what she's playing. When she flashes that familiar big, bright smile, her face is drawn so taut that she looks as if she's in pain. That smile gets to be like a nervous tic, a plea. Since Burns, who used to work on *The Mary Tyler Moore Show*, wrote the script for her, and the picture was produced by MTM Enterprises, she's not exactly in the position of an actress who takes an unsuitable role because it was

150

the best she could get. This role is tailored for her as she was fifteen years ago.

Christine Lahti walks off with the picture, and it's not just because of her savvy as an actress—it's also because she's at ease about her age. (She's in her thirties.) Lahti is like the audience's representative on the screen; she makes contact with us (the way Bonnie Bedelia does in *Violets Are Blue*). Her voice has a witty dryness, with deep resonances, and she plays the sophisticated newscaster with a modern, open brazenness. This newscaster is like a new, more plangent version of Rosalind Russell at her peak, in *His Girl Friday*—a woman who holds her own, who's too strong and too proud to turn helpless around men, and sometimes furiously regrets it.

May 5, 1986

DRIFTERS, DOPES, AND DOPERS

||||||||||||||||||||||||||||||||||||||||||||||||||||||||||||||||||||||||||||||||||||||||||||||||||||||||||||||||||||||||||||||||||||||||||||||||||||||||||||||||||||||||||||||

Agnès Varda wrote and directed *Vagabond*—in France, *Sans Toit ni Loi* (literally, *Without Roof or Law*)—a scrupulous, hardheaded film about an eighteen-year-old girl on the road. Mona (played by the eighteen-year-old Sandrine Bonnaire, who came to prominence in Maurice Pialat's 1983 *À Nos Amours*) is a deliberately homeless wanderer in a leather jacket. The movie begins with the discovery of her body in a ditch. Like other French drifters, she had headed south for the winter, but there was an unexpected cold snap and she froze to death in the countryside near the city of Nîmes. Varda presents the movie as if it were a documentary investigating how this happened. The characters are Mona and the witnesses to her last weeks, and we are put in the position of these witnesses—some of them envious of her freedom, others upset by her dirtiness, her sullenness, her vacant eyes. Some of them gave her rides or took her in, and though she hardly spoke at all, she was good company as long as she was given pot, or wine and cigarettes.

Mona is the solipsistic eighties version of what in the fifties was called a "rebel without a cause." She's numb, suspicious, indifferent—an extreme version of what in England now is called a "no-hoper." The American title for the film suggests something carefree and adventurous; it romanticizes her slightly—she's actually more vagrant than vagabond. Mona lives on handouts, thefts, a little prostitution, and the occasional odd job. She may flirt a bit, and she may have sex voluntarily or be forced into it, but the basic fact about this girl is that she gives nothing of herself—she's closed off.

Bonnaire, with her wide forehead and intelligent yet unyielding manner, plays the role immaculately; giving you nothing is her forte, and she has the strength and beauty to sustain your interest for a considerable stretch. She doesn't work like a trained actress; she works like a great camera subject, and Varda, a photographer turned moviemaker, renders her impenetrability as fully as a Cartier-Bresson might. Varda has based her film on observation of the new young drifters on the roads, and her approach here is a flat-out "This is how it is. This is what you see when you look up close." Emotionally, Mona is like a cagey infant, responding on the minimal basis of who gives her the goodies she wants this minute.

I can believe in the truth of what Varda shows us, and there's integrity in every frame of the film. Varda has a silly side that comes out in some of her work (as in *One Sings, the Other Doesn't*), but she's also a full-fledged visual moviemaker. The purity and boldness of her approach here may call Robert Bresson to mind, and it's perfectly evident why this film won the Golden Lion at the 1985 Venice Film Festival, was selected best picture of the year by the French Critics Association, and also won Bonnaire the French César for best actress. *Vagabond* is the work of a visual artist. But what Varda shows us isn't enough. The disadvantage of her neo-documentary approach is that we gain no more insight into the girl than we would have if we had actually been witnesses who encountered her. We see her strictly from the outside, the way the camera sees her. Varda appears to believe that the artist only needs to give you the facts. As in her 1965 film *Le Bonheur*, she gives you everything you want but the essential. We don't get what a great novelist or playwright or screenwriter can give us—an imaginative grasp of what has closed the young girl off.

In its own stubborn way, the movie (which is dedicated to Nathalie Sarraute) is admirable, but when you leave the theatre you're more likely to think of the social problem of the homeless than of Mona, because she never comes alive for us. Varda may have been attracted to the subject as a means of exercising her own closed-off, modernist temperament. She ends where she started, and in more than the visual sense of beginning

152

and ending with the frozen young body in the ditch. Sitting in the audience, we are turned into no-hopers—as if we had no means of understanding anything. Varda's flat-out—almost mulish—approach excludes the uses of the imagination, both hers and ours. If Tolstoy had looked at Anna Karenina as objectively as Varda looks at Mona, we would see her as no more than a frivolous, spoiled society woman. (Of course, Tolstoy flunks the modernist aesthetic.) If the outside of a life isn't used to reveal the inside, a movie turns to stone.

■

*W*ise Guys is a Mafia burlesque—a broad, slapstick Mafia farce, spattered with gross-out humor. The two heroes—Danny DeVito as the bumptious Italian Harry, and Joe Piscopo as the Jewish simpleton Moe—have been best friends since childhood and still live in adjoining working-class houses in Newark. They're on the lowest rung of the local organization; they're hangers-on who are treated contemptuously and ordered to fetch the godfather's groceries and dry cleaning, or start his car for him if he has reason to think there may be a bomb in it. Their duties don't require any brains, but they try to be smart, and they foul up: when they're given ten thousand of the godfather's dollars to bet on a horse, they're not told that he has fixed the race, and Harry, convinced that the horse doesn't have a chance, persuades Moe to put the money on another. When the godfather grills them and each takes the blame, he's indignant: these wise guys are loyal to each other, and not to him. The affronted godfather (Dan Hedaya), a New Jersey–style Machiavellian, tells Harry and Moe, each in private, that the other has ratted on him, and orders each to bump off the other. Then he arranges for his hit man, Frankie the Fixer—played by the retired professional wrestler Captain Lou Albano—to take care of the survivor. The movie is the account of the two friends' joint efforts to stay alive, their dash to Atlantic City in the Cadillac they steal from the Fixer, and his apoplectic rages.

The producer, Aaron Russo, has described the picture as *Laurel and Hardy Meet the Godfather*, and that's fairly close to the mark, except that it doesn't have a Laurel or a Hardy or much of a godfather. The turns and twists in the script (it's credited to George Gallo) suggest that Russo may have hoped for a slobby, knockabout *Animal House* Mafia movie, but Brian De Palma, who directed, sets up the old gags with no waste motion. Sometimes the gags have been around quite recently: Harry and Moe, in church with their pal (played by Ray Sharkey), are told to do as he does, and they go on imitating his movements after he has been shot—it's the same basic gag as the murder on the dance floor in *Airplane!* But De Palma stages these routines deftly, without any stress. He doesn't have to push you to laugh, because he knows how to pinpoint what he wants you to look at (and he adds a small zinger in the church scene, when the bullets hit the plaster statue of the Virgin).

De Palma's directing is canny and smooth, and he gives the picture a consistent texture; it's what he's directing that freezes my responses. I could hear the men around me in the theatre laughing. Not surprisingly, the audience was almost all male; women aren't likely to be attracted to a Mafia farce starring Danny DeVito and Joe Piscopo. The clownish archness of this kind of comedy must link up with young boys' cops-and-robbers games and all the "Bang, you're dead!" roughhousing that kids do. The gangster burlesque is a musty genre: it includes the 1971 *The Gang That Couldn't Shoot Straight*, Edward G. Robinson in the 1938 *A Slight Case of Murder*, films based on Damon Runyon stories, such as the 1933 *Lady for a Day*, its 1961 remake, *Pocketful of Miracles*, and the several versions of *Little Miss Marker*, and dozens of others. What they all have in common is childlike, warmhearted big-city hoods who talk ungrammatically (preferably in a croak or growl), rush around antically, and do plenty of mugging.

Some of these movies have their moments of humor, but even at best the stylization they require is very close to coyness, and they always end up as sticky fairy tales. (The thugs are lovable scamps at heart.) So fresh jokes and sharp, colorful personalities are desperately needed. De Palma doesn't get them. Danny DeVito, who often seemed inspired in the TV series *Taxi* but has been lethally over the top in some of his other film roles, isn't bad here. He uses his short frame confidently, assertively; it makes perfect sense that his Harry—a heavyset pixie who is carried away by his dreams and impulses—should be happily married. (Patti LuPone plays his wife.) DeVito is controlled and resourceful, and at times he manages to be touching without any hint of pathos, but he's a character comedian, not a star. It also makes some kind of sense that Joe Piscopo's pop-eyed numskull Moe should be living with his mother (played by Julie Bovasso). But Piscopo—familiar to TV viewers for the brash satirical impressions he did on *Saturday Night Live*—isn't quite an actor, and has no light or subtle side. (He's an abrasive performer—a bulldozer, like Jerry Lewis.) Possibly if his vaguely Stan Laurel–like role had been

154

better written, he could have brought some inflections to it. As it is, he's a blank. Most of the other mobsters are played so crudely that when Harvey Keitel turns up in the Atlantic City scenes he seems like a really classy actor.

The frankness of this movie's grubby anti-glamour is its only claim to charm, but maybe you'd have to be part of what is delicately referred to as the undemanding audience—say, somebody who watches every rerun of the Abbott and Costello pictures—to succumb and find it as uproarious as it's meant to be. Although the two underdogs come out on top, the picture doesn't have any real emotional payoff, because they don't get their revenge consciously. These two frightened clowns don't get to release their anger, and so De Palma doesn't get to release his wit. *Wise Guys* is for people who treasure the grossness in boyish humor and like it best when it's aged and has become mild.

∎

Hal Ashby's *8 Million Ways to Die* is about cops and robbers, coke and hookers. (These are the pillars of new American action movies— the ones that aren't about showing the Commies how mighty is our moral wrath.) The Ashby film is based on Lawrence Block's mystery novels featuring the detective Matthew Scudder; the best known of these books is *Eight Million Ways to Die*—which, of course, refers to New York City, where the stories are set. So it's a bit dislocating when the movie opens with a fine aerial view of traffic on the L.A. freeways. Scudder (Jeff Bridges) is now a narcotics detective for the L.A. County Sheriff's Department, and that first dislocation is one of many. The movie has an overlush pictorial exoticism, as if being coked out comes with the terri- tory. The locales, which include a cliff at Malibu with a tram that takes you up to a casino-bordello, and a cocaine importer's curvy, pseudo-Gaudí house, suggest an effort to find a dark, baroque beauty and sexiness in the corrupt city. (It's as if Ashby imagines himself shooting *The Third Man* in the bombed-out ruins of Vienna.) *8 Million* is both intensely visual and exhausted—"blown away." It's more enjoyable than the other pictures that Ashby has made in the last half-dozen years, yet it's per- meated with druggy dissociation and you can't always distinguish between what's intentional and what's unintentional. Plot points don't connect, as though they don't matter, the actors often sound as if they're making up their lines, and on three separate occasions Scudder and another man engage in lengthy, belligerent confrontations, exchanging obscenities and telling each other off. As far as the narrative is concerned, these macho shouting matches might be intermissions. What they tell us is that Ashby is less interested in the thriller aspect of the film than in men in a semi-stupor challenging each other. And the crazy confusion of these challenges is halfway amusing—you don't know what's going on, or if the director does, either. Violence and dreaminess are blended.

At the outset, Scudder, driven to drink after he has had to shoot a man, has taken a leave of absence from the Sheriff's Department and joined A.A. He's been free of booze for six months when a bright-eyed, coke-snorting young hooker called Sunny (Alexandra Paul) hires him to protect her. Sunny is one of a string of a dozen or so whores who are available to the patrons of the swank casino, and the film's grandiosity klonks a viewer on the head fairly early, when this fresh-faced sweetie takes off her clothes in Scudder's apartment and rhapsodizes about the glow of her pubic hair in the street light. Not in the moonlight but in the street light. Her words may be the ultimate in eighties film-noir self-consciousness. (Is there something in druggy subjects that encourages directors to make imitation film noir? Film noir itself becomes an addiction.) At first, Scudder thinks that Sunny is frightened of Chance (Randy Brooks), the black ex-convict who operates the casino, but after she is murdered his suspicions settle on a sleek Colombian-American racketeer, Angel Maldonado (Andy Garcia), who frequents the place and is enamored of Sarah (Rosanna Arquette), the top hooker of the bunch. The script, credited to Oliver Stone and David Lee Henry (other hands were also involved), is crude stuff, but it suggests more hardboiled narrative drive than Ashby delivers. (That might be what prompted the production company to fire him after the wrap—the completion of principal photography.) The story isn't filled in, and the spaces in the narrative contribute to the coked-out feeling. At times, Ashby might be waiting around for something in his brain to crystallize. He doesn't give the scenes the emotional shading that would make them play, and the actors are left exposed to ridicule, as if this were a cheap exploitation film instead of an expensive one. Except for Andy Garcia, the Cuban-born actor who was the trim, attentive homicide detective in *The Mean Season*, and who cuts loose here—he does Latino sleaze and volatility to hammy perfection, flashing his eyes like semaphores—the performances are negligible. That includes Bridges, and Arquette, too. When she's trying to be hard-edged, she chops her lines short and makes funny faces. (And the hopes that

156

people have had for her, on the basis of her work—and her look—in *The Executioner's Song*, keep withering away.) As for Bridges, he generally tries something different in each role, but he can't get hold of much this time; a passivity seems to engulf him, and the picture swings over to Garcia, who's simply more fun to watch.

8 Million Ways to Die is like a continuation of other drug-traffic movies that Oliver Stone has written (*Midnight Express, Scarface, Year of the Dragon*). It's pulpier and tawdrier than you might expect from Ashby, but it's also woozy, and it luxuriates in the glamour of being physically and emotionally spent, as if droopiness were sexy. Ashby seems to smear his materials on the screen; that includes such devices as blobs of color and breathy sounds on the track. He loves visionary, watery finales—he has Bridges and Arquette romping on the beach at the end, embracing and walking along, just two happy kids. And you feel as if you're seeing a mind shutting off in front of your eyes. He directs like a gonzo flower child.

May 19, 1986

FIZZLE/A*L*D*A

"I thought, 'My lord, one thing is certain, and that's that they'll make musicals one day about the glamour-studded 1950s.' " This prophecy by the hero of Colin MacInnes's 1959 novel *Absolute Beginners* is a bitter joke: his next words are "And I thought, my heaven, one thing is certain too, I'm miserable." This narrator-hero, a hipster photographer, is just a kid—he's in his last year as a teen-ager—but he's a smart, spirited kid (he has all the forty-four-year-old author's experience), and we see and feel street life in London in the summer of 1958 through his consciousness. The boy has no name in the novel, which is an inventive, slangy, poetic celebration of youth and jazz and the city, and a cry of disgust at the way teen-agers, who didn't emerge as a group with money to spend until the fifties, are already being commercialized and corrupted. He's called Colin in the ambitious, prophecy-fulfilling musical, directed by the thirty-one-

157

year-old Julien Temple. "Ambitious" isn't a dig. The movie goes to hell in its second half, and the first half doesn't really work, either, but it's trying for something. Temple takes on the large order of producing a total vision—a stylized, widescreen musical in which the streets and shops and houses are all part of the set, with the camera swerving around corners, and the whole huge cast performs like a troupe doing street theatre. At times, it's like a nightmare of Vincente Minnelli staging the Brecht-Weill *Threepenny Opera* at M-G-M. The staging is full of "ideas," but none of them are carried very far—they don't amount to anything more than distraction and diversion. Everything is kept in motion, though not exactly to the music, and, whether because of the fast-cutting style that Temple developed from his work in rock videos or because of the generally undistinguished choreography, it's peculiarly unlyrical and ephemeral—the images leave no afterimages.

The movie has an Expressionist vividness—a glossy immediacy. It's a total vision, but of what? You can feel the flash and determination that went into it. What you don't feel is the tormented romanticism that made English adolescents in the seventies swear by the novel the way American kids had earlier sworn by *The Catcher in the Rye*. In the movie we recognize that the teen-agers are the "absolute beginners" who are just starting to experience their freedom when they're snared by one group of exploiters or another, but there's no strong feeling attached to the recognition. And we experience little of the hero's deep love of London, or the pain of his disillusionment when street gangs attack the black immigrants from the West Indies and the authorities don't come to their aid—don't even condemn the attackers. Temple's teeming images have a look of their own but they're singularly short of emotion, and there are so many characters to keep track of and so much visual powie that the central story of Colin (Eddie O'Connell) and his love for Suzette (Patsy Kensit) doesn't have any dramatic weight. Partly, this is because the role of Colin is cast much too conventionally; what's needed is expressiveness, and Eddie O'Connell is just a good-looking kid, shallowly amiable, who can wear tight pants. With O'Connell in the role, Temple has no way to suggest the hero's quality of mind. So who cares when Colin sells out and becomes "a professional teen-ager"? That's what Eddie O'Connell is anyway. At first sight, Patsy Kensit seems a knockout. A blond dolly with babyish cheeks and a petulant mouth, she's a harbinger of the Swinging London that will arrive in the sixties. But you don't see anything more in Kensit after your first look, and you don't hear much to care about when she sings "Having It All." She's generic, like O'Connell, and she's playing a sullen postmodern version of Jayne Mansfield in Frank Tashlin's 1956 *The Girl Can't Help It*. So you don't feel bad about little Suzette's marrying for money and position rather than love.

The movie is slanted to youth, but it's the old pros who provide the entertaining little squiggles that keep it going. Some of the performers fit MacInnes's descriptions to a comic T. As Henley, dressmaker to the Queen, and the head of the Mayfair fashion house where the seventeen-year-old Suzette is a lowly assistant, James Fox is just as MacInnes described him—"looking like a superior footman on his day off." And he's funny at it. As the total cynic Vendice Partners, the advertising man whom Colin has dealings with, David Bowie, thatched with short blond hair, is "one of those young men with an old face, or old ones with a young one, hard to tell which." Bowie's Vendice has nifty gestures, like slicking his hair back over his ears with both hands—copping a feel of his own deluxe skull. As Colin's weakling father, Ray Davies (of the Kinks) brings a music-hall grunginess and bounce to his number "Quiet Life," and as the titian-haired gossip columnist Dido Lament the American Anita Morris has the wormy-rose beauty of a young Gabor sister—she definitely has "eyes [that] say she knows just how much your price will be." Julien Temple's work can be lively in the scenes where new characters are introduced. There are dozens of them (such as the talent agent, played by Lionel Blair, the psycho Flikker, played by Bruce Payne, and the amoral boy panderer Wizard, played by Graham Fletcher-Cook), who provide glints of humor and bits of grotesquerie but don't get a chance to do what you feel they could. Temple doesn't show any interest in developing them. He wouldn't have time anyway. The script, by Richard Burridge, Christopher Wicking, Don MacPherson, and probably others, tries to retain just about everybody in the book (which itself had more characters than MacInnes knew what to do with).

Sade appears in one sequence and sings "Killer Blow." She sounds just fine, and she has one real function here: she cools out the movie—the speeding images slow down and you get to rest your eyes on her. It may occur to you that her singing isn't right for the period, but everything is slightly off—the film isn't really set in the late fifties or any other period. It goes from one musical idiom to another, with the many performers singing in their own styles (and sometimes singing their own compositions) and the arrangements, by Gil Evans—sometimes more dissonant than you might expect in a pop musical—holding it all together. And it's impressive to see an attempt at a movie musical in which the songs carry much of the characterization and the plot. But it's as though the images were edited to different music. Despite Temple's background and his reputation, he doesn't seem to have a rhythmic style. You may register this at the beginning, when the camera and the cuts are at odds with the movements of the people in the street. And you may feel it quite acutely when Bowie has his big singing-and-tapping number "That's Motivation"—it's the only time in the movie that you're fully caught up in a performer's rhythm—and Temple gets jumpy and cuts away. The second half goes really bad: once the racial confrontations start and there's rioting in the streets, the music and the images seem to be coming from two different TV channels. The choreography is an inept homage to the high-kicking big rumble in *West Side Story*, and there's so much of this rumbling that you can't help thinking that Jerome Robbins has a lot to answer for. The street fighting also carries a moldy burden of political didacticism. In the movie (though not in the novel), the violence is instigated by Henley and Vendice Partners, who are co-conspirators planning to make millions with real-estate developments on the sites of the slum dwellings. They employ the terror tactics of slumlords like Rachman, and we get a fanatic Oswald Mosley–Enoch Powell speech delivered (by Steven Berkoff) to a meeting of hate-filled bullies. The movie becomes a self-important mess. It puts itself on the side of virtue by having the psychos and neo-Fascists marching through the streets shouting the slogan "Deport All Niggers." A sign is also displayed calling for an end to "Jews, homos, and blacks," though the film keeps encouraging you to laugh at Henley's twittish prissiness and Colin calls him an "old queen."

For all the scattershot energy that has gone into *Absolute Beginners*, it certainly doesn't give you the exhilaration of a musical. It's like a zippy, noisy commercial—all movement. Temple may represent a new phenomenon: a director perfectly attuned to rock videos—i.e., commercials that simulate the emotions of old movies, heightening them like crazy. In the book, the harshness of the material works because of MacInnes's strong poetic feelings; he's never just bitter—you always know there's love under the bitterness. Temple tries to make the harshness work by stylization; the result is a part-intentional, part-unintentional deconstruction of the Hollywood musical. There's all this fizz in his work and no feeling. Maybe only a director who came up via videos would stage a balletic race riot so confusingly that it's just about impossible to root for either side.

You may not be too distressed by all this unless you know the book—a precursor of Anthony Burgess's 1962 *A Clockwork Orange*—or give yourself the pleasure of reading it. This is a case where the movie's images

160

are so weak that they don't compete with the book's. Colin MacInnes imparts his love of jazz; he even imparts some of the sensations of dancing. (The title *Absolute Beginners* is taken from the lowest category of dance classes.) He has his young narrator-hero describe what happened one night when he was on the dance floor with Suzette: "there we were, weaving together like a pair of springs connected by invisible elastic wires, until we reached that most glorious moment of all in dancing, that doesn't come often, and usually, admittedly, only when you're whipping it up a bit to show the multitude—that is, the dance starts to do it for you, you don't bloody well know what you're up to any longer, except that you can't put a limb wrong anywhere, and your whole dam brain and sex and personality have actually become that dance, *are* it—it's heavenly!" MacInnes who was born in 1914 and died in 1976, is so emotionally unarmored that he makes you feel that blissful high, and perhaps recall times when you experienced it. MacInnes was an artist; Temple, at this point, is only a wizard.

■

There is a price to be paid for being likable in a TV series week after week, year after year: the only thing that can save Alan Alda now is to play bastards or weirdos, preferably in a heavy disguise. It's possible that nothing less than a gorilla suit and a voice box will do, but maybe there'd be some hope for him if he didn't write his own roles. In *Sweet Liberty*, which he wrote, directed, and stars in, he's a lump of laid-back complacency smack at the center of the picture, and since he writes his dialogue for his familiar vocal rhythms he's like a slightly stupid uncle who has been hugging us and boring us with his jokes for as long as we can remember. Of course, this is unfair. But being fair is what Alan Alda is all about, and it's clammy, it's oppressive. You might want to tear off his benign mask to see what was underneath if your instincts didn't tell you there's nothing different underneath.

You breathe stale air at *Sweet Liberty*, but this satirical comedy made me laugh quite a lot anyway. Alda plays a history professor whose Pulitzer Prize–winning book on the American Revolution has been bought by Hollywood and is to be filmed during the summer in the area where the events he wrote about took place—in and around the fictional college

161

town of Sayeville, North Carolina, where he teaches. He has been involved in a longtime affair with an attractive young member of the English Department, played by the unlucky Lise Hilboldt, who is required to be even nicer than he is, and to beam at him and stitch, stitch, stitch on a quilt, even in bed; these two representatives of solid and enduring American values have a soggy running argument about whether she should move in with him, and let's let it go at that. The fun in the movie comes from the Hollywood contingent of show folk who invade the community: Michael Caine as the star, Michelle Pfeiffer as the leading lady, Bob Hoskins as the scriptwriter, and Saul Rubinek as the director.

Caine plays a cliché—a skirt-chasing daredevil—as if it were a role in a classic farce, and he makes a near-classic out of it. His vocal rhythms may suggest a throwback to Errol Flynn, and his actions may stir a thought of his offscreen friend Sean Connery, but the light-headed aplomb is all his own. So is his supple attentiveness when he meets the wife of the college president. It tells us that he doesn't set out to make conquests—he's simply alert to the signals that women give out and other men aren't watchful enough to pick up on. The president's eager wife (Lois Chiles, with terrific comic verve) has been waiting for him for a long time; she sends out signals like the bells of Notre Dame. As a womanizer, he provides a service, and he seems to live in a state of grace. Caine convinces you that no harm can come to this foolish movie star— that he's beloved of the gods as well as of the public. (The moviemakers— or Caine himself—may have doubted no harm could come to him: a double seems to be standing in for him in some of his fencing scenes.)

Michelle Pfeiffer has the enchanting prettiness of a pink-and-white flower; she has no dark tones yet and no mystery (maybe her roles just haven't given her the opportunities to show them), but she's at ease in front of the camera, and she has a lovely streak of humor. She plays what amounts to a double role here. We first meet the starlet in her Revolutionary-period costume and speaking in an archaic mode, because she believes in staying "in character" as fully as possible. In costume, she has a chirruping sweetness; you think of her as a bit of a tweetybrain— a ditz. So it's a small shock—and the best moment in the movie—when the prof goes to see her at her apartment, where she's in modern dress, speaking on the phone. She turns to him and we see a faintly neurotic, career-centered young actress who hasn't the slightest confusion about what's real and what's illusion. (It's like the comparable scene in *The French Lieutenant's Woman*, but not so studied, and, I think, better.)

As the Hollywood Jewish writer who's always hungry for something

162

to chew on, the English actor Bob Hoskins is small, bald, and bearded, a lovable vulgarian with a voice as loud as his madras jacket. His American accent may not be altogether convincing (at times he might be a gay Cockney cowboy), but he's better than convincing—he's hugely funny. (And his role is a well-written broad caricature of an amiable hack.) Adorned with such artifacts of prosperity as a gold Rolex, Saul Rubinek does a very shrewd comic turn as the director who just wants to get the picture shot and get on with the next deal. He has the wily-politician look that you often see on directors, and he sizes up the professor in an unimpressed glance. Rubinek is wonderful in the scene where he sets up a battle the way he wants it fought, ignoring the local people, for whom the details of this battle have been a lifelong avocation. In the structure of the film, he represents Hollywood's mediocrity and aggressive vulgarity, which is pitted against the professor's passion for historical accuracy. This isn't a battle between bad and good, though. With the fatuous, outraged professor barging onto the locations and complaining about the color of the uniforms or the shape of the hats, our sympathy goes to the director, who's putting up with the star's demands and the leading lady's demands and now has this academic jerk to contend with. It's clear that Alda isn't trying to make the professor a heroic idealist. Probably he wants us to see the hopelessness of the prof's obsession with historical accuracy, and to see why compromises are inevitable. But he may not realize that we don't want to contend with this jerk, either; he isn't stylized enough to be funny. (It's too bad that we don't get to see Rubinek's rushes of the scenes where the professor has persuaded the starlet to speak his "authentic" dialogue; we need to be able to compare it with the little hack's dialogue—which might have been livelier.)

Alda shows a neat, light touch as a director in scenes such as the star's first moments in town. Caine signs an autograph for a young girl and presses her hand while giving her a smarmy, old-roué's smile that's like a pledge to the audience that there will be seductions coming. Alda does well, too, with the Hollywood stuntmen, who, out here in North Carolina (actually the film was shot on Long Island, around Sag Harbor and Southampton), are a race apart. If you just ride along with the movie's conventionality, there are enough enjoyable scenes to put you in a good mood. But though Alda's writing tends to be too explicit—he wants to be sure that everyone in the audience can follow the plot points—his basic intentions are foggy. I think he's trying to say, "These Hollywood high rollers are off in a world of their own, but we solid citizens—we're the real people." And I think he wants us to identify with the prof as a decent, ordinary man who's a bit of a pompous fool. This is that damned self-effacing liberal fairness of his. He wants us to see that the professor is smug and insecure but that he's right about the important things. What Alda doesn't seem to grasp is that this doesn't shape up as comic; all it is is limp. Alda's conception of the professor (and of himself) throws a wet blanket over his knack for writing and directing comedy. And the professor's naïveté about what Hollywood intends to do with his book is like something out of a movie of forty or fifty years ago. This brand of unworldliness is worn to the stump.

June 2, 1986

BRUTES

||||||||||||||||||||||||||||||||||||||||||||||||||||||||||||||||||||||||||||||||||||||||||||||||||||||||||||||||||||||||||||||||

The imperious black call girl Simone (Cathy Tyson) works on a strict schedule that requires a chauffeured car to take her to luxury hotels and private residences. One night, after she has finished her rounds, and her driver, George (Bob Hoskins), is heading for her apartment, she asks him to stop as they go past the rows of streetwalkers soliciting along a London bridge. Sitting half hidden in the back of the car, she stares at the battered, painted girls; her face looks pinched—haunted—as if she never slept, as if her memories were shadows that would never lift. In these shots in the new English film *Mona Lisa*, directed by Neil Jordan, an Irish novelist turned moviemaker, the streetwalkers are standing around the car. George sees Simone's face in the mirror swimming at the center of a sea of women's faces. It's an emotionally hypercharged image; it's hellish, yet it's also sensuous, dreamy, mythic. And in that moment we see him fall in love with her. When a pimp recognizes Simone and sticks his head in the car's open front window, shouting insults at her, George, in a fury, bashes the guy's head against the top and bottom of the open window and shoves the bloody mess out. As George drives on, the women's faces blur and disappear; they stay in your consciousness, though, throughout the movie, which is lurid in a beautiful way.

George is the central character. At one time an East End petty

164

criminal, he has just come out of prison; he took a seven-year rap in place of the vice lord Mortwell (Michael Caine), and has been given the chauffeuring job as his recompense. Neil Jordan (and David Leland) wrote the script with Hoskins in mind; he's in every scene, and he's tremendous. This short, chunky actor is a powerhouse, yet he doesn't wear you out, the way some powerhouse performers do. As George, he's a decent, simple guy and a romantic at heart, but when he attacks a couple of big bruisers and knocks them down, he's completely convincing. Jordan intends the movie to be an adult version of the fairy tale of the Frog Prince, told from the frog's point of view. But that isn't the image that comes to mind. Hoskins' George is a little like a Cockney version of Edward G. Robinson's tough guys and a little like Bruno Lawrence at his most impassioned and explosive in *Smash Palace*. He's intensely sympathetic, yet brutish—especially when he's trying to assert that he's as good as anybody—and he charges his enemies like a chesty bull terrier. When he starts work as Simone's chauffeur, he doesn't know how to behave in the fancy lobbies where he is to pick her up; being ill at ease makes him belligerent, and he calls too much attention to himself. Simone is furious. She does nothing but curse and complain, and that makes him touchier and more obstreperous. The friend sitting next to me summed him up: "He's like a testicle on legs."

When George shows his devotion to the uncommunicative Simone—the Mona Lisa of the story—she sets him to searching the red-light districts of London for the girl that she was hoping to find when she asked him to stop the car. She and this little blonde—a fifteen-year-old heroin addict who was her friend when she was working the streets—were in the control of the same vicious pimp. George makes his way through the strip joints and erotic shows and whores' hangouts, and is sickened when he sees defenseless young girls covered with bruises. He finds Simone's friend and breaks into the mansion where she's being used in a blackmail scheme; she's so strung out and wrecked that he has to carry her piggyback to the car. (At first, George doesn't understand what's the matter with her. The script sometimes requires him to be more thickheaded than seems plausible, and the audience grasps things faster than he does. But we can accept this as a convention.) We see the drugs and kinkiness and cruelty as the good-hearted, appalled George sees them. He also sees that his old boss Mortwell is in the rotten thick of it. In this movie, vice is pitiful and powerfully ugly, and hallucinatory, too.

Most of the picture was shot on location in London and Brighton, but Jordan's London and Brighton never look merely realistic; the lighting (by the cinematographer Roger Pratt) heightens their emotional resonances. And Jordan—this is his third movie, after *Angel* (1982), set in Northern Ireland and released here as *Danny Boy*, and *The Company of Wolves* (1984)—shows a gift for making the emotional atmosphere visual, and vice versa. He works in a heated-up rhetorical style that's something like a visual equivalent of Norman Mailer's method in *An American Dream*. It's thought-out pop, and Jordan is perhaps too aware of the mythic layers in the material—an awareness that comes out in old-movie conceits and symbolic touches and contrasts and balances. You get the feeling that Jordan has hovered over this garden of references (with its dwarf and its white horse) very lovingly. He may be one of those people who become so involved in dreams and the unconscious that they go at everything consciously, like a diligent graduate student. Even his playfulness is pointed. You hear Nat King Cole's 1950 recording of the Jay Livingston and Ray Evans song "Mona Lisa" during the titles; you hear it again (as in a forties movie) on George's car radio. When George visits his burly old pal Thomas (Robbie Coltrane) and you see a reproduction of the Leonardo painting stuck on the side of the refrigerator in Thomas's private junk yard, it may be a bit fussy. And when George and Simone run for their lives, racing through the carnival stands on the pier at Brighton, it may not be such a great idea for them to jostle a display of red hearts and make them fall to the boardwalk. But the way Jordan uses clichés they become part of a fluid, enjoyable texture, a melodramatic impasto with an expressive power of its own. It's his romanticism that pulls you along. And if there's an element of intellectual vanity or preciousness in the film's system of references Hoskins and Tyson and Coltrane and Caine redeem it. They haven't thought things out too much; they draw on their intuitions—and, yes, their unconscious. They do it naturally and confidently, and Jordan has made this possible. He may be overaware of how he wants us to read the film's meaning, but he goes with the performers. He appears to let them set the rhythms in some of the key dialogue scenes; the result is oddly irregular and lifelike (in this stylized thriller), and very pleasing.

Cathy Tyson was raised in Liverpool and is, at twenty, a member of the Royal Shakespeare Company. She's a head taller than Hoskins, and has a slender-faced poignancy that makes Simone's foulmouthed anger seem like a self-violation. Simone's anger is inseparable from pain and loneliness, and when she drops her haughtiness and shows some fellow-feeling for George a viewer experiences the scene as if it were a spring bouquet, even though the ambiguousness and tension in the atmosphere aren't dispelled. This is Cathy Tyson's first movie, and I think it helps that we've never seen her before: her Simone is as mysteriously stirring to us as she is to George. Tyson also has remarkable control: there are few feminist tags on her performance, but her beauty incarnates everything that the sadistic pimps beat down in the process of turning girls into dependent dumb cows. It makes perfect sense that Simone has no love left in her for men. (And it makes perfect sense that Jordan, who was born in 1950 and is the father of two girls, has the empathy that he shows here, and makes George the father of a girl as a way of deepening *his* empathy.) The faintly out-of-it character—Coltrane's big, blubbery Thomas—has a calming influence on George and on the picture. Thomas's eccentric sanity is lightly amusing, and very easy to take, even though it's apparent that he's a function of the plot; he's in the movie to be a true friend to George, to understand his follies, and to warn him about Mortwell right at the start.

The name Mortwell is a bit much and is probably intended to be, and so is the white rabbit that George gives this crime boss. (It provides the final baroque touch that, so to speak, fulfills the name.) But Mortwell is not a character you can just dismiss, and I can't recall a screen star of Michael Caine's rank who has had the talent and the willingness to play a man so foul and repugnant. It's said that all Caine's scenes were shot in four days, and there aren't really many of them, but they add up to a portrait of an abomination. Mortwell panders to the vices of the rich and the poor, and he does it in a routine, matter-of-fact way. His pallor and his fish-faced smile reveal that he knows he's not peddling nuts and bolts, but he views the girls he deals in as if they were something less than hardware. Mortwell is everything that the little mug George will never understand; he's what Simone has had to come to understand. And it's a scary performance: after more than fifty pictures, Caine still comes up with shocking surprises. As Mortwell, Caine is believably evil, just as Hoskins, as George, is believably kind yet violent. It may be no more than an accident of casting that these two actors are also onscreen together in *Sweet Liberty*, and that they were together in the 1983 *Beyond the Limit* (the film of Graham Greene's *The Honorary Consul*). But in some way that perhaps Caine and Hoskins—who are both playing Cockneys here—understand, they operate on the same energy level. They take paper conceptions and turn them into characters who are more alive than anybody else in their pictures. Caine manages to do this even when he's playing a piece of ordure like Mortwell.

167

Mona Lisa reeks of noirishness. Worse, it reeks of intellectualized noirishness. But the whole movie has some of the potency of cheap music that's represented by the title song. I succumbed.

■

The strapping Kelly McGillis spends her time in *Top Gun* sidling into rooms and leaning against doorways, or slouching or bending, so she won't overpower her co-star, the relatively diminutive Tom Cruise. In some scenes, she stands slightly behind him, resting on his shoulder with her body contorted into an S so their heads will be on a level. And all the while she does her full-blown best to leer at him sexily. The best part of the movie comes when he's suffering: he speaks in a little-boy voice and looks such a Nautilized, dinky thing. Trying to instill courage in him, she says throatily, "When I first met you, you were larger than life."

In Nabokov's *Lolita*, Humbert Humbert tortures himself with images of his nymphet in the arms of "kissy-faced brutes"; that's what *Top Gun* is full of. When McGillis is offscreen, the movie is a shiny homoerotic commercial featuring the élite fighter pilots in training at San Diego's Miramar Naval Air Station. The pilots strut around the locker room, towels hanging precariously from their waists, and when they speak to each other they're head to head, as if to shout "Sez you!" It's as if masculinity had been redefined as how a young man looks with his clothes half off, and as if narcissism is what being a warrior is all about.

In between the bare-chested maneuvers, there's footage of ugly snub-nosed jets taking off, whooshing around in the sky, and landing while the soundtrack calls up Armageddon and the Second Coming—though what we're seeing is training exercises. Photographed up close in a heavy make-believe fog, the planes turn into mythic beasts, the men in the ground crews are adjuncts of these beasts, and the high-powered music simulates a primeval storm. But once the planes are in the sky the jig is up. When aerial dogfights are staged with jets, the pilots are barely visible—you can't tell them apart—and it's all so quick and depersonalized there's nothing to see but hunks of steel flashing by.

What is this commercial selling? It's just selling, because that's what the producers, Don Simpson and Jerry Bruckheimer, and the director, Tony (Make It Glow) Scott, know how to do. Selling is what they think moviemaking is about. The result is a new "art" form: the self-referential commercial. *Top Gun* is a recruiting poster that isn't concerned with recruiting but with being a poster.

June 16, 1986

THEFTS

||||||||||||||||||||||||||||||||||||||||||||||||||||||||||||||||||||||||||||||||||||||||||||||||||||||||||||||||||||||||||||||||||||||||||||

Raw Deal starts, before the titles, in the Chicago railway station with an Amtrak train coming right at you and the music so hyper-assaultive that you feel as if you're being run over. The visual-aural hyperbole is sustained while a boat comes in to dock and a helicopter descends. Then the assassins, who have converged by land, by sea, and by air, come out of a stretch station wagon, with their stretch guns blazing, and they wipe out a nest of F.B.I. agents who are guarding a witness scheduled to testify against the head of Chicago's biggest "family." The grandiloquence suggests Sergio Leone's spaghetti Westerns, but it's Leone speeded up without lyricism, and, maybe because of that, much funnier. *Raw Deal* is reprehensible and enjoyable, the kind of movie that makes you feel brain dead in two minutes—after which point you're ready to laugh at its mixture of trashiness, violence, and startlingly silly crude humor.

This movie represents a just about inconceivable fusion of talents. The craftsmanship of the Englishman John Irvin, who, after ten years as a documentary filmmaker, directed *Hard Times* and *Tinker, Tailor, Soldier, Spy* for TV, and has been directing movies as disparate as *The Dogs of War* and *Turtle Diary*, is joined to a script cooked up by a couple of Italians (Luciano Vincenzoni and Sergio Donati), written by the erratic Norman Wexler, and then rewritten by Gary M. DeVore, but still retaining some of the rowdy spirit Wexler brought to *Joe* and *Serpico* and *Saturday Night Fever*, and the semi-parody *Mandingo*, with its wacko virulence. (Wexler is the writer who, back in the early seventies, made the sporty remark that he was going to shoot Nixon, and got himself arrested, because he was on a plane at the time.) Wexler's lowdown, crazily sophisticated humor is given a charge by the strength of Irvin's

169

staging, and Irvin directs as if he were on holiday, having the time of his life. The audience keeps erupting with laughter. What makes people laugh is that this fast-moving gangster picture doesn't take itself straight; it doesn't expect you to suspend disbelief—it includes the kind of jokes that are sometimes made by the derisive live-wire wits in the audience.

It's lucky that Irvin doesn't ask us to believe in anything on the screen: that solves the problem of how to react to its star, Arnold Schwarzenegger, as a lawman who infiltrates the Chicago mob. Schwarzenegger was ideally cast as the fearsome humanoid in *The Terminator*, but how can you make a hero out of a man who as an actor seems likably, harmlessly gaga, and who appears to have hams implanted above his elbows? And you can't really use him as a romantic figure—not with that diction. He speaks in a weird soft rumble, as if he had built up the muscles in his mouth, too, and couldn't get English words past them. But audiences enjoy him as a figure whose "unreal" physique gives a kind of left-handed credibility to his fantastic exploits. And that's how he's presented here: he's a puzzling, cartoon phenomenon, like a walking brick wall. Irvin sets the other characters to bouncing off that wall. When the tarty gambling-lady heroine, played by Kathryn Harrold, who's out to seduce Schwarzenegger, gets him to a bed and unbuttons his shirt, we're less interested in the spectacle of that chest than in watching her eyes pop. (It's lucky, too, that Schwarzenegger seems happy to laugh at himself; he's like a granite Teddy bear.)

Kathryn Harrold, who has usually been cast as a classy modern woman, gets a chance to show the physical abandon of a slapstick comedienne—she's an uninhibited whirligig, her long legs spinning in all directions. And as the gangland boss who hired the assassins, Sam Wanamaker has some juicy, egocentric moments—especially in the scene where, having had a hundred million dollars in cash and heroin taken away in a police raid, he's furiously self-righteous. His second-in-command (Paul Shenar) points out that he makes that much money every two weeks, but he can't say goodbye to it. He feels he earned it—it's *his* money and *his* smack, and he wants the stuff back. Steven Hill is entertaining as a Jewish mobster who golfs, and goes to the synagogue on the High Holidays, and Darren McGavin, Ed Lauter, Robert Davi, and Joe Regalbuto all come through with some humor. Irvin knows how to sustain the tone of a put-on in the midst of chases and bashings. There's a gleeful, flamboyant precision in the action scenes: when the globe-trotting assassins have finished with the F.B.I. men, they turn their attention to the witness, who pleads for his life. "Witness this," they tell him, and as he

170

looks in the mirror he sees a bullet make a hole right between his eyes. At the end, Schwarzenegger makes his ritual preparations for the climactic showdown, decking himself out in leather, packing up an arsenal of guns, and, as he leaves his apartment, copping a quick look of satisfaction in the mirror. It's his only love scene.

■

The most distinctive quality of *The Manhattan Project* is the rhythm and tone of its conversations, which are satirical yet intimate and affectionate. The writer-director Marshall Brickman and his co-writer, Thomas Baum, have a knack for capturing the way brainy people talk to each other, and how ridiculous and touching they can be. Big (slimmed-down) John Lithgow is Dr. Mathewson, a beaming, self-conscious nuclear scientist, the director of a secret government facility in Ithaca, New York, which is disguised as a pharmaceutical-research center. He's busy using lasers on plutonium, but he's a basically simple guy. The play of thought on his broad, placid face often suggests consternation at what he hears himself saying—the vacuousness of it depresses him. He's a mystery to himself: how can he be so smart and yet so embarrassed and boyish and gauche? Mathewson is an overgrown version of the innocent, prankish Paul (Christopher Collet), a seventeen-year-old scientific wizard. (It seems as if there's at least one boy genius allotted to each new sci-fi movie.) The story gets under way when Paul, irritated because the bumbling, enthusiastic Mathewson is courting his divorced mother (Jill Eikenberry), filches Mathewson's pass to the facility. (He knows what goes on there because Mathewson, trying to ingratiate himself with the boy, gave him a look at the laser technology.) Paul sneaks in at night and swipes the plutonium he needs to complete a homemade nuclear bomb with which he's sure he'll win the competition at the National Science Fair, in Manhattan.

The film takes its title from the Second World War Manhattan Project, where the first atom bomb was devised, by largely apolitical scientists, such as Oppenheimer, Teller, and Fermi. And I'm afraid that the movie sets up an analogous situation, where Paul and Mathewson consider themselves apolitical until they wise up and alert the Ithaca community to the danger of having a nuclear-research center in the area. The movie actually has Mathewson leaving his lab and going forth to join the people, saying, "There are too many secrets!" He doesn't mean scientific secrets—the movie is very explicit on this point. He means the government keeps too many plans and policies hidden from the citizenry. You don't have to disagree with this sentiment to be unhappy about the direction the movie takes. Its comedy spirit withers, and a bland moral rectitude takes over. Mathewson must face his culpability and change, in order to save the boy and everyone else.

On the positive side: Early on, there's a wonderful, courtly fellow in a white coat (Warren Manzi) who shows Paul into the lab when Mathewson demonstrates his work with lasers. The coolly self-possessed Cynthia Nixon—a teen-age Broadway actress—plays Paul's pretty blond girl friend, who helps him sneak into the facility by using her considerable wiles to distract the guards. (Cynthia Nixon has charm and her own sense of fun: it's as if she picked everything she said from the air.) The break-in sequence, which involves a series of ingenious, silent slapstick tricks, is the best part of the movie, and Sully Boyar's skillful turn as Ben, the puzzled night guard, is like a sober variation on a Barry Fitzgerald drunk routine. The kids at the Science Fair (which is the next-best sequence) are a choice collection of wizards, with projects that take you back to the looniest absorbing interests you ever had.

Brickman and Baum come through with terrific lines for these kids. *All* Brickman and Baum's lines are terrific, except when the dialogue makes its big points. Lithgow's Mathewson, who must become a responsible person, has the worst clinkers. But in the early scenes he's comic without ever losing his kindness or his dignity; the picture warms up when he's onscreen. So in the last twenty minutes, when the political issues reach their grand, banal climax, he's able to draw on the strength of character he's built up. It helps that his face is such a great, broad canvas; he's impressive, even after the movie has become a parable of a smart comedy director's foolishness.

■

The writing team of Jim Cash and Jack Epps, Jr., who receive the script credit for *Legal Eagles*, as they did for *Top Gun*, work a couple of thousand miles apart, one in L.A., one in Michigan, collaborating by computer terminal. Maybe they also let the computers work out the stories: their scripts are compendiums of old-movie gimmickry, with nothing developed or carried through. *Legal Eagles*, which is set in the New York art world, seems untouched by human hands. The scandal of how Mark Rothko's estate was managed might have been fed into the machine along with pieces of the plots of dozens of old romantic comedy-thrillers, like *Charade*, and maybe a courtroom comedy, like *Adam's Rib*. The revealing elements of the Rothko case—the exposure of the workings of the contemporary art world—have been completely lost; the movie is all melodramatic plot, except for a piece of performance art that has no particular purpose, except, maybe, to make the director, Ivan Reitman, feel swank and in the contemporary swim. (It's an inferno piece, reminiscent of Meredith Monk's 1966 work "16 Millimeter Earrings" but with Laurie Anderson–like sound.) What the picture comes down to is a matter of a couple of dozen gifted actors in search of some characters to play. All they've been given is labels, which might have come out of the computer, too.

As a New York assistant district attorney, Robert Redford bestirs himself more than he did in *The Natural* or *Out of Africa*; he's doing the affable, decent, manly fellow he played back in the sixties in *Barefoot in the Park*, only now it's an imitation and it takes more effort. (His acting style has become a form of airbrushing.) Disappointingly, Debra Winger, who in her earlier pictures seemed to be naturally sultry and showed the resources to be a great screen star, is confined in the prim, tailored-suit role of a dedicated young lawyer. She has some funny moments, but the part is an emotional straitjacket, and she's practically deadpan. She's a nice girl with neat, shiny hair, who looks small and ordinary, especially when she stands next to the girl she's defending—the tall, goddessy, vaguely libidinous Daryl Hannah, who is being prosecuted on the charge that she stole one of her dead artist father's paintings. Hannah is presented as the delectable one, but she has been pulped like everybody else, and she goes through the movie pouting, her long blond hair flowing, her eyes blank. Presumably, this girl was traumatized on her eighth birthday when she was carried out of her father's burning loft, where he perished, but the movie doesn't show any sympathy for her—it has no feeling of any kind for her. Terence Stamp (more assured every year and looking great), Brian Dennehy, Roscoe Lee Browne, Christine Baranski, Sara Botsford, Steven Hill, and many other gifted performers flit on-screen and off, with nothing to do but push the engine-less plot uphill. The movie is all plot, and the plot is all holes; it's not just that it doesn't add up right—most of the episodes don't quite make sense.

Film-school-trained writers have been raiding old movies for a couple

173

of decades now, but Cash (who teaches screenwriting at Michigan State) and Epps (who was one of his students) take this parasitism a step further: they don't bother with any kind of internal logic. Things happen with no consequences, or with consequences that don't flow from what happened. Redford, the prosecuting attorney, and Winger, the defense attorney, learn that the charges against the painter's daughter have been dropped; in crosscuts, we see them in their apartments that night—neither of them can sleep, and they're both watching TV, where Gene Kelly is doing his wet solo in *Singin' in the Rain*. What Reitman and the writers fail to do is to set up a reason for the crosscutting. Are the two lawyers thinking about each other? Has something about the case stuck in their minds? As far as we can tell, we're just watching two New York lawyers watch TV. In another sequence, these two lawyers secretly follow a gallery owner (Stamp) into a warehouse; he sets a bomb and goes out, trapping them inside. Does he know they're there? Maybe, maybe not. Nothing in the plot seems to connect with anything else. We don't even find out how the paintings that appeared to have been destroyed in the fire were saved.

Holes don't much damage a thriller if the director covers them with style, and if the personalities onscreen keep us amused. But Reitman— he made *Ghostbusters*—endows *Legal Eagles* with the visual excitement of a Rotary Club lunch. The most you can say for the square cinematography is that it's instantly scannable. And the actors are so tied down by plot they don't have a chance to establish personalities. All they've got to work with is the functional—and occasionally smooth, bright—dialogue. (The brightness may be the contribution of several uncredited writers—and actors—who are said to have done some polishing on the script.) I never thought I'd find myself praising David Clennon, but as a bug-eyed assistant D.A. with a mustache and an infant's high forehead he seems to be the only actor in the movie who knows exactly what he's supposed to be playing—a stinker. Everybody else is unformed or only partly formed. Winger is given nothing except glimmers of humor and a professional demeanor, and as the picture moves along her competence level goes down. After Redford leaves the D.A.'s office and teams up with her—to defend Hannah against a new charge of murder—she lets him do the talking. And she has a scene in which she sorts out the shipping papers for art works, filing them by the size of the paintings (while he protests that they should be filed according to the paintings' destinations). This bit of gimmickry might have been devised for a dizzy heiress in a thirties-forties screwball comedy, who would then have triumphed by making a discovery that couldn't have been made except by her lame-brained filing system. But in this movie the zingers don't arrive on schedule; they don't arrive at all. Winger files in her own way because somebody thought it would be frilly and feminine.

■

A few days after seeing the newly manufactured, disposable *Legal Eagles*, I noticed that Debra Winger's last picture to be released, *Mike's Murder*, was listed for Showtime in *The New York Times* TV schedule, and that the *Times'* advice was "Skip it." Please, don't skip it next time it comes around—or, if you can, rent it. I wasn't able to see this film during its unheralded, minuscule New York run in 1984, but I caught up with it on HBO last year. It's not a movie that had much likelihood of being a hit, but its view of the cocaine subculture (or culture) of L.A. is probably the most original and daring effort by the writer-director James Bridges, and it has two superb performances—a full-scale starring one by Winger, and a brief intense one by Paul Winfield. She's a radiantly sane young bank teller who has an affair with a curly-haired, clear-faced young tennis instructor called Mike (Mark Keyloun). She likes him—you can see her eagerness, even though she knows how to be cool and bantering with him. And when they're together you can believe that there's something going on between them. But it's a wobbly affair: she hears from him randomly over the course of two years. Whenever the mood hits him, he calls her, and once he asks her to drive him to an estate where he plans to hole up—he tells her he has been dealing, and that he's being chased for encroaching on some other guys' territory. One night, he's supposed to come over late, but he doesn't show. She gets a call from a friend of his telling her he's dead, and that he talked about her all the time. His death is abrupt, bewildering. She can't let go of him so quickly—not without understanding more about him—and she tries to find out anything she can. What she learns is that he scrounged off homosexual lovers (that's where Winfield, a record producer, comes in), and she discovers how slimy-paranoid the drug world is, and how quick on the trigger it can be with kids like Mike if they get just a little greedy. She learns a bit, too, about the pleasure-besotted underpinnings of the L.A. entertainment world. (Warner Brothers had been unhappy about the *Mike's Murder* project from the start, and the cast and crew took a thirty-per-cent reduction in salary to keep costs down and insure the film's independence. Then the Warner executives refused to release it until Bridges made some cuts and changes, and they probably breathed a few sighs of relief as they buried it.)

Winger has thick, long, loose hair and a deep, sensual beauty in this movie. Bridges wrote the role for her after directing her in *Urban Cowboy*, and you feel the heroine's expanding awareness in Winger's scenes with Keyloun and her scenes with Winfield. It's a performance that suggests what Antonioni seemed to be trying to get from Jeanne Moreau in *La Notte*, only it really works with Winger—maybe because there's nothing sullen or closed about her. We feel the play of the girl's intelligence, and her openness and curiosity are part of her earthiness, her sanity. There's a marvellous sequence in which Mike calls her after an interval of three months and wants her to come to him right that minute. She says, "How about tomorrow night?" He says, "You know I can't plan that far in advance," and gets her to talk to him while he masturbates. He says he loves her voice, and though we don't see him, we hear a callow sweetness in his tone; he wants to give her satisfaction, too. He talks hot, and she's sort of amused, and goes along with it. I don't know of anyone besides Winger who could play a scene like this so simply. She's a major reason to go on seeing movies in the eighties—but not in *Legal Eagles*.

June 30, 1986

TOADS

David Mamet's one-act play *Sexual Perversity in Chicago*, first performed in 1974, was, like the 1971 Mike Nichols–Jules Feiffer film *Carnal Knowledge*, taken to be a commentary on the sexual sickness of its time. These are works that encourage people to beat their chests. Each is constructed as a series of duologues, and each is about two perennial male adolescents—a monster and a weakling—who depersonalize women. In *Carnal Knowledge*, the men are of the educated upper middle

176

class; in Mamet's play, the two are a few social notches down. They're salesmen in restaurant supplies who hang out together, cruising the singles bars. Bernie, the major character, is empty and overbearing, a macho braggart; the passive Danny soaks up Bernie's poison—his obsession that women are out to trap them. The "perversity" in the title sounds jazzy and risqué; it's a come-on. What it refers to is the compulsive, repetitive singles scene where men find sex but back off from sex with feeling and women turn harsh from disappointment—it's a covertly moralistic title. The movie version has been given the innocuous tag *About Last Night . . .* because a number of television stations and newspapers refused advertising for the film under Mamet's more suggestive title.

Mamet's plays are pared down—he works to achieve a crackling tension, an obscene, lowbrow wit. (Bernie's jokes give him away.) The screenwriters, Tim Kazurinsky and Denise DeClue, retain much of Mamet's dialogue, but they piece it out, and then the director, Edward Zwick, punches up the breaks between scenes with rock music. It's like being pounded on the back every two minutes when your back is already sore. And it *is*, because the dialogue has been whacking you so hard.

Jim Belushi is a blastingly loud Bernie. He did a stint as Bernie on the stage, and his interpretation is a plausible (if monotonous) reading of the Mamet character, but he and the director haven't allowed for how the material has been altered in this version. In the play, Bernie is the lewd comic who fixates the audience, and Danny is his stooge. But in an attempt to bring the early-seventies text into the presumably more cheerful, optimistic eighties, Kazurinsky and DeClue make Danny (Rob Lowe) the major character—and a hero. He's intimidated by Bernie's know-it-all cynicism, but he's happy when he's with Debbie (Demi Moore), an illustrator for an advertising agency. *About Last Night . . .* is the story of Danny and Debbie getting off the singles treadmill and learning to trust their love for each other. Danny has to cast out the Bernie he carries inside him; Debbie has to cast out the doubts that are engendered by her roommate, the kindergarten teacher Joan (Elizabeth Perkins), who is a female equivalent of poisonous Bernie—she constantly undermines Debbie's faith in Danny. (Joan brings home a different man every night, because each time she begins to care about someone she's jilted.)

The story is much like that of the trivial 1969 movie *John and Mary*, in which Dustin Hoffman picked up Mia Farrow in a singles bar—sex came first and romance afterward, but John was afraid to make a commitment, and he had to overcome this block before he and Mary could be a couple. Except for the sex first, *About Last Night . . .* is close to being a conventional Hollywood romance—it's about the adjustments two people have to make in their first year of marriage (or, as here, of living together). What keeps it from being exactly that is the presence of Bernie and Joan. You don't know why Danny puts up with the yelling Bernie or why Debbie puts up with Joan's hatefulness. (Every time Joan opens her mouth, a toad jumps out.) The hostility between the sexes that gives Mamet's play its raucous dynamism becomes an abrasive nuisance—an intrusion on a boy-meets-girl movie that is clearly going to have a happy ending. Mamet's language has bite, but since that bite isn't the point of this movie and it gets in the way of the progress of true love it's mostly just unpleasant. Bernie and Joan are spoilers. And, of course, moving Mamet's singles-bars promiscuousness into the eighties doesn't work; AIDS has changed the scene. Bernie himself seems to belong to an earlier era. (So does the brassy, dictatorial boss at the restaurant-supplies company—he's like Bernie at a further stage of development.) As for Rob Lowe's common-man Danny, with his dreams of the future, he doesn't belong to any era. He comes out of the theatre and TV and movies; he's the confection of desperate writers.

There's a candy-man quality to Lowe himself. He has no weight, no density. It's not that he's a bad actor—it's that he doesn't suggest a real person. He's trying his damnedest to play Danny as an ordinary guy who doesn't like to shave and has mussed-up, funny-looking hair; you watch him, and, by God, he's acting, but what is it, exactly, he's doing? Suffering comes too easy to him; when his nostrils quiver he looks as if he's impressed by his own sensitivity. Maybe that's the clue: Rob Lowe acts Rob Lowe acting. The role of Joan is horrendous (she's forever putting everyone down), and so I wanted to be rid of her. At the same time, I thought that Elizabeth Perkins, a newcomer who has a lovely, piquant face for comedy and appealing, plaintive undercurrents, gave the most promising performance. Demi Moore is a hardworking but somehow impersonal actress; she has good vocal control, yet even her husky voice is reminiscent of half a dozen other voices. She isn't bad, but so far there isn't much that's distinctive about her—she doesn't make a role her own. As for Jim Belushi, if he's lucky he'll move on to some quiet roles—ones in which he doesn't have to be a rancorous pig from the word go. Maybe if he'd been able to suggest that Bernie had a genuine love of bawdiness— that he was an irrepressible porno fiend, that he was fun to be with— the character might at least seem colorful. But Belushi has been directed to show us that underneath the bluster Bernie is a pathetic, lonely mess— and that's intolerable.

Mamet wrote a screen adaptation of his play which wasn't used, and perhaps he found a way to expand it without adding bland slapstick scenes, like the ones here that are an insult to the audience, such as Debbie bringing mountains of possessions with her when she moves in with Danny. But would the play work onscreen if it were shot as it was written, and kept in its period? I don't think so. A great deal of what's the matter with *About Last Night . . .* is straight Mamet. The play has a virtuosic nastiness—Mamet writes with a whip hand. His dialogue is mannered, with calculated pauses and blackout effects to give the zingers their maximum explosiveness. The two salesmen aren't like the sharpers of Mamet's more recent *Glengarry Glen Ross*, but Bernie might be on his way to that. For the theatre audience, Mamet's vitality and assurance and the verisimilitude of his language can be a shock. Some of the people at *Glengarry* reacted as if they'd never heard hucksters talking—as if the play were an incredible revelation to them, a new kind of truth. Mamet is like Arthur Miller taken a step further and crossed with Pinter. His rancid, cruel characters don't have to be denounced; they incriminate themselves by their choice of words. His monsters are the vehicles by which he's *telling* us something, and the theatre audience is impressed. Mamet belongs to the much-honored blowhard tradition in the American theatre—he's the hippest of the bunch. But in a movie, with the characters up close, the insistent language of a grotesque male chauvinist like Bernie can be painfully obvious. And the playwright's skillful, worked-out stresses can make a movie an ordeal to sit through. At *About Last Night . . .* you feel as if you've been looking at an ant farm for two hours.

■

Alot of normally bright people seem to like getting dumbed-out when they go to movies in the summer. *Ruthless People* is a cheesy low farce with Danny DeVito as a thieving millionaire who wants to kill his heiress wife (Bette Midler) and is overjoyed when she's kidnapped. It was directed by the *Airplane!* threesome—Jim Abrahams, David Zucker, and Jerry Zucker—from a script, by Dale Launer, that's a reworking of an O. Henry twist. (Probably its last time around was the 1967 *The Happening*.) Launer provides a semblance of clever construction, but you see each complication being set in place. And the three directors don't have an eye among them; what they've got is some kind of affection for

179

pop culture of the past and an amateurish knack for "romps." I didn't actively hate the movie (they're blunt, innocently bad directors), but it's a little oppressive listening to people in the audience whoop with pleasure—it's alienating, like staring at the unfunny actors in a TV sitcom while the laughtrack goes wild. The kidnapped wife has a scene in which she realizes that her husband doesn't want her back and that the kidnappers who set her ransom at half a million dollars have reduced it to ten thousand. She cries out, "I'm being marked down!" What's worst about this movie is that it marks down Bette Midler's talent.

July 14, 1986

PIG HEAVEN

||||||||||||||||||||||||||||||||||||||||||||||||||||||||||||||||||||||||||||||||||||||||||||||||||||||||||||||||||||||||||||||||||||||||||||||

Oliver Stone expresses his pulp sensibility to the *n*th power in *Salvador*, which opened in New York in March and has just returned. He's probably aiming for a Buñuelian effect—a vision so intensely scummy that it clears the air. But if *Salvador*, with its grime and guilt, comes closer to suggesting a hyperkinetic, gonzo version of Graham Greene, that's still nothing to be ashamed of.

The Oliver Stone who made this movie isn't essentially different from the hype artist who wrote *Midnight Express* and *Scarface*, and co-wrote *Conan the Barbarian*, *Year of the Dragon*, and *8 Million Ways to Die*. *Salvador*, too, is a self-righteous nihilist fantasy, and even more sensationalistic than the others. Working with Richard Boyle, a free-lance foreign correspondent and photographer, as his co-writer, Stone presents the civil war in El Salvador during the years 1980 and 1981 as some kind of ultimate bad trip. What makes the picture different from those other movies is partly that he made it "outside the industry" (he raised the money—under five million—from British and Mexican sources); that he directed it himself, on location in Mexico, except for a few scenes set in this country; and that he used James Woods, perhaps the most hostile of all American actors, as the hero, who is called Richard Boyle but represents Stone's convictions, too.

Hostility oozes from James Woods' pores, and Stone anoints him with it. A whoring, freaked-out hipster, based in San Francisco, Woods' Richard Boyle has fouled up everything in his life, and he's scraping bottom. After getting fired from the news service he was working for, he's evicted from the apartment he has been living in with his family. His wife, who is from Italy, gives up on him—he's a hopeless liar—and she takes their baby son and goes home to her parents. All Boyle wants is to get back to El Salvador—he knows that things are busting apart down there. But he's arrested for speeding, and the woman cop's computer tells her that his license has been revoked and he has neglected a raft of parking tickets. So he's plunked in jail. He rounds up a buddy to bail him out—an unemployed disk jockey called Doctor Rock (Jim Belushi), who's in worse shape than he is, except that Doc has still got a couple of hundred dollars. Boyle feeds him a line about the wonders of Guatemala, and they go tootling down to Central America in Boyle's old red convertible, drinking and doping all the way, and complaining about women. Boyle just keeps going, with Doc in tow, heading for El Salvador; he tells Doc it's "pig heaven," where the drugs and the surfing are great and you can get a virgin for seven dollars, two virgins for twelve. He's a scroungy hustler who sounds like a mercenary and expresses contempt for just about everybody and everything.

At the border of El Salvador, there's a roadblock, and Boyle and Doc see a man in flames—only one leg still has flesh on it, and a remnant of trousers. They're pulled out of their car by some paramilitary thugs, and when Boyle shouts that he's a friend of a bigwig, Colonel Figueroa, they're shoved into a jeep. They watch a student being shot for not having his identification papers before they're taken to the Colonel, who actually does know Boyle. They've entered a world where no rules apply—where authority is in the weak hands of a military junta, and right-wing death squads are slaughtering suspected Communists at random and throwing their bodies onto dumps. It's chaos, and Boyle's own scurviness and corruption—his craziness—enable him to function in it. He's like a gambler who feels most alive at the peak of the action. The squalid confusion wires him up, and he feels on top of things. His loud Hawaiian shirts and his shades are his battle uniform. He knows how to bribe jailhouse guards (when Doc has been thrown in the clink for having marijuana on him); he knows how to placate a gang of riled-up toughs by buying them beers.

181

And, surprisingly, he knows how to wangle some work. (Richard Boyle, who was employed in El Salvador by NBC radio and Cable News Network, broke part of the story of the rape and murder of the three American nuns and the lay worker.)

The film moves so fast that it seems like no more than a matter of minutes after Boyle's arrival that he's at El Playón, a gigantic dump site, photographing the fresh bodies there; he works under the eyes of a big vulture and alongside Cassady, a dedicated photojournalist, played by John Savage (and based on *Newsweek*'s John Hoagland, who was killed in El Salvador). Boyle sees Major Max (Tony Plana), the Presidential candidate and head of the death squads (based on Roberto D'Aubuisson); he goes to a center run by the opposition party—it's for kids (many of them wounded or mutilated) whose parents are among "the disappeared." He talks to the principled but ineffectual American Ambassador (played by Michael Murphy), a Carter appointee, whose days in office are numbered once Reagan wins the election; he scraps with an American woman newscaster, a coldhearted bitch who parrots the official line; he argues with a pair of U.S. military advisers who are convinced that the opposition groups and the guerrillas are Communists, and that they'll take over if the Americans don't support the junta. And he visits the camp of the rebel army that is forming. Boyle is in the midst of it all, borrowing money wherever he goes, trying to dodge the beatings and gunfire, and, as the movie presents it, watching the forces of evil trample good, innocent people, and raging and suffering because he can't do anything to stop it. He is shocked into a different consciousness, or into getting down to a level of consciousness deep inside himself. And he keeps blurting out what he thinks—even at such official occasions as a press conference held by Major Max.

Boyle had a reason for heading back to El Salvador that he didn't disclose to Doc: he has a girl there—a peasant madonna, Maria (Elpidia Carrillo, who played a similar role in *The Border* and has grown even more beautiful). He finds contentment with the devoted Maria—he sets up house with her and her two small children—and he's determined not to screw up, the way he has always screwed up in the past. And because of her he sees things more sanely. When Carter's men are about to be replaced by Reagan's appointees, Boyle, the compulsive gadfly, challenges the U.S. military advisers. "What are the death squads but the brainchild of the C.I.A.?" he asks. Of all the modern movies that have dealt with U.S. complicity (or worse) in Third World repression—movies such as *State of Siege* (Uruguay), *Missing* (Chile), *Apocalypse Now* (Vietnam), *The Year of Living Dangerously* (Indonesia), *Under Fire* (Nicaragua), and *The Killing Fields* (Cambodia)—*Salvador* is perhaps the most visceral. It's also possibly the most politically simplistic. It shapes the issues so that we're seeing the primal battle of good and evil. When a guerrilla girl (in a single guerrilla departure from humane conduct) executes several prisoners, Boyle is there to point out that the guerrillas have momentarily fallen from grace and crossed over to the side of evil.

Like earlier movie madonnas, Maria doesn't get to speak much. The other people barely get time to talk, either; the movie is almost all Boyle hurtling from one emergency to another. It's not just that he stands in for both authors—he's really the only character. The movie is the story of his redemption. "Salvador" means "savior," and Woods' Boyle is the one who needs to be saved. It wouldn't seem out of place if he spoke Mickey Rourke's line in *Year of the Dragon*—"How can anybody care too much?" He might even deliver Al Pacino's line from *Scarface*—"Say good night to the bad guy." The film's most memorable scene is of Boyle, after a gap of thirty-three years—Christ's life span—going to confession. He hopes that this ritual will persuade Maria to marry him (though we know that he's still married, just as we know that that little thing wouldn't stop him). Woods is of Catholic background, and he plays this scene very boyishly: Boyle tries to strike a deal with his confessor, wheedling, and trying to settle for a minimum of promises, because he genuinely doesn't want to break them. It's probably the most touching scene Woods has ever played. Hustler that Boyle is, he's on the level with Maria—in his intentions, anyway. "If God gave me this woman," he says to his confessor, "then there must be a God." His long, thin, bony face softens as he speaks, and he wrings his hands nervously, helplessly.

The film's dialogue—it sounds like typical Stone, crude and profane—fits Woods; it seems an emanation of his character's speed-freak nature. And the hand-held camerawork, by Robert Richardson, and the jittery editing rhythms that keep the audience off balance all go together and give the movie a raw, pesky force. This isn't Stone's first time out as a director. After prep school and a year at Yale, he taught English to students in Vietnam, signed on a merchant ship, and, at nineteen, went to Mexico, where he finished a novel. Then he went back to Vietnam, in the U.S. Army; when he came home, with a couple of wounds, a Purple Heart, and a Bronze Star, he enrolled at the N.Y.U. film school, where he studied with Scorsese, made some shorts, and kept writing screenplays. In his mid-twenties, he directed one of them, *Seizure* (1973), on a low budget, and in 1981 he wrote and directed *The Hand*. Considering

Stone's scripts that were filmed, he has reason to see himself as having been a mercenary, and, considering the new political direction his work has taken, he may see himself as a man who has become responsible. But his romantic pulp thinking is so closely bound up with his idea of redemption that it's unredeemable. (Is he, for example, aware that the film's ideal woman, Maria—stunning as she is—has been idealized into a blank? She's like a schoolgirl in a silent movie. Even when she's in serious danger and Boyle is rushing around frantically trying to get her some identification papers or get her out of the country, she's passively unconcerned; she's more worried about the propriety of marrying a man who hasn't been a good Catholic.)

Stone takes a great many liberties in *Salvador*, such as showing John Savage's Cassady-Hoagland photographing the plane that strafes him, and dying despite Boyle's attempt to save him by performing a tracheotomy right there in the street. This wouldn't be offensive if Stone didn't have Cassady dying with an angelic triumphant smile, because he knows he got the kind of picture that his idol, Robert Capa, was famous for— the kind that, as he told us earlier, captures "the nobility of human suffering." The mixture of realistic death rasps and stale romanticism weighs the scene down. (What he photographed doesn't look as if it would be such a memorable shot, either.) There are also issues that go beyond aesthetic crimes. It's artistic license for Stone to show us Boyle and Maria at the Communion rail in the main cathedral, with the Host that Archbishop Romero has given them still melting on their tongues, when a man a few places down the line from them spits on the hand that offers him the wafer and shoots the Archbishop at point-blank range. But Stone goes way beyond artistic license in the earlier scene where Major Max is shown at a dinner table with a dozen of his key supporters and he designates the one who is to be Romero's assassin. (The scene is staged with enough villainous, melodramatic acting to suggest a posh, sinister version of *The Last Supper*, and Major Max formalizes the assassin's task by kissing him ritually on each cheek.)

Salvador has the tainted, disreputable, hardboiled surface we expect from Oliver Stone, and the sentimentality that goes with it. When the rebel army makes its big push, the Americans resume aid to the government forces (which would have fallen in a few days, because they were out of ammunition, and fuel for their tanks and aircraft). Then the guerrillas know they're doomed; they embrace each other before going out to fight to the death, and we hear a men's chorus swelling on the soundtrack—Stone is jacking up "the nobility of human suffering." He's working outside the industry, in freedom, but he's got all this Hollywood muck in his soul. It's there in the way peasant rebels are photographed to look plain and noble, and Major Max's followers are photographed to be lewd and brutish, or cold and cruel. And Stone has Woods' Boyle, who gets high on turmoil—a man for whom this civil war is like a great caffeine jag—making idealistic speeches to the U.S. military advisers about wanting human rights for "everybody on this planet," and then dickering with them, offering to swap worthless photographs of the rebels in exchange for papers for Maria.

The movie is as screwed up as its hero. As a revelation of a gifted filmmaker's divided sensibility, there's never been anything quite as spectacular as *Salvador*. Stone has a fine poetic ending, but he can't leave it at that—he tacks on explanatory titles that are inconclusive and raise questions about what was fictional and what was factual. What he has here is a right-wing macho vision joined to a left-leaning polemic. When the scenes are at their crudest, it's as if John Milius had joined Mothers for Peace, but Oliver Stone's gaudiness drives the film forward. He writes and directs as if someone had put a gun to the back of his neck and yelled "Go!" and didn't take it away until he'd finished.

■

Rodney Dangerfield is the King of Lower Slobovia, and a case could be made that the whole point of a comedy like his new vehicle, *Back to School*, is for it to be an ugly, inert mess—the kind of show at which the possibility of suspending disbelief never occurs to anybody. But this movie's inertia is too overpowering to be intentional. Its box-office success can only be due to the general affection for its star. Back in 1970, the popular culture critic Albert Goldman described Dangerfield's entrance on the TV talk shows: "The zooming camera sets you face to face with his moist, protuberant, bloodshot eyes, his impatiently pursed, irritably drawn mouth, his lugubriously heavy, self-pitying voice, and suddenly—you're staring deep into the soul of the Silent Majority." That underdog who was funny because he was so obnoxious has been cleaned up here; he's thinner, and his hair, which used to be sparse and sweaty, is now short and fluffy. (It's a Robert Stack coiffure.) The archetypal complaining loser—the man who was always a little berserk—is now playing a winner, a generous-hearted multimillionaire merchant. He's bucking the snobs, though, and he's supposed to be a common-man hero.

In a movie, directed by Alan Metter, from a script by four guys who can't have put much thought into it, Dangerfield is a swinging Santa Claus who discovers that his son (Keith Gordon) is miserable at college, and enrolls as a freshman so he can change things for the kid. The boy's only friend is his blue-haired punker roommate, played by Robert Downey, Jr., (of TV's *Saturday Night Live*, and the son of the writer-director of the sixties films *Chafed Elbows* and *Putney Swope*). Downey, a free-form physical comedian with the zapped big eyes and serene, dreamy smile of a true harlequin, gives the movie its only airy touches. Sally Kellerman helps out as a throaty-voiced literature professor; she starts the first day's class by reciting Molly Bloom's soliloquy—which mesmerizes Dangerfield, who cries out, "Yes! Yes!" Kellerman also has a funny moment or two with Paxton Whitehead, as her sniffy fiancé; and Sam Kinison turns up as a history professor—he does his winding-up-to-a-shrieking-rage specialty. (It's a high-concept version of the traditional slow burn.) But these are just marginal distractions. It's Dangerfield's movie, and when he can't say a line directly to the camera he seems worried that he's not doing enough, and so he does some eyeball mugging. He's so eager and persistent he breaks you down—I laughed a little. But I was still bored cuckoo. And after listening to his terrible jokes I've been hearing them again: they're being quoted by enthusiasts who know perfectly well that they're terrible jokes. That's what they love Dangerfield for. And they don't seem to mind the new, jovial avuncular Dangerfield or the cornpone script or the deadening moviemaking. It's like a beer bust to them.

July 28, 1986

PAIRS

The fire of adventure lights Andrea Martin's saucer eyes in *Club Paradise*. Even if your jaw sometimes fell open when you watched her on *SCTV*, you may feel that she transcends her earlier work in this first

186

screen appearance. She has a new exuberance; she's like a funky Gracie Allen, and she has her George Burns here in tall, gloomy Steven Kampmann. They play a vacationing couple hoping to put some zest into their fading marriage: Kampmann is a slack-faced plastic surgeon who's always at least half asleep, and his vest-pocket-sized wife wants to try anything, everything. When she goes on a para-sail and she gets caught, suspended from the limb of a tree, she beats her tiny chest like Tarzan, in sheer manic joy. When she steps into a shower and the water hits her with the force of Niagara, it's a new sensation and she gives in to it. Uninhibited, she embraces every shock or calamity. Andrea Martin turns her role into something like Martha Raye's part in *Monsieur Verdoux*—she's so avidly alive that nothing fazes her. Dark and vaguely exotic (she's of Armenian descent), this inspired comedienne has happy demons inside her.

The dauntless wife and her deadhead husband take the chartered plane to Club Paradise on the mythical Caribbean island of St. Nicholas in response to travel folders that the club's new social director (Robin Williams) and his girlfriend (Twiggy) have sent out—folders that promise swank, fun-filled days and languorous, sexy nights. But the social director's advertising skills are far in advance of his ability to cajole the Rastafarian staff and musicians to get the place ready. He has to deal with brainteasers like how to devise a hat for a chef which will cover hair five feet long. So when this first planeload of guests—the eager cartoon faces are familiar from *SCTV* and *Saturday Night Live*—make their bumpy landing, and the pilot (Joe Flaherty) kisses the earth in an ecstasy of relief, they discover that the tropical resort that sounded like nirvana on the cheap is a group of tumbledown cottages, plus a frowzy café with a reggae band, headed by the owner (Jimmy Cliff). There's a beautiful stretch of beach, though.

The movie is like those giddy, casual farces that Paramount turned out in the thirties—pictures like *We're Not Dressing*, in which Burns and Allen, Bing Crosby, Carole Lombard, and Ethel Merman goofed around on an island. Those pictures often got terrible reviews but kept audiences giggling cheerfully, and this seems to be the case with *Club Paradise*. Directed by Harold Ramis, from a script he wrote with Brian Doyle-Murray that at least two other sets of writers had had a share in earlier, *Club Paradise* has an offhand, lackadaisical ease. Apparently, members of the cast were encouraged to come up with gags and dialogue of their own (as long as they didn't improvise on camera), and this may explain why performers you've watched on TV, like Kampmann, are suddenly funnier than they've been before. Playing straight man to Andrea Martin,

187

Kampmann might have just discovered the pleasures of silliness. When Jimmy Cliff starts a revolution on the island, and there's shooting in the café, these two avoid the bullets by squatting and doing a duck walk across the dance floor together. They're a full-fledged comedy team—one of many pairings-off here.

Eugene Levy and Rick Moranis play businessmen, both named Barry, who are obsessed by the idea of scoring with women but terrified when women come close to them. Of all the nerdlings in recent movies, these two are perhaps the most desperately ineffectual—the nerdiest. They're a nightmare pair, yet endearing—their real attachment is to being miserable together. Moranis has a great solo gag, when he's proud of himself out wind-surfing and (to the sound of lushly orchestrated surfing music) is swept out to sea. But the film's romantic high point comes when Barry and Barry are reunited and—in slow motion—they rush to embrace each other, like long-lost lovers.

As the club's social director, Robin Williams is the picture's m.c., and his role is largely reactive. He doesn't have a chance to do the kind of acting he did in *The Best of Times* or *Moscow on the Hudson*, but it's surprisingly enjoyable to see him when he isn't charged up. He gives the movie a sane, low-key center. His lines are mostly asides or are given the sound of asides, and he's congenial—he has a graceful style that he adapts to each of his several partners. In the early sequences, he persuades Twiggy to leave the yachting party she arrived with and stay with him, and he does it without coming on strong. That's why she's attracted to him; he's honest and, in some unfathomable way, winning. Twiggy doesn't have running gags or terrific lines, but she does radiant double takes on Robin Williams' good lines—she's charming. In Williams' friendship and business partnership with Jimmy Cliff, it's taken for granted that we'll perceive what makes them trust each other, and we do. Perhaps most surprising is Williams' nifty teamwork with Peter O'Toole, who plays the governor-general of this flyspeck British island. When Robin Williams and the dulcet-voiced, eloquent O'Toole talk together, their two styles of acting mesh almost conspiratorially.

O'Toole has another partner, too—Joanna Cassidy, as a tough redhead who writes about resorts for *The New York Times*. She looks like nothing but trouble when we first see her, but after she meets the governor-general she lights up, and when they've become a pair and she looks at him her smile is big and dazzling. O'Toole certainly seems to have found the woman for him. She's a sexual powerhouse. There are other pairs: Robin Duke and Mary Gross as shy girls who make overtures to the Barrys; sets of male hunks and female hunks; and Brian Doyle-Murray and the late Adolph Caesar as a pair of finagling villains trying to take over the Club Paradise beachfront—they're the opposite numbers to Robin Williams and Jimmy Cliff.

The cinematography seems muddy at the opening (which is set in Chicago), but then the beach and the bright, aquamarine picture-postcard color—the island scenes were shot in Port Antonio, on the Jamaican coast—seem just right for a resort farce. (The light looks fake, which is how the light sometimes looks on ravishing beaches.) And Jimmy Cliff's songs have a relaxing, rolling rhythm that matches the lazy surf. Maybe Robin Williams took the cue for his performance from the reggae. The music doesn't come charging into your skull, like the high-pressure rock you get in most films now. And the movie itself doesn't pound or strain to impress you, either. It's tacky and unceremonious and as pleasant as can be.

■

*H*eartburn clicks along like a very expensive watch, and though many of the scenes don't point anywhere, they give off glints of sophistication and bitchery, and they have original edges. Directed by Mike Nichols, and written by Nora Ephron, who adapted her own 1983 novel (a jokey, fictionalized version of her marriage to Carl Bernstein), the film is rich in fillips—smart little taps and strokes. And the physical surfaces are so exact and polished that you feel as if you'd been brought into a special, artificial world. The sensation is similar to what audiences used to get from "smashing" productions of drawing-room comedies. It's cleverness raised to a principle—only now it's blended with what is generally referred to as "pain." Those who saw the Mike Nichols stage production of *The Real Thing* got the whole slicked-up package. Here you get the packaging, with visibly skimpy insides.

The movie is full of talented people, who, with the exception of Meryl Streep, have almost nothing to do. She is the protagonist, Rachel, a New York food writer and divorcée who may or may not want to get married again; whichever it is, she finds Jack Nicholson's Mark, a Washington columnist who's also divorced and has a naughty reputation as a ladies' man, irresistible, and says yes. Stockard Channing and Richard Masur are exceedingly likable as Mark's oldest friends; Catherine O'Hara is a

Washington newswoman and all-around gossip who breezes into the picture a few times (not as often as you might like: she looks as if she knows giggly secrets); Maureen Stapleton is Rachel's therapist, whose lips tremble with sentimentality during Rachel's wedding; Steven Hill is Rachel's acid-tongued father; Jeff Daniels, Miloš Forman, and Karen Akers also turn up; and John Wood does a sly, sweetly devastating takeoff of Alistair Cooke as host of *Masterpiece Theatre*. (Wood brings us up to date on Rachel's fantasies of herself as the heroine of a literary classic.) These performers are fun to watch, but after a while the scenes that don't point anywhere begin to add up, and you start asking yourself, "What is this movie about?" You're still asking when it's over, and by then a flatness, a disappointment, is likely to have settled over the fillips you'd enjoyed.

Streep's Rachel is blissfully happy as a wife and mother until, when she's seven months pregnant with her second child, she discovers that Mark is having an affair. She leaves him and goes back to New York; he comes for her and tells her that he isn't going to see the woman anymore, and she returns. But when she learns that he has broken his word, and probably never even meant to keep it, she pushes a Key-lime pie into his face at a Washington dinner party, and the marriage is over. This may be the only pie in the face in the history of movies that's flung more in sorrow than in anger. It's a bad mistake.

If the movie is no more than a semi-satirical view of a modern woman's ancient plight—that her husband is unfaithful—why isn't it more fun? In the book, Nora Ephron wants the hipness of treating Rachel's failed marriage as wiseass comedy; she wants us to feel the pain under the self-mockery, but the laughs are always on top. Though Ephron is a gifted and witty light essayist, her novel is no more than a variant of a princess fantasy: Rachel, the wife, is blameless; Mark, the husband, is simply a bad egg—an adulterer. And, reading the book, you don't have to take Rachel the bratty narrator very seriously; her self-pity is so thinly masked by humor and unabashed mean-spiritedness that you feel that the author is exploiting her life—trashing it by presenting it as a juicy, fast-action comic strip about a marriage of celebrities. Mike Nichols takes much of the cheapness out of the material, but the gossipy kick has gone out, too. Working with the cinematographer Nestor Almendros, he tries to make the story seem real; he shoots it in a tight, airless, neutral style. And with the heroine's life no longer treated as rowdy comedy, and the "pain" brought to the surface, the effect is like a weak mixture of *Carnal Knowledge* and a Woody Allen picture and Robert Benton's *Kramer vs. Kramer*. It's anorexic moviemaking.

In the film, Rachel and Mark first spot each other when they're guests at a wedding. He looks at her boldly—rudely. She turns to a friend and asks who he is. The friend tells her, and she asks, "Is he single?" The audience laughs, because we've just been given what we think is a direct pipeline to what's on Rachel's mind. And, as if to make her longings unmistakable, her eyes fill with tears during the ceremony. But a few scenes later, when it's Rachel and Mark's wedding day and the guests have arrived, everyone has to wait for Rachel, who hides out in a bedroom. She stays there for a long time, having doubts about whether marriage—*any* marriage—works; friends, relatives, her therapist all try to coax her to come out and march down the aisle, but she's absorbed in her Cassandra act until Mark finally stretches out on the bed next to her and convinces her. This not-wanting-to-get-married scene isn't directed comically as a celebrity princess's showing off her trepidation to the assembled crowd. The way the scene is directed, it could be taken as an indication that Rachel really doesn't want to get married, and that makes it a princess screenwriter's ploy. It was during this episode, with its cutaways to such random bits as two men caterers whiling away the time by discussing a recipe, that it first occurred to me that Mike Nichols didn't really know what he was doing and that the picture wasn't going to work. This was confirmed in the humdrum scenes about the renovation being done on the couple's Georgetown house, in the limpness of the reconciliation scene after Rachel leaves Mark for the first time, and in details, such as the way their infant is handled like a prop, and in the attempted poignancy of the closing mother-child theme music—Carly Simon's own version of "The Itsy Bitsy Spider."

A different screenwriter—one who approached the job of adaptation from the outside—might have treated the novel as a black comedy about two celebrity hustlers falling in love (mostly with each other's reputations) and trying to out-hustle each other, until the man is unfaithful to his wife with a socialite celebrity who outranks her. If this hardboiled screenwriter had carried the comedy through, it might have included Rachel's getting even: the publication of her book, and its being made into a movie. (Carl Bernstein had already been made a hero by the book and movie *All the President's Men.*) That's perhaps too harsh a satirical scenario. But Nichols and Ephron have come up with one that's soft and muffled. In the film, Rachel and Mark aren't even the heavy spenders they are in the book; they live more modestly. Mike Nichols decided to make *Heartburn* and then started looking for depth! So he tried to make the two more sympathetic, and he wound up without a story.

Nichols' technique—his moving the camera in for each significant nuance—makes us unduly conscious of the acting, and how studied it is. He turns us into connoisseurs of performance instead of giving us a grasp of character, and the movie appears to be about nothing except the signals and mannerisms that actors work up. Every twitch of Streep's seems to be recorded in closeup, and every shade of Nicholson's untrustworthiness is pinpointed. Except for a few showy scenes, Nicholson has so little to do that glowering or ambiguous expressions are almost all we get from him. The movie is about Rachel's heartburn, not Mark's; we don't know how he feels about anything, and he looks a little too middle-aged and confident. Streep's flair for comedy comes through intermittently, and if we had caught what she was doing out of the corner of an eye she might have come across as a funny woman. But her Rachel seems, finally, a joyless performance. Streep can't chew a bite of food without acting out chewing. And Nichols kills her with admiration.

Nichols' methods work for the lesser, purely comic roles here, but we see Streep and Nicholson in an assortment of moments, with nothing holding the moments together. Nichols seems to be trying to guarantee that each fragment will be perfect, and that we in the audience will see exactly what he wants us to see. That, I'm afraid, is all we see, and we feel starved.

■

*A**liens* is a very big "Boo!" movie. Long (two hours and seventeen minutes) and visually repetitious, this sci-fi action-horror film is scaled to be an epic, and it's certainly getting epic reviews. ("An authentic masterpiece!" "The scariest movie in the history of movies." "The most satisfying science-fiction shocker ever." And so on.) The writer-director James Cameron pumps up the familiar devices of the action and horror genres, and is acclaimed for imagination. (The praise suggests the Second Coming of John Carpenter.) An inflated example of formula gothic, this sequel to Ridley Scott's 1979 *Alien* is more mechanical than the first film—more addicted to "advanced" weaponry and military hardware. The movie is really a combat film set in the future, in space; Cameron pits a platoon of U.S. Marines (ethnically assorted, of course) against a family of monsters. He does it in an energetic, systematic, relentless way, with an action director's gusto. And though he writes bum dialogue, his images have a fair amount of graphic power; the movie has the look of a comic book for adults, and it achieves a fairy-tale horror when the queen monster looms up waving her tentacles, opening her metal jaws, and gnashing her switchblade teeth. She represents extraterrestrial primal evil, which might seem to be enough menace for one movie, but, to raise the ante, Cameron throws in the threat of a nuclear explosion.

As Warrant Officer Ripley, the only human survivor of the spaceship Nostromo, which voyaged forth in the earlier film, Sigourney Weaver is the one person who has looked into the face of evil and lived, but she's stricken with recurrent nightmares and the cold shakes. Weaver uses the trauma of this experience as the basis for creating what passes here for a character. Weaver's Ripley is different from other people: she's more intense; an angry, high-strung loner, she has been through too much horror to have any patience with small talk—she gets right to the point of things. Made consultant to a new expedition to the monsters' planet— its mission is to find out what happened to the human colonizers who have gone there—she sees that those in charge are lightweights, brushes them aside, and takes command. With her great cheekbones, her marvellous physique, and her lightness of movement, Weaver seems to take over by natural authority and her strength as an actress. Her surprisingly small, tense mouth holds all the suspense in the story. She's concentrating on the problems at hand when nobody else is. Weaver gives the movie a presence; without her it's a B picture that lacks the subplots and corny characters that can make B pictures amusing.

Cameron does include some B gimmicks, such as showing a crew member (Michael Biehn) training Weaver in the use of a huge, heavy gun and taking pride in her prowess with it. (This is the closest that the movie comes to romance.) And Cameron plays a few B games, such as having a Hispanic woman bodybuilder (Jenette Goldstein) among the rough-housing, muscular fighting Marines. (She wears a red headband, like a guerrilla.) But except for Weaver the film is short on inventive acting, and I would have thought that Cameron (who directed the Schwarzenegger picture *The Terminator*, and wrote the script for *Rambo: First Blood Part II* before Stallone reshaped it) would be too embarrassed to toss in the wraithlike, fey little girl, Newt (Carrie Henn), the survivor of the human colony on the deadly planet. Cameron actually gives Newt a forlorn remnant of a doll, so that it can float in brackish liquid when she has been captured. She is the kind of child you meet only in movies, where they're used to give plots some sentimental propulsion. Newt is out there in space to arouse Ripley's maternal instinct. That way Ripley's

193

final confrontation with the toothy monster will be the Battle of the Big Mamas.

Alien, with its horrible mutating creature (you never knew what form it would take), made you dread the scenes to come; it tied your innards in a knot. *Aliens* isn't that scary. There's an awful lot of claustrophobic blue-green dankness in the outpost that the colonists lived in, and when we see a tantalizing image, such as the Marines trying to find their way through a cavernous structure that looks like a sleeping giant's rib cage, the scene just leads to the use of battle weapons. Cameron is not a man for magic; he's more confident when he's showing off an armored personnel carrier or a cargo-handling machine with clumping feet. When Sigourney Weaver loads up with an arsenal of flame-shooting equipment and goes forth to fight the queen, she's no more than a smart Rambo. This movie has clumping feet.

August 11, 1986

ERSATZ

||||||||||||||||||||||||||||||||||||||||||||||||||||||||||||||||||||||||||||||||||||||||||||||||||||||||||||||||||||||||||||||||

The West German comedy *Men . . . (Männer . . .)* is lightweight and good-natured, and it moves along faster than most of the recent German imports but to no particular effect. What stirs interest in it is that it's about two men—dark, immaculately groomed Julius (Heiner Lauterbach), a prosperous and self-satisfied advertising executive in his late thirties, and blond, long-haired Stefan (Uwe Ochsenknecht), a bohemian, roughly the same age, who scowls with his lips, like Daryl Hannah—and it was written and directed by a thirty-one-year-old woman, Doris Dörrie. (This is her third feature.) The people lining up to see it are probably hoping for a new, different view of men. And what we get *is* different, but in a skewed way. The two men don't take hold—it's as if some essential element of masculinity eluded the director. Yet it's not just that: her women aren't all there, either. Dörrie's characters have no

194

substance; they're not quite human, and the picture is harmless and insipid, in the mode of French farces such as *Cousin, Cousine*.

When Julius, in his costly home in the suburbs of Munich, discovers that Paula (Ulrike Kriener), his wife of twelve years and the mother of his two children, has been having an affair with the slobby Stefan, it's a walloping blow to his ego. (He has been having dalliances with secretaries at the office, but he regards that as a male prerogative.) Julius can't think about anything but his wife's infidelity. He spies on her and her lover: he wants to know what Stefan's attraction is. So when he sees Stefan, who lives in the hippie and punkers' communal-living section of the city, posting notices of a room to rent in his apartment, he assumes a false name, and moves in with Stefan.

This is the kind of plot that was serviceable for musical-comedy films circa 1932 and is still serviceable, but Dörrie uses it without any under-pinnings. In 1932, it would have been clear that no matter how fatuous Julius was he loved his wife, and that more than his vanity was at stake; here, there's nothing at stake—it's just a game. Is Dörrie saying that men compete just to compete—that the object itself (the wife) is of little intrinsic interest? You can't tell; all you can be sure of is that Dörrie has a penchant for whimsical cuteness. When Julius, spying on Paula, sees Stefan drop her off and drive away, the only vehicle on hand to follow him with is a child's red bicycle; he doubles over on it and pedals like mad. The gag has a considerable lineage, going back to Jacques Tati, and back, back to Mack Sennett. When Julius is living in Stefan's apartment and Paula comes to lunch, he puts on a King Kong mask and boxing gloves. This isn't an homage to David Warner in his gorilla suit twenty years ago in *Morgan!*, any more than it's an homage to Mischa Auer's simian stunt fifty years ago in *My Man Godfrey*. It's just a gag, but at least this one has a payoff: Julius can see that Paula is intrigued—and a little aroused—by this unknown fellow's frisking about as King Kong. Most of these derivative "carefree" moments, such as a scene of Stefan and Julius taking turns playing with a toy car, don't come to much. They're tossed together with a jocular feminist exposé of men's attitudes toward women, and when Julius and Stefan become buddies there are ambiguous, sometimes sexually tinged romps. In one weirdly extended scene, Julius talks to Stefan while concealing a knife that's piercing his thigh, and the audience is invited to laugh at his pain. During all this, Julius, who has figured out that Paula is drawn to Stefan's lack of discipline, his frayed clothes that look slept in, and his general messiness, takes some kind of

195

revenge by turning Stefan into an orderly bourgeois with a regular job. Conveniently, Paula is just a sparkling creature whizzing by, so we don't ask what her motivation is. She might be trying out Stefan like a new flavor of ice cream.

In interviews, Dörrie has said that Julius and Stefan are meant to represent the divided sides of one personality. That may have been in her mind, but it's not what emerges onscreen. Dörrie's ideas are flotsam and jetsam; they bob up and then disappear. Does the trim, proper Julius find something to envy in Stefan—some freedom or originality? Does Julius become looser and more liberal because of his contact with Stefan? From what we're shown, the oafish, thick-skulled Stefan, who's eager for money, a good tailor, and a Maserati, is easily converted to a business-man's life, but Julius doesn't change. Part of the reason that the film wobbles about is that the two actors' physiques don't conform to what the dialogue says. Stefan tries to help Julius work off his white-collar softness and get in better condition, but in fact the actor playing Julius looks remarkably fit—so fit that when he puts on casual clothes he's sleek and stiff, like a mannequin showing them off. Having been cuckolded, he's supposed to be so full of self-doubt that he needs to ask a young woman, Angelika (Janna Marangosoff), who hangs around the apartment, whether he's attractive, but the question isn't convincing; this fellow is physically confident. And Stefan, with his messy receding hair and the petulant look of a babyish Siegfried, doesn't seem the sort of man who'd keep in shape, anyway. Something else is off: by the movie's logic, when Stefan's hair is cut and he's properly outfitted for success he should seem silly and castrated, but he doesn't. The vengeful Julius (who's by far the smarter of the two) may have got him to the point where he's repeating ancient sexist epigrams, like "A man is what he does; a woman is what she is," but he looks much better.

Men . . . isn't unpleasant. Dörrie's deadpan giddiness is likable enough. The picture is insignificant, though—a piece of fluff without the wit that you might hope for. And her little joke goes on too long; it sags in the middle, and then it collapses in an absurdist ending that suggests amateur theatricals. Possibly in Germany, where the picture has been hugely popular, audiences may see the two men (who were teen-agers during the late-sixties counterculture) as the two sides of what Dörrie, in inter-views, calls the "serious Teutonic soul" and identify with one or the other. But the writer-director doesn't seem to identify with either of them, or with Paula. (Perhaps she has a little sympathy for the forlorn Angelika waiting day after day until her boyfriend feels like going to Italy with her.) It isn't necessary for Dörrie to identify with men: it might be a happy binge for a woman movie director to turn the tables and view men as the Other—if she had something to show us about this Otherness. But Dörrie is using the technology of movies to cut out paper dolls. That may sound sexist, but it would be disingenuous to argue that if a man had made this picture I'd say the same thing, because a man isn't as likely to have made it. Men . . . have their own follies.

■

Consciously sensitive moviemaking is a sickly thing. *Stand by Me*, Rob Reiner's film taken from Stephen King's autobiographical novella *The Body*, is steeped in tenderness and understanding and nostalgia. It's the sort of movie that you're likely to see described as "a quiet little gem." It's ersatz art. Seeing it is like watching an extended Christmas Special of *The Waltons* or *Little House on the Prairie*—it makes you feel virtuous. (If there is any test that can be applied to movies, it's that the good ones never make you feel virtuous.)

On a summer weekend in 1959, four twelve- and-thirteen-year-old boys from the fictional Castle Rock, Oregon (pop. 1,281), go on an overnight hike in the woods outside town to look for a boy their age who has been missing for several days. They have reason to believe that the kid was killed by a train; so they stick close to the railroad tracks, searching for his body and hoping to become heroes by finding it. These four misfits could use a little glory. Gordie (Wil Wheaton), the quiet, sensitive one who will grow up to be a writer (presumably the not-so-sensitive Stephen King), is lonely at home; his father loved his older, star-athlete brother who was killed in a jeep accident, and Gordie has nightmares of his father saying that it should have been Gordie. The adult Gordie (Richard Dreyfuss), in 1985, narrates this account of the four boys' adventure. The leader of the group and Gordie's closest friend is Chris (River Phoenix), who comes from a family of lowlifes and is afraid that he won't have a chance to be anything else; the other two are Vern (Jerry O'Connell), who's short for his age, chubby, and fearful, and the reckless, unstable Teddy (Corey Feldman), whose father held his ear against a burner, mutilating him—his troubles are spelled out for us when a junkman they encounter along their way screams at him, "Your dad's a looney in the nuthouse."

197

The boys know that this is their last summer together—that in the fall when they go to junior high (Gordie for college-preparatory classes, the others for manual training) they will go separate ways. Their tree-house days will be over. These boys are very knowing; they keep intuiting one another's emotions, and they're plucky—when they get in tight spots, they stand by each other. They're like a pastoral support group, quick to perceive signs of trouble and to lay gentle firm hands on needy shoulders. That's what softens everything in the movie, purifies it, makes it lyrical and synthetic. The script, by Raynold Gideon and Bruce A. Evans, gives the boys some funny insults, and it doesn't push too hard on the theme (the boys' intimations of mortality). But the movie gives King's story a false refinement, a poetic glow. Every flicker of feeling is interpreted for you, and you feel as if you'd been here before. (At times, the boys' troubles suggest a genteel painless version of *Winesburg, Ohio*.) Audiences are supposed to laugh and cry at *Stand by Me*—and also *find it meaningful*. The narrator tells you what to think, and the film cries out, "Why can't grownups understand us the way other kids do?"

Stand by Me cooks up some crisis situations by having the little boys threatened by a gang of adolescent bullies. These scenes are hopelessly bad; if they're intended to indicate that the little boys may turn into hairy brutes in a few years, they fail, because these seventeen- and eighteen-year-old brutes aren't characterized. They're just a generic gang of ruffians who interrupt the story. It's the nostalgic fixation on the little boys at the time just before they (presumably) lose their innocence that gives *Stand by Me* its overdose of sincerity and finer feelings. At the end, the adult Gordie, with his word processor, types out "I never had any friends later on like the ones I had when I was twelve. Jesus, does anyone?" And you want to say, "Wait a minute, what's going on here? Are we supposed to believe that that was the last moment for true friendship?" This is like some crazy pedophilic idealization of life before puberty, or perhaps it's just male narcissism about what sensitive boys we were. (No women characters pollute this mythic vision; mothers are bit players. The only way we have of knowing that there's another sex is that when the nasty adolescents intimidate the little boys they call them "girls.")

The fifties and a man's vision of his childhood have been antiqued in this movie and held up as treasures. Five minutes after you've left the theatre, the picture evaporates, except for its one crude, repulsively funny sequence. At night in the woods, the boys sit around the campfire having a smoke as Gordie the storyteller spins a tall tale that's acted out for us. His story seems absolutely right for what a bright boy knows would delight other boys. It's about a blueberry-pie-eating contest in a town in an earlier America. A grossly fat boy known as Lardass (Andy Lindberg) enters the contest, downs an outsize bottle of castor oil, and, as the contestants aren't allowed to use their hands, proceeds to gobble and snuffle up the blueberry centers of dozens of pies, like a pig on a rampage. Then he avenges himself on the townspeople who have made fun of him, by barfing on them. Gordie doesn't have his facts right on what castor oil does. (It's a cathartic, not an emetic.) This is a delirious cartoonlike sequence, though; you gape at it as the action swells and involves the whole town. And maybe you wonder how moviemakers who had the spirit to stage this stupendous gross-out could have made such a vain, effete, self-coddling movie.

■

As David Basner, the hero of *Nothing in Common*, Tom Hanks uses his Peter Pan boyishness manipulatively. David, who has risen to be the creative director of a top advertising agency in Chicago, is a lovable smartie; his charm tempers his cockiness. He's a television baby—a quipper, fast on the uptake and fast to gauge how his wisecracks are going over. (He'll turn them against himself if he's in danger of giving offense.) David has found his niche in the lucrative, infantile world of devising concepts for commercials; he's cynical about what he does, but he loves it, too. He thrives on it—on the competitiveness, on his own ingenuity, on being an advertising ace. He grooves on his own shallowness.

The screenwriters Rick Podell and Michael Preminger, both former stand-up comedians, had a good idea for a character here. David Basner, who says, "It's economically unsound to grow up," is like an updated version of the brash reporter heroes of thirties movies. But the script puts him in a mawkish situation. After thirty-six unhappy years, his unworldly housewife mother Lorraine (Eva Marie Saint) leaves his garment-salesman father Max (Jackie Gleason). In recent years, David has shut his parents out of his thoughts and kept his visits home to a bare minimum (even though they live right there in Chicago); now he's thrust into the grownup role of being a mainstay to each of them, and though he has felt for a long time that he has "nothing in common" with his edgy, antagonistic father, he discovers that they have a strong bond. The writers seem to have worked up the mother's role strictly for schematic

199

purposes; the movie is really about David's relationship with sour, self-centered old Max, once a wizard at selling, who loses his job, and is losing his sight, too. The movie is *Death of a Salesman* as a sitcom, with the father's loneliness and his need for David used as a lesson to the swinging Yuppie son. Through helping his father—even when it means risking some of his standing in the advertising world—David grows up and develops a sense of values.

The theme would seem to require that the son begin to recognize himself in everything he can't stand about his father, and the tone of the advertising-agency scenes suggests that these recognitions would be ironic—that David would pick up on them ruefully, self-mockingly. But the writers don't follow through on their premises. David doesn't see himself in old Max (or Max in David). Instead, the movie turns into a generalized statement about the love-hate bonds between parents and children. And the director, Garry Marshall, goes at the subject in the blunt, unshaded manner of TV drama. (The father and son's coming together is much like the father-son reconciliation at the close of Marshall's 1984 film *The Flamingo Kid*.) Max undergoes life-or-death surgery, and David sobs in misery. In these scenes, you see Tom Hanks hard at work acting. When Hanks does comedy, his slightly blank quality is like a form of stylization. But when he's sobbing he's blank like Rob Lowe sobbing. (He does, though, have the grace to turn his head away when his mother reacts to the puppy he has brought her by exclaiming how wonderful it is to have something to love.)

In its mixed comedy-weepie intentions, *Nothing in Common* is similar to *Terms of Endearment*, which also featured sickness curing selfishness. But with all its emotional flip-flops *Terms* was at least skillfully acted. *Nothing* seems to be miscast in just about every major role, except for Hanks, and Barry Corbin, who plays the monstrous, egocentric head of Colonial Airlines, for whom David works up a presentation, and possibly Hector Elizondo, as the unimposing, considerate head of the ad agency. What looks like miscasting is probably a combination of the bone-thin banality of some of the roles—such as Eva Marie Saint's—and Marshall's misdirecting. The other women aren't much better off. The movie is an interlocking series of parallels, doubles, and contrasts. Lorraine is Catholic, Max is vaguely Jewish, and so on. And the young women are poles apart. As the new-style movie bitch, the aggressive M.B.A. who is the media director of Colonial Airlines, Sela Ward looks like a sneering, synthetic Ava Gardner; her makeup suggests a mask of heartlessness—she's meant to be the female equivalent of the pre-reformed David. As

200

her opposite number—an idealistic professor whose field is experimental theatre—Bess Armstrong stands for warmth and loyalty and integrity. But as an actress Bess Armstrong is like a machine-made emblem of TV—she plays her role exactly as it's written, without a whisper of individuality or temperament.

When the down-at-the-mouth Jackie Gleason heaves in sight, all hope for the movie disappears, anyway. We hear him before we see him: his raspy, boozy voice on David's answering machine has a sarcastic punch that cuts right through David's flippant invitation to leave a message. He's as grating as a bill collector, and he can make you laugh—not for long, though. The Great One is some kind of master comedian, but all his acting instincts play him false when he attempts suffering characters. Gleason stands outside his role, so he brings no illumination to the unpleasantness of this seamy, irascible old guy who thinks he's clever. And though the film practically diagrams the character traits shared by father and son, we never see a hint of what Max was like when he was young— the connection isn't made in a rakish attitude, an impudent, predatory grin, or a dirty laugh. So there's never an instant when we actually feel the dramatic point: "like father, like son." It's a dreary point, but it might seem less dreary if the movie made it via the acting, instead of stating it repeatedly through all these broad, obvious parallels. (Example: David drives a jeep; Max drives a gunboat-size old Cadillac.)

Nothing in Common has a good parody scene or two at the ad agency, and one hard-edged lampoon—the brainstorming sessions that lead to David's anti-high-tech concept for the Colonial Airlines account and the final presentation. (It features a loving family that's the reverse of what he grew up with.) But I hated the movie's mixture of glossiness and drabness—the clutter of David's overdecorated office, the gross swank of his bachelor lair, and the impersonal pastel dullness of the idealistic professor's apartment (which is meant to be tasteful). I hated the way Eva Marie Saint was photographed to look faded and wrinkled. (She's supposed to be about fifty-five, so Saint, who is actually sixty-two, is made up and lighted so that she looks seventy. She's turned into stale white bread.) I hated the insistent moralizing. David has to change because of his casual affairs with women, even though they're mutual conquests and nobody gets hurt. He has to learn to commit himself. (His father never did; when the young, inexperienced Lorraine didn't respond to his lovemaking, he decided she was frigid and took to philandering.) And most of all I hated it because just about everything in it is flagged for you. (Look, now David is going to feel bad about his father!) Is there anything safer than TV-style seriousness—i.e., delivering the conventional wisdom as if it were the deeply important truth?

As David's mild-mannered boss, Hector Elizondo keeps unveiling new hairpieces, hoping for David's approval. We see three of them, and David's mother, meeting the boss for the first time, stares at his rug, transfixed by it. She lived all those years with a portly man who stretches his few (probably dyed) hairs over his big bald head and tries to look dapper, and she can't take her eyes off this innocuous, fluffy little hairpiece? And, of course, Garry Marshall the TV-wisdom pusher has the decent-hearted boss discover the truth: that the deception of the rug doesn't work—that he feels better and looks better when he's honestly bald. This movie is a toupee made up to look like honest baldness.

September 8, 1986

OUT THERE AND IN HERE

||||||||||||||||||||||||||||||||||||||||||||||||||||||||||||||||||||||||||||||||||||||||||||||||||||||||||||||||||||||||||||||||||||

"Maybe I'm sick, but I want to see that again."
—Overheard after a showing of *Blue Velvet*.

When you come out of the theatre after seeing David Lynch's *Blue Velvet*, you certainly know that you've seen something. You wouldn't mistake frames from *Blue Velvet* for frames from any other movie. It's an anomaly—the work of a genius naïf. If you feel that there's very little art between you and the filmmaker's psyche, it may be because there's less than the usual amount of inhibition. Lynch doesn't censor his sexual fantasies, and the film's hypercharged erotic atmosphere makes it something of a trance-out, but his humor keeps breaking through, too. His fantasies may come from his unconscious, but he recognizes them for what they are, and he's tickled by them. The film is consciously purplish and consciously funny, and the two work together in an original, down-home way.

Shot in Wilmington, North Carolina, it's set in an archetypal small, sleepy city, Lumberton, where the radio station's call letters are WOOD, and the announcer says, "At the sound of the falling tree," and then, as the tree falls, "it's 9:30." Not more than three minutes into the film, you recognize that this peaceful, enchanted, white-picket-fence community, where the eighties look like the fifties, is the creepiest sleepy city you've ever seen. The subject of the movie is exactly that: the mystery and madness hidden in the "normal." At the beginning, the wide images (the film is shot in CinemaScope ratio: 2.35 to 1) are meticulously bright and sharp-edged; you feel that you're seeing every detail of the architecture, the layout of homes and apartments, the furnishings and potted plants, the women's dresses. It's so hyperfamiliar it's scary. The vivid red of the roses by the white fence makes them look like hothouse blooms, and the budding yellow tulips are poised, eager to open. Later, the light is low, but all through this movie the colors are insistent, objects may suddenly be enlarged to fill the frame, and a tiny imagined sound may be amplified to a thunderstorm. The style might be described as hallucinatory clinical realism.

When Mr. Beaumont, of Beaumont's hardware store, is watering his lawn and has a seizure of some sort—probably a cerebral hemorrhage—the water keeps shooting out. It drenches his fallen body, and a neighbor's dog jumps on top of him, frisking and trying to drink from the spray. The green grass, enlarged so that the blades are as tall as redwood trees, is teeming with big black insects, and their quarrelsome buzz and hiss displaces all other sounds. When Jeffrey Beaumont (Kyle MacLachlan), home from college to be near his stricken father and take care of the store, walks back from a visit to the hospital, he dawdles in a vacant lot and spots something unexpected in the grass and weeds: a human ear with an attached hank of hair, and ants crawling all over it. The ear looks like a seashell; in closeup, with the camera moving into the dark canal, it becomes the cosmos, and the sound is what you hear when you put a shell to your ear—the roar of the ocean.

Jeffrey's curiosity about the severed ear—whose head it came from and why it was cut off—leads him to Lumberton's tainted underside, a netherworld of sleazy interconnections. A viewer knows intuitively that this is a coming-of-age picture—that Jeffrey's discovery of this criminal, sadomasochistic network has everything to do with his father's becoming an invalid and his own new status as an adult. It's as if David Lynch were saying, "It's a frightening world out there, and"—tapping his head—"in here."

Wholesome as Jeffrey looks, he's somewhat drawn to violence and kinkiness. But he doesn't quite know that yet, and it's certainly not how he explains himself to Sandy (Laura Dern), a fair-haired high-school senior and the daughter of the police detective investigating the matter of the ear. She has become Jeffrey's confederate, and when she questions the nature of his interest in the case he speaks of being involved with "something that was always hidden," of being "in the middle of a mystery." Sandy tantalizes him with what she's overheard the police saying, and he tantalizes her with the strange, "hidden" things he learns about. During their scenes together, an eerie faraway organ is playing melodies that float in the air, and the sound italicizes the two kids' blarney. It's like the organ music in an old soap opera; it turns their confabs into parody, and tells us that they're in a dream world. Sometimes when Jeffrey tells Sandy what he thinks is going on it's as if he had dreamed it and then woke up and found out it had happened. Jeffrey himself is the mystery that Sandy is drawn to (perhaps the tiny gold earring he wears is part of his attraction), and you can't help giggling a little when she turns to him with a worried, earnest face and says, "I don't know if you're a detective or a pervert." She's still a kid; she thinks it's either/or. Jeffrey is soon withholding some of his adventures from her, because they're not just mysteriously erotic—they're downright carnal, and, yes, he's smack in the middle of it all. He has been pulled—with no kicking or screaming—into the inferno of corrupt adult sexuality.

Dorothy Vallens (Isabella Rossellini) is soft and brunette and faintly, lusciously foreign; she has had a child, and she's enough older than Jeffrey to have the allure of an "experienced woman." A torch singer in a night club outside the city limits, she wears a moth-eaten mop of curls and lives at the Deep River Apartments in musty rooms that look as if they'd sprouted their own furniture. The gloomy walls—mauve gone brown—suggest the chic of an earlier era, when perhaps the building was considered fashionable (and the elevator worked). Sandy has told Jeffrey that the police think Dorothy Vallens is involved in the mutilation case, and have her under surveillance. Jeffrey puts her under closer surveillance. The moviemaker doesn't do any interpreting for you: you simply watch and listen, and what ensues rings so many bells in your head that you may get a little woozy.

Hiding in Dorothy's closet at night, Jeffrey peeks at her through the slatted door while she undresses. She hears him and, grabbing a kitchen knife, orders him out of his hiding place and forces him to strip. When he has nothing on but his shorts, she pulls them down and begins fondling him, but sends him back into the closet when she has a caller—Frank the crime boss, Mr. Macho Sleazeball himself, played by Dennis Hopper.

Frank is an infantile tough-guy sadist who calls her "Mommy," wallops her if she forgets to call him "Daddy," and wallops her harder if she happens to look at him. All this seems to be part of their regular ritual; he demands his bourbon (as if he's sick of telling her), has her dim the lights, and he takes out an inhaler mask (for some unspecified gas) to heighten his sensations during sex. (The gas is probably a booster to whatever drugs he's on.) He also uses a fetish—the sash of Dorothy's blue velvet bathrobe. Jeffrey, in his closet, doesn't make a sound this time; he's transfixed by what he can just barely see. It's like a sick-joke version of the primal scene, and this curious child watches his parents do some very weird things. After Frank leaves, Jeffrey attempts to help the weary, bruised woman, but all she wants is sex. She's photographed in a clinch, with her face upside down and her ruby lips parted in a sly smile that exposes her gleaming front teeth—especially the one that has a teasing chip, as if someone had taken a small bite out of it.

When Jeffrey comes to see her again, he knocks on the door. She greets him eagerly—almost reproachfully—with "I looked for you in my closet tonight." (That line is a giddy classic.) The third night, they're on her bed after a round or two of intercourse. Trying to overcome his reluctance to hit her, she asks, "Are you a bad boy . . . do you want to do bad things?" We know the answer before he does. He's having trouble breathing.

Isabella Rossellini doesn't show anything like the acting technique that her mother, Ingrid Bergman, had, but she's willing to try things, and she doesn't hold back. Dorothy is a dream of a freak. Walking around her depressing apartment in her black bra and scanties, with blue eyeshadow and red high heels, she's a woman in distress right out of the pulps; she has the plushy, tempestuous look of heroines who are described as "bewitching." (She even has the kind of nostrils that cover artists can represent accurately with two dots.) Rossellini's accent is useful: it's part of Dorothy's strangeness. And Rossellini's echoes of her mother's low voice help to place this kitschy seductress in an unreal world. She has a special physical quality, too. There's nothing of the modern American woman about her. When she's naked, she's not protected, like the stars who are pummelled into shape and lighted to show their muscular perfection. She's defenselessly, tactilely naked, like the nudes the Expressionists painted.

Jeffrey, commuting between Dorothy, the blue lady of the night, and Sandy, the sunshine girl, suggests a character left over from *Our Town*. (He lives in an indefinite mythic present that feels like the past—

205

he's split between the older woman he has sex with but doesn't love and the girl he loves but doesn't have sex with.) Kyle MacLachlan is in just about every scene, and he gives a phenomenal performance. As the hero of *Dune*, he may have been swallowed up in the sand, but here he's ideally cast. His proper look is perfect for a well-brought-up young fellow who's scared of his dirty thoughts (but wants to have them anyway). And when Jeffrey and Laura Dern's Sandy first meet and they make each other laugh, you relax with them and laugh, too, because you know that the two performers are going to work together like magic. Laura Dern brings a growing-up-fast passion to Sandy's love for Jeffrey, and she has an emotional fire that she didn't get to demonstrate in *Mask* or *Smooth Talk*. Lynch takes a plunge when he stages the high-schoolers' party that Sandy takes Jeffrey to: the two of them begin to dance and begin to kiss, and can't stop kissing. "Mysteries of Love," the song that they're dancing to, is scored using an organ, but now the organ isn't mocking them—the music swells to do justice to their feelings. The sequence may recall Sissy Spacek's romantic whirl at the prom in De Palma's *Carrie*, but the tone is different: we're being told that these two are not going to let go of each other, that they're moving into the unknown together. And the song, with lyrics by Lynch and music by Angelo Badalamenti (who wrote the score), carries the emotion over to the later scenes when Sandy's belief in Jeffrey is tested. (The movie may frighten some adolescents, as *Carrie* did, though the violent images aren't obtrusive; you don't quite take them in at first—it's only as the camera is pulling back from them that you see them clearly.)

As the uncontrollable Frank, in his slick leather outfits, Dennis Hopper gives the movie a jolt of horrific energy. Frank is lewd and dangerous; you feel he does what he does just for the hell of it. (He uses his inhaler to heighten the sensation of murder, too.) And as Ben, one of Frank's business associates, Dean Stockwell is a smiling wonder; you stare at his kissy makeup, the pearly jewel that he wears halfway up his ear, his druggy contentment. Frank refers to Ben as "suave," but that's not the half of it. Miming to Roy Orbison's song "In Dreams," about "the candy-colored clown they call the sandman," he's so magnetic that you momentarily forget everything else that's supposed to be going on.

Actually, it's easy to forget about the plot, because that's where Lynch's naïve approach has its disadvantages: Lumberton's subterranean criminal life needs to be as organic as the scrambling insects, and it isn't. Lynch doesn't show us how the criminals operate or how they're bound to each other. So the story isn't grounded in anything and has to be explained in little driblets of dialogue. But *Blue Velvet* has so much aural-visual humor and poetry that it's sustained despite the wobbly plot and the bland functional dialogue (that's sometimes a deliberate spoof of small-town conventionality and sometimes maybe not). It's sustained despite the fact that Lynch's imagistic talent, which is for the dark and unaccountable, flattens out in the sunlight scenes, as in the ordinary, daily moments between parents and children. One key character is never clarified: We can't tell if Sandy's father (played by George Dickerson) is implicated in the corruption, or if we're meant to accept him as a straight arrow out of a fifties F.B.I. picture. Lynch skimps on these commercial-movie basics and fouls up on them, too, but it's as if he were reinventing movies. His work goes back to the avant-garde filmmakers of the twenties and thirties, who were often painters—and he himself trained to be one. He takes off from the experimental traditions that Hollywood has usually ignored.

This is his first film from his own original material since *Eraserhead* (which was first shown in 1977), and in some ways it's linked to that film's stately spookiness. Lynch's longtime associate, the cinematographer Frederick Elmes, lighted both films, and he has given *Blue Velvet* a comparable tactility; real streets look like paintings you could touch—you feel as if you could moosh your fingers in the colors. There are also reminders of the musical numbers in *Eraserhead*, which were like a form of dementia. (Lynch used an organ there, too.) With Rossellini singing at the club, and vocalists like Bobby Vinton on the soundtrack and tunes layered in and out of the orchestral score, *Blue Velvet* suggests a musical on themes from our pop unconscious. There are noises in there, of course, and Alan Splet, who started working with Lynch when he was doing shorts and has been his sound man on all his features (*Eraserhead* was followed by *The Elephant Man*, in 1980, and *Dune*, in 1984), combines them so that, say, when Jeffrey walks up the seven flights to Dorothy's apartment the building has a pumping, groaning sound. It could be an ancient furnace or foghorns or a heavy old animal that's winded. The mix of natural sounds with mechanical-industrial noises gives the images an ambience that's hokey and gothic and yet totally unpretentious—maybe because Lynch's subject is normal American fantasy life. Even that fetishized blue velvet robe is tacky, like something you could pick up in the red brick department store on Main Street.

Blue Velvet is a comedy, yet it puts us—or, at least, some of us—in an erotic trance. The movie keeps ribbing the clean-cut Jeffrey, yet we're caught up in his imagination. It must be that Lynch's use of irrational material works the way it's supposed to: at some not fully conscious level we read his images. When Frank catches Jeffrey with "Mommy" and takes him for a ride—first to Ben's hangout and then to a deserted spot—the car is packed with Frank's thugs, Dorothy, in her robe, and a large-headed, big-bellied woman in a short, pink skirt who has been necking with one of the guys. When Frank parks and he and his thugs start punching out Jeffrey, the pink-skirted woman climbs up on the roof of the car and, to the sound of that sandman song, dances aimlessly, impassively, like a girl in a topless bar. (She's in her dream world, too.) In a later scene, a man who has been shot several times remains standing, but he's no longer looking at anything; he faces a one-eared dead man sitting up in a chair, with the blue velvet sash in his mouth, and the two are suspended in time, like figures posed together in a wax museum, or plaster figures by George Segal retouched by Francis Bacon. Almost every scene has something outlandishly off in it, something that jogs your memory or your thinking, like the collection of fat women at Ben's joint, who look as if they were objects in a still-life. Or there may be something that just tweaks your memory, like the worrywart old maid—Jeffrey's Aunt Barbara (Frances Bay). Or a bit of comedy that's underplayed, like the shot of Jeffrey's mother (Priscilla Pointer) and Sandy's mother (Hope Lange) getting to know each other and looking interchangeable. (The only scene that feels thin—that lacks surprise—is Dorothy's lushly romanticized reunion with her child; for a few seconds, the film goes splat.)

It's the slightly disjunctive quality of Lynch's scenes (and the fact that we don't question them, because they don't feel arbitrary to us) that makes the movie so hypnotic—that, and the slow, assured sensuousness of his editing rhythms. This is possibly the only coming-of-age movie in which sex has the danger and the heightened excitement of a horror picture. It's the fantasy (rather than the plot) that's organic, and there's no sticky-sweet lost innocence, because the darkness was always there, inside.

The film's kinkiness isn't alienating—its naïveté keeps it from that. And its vision isn't alienating: this is American darkness—darkness in color, darkness with a happy ending. Lynch might turn out to be the first populist surrealist—a Frank Capra of dream logic. *Blue Velvet* does have a homiletic side. It's about a young man's learning through flabbergasting and violent experience to appreciate a relatively safe and manageable sex life. And when Sandy's father, speaking of the whole nightmarish business of the ear, says to Jeffrey, "It's over now," the film cuts to daylight. But with Lynch as the writer and director the homily has a little zinger.

Sandy, who may have watched too many daytime soaps, has dreamed that the morbid darkness will be dispelled when thousands of robins arrive bringing love—a dream that she tells Jeffrey (to the accompaniment of organ music twitting her vision). When a plump robin lands on the kitchen windowsill, it has an insect in its beak.

September 22, 1986

BODIES

||||||||||||||||||||||||||||||||||||||||||||||||||||||||||||||||||||||||||||||||||||||||||||||||||||||||||||||||||||||||||||||||||||||||||||||||

Jeff Goldblum has a gift for playing innocently self-absorbed goofs, and, luckily, he carries over a bit of the goof to the loner character he plays in *The Fly*—a brilliant, eccentric scientist whose intellect is always racing. As Seth Brundle, he wears his thick, curly hair Einstein-aureole style, and he delivers his lines as if queries were piling up in his mind about what he's saying—he does broken-rhythm double takes on his own dialogue. In the opening scenes, as the tall young Brundle is idly looking over the displays at a science exhibition he catches sight of the tall, pretty Veronica (played by Geena Davis), a reporter for a science magazine. Once he focusses on her, his enormous dark eyes don't take in anything else. He invites her to come back to his lab to see what he's working on—a discovery that will "change the world as we know it"— and she's too eager a reporter to pass up the invitation. After she gets to see this prodigy in his natural habitat—the lab, which is in a loft in an old brick warehouse—she's impressed by his work and charmed by his childlike directness, by his unworldliness, and maybe, too, by his muscular physique and remarkable height. Goldblum is six foot five, and Davis is a neat six feet; they both have masses of dark hair and "generous" mouths with similar occlusions (though he can't match her dimples or her cleft chin). Brundle and Veronica are a heroic pair. They become totally devoted to each other, and they look as if they could produce a race of giants. But when she becomes pregnant it isn't their offspring's probable height that worries her.

Brundle has two telepods spaced apart in the lab—machines that

209

Veronica accurately describes as looking like "designer phone booths."
He explains that he got carsick as a child and he has devised a method
of instant, painless travel: when an object is put in a booth, a computer
analyzes its molecules, disintegrates them, and reintegrates them in the
other booth. Brundle has no difficulty transmitting inanimate objects, but
he still runs into snags with the flesh of living creatures. He works with
baboons, and perhaps the scariest shock-cut in the movie comes when an
elegant, affectionate baboon is beamed from booth to booth and an error
is made in the reintegration process. In the 1958 version of *The Fly*,
which was based, like this one, on a short story by George Langelaan,
the lab animals were less photogenic—guinea pigs. The 1958 script (by
James Clavell) had more principal characters than this new one, which
was written by Charles Edward Pogue and then reshaped by the director,
the Toronto-based horror specialist David (*The Brood*) Cronenberg. Here,
surprisingly, there are only Brundle and Veronica and, generally in the
background, John Getz as her former lover Stathis, who is the editor of
Particle, the magazine she writes for. With so few characters and almost
no crosscurrents in the story, Cronenberg takes his time about setting
things up. He doesn't bother with the character of Stathis, who barely
makes sense; Stathis is needed just to explain why, at a critical point,
Brundle gets stupidly jealous and drunk and, alone in his lab, decides
that the time has come to transmit a human being. He pops into one of
the booths, too intent on the daring step he's taking to notice that he has
a fellow-passenger, a fly. Elated at his success, he strides out of the other
booth completely unaware that his genetic and molecular structure has
been fused with that of the fly.

This is the major departure from the 1958 version, in which the man
and the fly emerged mix-matched, with their body parts altered in size:
the little fly with the tiny head and arm of the man, and the man's body
with a big fly's head and foreleg. Here the fly takes over the man from
inside, and it's Veronica who first notices changes in her lover's body and
in his temperament. The opening half of the movie has had a romantic-
comedy edge, and it's still fun when Brundle is suddenly doing gymnas-
tics, jumping up and down out of sheer kinetic drive, and swinging around
in the high-ceilinged loft. But when his skin is mottled and his appetite
for sexual intercourse has become as insatiable as his new mania for
sweets it's less fun, and by the time he's walking on the ceiling and
scrambling down the side wall the quirkiness is gone and the shocks are
just about all that's left. By then, the computer has told him what has
happened—that he has become Brundlefly. He has enough of the scientist

left in him to keep a record of his physical changes and to collect the parts of his body that fall off; he's fascinated by them—he treasures them like a gloating miser. For the remainder of the movie, though, there is essentially nothing for the audience to watch except his hideous physical deterioration. The only other plot element is the matter of Veronica's pregnancy and her fear of giving birth to a pupal monstrosity. (Her gynecologist is played by Cronenberg; those familiar with his work—with his obsessions about flesh and biological disorders—will recognize this as a sick, sick joke.)

Probably the picture is having its huge box-office success because it's so single-minded. It's like a B horror movie given new weight by Cronenberg, and for what it is it's very well done. He narrows the film down to one man's decaying body, and concentrates your attention on one stage after another of poor Brundle's becoming bent over double and deformed. And although the successive jobs of makeup don't really make Goldblum look any more like a fly, the spectacle of ever-worsening rot has its own effectiveness. The movie can be taken as a metaphor for AIDS or cancer, or simply as a metaphor for what happens in the normal aging process. Yet on its own it has no real vision—nothing that lifts it out of the horror-shock category. There's humor in the early scenes between Brundle and Veronica, and the idea of their attachment's being so powerful that they go on loving each other even when he's rotting is funny and stirring. They're like Wagnerian superlovers, and Goldblum has some powerful, creepy moments. In the scene where Brundlefly tells Veronica to leave the lab—he says, "I'll hurt you if you stay"—there's pain in his voice, along with a breathy-buzzy sound. But the movie is extremely literal-minded about physical decay. Cronenberg wants to drive you to revulsion; that's his aim. It's as if *Rosemary's Baby* were remade without its nasty edge of satirical humor, or as if either Don Siegel's or Phil Kaufman's *Invasion of the Body Snatchers* were remade without the idea that the pods represented all the social pressures to conform and that when you closed your eyes and gave in to them they destroyed your soul, your individuality—as if the pods were just monsters who wanted to kill you.

The Fly is being called Kafka-esque, but the resemblance to Kafka's *Metamorphosis* is superficial. When Kafka's man woke up as a bug, it was an actualization of how he felt about himself, and the story stays with us because we all have our miserable, guilt-ridden moments of feeling like bugs. *The Fly* is just pulp that sets out to shock you. It features a love relationship, but that's not what it's about. If *The Fly* has a power, it's simply in our somewhat prurient fixation on watching a man rot until finally he's pleading for a coup de grâce. So, despite Goldblum's terrific performance and despite the graceful romantic teamwork between him and Geena Davis, moviegoers may not feel that they're having such a great time. *The Fly* is so determinedly concentrated that it certainly holds your attention, though. As a moviemaker, Cronenberg is a bondage freak; you feel that if he could he'd tighten the action until the screen burst, if not the heads of the people watching it.

■

In the past, moviemakers who were casting the role of a beautiful black woman generally looked for a black actress with perfect Waspy features; essentially, they were looking for a beautiful white woman with a tan. The twenty-nine-year-old Spike Lee, who wrote, directed, and edited the sex comedy *She's Gotta Have It*, breaks the pattern. Tracy Camila Johns, from the Negro Ensemble Company, who plays his pivotal character, Nola Darling, has almond-shaped come-hither eyes, a short nose with an inquiring tilt, full lips, hair that's cut like a wedge (it shoots up about five inches above the top of her head), and a smooth, sinuous walk. Nola, who works as a graphic designer and lives alone in the black bohemian world in Brooklyn—it's like a black Greenwich Village—is voluptuous and easygoing. She has no guile or deceit in her. She attracts men without working at it, and she's happily juggling three lovers when she's faced by a mock crisis: each of the three men has turned possessive and wants to be her one and only.

The movie is almost continuously quick-witted. This is one of those rare textbook cases of an artist's being able to use limitations to his advantage. Spike Lee wrote the script in a hurry, after the funding for a more complex project fell apart; he shaped the key roles for actors he already had lined up, and in order to keep costs down to next to nothing he had to write a script that wouldn't require sets or costumes and in which almost everything could be shot within a one-mile radius. The script also had to allow for several sex scenes, so that he and his friends in the cast and crew could be sure of eventually getting some pay for their work. He began shooting (in 16 mm.) in the summer of 1985 with only about $22,000 on hand ($18,000 from the New York State Council on the Arts and $4,000 from private investors); raising more money as he went along, he finished shooting in twelve days. The picture was completed on a final budget of $175,000, of which all except about $60,000 was deferred. Nola, her three lovers, and her family and friends explain themselves directly to the camera, because this is just about the fastest, most economical way of setting up a shot, and the film's basic set is Nola's bed—the story begins and ends with her alone under the covers. What makes this on-the-cheap method work is partly that Lee has a fine cinematographer—Ernest Dickerson, his close friend and former classmate at N.Y.U. film school. Dickerson's textured images (the film is in black-and-white) and the soft lighting he uses for the sex scenes help to give the film a lyrical, lilting feeling. And Lee himself is endowed with something more than training and imagination: he has what for want of a better term is called "a film sense." It's an instinct for how to make a movie move—for how much motion there should be in a shot, for how fast to cut the shots, for how to make them flow into each other rhythmically. (John Sayles has many gifts but not a film sense—he doesn't gain anything as an artist by using film—and this probably explains why Ernest Dickerson's work for him on *The Brother from Another Planet* looks stiff and pedestrian.) A great many movie directors don't have it, but when they find the right collaborators they can get by. When a director has it, though, it's as if nature intended him to make movies.

Spike Lee gives *She's Gotta Have It* a syncopated pulse, and he keeps it sparking and bouncing along. When Nola complains that most men's come-ons tell you that they're dogs, we get a quick comedy routine—a series of twelve sheiks looking into the camera and giving us their best shots at propositioning a woman. (She's right: they're dogs.) Lee is ingenious about varying the film's tempo, and he does it playfully—percussively—so that we enjoy his enjoyment of shooting and editing film. (It's scored to jazz by his musician father, Bill Lee, who also appears as Nola's father.) The director is pretty smart about the casting of Nola's three men: Jamie (Tommy Redmond Hicks), who's a conventional narrow-minded middle-class romantic; Greer (John Canada Terrell), a male model who's such a vain and pretentious social climber that he's sort of amusing—grooming is his religion; and Mars (Spike Lee himself), who wears oversize aviator glasses on his skinny face, has an arrow shaved out of the back of his hair, and flits about on his ten-speed bike in a satin baseball jacket. A gold nameplate around his neck spells out "Mars," which is where this jive artist seems to be from, and he talks so fast, using words

213

repetitively in a rat-tat rhythm, that he sounds like a scat stutterer. Mars, who's blithely unemployed, talks his way into Nola's bed (with his high-top basketball shoes on), and he makes her (and us) laugh.

Mars isn't a big role, but when he's wheedling Nola or rattling on telling her lies the rapster's push that propels *She's Gotta Have It* is incarnate. Lee doesn't get the same live-wire crackle from the other performers, and sometimes he lets their scenes run on into obviousness. (When Nola, doing exercises with Greer, flings herself on the bed eager for sex, and the clothes-conscious dolt takes so long folding his underwear that her passion burns out, Lee extends the scene so long that the joke burns out, too.) The movie also has a couple of bum patches: a switch to color for a dance number in Fort Greene Park that's as misconceived as the romantic duets in forties and fifties Hollywood musicals which it imitates, and the final stretch—fifteen minutes or so in which Lee takes the film's crisis situation too seriously. His idea seems to be that Nola can't choose among the three men because each has an element of what she wants in a man—and, besides, she likes sex with all of them. But Lee doesn't seem to know how to develop the story. He might have sustained his snappy, satirical tone. (If one or two or all three dropped away, others might have turned up to replace them.) Instead, he bears down on feminist issues. The picture starts going wrong in an ugly scene in which Jamie (who is the dreariest character anyway) goes into a rage about Nola's promiscuity and shows her how a tart should be treated by mounting her brutally from the rear. All the previous sex scenes have been sensuous and lighthearted, so this comes as a violation of the film's infectious spirit. After it, Lee fumbles around: Nola tries to define herself and considers celibacy before she and the picture regain their sanity in a rather perfunctory finish. (Lee doesn't get things swinging again until the closing credits.)

Part of what goes wrong is, I think, Lee's rather desperate stab at commerciality: he must have been so determined to have the film make some money that he gave the script the structure (and the title) of an exploitation film. Nola Darling (it's a porno-pic name) has three lovers and is courted by a leering lesbian, whom she pushes away; she consults a woman sex therapist, who tells her she's healthy; when she doesn't have a man around, she plays with herself; and so on. These are all standard ploys in the soft-core market. Most of this material, though, is handled with such grace that it transcends the attempt to play things corny and safe.

The movie's exuberance builds up so much audience good will that

214

you don't feel too let down by the fumbling at the end. Some of this good will comes out of Spike Lee's fresh, loose way of using the filmmaking itself as part of the subject (and the fun) of the movie: we can see how he's made do without funds. And a lot of the good will comes from his tapping a whole new subject matter. Whites don't exist in this movie. It's about the young black middle-class professional women and their new kinds of sexual problems with men. It's a screwball comedy of sexual manners set in a world that's parallel with the white world. For whites, it's like seeing how people sound and look in another country that's a mirror image of the terrain we know. For many young blacks, it must be like seeing themselves on the screen for the first time and liking what they see.

October 6, 1986

QUESTS FOR AMERICA

||||||||||||||||||||||||||||||||||||||||||||||||||||||||||||||||||||||||||||||||||||||||||||||||||||||||||||||||||||||||||||||||||

David Byrne's *True Stories* is laid out like a musical-comedy documentary about a town, except that the town—Virgil, Texas—is imaginary. It has been synthesized from streets and buildings in and around Dallas, and from studio-built sets. Most of the characters and events are based on people Byrne heard about or on news items he collected from sources as disparate as *The New York Times* and the tabloids that are found in supermarkets. These people—the bachelor (John Goodman) who has a "Wife Wanted" sign on his lawn, the rich woman (Swoosie Kurtz) who's so lazy that she doesn't get out of bed, the contentedly married civic leaders (Annie McEnroe and Spalding Gray) who haven't spoken to each other in about fifteen years, the kook (Jo Harvey Allen) who tells lies that put her in the middle of the most famous scandals of her time, the Hispanic worker (Tito Larriva) who thinks of his head as a radio transmitter-receiver, the plump, lisping woman (Alix Elias) who dresses in pink frills and wants everything to be cute as a puppy—are defined by their eccentricities, but they're also normal, everyday Americans. They're the kind of people who sit next to each other on the assembly

215

line at the microchip plant or at a revival meeting; they walk by each other at the shopping mall, and they're all preparing for the big day coming up when they will take part in the pageantry of the Texas Sesquicentennial. As Byrne, the narrator and observer, drives into the broad main street of this prairie town, he passes by the decorations for "1836–1986: Celebration of Specialness."

Byrne is looking for a true mythic image of America; Virgil is Our Town, it's Anytown, U.S.A. And as the characters interact in the days leading up to the big event you begin to get a sense of the community. It takes a while, though—a half hour or so—before you tune in to Byrne's deadpan presentations of the people and the setting. During these introductions, I thought he had come a cropper. His remarks to us presuppose our response, but it's only after his first throwaway gag lines are over that you get a sense of where the laughs should have come. So there's a feeling of discomfort in the audience. As a director, Byrne doesn't seem to have the timing for comedy, and his manner as narrator—his wide-eyed, immaculate blandness—doesn't cue us in. The imagery is calm and elegant, though. Working with the crack cinematographer Ed Lachman, Byrne brings a new visual sensibility to the screen—a respect for pared-down plainness, and an eye for how to place objects in the frame arrestingly, so that we always have something satisfying to look at. There are simple, rhapsodic images, like the sight of a string of 4-H Club kids in a field, in their bright-green T-shirts, moving in rhythm to the song "Hey Now." And there's a shot of the narrator's red convertible crossing the screen as smoothly as a toy car in a dream. The film is one superbly lighted frame after another in a relaxed, controlled pattern. And pretty soon the characters themselves begin to engage us—especially John Goodman as the big, friendly Louis Fyne, who wants a wife but describes himself as maintaining "a very constant panda-bear shape" and lacking the magical element that would make a woman love him. Louis is like the Scarecrow, the Tin Woodman, and the Cowardly Lion: he needs a wizard to do a little hocus-pocus for him. But he has the outgoingness to bring the picture partway to life. It may be Byrne's smartest move to have Louis and the narrator become pals, because their brief scenes together draw us in; the narrator's liking Louis makes it easier for us to accept the narrator himself. And the narrator is a good foil for Louis; he plays straight man to Louis and everyone else.

Aesthete and all-around multimedia artist, David Byrne, the singer and songwriter of Talking Heads, looks as if his feet had never touched earth; he may be the most distanced and the shiest of all the moviemakers who in the post-Vietnam years have gone on a quest for America. Wearing a black cowboy hat and a narrow-cut dark-green Western suit with a white shirt, Byrne as narrator materializes on a flat, bare landscape where—an image that seems intended to resonate more than it does—a little girl is playing on a road that disappears into the horizon. He's in the America of this movie but not of it. (He's like the mystical Stranger who has sometimes appeared in British plays and movies.) In his polite, formal, and slightly ghostly matter-of-fact way, Byrne is trying for something large-scale: a postmodern *Nashville*. And when you get the hang of the movie you see that his unworldly persona as narrator is of a piece with his vision. Altman's *Nashville* is imbued with consciousness of Vietnam and with the horror of the assassinations. *True Stories* stays clear of heated subjects; sex and politics (and even memories) are outside its design. Byrne is interested in American banality: in consumerism, in the manners and mores of the mall, where fashion shows are staged and miming contests are held to see who is best at lip-synching to records. (Miming is so popular it has spilled over from night clubs.) Byrne is interested in the paradox of "specialness" represented by twins—special because they come in pairs. They can be seen wandering around in the backgrounds.

Although Byrne worked closely with Jonathan Demme in 1984 on the triumphant Talking Heads-in-concert film, *Stop Making Sense*, and has directed several Heads videos, this is his first feature as a director. He attempts to organize the movie by a structure that owes as much to music as to traditional storytelling; it's risky and unconventional, and in general he brings it off. (He commits only one small visual barbarism: when he appears disguised by a dark mustache, he moves the camera in for a closeup, so that we won't fail to spot him.) *True Stories* wobbles between security and insecurity as the stories begin to mesh and the thematic-narrative logic becomes clear. Some of the performers break through Byrne's measured, clean restraint. Jo Harvey Allen's intensity gives her scenes a gleam of nuttiness. This lying woman's concentration on her whoppers has rage and abandon behind it; it's as if she were a composite of the fierce crackpots and fantasists who read the scandal sheets. And radio-head Tito Larriva's high-speed dancing has a comic dazzle. But the more normal eccentrics—the tame, peaceable ones—are duds, with less appeal than they might have in a Demme film or a film directed by Michael Ritchie. There's no comic payoff to Spalding Gray's scenes as the upper-middle-class husband who talks to his wife via their two children, and the rapidly-becoming-legendary Swoosie Kurtz, con-

217

fined to bed because the rich woman she plays can't think of any reason to get up, can't think of much to do with her role. The script, by Byrne, Beth Henley, and Stephen Tobolowsky, seems like a sly, tidy piece of work, but it flattens out the more normal crazies; the actors aren't provided with the kickers they need to point up their roles. The only one of the gentle characters who seems "special" is John Goodman's big, warm Louis the bear; he's the star of the movie, and he gets to sing the film's anthem, "People Like Us," in the one sequence that's really built up to. The song works in the movie, but what is Byrne saying in the words? "People like us/We're gonna make it because/We don't want freedom/We don't want justice/We just want someone to love." Is that meant as a parody of the woozy-mindedness of pop lyrics, or is it a preppy's observation about what "ordinary" people like Louis want? It may be both. (The nine songs by Byrne are conceived as rock or country, Tex-Mex or gospel, depending on which character sings them. The Heads provide the instrumental work, and can be heard now and then on the words; it's their voices that the lip-synchers weave and sway to.)

What's disappointing about *True Stories* is that Byrne's unconventionality is purely aesthetic. He set out to make a very precisely assembled collage, and the result suggests a mandarin's view of the Southwest. As the narrator, he shows his curiosity, but it's idle curiosity—he's looking for a droll subject and droll details. His view has no thrust, no subversion. It's as innocent as something made out of paper dolls. Is there a deep-rooted primness in Byrne, or is he so afraid of giving offense that he wouldn't let himself consider any seaminess or think any harsh thoughts about the characters—not even about the woman who has to make everything cute? His wanting to make everything odd yet benevolent is almost as limiting as cuteness. He sets up the material for satirical sequences—such as the fashion show with hugely fat, puppetlike models, with people dressed in banana leaves, Astroturf, and tiered wedding cakes, and with others in cloth that simulates building bricks—yet he doesn't give it a satirical spin. It's as if he refused to see any implications in what he shows us. His unacknowledged satire is like a soufflé that was never meant to rise.

In *Stop Making Sense*, when Byrne is working with the other Talking Heads, he's able to let go and let the music take over and transport them, and we share in their exultation. That's what Altman was able to do in movie terms in *Nashville*, and its zinging mixture of comedy, melancholy, and joyousness may waft back to you whenever you think of the picture. Byrne doesn't (yet) have that freedom as a moviemaker. The people in

True Stories have no independent life; they're pinned to the screen—all except Roebuck (Pops) Staples, as the wizard who heals big Louis Fyne by magic. Dressed in white, chanting his spells, and dancing and singing, the patriarchal Staples (who's eighty) has a juicy richness about him, as if he'd strolled over from *Nashville*. His song "Papa Legba" seems to go on its own, and when he's onscreen a viewer can be completely happy.

Not many films invoke comparison with *Nashville*. And not many new, young American directors invoke comparison with the best new directors at work now in England: Byrne, cool as he looks, may be right up there with them. *True Stories* has felicities that any director anywhere would be proud of. It's something to see, so that you can bask in its beauty and have your own complaints about it.

■

It's 1985, and Peggy Sue (Kathleen Turner), the mother of two grownup children, has recently separated from her high-school-sweetheart husband, who has been unfaithful to her. Distressed by her marital mess, she collapses at the twenty-fifth reunion of her high-school class, and when she wakes up she discovers that she has gone back in time to the spring of 1960. She enters the old house where she used to live, and sees her mother (Barbara Harris), who looks young and lovely and is amused by the way Peggy Sue overreacts to her presence. It's likely to be a blessed moment whenever Barbara Harris appears on-screen, but this moment—in Coppola's *Peggy Sue Got Married*—is bathed in special poignancy. Our pleasure at seeing the actress again is all mixed up with Peggy Sue's feelings about having her young mother restored to her, and with our imaginings of what that might be like—perhaps our own longings for the mother we've lost. This scene and a few others touch deep nostalgic fantasies before the movie settles down to the question of whether Peggy Sue, knowing what she does at forty-three, should make the same choices that she made before. Will she marry the same boy— passionate Charlie (Nicolas Cage), the only man she ever dated, and the one who got her pregnant on her eighteenth birthday—knowing that he won't go on to have the singing career he talks about, that he'll go into his father's business and turn into the man who introduces himself on television as Crazy Charlie, the Appliance King? There's never any doubt in our minds about what Peggy Sue will do, because, of course, if she doesn't marry Charlie her children will never be born.

Coppola doesn't bother much with the sci-fi aspects of the story; this is a dream movie, and it has a golden, romantic look. (Jordan Cronenweth was the cinematographer.) It has an emotional texture, too. After the hollow pyrotechnics of *One from the Heart*, in 1982, *The Outsiders* and *Rumble Fish*, in 1983, and *The Cotton Club*, in 1984, Coppola seems to be trying to get back to something more solid, something that the audience can connect with. But he's picked the wrong screenplay. This first effort by the husband-and-wife team of Jerry Leichtling and Arlene Sarner may have appeared to have the makings of an audience pleaser, but the writers haven't shaped the scenes for comedy, or for anything else—the script skitters all over the place. The plot lacks the mechanical ingenuity of a *Back to the Future* (the scenes don't snap into place), yet the characters are almost as superficial. Coppola's efforts to bring depth to this material that has no depth make the picture seem groggy. It's as if he were trying to reach through a veil of fog, trying to direct the actors to bring something out of themselves when neither he nor anyone else knows what's wanted.

Kathleen Turner gives her role a good try, but she's miscast, or, rather, it's an unwritten part—Peggy Sue doesn't exist except to worry about marrying the right man. And Turner looks self-conscious and embarrassed. She always seems to be doing something telegraphic—to be acting, acting. For most of the movie, she's supposed to be not quite eighteen, and she's trying to act young—one of the toughest things to do on camera. It's especially tough for her, because she's a womanly big woman poured into tight teen-age-schoolgirl dresses. I don't know why Coppola or the writers didn't slip in a few lines of dialogue to turn her height and fleshiness to a sexy, comic advantage. Couldn't her boyfriend have contrasted her with her petite-little-nothing schoolmates? The movie never acknowledges that she looks different from the other girls, and so we're acutely aware of it. (Turner is really good only when the joke is that Peggy Sue is much too experienced to put up with the behavior expected of her as a teen-ager.) Nicolas Cage isn't a facile actor; he works to get into his character, and he brings something touching and desperate to Charlie the small-town hotshot. But, matched with Turner's Peggy Sue, the rawboned Charlie is uncouth and callow, and his voice is funny, as if Daffy Duck had crawled into his mouth and got his teeth jammed up.

Coppola's efforts recall something that the cinematographer-writer Tom McDonough said recently:

A haunted nostalgia, sometimes sentimental, sometimes irritable, accompanies most quests for America. Perhaps memory—the genuine article, myth-piercing memory on the order of Marguerite Duras's or Gabriel García Márquez's—is a more strenuous enterprise than spinning stools in the old soda shop. Perhaps the problem is that we don't really feel nostalgic anymore; we just feel empty. Maybe America's memory is MIA.

Coppola does some nifty soda-fountain-stool spinning here when Charlie sings in a pop quintet (and winks at Peggy Sue), but he's too much of a director to be satisfied by effects like that. You feel that he's trying for something more and can't find it. The picture asks if given another chance Peggy Sue would marry Charlie again, but the question underneath that is: Should she reconcile with him, or go ahead and get a divorce? And the picture answers it the way Hollywood movies used to, by showing us that as teen-agers Peggy Sue and Charlie were physically attracted to each other—as if that meant that they were destined to live together forever, in the best of all possible worlds. I came away with the feeling that Coppola took on a piece of crap thinking he could do something with it, and when he discovered he couldn't it turned into sad crap. The tone at the end is maudlin and baffled.

■

Like Jim Jarmusch's 1984 *Stranger Than Paradise*, his follow-up film *Down by Law* is a low-key minimalist comedy about American anomie shot in black-and-white—this time by Robby Müller. The setting is the skid-row alleys of New Orleans, the hangouts of two harmless deadbeats—an ineffectual pimp (John Lurie) and an itinerant disk jockey (Tom Waits)—who become the victims of frameups and are sent to prison. Put in a cell together, they vegetate in hostile silence. They don't have the dignity of despair; they're passive and defeated, and we're meant to find their apathy (and the film's lingering over it) farcical in a hip, new manner. Everything changes when a little Italian, Roberto (Roberto Benigni), is put in with them. Roberto knows English only from the put-downs and slang phrases he has heard, and recorded in his notebook, but he misuses them comically, and he has such a hopeful expression that Jarmusch actually goes quite some distance on this, and on devices such as the little guy's getting hiccups. Jarmusch even yanks laughs by giving Lurie's pimp the name Jack and Waits's d.j. the name Zack and having Roberto get them mixed up. Jack and Zack seem interchangeable; they're so alike that they can't stand each other. But Roberto isn't anomic, like the Americans; he's a friendly, bighearted, life-loving fellow, and he tries to engage them in conversation. Pretty soon, the three of them are pals, grinning and talking together and playing cards. And soon this little life-force Italian devises a plan of escape.

The movie is like a comic reversal of those old Hollywood movies in which a high-spirited, enthusiastic American would show the dejected Europeans or Asians how to get something done. But the moviemaking itself shares in the lethargy of the two Americans, and that gives the film a cachet of modernism. (And something else does: we're meant to identify with them.) You can see Jarmusch's sentimentality peeping through. Before the arrests, Jack, at dawn, is in bed with a weary, rebellious black hooker (Billie Neal), who's partly covered by a satin sheet. (Müller knows how to light the textures of skin and satin.) Then we see another hooker on the porch of the shack, blotting out her sordid life by watching the light change. Jarmusch might deny it, but that's socially conscious poetry sneaking into his formula minimalism. A lot of other things sneak in, too, such as Roberto's recitations of Whitman and Robert Frost, in Italian. The best scene in the movie is the least characteristic of Jarmusch: it comes almost at the start, when Ellen Barkin, as Zack's girlfriend, throws a tantrum, quiets down, then gets sore again, and—wham-wham-wham!—his possessions land in the street. That's the most active the movie ever gets. When the story cries out for an action (how the men escape from prison, how Roberto skins a rabbit without a knife, and so on), Jarmusch fades away. He seems interested in the look of the actual world, but not in the world itself.

Jarmusch's passive style has its wit, but the style is deadening here until he brings in Roberto—a character out of folk humor (like old Aunt Lotte, who gave *Stranger Than Paradise* a jolt). And without the bore-dom of the first three-quarters of an hour Roberto wouldn't be so funny. Jarmusch must know he needs to expand; there are limits to how much lethargy audiences will sit still for. About the only peripheral attraction here is the writing on the walls of the cell and on just about every other wall we see; it adds up to a staggering amount of humorless graffiti until Roberto draws a picture of a window. Maybe the writing was all done by Jack and Zack.

October 20, 1986

SCORSESE'S SHOWMANSHIP

||||||||||||||||||||||||||||||||||||||||||||||||||||||||||||||||||||||||||||||||||||||||||||||||||||||||||||||||||||||||||||||||

At the end of Robert Rossen's 1961 film *The Hustler*, Paul Newman, as Fast Eddie Felson, defeated the poolroom champion, old Minnesota Fats, and then quit the game—the only thing he was really good at—rather than spoil it by truckling to the evil, crooked gambler who had staked him. Martin Scorsese's *The Color of Money*, in which Paul Newman is Fast Eddie twenty-five years later, starts off with one terrific scene after another. Silver-haired and fit-looking, Eddie is a Chicago liquor salesman who drives a white Cadillac and wears a neat mustache and natty duds; he has become a bit of a dandy (like old Fats himself). He's a likable cynical sharpie, who thinks he's a pretty shrewd judge of character and wants to give people the impression that he knows all the angles. It's the message he's trying to get across when he offers Janelle (Helen Shaver), a woman barkeeper he likes, a cheap, good booze that she could get by with if she uses the brand-name labels he can supply. And though he doesn't shoot pool anymore, that upstairs-backroom world has a tang for him that nothing else has, and he stakes young hustlers (for sixty per cent of their winnings).

The script, by the novelist Richard Price, which was shaped in confabs with Scorsese and Newman, is essentially an original screenplay using the Fast Eddie character developed in the earlier movie (and by Walter Tevis in his novel *The Hustler* and its sequel *The Color of Money*). Price's pungent lowlife dialogue makes it possible for Newman's Fast Eddie to be a sleazo who enjoys himself. Having drinks at Janelle's bar, he keeps an eye on the action at the pool tables, where a young guy he's staking is defeated in game after game by a cocky upstart—Vincent (Tom Cruise, with a thick head of hair standing up in a wedge cut), a clerk in

223

a toy store. Charged with excitement, Vincent is a kid who just likes to play; he jumps around the table and crows over his victories, while his girlfriend, Carmen (Mary Elizabeth Mastrantonio), who comes from a rough background, shows more interest in their loot. Eddie sees possibilities in Vincent the flake, and when he goes to work on Carmen, who is the kid's driving force, he has a charmer's energy. His voice is raspy—slightly sandpapery—and you can feel his snappy, rhythmic undercurrent of excitement as he tries to clinch a deal to train the kid as a hustler. He has to be a little dirty to do it: he makes Vincent feel that if he doesn't start making some dough he'll lose Carmen. Eddie the city slicker as teacher explains to them that playing pool isn't about winning and isn't about pool—"it's about money." And the three of them go on the road for a six-week tour of Midwestern pool halls, with the aim of hustling suckers, picking up a bundle, and then entering Vincent in the 9-Ball Classic, the big championship tournament at Atlantic City. Cozy in the Cadillac, Eddie tells them that the best is the one with the most money—in all walks of life.

During the first half, you may be a bit too aware of Scorsese's cold flamboyance, but Newman is like a great veteran tap dancer showing you how easy it all becomes, and the kick he gets out of acting is inseparable from Eddie's con artistry. The actor and the role carry the action along (despite some interference from an obstreperous score). And when Eddie observes the raw kid who's as dumb as he used to be, his disgusted expression helps to take us over the scenes of Cruise swaggering around during his pool matches. Cruise puts on a hotshot show that has about as much authenticity as Richard Gere's freaked-out display in *Looking for Mr. Goodbar*. Scorsese whips the camera angles this way and that and gives the kid's rock 'n' roll prancing a high-tech sheen, as if Scorsese imagined he was creating a razzle-dazzle big number. (For Scorsese, filmmaking is like popping amphetamines—which is what shooting pool is meant to be for Vincent.) But at least he keeps cutting back to Newman's reactions. In one scene, Eddie deliberately gets Vincent riled up during a match by petting and stroking Carmen in clear view of the pool table. It's perhaps the most assured piece of smiling deviltry that Newman has ever brought off; he has a wonderful lewd satisfaction—his hand moves over her backside so smoothly that you could almost weep for poor Tom Cruise, with his mousy voice and the way he overdoes poor insecure Vincent's anger.

The picture might have been a pop classic if it had stayed near the level of impudence that it reaches at its best. But about midway Fast

Eddie has a crisis of conscience, or something. It's signalled by a sudden change in his expression while he's watching Vincent during a match, and by a series of closeups in which Eddie's head seems to take over the screen. But what's going on is pretty blurry—we don't know exactly what has triggered it. And it takes a while before we gather that (a) Eddie realizes that his efforts to wise up the kid have actually been attempts to corrupt him, much like the attempts of that evil gambler who long ago tried to take the challenge and the beauty out of the game for Eddie, and (b) watching Vincent play gives him the itch again—he realizes that he hasn't been doing what makes him happy, that he wants to shoot pool, too. Stirred by these recognitions, Eddie locks his jaw, sets forth to become a man of integrity, and the joy goes out of Newman's performance, which (despite the efforts of a lot of good actors) is the only life in the movie. It's the only life, that is, except for a brief, startling performance by the twenty-five-year-old black actor Forest Whitaker as a pool shark called Amos, who talks about being a subject for experiments at a university. Whitaker might almost have been put on the screen by Cruise's enemies (if this sweet-faced kid had any). Cruise tries; he really works at it, and he's certainly a more active presence here than he was in *Top Gun*—he goes through the motions of a real performance. But there's nothing underneath his motions, and they don't mean anything to us. He's so wholesome and harmless he's like a cheerleader's idea of a De Niro flake. And he keeps flashing his big grin, but not to the effect desired. Whitaker is up there for a minute or two, and the movie vibrates. He has the inner qualities that Cruise lacks. What an actor! And what a mistake not to bring him back in the Atlantic City scenes! His reappearance was about all I was looking forward to.

Why don't we feel that itch that Eddie is supposed to be scratching? And why doesn't he look happier when he rediscovers himself and what he cares about? I think it's because Scorsese and Price have attempted to make a movie that, according to one approving magazine article, "with its themes of mortification and redemption," is linked to "many of the searingly personal Scorsese movies of the past." There's bughouse madness in this approach: Scorsese is trying to turn slick, amiable Eddie into a tortured, driven artist, suffering whatever temptations Scorsese is suffering, or—being a show-biz fantasist—imagines he's suffering. It's a bum idea, I think, to take Eddie Felson back to the tables that he swore off twenty-five years before, yet conceivably Eddie the sharpie might decide he wanted to shoot pool again and still be a juicy character—if he rediscovered the crazy elation of shooting pool to win, or if he just rediscovered the flukiness and fun of the game. But to have Eddie trying to redeem himself—to purify himself—through pool is just an artistic conceit. There's no grit in this plot development, no sleaze—nothing that Newman can turn into a tap dance. He's back to being the sodden lawyer of *The Verdict*, carrying the weight of the world on his shoulders.

It isn't really surprising that Scorsese, who tried for several years to get financing for *The Last Temptation of Christ*, should have instinctively tried to turn *The Color of Money* into a Jesus story. (Rossen lost perspective when he made *The Hustler*, too. It was swollen with windy thoughts, and George C. Scott's evil tempter seemed to be a Satan figure. But it had conviction; it was the movie that Rossen wanted to make, and it had a human scale. You could see all the picture's faults and still love it.) What's surprising about *The Color of Money* is how inexpressive Scorsese's visual style is. There has been considerable publicity about Newman's doing all of his own pool shots, and Cruise's doing all of his except one, but the way the picture is photographed they could be robots shooting pool. The matches are zap-zap mechanistic; they're impersonal, as if they'd been choreographed for the cameras without any consideration given to the players' individual qualities, and they all look the same. Scorsese is excessively conscious of his visual craft, and the images (the cinematographer is the celebrated Michael Ballhaus, who shot Scorsese's last picture, the 1985 *After Hours*) are handsome in a hyperkinetic version of the inflated, "classic" style that big-name Hollywood directors used in their prestige pictures. Scorsese shows off the dynamics of moviemaking, overdramatizing everything—punching it up. He gets high on camera movement: "Swish pan, swish pan—watch my camera go!" When Eddie and Vincent play each other for what may be the last time, the pool table is in a sumptuous mirrored salon that looks the length of the QE 2. Scorsese seems to feast on big pictorial effects, and he neglects the simple effects that might mean more to an audience. Carmen's feelings about Vincent—who's something of a simp—are never quite brought into focus. The beautiful young Mary Elizabeth Mastrantonio has a fascinating, humorous quality, but the framing makes her acting seem overcalculated. Is Scorsese so distanced from the characters that he doesn't notice that she has no light moments and that there's too much camera emphasis on her smirking-sneering wide mouth? And that Helen Shaver's Janelle has nothing to tip us to what Eddie sees in her—that she has nothing to do in the picture? Scorsese takes more care with the cue balls. It's a remarkably craft-absorbed, out-of-contact style, especially when you remember the heat and the vividness of the people in Scorsese's fevered, visionary *Mean Streets* and *Taxi Driver*. I don't think he himself believes in his "mortification and redemption" routines here. If he did, the second half wouldn't be such a letdown.

During the movie, I wondered why the sound mix was so irritating in the early sections. Richard Price's glibness is entertaining, and the audience was having a good time with Newman's small talk in the barroom—why did Scorsese have the score (by Robbie Robertson) up so loud that we had to strain to hear the wisecracks? Scorsese, who made the great rock-concert documentary *The Last Waltz* (1978) and was the supervising editor of the 1970 *Woodstock*, isn't somebody who'd be sloppy about sound. It wasn't until the picture was over that I understood the clamorous music. What was funny and likable in *The Color of Money* got jettisoned midway because Scorsese thought that that material was just marking time and setting things up. He had the music drown out some of the dialogue because he didn't think it mattered. Scorsese never got into the spirit and warmth and the beautiful canniness of Paul Newman's performance; he didn't take comfort from it, as we in the audience did. He saw Eddie's charm and slyness—what we enjoyed about him—as what had to be redeemed.

Scorsese tries to turn Eddie Felson into himself; he even tried to turn Rupert Pupkin, of *The King of Comedy*, into himself. He couldn't do it with the musicians of *The Last Waltz*, because they were right in front of him, and it's a magnificent film. But when he deals with fictional characters he carries identification over the top. Maybe he insists on making everything "searingly personal" because it's his only way of getting into a subject. Does he lack the imagination to become involved in other characters—characters with their own distinct individuality? I'd rather put it this way: his obsessiveness may be so strong that his imagination doesn't operate freely. And I'd speculate that Scorsese is still hung up on a New York street kid's confusion of aggressiveness and getting ahead and sexuality. The reason he doesn't get into the believable, appealing side of Newman's performance is that he isn't about to move into the things that come with experience. Even if he identifies with Eddie the con man, that isn't enough for him, because he sees himself as an artist. So Eddie has to be a candidate for purification. That's the purpose of the plot switches and reversals of the second half (which leave us with unanswered questions and feelings of being left out). Scorsese is probably the only greatly talented American director who can be schematic and crazily confusing at the same time. He mucks up Eddie Felson's story because he doesn't care about the fires within; when he thinks about art, he's still a downtown kid looking for flamethrowers and hard-hitting "integrity"—salvation.

But his obsessiveness has plunged him into some serious binds—like the psychodramatic morass of *New York, New York* (1977)—and so he doesn't go all the way with it anymore. He pulls back, or maybe he no longer has anywhere to go. The showmanship he exhibits here may be the only ground where he feels confident. When he plays with camera angles, he can feel like the Master he's being called.

November 3, 1986

DOUBLING UP

||||||||||||||||||||||||||||||||||||||||||||||||||||||||||||||||||||||||||||||||||||||||||||||||||||||||||||||||||||||||||||||||||||||||

For seven decades of romantic screwball comedies, sexy, smart, funny women have been waking up heroes who, through fear or shyness or a stuffy educational background, were denying their deepest impulses. The women perform a rescue mission. Sometimes, in earlier eras, they did it in the guise of dumb blondes (like Marie Wilson) or dizzy dames (like Katharine Hepburn in *Bringing Up Baby*), but mostly they were wisecracking broads, like Mae West and Joan Blondell, and Jean Harlow in *Red Dust* and *China Seas*, or they were kooks, like Shirley MacLaine, and Barbra Streisand in *The Owl and the Pussycat*. The theme of the repressed man being "brought out"—liberated—by the sexy woman is the male fantasy-equivalent of the theme of women's gothic romances, except that it's played for comedy, and that makes a big difference. (For one thing, it spares men's self-esteem: they aren't seen as yearning to be ravished.) Still, it has been worked up in so many movies that it's a familiar genre, and this may limit a viewer's initial interest in Jonathan Demme's *Something Wild*. But once you get past the disappointment of "Oh, it's a genre picture" (which can mean predictable and tame) you're likely to be struck by how authentically wild it is. The weekend spree that Lulu (Melanie Griffith, the porno star of *Body Double*) and Charlie Driggs (Jeff Daniels, the pith-helmeted explorer of *The Purple Rose of Cairo*) go on together takes the fantasy very far. This comedy isn't just about a carefree wacko-rebel heroine and a pompous man; it's about crossing over—about getting high on anarchic, larcenous behavior and then being confronted with ruthless, sadistic criminality. *Something Wild* is really screwball: it breaks conventions and turns into a scary slapstick thriller.

Charlie Driggs, who has just been made vice-president of a Wall Street firm, is gray-suited Yuppiedom incarnate. Lulu, who is done up as a bohemian vamp, in a dark, Louise Brooks haircut, a black dress, and bangles, pounces on him after she sees him pocket his check at a Manhattan luncheonette and stroll to the sidewalk. He gets a sneaky pleasure out of stiffing the restaurant: he's her man. Talking fast, she lectures him about the theft, scares him and teases him, then offers him a ride back to his office and heads in a different direction. When his beeper sounds, she throws it out of the car and tells him to take the afternoon off. Happy and hopped up, she goes into a liquor store, buys four pints of hard stuff, and, while the clerk climbs to the top shelf to get a bottle of Glenlivet for her, casually cleans out the register. Soon Lulu at the wheel and Charlie next to her are swigging down their booze, the music is on triumphantly loud, and before he quite knows what's going on he's in a motel in New Jersey, she has thrown him onto the bed, and he's manacled and chained, with her writhing in S&M gear on top of him. She's like a freakier young Shirley MacLaine; we don't know how far she'll go. But by the time she tells him that he can return to the city by bus—that she's going on to Pennsylvania—we know that he is never going back to his Yuppie life. That's about the first ten minutes, and I won't discuss the plot beyond that point, because part of the fun of the movie is in the surprises it springs. The script—a first by a former N.Y.U. film student, E. Max Frye—is like the working out of a young man's fantasy of the pleasure and punishments of shucking off middle-class behavior patterns.

Melanie Griffith's dark Lulu turns into blond, fresh-faced Audrey, who suggests Kim Novak and, a bit later, Ginger Rogers, but Griffith's tarty, funky humor is hers alone. She has the damnedest voice; it sounds frazzled and banal—a basic mid-American-girl voice—but she gets infinite variations into its flatness. She can make it lyrically flat. That voice keeps you purring with contentment. It can be as blandly American as Jean Seberg's voice was when she spoke French, and Griffith has a bland American prettiness, too. But her delicate head is perched on an intimidatingly strong neck, and she never seems innocent. (Has anybody ever looked better in smeared lipstick?) Her role ranges from confident kook to girl with misgivings to terrified woman, and I thought her amazingly believable—even in the first section, when that dark hair looks as if it could stand up without her. Jeff Daniels' performance isn't as much of a showpiece, but he brings off difficult, almost imperceptible transitions. Charlie begins as a fearful, skunky guy and then is so excited and keyed up and soused that he doesn't take in the warning signals that Audrey sends him; by the time he's in real trouble he's too exhausted to function. Daniels is playing the kind of square that we in the audience are eager to laugh at and dissociate ourselves from. Later, he has to let us understand what was inside Charlie's self-protectiveness—what an unhappy, pathetic fellow he was. And he has to do it without its ever being made explicit—without his ever asking for sympathy. (The middle-class Charlie becomes a real hero: he isn't just liberated—he's also tested.) In a third major role, Ray Liotta makes an impressive film début as Audrey's dangerous old flame Ray, who she thought was safely tucked away in prison. Demme directs the dark and handsome Liotta so that he's threatening yet you can see how appealing he could have been to her. Ray isn't just a villain. He still has the dimply charm of a delinquent who can smile and get by with a lot. He still loves Audrey, and, having lost her, he thinks he was robbed. There are suggestions of underclass anger in his menace; attempting to reclaim her, he feels righteous, justified. But even when you're frightened of Ray you don't hate him; you hate his streak of ruthlessness. Max Frye's script provides the characters with some nifty spins, such as the moment, just after Charlie has met Ray, when Ray compulsively asks a leering, needling question about Audrey's sexuality. Offended, Charlie reproves this psychopath for not behaving like a gentleman. And the psycho backs off.

Demme has a true gift for informality. It shows in the simple efficiency with which he presents these three; it shows even more in the offhandedness with which he fits in dozens of subsidiary characters. And, working with the cinematographer Tak Fujimoto (it's their sixth outing together), Demme somehow enables each of the small characters to emerge as a comic presence. I can't think of any other director who is so instinctively and democratically interested in everybody he shows you. Each time a new face appears, it's looked at with such absorption and delight that you almost think the movie will flit off and tell this person's story. And, though Demme doesn't flit off, his best movies are many people's stories. Some of the people here have sizable roles, like Dana Preu, as Peaches, Audrey's affable, pleasant-faced mother, who lives in a comfy little house in Pennsylvania and plays the spinet. Peaches has a remarkable, weirdly calm scene in her kitchen with Charlie, whom Audrey has introduced as her husband; the mother makes it clear that she isn't taken in—that she knows it's one of Audrey's games. As Dana Preu plays her, Peaches is a gloriously bland cartoon mother of us all, who is such a fount of love that she acquiesces in every folly we can dream up. Margaret Colin is striking as bitchy Irene, so envious of Audrey that she propositions Charlie. And one character in this Pennsylvania town has a shock effect on the audience: when Jack Gilpin's Larry appears and recognizes Charlie—he works in the New York firm that Charlie has risen in—it's a collision of worlds. Larry and his dour pregnant wife, Peggy (Su Tissue), who went to high school with Audrey, are a harmless enough pair; they're cartoons of a more limited nature than Peaches. (Larry is a little turned on when he sees Charlie with hot-tootsie Audrey—he thinks she could be one of the rewards of a vice-presidency.) But this surprise meeting is like something that happens in a bad dream, and we recognize how far we've got into Charlie's fantasy. Larry doesn't destroy it, though; it doesn't collapse until Charlie is in Ray's run-down motel cabin and he hears the ugliness of Ray's tone as he yells at somebody next door, and bangs and stomps on the wall. (Charlie's liberation begins with the kook; it isn't completed until he clashes with the psycho.)

Demme's spirit shines through most clearly in the bit parts, which are filled by people from his earlier films (such as Charles Napier, who turns up here as an enraged chef), friends and relatives, his production staff (his co-producer, Kenneth Utt, appears as Dad), other filmmakers (John Sayles as a motorcycle cop, John Waters as a used-car dealer), assorted actors (such as Tracey Walter, climbing up for the Glenlivet), and singers, rappers, musicians—lots of them, many black or Hispanic. The bit players are always there, in service stations and convenience stores and wherever people gather; they're in the background or at the side of the screen, providing a counterpoint to the main action. It's as if Demme were saying, "Sure, it's a genre picture, but there's all this life going on around Lulu and Charlie. They're part of something. So is Ray." And as Lulu and Charlie—with rock and reggae booming out—drive from New York to New Jersey and on to Pennsylvania and Virginia, and then head back, you get a feeling of being part of the pop life of the country, and of loving it. You don't forget that Yuppie boredom with bounty coexists with deprivation and with underclass rage at being deprived of booty—how can you, with Ray at your heels? But the movie gives you the feeling you sometimes get when you're driving across the country listening to a terrific new tape, and out in nowhere you pull in to a truck stop and the jukebox is playing the same song. Demme is in harmony with that America and its mixture of cultures.

Starting with David Byrne and Celia Cruz singing Byrne's "Loco De Amor" during the opening credits, and ending with a reprise of Chip Taylor's "Wild Thing" by the reggae singer Sister Carol East, who appears on half of the screen while the final credits roll on the other half, the movie has almost fifty songs (or parts of songs)—several of them performed onscreen by The Feelies. The score was put together by John Cale (who did the track of Demme's first picture, *Caged Heat*, in 1974, for Roger Corman); Laurie Anderson worked on this score, too, and it has a life of its own that gives the movie a buzzing vitality. Some years back, and long before Demme made *Stop Making Sense* or his videos, he said, in an interview in the now defunct *Soho News*, that "music was my first love; movies came second." He brings them together here in a light-hearted way. It's a little reminiscent of the use of music in *Easy Rider*, but it's more of a rap. The singing voices keep talking back to us in the way that they often do from car radios and tape decks, or at noisy parties. I like the doubling up of the energy sources; it turns the film into a satirical joyride. *Something Wild* is a road movie, and car music is primal American pop. How else could we live through the distances we travel? Shallow entertainment helps keep us sane. This kind of music is, in its way, the equivalent of the genre movies that are often just what we want and all we want.

Something Wild is rough-edged. It doesn't have the grace of Demme's *Citizens Band* and *Melvin and Howard* or the heightened simplicity of his *Stop Making Sense*. It has something else, though—a freedom that takes off from the genre framework. And Demme has used it to weave the stylization of rock videos into the fabric of *Something Wild*. Probably no other director could have performed this feat so spontaneously or unself-consciously; the doubling up works integrally for him—it fulfills impulses that were there in Demme right from the start of his career. And he's made something new: a party movie with both a dark and a light side.

November 17, 1986

232

FAMILIES

||||||||||||||||||||||||||||||||||||||||||||||||||||||||||||||||||||||||||||||||||||||||||||||||||||||||||||||||||||||||||||||||||||||||||||||||||||||||||||

Beth Henley's play *Crimes of the Heart* may suggest a quaint variation of early Tennessee Williams (*The Glass Menagerie* especially) or William Inge, or even Paul Zindel or Horton Foote, but it isn't bad. It has a goofy charm. Henley has a streak of campiness in her, and she curls the edges of the dialogue with Southernisms, or what we take to be Southernisms. ("How's my hair?" "Fine." "Not pooching out in the back, is it?" "No." That same non-pooched-out woman complains of a polka-dot dress she was given for her child: "The first time I put it in the washing machine, I mean the very first time, it fell all to pieces. Those little polka dots just dropped right off in the water.") The three actresses who star in the movie version—Diane Keaton, Jessica Lange, and Sissy Spacek—bring it such overflowing wit and radiance that they waft it up high. The play is thin, and the playwright's screen adaptation is just the usual "opening out," but the actresses put so much faith in their roles that they carry the movie, triumphantly. It's too bad that the director, Bruce Beresford, didn't know how to give it a push and make it spin. With these three actresses sparking off each other, he might have caught something like the whirling magic of Robert Altman's *Come Back to the 5 & Dime Jimmy Dean, Jimmy Dean*. But the movie has some élan anyway, because these women working together are something to see. They giggle over the stagy exposition, treating it like choice, well-loved gossip.

The sweet and dippy Babe (Sissy Spacek), the youngest of the MaGrath sisters of Hazlehurst, Mississippi, has shot her rich lawyer husband and faces trial. The oldest, Lenny (Diane Keaton), has been too shy to have boyfriends; at thirty, she takes care of Old Granddaddy, has a routine job, and keeps up the family home. The middle sister, Meg (Jessica Lange), may have had a few too many boyfriends; she started smoking and drinking at fourteen, and the town regards her as a tramp. Now Lenny sends word of the shooting to Meg, in Hollywood, where she has tried to make a career as a singer, and she returns. The three are united in the house they grew up in, and their childhood alliances and petty jealousies start up all over again, along with a fierce, us-against-the-world family loyalty. A friend of mine in Oregon went to see Diane Keaton in *Mrs. Soffel* at my urging, and then wrote me that "at its best *Mrs. Soffel* is about the mystery of where love and courage come from." I think it could be said that at its best *Crimes of the Heart* is about the comedy of where love and courage come from. Its goofiness is integral: it's a comedy about wacked-out normality. The characters say dumb things with such simple conviction that they seem to have a glimmer of truth. When Babe wonders "why Mama hung herself," Meg says, "I don't know. She had a bad day. A real bad day."

It's no surprise that Keaton and Lange are full-scale funnywomen; the news here is that Spacek, after all the tiresome studied acting she has been doing in recent years—she's dull as an achiever heroine or a suffering heroine, she's dull when she searches for depth—can still play on instinct and be terrific. (Yes, she was lovely and gave a fine performance in *Raggedy Man*, but it lacked the oddball zing of what she does here.) Spacek looks as if she'd rediscovered how much fun acting could be, and she isn't afraid to play a character as weird as her Carrie was. Babe verges on the bizarrely unbalanced, and the trick in playing her is to make her human—to make her motives accessible. Spacek empties the foxiness out of her face and plays this zany Babe with a propulsive sureness. Her twang gives a flourish to her lines, and when she has her star turns—a series of slapstick disasters that she has to bring off all by herself—she's *up* for them. She has real voltage here; she holds her own with big Jess and gurgly, wild-eyed Keaton—and with energy to spare.

Lange must have gained something from playing the forthright Patsy Cline in the 1985 *Sweet Dreams*. She seems liberated from the "image" fears that constrict the acting of so many stars, and any anxieties about the self-exposure in screen acting seem gone, too. It's a strong, unabashed performance. She's as confidently sexual as any American screen star past or present, and when this woman gets to shake her chassis it's some chassis. From our first view of Meg, on the bus heading back to Hazle-hurst, we know she's had some rough times. What we're not prepared for is the gusto that Lange brings to Meg's schoolgirl meannesses. Meg can't resist showing Lenny that she knows her one poor little secret, and she has no compunction about doing the dirty to Babe, who told it to her. The way Lange plays this scene, Meg enjoys her sisterly one-upmanship so much that she's rather lovable when she spills the beans. Underneath, she conveys the feeling that keeping a secret is just a piddling convention anyway. And Lange goes beyond the individual character: she leaves us with the image of a smiling tough cookie in a blue denim jacket and a short skirt that sets off her long legs—a rowdy, down-to-earth American archetype, everybody's favorite waitress. (I came to like her faded denim better and better; she wears it like a badge of honor.) Lange seems an effortless comic virtuoso here—there's no fussiness in her acting. Her soft voice has a defiant edge, and she's economical even in her delivery of the film's best line. When Babe is worried because the husband she shot has threatened to send her to an insane asylum, Meg reassures her by saying, "Why, you're just as perfectly sane as anyone walking the streets of Hazlehurst, Mississippi."

Keaton's Lenny is abashed about everything; she has so many timidities she's in a constant tizzy. Keaton is a master of high-strung unsureness; when she plays comedy, she has a miraculous gift for fumbling in character—for showing you the emotional processes that lead the character to say what she does. What makes Warren Beatty's performance in *McCabe & Mrs. Miller* stay in the mind in a way his other performances don't (not even his Clyde Barrow) is that he shows you McCabe fighting through his own clumsiness and confusion, trying to express what he doesn't fully understand. That's what Keaton's Lenny does. Her tangled feelings spill out in all directions, and what makes her a great comic presence is that she always reveals more than she means to. Babe and Meg talk about how she has been turning into Old Grandmama—Lenny wears her grandmama's sun hat and gardening gloves, and she huddles, and hides her body in shapeless pinafores. (In some ways, the play, which was first performed in 1979, is Beth Henley riding the 1977 *Annie Hall* down South.) Keaton's nervous old-maid Lenny is a much richer character than you could guess from reading the play. She's a wonderful mixture of raw shyness and unconscious, eye-batting flirtatiousness, and her "fumbling" lifts the character right off the page. Even her feeling her way into a Southern accent seems to become part of the character. And Keaton is great at playing a sense of injustice for laughs: Lenny's resentment of Meg for having been granted childhood privileges denied to the two others wells up in her uncontrollably, as if she were still thirteen. She's had so few experiences as a grownup that she keeps their childhood alive all through the movie. She's the responsible sister—a thirty-year-old hopelessly good little girl longing to be naughty.

As a cousin of the sisters—an officious bitch who's so much like Mae, the mother of the no-neck monsters in *Cat on a Hot Tin Roof*, that she comes across almost as an homage to Tennessee Williams—Tess Harper gets laughs with a minimum of waste motion. They're stagy, predictable laughs, though, and in these moments that the stars don't dominate, you can recognize how much they bring to the material. Without them, the fluidity is gone, and there's nothing but artifice; the movie stops. The director's work seems negligible (he doesn't show any flair for slapstick in the scene of Lenny flapping a broom and chasing her cousin out of the house), but it's inoffensive. David Carpenter is likable as Babe's impressionable yet hardheaded young lawyer. And Sam Shepard appears in the small part of horn-rimmed Doc—the fellow Meg ran out on when she went to Hollywood to satisfy her granddaddy's idea that she had a big career ahead, and the fellow Lenny has always had a crush on. Shepard plays his scenes with the drab seriousness of a weak man who was left in the lurch once and holds no hard feelings but doesn't intend to let it happen again. When Doc and Meg talk together, their voices are in quiet, lovers' tune; you can believe that she might have been happy with him, and that strengthens the importance of the mostly offscreen Old Granddaddy (Hurd Hatfield), who raised the girls and screwed up their lives.

The movie has a bad opening: the first scene, in which Lenny picks up Babe's things at the mansion where she shot her husband and carts them back to the MaGrath house, does more to dislocate us than to give us our bearings. And when we get our first view of the MaGrath place it's perhaps more architecturally pixillated than seems appropriate to the emptiness of the sisters' lives there. But though the moviemakers' efforts to make the play "visual" fail, the actresses give it their vitality. And they avoid the danger in Beth Henley's material—the trap that *Nobody's Fool*, which is based on Henley's autobiographical script, falls into. At her worst, Henley turns the heartbreak and boringness of small-town life into cute tics. In *Nobody's Fool*, the young heroine (Rosanna Arquette) behaves as if she were brain-damaged, but we're supposed to take her sickly romantic carrying on as an indication that she's going to become an artist. The picture dotes on her; it swoons over her while we in the audience stare numbly. *Crimes of the Heart* has some of the same mixture of looniness and lyricism, but the actresses are smart and generous and inspired. So the three women's looniness really is lyric. Lenny's *hysteria* is lyric. It's as if the three actresses said to the director and the rest of the cast, "Just back off, and let us become sisters." And they became sisters.

■

The Decline of the American Empire, written and directed by Denys Arcand, a veteran French-Canadian moviemaker, none of whose other films have been released here, is smooth and harmonious. It has an up-to-the-minute melancholy high chic, but that's also what this comedy is about, and if it leaves a viewer with mixed reactions, that may be an appropriate response, because Arcand himself has mixed emotions about what he shows us. His subject is sex in a period of social change, without the binding ties of family and religion, without sacrifice for the community or strong commitments to the future. It's sex in a period when people—aging middle-class intellectuals, at least—no longer believe in postponing pleasure. The eight principal characters—four men and four women connected with the History Department of a Montreal university—belong to a new, loose form of extended family, which includes spouses, lovers, and co-workers. On this Friday afternoon in autumn, the women, who need to keep in shape in order to appeal to men, work out together at a gym in the city while the men, gathered at a lakeside cottage, prepare trout coulibiac for a festive dinner. Both groups talk about sex, and when they're together in the long evening they go on talking about sex, but more discreetly—with less bravura.

There is only one married couple in this intellectual fellowship: slender, fastidious Louise (Dorothée Berryman), who looks like the stunning Parisiennes in old French movies and is the most conventional of the women, has been married to the pudgy, affable professor Rémy (Rémy Girard) for fifteen years. At the gym, Louise (who isn't an academic) talks about her husband as if he were a comfortable, faithful Teddy bear. Her unmarried companions—a prof, an assistant prof, and a graduate student—listen politely, though two of them know she's deceiving herself, because they've both had affairs with him. Meanwhile, the highly sexed Rémy, drinking wine and puttering about in the kitchen of the cottage (it belongs to him and Louise), is the most spirited of the conversationalists there. He may lie constantly to Louise, but he doesn't seem to lie much to himself or his friends; he's a man who lives to philander, and though the men aren't great wits (nor are they meant to be), he's very funny about his monomania.

Rémy and his buddies raise the kind of blustering questions that heterosexual men talking about sex are very likely to raise. Why do men have to go through so much hell on the dance floor, trying to come up with the right conversational inanities? Why are homosexuals so much better-looking than *they* are—or, rather, why do so many good-looking men turn out to be homosexual? They point to Claude (Yves Jacques), an art-history prof—a handsome homosexual member of the group, who, like the women, keeps himself in good shape, though he's rather listless. (Claude is perfectly convincing when he says, "The only time I feel alive is when I'm cruising.") The conversation is bawdy and enjoyable. And though Rémy is the sort of cheerful seducer that movies generally expose as spiritually empty, he doesn't appear to be a bad guy. Arcand seems to be saying, "This is how some men are. I'm not giving Rémy a vote of confidence, but I'm not putting him down, either. I'm simply saying, 'Let's get a truthful look at each other.'" And maybe he's also saying that men like Rémy and Claude aren't just led around by their sex organs—that it's their romantic imagination, their sense of possibilities, that leads them to take risks.

There are a great many crosscurrents in the story. Diane (Louise Portal), the assistant prof, feels that the early marriage she finally got out of was a setback to her career. (She cries "I'll never get tenure!" and it has a moaning echo—it's the tragedy of her life.) Diane is having a sadomasochistic relationship with a rough-guy drug dealer (Gabriel Arcand); he has covered her back with whip marks, which she displays at the gym as if they were jewels of sexual liberation. Her rough guy (this outsider is the ninth member of the cast) shows up at the cottage. And there's the pedantic Pierre (Pierre Curzi), a lazy-minded professor, who since his divorce has been lucky in his sex life: he has taken up with a beautiful graduate student (Geneviève Rioux), whom he met when she serviced him at a massage parlor.

Arcand slips in flashbacks without breaking the flow of talk or jostling the ravishing natural changes in the light at the lake. There's nothing weighty in his approach and nothing that he insists you look at. It may take a while to sort out the characters' interrelations, and those of us who are dependent on the subtitles may be a little perplexed by the nuances of the women's conversation at the gym. A couple of them rattle on amusingly, comparing the prowess of men of different nationalities around the globe, and it isn't quite clear when they're kidding and when

238

they're boasting. But these are minor inconveniences. The film is structured like a concerto for nine instruments.

Its high point comes in an act of treachery at the cottage—a case of motiveless malignity (which doesn't mean that the perpetrator has no reason for his action but that the victims haven't consciously wronged him). Dominique (Dominique Michel) is the head of the History Department and the author of a new book, *Changing Concepts of Happiness*, in which she enunciates the theory that gives the movie its misleading, ironic title—the theory that the satisfaction of personal desires becomes more important as a civilization declines. The oldest of the group, Dominique is one of the women present who have had affairs with Rémy, and, for no apparent reason beyond pique at Louise's smug conviction that the old values are intact, she mentions his adultery in front of the whole group, in very precise tones. Louise is stung and humiliated. A little later, when a young doctoral candidate, Alain (Daniel Brière), asks Dominique why she spoke up that way, she informs him—as if this answered his question—that Rémy has slept with hundreds of women, including Louise's own sister. And Louise, who overhears her, is destroyed.

That's the drama at the center of this talk film, and we understand that a subtle shift in all the relationships will now be necessary. We feel the foreground action and the flashbacks that have been providing the background begin to merge. Tennessee Williams is a touchstone for this movie, too, because in a Williams play Dominique's act would be regarded as deliberate cruelty, and hence a sin. Here her puncturing of Louise's pride and her betrayal of Rémy (which is perhaps her way of punishing men in general) are treated as part of the texture of modern promiscuity. Nobody is being judged—not even the American Empire is being judged. It's a very unassuming picture; it doesn't even suggest that imperial decline is such a bad thing.

Yet you feel a chill. The movie leaves you sad, chastened. The revelation that affects the brisk, brittle Louise comes in the evening, and, with the exception of Diane, who has left with her bruiser, the members of the group go off to their beds—Rémy with two sleeping pills, Pierre with his luscious masseuse, the tireless campaigner Dominique with her new conquest, Alain—and are all there in the morning. Louise spends the night weeping, held and comforted by Claude. It's as if she had just been forced to grow up and face what the other people there who have reached her age have come to know—that the old dreams won't hold.

The morning is calm, with Louise in dark glasses to hide her red eyes, and Rémy coming out of hiding, and their friends providing support.

Louise has been deprived of her illusions, that's all. The others lost them, too, and they're having a good time—they're not suffering. But a viewer can't shake off the lonely feeling in the air.

December 15, 1986

THE GOOD, THE SO-SO, AND THE UGLY

Carroll Ballard's new *Nutcracker, The Motion Picture* is poised at that moment in childhood when a little girl longs to go to the adults' parties and be treated as a lovely young lady but also wants to escape and run upstairs to play with her toys. It's set inside the mind of a child as she teeters between one world and the other and gets them magically scrambled. It's a fairy-tale Christmas-party movie that avoids the confectionary innocuousness we may be afraid of when we hear the words "The Nutcracker." We're saved because the designs, by Maurice Sendak, have his lowdown, bad-boy klunkiness. We're saved because Ballard has a marvellous sense of proportion and of scale. He doesn't try to turn this holiday show into an ethereal transcendent experience. He doesn't enlarge Dr. Stahlbaum's household to infinity; he retains the stage frame and two-dimensional sets, using them for their own comic, cardboard appeal. So you're never in doubt about where you are: you're watching a mime-ballet, a piece of theatre. And for the first half you're in the rooms where the good bourgeois Stahlbaums are celebrating Christmas, and where the little Clara (thirteen-year-old Vanessa Sharp) is delighted by a nutcracker, in the form of a grimacing, toothy soldier, that falls from the tree.

After the old friend of the family, the one-eyed toymaker Herr Drosselmeier (Hugh Bigney), has distributed his gifts for the other children, he brings in his big surprise for Clara: a doll house—a miniature Byzantine palace. She peers into its chambers and sees a ballerina doll in a tutu. Drosselmeier winds it for her—the dancing doll is Clara grown up (the tall young Patricia Barker, as princesslike as any young girl's dream of herself). Clara and her brat of a brother, Fritz (Russell Burnett), who is a chubby little terror, both peer into the palace as a handsome soldier doll does a sword dance. When the party is over and Clara is asleep, she and her nutcracker-cavalier, a mustachioed, swashbuckling fellow (Wade Walthall), sail over make-believe seas on which a toy fish frolics, and arrive at the palace, where the second half takes place. It's ruled by Herr Drosselmeier—only now he's the Pasha, in a gigantic, funhouse turban, who controls the universe. He entertains Clara with such pleasures as dervishes and commedia clowns and a sinuous dancing peacock, who is Clara's mother (Maia Rosal) and is like an erotic essence. Best of all is a dancing tiger with clumping paws and the big head of a stuffed animal; it's crowned by a gigantic fez.

Drosselmeier is the key figure in this interpretation of the E.T.A. Hoffmann story—which is danced by the Pacific Northwest Ballet, and is based on the production, choreographed by its artistic director, Kent Stowell, and designed by Sendak, that had its première in Seattle late in 1983. Tall, skinny old Drosselmeier, with a bumpy long nose, a witch's jutting chin, and wisps of white hair flying, doesn't do anything threatening to Clara; he's her godfather, and he'd do anything to please her. Yet he frightens her. He's eccentric, he's careless of his appearance, and he wears an eyepatch—that's scary just on its own. There's something more, though, that makes the little girl, with her expressive face and rabbity grin, shy away from him: this man who labors to make her wonderful gifts wants to please her too much. She senses the intensity of his feelings. At a time when she's beginning to feel romantic stirrings for cavaliers and princes, this creepy old man's devotion makes her uncomfortable in a way it didn't when she was smaller.

There's nothing lustful or sexual about Drosselmeier, but Clara's fearful feelings help to darken the film's tone. We begin to wonder: Is he perhaps malevolent? No, he's tender and uncertain around her, and no more than a little spitefully prankish upon occasion. He's just a solitary, strange-looking old craftsman. But what freezes her smile when he's around isn't just imaginary: she's responding to the needs he satisfies by making toys. This *Nutcracker* has its Mouse King and plenty of other Fritz-size rodents, and its waltzing Flowers and whirling Snowflakes and batteries of toy soldiers. It also has some of the confusions that are part of growing up. They're stylized and played out on a proscenium stage, so they're not fearsome to the audience. (They're not fearsome in Sendak's books, either.) But they give this dance movie a more suggestive emotional texture than you expect from a *Nutcracker*. Clara clings to childhood (with its perils), has her dreams of romantic fulfillment—but only

241

as a princess—and fights off the kinds of recognition that growing up involves. And you can identify with her in a way that you didn't expect to.

Despite my admiration for Carroll Ballard's films, I didn't look forward to this one: the music may be (as we've all been informed) a great ballet score—perhaps the greatest—but it's familiar to the point of pain. Yet Sendak's tiger in his fez and the dancers' luminous floating tulle skirts and the many cheerful felicities of well-trained performers who seem too engaged in what they're doing to worry about perfection make it all seem fresh. (And I didn't mind the music when its candyland associations were gone.) There's a sensuousness about seeing ballet on a big screen; Ballard's camera seems weightless, but the dancers have more weight than dancers have on TV—where they're disembodied. (There isn't enough gravity on that light little planet.) And this filmed *Nutcracker* has an enchantment that's distinct from that of the stage versions—even, no doubt, from that of Stowell's production. Although Ballard had only two weeks with the company in which to shoot the movie, the way he cuts into the dancing leaves you feeling that you know what the bodies are doing when you're seeing just the faces. It's as if you saw the dancers up close without any interruption of the movement—the dancing is in suspension. That's another way of saying that he has prepared you. He keeps the whole production moving the way the dancing moves, and you become familiar enough with the film's choreographic pulse to carry the awareness over: you see the dancing with your sensory memory even when it's interrupted.

This *Nutcracker* is about transformation, and maybe we need the cut-ins: Clara the sprite is watching herself being transformed, and watching her way of seeing the world change. The dance is what is being lived through, and we need to see the faces—to see the characters react to what is happening to them. Maybe that's why when we see a full-screen image of the little girl sleeping, with the figures she's dreaming about superimposed on her, the movie seems to be saying it all. Clara is a caterpillar watching herself turn into a butterfly.

Ballard doesn't distort his vision to get into the spirit of a child teetering between worlds—that's how he sees. That's how he was able to make *The Black Stallion*. In that film, the boy's Bucephalus storybook formalization of what he experienced was a process comparable to Clara's. But there it was the world of nature—of water and sunlight and a horse that was transformed magically. Here, it's an inner world represented by painted sets and costumes. Ballard's child-adult sensibility gives the

Sendak designs a quality that's different from the humor in Sendak's books: Ballard's is a more formal yet more mysteriously chaotic sensibility, pre-verbal, somehow—an ideal sensibility for a movie that tells its story primarily in non-verbal terms. The landscape of this film is childhood before the hormones begin to rage. Yet your responses to things are already being affected. You have strange thoughts about dirty old men who compete with princes, and you accuse the old men of putting rodents in your dreams. But the accusation itself is part of a dream.

■

There was a flash of the earlier Jane Fonda—Jane Fonda the actress—in her last picture, the 1985 *Agnes of God*, right in the middle of the porridgy wars between reason and faith. Fonda, a psychiatrist, is at a sanitarium visiting her fuddled, disoriented mother, and the old woman mistakes her for her other daughter, Marie—her favorite, who died in a convent. The level, dry tone in which Fonda corrects her—"I'm Martha, Mama"—has enough scratchy desperation in it to nick your insides. That bit of acting was token evidence that even after almost ten years of dull, constricted performances (in *Coming Home, Comes a Horseman, California Suite, The China Syndrome, The Electric Horseman, Nine to Five, On Golden Pond, Rollover*, and, for TV, her misguidedly noble *The Dollmaker*) Fonda wasn't to be written off. In Sidney Lumet's *The Morning After*, she shows that her talent may be intact. The movie is far from a first-rate vehicle, and her role doesn't allow for much range; it doesn't do her justice. But her down-in-the-dirty performance has some of the charge of her Bree in *Klute*, back in 1971 (when she was only thirty-three), and her Gloria in the 1969 *They Shoot Horses, Don't They?* and her Lillian in parts of the 1977 *Julia*.

Fonda's Alex is a bright woman who has squandered her life. A former screen actress whose career blew up in scandal, she still has her face and her figure, but she has a hard, tortured look under the fluffy blond hair. She's a lush, with an ugly temper and an angry, defensive humor that's directed against everything. (Fonda has said that she modelled the character on the starlet Gail Russell, who, at thirty-six, was found dead in her apartment, among empty liquor bottles.) Hanging on in L.A., Alex drinks so much she has blackouts, and in the opening scene she wakes up in bed Thanksgiving morning with a man she can't remember ever meeting. The sheets are soaked with blood, and there's a knife sticking out of his heart. Shaken, she goes into the next room—the dead man's streamlined photography studio, decorated with pictures of women bodybuilders, who were his specialty—and then Fonda does something that's so right it's beautiful. Seeing a white kitty there, Alex says "Hi" and makes a move toward it, as if to pet it or take it in her arms. This instinctive, yearning movement toward the ongoing normal world—it's as if the cat could wake her from the horror in the bedroom—lasts only part of a second, but it alerts us that Fonda is using her imagination, along with the rest of her acting equipment. She moves with a tense grace, and her slender body (no one could accuse her of not being in shape) suggests Alex's cowering devastation: her life is in ruins over someone she doesn't even recognize. Fonda seems smaller in this role— maybe because tough, knowing Alex is frightened from the moment she opens her eyes, and maybe also because she's working opposite the sizable Jeff Bridges. He plays a former Bakersfield police detective now down on his luck who (literally and symbolically) fixes things that people have thrown out; he gives her a lift in his low-rider '56 Chevy when the police have taken her Mercedes.

Fonda is terrific to listen to; her crackling precision carries a number of the scenes. And she has a great lower register. She gives Alex a husky barroom voice, with low tones so raucous that they rival one's memories of the suggestiveness of Tallulah Bankhead's baritone. At one point, though, she uses a virtuosic voice change for a misdirected, cheap effect. Panicked about the murder, Alex tries to buy a plane ticket for San Francisco, but the holiday traffic is heavy and there are no seats. She begs an airline supervisor for help, claiming that she must get there to be with her child who's dying, and she has him fooled. But when he's stewing about how he's going to find space for her on a San Francisco flight she suddenly drops her voice down to a whorehouse madam's belly button and says, "How about Vegas?" She's probably supposed to be so fed up with her own maudlin fakery and the supervisor's compassions that she just cuts through the crap. But the way it comes across, just flat out, you say to yourself, Why is Alex deliberately destroying her own credibility? Is it just so the picture can get a laugh? In this sequence, as in many others, the actors seem to be playing to the audience rather than to each other.

The Morning After moves along, and so it seems fairly efficiently directed—up to the last half hour or so. Then there are some scenes that are staged miserably, and you realize that Lumet has been coasting on Fonda's performance and the tart, tawdry dialogue. The script, attributed to James Hicks (a pseudonym for the actor turned movie-and-theatre producer turned writer James Cresson), carried Jay Presson Allen's name as co-writer at one point, carried David Rayfiel's name as sole author for a while, and was probably worked on by others as well. Much of the dialogue has a polished bitchiness, but the talk doesn't go anywhere. (Is this because of the many hands?) When the characters say bright things to each other, they seem to be treading water. And when the film tries to supply an emotional background for Alex and her Bakersfield boyfriend—as in the revelation that he collects junk-store secondhand books, including the Nancy Drew stories, which she once loved—what does it mean? That they're both lost souls? You can't even be sure that scenes like this are false notes, because who knows what they're being false to?

The director has missed too many chances to shape the scenes. He hasn't built the thriller elements that would give the film the kick it needs, and he fails to establish a couple of the important characters: Raul Julia as the Hispanic owner of a swank beauty salon, and Diane Salinger as a Bel Air socialite. (It doesn't help that they're both miscast.) Raul Julia doesn't show the drive that his role calls for; he seems phlegmatic, blobby. As for Diane Salinger's socialite, the structure of the plot suggests an L.A. heiress out of Raymond Chandler, but the part is played as if Lumet's vision of "society" were fixed forever by the upper crust he saw as a child, in thirties movies. When he's called upon to stage a dinner party of socially prominent people, he gives us a frozen-faced collection—stiffs in full formal regalia. This dinner party isn't just misdirected, it's completely undirected; the actors might be sleepwalking. Some of the film's ideas are stiffs, too—such as the underlying notion that a rich socialite will just naturally be believed in court. (Like Patty Hearst?) And the picture features a Sergeant Greenbaum (Richard Foronjy), a wheezingly good-natured Jewish cop—another antique. Among the minor players, the good, muted performance by Kathy Bates, as an artist neighbor of the dead man, is a rarity.

All the forced, phony elements come together at the end and bring the picture down. Jeff Bridges, with his solidity, could be a good foil for Fonda's flare-ups, and if their relationship had been developed maybe they would be more vivid and resonate a little, and would survive what was happening around them. But too many of their crucial scenes go by in a blur. And there are too many gaffes. When the Bakersfield deadbeat

245

is injured and Alex visits him at the hospital, he's alone in a semi-private room. It's in this spacious room that we're supposed to grasp that their feeling for each other is based on the affinity of people who have hit bottom.

■

The Marine Corps has been getting a bit of a tweaking from the press for refusing to give its imprimatur to Clint Eastwood's *Heartbreak Ridge* and for its decision not to use the film as a recruiting tool, as the Naval Air Force used *Top Gun*. But no doubt there'd be a full-scale ruckus in the press if the Corps had approved this orgy of baroque obscenity. It's well known that many people have strong feelings about anal intercourse, but it's doubtful if a whole movie had ever been devoted to the expression of those feelings until now. And the scriptwriter, James Carabatsos, comes up with phrases so florid and complicated that Eastwood, the director and star, has trouble getting his tongue and lips around the ornate threats he spits out. Eastwood plays (so to speak) a Medal of Honor winner from the Korean War and a decorated Vietnam vet—a Marine gunnery sergeant whose abhorrence of being put in a passive sexual position seems to be what makes him super-tough and manly. The marines in his platoon stand waiting while Old Gunny wraps his jowls around witless scurrilous insults, all involving what he's going to shove up their orifices. When he's at his most refined, he addresses them as "ladies"; you can hear the depth of contempt in his tone, and see his canny, satisfied look—the poor devil thinks he's being clever. This should be the portrait of a pathetic vulgarian militarist with terrible anal-aggressive problems, but Eastwood presents him as a great fighting man, a relic of a time when men were men.

Gunny wants to turn his "ladies" into fighting marines—so they won't lose the next war. And when Grenada comes along, in 1983, they're ready. The enemy are faceless Cubans with Russian rifles. Gunny shoots one of them, who falls face down. Our warrior hero finishes him off with shots in the back, takes a cigar from the dead man's breast pocket, says "Cubans," and puts it in his mouth. And when Clint the realist sees that his men have fought like true marines he lights it, and smokes it luxuriously. The picture celebrates Grenada as a victory that evens the score, after a tie in Korea and a loss in Vietnam. It would take a board of inquiry made up of gods to determine whether this picture is more offensive aesthetically, psychologically, morally, or politically.

Variety, which says of *Heartbreak Ridge* that it "will satisfy Clint Eastwood fans," doesn't make any mention of Gunny's scatological obsession, but Marsha Mason, who delivers a few standard epithets, is described as "his foulmouthed ex-wife." The reviewer seems as benighted as Gunny, who reads such magazines as *Vogue* and *Harper's Bazaar* in order to become more sensitive about women and win this ex-wife back. As a director, Eastwood shouldn't bring up issues of sensitivity. In one scene, Gunny, on a bus trip, loiters too long at a bus-stop coffee shop, and is left behind. The waitress can hardly believe her good luck; she unbuttons her blouse and when he goes outside follows him, licking her lips in anticipation.

December 29, 1986

LITTLE SHOCKS, BIG SHOCKS

*L*ittle Shop of Horrors is jivey, senseless fun. The stupidity is appealing, the way it is in great comic strips. These moviemakers aren't trying to edify us or make us see beauty in the skid-row settings—they're just out to make us feel brainlessly slaphappy gaga. The film is taken from the Off Broadway musical that was based on Roger Corman's 1960 quickie—he is said to have shot it in two days and a night, from a script that Charles Griffith threw together. (Corman's picture didn't originate in a flight of imagination; it came out of sheer expedience—he was offered the set.) It's impossible to guess what made Howard Ashman (words) and Alan Menken (music) think there was the basis for a stage show in this junky travesty of sci-fi genetic-mutation pictures, but they had a historic Pop insight: they understood that the show's appeal would be in its undisguised mental deficiency.

Nothing in the new movie, directed by Frank Oz, is realistic. This is still a stage musical on exaggerated sets with exaggerated people. It takes its period from the date of the Corman movie, and its setting is the downtown-Manhattan skid row of reddish tenements and overstuffed garbage cans, with singing winos curled up in doorways, and vocalizing bag ladies, and a Greek chorus of three cheeky black girls—teen-agers who hang out on the streets, wiggling like chorines and commenting on the action in the Motown-Supremes sound of the period. Smooth and knowing, these lollipops like to view the street action from the corner in front of Mushnik's Flower Shop, but Mushnik (Vincent Gardenia) chases them away, even though there are no customers for them to annoy. Business doesn't pick up until Mushnik's assistant, Seymour (Rick Moranis), puts in the window a strange little flowering cactus, potted in a coffee can, that he bought from an ancient Chinese after a total eclipse of the sun. The plant, which lures customers and changes the fortunes of Mushnik, Seymour, and the shop clerk Audrey (Ellen Greene), is a carnivore, but only Seymour, who takes care of it—and lets it suck blood from his fingertips—knows that. This suggests musical Grand Guignol, but the Guignol aspects are tame. The movie isn't out to horrify you; it uses humor to turn shock into bliss.

Ellen Greene's platinum-blond Audrey arrives for work with a shiner, and in her idea of proper attire for a salesgirl: stiletto heels and the black femme-fatale dress of forties thrillers, with neck scooped low. Her clothes look laminated to her body, which is so frail, narrow-shouldered, and tiny-waisted that you can't believe the fleshy boobs that puff out of her décolletage. She might be a mutation, like the ravenous plant, and Seymour, who adores Audrey, christens his prize specimen—which has a shark mouth, like hers—Audrey II.

Ellen Greene seems to have created the sexpot-waif Audrey out of some dreamy dementia—she's not like any other heroine you can think of. Audrey is so romantic she isn't quite all there. She "dates" a biker-dentist, played by a dark-haired Steve Martin—a sadist who leaves her battered after every encounter. But she pines for considerate Seymour— the gentleman nebbish. (When he's overexcited, she slaps him smartly and lisps, "You're hysterical.") Ellen Greene originated the role, and played it for eighteen months in New York and Los Angeles and six months in London; it has perhaps got overly stylized—it's a little rigid. Frank Oz might have helped to compensate for her familiarity with the part by suggesting the kind of subtlety and nuance that the camera can pick up (and he might have compensated for the general airlessness of the studio-set musical by more fluidity in the production). But this is niggling; in its own broad, blatant terms, the movie works. And Ellen Greene is a weird little wow. Ever since I saw her in Mazursky's 1976

Next Stop, Greenwich Village, I've been in thrall to her talent. "Thrall" may be the word for it, too, because she seems to wrap a hypnotic state around herself; watching her, you just about enter into it. When she shifts from her mousy little-Audrey manner of speech to her big Broadway singing voice (it's like pent-up passion being released), you're even more transfixed—you don't know where that sound can be coming from.

Greene in her trance-state cocoon gives the movie its peculiar aura. She's an authentically peculiar diva, like Bernadette Peters. With a more conventional ingénue—one who didn't twist knots into the dumb-blonde stereotype—it might collapse. Audrey is oddly valiant, and she's matched up well with Moranis, who's very appealing here. It seems right that when these two look at each other they see their romantic ideals. And though the picture might have gained if the naïveté of their romance, which is fine at the start, had developed, the cartoon characters that don't change are O.K., too. These two are balanced against the much wilder cartoons played by Steve Martin and, in a brief but glorious turn, Bill Murray. Their sequence together is a classic encounter between sadistic dentist and pain-freak patient; when you see it, it's like stumbling on a piece of historic footage, like an encounter between legendary crazies such as Bert Lahr and Joe E. Brown. Martin's dentist is a confident brute until this scene. He plays his status-conscious professional man like a mad satire of Elvis Presley in his concert entrances, when he stalked onstage as if to assault the audience. But when this sadist comes up against Murray, who's even more bughouse than he is, he's undone. And when Murray, in the dentist's chair, climaxes and grabs Martin's shoulder Martin is enraged and disgusted. Furious that the patient enjoyed the pain, he throws him out. It's a piece of transcendent slapstick. Murray plays the masochist so tenderly that through sheer force of imaginative lunacy he's practically the star. (And Martin helps to redeem himself for *Three Amigos!*)

At first view, Audrey II is small and rather feminine: it has something creepy yet coquettish and alluring about it. And it seems to have its own light source—it suggests star quality. Seymour talks to plants, of course, and this one answers. It demands "Feed me! Feed me!" and Seymour, suckling it with his blood, shows a screw-loose humility. Audrey II grows quite a bit before it's unmistakably male and orders Seymour around in the deep, rumbling basso of Levi Stubbs, the lead singer of the Four Tops; it's a threatening big black bopper that sings, "I'm a mean, green mother from outer space." As the plant grows bigger, the joke doesn't, and Audrey II becomes more mechanical-looking. But Stubbs' growl is

249

awesome. And there's at least one neat gag: Audrey II uses a tendril to dial the telephone. And there's a wonderful comic-strip image of Audrey II surrounded by its offshoots, all of them singing, "I'm a mean, green mother."

Oz, the Muppeteer, isn't an experienced or, from the evidence here, an especially talented film director, and you have to be willing to accept a movie that's all smack in front of your face; you might almost be glued to a puppet theatre. But it goes from one plot-advancing smash number to the next, and it has wonderful details. There's a skid-row parody of Busby Berkeley with the street people definitely not in symmetry—they're all askew. And a shot of the dentist seen from inside a patient's full-screen mouth—Steve Martin is like a little devil with his pitchfork tools. The three streetwise teen-agers (Tichina Arnold, Tisha Campbell, Michelle Weeks) wear witty girl-group dresses and girl-group smiles; they prance right into the shop where something awful is happening and slink out again, carefree figures of doom. Comic actors drop in for bits: John Candy is almost terrific as a Wolfman Jack–style radio host; as the first customer to be attracted by little Audrey II in the window, Christopher Guest flashes a bright, sweet smile.

The movie has an elusive midnight-movie feeling to it. It's nothing but blown-up cartoon-style friskiness, and it keeps slugging you. But it makes you feel as inexplicably sappy and contented as a kid used to feel on Sunday morning lying on his stomach reading the funnies. Only, this is bigger, brasher, with its own kind of higgledy-piggledy ecstasy.

■

Oliver Stone, who wrote and directed *Platoon*, based on his own experiences, dropped out of Yale at nineteen, taught Chinese students in Vietnam, did a stint in the merchant marine, and finished a novel (in Mexico), which he couldn't get published. Feeling, he says, that he needed to atone for his life of privilege and his individuality—that he had to be an anonymous common soldier—he enlisted in the Army, and on his twenty-first birthday, in September, 1967, he was on his way back to Vietnam, where he saw action with the 25th Infantry along the Cambodian border. In the next fifteen months, he was wounded twice and decorated twice. He came home, he acknowledges, a freaked-out pothead;

at one point, his stockbroker father paid off some people to get him out of jail for marijuana possession. In 1969, he enrolled in the N.Y.U. film school, where he had Martin Scorsese as a teacher and pulled himself together. "Scorsese gave me film as a way to use my energies," he said to Peter Blauner in a recent interview in *New York*. We can surmise that Stone became a grunt in Vietnam to "become a man" and to become a writer. As *Platoon*, a coming-of-age film, demonstrates, he went through his rite of passage, but, as *Platoon* also demonstrates, he became a very bad writer—a hype artist. Actually, he had already proved this in his crude scripts for *Midnight Express* and *Scarface*. (He was also co-writer of *Conan the Barbarian*, *Year of the Dragon*, and *8 Million Ways to Die*.) Stone has an action writer's special, dubious flair: his scripts have drive— they ram their way forward, jacking up the melodrama to an insane pitch. Luckily, he's a better director than writer.

Salvador, the early-in-1986 film that Stone directed and co-wrote, had a sensationalistic propulsiveness, and a hero (James Woods) whose hipster hostility was integral to the film's whole jittery, bad-trip tone. I don't think *Platoon* is nearly as good a movie. Although Stone was born in 1946, this is like a young man's first, autobiographical—and inflated— work. Written in 1976, eight years after his war experiences, the script is swamped by his divided intentions: he's trying to give us an account of what it was like to be an infantryman in Vietnam in 1967–68, and to present this in all its immediacy and craziness, but he's also trying to compose a requiem for that war. The results are overwrought, with too much filtered light, too much poetic license, and too damn much roman-ticized insanity.

The picture begins with an epigraph from Ecclesiastes ("Rejoice, O young man, in thy youth!"), and then the music, Samuel Barber's "Adagio for Strings" (which was used so chastely in *The Elephant Man*), comes on in a soupy orchestration by Georges Delerue—and the movie is gran-diloquent before it even gets rolling. The first images draw us in, though: Charlie Sheen's twenty-one-year-old Chris Taylor—the Oliver Stone character—arrives in the confusion of Vietnam, and the plane that brought him is loaded with body bags for the return trip. Just about everything to do with Chris's initial disorientation, his getting to know the men in the platoon, and the pre-dawn jungle ambush in which he sees the enemy advancing but is paralyzed with fear and can't warn the other men, and then is wounded, has dramatic life in it. So does the small talk. There's a good, if perhaps too eloquent, sequence with the men in a hooch, drink-

251

ing and doping, listening to rock 'n' roll and dancing; in a psychedelic, homoerotic bit, an older soldier blows pot smoke through a rifle and Chris inhales it—it's like the seductive smoke-through-the-prison-wall in Jean Genet's *Un Chant d'Amour*. And there's a fine, scary scene in which the men are attacked in their foxholes and the bursts of fire are like a light show in the middle of a nightmare.

There are scenes unlike any I've seen before, in which we can see the soldiers' frustration, and how they're caught in a revenge fever. Then, when they take a small village suspected of aiding the Vietcong, their rage against the villagers builds in waves and finds release in violence against animals, a helpless grinning idiot, women, children. The film shows Chris taking part in the cruelty and then gaining control of himself, and grasping at first hand what many of us at home watching TV grasped—that whether the Vietnamese won or lost in the fight it was what we were doing to them that was destroying us. The film is about victimizing ourselves as well as others; it's about shame. That's the only way in which it's political; it doesn't deal with what the war was about—it's conceived strictly in terms of what these American infantrymen go through.

Platoon has many things to recommend it, but its major characters aren't among them. Chris is a pleasant-faced blank—not the actor, the character—and, regrettably, he narrates the movie by reading aloud the letters he writes home to his grandmother. You might think that Stone would be too hip to add the explanatory emotions this way—particularly after Sheen's father, Martin, recited the tormented, purploid prose that Michael Herr wrote for the narration of *Apocalypse Now*. The voice-overs here are perhaps even more stupefying, since they're easier to comprehend. They're populist sentiments reminiscent of the Joad family conversations in *The Grapes of Wrath*.

Well here I am—anonymous alright, with guys nobody really cares about—they come from the end of the line, most of 'em small towns you never heard of—Pulaski, Tennessee, Brandon, Mississippi, Pork Bend, Utah, Wampum, Pennsylvania. Two years high school's about it, maybe if they're lucky, a job waiting for 'em back in a factory, but most of 'em got nothing, they're poor, they're the un-wanted. . . . They're the best I've ever seen grandma, the heart and soul—maybe I've finally found it way down here in the mud—maybe from down here I can start up again and be something I can be proud of, without having to fake it, be a fake human being. Maybe I can see something I don't yet see, learn something I don't yet know.

252

It's like some terrible regression. Stone's gone back to being a literary preppy.

He's thinking like a preppy, too. Chris finds two authority figures in the platoon: the two sergeants, who were once friends, and are personifications of good and evil. Willem Dafoe's Sergeant Elias is a super-sensitive hippie pothead, who cares about the men—he's a veteran fighter who's kept his soul. Tom Berenger's Sergeant Barnes is a kickass boozer—a psycho, whose scarred, dead-eyed face suggests the spirit of war, or the figure of Death in a medieval morality play. The movie is about the miseries of Nam, but it's also about the tensions that develop between the factions in the platoon who line up with one or the other—Love or Hate, Life or Death, Christ or the Devil. And it's about Chris's learning—and, worse, telling us—that "we weren't fighting the enemy; we were fighting ourselves," and, yes, that he feels "like the child of Barnes and Elias."

This melodramatic shortcut—and Stone's reduction of all the issues of the war to make them fit the tags "good" and "evil"—may make you wonder if he is using filmmaking as a substitute for drugs. (The picture itself, in representing the heads as the good guys, makes a case for the socializing, humanizing qualities of dope; God Himself seems to be on the side of the dopers.) Stone is in such a hurry to get a reaction out of us that he can't bother to create characters with different sides. The two sergeants are posed and photographed to be larger than life, but the roles are underwritten. Dafoe's tough, courageous Elias is like a young Klaus Kinski playing innocent miss, and Berenger's glamorous, scarred-up Barnes, who has been shot seven times but can't be finished off until he wills it, looks as if he were a killing machine carved out of jagged rock, though he moves with a slithering grace. The two are mythic figures out of nowhere—Elias who's high only on drugs and goodness, Barnes who's high on war. The men in the platoon may suddenly be trashed by a line. Round-faced Forest Whitaker, who plays gentle Big Harold, is going along all right until after the atrocities against the villagers, when he has to say, "I'm hurtin' real bad inside." That's the end of his performance.

Stone tries for bigger effects than he earns. When he doesn't destroy things with the voice-over banalities or a square line of dialogue, he may do it with a florid gesture, such as having the Christus, Sergeant Elias, run away from the Vietcong who are firing at him, run toward a departing helicopter, which is his only chance for life, and lift his arms to Heaven. There are too many scenes where you think, It's a bit much. The movie crowds you; it doesn't give you room to have an honest emotion.

253

You knew you were getting pulp in *Salvador* because it was grungy; here the pulp is presented pedagogically, and it's made classy and meditative, but it's laid on thick—that idiot gets his head bashed in by Americans trying to wipe the grin off his face. Is it powerful? Sure it is. (This kind of routine played well in the twenties and thirties, too, when the bad guys in Westerns did it, and it wasn't as graphic then.) Stone has talent: he shot this epic in the Philippines on a tight budget—roughly six and a half million dollars. He's a filmmaker, all right, but he lacks judgment. Just about everything in *Platoon* is too explicit, and is so heightened that it can numb you and make you feel jaded. You may suspect that at some lowdown level Stone (he appears as the major blown up in his bunker at the end of the film) is against judgment. Elias is supposed to represent true manliness, but if Stone's other films tell us anything— if this film tells us anything—it's that he's temperamentally more on the side of the crazy stud Barnes. The preppy narration extolling the nobility of the common man is worse than a "privileged" boy's guilt—it's a grown man's con.

Stone's moviemaking doesn't suggest that he was a young, idealistic Chris Taylor going to war to find himself in the comradeship of the anonymous but, rather, that he was a romantic loner who sought his manhood in the excitement of violent fantasy. Stone seems to want to get high on war, like Barnes. The key scene in the movie is directed so that it passes like a dream. In a remote area, Chris calmly, deliberately shoots a fellow-soldier. There is no suggestion that Chris is an innocent corrupted by having got used to violence. The murder is presented as an unambiguous, justified execution. This oddly weightless pulp revenge fantasy is floating around in Stone's requiem, along with a lot of old-movie tricks.

I know that *Platoon* is being acclaimed for its realism, and I expect to be chastised for being a woman finding fault with a war film. But I've probably seen as much combat as most of the men saying, "This is how war is."

January 12, 1987

254

AT FIFTEEN

||||||||||||||||||||||||||||||||||||||||||||||||||||||||||||||||||||||||||||||||||||||||||||||||||||||||||||||||||||||||||||||||||||||||||

Alain Cavalier's *Thérèse* is undoubtedly a feat of some sort. The life of the young upper-middle-class nun from Normandy who died in 1897, at twenty-four, and then became a kind of ingénue saint is told in brief, mostly stationary scenes, in a richly austere visual style. The picture was shot in a diorama that doesn't have the depth of a theatre stage; it's more like a shallow platform, and the actors appear against a mottled, opaque backdrop. Except for a suggestion or two, there are no surroundings, no locations. The effect is like a series of ghostly classical paintings: illumined faces, hands, and parts of bodies, and a few objects appear from nowhere, and are then blacked out. The movie is a closed world, like that of the convent, or of a photographer's studio swathed in dark draperies.

Catherine Mouchet, a plump-cheeked twenty-seven-year-old Paris stage actress, plays Thérèse, who at fifteen was cheerfully determined to join her two older sisters in the Carmelite order. When her priest and the bishop told her she was too young, she persuaded her father to accompany her to Rome; there she petitioned the Pope, and soon afterward got permission. But some may feel that she *was* too young: the privations of convent life—she lived in a stone cell—and her own self-denial were possibly what led to her contracting tuberculosis. The mother superior had instructed her to keep a diary of her thoughts; after her death it was published, and in 1925 she was canonized and became—well, popular, as St. Theresa of Lisieux, the Little Flower of Jesus, and the model of the pure woman. (This is at least the fourth French movie she has inspired.)

What's unusual about her sainthood is that it's not about good deeds or miracles; it seems to be about her obscurity, her childlike faith, and about how gratefully she adapted to hardships—to doing without. What the movie gives us is the beaming eagerness of this girl who seems born to be a nun. She takes completely literally her marriage to Christ, and burns with love for her bridegroom. For Thérèse, carnal passion and spiritual passion seem fused. She quite explicitly wants a love higher and more intense than a mortal man could supply: she becomes a nun for the ecstasy of marrying Christ's perfection. And she appears to achieve fulfillment.

How we are meant to react is another matter. The film has a cool, objective manner; it's as detached as a case study. Yet I've never seen anything more composed, hushed, and art-conscious. It concentrates our attention on the bare, masterly images (lighted by Philippe Rousselot) that come out of the darkness, and on tiny sounds and whispered bits of conversation. The director, who wrote the script with his daughter, Camille de Casabianca, has eliminated almost everything that most movies are made up of, and what's left seems rationed—like the nuns' few possessions. In material terms, they live a minimalist life, and the film's method is almost minimalist. It, too, seeks purity and simplicity. There's almost no movement on the screen, and Cavalier rations even the colors. Blue eyes are made to look dark. Black and white, grayish green and brown, flesh tones—that's all you get, except for special emphasis, like a swatch of deep red when Thérèse bleeds at the mouth. In a scene that's unlike anything else in the film, Thérèse's father puts a glass bubble over her head. He seems to be commenting on her lack of interest in worldly matters, on the single-mindedness of her quest for sainthood, on her being sealed inside her obsession. And the whole movie is a glass bubble placed over her head.

Mouchet—she resembles the young Sally Field—is convincing as a fifteen-year-old, and seems to have the plain, open face of a guileless farm girl. Actually, her cannily underacted performance leaves almost every mood or expression of Thérèse's open to interpretation. We can't read her benevolent, straightforward look; we're kept at a distance. Her Thérèse is alive with enigmatic feelings, but after a while you know they're going to stay enigmatic. It could be thought that there's something perversely ambiguous in Cavalier's method—that the picture is an agnostically detached examination of a young teen-ager's crush on Jesus and how it kills her. Certainly there are scenes that can't make the religious-minded very happy—a reference to washing lepers and drinking the water, a close view of a nun who's in love with Thérèse as she picks up a container of the dying girl's bloody sputum and delicately dips in a finger and puts it to her mouth. Yet Thérèse herself, with her satisfied smile and the rapture she takes from her own martyrdom, has such a girlish fervor—a conviction of sublimity?—that you almost can't make fun of her; it would be like making fun of a happy afflicted child. (You may be put off, though.)

The other nuns have more worldly, grownup faces; Thérèse's cloistered older sisters, and another older sister, at home (whom she persuades to enter the order after their father dies), all have an element of sophistication about them. But Thérèse, having entered the convent so early, still has the bloom of youth on her cheeks when she dies. A doctor who is called in—too late—to examine the pain-wracked girl listens to the mother superior talk about the nuns' being *supposed* to suffer, and says, "They ought to burn this place down." Cavalier keeps scenes like this moving along fairly briskly; he never tips his hand. Still, if he weren't deliberately raising questions about the Church's glorifying young girls' infatuation with the idea of becoming the bride of Jesus, why would his presentation of Thérèse's passion be so detached? And why would a Christmas scene of a nun cradling a wooden Christ child in her arms be so creepy? It might even be thought that the convent suggests a deranged girls' boarding school with middle-aged women dedicating themselves to a perpetual adolescence. All this could, of course, be projection. Perhaps he means to tell us that if we have simple faith we can all be saints, though we remain as obscure as Thérèse. But he walls off her inner struggle (to overcome her stubbornness—what she called her "difficult" personality), and since nothing happens to her outwardly, she becomes only an aesthetic or possibly erotic object. A movie as objective as this isn't ultimately about anything—at least not anything religious.

It's perhaps a matter of temperament—rather than of religious belief—whether a viewer will find *Thérèse* a soaring, exalting experience or, more simply, an art curiosity. I'd call it an art curiosity. I was glad I saw it, but after a while its austerity began to seem as repressive as the cloistered life. Cavalier's formal, noncommittal style is too measured for you to get any sense that you're observing life in a convent. Watching *Thérèse* is more like looking at a book of photographs of respectfully staged tableaux and not being allowed to flip the pages at your own speed. You have to sit there while Cavalier turns them for you, evenly, monotonously, allowing their full morbid beauty to sink in. You're trapped inside his glass bubble.

■

Neil Simon's play *Brighton Beach Memoirs*, the first of a semi-autobiographical trilogy, had its première in Los Angeles at the end of 1982, opened on Broadway early in 1983, ran for three years, and has been licensed for over five hundred professional and amateur productions in this country alone. It has won prizes, too, and been honored in the press—in *The New York Times*, especially—as a deepening of Simon's talent, a move beyond wisecracking Broadway entertainments to something true. Now it is a film, directed by Gene Saks, who staged it for L.A. and Broadway, and some who might be expected to give it a skip may be drawn to go—as I was—by the chance to see Blythe Danner, Bob Dishy, and Judith Ivey. They certainly help. But the whole experience of this lower-middle-class-family drama set in 1937 is so drab that even these performers finally fade into the dark wallpaper. The movie is ineffably fuddy, and not just because Saks has never learned the craft of using the camera in the storytelling process. The material itself is tired.

Brighton Beach Memoirs doesn't have the noisy abrasiveness of many of Simon's earlier plays-into-films; you're not subjected to verbal exchanges that beat a tattoo on your skull. But that doesn't mean this text is an advance over those more stylized plays. In a sense, it precedes the farces: this is closer to the stale raw material that went into them. Now he's giving us near-realistic misery—what you expect from a young writer trying to be faithful to his limited experience. This could be Simon's idea of how great playwrights work: the fifteen-year-old boy who represents Neil is called Eugene, and he's the smartmouth Jewish kid as aspiring writer.

Jonathan Silverman, only nineteen when the picture was shot, plays the part, fits it, and strongly suggests a young Neil Simon; the boy gives very believable and precise readings of his lines—he's a "natural." But he's not an exciting presence. I think that he's a mistake in the role, and that the movie would gain from an actor who would bring it something different from Simon's view of himself as a stereotypical Jewish kid: an actor who would give the role some layers, maybe something strange and goony and introspective—or, at least, angry. Silverman's Eugene is too pat, too sitcom-likable and right-down-the-middle. There's no mystery in this kid—nothing that suggests the willingness to be lonely that goes into writing. Silverman certainly stays in character, though, and it's doubtful that any actor in the role would have been allowed to show any scarring. Simon and Saks seem desperate for us to see what a normal kid this is.

Eugene, who tells us the story of his life as a horny adolescent in Depression Brooklyn, lives in a small single-family house, with his mother (Blythe Danner), his father (Bob Dishy), his mother's widowed sister, Blanche (Judith Ivey), and her two daughters, and his older brother. These seven major characters include three sets of prickly siblings, but there's only one full-scale eruption, and that comes after the family, which has been scraping by, is subjected to a series of calamities: Father, who has been holding down two jobs, has a heart attack and can't work; the older brother loses his salary at the pool table; and Aunt Blanche's gentleman friend (who has seemed ready to take on supporting her and her girls) lands in the hospital. When things are at their worst, Eugene's mother suddenly blows up at Blanche and blames her for all the family's troubles. It's a venomous outburst; it poisons the atmosphere, even if it eventually "clears the air."

The real horror in this family isn't its desperate lack of money—it's the mother, in all her ghastly ordinariness. (Like her younger son, she lacks imagination.) She's lawmaker, disciplinarian, and mind reader—Eugene can't put much over on her. She's a hard woman, closed-minded and suspicious, and her suspicions generally turn out to be correct. She's a poisoner in the kitchen, too: she spends her time preparing inedible meals and insisting they be eaten. Blythe Danner, with her magnificent eyes and limbs and the intelligence of her interpretation, is a blessing in the role. She gives it a tartness and edge, and she manages to show glimmers of proprietary affection for Eugene when he sasses her. Danner dries out some of the mother's tyrannical self-righteousness and her distrust of Gentiles. And she doesn't make her too vivid. (If the role were played as warm and bosomy, you might want to retch.)

This woman who kills any possibility of domestic pleasures—it's like living with a hanging judge—would breed rage. And by any kind of dramatic logic her steaming ahead and imposing her narrow, limited world view on everyone around her would have to collide with something. But, maybe not altogether surprisingly, Neil Simon doesn't seem to know what to do with her (or with Eugene's responses to her). There isn't even a suggestion that she resents the family she dedicates herself to. The mother simply runs right over her husband, and her two sons don't even form an alliance against her. All three accept her domineering, as if that were the way home is meant to be.

On the stage, Bob Dishy has made me weep from laughing, but he has no chance to show his gift for comedy here. I was moved, though, by his ability to envelop the father in a bowed-low dignity. I wouldn't have thought it possible to give the slim part so much fullness and conviction—it's a very fine performance. And Judith Ivey brings a sniffly, comic insecurity to Blanche that's entertaining in the early sections. (The character collapses in a misshapen scene with the mother of Blanche's Irish date, and goes further downhill in anxieties about her older daughter, who has become resentful. After a while, Blanche merely serves the plot, and Ivey is left with nothing to play.)

The film's tone is jokey nostalgia. Eugene sees the lunacy in his mother's behavior, but he sees it humorously, as if it gave him no pain. Simon is being "serious," but his techniques are like reflexes: he instinctively makes things easy and palatable. When Eugene and his brother talk about masturbation, we're supposed to be charmed by their naïveté. The gags about Eugene's sexual innocence are so ingratiating they nudge the audience to think, How things have changed! Simon makes adolescent miseries lovable, the way movies did fifty years ago. He wins over a sizable portion of the audience, but there's a penalty for making people so comfortable: it's the retrograde, pepless snooziness of the picture. You come out feeling half dead.

January 26, 1987

KILLER-DILLER

||||||||||||||||||||||||||||||||||||||||||||||||||||||||||||||||||||||||||||||||||||||||||||||||||||||||||||||||||||||||||||||||||||||||||||

Young kids often think that a lunatic is a horrible-looking bogeyman coming at them out of the darkness. But as you get older the psychopaths who plague your imagination are the smooth-faced Ted Bundys and the bland ones, like John List, the New Jersey accountant and Sunday-school teacher who arranged his 1971 disappearance so fastidiously that the five members of his family whom he left dead in his house weren't discovered for a month. He himself was described in "Wanted" posters as "6-1, 185 lbs Caucasian male, with no distinguishing features." The imagined scene of carnage at the List home provides the starting point for *The Stepfather*, which Joseph Ruben directed, from a dandy screen-play by the crime novelist Donald E. Westlake that devises a logic for the killer and follows him as he goes on his way to a new life. Jerry Blake, as he calls himself in the town he moves to, wants to be the head of an ideal family. He's an obsessive conformist, who's attracted to widows with children, in picture-postcard houses. As Terry O'Quinn plays the part, Blake has a waxen handsome ordinariness; a realtor now, he could be your trustworthy realtor in a TV commercial. But with any strain in the middle-class surface of his life—the troubles that his sixteen-year-old stepdaughter (Jill Schoelen) gets into at school, the unexpected willfulness of his wife (Shelley Hack)—his idealized vision is imperilled. And since he's a perfectionist who sees anything less than the ideal as total failure, if he can't restore an even tenor he's furiously, self-righteously angry. And he prepares to move on.

The Stepfather is a cunning, shapely thriller—a beautiful piece of construction. But it could easily be overlooked, because it has a placid surface that resembles B-picture banality. Ruben—his last film was the 1984 *Dreamscape*, with Dennis Quaid—is a craftsman, who uses this banality for a purpose. The movie is all implication: everything that's going on is held in check, and the restraint is menacing, with each scene moving quietly into the next. Jerry Blake's persona has a narrowly limited capacity for expressiveness. Ruben presents this subject by making what could be said to be a repressed movie; the excitement here is deep down—and the fun of the movie is deep down, too. Nothing is withheld from you, yet nothing happens quite as you expect. (The surprises all fit together, though.) The atmosphere suggests a Joyce Carol Oates twist on the American dream. Jerry the model citizen who's out in the open whistling "Camptown Races" becomes more frightening the more we see of him. The horror is there waiting all the time. It's in what's missing from the man we see, and the skill of the picture is that it keeps us creepily conscious of what's missing.

Ruben, whose first movies after he'd taken theatre and film courses at Michigan and got a degree at Brandeis included *The Pom-Pom Girls*, still has his affinity with teen-agers, and the sixteen-year-old girl who recoils from her stepfather's touch on her arm has healthy instincts that she can't explain. She knows right down to her toes that he's got some kind of fix on her and that he doesn't love her bamboozled mother. The scenes between the girl and smarmy Jerry have a special tension, because of her not covering up the revulsion she feels for him and because of his soft-soaping attempts to win her over. She stands between him and his dream of a perfect family life. It's a battle to the death.

They're the two main characters, and I didn't see a hitch in either performance. Jill Schoelen, a spirited, dark young beauty, has been acting since she was a child and has appeared in lots of TV and in several movies; O'Quinn has put in his time on and off Broadway as well as in TV and films. She comes through with the right raw freshness, and he with hypercontrol. We become so familiar with Jerry's steady gray-blue eyes and his eerie intuitiveness that if he momentarily flips out and loses track of which identity he's using it's like a crazy crack in a frozen lake. We're shocked: we know—just as he knows—that it can't be sealed up again. At one point, when a fissure appears he grins so foolishly it's like a giggle. At moments, he parodies his own unctuousness: strapping a corpse behind the wheel of a car, he says, "Buckle up for safety," as if he were a grammar-school traffic officer.

Jerry attempts to win his stepdaughter's affection by giving her a puppy; he's doing what the father figures on the old *SatEvePost* covers would do. His hobby is building birdhouses that are painted and divided like doll houses—he evidently intends them for birds who live respectable family lives. His carpentry tools are arranged methodically in his good-manly-dad shop in the basement. That's a *SatEvePost* cover, too, although not when he's incensed about the girl's suspiciousness and talks to himself about what a sweet little girl she is while he handles those lethal instruments. And when we get a look at a practically identical arrangement of tools in the basement of the house he lived in earlier, everything important about him seems to be buried. He seems to be alive only in these dark areas—in what's underneath "no distinguishing features."

Westlake's way of using the carnage at the start—to foreshadow what may happen—is a daring stunt. And he introduces the girl's therapist (Charles Lanyer) and Jerry's previous wife's brother (Stephen Shellen)—characters you expect will serve mechanical plot functions—and then throws you curves. (He has written a pip of a meeting between Jerry and the therapist in an empty house, and a quick collision between Jerry and the brother that's even better.) Working with this sharp script, Ruben sets up a scene between the mother and the daughter so that we see the solidity of their affection for each other and understand how muddled they both get when Jerry comes between them. Ruben uses the girl's boyfriend (Jeff Schultz) to demonstrate how sound of head the two kids are, in contrast with the fantasy-driven Jerry, who catches them in a chaste goodnight kiss and yells rape.

The Stepfather doesn't have the cocky zest of *Dreamscape*; the subject doesn't allow for it. This is closer to the genre of the Hitchcock–Thornton Wilder *Shadow of a Doubt* (though the killer here isn't a charmer, like the Joseph Cotten character, and the mood is very different). With the Vancouver area doubling for Seattle in the opening section, and then for the fictitious towns nearby, Ruben uses everyday settings. They could be called plain, but they're well lighted (by John W. Lindley), and this young director turns plain into precise—the appurtenances of middle-class life become a bit crawly. And the picture's submerged sexual content goes way beyond the usual scare movie. *The Stepfather* is almost cruelly plausible; luckily, Ruben and Westlake are entertainers.

■

*T*ouch and Go, which just opened in New York, was made so long ago that Michael Keaton still has some hair in front, and there's a general tendency for reviewers to dismiss a movie when they know that the company (Tri-Star, in this case) hasn't been eager to release it. What's wrong with the picture is pretty obvious, and it was there right from the start, when the executive producer, Harry Colomby, watched a commercial that showed a retarded youngster being helped by a professional athlete, and thought he had the idea for a movie. Mercifully, the retardation was dropped, but the story was "developed" (by Alan Ormsby and Bob Sand, with Colomby) into that of a tough eleven-year-old "ethnic" boy (Ajay Naidu), who's economically handicapped, and the career-centered all-star forward (Keaton) of a Chicago hockey team, and how they change each other's lives. It's a terribly virtuous idea. But the director, Robert Mandel, who finished the film in 1984 (after his first, *Independence Day*, and before his third, *F/X*), doesn't allow it to become a tearjerker. Mandel was directing plays in New York before he went to the American Film Institute in the late seventies to learn filmmaking, and he has a gift for modulating performances. He's an honest director; he takes the drivelling story and turns it into something that has moments of likable, believable emotion.

Keaton's performance is easily the best acting he's done on the screen. I retain an affection for the wound-up idea man he played in his first movie, *Night Shift*, but that was stand-up impishness—an inspired routine—rather than the kind of straight acting he's doing here: a grownup-male performance of a kind you don't often see. As the hockey star Bobby Barbato, a local boy from the South Side who is known as the Hornet, he's in fighting trim, and he's quick and impudent in conversation. He gets up early and works out, and, high up in his expensive lakefront apartment, he watches the VCR, studying replays of his moves. He's a real pro, and Keaton's on top of the role. He got into shape for it, and it's obviously he, and not a double, in most of the scenes on the ice—you see his concentration and his excited interplay with his teammates. And the physical confidence that Keaton gained from the exercise makes him different from the rather limp fellow of movies like *Mr. Mom*. Keaton shows a wider range here. Bobby's impatience and cool, light-blue-eyed irritability seem earned: they're the consequence of all his training to keep at his peak. He doesn't have time for extra words; he's proud of his athletic ability—he radiates pleasure in it—and he wants to stay a star as long as he can. Bobby's no hypocrite: he likes his Jaguar, he enjoys the one-night stands with glitzy groupies and being unencumbered. And the movie isn't preachy about his single life. But when Bobby is ready to change, Keaton shows us the deepening of his feelings.

If the kid were a heartwarming, dear little tyke (or if the cinematographer, Richard H. Kline, had lighted him to soften his features), we wouldn't understand why Bobby would be drawn to help him. But Ajay Naidu isn't childlike—in movie terms, that is. He already has a man's mug. And this kid, who fronts for a gang of street hoods that try to rob Bobby, is a bold, grubby little con whose inventiveness has a fascination. He knows the trick of making himself seem the injured party—Bobby is sucked in to find out how much of his tale of hardship is true. And when Bobby meets the kid's mother, in the person of the volatile Maria Conchita Alonso, he meets a just about irrepressible force of nature. Alonso, the Venezuelan beauty who played opposite Robin Williams in *Moscow on the Hudson*, isn't like any other comedienne on the screen. She has wild, impulsive fingers that are always moving and dark eyes that click like castanets. I've heard her on television telling David Letterman that she "could be a grreat movie star," and she's right. She brings a happy sizzle to the role of the openhearted single mother who's never been able to make a decent living but knows how to enjoy life; she's so eager for experience that she walks tilted forward, almost at a run. Alonso has the uninhibited sexiness of the young Sophia Loren (and she's a better actress). A performer with her vim and momentum should never have to play the kind of stretched-out-in-the-hospital scene she has here, but she and Keaton aren't degraded, because you can feel that the director appreciates what they're gifted at. Their funny scenes have a lovely, spinning rapport. *Touch and Go* is stuck with its bad idea and with plot turns manufactured to give it an action finale that brings the lovers together, but it has real sensibility.

■

Curtis Hanson, the writer-director of *The Bedroom Window*, started with a good premise (adapted from the English novel *The Witnesses*, by Anne Holden). A young architect (Steve Guttenberg), who works for the leading construction-and-restoration firm in Baltimore, is visited late at night in his Mt. Vernon Place apartment by his boss's wife, Sylvia (Isabelle Huppert). While he's in the bathroom, she hears screams, gets out of bed, and goes to the window, from which she has a clear view of a tall, carrot-haired man beating a young woman and trying to drag her into the park. She pounds on the window while staring at the attacker, and he stares back at her (she's naked); then the victim yells some more, and he's frightened off. But the next day the two lovers discover that another young woman was raped and strangled close by just a short time afterward, and they worry about whether they should get Sylvia's description of the man to the police, as it could reveal their affair. She won't take the risk, so her lover goes to the police, reporting all the details she has given him but pretending that he was the observer.

Hanson, who wrote the script for the 1978 Canadian film *The Silent Partner*, a tip-top nasty thriller starring Elliott Gould and Christopher Plummer, and did a pleasant, unaffected piece of work as director of the 1983 Tom Cruise–Shelley Long picture *Losin' It*, is so surefooted in some scenes that the film's patchy surface suggests that he didn't have the control he needed. The leading part is written as that of a man-about-town, a ladies' man who wears Italian suits and drives a chic 1963 Mercury Comet convertible, so it doesn't seem likely that Hanson had anyone like Guttenberg (a specialist in smirking, fatuous comedy roles) in mind. Guttenberg brings about as much to a sophisticated thriller as Robert Cummings did in the forties. His going to the police seems to be his way of acting smart, of grandstanding; his puerility serves a purpose in the first third of the story, but then Guttenberg simply can't work up enough sex appeal to distract us from the holes in the plot and enable the picture to have the adroitness and dazzle it needs. When the architect meets the girl who was attacked, a cocktail waitress (Elizabeth McGovern), and she tells him that he's "either a romantic fool or an idiot," you think, Fool, yes, idiot, yes, but romantic, no. And surely Hanson couldn't have meant Sylvia—the sort of shallow, bitchy woman who used to be called "a woman of the world"—to be played with Huppert's flat, phonetic readings. Huppert can play a cuddlebug (she's delectable when she goes to the bedroom window), but her cool, hard petulance has no authority, no style. (She's so inert that the audience might have cheered when she's kissed off if Hanson had pointed it up a bit more.) With two of his three leads miscast, Hanson is in trouble, and there are all sorts of other oddities. As the socially prominent cuckolded boss, Paul Shenar starts out with suggestions of power and an overly amiable, egotistical manner; he's almost lewd in his teasing of the younger man. But his position in the community and the hints that he has unusual standing with the Police Department are never filled in—the role just dwindles away. The cinematography, by Gilbert Taylor (who also shot *Losin' It*), has a snazzy verve; the Baltimore locations, and the scenes in Wilmington and Winston-Salem, North Carolina, doubling for Baltimore, provide a colorful architectural mix, and we can gather that all this relates to the husband's prosperity and the lover's slightly awed treatment of him. But the murder mystery itself seems to be taking place in a void, as if the movie had been put together before it was really finished.

It's an erratic and, finally, disappointing picture (it loses its snap), yet you keep rooting for it, because of that premise, and because it has some visual life to it, and some clever ideas, too. For example, there's the lover's confusion when he's asked to pick the attacker out of a police lineup. And there's the high point of the movie, which, unfortunately, comes fairly early, when the attacker is on trial, and the lover, who is the prosecution's chief witness, has his credibility demolished by the defense attorney—a part played by Wallace Shawn with a witty suavity he hasn't had a chance to demonstrate onscreen until now. The courtroom sequence has an amusing texture, because Sylvia, who is among the spectators, tries to coach her lover when he's on the witness stand faltering in his answers. Her signals are spotted by the two people who care the most about the trial: the pale-faced, carrot-top defendant (the chilling, well-cast Brad Greenquist) and McGovern's cocktail waitress, who grasps immediately that it was Sylvia who was the witness. McGovern is playing a straightforward, no-nonsense girl, and when she's disgusted with the deception and tells off the Guttenberg character she's so much the stronger actor that poor Guttenberg seems to wilt before our eyes. McGovern's performance takes over the second half of the movie. Possibly the scene in the pool hall–barroom, where she's disguised as a seductress in a wig, a skimpy black leather halter, and purple spike shoes, is played a little too slowly and deliberately to be hot fun, but by then she's all that the picture has left. *The Bedroom Window* is almost over before you become aware that Hanson has brought off a little trick that demonstrates a real flair for the suspense genre: the pale, ghoulish killer speaks only one emphatic word in the entire movie.

February 9, 1987

VIRGINS, VAMPS, AND FLOOZIES

||||||||||||||||||||||||||||||||||||||||||||||||||||||||||||||||||||||||||||||||||||||||||||||||||||||||||||||||||||||||||||||||||||||||

Every so often, you're watching a movie about ordinary, deprived, unlucky people and something numinous happens and they're no longer ordinary. You may feel that transformation at De Sica's *Umberto D.* and *Miracle in Milan,* at early Fellini, and at the work of the Taviani brothers. You may feel it at Jacques Demy's *Lola* and Hector Babenco's *Pixote.* It's as if the characters' souls became magically visible, and when that happens the movie becomes piercingly close to you. You feel protective of it, and momentarily alienated from people who don't respond as you do.

So it's not a good idea to see *The Hour of the Star* with the wrong companions. A lot of the scenes don't quite work, but the transforming power of art is very strong in this movie, a first feature by the Brazilian Suzana Amaral, the mother of nine, who, at the age of fifty-two, shot it in four weeks, in 1985, for $150,000. Amaral didn't suddenly turn primitive moviemaker. She's from a family that is well known in the arts, and though she had quit college to marry she began to study film at the University of São Paulo when she was in her late thirties, and she worked in television and made more than forty documentaries and short films before coming to this country and enrolling in the graduate program at

267

N.Y.U. film school, where she took a master's degree in 1978. She's a knowledgeable artist, and it's so rare for anyone to attempt what she's trying for here that I can feel myself wanting to overpraise the results. What I can say with honor is that at moments the picture comes very close to the effects achieved by De Sica and the others.

Working from a script that she and Alfredo Oroz adapted from the 1977 novella by Clarice Lispector, Amaral tells the story of Macabéa (Marcelia Cartaxo), a nineteen-year-old orphan from a depressed rural section in the northeast, a girl with no skills or education—without looks or personality, or even training in keeping herself clean—who comes south to São Paulo, a city of fourteen million. It wouldn't occur to this girl that the world could be changed; she probably wouldn't notice if it were. She barely knows what people are saying to her: her dialect is different from theirs. She lives in a rented room in the slums with three other girls, all named Maria; she absorbs trivia from radio shows, goes to her job as a typist, and mimics the behavior of her co-worker Gloria (Tamara Taxman), a veteran of the dating wars, whose five abortions are her battle stripes. Macabéa apologizes politely to her boss for her hopelessly inept one-finger typing, for the smudges on the paper and the holes she makes; he can't bring himself to fire her. So she hangs on. The distance between her timid, passive existence and her fantasy life is so vast as to set off poetic reverberations. Wrapped in the isolation of ignorance, she doesn't think about things like improving her typing; she simply wants to be a movie star.

Amaral has been quoted as saying, "My film is not a feminist film; it's a feminine film." And that's what gives it its special qualities of heartbreak and revelation. It's as if *Umberto D.* had concentrated not on the old professor but on the young servant girl. It's like a fuller version of the story of the Sicilian girl killed by the German soldiers in *The Night of the Shooting Stars*. Amaral has taken a character who might be considered far more marginal than either of those girls, put her at the center of our attention, and made us feel what it's like for her when she looks at men with hopeful interest, trying to make eye contact with them. Later, we feel what it's like for her when she's dating Olimpico (José Dumont), a vain—and mean—metalworker, who's almost as ignorant as she is but puts her down because he's embarrassed that he can't get a snappier girlfriend. He's the sort of man who turns nasty when a woman asks questions he doesn't know the answers to. Macabéa has a little of Gelsomina (from *La Strada*) in her. When she sings an aria that she's heard on the radio, Olimpico hits her on the head because it annoys him and then lifts her high in the air, gyrating with her; he's playing the strongman, just like the brute Zampanò.

Macabéa is clumsier than Gelsomina, heavier-spirited; she seems more enduring. She's devastated, though, when she experiences a betrayal. Macabéa has hooded eyes, and when she suffers they become the eyes of a forest creature at bay: she loses all hope. Gloria, who has thoughtlessly betrayed her, tries to square things by paying for her to go to Madame Carlot (Fernanda Montenegro), a *macumbeira*—an illegal witch doctor–fortuneteller—whose flashy old-whore makeup and bangles seem to lend color to Macabéa. The *macumbeira*, who is fascinated by the girl's innocence, gives her ready-made dreams, and the film completes its trajectory from neorealism to magic realism. Like *Umberto D.*, *The Hour of the Star* has moments of uncanny humor and painful intuition, but at the end it has a plunging happiness that is inseparable from horror. The hallucinatory effect seems somewhat alien to Amaral's temperament; she's better at the plain, level scenes—they have a truer magic. Still, this Latin-American mash of dreams and reality and American advertising art and images from the movies—a vision similar to what you get from Manuel Puig's novels—has an awkward, mystic sanctity. All the moldy colors seem to come together and to be struck by sunshine. It's contrived with too much trickery (flash-forwards and slow motion), yet it's affecting.

Visually, the movie has a trancelike quality right from the start, when Macabéa, looking in a mirror, moves her hands over her face, as if connecting the sense of touch with the image. As the unloved girl, the twenty-three-year-old Marcelia Cartaxo, who was performing with a regional theatre group when she was selected for the role, is grim and lumpish—she seems misshapen—and you can't believe she could look any other way. Then, in a scene where Macabéa has wangled a day off from work and is luxuriously alone in the rented room, she dances to the radio, watching herself in the mirror and swirling a sheet around her as if it were a bridal costume, and, yes, she seems to be what she longs to be— a pretty girl who could please a man. But when she's there with the Marias or is out in the city she's like a lost member of an ancient race. She's a misfit—her dinky white barrette a badge of her miserable virginity. Yet she accepts her life, accepts the slums, accepts her failure to please her boss, with a stolid meekness. She has inarticulate yearnings but no consciousness; she's all unconscious. She's simply *there*, looking to be a slave to a pathetic, twisted Olimpico. (Amaral doesn't extend much sympathetic imagination to Olimpico.)

Macabéa's story can be perceived many different ways; it's certainly a metaphor of male-female relationships and of the barely literate poor in the burgeoning big cities of the Third World, such as Mexico City, São Paulo, and Seoul. And to some degree Amaral is working inside the skin of her subject. The story connects at all sorts of points with the life of a woman who in her childhood wanted to be a movie star and, after raising nine children and divorcing her husband of twenty years, has become a star in the world of movies—the picture has been gathering major prizes at festivals. It's not a great movie, but it's good enough to get to you, and the image of Marcelia Cartaxo's Macabéa is what does it—the terrible aloneness of this mass woman, this nothing of a woman whom you wouldn't notice on the street. Umberto D. stood for all the proud, angry old people who couldn't live on their pensions, but he was himself, too—his own ornery old man. Macabéa is most herself in her moments of contentment: she smiles serenely as she celebrates her Sunday by taking a ride in the subway. It's Suzana Amaral's triumph that this girl gets away from her. Numbed as she is, she's as alive as Amaral or you or I, and more mysteriously so.

■

Some directors have got audiences heated up by shooting a sex scene against a blazing fireplace. Bob Rafelson is the kind of director who gets the audience primed with a raging volcano in Hawaii but then doesn't put a sex scene in front of it. His new movie, *Black Widow*, is about a slinky cat-eyed dame (Theresa Russell) who is somehow driven to marry a series of the richest millionaires in the country and murder them. It sounds irresistibly succulent and trashy. And with Debra Winger as the investigator at the Justice Department who notices the pattern in the string of sudden deaths and gets on the widow's trail the picture should be pop bliss. But Rafelson can't seem to give trash its due; he conveys the impression of being superior to it. He doesn't fulfill the genre he's working in—or transcend it, either. He intellectualizes it.

The picture is being referred to as a "psychological thriller," but the psychology is missing. At one point, we're told that nobody knows why anybody does anything, and that has a rather chic sound. (The picture may go over big with the French.) That bit of dialogue is the moviemakers' way of telling us that they disdain motivation; it's also their excuse for not developing the characters. Theresa Russell's hair had a beautiful shine in the 1984 *The Razor's Edge*; she was pretty shiny all over. And it's fun to see her as a mercenary femme fatale; she seems to be playing a movie star, or, rather, a near-star—Gloria Grahame, to be precise. She almost has that thin-lipped icy-bitchy petulance down pat, but Rafelson and the screenwriter, Ronald Bass, seem to have beguiled themselves with the conceit that this black widow suffers after the killings. We see Russell squeezing out a few tears even when there's no one around to appreciate her grief—it's as if black widowism were a disease. Winger the investigator has some blurry, unspecified block about men and sex; she's a workaholic who keeps refusing to go out with guys, and she can't get herself together—she's swathed in bulky clothes, and her messy hair flies behind her.

Russell dispatches husbands, such as Dallas toy manufacturer Dennis Hopper and Seattle philanthropist Nicol Williamson, in a few quick scenes (though both actors are amusing and you don't want to lose them). This is handled so economically that it seems to be preparation, and you expect the movie to be about the attachment that develops between the seductress and the frump. And, of course, you expect to get some inkling of why Russell kills when she's got fortunes piled upon fortunes, and why Winger is drawn to her. What is it in Winger that makes her spot the murderous pattern and become single-mindedly absorbed in this killer, whom she gets to know? Then other questions come up. Why can't Winger show herself off except in Russell's clothes? And what keeps her out of men's embraces until Russell designates a lover for her (Russell's own new suitor, Sami Frey) in Hawaii? You expect the women to share identities, or the picture to go lesbian, or *something*. But you're wrong. This is postmodernist film noir.

Rafelson can't be bothered with anything so mundane as suspense; he doesn't seem to *believe* in suspense. He believes in high-tech swank, though. He provides an imitation of the fringe elements that used to go into star vehicles—the gowns, the cars, the on-the-move use of wouldn't-you-like-to-be-there locations. The glossy format sets off Russell's sly glamour puss, and there's a prickly challenge in her I-am-desirable manner. Her expensive look—the coiffures, the tanned, waxed limbs, the form-fitting clothes—suggest a stage set, ready for action. Even Russell's tight, narrow-range voice—the voice of a sorority girl more than of an actress—doesn't work against her here; it goes with her pampered sheen. But Winger is disappointing, because her role de-sexes her. It doesn't call upon what she's best at: a fearless hypersensuality. She's too clear-eyed and too much of an actress to be dull, but her character can't compete with a siren who angles with a platinum hook. Playing a detective, Winger has to put on a deadpan, and her husky voice is played down—maybe because the moviemakers realized that in terms of their plot it was coming out of the wrong woman.

The picture doesn't give you any shivers; it's muted, with an occasional near-pornographic texture—as in a nighttime swimming scene. (You hope for something more pornographic in Russell's personality than you get.) The writer and the director don't seem to have toyed with the possibilities in the black-widow idea. Couldn't we have had the fun of *wanting* the guys to be bumped off? There are bits that stand out, such as moments of sleazy comedy provided by James Hong as a drugged-out private investigator—a Hawaiian variant of Denholm Elliott's gutless, seedy Englishmen. But underneath the picture's studied air it's merely a caper film (like *Body Heat*), and the roles are so tawdry and under-developed that you may want to giggle at the fanciness. The whole thing is a very literary notion; Rafelson must talk a terrific movie.

■

A few decades of TV have conditioned audiences to laugh on raucous cue. But it would be stupid to try to convince people who are roaring at *Outrageous Fortune*, the hit starring Shelley Long and Bette Midler, that it isn't funny. The most I can do is to tell those who aren't laughing that I don't think they're deadheads. *Outrageous Fortune* should be elemental belly-laugh farce, but most of it is flattened out and rackety, an old-Hollywood chase comedy repackaged with what is being called "female raunch"—i.e., comparative anatomy. The picture is getting the same kind of laughter that *Ruthless People* did. Only now people laugh before Bette Midler does anything—they laugh in anticipation of her cute waddle walk. And this great bawdy woman who gave a heroic performance in *The Rose* and inflected everything from her hippety-hop to the gleam in her eyes in *Down and Out in Beverly Hills* is herself anticipating how bumptious and darling she's going to be. Pregnant when the picture was shot, she sticks out her chest and charges into her scenes; she's playing the Three Stooges—all three.

The setup is very simple: two young New York actresses of contrasting types—Long is a tall, blond élitist and Midler a vulgarian-sexpot Kewpie doll—discover they've been sharing a lover (Peter Coyote); when he disappears, they chase him across the country to the cliffs and mesas of New Mexico, becoming friends along the way. Shelley Long's role has obviously been shaped by someone who has watched her in her TV series, *Cheers*, because once again she's playing a prissy pill and making her likable by exposing her as all screwed up. Shelley Long showed some range in pictures such as *Caveman*, *Losin' It*, *Night Shift*, and *Irreconcilable Differences* (as well as more heaven-reaching neck than anyone in movies since Audrey Hepburn), but now that she has done a series she's in danger of seeming used up, and this performance conveys the impression that a lofty ditz is all she can play. And to some extent she's playing on our memories. Long had a blushing primness when she first did her pretentious hoity-toityness in *Cheers*; prattling about high art, she was so pleased with herself that she was rather fetching. Here the character is too brittle. This must be partly the fault of the director, Arthur Hiller (never a master of spontaneity), and partly due to the writing, which doesn't take her beyond what she's already done.

It's not hard to believe the report that the Disney-Touchstone executives swooned with pleasure when they read the script by the young woman screenwriter Leslie Dixon, who took on the assignment of devising a female-buddy-buddy picture after a couple of male teams had failed. Dixon has put the two women in the middle of a claptrap plot about spies and terrorists, with upright C.I.A. guys and devious K.G.B. guys falling all over each other, and such feminine touches as the women's stopping to try on clothes while they're running for their lives. Near the start, there are a few snappers for Midler, and she gets to shoot some wonderful derisive looks at Long. Though the gags aren't fresh, Dixon knows how to construct them. With a director who had an appetite for broad comedy, this script might have been turned into a movie that had something like the self-mocking giddiness of Robert Zemeckis's *Romancing the Stone*.

With Hiller in charge, much of the dialogue turns into squawking, and the tiresome escapades—scrambling through airports and clutching at the sides of mountains—take all his attention. He leaves the promising lesser characters to wither away. Robert Prosky's role, as the famed Russian acting teacher that both women study with, doesn't have a comic payoff; George Carlin appears, in flower-child Indian drag, as a leftover sixties burnout who lives on a reservation, but he doesn't do anything special—it's just supposed to be funny that he's up there in the movie. Peter Coyote stands out as the smoothie—eligible, solvent, and hetero-

273

sexual—who is both women's dream lover come to life; he gives a polished and wily performance. But that's only in the first section; then he gets lost in the noise. And though the two women go through the motions of becoming devoted to each other they're not much of a team: they don't bring out anything in each other. Hiller depends on Midler to pump sass and energy into the picture; that's better than nothing, but it's not enough. And Hiller avidly touches the audience's soft spots. Midler's gutsy broad is shown to be all heart, and to be thin-skinned. The most exuberant woman lech we've got is reduced to being a conventional good girl.

The audience whoops it up; the audience loves this cartoon version of Bette Midler. In the Paul Brickman–Jonathan Demme *Citizens Band*, which came out ten years ago, two contrasting women (softheaded, gaga Ann Wedgeworth and hard-bitten Marcia Rodd) weren't just having affairs with the same man, they were married to him, and each of them had kids by him. That picture had the idiosyncratic, loose-screw American humor that this picture lacks, but it didn't cue people when to laugh. It was a commercial flop, of course. The wide movie audience appears to resent American pictures that aren't in mainstream style. In some angry, instinctive way, the audience seems to be saying of the artists, "How do *they* dare to be different?" The rewards for not being different have never been higher.

February 23, 1987

NICENESS

||||||||||||||||||||||||||||||||||||||||||||||||||||||||||||||||||||||||||||||||||||||||||||||||||||||||||||||||||||||||||||||||||||||||||||

Woody Allen's *Radio Days* starts high and, with its warm, amber colors (soft-toned reds and yellows and browns), it casts a spell. The picture is so likable and lulling that it may be a half hour or more before you say to yourself, "Is this smooth, anecdotal texture all there is? Is the whole thing just going to be Woody Allen looking back fondly?" It's based on Allen's recollections of his childhood (as well as on radio stories he's heard or dreamed up), but it's as if he had distanced himself from himself, because the childhood he shows us here isn't the genesis of his early choppy, fitfully funny movies. The protagonist of those comedies was fuelled by hostility and neurosis, and he had a boyish affection for dirt. Now Allen is like a radio narrator summing up the images. Speaking in a strong, confident voice-over while a slight, eleven-year-old redhead, Joe (Seth Green), acts things out, Allen makes his childhood innocuous. He seems to be saying, "I've grown past all that angry immaturity," and in this account his memories of what radio meant to him and his family at the start of the Second World War are converted into nostalgic "poetry."

Allen has learned how to work with a large cast and get the texture he wants. The performers who make up Joe's lower-middle-class Jewish family in Rockaway Beach are presented as comic-strip homilies, but they're wonderfully affable. His parents are said to squabble, but it's not about anything vital, and they do it in a familiar, comfortable way. His father (Michael Tucker) is a low-key, smiley joker, and Julie Kavner, youthful and bouncy, is near-miraculous as the practical-minded, dreamy, goofy mother—at least, she is at first. Allen doesn't do enough with her, and by the end you've forgotten her. In one way or another, that happens to just about everyone in the movie, and you become aware that that's how Allen wants it. It happens to Joe's big-bellied uncle, played by Josh Mostel, a whiz at naturalistic timing (and the screen actor his father, Zero, never was), and to his stocky wife, played by twinkle-eyed Renee Lippin—she pumps her elbows as she bustles about. Their teen-age daughter (Joy Newman), who loves to mug, has only one full scene, but it's a beauty: miming a Carmen Miranda song that's on the radio—"South American Way"—she's joined by Tucker and Mostel, who perform as backup singers. Dianne Wiest is an unmarried aunt, a bespectacled book-keeper eager to find a husband—she's Joe's special pal. Yet the role has no edge, and she always seems to be across a room, never up close, at the center of our attention. This is part of our disappointment: the strategy of the movie is that nothing is up close. Allen has everything receding into the past.

The characters only come half awake, half alive. They go back to being "little people." And this may be the big weakness of *Radio Days*. Feeling that he's outgrown the early tensions and can now see his family's funny side, Allen has reduced everyone to harmlessness. It's pure nostalgia—the past sweetened and trivialized. We in the audience want to see the actors show more of what they can do; there are real comedians here, and it's a turn-on. Allen cares about the total artistic effect. Yet he can't compensate us for the loss of the performers, because most of the moviemaking skills he has acquired have nothing to do with comedy. His total artistic effect is studied. Commenting on the old neighborhood, he's like the curator of Woody's childhood.

Toward the end, Allen serves up poignant thoughts about the transience of popular culture: Wallace Shawn, as the actor who plays radio's Masked Avenger, says "I wonder if future generations will even know about us." This might be touching if it were played for a hack actor's fatuousness—and there has been nothing to make the radio celebrities look impressive—yet Allen directs it straight. As he spells it out, the public's memories of the stars of radio become dimmer each year. The question the film asks—its theme—is "Will our fame last?" Implicitly, Allen's saying that we movie stars (and TV stars) must learn humility. But the fleetingness of fame doesn't sadden the audience as it saddens him; the audience isn't distressed about his slim chances for immortality. And so at the climax the aching melancholy seems to be misty eyes in a void.

The picture goes soft on itself. It's a celebration of what Allen was addicted to when he was a boy. But then he treats his boyish tastes in popular culture as the good things in life, and as a stick to hit contemporary pop culture with. He described the period to a *New York Times* interviewer in these terms: "It was a simpler age, and the music one heard on the radio was not earsplitting, pretentious rock music. It was very lovely." (Big-band music not pretentious?) Woody Allen is an aesthetic conservative—a fogy. It's understandable that he might prefer the more inhibited, romantic pop of his early years to contemporary pop, but by the fifties it had gone stale, and the fun of pop culture is that it's disposable. Why all this regret? Allen treats the old songs (the film incorporates a generous assortment of hits) as a value that we've lost. That's a way of killing the pleasures of pop. Too bad he can't feel what we've gained, because it correlates with everything that's missing from *Radio Days*: immediacy, exhilaration. (He wants life to back off.)

The character most affected is doll-like Sally White (Mia Farrow), the pert little bimbo from Canarsie—the one character whom we follow over a period of years, as she rises from cigarette girl to jewel-decked radio star. Mia Farrow is presented as the essence of prettiness, and it's perfect casting. But she's also supposed to be the subject of a million dirty jokes, and Woody Allen can't bring himself to tell even one. He's so protective of the actress (and the picture) that Sally may be a first: a sexless bimbo. And though she's meant to be a nincompoop who obliges any man who asks, Allen denies her even the little bit of consciousness she'd need to boost herself up. So she has no satirical kick. (The movie is centered on a pre-adolescent boy, and there are places where you think he directed it.)

It's a relief whenever somebody seems to go all out. In one scene, Danny Aiello, as a Mafia hit man who means to kill Sally, has her in tow when he stops by his house. His ripsnorting, gnarled old mother tempts the cutie to eat great heaps of pasta and, delighted by her face and her appetite, tells the son that it would be a waste to kill her. Gina DeAngelis, who plays the mother as if she'd trained Anjelica Huston in witchcraft, gives the audience a lift. So does a Latin singer (Denise Dummont) who wiggles and sways. And so does Diane Keaton, appearing at the finish as a sophisticated song stylist with a band on New Year's Eve, 1944. The movie features skyscraper rooftops and the lighted signs of Times Square in the forties, but the art design has no streamlined playfulness, no sense of caricature. And such men-about-town as Tony Roberts and Jeff Daniels don't seem intended to have much comic dash; they're just there, for no particular purpose. Keaton, though, with her glittering snood, her demure naughty smile, and the subtle languor of her rhythm as she sings Cole Porter's "You'd Be So Nice to Come Home To," momentarily makes you feel the radiance of old Manhattan. And Farrow's Sally, pulling her sequinned cape around her, makes you feel the satisfaction that she takes in being a celeb.

Radio Days has its moments, but it's a museum piece. It has charm but no revelations, no excitement; the jokes don't go anywhere. It's like an analysand's nightmare of what his shrink might do to him: level his emotions and make him accept everything banal in the society. ("It was very lovely.") This is Woody Allen, the sexually obsessed upstart hero of the sixties and seventies, looking back to a golden age of niceness. (Young audiences may not find much in the movie to plug in to.) The film's sentimentality comes through fairly overpoweringly in a set-piece episode in which a little girl has fallen into a well and the American public is glued to its radios, hoping for word that she has been rescued. The sequence is presented without irony, as an indication of how radio used to bring us all together. As Allen tells it, people's feelings came out at a time like that. I'm not sure that I can pinpoint exactly why this sequence is slightly sickening, but it just about cancels out the best crazy-comedy routine in the movie, in which the rabbi (Kenneth Mars) and Joe's father and mother argue about who has the right to discipline the boy while they take turns smacking him. With just a twist—say, the nation coming to a standstill while a broadcaster describes the frantic efforts of firemen

277

to get a cat down from a very short tree—the movie would gain some tartness, some perspective.

Woody Allen has fought hard to keep his individuality as a moviemaker (this is the fifteenth film he has written and directed), and he takes chances: this picture probably won't succeed with a wide audience, because it's a reminiscence rather than a conventional story. Yet while you're watching it you feel that he wants too much for you to like it. What the country unified by the plight of the little girl suggests is that Woody Allen has found in himself the heartfelt coyness of Louis B. Mayer—without the (often redeeming) vulgar joyfulness. Allen goes for the lump in the collective throat, carefully, tastefully.

∎

The English political thriller *Defense of the Realm* is hushed and complicated; events go by very fast. I was intent, my face resting on my left fist, as I concentrated on what all those low-voiced Britishers were up to. Suddenly I became aware of a loud, percussive sound, and, wondering what new element was being introduced, I strained to make it out. It was my Swatch ticking. Directed by the talented David Drury, from a script by Martin Stellman that's just about all plot, the picture demands too much close attention; you don't have time to think about what's going on—you're locked into just finding out what it is. And there's no fun in putting the puzzle together. Yet the movie leaves you with something—a sci-fi vision of an octopus state.

In subject, it's probably the closest English equivalent of *All the President's Men*, but the atmosphere is much darker and more oppressive. It deals with a rising young Fleet Street journalist, devious, amoral Nick (Gabriel Byrne), who goes after a scoop, gets some hot tips, and writes stories that destroy the career of an Opposition leader, a Labour M.P. (Ian Bannen)—he's exposed as the patron of a call girl, and as possibly a Communist passing information to the K.G.B. An elderly journalist (Denholm Elliott) at the paper tries to persuade Nick to wait and check further before publishing the data, but this rumpled old duffer with his conscientiousness is a bit of a joke in the newsroom, and it isn't until his sudden death that Nick discovers that the tips he acted on were phonies, engineered by the Tory government. That's when he begins, with the help of the M.P.'s assistant (Greta Scacchi), to penetrate the conspiracy, and to discover how the paper itself is implicated, and how little he can do about it. (The fluke that sets things off is an attempt by a couple of juvenile delinquents to break out of a Borstal institution; one of them blunders into an American military base where nuclear weapons are stored and, in the middle of a nuclear alert, is killed—but all this is, of course, concealed. The M.P. learned these secrets, which the government considers vital to the "defense of the realm," and was framed to silence him.)

Shot by Roger Deakins (who also shot *1984*), *Defense of the Realm* suggests a color version of the dark-night-of-the-soul baroque of *The Third Man*, and it's a measure of the director's skill that you accept the overcast skies as a spiritual condition. The movie is about pervasive bureaucratic rot. It's a new-style acrid thriller, an Orwellian coffee jag rather than a Graham Greene entertainment. Even the dawns are gray.

The initial focus is on the journalists—on Nick, who knows how to get a story but hasn't had the intellectual reach to form a clear picture of how the society works, and on the rival newsmen (Robbie Coltrane is among them) and the editors (Bill Paterson shines) and the mighty owner (Fulton Mackay). The picture gets weaker as it goes wider and takes in the whole power structure. And it doesn't go far enough into the characters—into Nick, especially. But it's restless and adventurous in its camera moods. An example of paranoiac realism, it infuses cinéma vérité shooting with a spirit of grim fantasy. The whole production has an alert intelligence. It has everything but the basic storytelling astuteness to give you a good time; after a while, you feel charred.

March 9, 1987

NOT FOR THE AGES

||||||||||||||||||||||||||||||||||||||||||||||||||||||||||||||||||||||||||||||||||||||||||||||||||||||||||||||||||||||||||||||||||||||||||||||||

Tin Men—the term that Barry Levinson uses for the title of his movie about aluminum-siding salesmen in Baltimore in 1963, the year that the state cracked down on them—is new to me. I had always heard this breed of wise guys referred to as shinglemen or shinglers. They were compulsive, rhythmic talkers—spritzers—and when they travelled in groups (so they could spread out over a neighborhood) they were like comedy clubs of bunco artists. They worked with partners during the sales pitches; the partners were their audience, and could verify their exploits when the group got together at night. Shinglemen often moved to and from the lower rungs of show biz. When the young Rodney Dangerfield freaked out during a club engagement, he became a contractor selling aluminum siding; he hired his out-of-work, often unemployable pals—comics, dancers, jazzmen—and transported them, in the afternoons, from Broadway to New Jersey. He had five offices going and a sales force of fifty crazies when he began working the clubs again. The hipster Joe Ancis, whom Buddy Hackett called the original version of Lenny Bruce, whizzed around the country with a troupe of shinglers, and in the early fifties Bruce himself canvassed with crews around L.A.

Although Levinson, who both wrote and directed *Tin Men*, has a real facility for creating in-group small talk, the talk he provides is smaller and tamer than you might hope for. It's unresonantly funny; tameness may be Levinson's idea of realism. His shinglers aren't pot-smoking show-biz maniacs covering the country looking for home-owning saps. They're crumbum businessmen who stay put in Baltimore—supersalesmen who can't resist the double-dealing that will make a story when they're back with their cronies at the office or the bar or the diner. Levinson uses the same hangout that he used in the 1982 film *Diner*, and he's making essentially the same point here—that guys relate better to guys than they do to girls. The men are inside each other's heads. They accept each other's limitations; they're entertained by them and at the same time bored by them. (Their get-togethers are a form of consciousness-lowering.)

Levinson's basic theme here is the stunted imaginative life of the businessman who hangs out at the race-track because he can feel good about himself when he's joking with his business pals. But shinglemen in the unregulated glory days of the fifties and the early sixties were, according to legend, explosively energetic. They put so much imagination into their grifting that they were hopping up and down with glee. The movie might have been more exhilarating if it had opened up the possibilities in the whole salesmanship-show-biz connection. And although it can get along without the cutthroat rancor of the real-estate scavengers who sell Florida swampland in David Mamet's play *Glengarry Glen Ross*, it could have used some of the tingling heartlessness of the farcical selling schemes in the Zemeckis-Gale film *Used Cars*. *Tin Men* is too middle-of-the-road; the subculture it presents isn't distinctive enough, or callous enough. Levinson was himself inside the characters of *Diner*—they were his own generation. These men are his sometime tin-man father's generation, and he doesn't share their pleasures.

At the opening, the camera nuzzles the grille and fins of a gleaming new Cadillac that's on display. Wooed and won by this turquoise, twenty-foot number, BB (Richard Dreyfuss), a small, dapper know-it-all, backs out of the showroom driveway and is smacked by a yellow Caddy, driven by Tilley (Danny DeVito). That's the beginning of a feud between the two strutting tin men who work for different outfits. They start by shouting insults at each other while straightening their gaudy ties on their puffed-out chests. For a few scenes, they attack each other's enormous cars, using hands, feet, and a crowbar—it's a standard screwball version of a Laurel & Hardy destruction orgy. In between the smash scenes, BB and his partner, Moe (John Mahoney), pull a sweet scam: it starts when they convince a woman that they're photographers from *Life* taking pictures of her house to use as an example of deterioration. By comparison, Tilley's maneuvers are desperate and crude, though it's a pleasure to listen to his partner, Sam (Jackie Gayle, whose cracked, tired cadences evoke con artistry throughout the ages). Soon Dreyfuss's BB, who has had enough of battering Tilley's car and hauling his own in for repairs, raises the stakes: he seduces Tilley's wife, Nora (Barbara Hershey), a frustrated, pining-for-some-fun woman who works at a Social Security office. After BB phones Tilley to gloat about his conquest, it becomes clear that Levinson has a game plan that runs deeper than funny feuding.

DeVito's Tilley feels liberated when he hears of his wife's infidelity. He picks up her clothes, her trinkets and toiletries, and anything else he can think of, and throws them out the windows onto the front lawn. And he yells, "I'm a free man!" Stunned and homeless, Nora asks BB if she can stay with him for a day or two, and BB, an ace salesman—a Don Juan who has never awakened with the same woman for two consecutive mornings—is amazed to discover that he likes having her there, likes the companionship. His partner, Moe, has had a heart attack (at the climax of a con), and BB has been doing some thinking. A much more observant fellow than Tilley, he recognizes that the Maryland Home Improvement Commission is going to clamp down on their hustling, and he's fed up with it anyway. He keeps noticing the Volkswagen bugs on the streets while he's rolling by in his turquoise hulk. The idea of the movie is that BB is growing up as well as changing with the times. Tilley, meanwhile, is becoming more infantile, and things are falling apart on him.

Levinson sets up a logic in which BB is the winner and Tilley is the jerk, but he doesn't want to leave Tilley high and dry. All that's necessary is to see that the shinglemen share a demented creativity, and that when BB no longer joins in the hysteria—when he *thinks* he feels most like himself with Nora—it's time for him to start selling Volkswagens. But this straightforward idea for a comedy is presented as if it would be too strong for an audience, and the two men had to be made buddies. So the action is prolonged with limp, wavering scenes (BB's discovering who the commission's informer is, turning himself in, and being called to testify, and his going to Tilley's house at night, meeting him for breakfast, and, finally, giving him a ride). Levinson wants to be on the humane side of every issue. Nora gets to express her indignation at being treated like a chattel, and she does it in speeches that are way too explicit. Levinson doesn't leave anything to the viewer; he has warmth and sympathy spilling over—enough for the both of us.

The casting of Dreyfuss and DeVito was a gamble that didn't quite pay off. Dreyfuss is resourceful, but when he's in love and should be adapting his salesman's tactics to the campaign to convince Hershey's Nora of it, he gets boyishly ingenuous. (The writing is blatantly sincere in these scenes.) Dreyfuss seems a little too young for the role; it would be funnier if he were more jaded. And with DeVito as Tilley there's no tension in the latter part of the movie—you know that Hershey won't go back to him. (The writing is off here, too. If Tilley cared more about his wife, the plot would have some snap.) Talented though DeVito is, he gives his role away in the first five minutes; he has nothing more to reveal. He doesn't mug; he gives an honest performance as a man with a full-blown gift for deluding himself, but it's not a star performance.

Shinglers and their snow jobs could be such a great subject that you keep wanting the picture to be better. If it's moderately absorbing, that's largely because of the two crews of featured players. Mahoney and Gayle seem effortless, and, to a lesser degree, so do Stanley Brock and Seymour Cassel, and Michael Tucker and J. T. Walsh as the two managers, and Bruno Kirby, Matt Craven, Richard Portnow, and Alan Blumenfeld. They carry a whole way of life in their salesmen's suits. If only the writer-director would stop leaning over our shoulders saying, "They're just limited middle-aged guys trying to make a living." That's not a great subject.

■

Mike Newell's *The Good Father* has the festering gloom and dissatisfied-with-itself hatefulness that seem to be the current English badge of integrity. Anthony Hopkins appears in the starring role, and the whole movie is summed up in his face. He has taken over the Peter Finch crown of middle-class suffering. Quoting various critics, the ads say that Anthony Hopkins is spectacular, brilliant, stellar, riveting, high-voltage, terrific, a smoldering fury. Those are all the things he isn't. Hopkins is Hopkins—thoughtful, masochistic, a man whose emotions are convincing within a small, dark range. Hopkins never dazzles you; he never dazzles himself.

As Bill Hooper, who was once a college radical and aspiring writer, and is now a grimy-souled marketing executive with a publishing house, he vents his general rage on the wife he has left, and has horrible, guilty dreams of murdering his tiny son. He becomes close friends with Miles (Jim Broadbent), a schoolteacher whose marriage has also collapsed, though for very different reasons—Miles' wife is a lesbian who has left him for an Australian woman and is about to move to Australia, taking the child, whom Miles adores. Miles' situation is so much more clear-cut than his own that Bill springs into action, urging Miles to use the law to block his wife's move. Then he watches in horror as Miles perjures himself in court and, pretending to be shocked by his wife's lesbianism, gains the upper hand.

Based on the 1983 novel by Peter Prince, this is an attempt to get at the new complications in the sex wars and perhaps at the whole modern English muddle. Bill came of age in the sixties, believing in equal rights for women; he's still pro-feminist. But when he thinks of Miles' wife or his own he hears himself muttering "Bloody bitch." At some level, he wants power over women, yet when he gets close to it—when he has an affair with a docile young girl, and when he sees Miles exercising his new power over his wife—he's depressed by it. He's still a man of principle, even though his feelings don't match his principles. Bill feels monstrous: he's confused about his own motives, and he can't trust himself.

The novel has impetus, and the adaptation, by Christopher Hampton, follows it closely; yet the movie is all at the same level of anxious intensity. Mike Newell (he also directed *Dance with a Stranger*) never lightens up. He's monotonously skillful in the same way that Hopkins is. Hopkins is a highly theatrical actor, but in realistic roles like this you don't get the fun of theatricality. You never see Bill Hooper (or Mike Newell) take pleasure in anything. Newell keeps showing you what lice Englishmen are; Englishwomen seem exempt from the moral pollution—they've been

made a shade too tender and decent. A few small bravura performances—
Simon Callow as Miles' beady-eyed little devil of a barrister, who loves
to outsmart the opposition; Miriam Margolyes as a feminist lawyer up
against a reactionary judge—help things along. But the dialogue is often
spoken with ominous slowness, and everything seems blue and damp and
constricted (the picture was financed by British television); nobody has
a loose impulse or a vagrant thought. There are glimmers of truth in this
movie, and it holds you, but there's no clarity or relief in its truth. If
Newell has a goal, it seems to be to leave you with a sense of impacted
bleakness.

■

Spalding Gray has wild blue eyes and a bland, foxy-naïve deadpan. An actor who has made a career Off Off Broadway as a performance
artist, he's a singular phenomenon. He gives you old news as if it were
the subject of an investigative report. (It's new to him.) In his most
celebrated dramatic chronicle, *Swimming to Cambodia*, he presents a
vaguely stream-of-consciousness report of his life as an actor, and of how
he happened to audition for the small role of an American diplomat in
The Killing Fields, and of his getting the job and becoming part of the
well-fed, pampered company enjoying the beaches of Southeast Asia.
This was in 1983—he's in this world of lavish, imperial moviemaking, and
he loves it. But then he tells us the truth he found when he became
politically aware. The high point of his monologue comes when he hears
for the first time about our secret bombing of Cambodia, and what the
Khmer Rouge did to the Cambodian people in 1975, driving them out of
the cities and to their deaths. Mostly, his tone has been gentle mockery
of himself and everyone else, but now he's upset, indignant. He's in-
credulous and horrified as he describes the exodus; he's an actor who has
just discovered strong material, and he builds the tension. His words
come faster, his voice gets louder—he's telling you, "This is incredible
stuff and it really happened. We're an aggressive, psychotic nation—our
moviemaking is as decadent as our warmaking." Is he effective? To judge
from reactions to his stage appearances and to the new concert-film version, definitely. Yet I can't be alone in feeling that he's a total opportunist,
and so unconsciously that it never even occurs to him that there's anything

wrong about using a modern genocidal atrocity story to work up an audience.

Wearing a plaid lumberjack shirt—he rolls up the sleeves when he gets going—Gray does his raconteuring while seated on a chair behind a small table that holds a microphone, a glass of water, and a notebook he's carried onto the stage. Occasionally, he uses a pointer to refer to one of two maps on stands behind him, and now and then we see a slide—just blue sky with clouds. He uses his few bare props with an ironic awareness of their simplicity. His observations are not very sharp, but what he notices is told in a quiet, responsible, droll way—as if he were locked in with this information and had to unravel it—and the audience responds generously. Gray calls himself a "poetic reporter," and that's probably meant to indicate a deeper savvy than that of ordinary reporters. The material he prepares doesn't come out of a writer's mind; it comes out of an actor's mind, an audience lover's mind—these are observations to seduce, to tantalize an audience. And his vocal rhythms are lulling—they're a tide pulling you along. (He's like Alan Watts without mysticism.) What it comes down to is semi-confessional commentary plus great fly-away eyebrows and a bemused, quizzical manner. He's cagey in his use of his naïveté: he seems to be saying, "We're all in on this, and I'm as harmless and inept as you are." He's a bit simple, and that has its appeal. And some of his material (his firsthand observations, his voice mimicry) is legitimately effective—maybe about fifteen per cent at this point, but as his career advances he seems to be on a sliding scale downward.

Jonathan Demme directed the film of Gray's stage performance—it was shot before live audiences during three consecutive evenings (and one day) last November at The Performing Garage, in lower Manhattan—and it's a classic case of a split between form and content. The film is serenely assured and elegant. In his last two movies, *Stop Making Sense* and *Something Wild*, Demme showed a new grasp of visual dynamics. The way Sister Carol East was placed on the screen in the last sequence of *Something Wild*, she was still dancing around behind your eyes after you left the theatre, and maybe the closing titles that switched around, as in a hip children's game, were still switching around, too. Demme's graphics have become more abstract yet more jazzy, and there's a new goofing-off playfulness in his use of the film frame. Working on a minimalist basis here, with nothing but Spalding Gray and his props, Demme uses the lighting and shifts in camera angles and a musical score by Laurie Anderson to virtuoso rhythmic effect. Demme (who made the film for $485,000) endows Gray with a dramatic presence he didn't have when I saw him last year in a live performance. What we're seeing here is the apotheosis of Spalding Gray. The monologue acquires contrasts, and he seems an imposing actor with a fine camera face. Speaking fast while smiling, he has a quirky glint in his eyes, his voice keeps changing volume, and his hands move in the air. He's acutely "on."

It's a superlatively skillful piece of filmmaking, but at its center is a man who doesn't know that heating up his piddling stage act by an account of the Cambodian misery is about the most squalid thing anyone could do.

■

Alan Parker has technique to burn in *Angel Heart*, and that's what he should do with it. This film, which he adapted from the novel *Falling Angel*, by William Hjortsberg, and directed, was initially given an X rating, and that has created the false impression that it's hot and sexy. Actually, it's a lavishly sombre piece of hokum—*The Exorcist* for people who haunt bookshops specializing in metaphysics. It's the sort of movie that makes you think better of Ken Russell's hyperbolic perversity—at least, he was outrageous. (Russell was saying "Yum-yum.") And Nicolas Roeg, for all his twerpy decadence, does manage to suggest a silken sort of tactility. The Parker of *Angel Heart* broods while serving up slit throats, bodies with hearts cut out (and placed nearby for your delectation), a man plunged face down in a vat of scalding gumbo, chickens being drained in voodoo rites, and assorted solemn mutilations. He also serves up Mickey Rourke as a 1955 private eye with an office on the Lower East Side who is summoned to meet with a client (Robert De Niro) in a Harlem mission. De Niro hires him to search for information about a crooner of the prewar era who has disappeared, but it's amazing that he turns up anything, because the whole picture must have been shot during an eclipse. Rourke searches in the murkiest holes in America—New Orleans is almost as dim as the New York slums. (The primary colors have been desaturated, even from the clothes; what's left is leaden grays and browns and overcast skies that give you deluxe forebodings.)

Every place Rourke goes is artfully arranged to be scuzzy, and *he's* scuzzy. Though he has plenty of money, thugs throw him out of a bar and into the gutter, he vomits after seeing a particularly bloody stiff, he's attacked by a fierce pit bull that won't let go and by an old man wielding a straight razor—and he doesn't change his clothes. Sweaty and unshaven, he wears baggy pants that might have been used to wipe the grease from a ship's engine, and there's no indication that this is meant to be funny. But then this is a movie in which a man sitting alone at Coney Island in winter (so there's nothing else on the screen to notice) juggles his genitals at the camera—for no particular reason—and then does it again. This doesn't seem meant for a laugh, either. I listened to the plot resolution at the end, but it didn't explain Parker's funereal, loony style. He edits like a flasher. Why are ceiling fans used as portents of death? (Why not licorice drops or mayflies?) What is the significance of the frequent quick images of a moving elevator making a Constructivist pattern? (Is this just another descent into Hell?) Are the black religious sects that keep popping up meant to be scarily exotic? That's all that comes across. Is the unidentified corpse in the opening scene just a teaser? There's no way to separate the occult from the incomprehensible.

Most of the time, Rourke seems to be engaged in a private performance, as if he were chewing over his character with himself, but there are some almost amusing moments in his slobby interpretation. He uses one of his tricks from *Diner*: when he's with an attractive woman, he has a cajoling, intimate way of talking to her. This happens with Elizabeth Whitcraft as a ready-for-action blonde, with Charlotte Rampling as a sullen psychic, and, especially, with the screen's newest sexpot, Lisa Bonet, as a teen-age Mambo priestess who has a penchant for smearing herself with chicken blood. Rourke leans toward each one as if she were the only woman he'd ever cared about. (But don't they notice that he has enough dirt on him to sprout mushrooms?) De Niro drops in from time to time; it's the sort of guest appearance that lazy big actors delight in— they can show up the local talent. God knows he's welcome, but he isn't quite the comic-strip life of the party that he was in his cameo in *Brazil*, and this picture's no party. Parker doesn't have the gift of making evil seductive. He delivers a few Roegish images: a woman scrubbing the wall where her husband put a gun to his head; two dusky-brown nuns in beige habits sitting together and moving their heads in unison. But every shot looks weighted and fussed over, and he can't resist throwing in a cockfight on top of everything else. Parker says, "I have very eclectic tastes"; they seem to encompass braining the audience. What was he thinking of? Did the Devil make him do it?

April 6, 1987

MANYPEEPLIA UPSIDOWNIA

Big-bosomed, short-waisted, and long-legged, Tina (Carmen Maura) has a hot, roiling temperament; after she has given her nightly performance in Cocteau's monologue-play *The Human Voice*, which her famous brother Pablo (Eusebio Poncela) directed, she walks toward a café with him and her daughter Ada, and, seeing a couple of street-cleaners who are busy with their spraying, she calls out to them to hose her down. Soaked, her short knit dress clinging to her wide hips, she's deliciously happy at the café, until the cool, chic Pablo tells her that she overacted. Overacting is what she's all about; it's what the Madrid writer-director Pedro Almodóvar's *Law of Desire* is all about. Tina has a slutty splendor: she swivels around on her clicking high heels, prays to the Virgin, and fills little Ada's head with her sentimental gabbing. She's overacting womanhood, which is the role of her life. She started out as Pablo's brother; as a teen-ager, she ran off with their father and had the operation to please him, but he finally left her, and she hasn't had anything to do with a man since. Little Ada is actually the daughter left behind by her lesbian lover. Almodóvar adds another layer of topsy-turvydom: Carmen Maura, the transsexual here (and the slum mother in his *What Have I Done to Deserve This!*), is a powerful actress in the manner of the early Anna Magnani, with the trippiness and self-mockery of Bette Midler; the strikingly beautiful lesbian is played by a low-voiced male transvestite.

If Tina lives in make-believe, so does the less flamboyant Pablo, who adores her. In story terms, Pablo, who imagines himself a discreet homosexual, is the protagonist. The sexual effrontery of his stage productions and his classy homoerotic films (which delight the public) have made him a glamorous celebrity, with a wide choice of lovers. (His sleek dark-blond hair, cleft chin, and steely-blue eyes help him along.) Pablo's liaisons don't make him happy, though, because he's in love with a curly-haired young workingman, Juan (Miguel Molina), who values his companionship—a rather steamy companionship—but isn't fully committed to homosexuality, or to Pablo's upper-bohemian style. One night, Pablo takes home Antonio (Antonio Banderas), a government minister's son, who has been stalking him; by morning, Antonio loves him and is determined to possess him completely. Determined also to possess anyone dear to Pablo, Antonio becomes the central horror of Pablo's life. And the film winds up in a demonstration that Antonio's desire, which is grotesque, uncontrollable—crazy—simply can't be denied. It gets so all-encompassing that Pablo has to respond to it. This will come as no surprise to people who have found themselves in bed with people they despise, or with ex-spouses or ex-lovers whom they have fought to get rid of—a sexual paradox that can have a passionate, oh-well-what-the-hell quality on the screen.

Almodóvar's tone is not like anyone else's; the film has the exaggerated plot of an absurdist Hollywood romance, and even when it loses its beat (after a murder) there's always something happening. This director manages to joke about the self-dramatizing that can go on at the movies, and at the same time reactivate it. The film is festive. It doesn't disguise its narcissism; it turns it into bright-colored tragicomedy. (Almodóvar is the director who might have brought off the sultry spirit of Manuel Puig's *Kiss of the Spider Woman*.) I've never been to Spain, but the temperament of Almodóvar's Madrid—*his* temperament—goes with the world I know. Partly, this may be because his sensibility is steeped in Hollywood movies and underground films, but it's more than that. In a recent interview in *The New York Times* he said, "My rebellion is to deny Franco. . . . I refuse even his memory. I start everything I write with the idea 'What if Franco had never existed?' " Well, that's America.

He opens with a metaphor of moviemaking—an autoerotic film is being shot in a studio—and he goes on side excursions that are also metaphorical. Some of these are the best jokes in the movie—such as Tina's taking Ada to the church where she used to sing as a choirboy, and introducing the child as her daughter to the courteously befuddled, somewhat pained choirmaster priest. And straight-faced gags keep popping up, such as Pablo's telling Tina she should get a guy and go straight. Even better: the ten-year-old Ada, worried about her developing body, asks Tina whether she'll soon grow breasts, and Tina says, "Sure. At your age, I was flat as a board." This gagster-artist Almodóvar loves Tina's religious view of herself as a woman; she has surrendered to the movies she saw as a boy. Her eyes shine when her sentimental fantasy of herself as a woman and a mother is intact; when some guy rudely

289

disturbs it, she unconsciously throws a punch like a man. Carmen Maura, whose plumpish figure is baffling, succeeds in looking neither masculine nor feminine—her Tina is a great satirical flip-flopping creation.

Almodóvar seems to have skimped on the three men. They're wonderful romantic types, but they're involved in the more conventionally melodramatic side of the story, and in some fairly conventional homosexual romanticism. And they're almost too sensually handsome, too well built. Eusebio Poncela's Pablo lacks a goosey, comic side; he's stone-faced in scenes involving letters to Juan and Antonio—scenes that could have a flaky vivacity. (His porno movies can't be as much fun as we're led to think they are.) And Miguel Molina's Juan is boringly, honorably straight and decent. (Is Almodóvar, who comes from a rural, working-class background, taking this hardworking lad more seriously than he should?) Luckily, the well-heeled Antonio isn't held down by virtue, and the actor Antonio Banderas gets to suggest a little of the spoiled-rotten instability of Bellocchio's pug-dog hero (Lou Castel) in *Fists in the Pocket*. Banderas has a sly, funny side: when Antonio first goes home with Pablo, he explains that he's never been with a man before, and when Pablo mounts him he has a comedian's chagrined, quizzical look that says, "This isn't going to work." (Pablo makes it work, all right.)

Antonio has already interrupted their lovemaking to ask Pablo if he has any diseases. Pablo answers contemptuously, implying that if you care about sexual pleasure you can't worry about such matters. His manner says, "Go home, little boy, if you're worried about syphilis." It's the grand attitude of an earlier era. *Law of Desire* is a homosexual fantasy— AIDS doesn't exist. But Almodóvar is no dope: he's a conscious fantasist, and the movie is as aware of AIDS as the audience is. This wild man has a true talent. When Tina gives to the poor, her expression is exalted— she's Jesus and she's Eva Perón.

■

*R*aising Arizona is a monkeyshines burlesque of people who feel they can't live without an infant to cuddle; it's about baby love. At first, Edwina, or Ed—played by Holly Hunter—seems the sanest person around. Then she discovers she can't have a child, and she's a wreck until she hears about male quintuplets that have been born to a woman who took fertility drugs. Now a huffy little pixie with a quivering pout, Ed torments her husband, Hi (Nicolas Cage), until he goes to steal one of them. As soon as Hi plunks a quint into her arms, she yowls, "I love him so much!" The compliant Nathan Arizona, Jr., has this effect on everyone. Hi's plant foreman comes for a visit, bringing his wife (who's Ed's best friend) and their gang of children; ignoring their own kids, who attack everything in sight, the couple coo over the baby covetously, and plan to steal him. But two escaped convicts—backwoods brothers played by John Goodman and William Forsythe—make off with Junior, and they turn mushy and won't part with him even while they're robbing a bank. These two have deep, big-bellied voices, but they look like babies. They get so wrapped up in the gaga emotions of parenthood that they keep misplacing their snugglebug, leaving him on the double yellow line that divides the highway. Each time they discover he's missing, they wail in grief.

This broad satire has a cornpone-surreal quality. It kept reminding me of the 1945 hillbilly farce *Murder, He Says*, in which Fred MacMurray was an insurance agent who stumbled into a houseful of homicidal maniacs headed by Marjorie Main as a matriarch with a whip, and at times it has a Preston Sturges spirit crossed with the cartoon abandon of the early Gene Wilder and Mel Brooks comedies. It's an apparition of a movie: Hi and Ed live in a yellow mobile home with rooms that are huge—big enough for Sergio Leone to shoot in—and the home sits in a Tempe, Arizona, trailer park at the edge of a Pop-art version of the desert. The cacti in the background look artificial, and everything is warped and flipped out; the light seems fluorescent, as if the world were a twenty-four-hour supermarket. Joel and Ethan Coen, who did the writing together—Joel directed and Ethan produced (with Mark Silverman)—have a knack for hick-suburban dialogue. The characters speak a stilted slang to the accompaniment of banjos and, sometimes, a yodeller. The film has a galumphing tempo; storyboarded like a comic strip, it races from one sight gag to the next, from punch lines to double whammies.

As a compulsive fellow who once robbed convenience stores simply because they were conveniently on his route home from work, Nicolas Cage is a hound dog with goo-goo eyes—a flirty guy with a woebegone mustache, long sideburns, and a lamebrained barber's idea of a punk cut. Cage has sometimes been expected to carry roles that he wasn't ready for, but his youth works for him here. He's a lowlife caricature of a romantic hero, trying to do the right thing by everybody. Even when Hi robbed stores, his gun wasn't loaded, and once he's fallen for Ed (she was the policewoman who took his mug shots three times) he becomes a responsible person, a model husband. After the kidnapping, a hairy, demonic biker, played by Randall (Tex) Cobb, materializes out of Hi's scared dreams—he's an evil Road Warrior (even his boots are hairy) who blows up a bunny rabbit and sets fire to a daisy. Hi's apologetic expression when he dematerializes this monster is Nicolas Cage at his most winning. (Actors have made big reputations as farceurs on less talent than Cage shows here; his slapstick droopiness holds it all together.) Hi and Ed are a funny pair of lovers because they have such ordinary middle-class family aspirations; what makes them appealing (and redeems the banality of those aspirations) is that they lose out.

Raising Arizona should probably be a little shorter, and a few scenes (such as Hi's hanging around the quints' nursery trying to decide on the pick of the litter) aren't precise enough. Others (such as the jailbreak, with the brothers emerging from their tunnel during a rainstorm, as if coming to life out of primeval ooze) are of a likably silly too-muchness. The Coens (whose first film was the 1984 *Blood Simple*) are going with their strengths. They're making a contraption, and they're good at it because they know how to make the camera behave mechanically, which is just right here—it mirrors the mechanics of farce. *Raising Arizona* is no big deal, but it has a rambunctious charm. The sunsets look marvellously ultra-vivid; the paint doesn't seem to be dry—it's like opening day at a miniature-golf course.

■

Is Morgan Freeman the greatest American actor? Back in 1980, in a late-night-over-drinks conversation, a friend and I wound up agreeing that maybe he was. That was after seeing him in plays and on television and, earlier that night, in *Brubaker*. As a death-row prisoner who broke out of his hole and started to strangle another convict, he gave the film a sudden charge that the moviemakers didn't seem to know what to do with. Freeman just shot out onto the screen, and then his character was dropped from the story. After seeing him in the new Jerry Schatzberg film, *Street Smart*, I don't think that my friend and I were too far off. This is probably the first major screen role he's ever had, and he turns a haphazardly written Times Square pimp into something so revealing that it's a classic performance. Tall and slim, and looking like a very handsome, elongated Richard Pryor, he gives the role of Fast Black a scary, sordid magnetism, and he gives the picture some bite. Fast Black is old for a pimp; he's heading toward fifty, and he has watchful eyes; they're weary and shifty—you wouldn't want to look into them. This man's coiled power is in his complete lack of scruple; it's in his willingness to resort to violence. So it's best not to make the mistake of thinking that you can put anything over on him. He's seductive—he has a veneer of affability—but he's all contradictions; you never know where you are with him except right this minute, and the minute can be cut short. Magically, Morgan Freeman sustains Fast Black's authenticity; it's like sustaining King Lear inside *Gidget Goes Hawaiian*.

Christopher Reeve plays Jonathan, a privileged young man trying to be a smooth hotshot; he has gone from Harvard to free-lance writing for a weekly "lifestyle" magazine like *New York*. Lately, his facility has been failing him, and when he pitches ideas the editor (André Gregory) barely listens to him, until he comes up with "twenty-four hours in the life of a pimp." The editor jumps at it and wants it fast; Jonathan assures him that he has the contacts, and then he goes out to try to find them. He can't, so he fabricates the story—that's what the screenwriter, David Freeman, did when he published "The Lifestyle of a Pimp" in *New York* for May 5, 1969. It created no big stir; there were no dire results, and no big-time benefits, either. In the movie, though, we get the screenwriter's fantasies of all the things that could or should have happened. Doggedly, he piles them on: Jonathan's fiction appears as a cover story and is such a wow that he becomes the editor's pet and a celebrity; he's hired to appear on the local TV news as a roving reporter specializing in street life; his apocryphal pimp is somehow thought to be based on Fast Black, who is facing a murder charge; Fast Black seeks Jonathan out and gets to know him, and when the editor wants to meet the pimp it's Fast Black that Jonathan introduces; both the assistant D.A. and Fast Black's lawyer are now on Jonathan's tail; a judge orders him to turn over his nonexistent notes, and he goes to jail when he refuses. Eventually, after Jonathan's girlfriend (Mimi Rogers) has been knifed and a prostitute called Punchy (Kathy Baker) has been killed, the new, wised-up, devious Jonathan gives in to Fast Black's pressure, fakes notes that clear the pimp of the murder charge, and then, in the screenwriter's final (most synthetic) twist, outwits Fast Black for all time.

Often underrated, Jerry Schatzberg can make viewers feel the beauty and excitement of everyday grit. (He even brings off the trick of using Montreal for most of the Manhattan locations.) Schatzberg knows how to tell a story visually: in a hotel-room scene between Jonathan and Punchy, the movements of the actors and the camera show us layers of sexual gamesmanship building up. He makes the script look and play better than it deserves to. But he can't give it conviction, rootedness. He can't conceal the author's thin, brassy attitudes: this screenwriter is out to show that everybody is corrupt, that everybody uses everybody, and so on. Most of the performers do their damnedest. Kathy Baker's Punchy looks as if she'd be called Punchy; at times she's as forlorn as an alcoholic who has been falling face down. Baker's face seems to go out of focus, as if her expressions had changed too fast for the camera—but in sexual situations her face takes on an all-out intelligent sexiness. As a hooker, she makes you feel she's a pro who delivers pleasure. (She even gets by with seducing Jonathan to Aretha Franklin singing "Natural Woman.") André Gregory is terrific as the heartless, dryly self-amused editor. Trim and dandified, he's more than pleased with himself: he's his own yes man. Gregory is some kind of eccentric genius: this editor inflects smugness, cackling at his own cleverness, leaving a trail of media slime.

Morgan Freeman wears long fingernails (proof that Fast Black is not a laboring man); he has the accompaniment of funky music and Miles Davis's trumpet; and he's terrifying in a battle of wills with Punchy, who has made the mistake of thinking they're friends. But Christopher Reeve has no peculiarities, no distinctive musical backup, and no threat. He's a big nothing. Reeve is willing to play Jonathan as a suck-up who's trying to make his name. But as an actor he's physically too inexpressive to play inexpressiveness; it isn't the character who's a lug—it's Reeve. (When Jonathan's girlfriend marvels at his wonderful article and asks where the material came from, he crooks a finger to his skull. I blinked, expecting the finger to go right through.) Reeve has a personality when he's Superman; here, though, he doesn't seem to do anything but play what's on paper (diffidently), and it isn't enough. In the scenes where Jonathan thinks he can hold his own with Fast Black and discovers he's a helpless babe, Reeve isn't bad. His clumsiness works when he's up against Morgan Freeman's dancerlike swiftness; this taut actor can whip him with an eyelash. But when Jonathan gains the cunning to out-street-smart Fast Black it's a joke—an Ivy League white boy's dream of glory. We're supposed to take his victory as proof that he's learned his lesson and become a dirty realist. Actually, it's just a confirmation that the plot is a sham. Screenwriters who come on with the scoop that we're all pimps should just speak for themselves.

April 20, 1987

VAMPS

||||||||||||||||||||||||||||||||||||||||||||||||||||||||||||||||||||||||||||||||||||||||||||||||||||||||||||||||||||||||||||||||||||||||||||||||||||||||||||||||||||||||||||||||||||||||||||||||||

*P**rick Up Your Ears*, the English movie about the star playwright of the anarchic sixties, the disreputable farceur Joe Orton, shows dedication, courage, forethought—all the wrong qualities. The movie is a dud—honest and watchable, but not more than that, though the people involved might seem just about the best imaginable. It was directed by Stephen Frears from a screenplay by Alan Bennett, based on the literary biography of the same name by John Lahr. And it stars Gary Oldman, the rag-doll Sid Vicious of last year's *Sid and Nancy*, who looks so much like Orton that at a superficial glance you can't distinguish stills of him from the sixties photos. Yet the film has the wrong temperament: unlike Orton, it takes no real delight in misbehaving. Possibly the central mistake was to start from Lahr's book and to treat Orton's life in fractured biographical terms. Wallace Shawn, as Lahr, questions Vanessa Redgrave, who plays Orton's agent and close friend Peggy Ramsay, and who more or less tells Orton's story, which is presented in flashbacks, in the manner of *Citizen Kane* and *All About Eve*. This flashback machinery doesn't release Orton's snickering impudence—his inspired provocations. Mostly, it gets in the viewer's way. And though the film doesn't try to conceal the facts of Orton's sixteen-year union with Kenneth Halliwell (Alfred Molina), it uses them for a new kind of psychosexual moralizing.

By the time Frears and Bennett got to do the movie, Lahr had chewed over the material and solemnized Orton as a major, major artist. Lahr wrote a scholarly introduction to the collected plays, and he edited *The Orton Diaries*, which is pretty funny stuff—Orton does the buggering, Lahr does the footnoting. Frears and Bennett appear to have let Lahr, who uses Olympian tones for Pop figures, condition their thinking. We're not even made to laugh at the comedy of Orton's lewd antics with public-library books. After he and Halliwell had lived and worked together in claustrophobic conditions for almost a decade and couldn't get

295

their pseudo-Firbankian novels into print, they showed their contempt for public taste by stealing library books, redesigning the book-jacket artwork, typing up new blurbs on the inside flap, and then returning them. They defiled such work as books by Dorothy Sayers and books on John Betjeman and Sybil Thorndike; they did it with vengeful bawdiness. It was a preparation for the abominations Orton put into the plays that he worked on when he was separated from Halliwell for six months— the length of the jail terms they were given for their desecration of library books.

Presented differently, this episode, which was a formative event in Orton's life, could have pulled us all into the story. Who hasn't, at some point, wanted to befoul a book that angered him? And who but a scabrous, frustrated artist would give his energies to this defacement for three or four years, using meticulous collage techniques to turn library books into works of furtive, hilarious art? The movie treats the upset librarians as if they were Victorian prigs; this diminishes Orton's (and Halliwell's) satirical compulsiveness by making it seem as if only outdated, prissy people would be upset by it. If the moviemakers had got into the Orton spirit and made examples of his art clearly visible to the audience, we would be driven to giggling like dirty schoolkids.

Orton's life was a black farce, and a straightforward narrative might have been helplessly funny. The shifting flashbacks prevent us from getting a grasp on his character, or even caring to. Oldman's Orton seems outside his own story—an onlooker. We don't feel the process by which the poor, ignorant, stagestruck boy from Leicester, who learned so much from the older, better-educated Halliwell, found his independence in jail, in 1962. We don't follow the process of his self-invention: the transformation of a frail, scrawny, bookish kid into a bodybuilder who got into tough-guy outfits for cruising and had the cocky chic to know that they were more fetching on him than expensive tailoring would be. First, Orton scraped the money together for elocution lessons, so he could get rid of his working-class accent; later, he affected a laborer's speech. And he was shrewd enough to win grants and accept awards while playing the poor-boy outcast. The moviemakers seem to believe that their real material is in the sections that deal with Halliwell's inability to adapt to Orton's success. The facts are certainly sensational: as Orton's playwriting gift was recognized, Halliwell fell apart, and in 1967 he bludgeoned the thirty-four-year-old Orton to death and killed himself with sleeping pills. But in the movie the relationship between the two isn't convincing.

The actual Halliwell may have been even more jealous and tortured than the Halliwell of the movie, but physically he and Orton were about evenly matched. The casting of the large, heavy Molina as Halliwell puts a sad lump in the middle of the movie, and, with Molina's head shaved (Halliwell was bald), his bulging eyes are emphasized; he's a huge version of Peter Lorre in *M*. Halliwell's misery and grotesqueness seem to suck all the energy out of his scenes, and they affect our feelings about Orton: why is he so passive about getting clear of this guy? If the film had shown that the once assured, rakish Halliwell had become withdrawn during all the years of social isolation when they were a unit, and that he couldn't come out of his melancholy and connect with anybody else, maybe we'd feel a sympathetic involvement with him. And if we did maybe we'd understand Orton's commitment to him, especially after Halliwell's suicidal response to the shame of imprisonment. But the interaction of the two isn't well dramatized—it isn't quite there—and this also affects one of the subtexts of the movie: the cranky suggestion (it's quite explicit at the beginning) that we're seeing a symbolic marriage, and that the relationship between the Lahr character and his resentful wife, Anthea (Lindsay Duncan), is parallel to that of Orton and *his* resentful "wife," Halliwell. Frears and Bennett may have found this notion irresistible: Orton had dedicated his first big play, *Entertaining Mr. Sloane*, to Halliwell, and Lahr's dedication of *Prick Up Your Ears* to Anthea—the real one—was accompanied by unusually fulsome acknowledgments. (Imagine what Orton might have done to the jacket copy on Lahr's tomes.) It's quite possible that it was for the sake of this subtext (which fizzles out) that the moviemakers employed the device of Shawn's Lahr as inquiring author. It's a numbing device: it emphasizes the pastness of the bio form, and makes the material respectable.

You keep waiting for this movie to find its pitch, and it seems about to in the Moroccan scenes where Orton and Halliwell laze about with troupes of native boys, and in a balletic orgy in a public lavatory in London, but the staging is tasteful and unerotic. Frears provides an unsuggestive view of uninhibited sex. The cinematographer, Oliver Stapleton, gives the images a toilet look that's compelling—if only the Dionysian farce spirit were there. (After the Moroccan footage, the film seems to give up on any kind of rhythm.) Throughout, rough language is reproduced without the racy zest that would make it funny. (The only tease is in the title, which Orton was planning to use for a play; unscrambled, "ears" turns to "arse.")

Gary Oldman's Orton always seems to be in the middle distance, and he has no special priapic quality. This boyish fellow isn't much more than a series of reflexive cute smirks. Were Frears and Bennett deliberately trying not to get Orton's exuberance or any of his anger or intensity? For whatever reason, you don't feel his pulse. Vanessa Redgrave's smart, ribald Peggy Ramsay is the one with life. Redgrave has never been more physically witty than she is here in a scene where she's just sitting and talking and rubbing her shapely leg. She's fifty, and she's never been sexier or more spontaneous. The combination of her size and the light in her eyes is enough to heat up the theatre. But you could come out of *Prick Up Your Ears* without any sense of what Orton's farces were like. You wouldn't even know that he reinvented the epigram.

What you come out with are some post-Freudian banalities about how Orton's pansexuality liberated his talent whereas the inhibited Halliwell was driven to murder. Halliwell's motive is supposed to be envy of Orton's literary success and freer sexuality—which is defined here as anonymous sex in dangerous places. The film moralizes about sexuality in the political manner of the *Village Voice*. It may make you wonder why so much orgiastic sex has produced so few works of art.

■

It can be a little embarrassing to hear yourself laughing at *The Secret of My Success*, because the picture is stupid and often perfunctory. At the same time, it's moderately enjoyable. It has a let's-try-it cheerfulness, a knockout performance by Margaret Whitton, who's like a Lubitsch vamp, and nonchalant bits of artifice that are like Lubitsch touches. The director and onetime choreographer Herbert Ross has never been as freely kinetic as he is in this, his twentieth movie. He seems to take the derivative, jumbled material as a challenge, and he gives the adventures of a polite Yuppie hustler a spinning, light-headed quality. Michael J. Fox plays the farm-bred Brantley, a business major fresh out of a Kansas college and eager to storm Manhattan. His distant uncle (Richard Jordan), chief executive officer of the Pemrose Corporation, gives him a lowly job in the mailroom. Brantley reads the interoffice communications, sifts through the bureaucratic chaos, and, inventing an executive identity for himself, is soon issuing orders. Within a matter of weeks, he takes over his uncle's wife (Whitton), mistress (Helen Slater), and conglomerate. Yet the line between Brantley's guile and his guilelessness is blurry, and there's no follow-through on the orders he gives, or on much of anything else. The movie seems to be made of spare parts and assorted polishes.

It started with a script by A. J. Carothers, which was rewritten by the infamous Jim Cash & Jack Epps, Jr. (the cross-country-by-computer collaborators, whose reputation is based on *Top Gun* and *Legal Eagles*); the Writers Guild assigned these three the credit, though the dialogue was reworked by others—principally by Peter Stone, who is known for his dapper repartee (as in *Charade* and *Who Is Killing the Great Chefs of Europe?*), and by the sacred-monster playwright Christopher Durang. (He appears as the most petulant member of the Pemrose board, a twit with a glowering baby face.) The movie has nutty glories (much like those in Durang's plays), and Ross does a lot of visual ad-libbing; the movie isn't coherent, exactly, and it certainly isn't inventive enough, but it's frictionless—it has an easy flow. The cinematographer, Carlo Di Palma, puts a shine on the New York skyscrapers. They're the architecture of Brantley's dreams. When he sits up on the window ledge of his purloined office (it's actually the forty-third floor at 77 West 45th Street, south of Rockefeller Center), the image suggests a piece of calendar art; all that's missing is a friendly mutt. The editor, Paul Hirsch, may have the best sense of rhythm in his trade, and, with the action skidding around the corridors of power or twirling off to a country estate, the picture is surprisingly painless. (Well, not altogether. The music track, which features a basso's lascivious moans, starts up loud over and over again. It's nightmarish.)

As an executive at Pemrose, Helen Slater, who's also an architectural dream, has an introductory scene so quintessentially romantic that it's comic. She bends down over a drinking fountain, the water trickling from her mouth, and Brantley, staring at her in lovestruck slow motion, sees a goddess with great, heavy blue eyes, blank as those of a statue. This standoffish, ladylike executive (and mistress of the boss) has a refrain; she's a bimbo who keeps complaining about being called a bimbo. The line should be funnier than it is. Slater doesn't give much to the audience; she's deadeningly fatuous here—you don't even feel a commitment to acting. And maybe that's why when this executive was hurt and began to weep the audience laughed. Besides, we don't want to be reminded that Yuppie robots have feelings.

Michael J. Fox doesn't commit that kind of howler: when he's playing comedy he doesn't "go for real." Nothing is at stake when he's the protagonist; he doesn't pack the weight of an adult consciousness, and his boyish inconsequentiality may be part of his appeal to the audience. Fox gave a fine, staying-in-character performance in his last film, Paul Schrader's *Light of Day*—a performance that was completely different from his work on TV and in *Back to the Future* and *Teen Wolf*. But Schrader's cheerlessness infects his movies. This rock 'n' roll picture about family, religion, and death was a lugubrious working-class variation on *Terms of Endearment*—one in which the mother (rather than the daughter) died. Fox, in the backup role of son and brother—the stable member of a high-strung family—was wasted. Here, as bland, benign Brantley, Fox is back to doing what he does on TV, but he isn't monotonously "on"— he's relaxed at times, and he's jaunty when he's swaggering around the halls. His role is much like that of Robert Morse in the musical satire *How to Succeed in Business Without Really Trying*, but the pointedness is gone. The film's only goal is movement that makes you laugh. Luckily, Fox is a very supple performer; he slides through the cracks in the script.

The picture is sprinkled with standout "character" performances (Elizabeth Franz as Brantley's mother, John Pankow as his mailroom pal, Christopher Murney as the boss of the mailroom, Susan Kellerman and Carol-Ann Susi as secretaries, Mercedes Ruehl as a waitress). And there's Richard Jordan as the heel. Jordan is too sly and mellow an actor to be merely a heel. As the big boss, he's wonderfully oblivious and so self-absorbed he's slightly, casually paranoid. He's an ideal foil for Margaret Whitton as the sex-starved wife whose existence he has almost forgotten. It's quite believable that he loses track of her even when she's sitting next to him; he has lost track of his business the same way. (But this triple cuckold is confident that he's on top of things, and when he innocently asks, "You like to sweat, don't you, Brantley?" we share Brantley's momentary confusion.)

The artful Whitton enters the movie as if from a side door, and suddenly she *is* the movie. She was Darla, the hooker whom Robin Williams turned to for psychiatric counselling in the 1986 *The Best of Times*. Here she's Aunt Vera, the seductress who chases Brantley into the swimming pool and pulls off his shorts; she's what Anne Bancroft's Mrs. Robinson was at the start of *The Graduate*, before she turned crazy and vindictive. Whitton adores playing comedy; you can see her glee in those flirty, almond eyes. She gives her scenes a bedroom-farce zinginess that the other scenes just don't have. Ross must appreciate what he's got here. When Vera is in bed next to her husband, with her paperback of

Chéri and *The Last of Chéri* open on the quilt, the camera moves to her face and she looks like photographs of Colette—it isn't just the frizzy curls that are right, it's the expression. In one scene, Vera wears a little pointy hat, and she does it with an insouciance that suggests there's a little pointy head inside. That's comic style.

May 4, 1987

NANNIES AND NONCOMS

||||||||||||||||||||||||||||||||||||||||||||||||||||||||||||||||||||||||||||||||||||||||||||||||||||||||||||||||||||||||||||||||||||||||||||||||||||

As the brothelkeeper Christine Painter in *Personal Services*, Julie Walters is indulgent, like a bawdy nanny. She treats her customers like dirty little boys, and they love it, because that's what they feel themselves to be. Christine herself thinks that sex is dirty but it's like changing diapers—it has to be done. And she has a rude sunniness. She seems to free-associate to herself while talking to other people; she doesn't censor what she says—her unconscious associations just pop out. She keeps you laughing even when you can't quite hear what she's saying or tell what she's implying. It's her gleeful practical-mindedness that does it. When she thinks about the undignified actions that her dignified old gentlemen like to engage in, she giggles, and she carries you along with her. Her giddy hysteria seems the only appropriate response to the sexual habits of the English—it seems a higher normality.

Watching the movie is like being at a slapstick, slightly naughty party, and, sure enough, the picture has been banned in Ireland. The madam, Christine Painter, grounded on Cynthia Payne, London's famous Mme. Cyn (who acted as consultant to the film), is a great subject for the director, Terry Jones, of the Monty Python group. His first solo job of directing, Monty Python's *Life of Brian*, was condemned as blasphemous by Catholic, Jewish, and Protestant spokesmen—a clean sweep. Based on a script by David Leland (who co-wrote last year's *Mona Lisa*), this new Jones film is a cheerful piece of surreal vaudeville about British kinks. Alec McCowen plays one of Christine's regular customers—

301

ex–Wing Commander Morton, a ruddy-faced veteran of the Second World War who claims that he flew two hundred and seven missions over enemy territory in "bra and panties." Wing Commander Morton is so enthusiastic about the homey services that Christine provides—orgies are followed by tea and poached eggs on toast to replenish the old gents' strength—that he backs her financially. And he's like the brothel's m.c.

In the Python films, the shagginess could become exhausting, but this movie has Christine's story to link the skits, and it has Julie Walters' manic, inspired vulgarity. At times, she's as spirited as Mel Brooks on a good day. Like him, she's incredibly quick; you know that her Christine never once stopped to think—not in her whole life. She's a human carnival: you're seeing everything right bang at the instant it's happening. The whole film seems energized by Julie Walters, though she actually gets a lot of help. Shirley Stelfox is the cool dominatrix who does teamwork with Christine; they're at their funniest dressed as schoolgirls and sitting on both sides of a prim, guilt-ridden barrister who's also dressed as a schoolgirl—it's his fantasy that they're all three lesbians. Danny Schiller's Dolly, the elderly, gray-haired maid at the brothel, is perhaps the most paranormal of the characters. (It will be remembered that in *Life of Brian* Jones himself played Brian's mother, Mandy. Dolly looks rather like Ed Wynn.)

Leland and Jones take too much for granted: it isn't clear at first that Christine, who begins as a waitress, is trying to earn extra money by subletting rooms to prostitutes, or that when they don't pay up she has trouble meeting the rent of the flats she's trying to profiteer on. And later the film goes too soft when the moviemakers attempt to use Christine's story to represent a full range of English follies by showing us her posh romantic dreams and the hurt she feels at how she's treated by her father and her sister. But when the action sticks close to the brothel and its customers' requests, the film has a screwball fizziness and a sympathy for Christine's elderly clients—bank managers, magistrates, and other eminences. Christine services such a distinguished clientele that during the Christmastime raid that closes her down the police have to be careful to sort out the diplomats and let them go home. The other patrons are detained for only a short time, yet when they emerge from the police station they've been shocked sober and they look desolate. Their revels now are ended.

■

Gardens of Stone, the title of Francis Coppola's new film, refers to Arlington National Cemetery and, by extension, to all our soldiers lost in Vietnam. This isn't a combat film, though—it's a home-front film, set in 1968 and 1969, in the Washington area. Most of the characters are stationed at Fort Myer, Virginia, where they serve in the Old Guard, the Army's official ceremonial unit; they're precision-drill soldiers—show soldiers, used as Presidential escorts and to impress foreign dignitaries, used for outdoor concerts, for maneuvers at the White House and the Pentagon, at the Tomb of the Unknown Soldier, and, during the Vietnam War, for as many as fifteen burials of young men a day. The film is about this unit and its rituals, and the messy feelings of the show soldiers themselves and all the rest of us. *Gardens of Stone* is far from being a seamless work of art, but it probably comes closer to the confused attitudes that Americans had toward the Vietnam War than any other film has come, and so its own messiness seems honorable.

As Sergeant Clell Hazard, James Caan, returning to the screen after an absence of several years, looks older and, with an Army haircut that extends halfway up the back of his head, tougher and beefier. Caan's sergeant has spent eighteen years in the Army, and he loves it—he loves it the way Prewitt in *From Here to Eternity* did—and even though he doesn't believe the war can be won, he's hostile to the war protesters and he wants to get back into combat. Blocked from that, he becomes obsessed with trying to give the trainees a simulation of jungle warfare, so that they'll stand a better chance of surviving if they're sent to Vietnam. The story centers on his efforts to wise up a young trainee, Jackie Willow (D. B. Sweeney), who's the son of an old buddy of his in Korea. The kid thinks a good soldier could make a difference in Vietnam, and is eager to see action. He has kept his boyhood dreams of being a military hero—he feels that his manhood depends on it.

Caan has never given a sturdier performance, or a more demanding one—at times, he's as brusquely hypermasculine as James Whitmore—and yet it adds up to a flabby literary conception: a good soldier in a bad time. Coppola and Caan worked well together in *The Rain People* and the *Godfather* movies, but in those pictures Caan didn't have to negotiate the obstacle course that he's up against here. The screenplay, by Ronald (*Black Widow*) Bass, was adapted from the novel by Nicholas Proffitt, a self-described Army brat, who served in the Old Guard for three years before becoming a *Newsweek* correspondent in Vietnam. Since there was also considerable improvisation on the set, it's difficult to assign credit or blame, but it's clear that Coppola doesn't have the daring sureness of taste that he had in his *Godfather* days. He used to know the difference between rich material and junkiness, but something in him has got blunted— he goes right from robust comic scenes to vague searching and groping among platitudes. When Caan's Sergeant Hazard and James Earl Jones, as the sergeant major who's his best friend, express their profane disgust with the Army bureaucracy and the Vietnam War (Hazard had four years of action), the picture is a virtuosic service comedy. And when the sergeant is giving a dinner party to impress the woman he has just met, a *Washington Post* reporter, played by Anjelica Huston, and the sergeant major is there with his steady womanfriend, an aide to Senator Ervin, played by Lonette McKee, the conversational crosscurrents are explosively funny. The *Washington Post* war protester doesn't expect anything like the anti-war attitudes she hears from the veteran noncommissioned officers, or the right-wing views she hears from the radiant, sexy congressional aide.

Maybe it's inevitable for elements from old movies to crowd into a story like this one. The novelist, Proffitt, may have felt he was drawing upon his own experience of noncoms as father figures, but he was also drawing upon generations of lovable toughs. The movie's two jug-eared, bullnecked heroes are descendants of Louis Wolheim in *All Quiet on the Western Front*, of Edmund Lowe and Victor McLaglen and all the other actors who have played the brawling Flagg and Quirt in various versions of *What Price Glory?*, of Burt Lancaster in *From Here to Eternity*, and of dozens of more recent battlers. There's juice in the rousing characters Caan and Jones play; it gets diluted when they turn into idealized father figures, but when they can stick to comedy they're great together, overacting joyously.

Some of the best comic gimmickry in *Gardens* doesn't come from "life"; it comes from the movies. But some of the worst stuff—the serious stuff—also derives from the movies. There ought to be a way to give it a spin, to shade it as irony rather than try to pass it off as archetypal. That's how Coppola fouls himself up. He has lots of feeling, but he's short on resources, on cunning. And your respect for Coppola is shaken when you hear Caan saying that a man's gotta do what a man's gotta do and hear Anjelica Huston reply that a woman's got to do what a woman's got to do. Coppola may think that a scene in which a man and a woman define themselves has an aura—that it also defines our movie heritage. But what we feel is the sudden pulpiness of the two characters and the dispersal of the film's energies.

Coppola has been a first-rate scriptwriter, and so it's puzzling that he settles for scripts that are sketchy, rudimentary. This one isn't as fogged over as *Peggy Sue Got Married*, but after getting us involved in the story of the two noncoms and their stunning, tall women it shifts to Sweeney's Jackie Willow and his petite Rachel (Mary Stuart Masterson), who recognizes how gullible he is about the war. Coppola used to be confident that the audience would accept some complexity; now he throws us starry-eyed young lovers. He gets a smart, alert performance out of Sweeney, and Masterson, who has the jawline of a skinny angel, would be fine if the editor hadn't left in too many frames that show her quivering and shaking in grief. But these characters come from thin, slick movies. So does the central father-son relationship of the sergeant and Willow, which seems naïve and straggly; it doesn't draw us in, and most of it is consigned to the narration.

You'd think that after *Apocalypse Now* Coppola would avoid voice-overs. But Willow is on the soundtrack here, and if his letters from Vietnam (to the sergeant) are not as flossy as the letters in *Platoon* they're still a feeble device—they point up the weaknesses in the movie's construction. *Gardens of Stone* was underdeveloped in its thinking stages; it's too generalized and emblematic. So all the skill that has gone into the acting, the directing, and the cinematography (by Jordan Cronenweth) adds to the impression of incoherence that it gives. And there are embarrassments such as an embassy reception at which Bill Graham, playing an anti-war activist, goads the sergeant into breaking his jaw. (You almost wish it had been broken before Graham gave this performance.)

Coppola seems to have lost the ability to differentiate between what plays and what doesn't, yet the picture has some of the best-detailed work he's done in years. He has the show-biz zest to make that first dinner-party scene whoppingly entertaining. The picture establishes his talent for comedy: somehow he gets by with the tough-on-the-outside, caring-on-the-inside sergeants, probably because they're conscious of being tough-on-the-outside, caring-on-the-inside. The two sergeants are tired of the purely ceremonial aspect of their unit, tired of the empty masculine rituals. Caan and Jones embody the film's unarticulated theme: what it costs to keep up an appearance of strength. They bring an unforced depth to service comedy. James Earl Jones is the more engaging of the pair. When he laughs infectiously, you can't fight him off—he's a male Ethel Waters. He's playing a happy man, and his strange gray eyes have a dancing wit. He seems at ease; his Darth Vader tones are under wraps—

he uses a smaller rumble, which has its own comic range. Coppola keeps you attentive to the actors. You register the way the sergeants' stiff collars push up their flesh, making them look thick all over, and you register that McKee and Huston wear their period clothes like thoroughbred clotheshorses. The women don't get enough to do, but they're certainly physically imposing. I kept wanting to see lanky Lonette stand next to the towering Huston. Coppola doesn't grant us that diversion, but we do get to see Huston in a series of sleeveless, tight late-sixties minidresses, and—*oooee*—she's a harlot, she's a princess.

Dean Stockwell's nervy, doodling performance as the captain who knows how to use the skills of the sergeant and the sergeant major for the benefit of the Old Guard has a snap to it. With a big cigar for a prop and a gleam of infernal humor in his eyes, Stockwell is pure acting magic— i.e., imagination plus technique. A star at M-G-M when he was nine, he grew up to play the D. H. Lawrence character in *Sons and Lovers* (1960) and the Eugene O'Neill character in *Long Day's Journey Into Night* (1962); that means he went from being Wendy Hiller and Trevor Howard's son to being Katharine Hepburn and Ralph Richardson's son. He survived that lineage and *Blue Velvet*, too. It took resilience like the captain's.

Coppola (who may have thought of the Caan character as a movie director) is also becoming resilient. He has gone from great director to vacuous stylist to good-and-bad director. He seems to be fighting his way back—if not to greatness, at least to substantial, workmanlike moviemaking. In *Gardens of Stone* he's about halfway there.

May 18, 1987

NOODLES

||||||||||||||||||||||||||||||||||||||||||||||||||||||||||||||||||||||||||||||||||||||||||||||||||||||||||||||||||||||||||||||||||||||||||||

The title *Tampopo*, which is Japanese for "dandelion," is the name of a fortyish widow (Nobuko Miyamoto) who is trying to make a go of the run-down noodle shop on the outskirts of Tokyo that her late husband operated. The name—it's the name that the restaurant acquires, too—fits her. She's a weedy sort of flower—a meek, frazzled woman raising a young son and doing her best to please the customers. She can't, though, because she's a terrible cook, and knows it. One day, a courtly truck driver, Goro (Tsutomu Yamazaki), and his helper eat at the shop, and Goro, who wears a dark-brown cowboy hat straight across his brow, like the righteous hero of a solemn Western, gets into a fight on her behalf. Seeing him take on five men, she is inspired by his courage. She tells him that meeting him has made her want to be a real noodle cook, and, in his formal, majestic way, he makes it his mission to teach her.

Juzo Itami, who wrote and directed this flapdoodle farce, is the son of a pioneer director. Born in 1933, he spent time as a commercial artist before becoming a well-known film actor (he played the bank-executive husband of the oldest sister in Kon Ichikawa's *The Makioka Sisters*), and he's also a popular essayist. He turned to directing in 1984 with *The Funeral*, a prize-winner in Japan, which also starred Nobuko Miyamoto (who is his wife). *Tampopo*, his second film, has its own brand of dippiness. The subtexts connect with viewers' funnybones at different times, and part of the fun of the movie is listening to the sudden eruptions of giggles—it's as if some kids were running around in the theatre tickling people.

The picture is made in a free form, crosscutting between two sets of food adventurers. The main story is that of Tampopo, the cowboy-samurai Goro, and their band of friends as they penetrate the secrets of other noodle shops, bribing and finagling to get hold of valuable recipes. The secondary story takes up the culinary-erotic obsessions of a pair of lovers: a gangster (Koji Yakusho), in a white hat and suit, and his ready-for-everything cutie (Fukumi Kuroda). These two demonstrate that eating and sex can be the same thing. The proof is in the orgasmic moment when they pass a raw egg yolk back and forth from his mouth to hers, over and over, until it bursts and dribbles down her chin. This is undoubtedly one of the funniest scenes of carnal intercourse ever filmed, and it's shot in hot, bright color that suggests a neon fusion of urban night life and movie madness.

Itami uses his background in commercial art: every now and then, the characters assume shiny Pop poses, and the images have the slightly crazed look of heightened reality. (It's a little like the heightening in *Blue Velvet*.) The whole movie—an understated burlesque of Westerns, samurai epics, and gangster films—is constructed like a comic essay, with random frivolous touches. (Goro wears his hat in the bathtub, like Dean Martin in *Some Came Running*, and it works on its own—it's entertaining.) The characters are agreeable monomaniacs: they often speak in the stiltedly civilized language of food critics. (A noodle may be profound or synergetic; it may have depth without substance.) Itami loves filmed anecdotes. He shows us a woman dying just as her kids have sat down at the table, and her husband telling them excitedly, "Keep on eating! It's the last meal Mom cooked! Eat, eat while it's hot!" The scene is a brief sacramental black comedy. On the rosier side, there's a disconsolate little boy whose parents have decreed that when he's out playing he must wear the sign "I only eat natural foods. Do not give me sweets or snacks." When a man gives him an ice-cream cone, you get the feeling that the man wants to spite the parents more than he wants to give pleasure to the child. And there are such diversions as a restaurant scene with a class of young ladies being instructed in how to eat spaghetti without slurping. Elsewhere in the restaurant—in a private room—the man in the white suit is supping on crawfish in cognac, from his cutie's navel.

The film dawdles at times, and it has its lapses: Goro gives Tampopo her cooking lessons to the accompaniment of too much triumphal music; later, the jocular use of ragtime is a bit of a pain. And when Goro is giving Tampopo her workouts, to toughen her up for cooking, the spoof of *Rocky* is cloddish. But the lapses don't last long, and the picture has a frisky texture. Reminiscences of *Shane* and *Pépé le Moko* and Kurosawa's *Yojimbo* and films by Godard, Sacha Guitry, John Ford, and Sergio Leone may slip in and out of your consciousness while Tampopo struggles to get the broth right and goes to visit the Old Master, a chef who is surrounded by shaggy-haired vagrants discussing French food and wine. The Old Master decides to rally to Tampopo's cause, and his gourmet bums (they're like Japanese Hell's Angels) sing him on his way. When the skinny-necked, fine-featured Master joins up with Tampopo's other noodle warriors, the image seems posed as if for a calendar.

The film's greatest charm is in Juzo Itami's delicate sense of fatuity. He may have developed it during his years of acting. (He was in the American films *55 Days at Peking* and *Lord Jim* as well as in Ichikawa films and, more recently, *The Family Game*, by Yoshimitsu Morita.) Tampopo, who seems to transform from within, like the American heroines of the thirties, weeps for joy when her band of friends and teachers pronounces her cooking perfection. Goro lives by his code, and he beams with satisfaction at a task accomplished. He's as proud of the refurbished restaurant, Tampopo Noodles, as he would be if he'd saved a medieval village. He looks at the throng of customers waiting to get in and knows he's no longer needed. Stately as ever, he heads out to his truck; the Old

Master gets on his bicycle; and the whole group of mother's helpers disbands.

Itami's movie background is a satirist's treasure trove. There's a startling scene in which the white-suited sensualist buys a huge oyster from a woman diver; he tries to swallow it right out of the shell to which it's still attached and it bites him on the lip. Stirred by his appetite, the diver feeds the rambunctious oyster to him out of her palm, then licks the blood off his mouth. The gangster—the movie's dream hero—comes to the classic gangster finish. But even after he's shot down in the streets on a rainy night and his loyal moll pleads "Don't die!" he won't stop talking about what he wants to eat. He's got a recipe for wild boar stuffed with yam . . . And, with the whole history of movies reverberating in her voice, the moll says, "We'll eat wild boars in winter," as the gangster relinquishes his white fedora and puts it on her perfectly beautiful head.

■

Acomedy creator trying to work up fresh gags can lose his equilibrium. This helps explain why so many movie executives would rather deal with hacks than with artists. The hack brazens his way through, without knowing or caring that what he's getting is stale. The artist can have so much trouble getting his footing that he sometimes comes out with less than a hack might have.

Elaine May is one of the most gently nutty of comedy writer-directors. When her timing is on target, the target itself is faintly blurred and a double take is built into the viewer's response. When her timing is off, as it is in most of *Ishtar*, the viewer is left thinking Huh? The movie certainly isn't dislikable; you observe the fine touches. But you feel as if your mind is wilting.

Ishtar must have started out to be a casual, tacky *Road to* comedy about two aging nonentities—singer-songwriters who can only be booked into faraway night spots; dreaming of show-business success, they arrive in the Middle East and get caught up in revolutionary politics they don't know a thing about. This is the kind of musical-comedy burlesque of adventure movies that thrives on looking like an imitation B picture, as if the actors had wandered onto sets left over from straight-faced epics. The jokes call for papier-mâché Moorish castles, and spies in moth-eaten burnooses trudging around Palm Springs, with a caterer's wagon just out of frame. But *Ishtar* has been shot (by Vittorio Storaro) in a glamorous romantic style featuring authentic African sunsets, and Isabelle Adjani's pure, childlike face peeping out of the Moroccan clothes she's swathed in. All this misplaced visual gloss doesn't compensate for what's missing: comic energy. May comes up with clever script ideas, and the two male stars—Warren Beatty and Dustin Hoffman—give her lines a shine. They do everything they can *as actors* with the jokes that come their way. Her directing is passive, though. The stars get their laughs, but she doesn't build on them, and the laughs die away. The audience sits uncomfortably waiting for a sustained routine, waiting for the picture to get going. All that happens is another laugh followed by another dead spot. (May doesn't do the obvious, but sometimes she doesn't do anything else, either.)

The *Road to* genre calls for entertainers with the kind of sketch-humor savvy that passes for goofing off. The two roles could be handled more easily—and probably more energetically—by, say, Steve Martin and Bill Murray, or the *SCTV* performers. When Beatty and Hoffman play small-timers, it's a reverse conceit, a form of affectation. (And it's a big production.) As a bashful hick from Texas who drives a Good Humor truck in New York and wishes he were attractive to women, Beatty has his larkish moments, but he's playing against the grain. He muffles his personality; he makes himself so much less talented than he is that it's as if he were trying to take himself out of the picture. Hoffman, flexing his muscles and watching himself in the mirror, is effective in the early scenes. He's a preening vulgarian, a singer–piano player in a restaurant who belts out "That's Amore" and considers himself a ladies' man. But just when you think Hoffman is going to skip away with the movie, he appears to decide that he wants to be a sweet simp, too. The little muscleman confesses that his show of confidence was a fraud, and he begins to blubber. Hoffman, who can be funny when he's mean and vain and self-centered, is at his worst when he wants you to like him for his weakness and his innocence. These two major stars with a combined age of ninety-nine are both playing ten-year-olds.

They do have a great desert scene with a troupe of unusually handsome, well-groomed vultures. And there are performers who bring some charge with them: Jack Weston, as the team's two-bit hustling agent; Rose Arrick, in a tiny role as Hoffman's mother. And Charles Grodin manages to be fairly amusing because of his bland, whiny *lack* of charge. (He may be the only comedian to have made a career out of complacent affectlessness.) Grodin is a soft villain, despicable without being menacing—just right for Elaine May movies. He plays the C.I.A. man whose machinations force the two shlubby heroes to go out into the Sahara with a blind camel, and force the swathed beauty—a revolutionary—to go after them. (I admired Grodin, and I admired the camel, but both of them have given this performance before.) The plot involves too much exposition, and then doesn't add up. *Ishtar* is like a comedy act by a depressed person who keeps losing track of what's meant to be going on. The premise of the story is that the people of (the mythical) Ishtar will accept the two songwriters as the two Messengers of God who have come to fulfill an ancient prophecy. But there's no follow-through; the idea seems to have been abandoned. Other ideas aren't abandoned, exactly; they just aren't directed with much vitality. An American goes to a camel bazaar and asks for Muhammad; that should be funny, but the joke fizzles out in the amorphous staging. And it's disappointing that there's no snapper in the hoary device of the mysterious map that's supposed to alert the people to rise up, and no comic twist to Adjani's ardent chitchat about overthrowing the evil (American-supported) Emir of Ishtar. (An inside joke: When the knavish Emir offers the C.I.A. bozo a drink, it's a Pepsi. The movie was financed by Columbia; i.e., Coca-Cola.) Some scenes look scheduled for a payoff. Adjani gives Beatty necklaces of seeds to mark his path in the desert; she tells him they'll shine in the night. They don't, of course, and he and Hoffman get lost. But when she turns up he doesn't ask what happened. And the viewer's expectations shrivel and blow away. The plot finally hinges on the Jack Weston character's pressuring the C.I.A. into turning his two clients into stars. But May somehow fails to give the whole burlesque a satiric kick by pointing up that when it comes to cutting a deal, the C.I.A. is no match for even a penny-ante show-biz agent.

The movie has unusually clear sound recording—the kind you get from Godard or Robert Altman. But most of the music is a washout (even though some of the batty lyrics almost click). Sinatra's record of "One for My Baby (And One More for the Road)" is used for an extended sequence, and it gives the film a rhythmic blissfulness that you miss the rest of the time. When Beatty and Hoffman do their (deliberately hopeless) singing numbers, jerking like mechanical men, phrasing unmusically, going off-key, they don't have the slapstick skills for it. That's when you long for Martin and Murray or some other comics. (Beatty and Hoffman are pretty funny near the end, singing "How Big Am I," but it's too late.) When real comics make fools of themselves, you don't feel they're being good sports. You feel that foolishness is built into them—that it's natural to them. That's what you miss with Beatty and Hoffman. *Ishtar*, a burlesque without a subject, becomes, by default, a burlesque of their stardom.

June 1, 1987

HAPPY FEET, DEAD HEADS

||||||||||||||||||||||||||||||||||||||||||||||||||||||||||||||||||||||||||||||||||||||||||||||||||||||||||||||||||||||||||||||||||||||||||||||||||||||

Steve Martin is improbably light on his feet in the love comedy *Roxanne*. He's C.D., the fire chief, whose agility expresses the ticktock workings of his mind. C.D.'s body seems able to do anything his mind wants it to, and with the speed of thought. But he has an anomaly: a nose so long that birds can perch on it and he can sniff out distant fires. When he bangs this meta-nose into things and he shakes his head as if to clear it, he's suddenly W. C. Fields. As he saunters through the streets of the ski-resort town of Nelson, Washington (nestled against the mountains, it seems a dream-built town, but it's actually Nelson, British Columbia), he may do a precise little hop and a skip or waft himself in the air. The man and his timing are the same: he has a snap to him. And everything he does—like fighting two bullies—is a routine: assorted spins, kicks, whacks, and the bullies are knocked unconscious. Each routine is completed, and clicks into place. Early on, he puts a coin in a newspaper-vending machine, looks at the front page, screams, puts another coin in, and puts the paper back. And the gag tells us how lucky he feels to be high up in this town, far from the horror. His willingness to pay money to make the gesture tells us something else about him. He dances down the street because he craves movement, he loves gestures.

As C.D., Martin seems to crossbreed the skills of Fields and Buster Keaton, with some Fred Astaire mingled in. He's a wonder, which is what he should be, because C.D. stands for Cyrano de Bergerac. The script is Martin's updated version of the play that Rostand wrote in 1897, for Coquelin. Film footage of Coquelin in the role shows him tossing his sword about and juggling it in the duel-of-wits scene; he uses his physical dexterity much as Martin does. But Martin, who tells the story in a modern vernacular, isn't dashing—he's jaunty. His tart, low-key script

312

solves the updating problems tactfully, buoyantly. (The scene that explains why C.D. can't have his nose bobbed also gives him a chance to see himself in the mirror while holding up cards with different noses.) And, as a comic, Martin is in a conspiracy with us to stay a beat or two ahead of us. That's what we pin our trust on, and he does it more than ever here. His timing has Buster Keaton's inspired airiness. Nothing Martin does in this movie seems familiar, yet he's always the man we've come to see. He's in character as Steve Martin, only more so.

His lightness is a form of purity. It cuts down on the mawkish appeal of *Cyrano*—that it's shaped as an actor's masochistic fantasy. (In the play, the star can wallow in the feeling of being unloved because of "fate.") Yet he keeps the romanticism. Daryl Hannah is the stargazer Roxanne, a graduate student in astronomy who has rented a house in Nelson for the summer so she can study the skies. This new Roxanne isn't chaste, but she's not sullied, either. The experience she's had makes her seem more desirable, more voluptuous. And Daryl Hannah's height, the confident swing of her walk, and the fullness of her mouth and chin make her a spectacular Roxanne—a convincing embodiment of a flawed man's ideal. Wearing white clothes, she gives off a womanly radiance—a combination of carnality and moonglow—and in one sequence she wears two little Christmas-tree angels as earrings. Somehow, these dangling angels become emblematic; they take over for the white plume in the play. They stand for the unabashed ingenuousness of the film.

C.D. is, of course (as just about everybody will remember from high school, or earlier), too nose-conscious to tell his new friend Roxanne of his love for her. It's a measure of the success of this adaptation that when Roxanne impetuously takes a fancy to young Chris (Rick Rossovich), the strapping new firefighter brought in by C.D. to raise the level of the volunteer squad, it isn't distressing. By then, we have enough confidence in Martin's script and the verve of the director, Fred Schepisi, to know that the movie won't go clammy on us. And when the dumb lug Chris inveigles C.D. into carrying on his courtship rites for him—reciting speeches to Roxanne, writing impassioned letters—and Roxanne falls in love with C.D.'s words, thinking they're Chris's, the deception never gets a chance to be sickly. For one thing, Martin has had the script inspiration to whip up a character, the barmaid Sandy (Shandra Beri), who doesn't awe Chris the way Roxanne does. Chris doesn't need to be poetic and intense for Sandy, and as soon as we hear the easy way they talk together we know they're a perfect match. His attraction to Roxanne has been a mistake, like hers to him. And Martin's adaptation, without wrecking the play, speeds up Roxanne's coming to her senses. The moviemakers know that Rostand's idea of beauty (in the Brian Hooker translation) is too limited for an age that encompasses punk, an age in which looking unusual may be taken for an achievement, or, at least, a "statement."

Schepisi is a fluid yet right-on-the-button director, starting with the first scene, in which the spruce, angular, gray-haired C.D. jumps out of his front door and greets the day with a twist of his hips. It's like the beginning of oddball classics such as *The Bank Dick*, which didn't fuss around with overtures—they just got on with it. It's like that, but it keeps going more gracefully, without the jerky starts and stops. Schepisi's control probably helps to account for the warmth and likableness of Daryl Hannah's performance and for the quality of surprise in the scenes between Chris and Sandy; these two have the conversational rhythm of good-natured dopes. (Shandra Beri gives her idle talk just the right weight, and she's got a barmaid's sociable smile down pat.) Schepisi does well by the encounters in the town café. (Its owner is played by Shelley Duvall.) His blitheness comes through at the firehouse: the squad of volunteer firefighters are this movie's Keystone Cops; they're fumblers, unromantic clowns. (C.D. is a clown *because* he's romantic; he makes every day different for himself.) Schepisi uses the town of Nelson as if it were the firefighters' playpen. It's also a safehold, a haven for lovers. As the director uses it and as Ian Baker shoots it, this otherworldly, lost-in-a-trance locale is a major contributor to the film's mellow, dotty charm. You want to go to the town; you want to go back to the movie.

A false nose in closeup is riveting, of course, and we in the audience can't help looking for signs of where this thingamabob is attached to a real nose (and in at least one scene—with the bird—the joining makeup is visible). But the moviemakers do something very smart: Steve Martin makes his appearance as C.D. and we laugh at his quick-thinking moves before he turns his profile and we see the extension of the nose that sticks straight out. It doesn't do what the bandage did to Jack Nicholson's nose in *Chinatown*—it doesn't uglify him. This is a funny nose, an absurd nose, and it never really seems to mar his face.

In Hawthorne's story "The Birthmark," a magnificent woman's tiny defect is the source of tragedy because her husband can't accept it. Here C.D.'s aberration is comic because Roxanne isn't bothered by it. The movie is finally as simple as that: a love story about two sane people. It's like *Annie Hall* without anhedonia.

■

314

$\mathbf{S}$creenwriters: Beware of thesis sentences. They give the amateur away. (Though they enter consciousness through the ear, they can
make a moviegoer drop his eyelids in misery, as if to shut them out.)
How do we know that *River's Edge* is about teen-age anomie and the
indifference of selfish, corrupt adults? Because the movie keeps telling
us how to interpret what it's showing us; it interprets more than it shows.
Big-bellied John (Daniel Roebuck), a slugged, uncommunicative high-
school pothead, strangles his girlfriend, Jamie, and leaves her lying nude
on the riverbank; he mentions it—trying to sound casual—to a couple of
the boys he hangs out with, and when they refuse to believe him he takes
them to the spot and shows them her body. Soon all the members of his
pack of six or seven stoned, lost kids have viewed their dead friend,
whose body is beginning to look like pale-blue marble, her glassy eyes
wide open, her lips violet. Nobody makes a move to cover her. And nobody
speaks of notifying the authorities, because Layne (Crispin Glover), the
high-strung leader of the group, pressures them to believe that it would
be a violation of their code to let any adults know about what happened.
He argues that they can't help Jamie—she's dead. They've got to help
John, who's alive.

Taking off from an incident in Milpitas, California, in 1981, the film
uses each of the high-school-student characters to illustrate his own form
of deprivation and a generalized need for love and approval. This might
suggest a movie made for TV if it weren't for the explicitly sexual pulp
elements and the woozy poetry. Dennis Hopper plays an ex-biker dope
dealer who supplies the kids—a scroungy psycho who talks about having
killed a woman twenty years earlier. You may hear yourself sigh when
Hopper takes off a false leg. This cripple waltzes with an inflatable sex
doll he calls Ellie—she has the lewd round mouth of a piranha. In the
film's most pastoral sequence, he takes Ellie for an outing on the riverbank. She's part of the baroque live-girl/dead-girl/toy-girl symbolism. The
most courageous of the kids, Matt (Keanu Reeves), who is upset about
Jamie's being left out there on the grass (like a doll), has a younger
sibling, a twelve-year-old, who drops a doll into the river. At first, it isn't
clear what his sibling is: A girl? A boy? A hermaphrodite? It turns out
to be a malicious, twisted little boy (Joshua Miller), who has deliberately
drowned his baby sister's favorite plaything. This miniature sociopath,
whose only goal is to be accepted into the pack of teen-age dopers, is
designed to show us that the dullness of the adolescents is being super-
seded by something worse—little kids who don't feel anything. (Then it
turns out that he, like the older kids, can be saved by love—in his case,

brotherly love. If ever there was an unconvincing change of heart . . .)

The script, by Neal Jimenez, which began as a screenwriting-class assignment at U.C.L.A., appears to have been conceived as an exploitation melodrama, with Matt challenging Layne's leadership, and Matt and the dead girl's friend Clarissa (Ione Skye) finding strength in each other, finding someone to believe in and a reason to stay alive. But the director, Tim Hunter (*Tex*), has a fuzzy naturalistic approach, and *River's Edge* is a slack mixture of "important" and mediocre. I have been reading quotes in the ads about the film's "raw power," but power is what it doesn't have. It might have had it if we could feel how Layne dominates the others, if we could feel their admiration and their fear. That seems to be the dramatic logic in the script, but what comes across is that Crispin Glover is all actor. Is he being a contorted James Dean or a contorted early Brando? He's giving an expressionist performance in a movie that's trying to be "real." (The other adolescents are played very simply.) Glover's Layne is neurotically dependent on his hands: they want to talk. Or is it that Glover just waves his hands if the director doesn't stop him? Hunter doesn't seem to know what to do with this weirdo (who looks stimulated by his first sight of the corpse), and leaves him wandering around the screen grimacing. Glover certainly gives us more to watch than anybody else does (except for the scary, evil little doll-drowner). But the character he plays has no force as a leader: Layne doesn't connect with anybody, and when he's brushed aside nothing major seems to have happened.

River's Edge is being touted by some of the press as a cautionary movie about the "blankness" of youth. The kids we see aren't blank, though. They have raging feelings that they don't know how to put into words. And they don't know where their loyalties should be. They're confused. Part of the reason they can't articulate what they feel is that they smoke dope all the time, they've been smoking it heavily for years, and they're apathetic about what's being taught in school. But most of them aren't callous about Jamie's death; they just don't know what to do about it. In this movie, it's the adults who are blank. The parents are cartoon figures. Matt's mother isn't worried about his smoking pot; she just wants to be sure he doesn't swipe any of hers. And she's too involved with her lout of a lover to care what her kids do. She says feebly, "Where do my children go at night?" (That's a thesis question.) Clarissa's mother is barely aware of the girl's presence or absence. A teacher talks to his class about Vietnam and his part in the demonstrations of the sixties, but what he says is beside the point; the kids aren't educated enough to grasp how it might relate to them, and he puts them down for their squareness. And the cops are hostile to the kids, and think the worst of them. The clincher is that when Jamie's body is finally laid out in a casket there's no adult grief. (Nobody from the adult world even noticed that she was missing.)

This movie has something of the sensibility of a John Hughes picture—*The Breakfast Club*, for example—and of movies like *Tex* and *The Outsiders* that were based on S. E. Hinton novels. That is, kids can only trust other kids; adults belong to a rotten, materialistic world. This is terribly naïve, obvious stuff, but it seems to get audiences (and reviewers) just about every time. It expresses how adolescents feel and lays guilt on parents, who almost always know that they've earned some.

Hunter, by soft-pedalling Jimenez' melodramatic, often garish material, creates a blur that viewers can project onto. *River's Edge* doesn't deal with the facts of the Milpitas case (where the murderer was black). It tells us next to nothing about why John killed Jamie and shows us very little of how the other kids react to her death. Then this vacancy at the heart of the film is used as proof of the kids' heartlessness. By now, hundreds of reviewers and commentators must have quoted Clarissa's line "I cried when that guy in *Brian's Song* died; you'd figure I'd at least be able to cry for someone I hung around with." It has been cited as an indication of how unfeeling Clarissa is. But Brian's death was packaged for us to cry. Jamie's death is sudden and unreal; reactions to it come more slowly. *River's Edge* packages "thoughts" for us: when the little girl whose dolly was drowned erects a tiny cross for her, the moviemakers are pushing us to recognize that the older kids didn't do as much for their real-life friend Jamie. This is the same kind of flashy thinking as the allusion to *Brian's Song*. (It's also a ripoff of *Forbidden Games*.) And when Matt is grilled by the police he echoes Camus's Meursault; alarms go off in viewers' heads—these kids are Strangers.

River's Edge makes it possible for adults to cluck over what's happening to youth. (Clarissa says, "Sometimes I think it'd be a lot easier being dead," and her boyfriend answers, "Aw, that's bullshit! You couldn't get stoned anymore." That's a thesis joke.) At the same time, the picture endorses the kids' rejection of the adult world by showing that the adults who should be closest to them don't give a damn about them. And these adults aren't full of raging feelings. If they were, there might be some dramatic collisions in the movie. Instead, it reinforces the self-pity of adolescents and the audience's love of pathos. (What could be more pathetic than Clarissa's not being able to cry for Jamie?) When Hopper delivers soliloquies about how he loved the girl he killed and so is morally superior to John, who (apparently) killed passionlessly, are we meant to think he's making a valid point? Are the sixties being invoked as a holy time, because the young weren't apathetic then? Probably so. Why else would the dealer be set up as a parallel figure to John? The picture appears to be saying that the dealer may be crazy but he has got feelings, and John doesn't. This movie is so balled up it's using a catatonic boy to indict the children of pot and permissiveness. It's saying that they don't make psychopaths the way they used to.

June 15, 1987

BROAD STROKES

||||||||||||||||||||||||||||||||||||||||||||||||||||||||||||||||||||||||||||||||||||||||||||||||||||||||||||||||||||||||||||||||||||||||||||||||||||||

Chicago circa 1930—Al Capone's capital of crime—looks so much better than New York City looks right now that local audiences for *The Untouchables* may feel somewhat chagrined. Chicago still has solid traces of Louis Sullivan and Frank Lloyd Wright, and these and the other architectural remnants of the era that have been refurbished for the movie are a swaggering showcase for the legend that the screenwriter, David Mamet, and the director, Brian De Palma, present. It's the legend of the Prohibition era, and of a gangster who lived like a swell and almost got away with it. Assigned by the federal government to break Capone's hold on the city, Special Agent Eliot Ness (Kevin Costner) is a fresh-faced young innocent who doesn't even understand that bootlegging couldn't flourish without the collaboration of the police, and that the mobsters have bribed the officials, the judges, the mayor. At first, we wonder how anyone could think that this stiff is up to the job (or that Costner is up to playing the role). That's part of the film's plan: Mamet and De Palma want us to recognize that Ness, in his neat gray suit, is too clean to be able to clean up Chicago (and they've worked out how they mean to use Costner's blandness, too).

Ness is inexperienced, but he's dogged. Encountering a smart, ornery veteran cop, Jim Malone (the name rhymes with Capone), he asks the fellow to join up with him. Malone, played by Sean Connery, has had two aims: to stay honest and to stay alive. So he's still walking a beat. But he's sick of watching policemen get their palms tickled, and he starts teaching Ness how the city operates. At this point, the movie picks up. Ness and Malone find two other men who don't owe allegiance to Capone: a rookie-cop sharpshooter (Andy Garcia), who is an Italian-American and regards Capone as a stain on his people, and a small, middle-aged government accountant (Charles Martin Smith), who's an amiable crank with a fixation—he thinks that the gangland chief can be nailed for failure to pay income tax, if only the evidence of his business profits can be found. The movie is about the interaction of these four, and their fight to restore the honor of a corrupted society. They're designed to be true heroes, because they resist corruption in a situation where that takes supreme courage. And they're designed to be entertaining heroes, because they're such an unlikely group.

The Disney moviemakers knew that Snow White alone would be stupefying; she needed the Seven Dwarfs. And Mamet and De Palma know that the way to set off the Waspy-white Eliot Ness, the family man, is to surround him with misfits who are unlike him in everything except loyalty, courage, and a belief in justice. These qualities seem strongest in Connery's Irishman, Malone. At fifty-six, this grizzled Scots actor has an impudent authority that's very like Olivier's, except that Connery is so much brawnier. His performance here is probably his most sheerly likable turn since *The Man Who Would Be King*; it's a far less imaginative role, but he gives it a similar straightforward bravura. Mamet has provided him with lines that have a Biblical simplicity, and Connery delivers them with a resonant underlayer—Malone is always thinking and feeling much more than he's saying. In one scene, this aging man has a fistfight with a heavy, powerfully built white-haired cop on the take; we watch in horror as these two pound each other, and punches land on flesh that has lost its resilience. Somehow, Connery's Malone, while fighting with all his strength, never loses his sense of irony about his opponent's being an old man; his awareness makes the fight a comic horror. In a later scene, Malone, registering in a glance that he has been outfoxed by a killer, makes you feel the full, pulsing force of life in him. It's the force that holds this movie together. It transcends the pitches to the audience that are built into his role—tired gimmickry, like having him carry a St. Jude's medal that is passed along in the group.

The magnificent wide-screen vistas require a villain on a grand scale, and Robert De Niro's Alphonse Capone is a plump peacock with receding hair and a fat cigar in his mouth who wants everyone to jump at his bidding. He's also a ham who wants to be admired. In the first scene, photographed from overhead, he sits on his barber's-chair throne and is shaved and manicured and shoeshined while reporters ask questions and his underlings laugh appreciatively at his jovial answers. The scene suggests a windbag king's levee, and later, when Capone, surrounded by his retainers, comes down the main staircase of the hotel in which he has his baronial apartments, he exudes opulence. De Niro isn't in many scenes, but his impact is so strong that we wouldn't want more of him. Right after Ness's first successful raid of a Capone warehouse (it's in a post office), Capone, in full evening dress, stands pontificating about teamwork to his seated lieutenants, also in formal attire. They're at a huge, round banquet table set in a ritzy hall—the table suggests that this is his Camelot. (Here, and elsewhere, too, the palatial rooms are reminiscent of the vast spaces in Sergio Leone's *Once Upon a Time in America*.) All swanked up, and smiling at his own wit, Capone suddenly does something so grotesquely violent that we are as stunned as the men at the table. (His victim's crime is that he was in charge of the warehouse that got busted.) A movie doesn't need many scenes as shattering as this one; *The Untouchables* has all it can contain. Capone's stink is palpable. In his box at the opera—it's *Pagliacci*—he's brimming-eyed from the beauty of it all as the tenor, laughing through his tears, sings "Vesti la giubba." Capone's enforcer, Frank Nitti (Billy Drago), comes into the box to whisper that he has carried out his instructions to kill an enemy, and a grin breaks through Capone's beatific expression. When his lips part, a beam of light bounces off his teeth, and his face is a cartoon of obscene satisfaction. Later, in a courtroom scene, Capone displays a low-comedy belligerence: goaded by Ness, he lunges at him like a maddened beast, and has to be pulled back. He's ludicrous yet terrifying; he'd pull Ness apart if he could get his hands on him.

The Untouchables is a dream of gangsters in Chicago. It isn't De Palma's dream, though. This isn't a "personal" movie. He isn't the voluptuary satirist here that he is in *Carrie* or *Dressed to Kill* or the hallucinatory *The Fury*; he isn't the artist that he is in *Blow Out*. And *The Untouchables* doesn't have anything comparable to the romantic lushness or the obsessive, sensuous rhythms that Leone brought to *Once Upon a Time in America*. The picture is more like an attempt to visualize the public's collective dream of Chicago gangsters; our movie-fed imagination of the past is enlarged and given a new vividness. De Palma is a showman here. Everything is neatly done in broad strokes—the gangsters' bulging bodies in their immaculately tailored suits, the spats and fedoras, the tommy guns and gleaming cars, the gilt on the furniture, the deep, plushy reds of the blood. And the slight unbelievability of it all makes it more enjoyable.

De Palma has been developing a great camera technique, and in this movie—it's his eighteenth—he uses it more impersonally than in the past. He's making a self-consciously square movie. He works within the structure of Mamet's moral fable, and Mamet is a master of obviousness. This writer is all deliberation—his points are unavoidable. Yet his characters have a fullness: you get what you need to know about each one. His dialogue is pointed; it has tension. And the scenes have a satisfying economy. He's a good engineer, and his construction provides De Palma with the basis for reaching a broad audience. De Palma employs this engineering without being false to his own sensibility. He puts almost no weight on Mamet's moralism. (The film isn't at all like the Mamet-Lumet *The Verdict*.) De Palma doesn't press down on the scriptural language— he uses it as much for its rhetorical color as for its import—and when Ness makes a speech about how the war with Capone has changed him, De Palma glides over the words.

De Palma's resistance to Mamet's heart-tugging devices results in a neutral tone in some of the scenes. (The mother of a little girl who has been killed by a gangland bombing comes to see Ness to encourage him in his efforts; there are interludes of Ness at home with his wife and small daughter to show us the domestic tranquillity he's trying to protect; and his wife puts little notes in his lunch bags telling him how proud she is of him.) But if De Palma's cool neutrality is infinitely preferable to the cloying emotions that other directors might have piled on to scenes such as the one where the little girl is killed by the bomb (she might have been a bonny little lass), it nevertheless creates dead spots. At times, you feel that he's going through the motions pro forma, in order to preserve Mamet's structure. Yet De Palma takes such pride in camera angles and the organization of the shots that even the dead spots are likely to have some visual life. (The cinematographer, Stephen H. Burum, uses Panavision to spectacular effect. The imagery, though, isn't always backed up by the music; every now and then you wonder what Ennio Morricone's throbbing disco-synthesizer beat is doing in this period.)

De Palma demonstrates his technical command in a stakeout on the marble staircase of Union Station, where Ness and his sharpshooter have gone, hoping to grab Capone's bookkeeper. They've been tipped off that he's going to try to slip out of town, and they know that he'll be escorted by gunmen. A young mother is struggling up the steps with two suitcases and a child in a cumbersome old-fashioned baby buggy. Ness, positioned at the top of the stairs, keeps looking down at her progress, knowing that she's going to be right in the line of fire, and De Palma has the beautiful effrontery to make us experience Ness's anxiety in suspended time, as in the instant of a car's skidding into a tree. He holds sound in suspension, too: the shooting is punctuated by the noise of the buggy as it rolls down, clattering slowly, step by step. The sequence deliberately evokes the Odessa Steps montage in *Potemkin*. It doesn't involve crowds and armies, though—only a small number of people—and it isn't meant to be taken as real life. It's a set piece, and when it's over, you want to applaud De Palma for having the nerve to bring it off.

The Untouchables uses only a few historical facts, and embroiders those; it's a rehashing of the 1959–1963 TV series (which starred the imposing, fine-voiced Robert Stack) and of countless movies. But it has a pulp grandeur, like the big, magisterial Westerns made by John Ford. De Palma includes an homage to those epics in a sequence set on the Canadian border, where a truck convoy carrying liquor is expected, and Ness and his three friends are on horseback, working in cahoots with the Mounties, who are lined up on the horizon. But the follow-through of that lineup image is disappointing, and the sequence wouldn't be very effective if Charles Martin Smith's little, half-bald accountant weren't there to be the hero of the occasion. Smith has never before had the glory moments onscreen that he has here; when he charges the enemy, you feel the joy rise in him, as it does in the gunfighters of *The Wild Bunch*. It's a crazily exhilarating performance, helped by the fact that the accountant is no longer young; he never expected to be a hero—it sneaked up on him.

There's no getting around it: though *The Untouchables* is De Palma's only measured film, it's a blood thriller. It works for an audience because of the excitement you feel when the four heroes overcome their misgivings and their tremors, and go in for the kill. The Old Testament language is, finally, preparation and justification for attacking the mobsters with the only means at hand. And when, near the end, Ness arrests the mob's white-suited enforcer, Frank Nitti, and Nitti taunts him, saying that he'll be let out by the courts, and then tells a spiteful lie about Malone, we can see Ness's need to release his anger. The scene is directed so that the audience wants it to happen, *needs* it to happen. Ness says at the beginning that he will do anything "within the law" to destroy Capone's grip on the city; the point of his character is that as he gets to know himself better he learns he'll do more. This is too programmatic. The way Mamet designs his celebration of law enforcement, Ness's giving in to his vengeful impulse completes the plan. It's what is supposed to show that he's human—that he's grown. For some of us, this takes the air right out of his actions, and he's left a little wooden. Mamet doesn't allow the characters enough free will. But, in an impressive, four-square way, he fills out the audience's expectations. He gives you revenge—an eye for an eye—and makes it seem just and righteous. It's a relief when the film doesn't take itself so seriously—when it tosses in such burlesque stunts as a judge's ordering a jury that Capone has suborned to switch places with the jury in the courtroom next door, and then has Capone's counsel changing his client's plea from not guilty to guilty without consulting him. It's as if the stern Mamet had left the room and the kids were playing.

The Untouchables is not a great movie; it's too banal, too morally comfortable. The great gangster pictures don't make good and evil mutually exclusive, the way they are here. (Even Ness's deliberate violence, when he turns judge and executioner, is meant to be good: he's carrying out Biblical law.) But it's a great audience movie—a wonderful potboiler, like *Pagliacci*. It's a rouser. And if people laugh and cheer when the gangsters get their heads blown off they're probably not cheering real death. These gangsters aren't the lawless aspect of ourselves—the sly, manipulative part, the killer part. They're just sleazeball monsters.

■

Jack Nicholson entertains himself in *The Witches of Eastwick*: he snuffles and snorts like a hog, and he talks in a growl. And damned if he doesn't entertain us, too. As Darryl Van Horne, who describes himself as "your average horny little devil," he has half-closed piggish, insinuating eyes, and his big, shaggy head doesn't look as if it belonged on those small, fleshy shoulders. His wardrobe is an astonishment: it suggests a pasha or a samurai, and he changes garments in the middle of his conversations. He seems to have given more attention to assembling

323

his flowing brocade robes than he ever gave to assembling his body. He's so repulsive he's funny.

The movie wavers between satirizing a hyper-sexed male's misogyny and revelling in it. Directed by George Miller (of the *Mad Max* movies), from a rickety script credited to Michael Cristofer, it's a farce that resembles its source, John Updike's 1984 novel, only in its high gloss, the general outlines of the leading characters, some purloined lines of dialogue, and Darryl's entertainingly uncouth turns of phrase. When Nicholson has a dirty word to deliver, he punts it right into your face. And he has invented some furiously demented slapstick; he's an inspired buffoon. (Nobody is likely to fall asleep at this movie.)

The three women in the fictional New England town of Eastwick—Cher as a sculptor, Susan Sarandon as a cellist and music teacher, Michelle Pfeiffer as a reporter on the *Word*—aren't the busy adulteresses that they are in the novel. They're three good-hearted beauties (a brunette, a redhead, a blonde) who have lost their husbands by death, divorce, and desertion. They're lonely, and they practice a little harmless magic just to keep from being bored. It turns out that their combined longing for a man is potent enough to lure Darryl the lech from New York City. Once ensconced in a comically vast mansion, he seduces each of them, and soon they're all frolicking together in his indoor swimming pool. But though the women are in sexual bliss with Darryl, they're so upset by his cruel tricks (he causes the death of a puritanical local woman, the owner of the *Word*, played by Veronica Cartwright) that they decide not to have anything more to do with him. When he starts punishing them, they turn to witchcraft, in self-defense, to get rid of him. Except for this mechanical structure, nothing is carried through; about half the scenes don't make much sense, and the final ones might as well have a sign posted: "We're desperate for a finish." But even at its trashiest the movie keeps bumping along. It has its moments, such as the townspeople's initial inability to remember Darryl's name.

And those three beauties *are* beauties. Cher, though, mysteriously ravishing as she is, has too many closeups. The camera feasts on her heavy-lidded exoticism for so long that we can't help noticing that she isn't playing a character. And she doesn't relate to anyone else: she might be acting in front of a mirror. Sarandon is more luxuriantly physical, and she makes contact with the other performers—especially with Nicholson, in a scene where he accompanies her cello playing and she gets so hot her instrument starts smoking. Sarandon's huge eyes are made for batting, and she knows it. She has become a terrific comedienne. (A friend

324

of mine says she wears her eyes on her sleeve.) Pfeiffer has less to do, but her kitty-cat comedy style is soft and fluid; she blends right in with the others. They're a supple trio—not a brittle bone among them. Nicholson has waited all his acting life for a harem like this.

June 29, 1987

PONDEROSO

||||||||||||||||||||||||||||||||||||||||||||||||||||||||||||||||||||||||||||||||||||||||||||||||||||||||||||||||||||||||||||||||||||||||||||||||||||||||||||||||||||

Chances are that when Stanley Kubrick's Vietnam film *Full Metal Jacket* is at midpoint a lot of moviegoers will be asking themselves what it's going to be about, and when it's over they still won't know. The picture stays reasonably close to its source, Gustav Hasford's compressed, white-hot Vietnam novel *The Short-Timers*, which came out in 1979; much of the dialogue is taken directly from the book. Yet the short, spare novel has an accumulating force of horror and the movie doesn't, though it prepares for it in the long first section, set in the Marine Corps training camp at Parris Island, South Carolina. Private Joker (Matthew Modine) and the other recruits are methodically brutalized by the hateful gunnery sergeant (Lee Ermey), whose small-mindedness and impersonality are faintly funny. The man shouts abuse at us just about nonstop for three-quarters of an hour, and he punctuates his shouting with slaps on the trainees' faces, punches in the gut, and other assorted punishments. This section is basic training stripped down to a cartoonish horrorshow; it's military S&M. Kubrick seems to know exactly what he's doing here. He's so narrowly geared to the immediate purpose that he fails to establish the characters who will figure later in the film, but he achieves his effect: the process of turning young boys into robots has a sadistic, pounding compulsiveness. The moviemaking suggests a blunt instrument grinding into your skull. This can easily be taken for the work of a master director.

At the beginning, Kubrick's photographic style is oppressively close in; he holds the camera so tight on the actors' faces that he doesn't give them room to act. When the recruits' heads are shaved, they're shot like Falconetti in *The Passion of Joan of Arc*, only no emotions are being

325

expressed—that's a big "only"—and so there's no beauty in the imagery. The boys are under a microscope. When the sergeant tells them that they're "maggots" and all "equally worthless," there's nothing in Kubrick's approach to suggest anything different.

The lean, mechanical-man sergeant has a pet victim: a slow, overweight recruit whom he calls Gomer Pyle (Vincent D'Onofrio). The sergeant degrades him mercilessly, and pits the other men against him by penalizing the whole platoon for Pyle's failures. And Kubrick concentrates our attention on poor, doughy-faced Pyle; he's a fatty, like Dim the droog in *A Clockwork Orange*. (D'Onofrio had to put on sixty pounds to get the role.) But Kubrick isn't a psychological director; he doesn't seem to care anything about motivations. And so Pyle, whom Kubrick uses to demonstrate that the system for turning kids into killers can spin out of control, is no more than a comic horror, like a sad, fat crazy in an exploitation film.

In the novel, when Joker, who has tried to help the slow learner Pyle, joins the rest of the platoon in beating him while he yelps and moans, a scary-sick ambivalence gets its grip on the reader, and all the action in Nam that follows intensifies that ambivalence. The Joker of the book is like a living Catch-22: he's telling the story (it's a first-person narrative), and when he discovers that the war is turning him into a vicious racist killer we're right there inside him, as baffled by his emotions as he is, yet never doubting them. He has been brainwashed, like the others, and he becomes part of the fighting machine that the sergeant has built. In the movie, Joker joins in the beating but nothing in the second section seems to follow from it. And although the subsequent material is episodic—almost random—as it follows Joker, who eventually finds someone he knows from boot camp, we don't see through his eyes. Angular and sharp-featured, he's remote, spectral—he's supposed to be smart, but he, too, seems dim.

After the first part reaches climax, the movie becomes dispersed, as if it had no story. It never regains its forward drive; the second part is almost a different picture, and you can't get an emotional reading on it. Joker serves as a combat correspondent with the 1st Marine Division, and is assigned to write upbeat, "public relations" stories about the American soldiers' kindness to the natives, and to invent anecdotes that show we're winning the war. When he meets up with his buddy from Parris Island, he goes out on a patrol with him. They're part of a squad that sticks together during the Battle of Hue, the final round of the Tet offensive, in 1968. But when a sniper picks the men off, shooting them limb by limb, like a gourmand saving the tenderest bits for last, and we hear the men's cries, we can barely remember who they are. And we don't know why we're following Joker. His streak of humor seems ornamental—a curlicue, like the Peace button he wears on his uniform (to contrast with "Born to Kill," which he has painted on his helmet).

A Vietnamese hooker flips up her miniskirt, the better to show off her bottom for a marine's camera. That's the only suggestion of spontaneity in the film. Kubrick has become a hermetic, deliberate director, who painstakingly records scenes over and over again until he achieves—what? It can't be performances he's after. He shows so little interest in the actors that they come across as the dullest cast he's ever worked with. Only the sergeant and Pyle leave any visual recall, and that's not because of their performances—it's their physiques, their faces. A sequence in which the men in the squad encounter a television crew and are asked to talk about what they're fighting for is flabby, because Kubrick doesn't discover anything in them to reveal. And it can't be the atmosphere—the feel of the place—that he's after. He began as a photographer shooting pictures for *Look*, but now he lives near London, and he didn't go to Southeast Asia or the Philippines—Asia was brought to him. (The movie was shot in England.) So our vision of the war is changed. We don't get the image of a handful of black and white intruders in a land of Asians; it's a handful of Asians who are the intruders. There they are in the rubble of Hue under gray, lowering English skies, with some imported palm trees in the distance. Even when the marines are being trained it's disorienting to hear someone refer to the Island, because we have no sense that the men we're watching are on an island, or anywhere in particular. Yet it isn't so much the English locations that are the problem—it's the spirit behind using them.

It must be ideas that Kubrick is trying to get at. The screenplay, by Kubrick, Michael Herr, and Hasford, has attitudinizing speeches—the kind that sound false no matter how true they are. When a marine talks about how "we're killing fine human beings," his language is inert. Generally, the men talk in a profane military slang that can't always be deciphered but makes its point: that clean English can't express how they feel. The themes are familiar. The sergeant's boast that before basic training is over, the men will be able to shoot as well as Charles Whitman and Lee Harvey Oswald, who learned their marksmanship in the Marines, is in the novel, but in the movie it becomes a *Dr. Strangelove* joke. And the whole theme of the reprogramming of human material recalls *Clockwork Orange*—except that there it was from sociopathic to social, and here it's the reverse. But somehow the book's overriding idea—how these brainwashed men were destroyed from within—gets lost. This war was more intensely confusing than earlier wars (in which marines were also trained to be a fighting machine). Second World War books and movies seem reasonable compared with the psychedelic, acid-rock horror that you find in accounts of Vietnam, where the emotions of combat are heightened by a druggy poetics of guilt. The Joker of Hasford's book hated the helplessness of an old Vietnamese farmer the way he hated the infantile, blubbering Pyle. He was shooting at his own helplessness. It was his fierce revulsion that made him do horrible things; some part of him protested against being turned into a killer.

In the movie, Kubrick doesn't allow his "hero" to do those horrible things. So we don't get a sense of his inner conflict. Joker just seems a detached sort of wise guy, with a superior manner; perhaps his mocking attitude is supposed to help the hip young audience identify with him. He doesn't really connect with anything. And the Peace symbol he wears isn't a sign of the protest he can't quite acknowledge; it's explained as a symbol of the Jungian duality of man. What is emotional in the book is made abstract. The movie has no center, because Kubrick has turned this hero into a replica of himself: his Joker is always at a distance—he doesn't express his feelings. So the movie comes across as not meaning anything. But it has a tone that's peculiar to Kubrick. His cold-sober approach—the absence of anything intuitive or instinctive or caught on the wing—can make you think there's deep, heavy anti-war stuff here. The gist of the movie, though, seems to be not that war makes men into killers but that the Marine Corps does. (In *2001*, we were told that it was enough to be a man to be a killer.) Here's a director who has been insulated from American life for more than two decades, and he proceeds to define the American crisis of the century. He does it by lingering for a near-pornographic eternity over a young Vietnamese woman who is in pain and pleads "Shoot me! Shoot me!" This is James M. Cain in Vietnam.

It's very likely that Kubrick has become so wrapped up in his "craft"—which is often called his "genius"—that he doesn't recognize he's cut off not only from America and the effects the war had on it but from any sort of connection to people. (The only memorable character in his films of the past twenty years is Hal the computer.) What happened to the Kubrick who used to slip in sly, subtle jokes and little editing tricks? This may be his worst movie. He probably believes he's numbing us by the power of his vision, but he's actually numbing us by its emptiness. Like a star child, Kubrick floats above the characters of *Full Metal Jacket*,

328

the story, the audience. Moviemaking carried to a technical extreme—to the reach for supreme control of his material—seems to have turned Kubrick into a machine.

■

*J*ean de Florette is set in a wide-screen Provence in the early nineteen-twenties. Clearly, man is the viper in this harsh paradise—man in the form of the tough, greedy old peasant César Soubeyran (Yves Montand), called Le Papet, the grandpa, though he has never married and has no descendants. Le Papet wears a smile of self-satisfaction, even when he causes the death of a neighbor, whose land, with its spring of fresh mountain water, he covets for his dull-witted nephew, Ugolin (Daniel Auteuil). To make sure that those who inherit the property will sell out fast, Le Papet and Ugolin hide the spring under a load of cement. A poacher sees them doing it, and just about all the men in the area know that there has always been a source of water there, but they are a close-mouthed, tight group, and when the new owner, the hunchback Jean de Florette (Gérard Depardieu), turns out to be an educated city fellow, who has learned about farming from books, nobody tells him about the mountain spring. This nature-loving dreamer has a devoted wife (Elisabeth Depardieu), who used to sing in opera, and a delicate little daughter named Manon. Depardieu wears "GOOD MAN" in capital letters across his wide brow; in smaller letters we can read "He has poetry in his soul." And for slightly over two hours we watch him trudge across his land hauling two barrels of water that are fastened across his hump. When there's no rain and his plants shrivel and his rabbits die, it's our doom. Our only relief comes when the director, Claude Berri, cuts to Le Papet and Ugolin, who monitor Jean's misery, plot against him, and gloat. Their dinnertime talk, in the darkness of an old stone house that is partly sunk in the earth, is the film's regularly scheduled den-of-thieves time.

Adapted from the first volume of Marcel Pagnol's two-part novel *The Water of the Hills*, published in 1963 (it was derived from a picture he made in 1952), *Jean de Florette* is to be followed, later this year, by *Manon of the Spring*. Both films have been much honored in France, and the New York opening of *Jean de Florette* has been preceded by respectful—even awed—publicity. It isn't hard to see why. The scheming Le Papet and Ugolin stand for the dark, elemental forces. Clear-eyed

329

Jean is no match for their mingy-mindedness. We're seeing a big theme about "fate" being played out—the fate that used to be dramatized in silent-film epics and in sprawling realistic novels. But those works often had an unruly imaginative power. Berri, who did the adaptation with Gérard Brach, has conceived of his two films as a majestic, faithful version of the Pagnol books. He has said that it was his task to give the material "a cinematic rhythm," but "there was no need for imagination." That's what *he* thinks. *Jean de Florette* doesn't have the motor of a work conceived as a film. It's a copy, with no life of its own.

The movies that Pagnol himself made from his own material didn't have much life, either. As a scriptwriter, Pagnol drew upon many sources; Zola and Alphonse Daudet were among them, and several of his finest films, including *Harvest* (1937) and *The Baker's Wife* (1938), are from stories or novels by Jean Giono. The young Orson Welles cited *The Baker's Wife*, starring Raimu, as proof that "a story and an actor, both superb" can result in "a perfect movie" even if the directing and the editing are not "cinematic," and many of us would agree. But in the movies that Pagnol produced from his own plays the emotional texture is thinner and the talk is talkier (to American ears, anyway). The films in the famous Pagnol trilogy—*Marius* (1931), *Fanny* (1932), *César* (1936)—are static and seem to last forever. Whether the director is Alexander Korda, who did the first, or Marc Allégret, who did the second, or Pagnol himself, who did the third, the director is the caretaker of the text, and that's all he is. These are writer-controlled movies; literal-mindedness and pedestrianism are built into them. (It was no accident that Pagnol was the first moviemaker to be elected to the Académie Française.) And Berri, in some sort of ultimate homage to Pagnol, has honored his shallow, academic side.

One of the French film traditions that the New Wave seemed to have washed away for good was the folklore of greed in which the ignorance and meanness of the peasants were supposed to be cosmi-comic. Ugolin (that name!), who actually rather likes Jean and his family and half wants to be their friend, is a figure right out of those rustic fables. He and Le Papet and their opposite number, the sainted hunchback, are characters without any subtext. Berri seems dedicated to these people who live by the seasons and have rich earth under their fingernails. But his sincerity doesn't live up to Verdi's "La Forza del Destino" on the soundtrack. The actors say the lines that Pagnol wrote decades ago, and then time passes and they say some more lines. (It's *Masterpiece Theatre* with subtitles.) Montand, in his wide-wale brown corduroy jacket, is a pillar of peasant chic. And though Berri may have felt courageous making a movie about a hunchback, this hunchback is Gérard Depardieu, who's a six footer. His hump was made in box-office heaven.

July 13, 1987

A LADY SURRENDERS

||||||||||||||||||||||||||||||||||||||||||||||||||||||||||||||||||||||||||||||||||||||||||||||||||||||||||||||||||||||||||||||||||||||||||||||

*W*ish *You Were Here*, an English comedy about an uncontrollably ribald girl, is shot in warm, sunny flesh tones, in orange and pink and russet, with interiors that have the lived-in look of the wallpapered rooms of Bonnard and Vuillard. The colors seem to radiate from the willful Lynda—from her fair skin and strawberry-blond hair, from her frankness. Lynda blurts things out. If she thinks a woman is an old bag, that's what she calls her. Lynda, who lives in a seaside town on the south coast of England, has been contemptuous of sham since her childhood, during the Second World War, and her language has always got her in trouble with her tidy, stiff-necked hairdresser dad. It wasn't so bad when he was serving in the Navy, but it's 1951 now, her mother has died, and he's operating a barbershop. A proud Freemason, he doesn't understand why she can't behave like a demure, proper young lady—why does she have to shock people? At fifteen, the snappy girl flaunts her sexuality the same way she flaunts taboo words. She lifts up her skirts to show off her Betty Grable legs and gives men a good look at her knickers.

Written and directed by David Leland, the movie has a satirical yet dreamlike texture and an elusive grace. This is the first feature film Leland has directed, but it has some of the boardwalk atmosphere of *Mona Lisa*, which he co-wrote, and it's related to his script for *Personal Services*. Cynthia Payne, who was the inspiration for the madam in that movie, inspired this one, too. It's based on her early life, as the daughter of a widowed hairdresser father. As Lynda, dimply, curly-lipped Emily Lloyd, who turned sixteen on the first day of shooting, has something of the fluffy pertness of a newly hatched chick. (A friend of mine described her as a cross between Molly Ringwald and Laura Dern.) She embodies

331

everything that Leland is trying to say about the spontaneity, the honesty, and the happy, rude extroversion that kids have pressured out of them. She makes Lynda's tactlessness—which would be somewhat monstrous in life—seem a cosmic expression of truthtelling. And she has the kind of freshness and youthfulness that can't be faked on camera.

It's an entrancing performance, especially in the set-piece scenes that demonstrate Lynda's enthusiastic spirit. Ashamed of her cussing and her exhibitionist displays, her father (Geoffrey Hutchings) takes her to a psychiatrist, played by Heathcote Williams in a haircut that gives him a high-top resemblance to the title character of *Eraserhead*. The session in which the prissy, weirdo doc supplies her with words he considers provocative and tries to get her to associate freely is a high-camp vaudeville routine. It's perfection of its kind. She doesn't respond by the book, and the doc is stymied; Lynda feels she's the winner. But the townspeople don't ever regard her as a winner; they feel superior to her, because she's so obviously available. There's a sexual-initiation sequence that's a vaudeville skit, too. Dancing at the Rex Ballroom with a young bus conductor (Jesse Birdsall), Lynda is so elated that she eagerly goes home with him. Their night of lovemaking leaves her feeling that she's still practically a virgin. She wants a boyfriend so badly she could forgive him that, but her father leans on him and he doesn't ask for a second date.

You can see that this girl, in her long, full skirts, feels pretty and sexy, and that the townspeople almost fear her sexiness. The one who doesn't—the one who sees her eagerness as his opportunity—is an unsavory middle-aged pal of her father's, a bookie with a game leg. She cruelly calls him Long John Silver. And as Tom Bell (grown hawklike) plays him he's a loner with nothing to offer a young girl except his sensual expertise. Bell gives a fine morbid performance as a burned-out, self-protective man so ingrown that he can't loosen up and respond to Lynda. He devalues her because she accepts him. It's a seamy relationship; he exploits her youth and inexperience.

There doesn't seem to be anything in the culture to help Lynda get her bearings. When she goes to a movie with a teen-age boy, it's the swank spectacle of *Love Story* (known here as *A Lady Surrenders*), a 1944 film reissued in 1949, with Margaret Lockwood hilariously awful as a classical pianist who doesn't have long to live and Stewart Granger as an R.A.F. pilot who's going blind. The cutting between the petting teenagers in the audience and the noble, grimacing Lockwood (with a pure-white bow in her dark hair) is a short, full essay on high-flown British kitsch of the era. (*Wish You Were Here*, like just about everything of interest that's come from England recently, is from Channel Four, which doesn't go in for salutes to the Empire.) Lynda falls into the traps that rebellious, sassy girls have fallen into for decades, for centuries. She does it with a toss of her bright hair, but when she's pregnant and down, the picture loses its comic rhythm. Leland has a knack for dream-logic non sequiturs and batty, reminiscent details (the bus conductor has the kind of ear-lowering haircut that makes him look a total jerk), but he also has an earnest side: he puts unnecessary limits on the sexual-rebel theme by explaining the reasons for Lynda's behavior. She wants her father's attention, and since she thinks she isn't getting it she tries to get everybody's attention; she wants all eyes to be on her. This sort of thing isn't much more to the point than the doc's word games. And Leland doesn't hit many resonant notes in his efforts to link Lynda's troubles to the death of her mother. (That's what the title refers to.)

The picture makes its feminist points comically, then becomes diffuse when it turns into a poignant melodrama. But its banalities and simplifications are generous, and Pat Heywood's performance, as Lynda's aunt who comes to her aid, transcends the explanations. And the action is never visually banal. The cinematography, by Ian Wilson, makes you feel as if you could touch the shafts of sunlight and Lynda's pink clothes. Even when the film isn't completely effective, it has its feeling for the dance at the Rex, where a male vocalist whose ears stick way out sings the film's theme song, "Lost in a Dream"; the van on the beach where Lynda works selling fish-and-chips and sees the bus conductor queuing up with his new girlfriend; the Dome Cinema, with its outsize figure of Betty Grable and, above the theatre, the room with large, arched windows, where the bookie lives.

Lynda goes to Bournemouth and works as a waitress at the staid, upper-class Paris Café Tea Room that suggests a mausoleum for meals. Riled up when she's fired, she climbs onto a table, addresses the guests on the subject of sex, and denounces the hypocrisy of the management. (After she finishes spouting off, an ancient lady in a lace floor-length tea gown who plays the piano for the guests applauds her enthusiastically. This desiccated old dame still has her own spark of rebelliousness.) When Lynda returns to her home town, she holds her head high and walks about briskly in an attention-getting bright-yellow dress that says "I'm here, everybody." She'll find her bearings by herself.

■

Eat the Peach is whimsical, but it has an element of desperation underneath. (The title is from "The Love Song of J. Alfred Prufrock," with a switch in meaning.) The story takes place in an Irish village just a few miles across the border from Northern Ireland. When the local Japanese computer factory closes down, the principal employer in the area seems to be the mob that runs the smuggling. Vinnie (Stephen Brennan), one of the men thrown out of work, is tall, handsome in a morose way, and obsessively ingenious. You may think that he's the sort of man you'd want with you if you were a pioneer heading out into the wilderness, or if you were cast up on an island and needed someone to figure out how to build a shelter and construct a boat. He seems a natural leader of men who's stranded in the peat bog, with nothing to do and nobody to lead except his amiable brother-in-law, Arthur (Eamon Morrissey), who seems a natural follower. One of the departing Japanese executives hitches a ride with Vinnie and Arthur on their motorcycles, and, already nostalgic, he shouts to the wind, "I love this place! . . . You're free here!"—which, in terms of the movie, is both irony and simple truth. *Eat the Peach* is about Vinnie and Arthur's freedom, but we retain the image of the beautiful green helicopter that lifts their Japanese friend off the spongy earth through overcast skies. That copter is the last piece of shiny, dream hardware to be seen in this movie.

Killing time in the village bar, Vinnie and Arthur watch a cassette of Elvis Presley in the 1964 *Roustabout* and see a cyclist ride in a carnival Wall of Death—a round, high, barrel-like track where centrifugal force keeps the rider up in the air circling. Vinnie immediately starts diagramming and measuring, and clearing a patch of land near his house. Despite the protests of his wife, Nora (Catherine Byrne), who packs up their little girl, Vicky, and goes back to her mother's, the two men begin sinking tree posts into the ground and putting up a huge cylindrical construction. Now that they have their "project," as they call it, they become energetic and resourceful—scavenging wood, talking villagers who have machinery into helping them, and smuggling booze, so they can buy the lumber they can't steal. Vinnie is the man he might have been in a different place at a different time, and his enterprising manner persuades Nora to return. He convinces himself that his Great Wall of Death will be a source of income—that people will buy tickets to stand on a gallery around the top of the rink and watch him and Arthur give daredevil performances. Then they can build another Great Wall, in sections, and take it on tour to carnivals.

The movie is actually about the deep-seated eccentricity of a man like Vinnie, who doesn't use his problem-solving ingenuity in order to make a living or to provide decent quarters for the wife and child he loves or to give his wife the kitchen she longs for. He's an impractical man who solves only those problems that tease his imagination, and his wife learns to value him for what he is. Her brother Arthur is more than a follower: he's a man with a gift for companionship—he has riches inside. He eats the peach all the time.

Just about everything in the picture is based on actual events. The director, Peter Ormrod, who stumbled on the story when he was searching out items for Irish television and saw a huge, wooden tank just off the road, co-wrote the script with John Kelleher, who arranged the financing through Channel Four and his own new Irish production company. (Many of its subscribers are in the crowd of ticket buyers who stand on the rattling, swaying Wall at the first public performance.) Ormrod and Kelleher tell the story as if it were a simple one, taking care to let it expand in our minds. The three leads, who are well-known stage and TV performers, are backed up by Niall Toibin as Boots, a local fellow who wears a cowboy hat and Western footgear and tries to pawn himself off as an American-style promoter. Boots signs on as the manager and publicist for the Wall (and tries to make time with a blond barmaid, played by Bernadette O'Neill, by telling her that he'll turn her into a singing star). The other characters include the brutish head of the local mob and his suave younger brother—a politico who's the elected official of the region. This engaging film gives you a pretty clear sense of the accepted level of corruption in the countryside and, more centrally, of how a "project" can keep a man's brains and hopes from rotting.

It has wonderful, uninsistent images. Hauling a truckload of Smirnoff across the border, Vinnie tells the guards it's pigs, and Arthur sits in the middle of the cases playing a tape of pigs squealing. After Vinnie's first test ride on the Wall, he and his buddies celebrate just outside his house: he plays the guitar and they all sing "Heartbreak Hotel." And then, after Nora has put Vicky to bed, she comes out and he takes her for a lovers' spin and rides the cycle right into the house. This is poverty-row filmmaking, and often the shots don't match. (Sometimes you can't tell whether the action is meant to be at dusk or night or dawn.) But it's the kind of movie in which you rather enjoy the shots' not matching. It draws you into the moviemaking process; the informality is likable, and, with your head cleared of the usual expectations (this is not like any other

335

film you've seen), you respond to the way the characters go about living their lives. At times, you may feel a little tuned out, but then the vision comes together.

After little Vicky has watched her father flying around the tank (he loves it, he's completely happy), she, too, becomes obsessed, and there's a quick shot of her, her face as determined as his, as she rides her tricycle along the Wall, trying to climb it. There's nothing coy about this kid. She wakes up one night hearing the crackling sound of burning wood; she rushes out the front door and sees her parents and her Uncle Arthur watching a fire, and she stares at the spectacle without a sound, the flames lighting her awed, startled face. For an instant, with her hair streaming back from her head, she's the soul of Ireland, the way Sara Allgood was when she played in *Juno and the Paycock*.

■

In *Innerspace*, Dennis Quaid plays a frisky, brawling Navy test pilot who loses the girl he loves, a San Francisco reporter (Meg Ryan), because he can't seem to get it through his head that it's time to grow up. A lush who talks back to his superiors isn't going any higher in the Navy, so, just for the hell of it, he volunteers for a top-secret Silicon Valley human-miniaturization experiment that nobody else is willing to take on. It involves the use of two microchips—one for the reduction, the other to reverse it. Quaid becomes a germ-sized pilot in a tiny pod that's meant to be injected into a lab bunny (called Bugs), but industrial spies break in, the reversal chip is stolen, and, in the ensuing chaos, he is injected into the backside of a fretful hypochondriac supermarket clerk, played by Martin Short. This fellow is ready for a nervous breakdown even before Quaid starts talking to him and he thinks he's possessed— as, in a sense, he *is*.

With one guy floating around in the other's bloodstream, this sci-fi buddy-buddy comedy sounds stupid-crazy-funky, and at its best that's what it is. But mostly it gets by on being good-natured enough for you to accept its being clumsy and padded and only borderline entertaining. The director, Joe Dante, made his reputation by the subversion of cuddly themes. Here, working from a script by Jeffrey Boam (and Chip Proser) that's a synthesis of the 1966 *Fantastic Voyage* and the 1984 *All of Me*, he seems to be slogging through pages of plot, dutifully trying to set up the mechanics for the gags to pay off. And a lot of the time he's setting up the emotional apparatus to give the movie "heart." The gimmick is that the Quaid character is a rooster with, as he says, "zero defects," and the Short character is a harmless hysteric who sees himself as a catalogue of malfunctions. Quaid has to coach Short to develop the courage necessary to fight the spies and help Quaid get out before he exhausts his twenty-four-hour supply of oxygen. Short is changed from a neurotic pipsqueak into a confident man of action, and Quaid learns to value life, and that allows for a reconciliation with his girlfriend. The picture strains to be inoffensive.

Luckily, the three leads are just about everything they should be. Dennis Quaid has the leering big smirk of a smartmouth satyr. He may be the only actor who can be infectiously free and breezy while scrunched up inside a pod. He got some practice as Gordo Cooper in *The Right Stuff*; this role is a continuation of Gordo's brief in-pod sequences, but here it's an almost totally encapsulated performance. Quaid and Short are rarely in the same scene, yet Quaid's personality leaps out and they seem to be together. When Short, at Quaid's urging, has a drink, so that Quaid can get a tingle, and Rod Stewart singing Sam Cooke's "Twistin' the Night Away" blasts forth from Quaid's stereo deep inside him, Short reacts with the euphoria of someone who isn't used to alcohol, and dances. It's a nerd's letting-go Twist. Gluey-legged, he's like an insect in convulsive ecstasy. A terrific yet familiar insect: Short moves like his Ed Grimley getting carried away on *Saturday Night Live*. But *Innerspace* is held down by so much slow-moving script that it's starved for craziness, and this dance is its high point.

In one scene, Short goes to his doctor's office; in the waiting room, he sits between his old *SCTV* cronies Joe Flaherty and Andrea Martin, and, hearing Quaid's voice, thinks they're talking to him. These *SCTV* troupers know how to respond to each other's rhythms—it's as if they were all inside each other. The scene is just a doodle—it isn't developed— but it can make you register that the movie needs more doodling (and needs to run with it). And it makes you conscious of how little comedy Dante is able to squeeze out of his character actors and his supposedly comic villains. (The problem isn't that they're cartoons but that they're pointless, impersonal cartoons.) Meg Ryan's blitheness gives the picture a lift; she brings a quirky, resilient spirit to the scenes in which she and Short have to chase after the thieves in order to locate the tiresome microchip and save Quaid. But the movie is too commercially clever in its notion of having Short fall in love with her. Short is a wild-eyed,

337

furiously inventive performer; he shouldn't need this trumped-up tenderness and pathos. This movie puts him among the screen's ranking
comic actors, but the danger looms that he could become elfin-lovable—
a darling. Dante is already tapping that possibility.

July 27, 1987

SIBLINGS AND CYBORGS

||||||||||||||||||||||||||||||||||||||||||||||||||||||||||||||||||||||||||||||||||||||||||||||||||||||||||||||||||||||||||

*G*ood *Morning, Babylon*, the first film made in English by the
Taviani brothers, seems to shed its humor as it goes along. It's amiable
at the start, when it shows us the exalted ideas of themselves that Italian
workmen have. Two teen-agers (Vincent Spano and Joaquim de Almeida),
the youngest of seven boys in a family of Tuscan plasterers and masons,
are the favorite sons of their patriarchal father (Omero Antonutti) and
think no harm can befall them. They're happily at work restoring the
façade of a Romanesque church, but when that job is finished the family
business collapses, and these two bumbling innocents, told by their father
to remain equal always, go off to seek their fortune in the New World.
The period is the years before the First World War, and there's a charming, folklorish shot of the boys' first sight of the lights of New York
through a porthole: they see the city as a Christmas tree. Eventually,
they find jobs as plasterers in San Francisco, working on the Italian
Pavilion of the 1915 Panama-Pacific Exposition, and then in Hollywood,
working for D. W. Griffith (Charles Dance), building the elephants—
which are poised on their back legs—for the vast Babylonian set of *Intolerance*. But the Tavianis' movie has gone down in defeat long before
the immigrant brothers are hired by Griffith. It takes them too dismally
long to get to the West Coast: the film slumps into masochism during
their hardships in this country, when they work at bizarre, humiliating
jobs along the way, like tending pigs in the Grand Canyon. (What are
they doing there? What are the pigs doing there?) And even after they
reach L.A. and meet the people associated with Griffith they seem piti-

338

able, and it takes forever (and more humiliation) before the great man gives them the nod.

The L.A. scenes are meant to be an affectionate tribute to early moviemaking, yet they don't show much respect for the facts. The two girls that the brothers marry (Greta Scacchi, Desiree Becker) are extras who get jobs dancing a modified hoochy-koochy at Belshazzar's court; this is an insult to Griffith, who used dance as part of the lyric, flowing strength of his conception, and to the dancers in *Intolerance,* who were specially trained by Ruth St. Denis and Ted Shawn. (Most of them were from the Denishawn troupe.) And though Griffith was meticulous in his use of dyes and beams of color, when we're shown the première of *Intolerance,* in 1916, it's in black-and-white. It's understandable that the Tavianis couldn't afford a set with the depth or dimensions of the one that Griffith built, but surely they could have done better by the elephants, which are a key element in their story. These elephants look as if a not too talented child had carved them. (Was the intention, perhaps, to turn film history into a child's fable?) The sum total of the early-moviemaking scenes isn't so much a desecration as an embarrassment. The Tavianis try for a fanciful, naïve tone and almost always miss, though there's a lovely pictorial effect when the two boys court their girls by handing them fireflies, and another when they're in charge of the panels releasing sunshine onto a set and they flood the girls in light. The score, by Nicola Piovani, adds to the poetic texture of moments like these.

The film goes completely to hell in its sections about sibling rivalry. When a movie is about two brothers who work together in pictures, and is made by a team of brothers, you expect some linkage. But you don't expect the sudden, jarring craziness you get here, when the Spano character's wife dies in childbirth and, the parity of the brothers' relationship being destroyed, he is enraged, irrationally blames his brother for his loss, and goes off to fight in the war. The two meet again, one in the Italian Army, the other in the American Army, on a battlefield near the church we saw them repairing. This piling up of coincidences is probably meant to suggest the storybook symmetry of movie plots, but it just feels silly.

The reduced scale of the Babylonian set makes it obvious that the Tavianis' huge undertaking was undercapitalized, and the fact that L.A. was re-created in Italy and the Grand Canyon sequence shot in Spain doesn't help. The Tavianis' not speaking English is certainly a factor in their misjudging their effects; they were hampered, too, by the international cast, with actors playing Americans who aren't remotely Amer-

339

ican. But maybe the whole idea was at fault. (It came from an American, Lloyd Fonvielle; was turned into a script by the Tavianis, assisted by Tonino Guerra; and was then translated into English.) It sounded wonderful to me when I first heard about it: the Tavianis were going to make a movie about two Italian brothers who go to Hollywood and work on the construction of the Babylonian set for *Intolerance*. My eagerness was tempered when I heard that the two boys came from a long line of builders who worked on churches. One of the most tiresome myths about movies is the identification of movie crews with the "anonymous artisans" who labored on the great cathedrals. Ingmar Bergman is responsible for giving it intellectual respectability, and all over the world moviemakers who battle for credits love this phony view of themselves. (They may seem to be saying something modest and self-deprecating, but if you listen closely they're claiming for movies the status of enduring works of art and spiritual monuments, and they're claiming for themselves the highest and most dedicated functions.)

This democratic sentimentalization of moviemaking—as if the replaceable plasterers made the same contribution as the irreplaceable writers and directors—is at the center of *Good Morning, Babylon*. The two artisans express their pride in their heritage, shouting to the Hollywood paper pushers, "We are the sons of the sons of the sons of Michelangelo and Leonardo! Whose sons are you?" This may be meant to be funny— meant to parody the boys' passionate, Italianate self-regard. But it's a singularly infelicitous challenge, since Michelangelo and Leonardo were both homosexual and are not known to have fathered children. More to the point, it confuses craft and art. The idea of *Good Morning, Babylon* probably appealed to the Tavianis because, as the major artists they showed themselves to be in *Padre Padrone, The Night of the Shooting Stars*, and parts of *Kaos*—artists who are also idealistic egalitarians— they could use it as an opportunity to try to reconcile art and Marxism. They sought to demonstrate that the magic of movies comes out of teamwork. The whole film is like a speech a director might make to his crew or a coach to his team: it seems to be saying that movie magic and team spirit are the same thing.

There's a little bit of truth in this, and the Tavianis toy with this truth, romanticize it, try to give it some iconic substance. They have Griffith explain to the boys' father, who has come over for their double wedding, that their work in movies is part of the same collective dream that built the cathedrals, and that movie work is done in the spirit of anonymity. All this makes *Good Morning, Babylon* somewhat repugnant:

the celebration of moviemaking and team spirit makes your tongue feel coated. In the middle of the piousness, there's the towering, autocratic figure of D. W. Griffith to give it all the lie. And, from the shifting tone of the film, it appears that the Tavianis know that what they're saying is absurd. But they hope their storybook maneuvers will whirl us past the absurdity and make us feel that at some deeper level it's all true because it should be, the same way New York should be a Christmas tree. It has probably occurred to the Tavianis that at times they themselves are bumbling innocents.

■

*L*a *Bamba* is the life story of the Chicano rock 'n' roller Ritchie Valens (Lou Diamond Phillips), who had three hit records before he died at seventeen in a plane crash, in 1959. But the writer-director Luis Valdez (who also made *Zoot Suit*) isn't primarily concerned with Ritchie Valens as the bullet of talent he must have been. The film's Ritchie has no special drive. Phillips is playing a Latino version of the boy next door; he's warm and friendly and rather simple. Valdez's aim seems to have been to create a positive image, and to transmit the message that you can have dreams even if you're Hispanic, live in a migrant camp, and pick fruit. But movies have a way of cutting through high-mindedness: Ritchie Valens' music, as it's performed by the group Los Lobos, with David Hidalgo singing for Phillips, is what carries the movie along. And, even with the music, this is a feeble, lachrymose piece of filmmaking. Phillips has nothing to play but dewiness, while a fiery, hammy actor, Esai Morales, plays Ritchie's tormented, bad-boy half brother, Bob. The director overworks the torment: whenever Ritchie is praised, Bob's eyes flash, signalling his jealousy and his misery. Bob keeps having snits and tizzies, but the innocent Ritchie doesn't seem to notice that he's the cause. It isn't until late in the film that he asks Bob, "What's your problem, man?" By then, you want to hide your face.

No doubt many people are susceptible to the film's mythmaking; you can hear their enthusiastic weeping in the theatre. Others will find that except for the score the pleasures the movie provides are almost all incidental. As Bob's young wife, who can't stand his constant demands for sex, Elizabeth Peña has only a few lines (and those are stale), but when she whacks at Bob the stud or pushes him away, or just looks at him with disgust, you want to applaud her. And several of the singers who play singers are jovial and assured: Stephen Lee is the Big Bopper (who was killed in the crash along with Ritchie and Buddy Holly); Brian Setzer is Eddie Cochran and sings "Summertime Blues"; the terrific Howard Huntsberry is Jackie Wilson. They have a sensual, rhythmic ease that livens up the picture; they move like performers who are used to holding an audience. That's also the case when we see Los Lobos as a band in a Tijuana café—when Ritchie gets his first look at Mexico. But these moments only make us more aware that Lou Diamond Phillips is just gesticulating when he pretends to be singing in front of a crowd. Jessica Lange gave herself over to Patsy Cline's happy, rowdy belting in *Sweet Dreams*: her strong body and Cline's exultant voice became one. And she was a hot creation. But Phillips is an inexperienced actor going through the motions of being the young fireball who was one of the innovators of Latino rock. A teen-age performer with Ritchie Valens' energy would have been powerfully attractive, but you don't feel any heat from Phillips—just likability.

Valdez has made the kind of sincere, leaden movie that can be acclaimed as the story of a Chicano boy asserting his heritage. Or it can be acclaimed as the story of a poor Chicano succeeding in America by ambition and hard work, and rising to the top of the charts. Valdez appears to be saying both; it's a very affirmative movie. Ritchie's brother takes him down to Tijuana to be deflowered, but he's more interested in the band than in the girls—he responds to the risqué folk song "La Bamba" that the band is playing. Once home, Ritchie adapts it to a rock beat, and learns it in Spanish, which he doesn't speak. In *The Jazz Singer*, back in the twenties, the hero had a conflict between his cantor father's religious music and the black man's jazz he loved to sing. But Ritchie has no conflict: he likes the song "La Bamba," he sings it and records it, and everybody's delighted. Basically, this Ritchie is the best-adjusted kid you've ever seen—except for the bad dreams he has about an air collision that took place above his elementary school.

Implicitly, Valdez appeals to your good will: he's making a film about poor, hardworking people who love their families. So a lot of people are disposed to accept his ineptness and shamelessness. He throws in mystical portents (a winged tattoo, a Thunderbird) and everything from Ritchie's having premonitions of planes falling to the two brothers' having an encounter with a Mexican sage—ancient, of course—who feeds them a snake and mutters words of wisdom. Valdez has this seer give Ritchie a good-luck charm, which he wears around his neck until Bob, who is fight-

342

ing with him, breaks it off—just before the fatal plane trip. The movie may be about roots; it's definitely about hocus-pocus.

Ritchie does experience prejudice: the Waspy car-salesman father of the blond schoolmate he falls for—Donna, who has Mamie Eisenhower bangs—is hostile to him. But this isn't the kind of movie that asks why he's drawn to this Waspy blonde. His attraction to her comes across as his aspiring to American niceness; the Ritchie of this movie seems Waspier than anybody else. He's an imitator of Elvis, but he's such a good boy that he takes all the sexual aggression out of rock. The way Valdez shapes the movie, Bob is the sinner and Ritchie is the virginal schoolboy saint, crooning his song "Donna" to his unattainable sweetheart. He can be the pride of the Latino community (and still be innocuous enough to be liked by the larger public). The picture is a hangover from the fifties: he's a credit to his ethnic group.

■

When the sounds of *RoboCop* came at me, amid the yells of the boiling-over audience, I attributed the bludgeoning line readings to the fact that the Dutch director, Paul Verhoeven (*Soldier of Orange, The 4th Man*), doesn't have a particularly subtle ear for English. But something bigger may be involved: maybe, working with only a rudimentary knowledge of the language, he embraced a mass-audience obviousness that he couldn't—or wouldn't—have settled for in a culture where he knew the nuances. In interviews, Verhoeven has spoken of wanting to make an American movie, and his idea of what's American turns out to be a punk sci-fi revenge fantasy that gets people in the audience so worked up they shriek louder than they did for Charles Bronson or Clint Eastwood. The thing that's distinctive about *RoboCop* is that its gloomy, frightening vision of the future is played for depravity, for kicks. Set in a Detroit of cloud-topped skyscrapers and a decaying older part of the city where rapists and vandals run wild and every day is open season on cops, the movie is shot in a deliberate sicko-sleazo comic-book style. (Body parts are treated as if they were auto-body parts.) Essentially, it's just a hipper, more bam-bam version of the law-and-order action hits of the seventies. The ads feature the enthusiastic quote "A stainless steel unstoppable Clint Eastwood."

At first, the hero is Murphy (Peter Weller), a dedicated young cop employed by the all-powerful conglomerate OmniConsumer Products—OCP—which has a contract with the city to operate the Police Department. When Murphy is blown apart by a gang of scummy sadists, OCP's scientists use his remains as part of a cyborg—an experimental model for a new kind of organic, automated cop that requires food but is virtually indestructible and is programmed to keep order. Part man, part tank, this virtuous knight in heavy metal clumps through the picture. What gives viewers a rooting interest is the spark inside this prototype. Murphy had a woman-cop partner (Nancy Allen) when the hoods used him for target practice, and she recognizes him in his new, armored form; she talks to him as if he were still a person—still Murphy—and he responds. Despite RoboCop's metal plating and his circuitry, some human memory remains: he has dreams in which he reëxperiences his death, and he goes out to get the giggling coke freaks who killed him.

Nancy Allen's short, efficient-cop haircut makes her look a bit apple-cheeked, but she has a great, wobbly run, and she's a quiet blessing here. She has the right soft tones to give the movie a little differentiation; it makes sense that she would get through to RoboCop's human memory. And he rediscovers his humanity in the nick of time. (You can get tired waiting for him to show something besides armor.) Weller's delicate-boned face is wan in the early scenes, and during the middle section he is steel-hooded. But then his face is revealed again: his skin is stretched back and his features are sunk in a big, no-neck face that's attached to coils of metal brains. This face seems tense, pained, ethereal. It has the imaginative beauty that stirs audiences at classic horror films. And, on a simpler level, Weller and Allen suggest a rapport without overdoing it; their chumminess is the only relaxed, pleasant touch in the movie.

In general, *RoboCop*, which was written by Edward Neumeier and Michael Miner, is a compendium of gimmickry from *The Golem, Frankenstein, Death Wish, Westworld, Superman, Rambo, Mad Max, The Terminator, Blade Runner, A Clockwork Orange, Escape from New York, Streets of Fire*, and dozens of other sources. What gives it its box-office cachet is its romantic plot device (man's soul survives death) and its kinky, leering tone. The picture keeps telling you that its brutishness is a terrific turn-on, and maybe it is if you're hooked on Wagnerian sci-fi comic books. (The movie company has already spawned a Marvel version of *RoboCop*.) But if you're not you may keep flinching at the clumsy, heavy-metal vigilantism, as RoboCop dispatches one lowlifer after another. Some directors can make the distasteful witty; they can be nastily decadent, as Verhoeven was in *The 4th Man*. But here, working in English, he doesn't have the timing or the spirit for that. This isn't gallows humor—it's just gallows pulp. When a huge, lumbering pre-cyborg robot is being tested and goes on the fritz, it does just what you expect. And even when a scene has some fast, quirky tracking or when it employs a flashy effect, Verhoeven's directing goes clump, clump.

In this near future (the nineteen-nineties, say), the TV news is delivered by trashy, gossipy anchorpersons (brunet male, blond female), and it comes in three-minute "Media Breaks" that interrupt a sitcom (or maybe it's a commercial; you can't tell the difference anymore). The news reports are gleefully cartoonish about nuclear threats and a space-weapons disaster, but there's no vision behind the film's two-bit nihilism. We're told that OCP has a contract to run the police. A contract with whom? Clearly, OCP (an anagram of "cop") is the city's only government. After sketching this society, with its sleek corporate wealth and its pervasive rot—the corruption is at the top, among the aging Yuppie executives, as well as at the bottom—the picture goes for a pseudo happy ending, brought about by the chief executive officer of OCP, who's a fine, socially responsible fellow. He's at the helm of a viciously corrupt totalitarian society, yet he isn't drawn satirically, as a front for the guys who run the whole works. He's the real thing: white-haired Daddy-God. This stuff is being called satire. That's a glorification of comic books, which may have a sharper reputation than they deserve.

There are a few neat ironies surrounding the picture. The film's Detroit of the future is actually Dallas, with the help of some matte paintings. (The added skyscrapers look like robot buildings.) This Detroit's creepy section, where RoboCop and the woman cop hole up, and where one of the psycho villains is splattered by toxic waste (we see him in various stages of meltdown), is a rusted abandoned steel mill outside Pittsburgh. In interviews, Verhoeven, who had a failure with the 1985 English-language film *Flesh & Blood*, has been explaining that *RoboCop* deals with "a very Christian thing," that it's "about a philosophical situation: death and resurrection." Of course—the resurrection of his career. He's come back as a man without sensibility, RoboDirector.

August 10, 1987

TENDER HOOEY

|||||||||||||||||||||||||||||||||||||||||||||||||||||||||||||||||||||||||||||||||||||||||||||||||||||||||||||||||||||||||||||||||||||||||||||||||||||||||||||||||||||

Slowed down and seen in stop-motion, the dancing during the titles of *Dirty Dancing* turns into writhing and groping. It's so sexual it's funny, and it's a promise of giddy good times ahead. Set in the summer of 1963, this bright dance musical is about the role that dancing had in the embryonic counterculture. Baby Houseman (Jennifer Grey) is a serious-minded seventeen-year-old with a mop of curly blondish-brown hair. She has intentions of joining the Peace Corps, but that's still a few years away. So here she is on vacation with her family at Kellerman's Mountain House, a resort in the Catskills. Not much interested in the sports and other activities that occupy her doctor father (Jerry Orbach), her complaisant mother (Kelly Bishop), and her square older sister (Jane Brucker), she wanders about alone, and on one of her nighttime explorations she chances on a party in the staff's quarters where couples are wriggling orgiastically to the loud sound of the hot Motown record "Do You Love Me?" Their erotic dancing—a sultry form of moving while holding each other close—is a shock to Baby. She's scared of it and drawn to it, and when Johnny Castle (Patrick Swayze), the resort's muscular young dance instructor, reaches out for her and shows her how to move with him she adores it. A new world of physical sensation is opening to her. But Max Kellerman (Jack Weston), who is all foxy smiles to the guests, is a hard-eyed businessman, and he has issued an edict that the help (the working-class ones) should not become involved with the daughters of his (prosperous, middle-class) customers. So after sweeping Baby into his arms and getting her to loosen up, Johnny Castle thinks better of it and abruptly leaves her on the dance floor. Stirred, excited, she goes on moving alone for a second before she knows she's alone. It's coitus interruptus.

The movie is ruefully perceptive up to this point. Jennifer Grey has the soft manner to make Baby's chagrin gently comic. We feel that we're

346

seeing a movie written from memory and imagination, and that we're seeing this girl as the innocent, protected fool the screenwriter now realizes her to have been. And though the dance scenes don't knock you out or get you wildly elated, they seem just right—even if this close dancing was actually more popular in the late fifties. (By the early sixties, the Twist was in, and couples were already separate and gyrating.) The director, Emile Ardolino, has a background in dance documentaries, and the choreographer, Kenny Ortega, is experienced in music videos, theatre, and films; they've given the dance sequences a growing-out-of-the-story feel yet made them brisk and rousing. When Swayze's Johnny Castle and his blond partner, Penny (Cynthia Rhodes), are trying to sell lessons to the guests, they do exhibition dancing that's very different from their dancing at the staff party. And when Baby, who has befriended Penny, goes through a quick intensive training to fill in for her and serve as Johnny's partner at a public performance you can see that the plot is getting rigged, but Jennifer Grey's natural-looking acting and her tentative dancing carry you along. This young actress—she's Joel Grey's daughter—is tiny, but all of her is expressive; she's affecting right from her first scene. As Grey plays her, Baby is convincingly scared and awkward, yet it doesn't take long to realize that she leads a charmed life. At a training session, Baby follows Johnny's strong lead while Penny dances behind her with her hands on Baby's hips to give her more of a sense of the movements. The scene has the texture of a dream; Baby, in the middle, is safe.

Dancing here is a transparent metaphor for Baby's sexual initiation, and when she goes to bed with Johnny—who's written as experienced, sensual, and loving, an honorable working-class youth with a streak of early-Brando alienation—he's as ideal a partner as he is on the dance floor. By then, you know that the gifted but self-romanticizing screenwriter, Eleanor Bergstein (the daughter of a doctor, and a competitor in "dirty dancing" contests), still shares the view that Baby the seventeen-year-old has of herself. Ardolino does a steadfast job of directing, and the movie never loses its energizing spirit, but the material turns into something like a young-adult novel. Baby wears a halo of good motives. Her love for Johnny is strong and sure; she has the nobility to see the baseness of class distinctions and rise above them. Johnny recognizes her qualities; his love for her is deep and honest. And everybody comes around to recognizing what a wonderful girl she is. By the end, the whole world is collaborating in Baby's (and Bergstein's) fantasy: parents and children

347

and staff are all dancing together in the main dining room, and Baby, high up on the stage, nods in approval.

What Bergstein has written is a girl's version of that old phony: the-summer-I-grew-up-and-everything-changed. In the boys' versions, the hero typically had a bitter revelation: his eyes were opened to the weaknesses of the person he'd idolized—the older brother (Warren Beatty in *All Fall Down*) or the uncle (Paul Newman in *Hud*) or the father figure (Richard Crenna in *The Flamingo Kid*). Typically, the boys in these coming-of-age movies came down to earth with a jolt. But this is a girl's coming-of-age fantasy: she ascends to spiritual and sensual perfection. For Baby, the change occurs as the result of self-discovery through dancing and then through her sexual initiation and her full and open commitment to Johnny. He has been treated as nothing and he has come to believe he's nothing; Baby the fearless changes all that. Soon Johnny is telling the assembled guests and staff that she has taught him the kind of person he wants to be. Too many life lessons are learned in this movie, and, of course, its wish-fulfillment aspect makes Baby and Johnny and all their dirty-dancing friends pure of heart—it defuses any possible explosiveness in the material.

Dirty Dancing starts smart and ends dumb, with Baby having made the transition into an independent woman who will now be called Frances. It even has scenes that you can hardly look at, like one in which Baby's father (also an honorable, loving man), who has misjudged Johnny and refused to shake his hand, apologizes to him. It's lucky that Bergstein writes light, rumpled dialogue; it helps you over the hooey. So do Grey and the other performers. Cynthia Rhodes is very appealing as the hard-luck Penny, whose dancing has a professional sheen; Penny moves in keeping with what she says—that dancing is all she has ever wanted to do. Lonny Price is impressively skunky as Max Kellerman's bustling, officious grandson. Jack Weston plays knowingness like a master—he should change his name to Max. In the role of a 1963 bandleader, Honi Coles doesn't get much of a chance to tap, but he blends in neatly, and he and Weston have a moment of goofing off together. (The two-faced Max is light on his feet.)

Patrick Swayze was a principal dancer with the Eliot Feld troupe and danced on Broadway before he entered movies (*The Outsiders*, *Red Dawn*, *Uncommon Valor*, and, perhaps his best performance, *Grandview, U.S.A.*). And though we're made too conscious of his broad, gladiator's chest, especially when it's bare and Baby says urgently, "Dance with me," he gives the film a masculine dance strength. (Baby's like a soft child holding on to big, virile Daddy; the picture seems subconsciously shaped to the reveries of teen-age girls.) Swayze isn't much of a singer, though, and his rendition of his own composition, "She's Like the Wind," is a slack spot. The score has half a dozen new numbers, but it's mostly period "classics"; and songs like the Shirelles' "Will You Love Me To-morrow?" and Maurice Williams & the Zodiacs' "Stay" and the Blow Monkeys' "You Don't Own Me" and Otis Redding's triumphant "Love Man" have a pop ardor—they heat up the images. Some of the songs have synthesizer effects laid on them like a slime, but even so the score has verve, and Ardolino knows how to edit dance to music. The dancing here brings out the sensual dreaminess of the songs. *Dirty Dancing*— what a great title!—is such a bubbleheaded, retro vision of growing up in the sixties (or any other time) that you go out of the theatre giggling happily.

■

You have to hand it to John Badham: he's no shirker. After *Blue Thunder* and *WarGames* and *American Flyers* and *Short Circuit*, he trots right on to *Stakeout*. What keeps him going? What could possibly interest him in these projects? Yet there's no rage in them. Impersonal as they are, each is brought off proficiently, with the shots attentively angled and the whole film marked by careful, studied effects—by what at the Kennedy Center is called "excellence." The body of work he's been building up represents an immense amount of effort. But there are no signs of the funkiness of his earliest films—*The Bingo Long Traveling All-Stars and Motor Kings* and *Saturday Night Fever*. They were the work of a man who had some belief in what he was doing, who got excited about it. *Stakeout* is the most entertaining of his recent string of cold, craftsmanlike films, but he was a better director when he knew less about moviemaking; he was a more promising artist when he was less of a craftsman. Now he takes a piece of recycled garbage—like this shrewd Jim Kouf script about two Seattle police detectives (Richard Dreyfuss, Emilio Estevez) who are assigned to the night shift on a stakeout, watch-ing the former girlfriend (Madeleine Stowe) of an escaped convict (Aidan Quinn)—and he thinks about all the technique he can use on it. He works dedicatedly, painstakingly, and he comes out with a piece of first-class, polished garbage.

If you've been going to many recent movies, this one is so much more cleverly put together than most that you can say to yourself "It's a hit." You can even say—though that's a bit obscene—that it's one of the better American movies of the year. What you can't say, though, is that you truly enjoyed it.

Always a skillful comedian, Dreyfuss has an unusual, empathic warmth, but it has its downside: he's often a shade adorable. That was true back in his *Goodbye Girl* days, and it's still true. Yet wanting to be loved isn't necessarily the worst thing in an actor; Dreyfuss makes his adorableness amusing here, and gives his most confident star performance. *Down and Out in Beverly Hills* had a genuine sunbaked satiric vision, but Dreyfuss's role was limited: he was the henpecked husband, the patsy. And in *Tin Men* he was a little smarmy and ill at ease in the courting scenes. He's more assured in the man-woman relationship here, because it has a comic booby trap. He plays a veteran cop who knows better but finds himself falling in love with the woman he's spying on, and when he breaks the rules and spends time with her he's aware that his partner, Estevez, is watching him. Hypnotized by the soft-lipped Irish-Mexican beauty played by Stowe, he's also mugging for the benefit of the young worrywart Estevez, who's afraid that this infringement of the rules is going to get them both in trouble. Estevez' innocent-eyed dopiness here is rather endearing. He and Dreyfuss, both short, wear matching mustaches, and Estevez is a nagging, wifely stooge to Dreyfuss—partly a put-on that the cops engage in to while away the dull stretches of the twelve-hour shifts, and partly an expression of the younger cop's loyal, dogged nature. Stowe, meanwhile, conveys the sense that, having spent too much of her girlhood admiring defiant, volatile studs like the convict, she now finds Dreyfuss's soft-spoken unaggressiveness infinitely appealing. Stowe has a tantalizing quality, and plays these scenes just right: she's desirous, she's more than willing. And the Dreyfuss character, surprised to discover that she's attracted to him, and conscious that he's being seduced in front of an audience across the street, can't help feeling tickled.

All this is a jolly setup for amorous farce, and Dreyfuss has a Chaplinesque glee in some of the scenes; he's fun to watch. But when, having overslept at Stowe's place, he tries to escape the eyes of the day-shift team of detectives by borrowing a pink hat and a scarf and running through the neighborhood, the chase, complete with a dog at his heels, degrades the farce scenes. So do the pranks that the two shifts of detectives play on each other. And even in the moments of improvisatory cheerfulness you feel the pressure of engineering underneath. You know that the movie is scheduled to deliver action, and Badham keeps everything dark and grungy, with frequent cuts to the cop-hating escaped convict, who is committing a few murders as he makes his way to Seattle. You feel the mechanical format despite Aidan Quinn's flame-breathing, paranoiac performance. It was a smart move to cast the handsome young Quinn as the psycho: his high-keyed unpredictability makes it clear why the girl would have been drawn to angry outlaws and also why she has had enough of them. Quinn, who first appears heavily bearded, has a dashing, bulging-blue-eyed scariness. He's not afraid of touching emotional depths. His performance on TV as the AIDS victim in *An Early Frost* was an intense, restrained piece of work, and then, in Jack O'Brien's PBS *American Playhouse* production of *All My Sons*, early this year, he sprang some real surprises—he was spectacular. (So was the show; it's the best Arthur Miller I've seen—far superior, I think, to the more widely publicized Dustin Hoffman *Death of a Salesman*.) Quinn keeps his role here from being that of a standard brutal villain; still, his function is to provide the movie with periodic moments of terror and a big climax. And the desperately calculated zing of the action scenes, culminating in a sawmill sequence right out of silent serials, is parody played straight.

Badham doesn't have the temperament of the early action directors, who could take some lowdown joy in staging a scene like the one of Dreyfuss chasing a suspect through a fish-processing plant and falling into a conveyor belt full of thousands of pounds of herring. (The picture was shot in and around Vancouver.) Badham lacks the instincts and the common touch of those directors. Even in the best-staged big scene— the prison riot that's instigated so the Quinn character can break out— the jangling fast cutting is *too* terrific. It's like a metronome running amok. This scene has a potentially memorable device: the inmates hold mirrors out through their bars so they can see what's going on in the corridor and in the cells near them. The area is alive with flashing mirrors. But Badham doesn't follow through: we don't get to see what's reflected, or how it determines what the inmates do next, or even their disappointment at how little they can see. For all the nippiness in the dialogue, and the comic interplay of the actors, *Stakeout* isn't meant to affect you or leave you with anything. It's an example of high-grade commercial formalism. It's hip, it's violent, it's funny. These pictures begin to add up: you laugh in the theatre, but you take the chill home in your bones.

■

While you're watching *Nadine*, you have to keep reminding yourself that you're not just watching the trailer. It features such faded thrills
as a shack full of dynamite, a box packed with rattlesnakes, and an
ancient, rickety ladder stretched horizontally between two rooftops. You
never quite get involved. Nadine, a manicurist in a beauty parlor in
Austin, Texas, in 1954, is played by Kim Basinger, a lusciously pretty
woman with a stunning figure (especially when it's in motion), who's
peculiarly muted as an actress. She's livelier here than usual—she obviously enjoys her Southern accent, and her line readings have some
humor—but she's still vacant and she doesn't seem to play off anybody.
(It's as if she did her scenes alone, and then the other actors were put
in at the lab.) Nadine stalls on giving her small-time dreamer husband
(Jeff Bridges) a divorce, because she still loves him, and the story has
her running around trying to outsmart him. We're given to understand
that that isn't difficult. Nobody in the movie seems meant to be hefty in
the brains department. They're all jes' folks—comical and kooky. Nadine
has been at the scene of a murder and, by mistake, got hold of copies of
state plans for a superhighway—inside information that real-estate spec-
ulators could parlay into big money. She turns to her husband for help,
he swipes the plans, and then they're both trapped by the local crook
(Rip Torn) who arranged for the copies in the first place. They escape,
and the crook's dimwit thugs chase them. That's the movie. They release
the snakes, crawl and crawl across the collapsing ladder, and explode the
dynamite.

Some members of the press seem to be taking the writer-director
Robert Benton's word for it that *Nadine* is about marriage, and the
mechanism of the Basinger–Bridges relationship is modelled on that of
Rosalind Russell and Cary Grant in *His Girl Friday*. The picture, though,
is more like a genteel variant of a redneck, hillbilly burlesque about how
it pays to be lucky and dumb. Basinger doesn't have star presence, and
Bridges doesn't have it here, either. (He no longer has the manic, boyish
spontaneity the role calls for.) As a scuzzball photographer, Jerry Stiller,
who has just one scene before he turns into the murder victim, conveys
a lifetime of self-disgust—that's more felt life than anyone else shows.
(He would have fit into the world of Benton's *The Late Show*.) About the
only image you take away is Basinger on that ladder in a body-hugging
deep-pink suit with a wiggly flounce on her rear that looks as if it would
light up like a clown's nose. Despite Benton's statements, he has made
a cuddly romantic piffle about two people who *really* love each other.

Nadine is revealed to be (secretly) pregnant. This gives her an extra layer of pluck and darlingness. It's extras like this that shake your respect for a filmmaker.

NO SHELTER

||||||||||||||||||||||||||||||||||||||||||||||||||||||||||||||||||||||||||||||||||||||||||||||||||||||||||||||||||||||||||||||||||||||||||||

*H*amburger Hill tells the story of a squad of fourteen American soldiers from the 101st Airborne Division who on May 10, 1969, encountered the North Vietnamese at the base of a jungle hill known as Dong Ap Bia. Ordered to take the hill, they made eleven assaults on it during the next ten days while the Air Force made two hundred and seventy-two sorties and dropped a million pounds of bombs, including a hundred and fifty thousand pounds of napalm. When the battle was over and the Americans held the peak, the survivors gave it its new name. What makes the film distinctive is that it doesn't provide the viewer with any shelter. You don't get melodrama to fall back on; you don't have the reassurance of plot. *Hamburger Hill* doesn't offer the jingo heroism of *Rambo*, or the impassioned metaphorical good-and-evil of *Platoon*, or the neat parcel of guilt supplied by *Full Metal Jacket*. It's a straightforward, unblinking account of the interrelationships of these young men—most of them boys of nineteen.

The director, John Irvin (*Tinker, Tailor, Soldier, Spy; The Dogs of War; Raw Deal; Turtle Diary*), was born in Liverpool, of Scottish parents, during the blitz; in 1969, he was in Vietnam, shooting a documentary. The scriptwriter, Jim Carabatsos, served in Vietnam, and has been trying to write about it ever since (in *Heroes* and the vandalized *Heartbreak Ridge*). The writing here is sometimes a shade too heartfelt, but Irvin doesn't let the young actors sentimentalize—he keeps things as plainspoken as he can. Every now and then, the medic (Courtney B. Vance) will overarticulate a line or hype his character, but most of the talk is lifelike. The black soldiers bitch about the unfairness of their having

353

to be in Vietnam, but they're bitching to the wrong white kids—grunts who are just as trapped as they are (though the blacks don't see it that way). Many of the kids are bitter about the way the war protesters at home look down on them; some of them imagine that while they're sweating in the jungle the peaceniks are making out with their girls. The soldiers are uncomprehending and confused. Perhaps the most naïve is Sergeant Worcester (Steven Weber), who is convinced that they're there to help the South Vietnamese fight the Communists; in the introductory scenes, he gets sore and upset when a girl in a brothel refers to the war as the Americans' war. These tensions almost break up a hot-tub party, but Worcester's pal Sergeant Frantz (Dylan McDermott) calms things down by blandly assuring him that the war is everybody's. Later, though, when the men are dying, the lieutenant (Tegan West), talking to headquarters and ordered to proceed, tries to indicate what they're up against. He's told that he's being paid to fight this war, not to discuss it. The men at headquarters aren't going to see what they're ordering the grunts to do—they're not engaged in the same war.

Most of the film's power isn't in the talk; it's in the terror and the foreignness—the far-from-homeness—of the imagery. Just after the opening, a wounded grunt is carried through tall grass onto a copter; he dies and the air is filled with a white spray of sparks. Is it a shell bursting? It has no right to be so incredibly lovely. The film cuts to a shot of a little Vietnamese girl sitting under a green umbrella—just sitting there. The shots of copters in swirling skies and of downwash in the grass leave a viewer a little stunned—dislocated. So does the sense you get of how random the casualties are. The fireworks in the sky take an indiscriminate toll of the men in the jungle below. After one of the boys is hit, there's no body to be found; the huge leaves of thick, strange plants are spattered with blood and flesh.

The men keep going up the hill, and being driven back by enemy fire; when it rains, they slide down the mud while the North Vietnamese throw grenades at them. Crawling along through the mud, one grunt finds himself lying on top of another, who has been hit. At times, the task assigned them seems hopeless—Sisyphean. The medic, wounded, complains of the enemy, "We've been up that hill ten times, and they still don't think we're serious." When, in the eleventh attempt, the men "take" it, the moviemakers are under no illusions about the accomplishment. The taking of this pile of mud, blasted trees, and bunkers is about on the level of building the bridge on the River Kwai. (The Americans soon abandoned the hill.) Yet taking it is what these grunts' world has been reduced to. They follow orders; they fight because their country tells them to fight. And the movie—without illusions—respects their loyalty to one another and their suffering. The casualties are seventy per cent; most of the squad give their lives to the hill. We see them doing it, but the brutality is never lingered on. When a young man (M. A. Nickles) whom we first notice because he is wearing a Band-Aid and looks like an actorish Greg Louganis suddenly has no head, or the lieutenant, reporting back to the base on the phone, stands in shock with one arm shot off, you hardly see it—you absorb it almost subliminally. And it's more powerful this way. The terror is deeper—you don't just write it off as special effects. There's nothing "dramatic" to write off, either. John Irvin keeps the virtuosic effects in the mud sequences lean and controlled; he has the pride of a director who knows what he's doing. Almost inevitably, the hill comes to represent Vietnam, but it does so without histrionics.

Irvin and Carabatsos are aware that the grunt's-eye view won't help us understand what the United States was up to in Vietnam. (For that you'd need a movie about the brightly lighted offices where military strategy and military careerism intertwine.) What the moviemakers offer is admiration for the Vietnamese as fighters and grief for the Americans who left their bodies or their youth in that incomprehensible terrain. The movie isn't an inspired work of art. The script is no more than proficient; it merely touches the appropriate points to achieve a balanced view. And it's perhaps too superficially accurate about our baffled, ignorant young men. They don't make an abiding impression. We don't remember our glimpses of their lives—only their manner of leaving them. But the movie is a scrupulously honest memorial. It has great decency; it joins together terror and thoughtfulness.

■

Most of us would probably agree with Cocteau that "the privileges of beauty are enormous," but do they include Sean Young's bad acting in *No Way Out*? She smirks when she means to be suave, and bares her teeth and jumps up and down when she means to be daring; she emits peals of phony laughter when she's being delightful. The audience seems perfectly content to have her put away early in the movie. (She may look like Kay Kendall, but she acts like a nutbird Ali MacGraw.)

No Way Out doesn't have an ounce of credibility, but the director, Roger Donaldson, whips the action along, with camera angles changing so fast you hardly have time to ask what the chases are for or why the story points don't follow through. The movie starts with booming timpani under the titles, and it keeps slamming ahead and never lets up. If it could, it would tear your clothes off. Instead, it semi-strips the bored cynic—Sean Young—and the smooth, deadpan lieutenant commander (Kevin Costner), who, having eyed each other at the President's Inaugural Ball and exchanged a cutting remark or two, make a dash for her stretch limo. They're meant to be recklessly, frantically hot; they seize each other. One kiss, and he undresses her, starting at the top; she tugs at her scanties, then helps him get out of his things, and they go at it while the driver coasts around the historic buildings, with special emphasis on the Washington Monument. (This is kiddie comix compared to the byplay between the taxi-driver and the couple in De Palma's *Dressed to Kill*.) Sean Young is supposed to be a super-classy kept woman—the mistress of the Secretary of Defense (Gene Hackman)—and the plot hinges on her longtime connection with him being as secret as her brief dalliance with the lieutenant commander. But, considering the telegraphic, knowing glances that Young and Hackman exchange at a cocktail party, you'd expect these carryings on to be reported in every scandal sheet in America.

The movie swings into its gaga plot when Hackman finds out that she has a lover (though not who it is) and, in a rage, accidentally kills her. He tells his aide (Will Patton) what has happened; the aide dreams up the idea that the lover is an as yet undiscovered—perhaps only hypothetical—Russian agent named Yuri, who can be blamed for the murder. Needing a front man for this coverup, they arrange to have Costner put in charge of the search to find the lover and "neutralize" him. Does this sound as movieish as it is? The picture is a remake of *The Big Clock*, which starred Charles Laughton as a Henry Luce figure; in the 1948 film, the action was set in something like the Time-Life headquarters. Now the chasing around takes place in the glass offices and corridors of the Pentagon—actually Stage 27 at the old M-G-M studios in Culver City. The new script, by Robert Garland, is metallic, and many of the performances rate a blank stare. Donaldson had an unconvincing central figure in his last film, *Marie*, but the characters who filled the edges were an engrossing bunch; they gave the movie some feeling. Here the actors have almost nothing to work with. You have to keep your eye on the action, which is wherever Costner is; his peril is what the movie is about. The chief villain isn't Hackman, who begins as a supposedly flamboyant political tactician—an intellectual powerhouse—and then falls apart after the girl's death. (This doesn't come across as the Secretary's falling apart: rather, Hackman seems to be nullifying himself—saying, "I wish I weren't in this picture; maybe I can just pretend I'm not here.") The villain is Will Patton, the wormy yes-man aide, who's an old-time movie homosexual—unctuous, ruthless. And, what with this aide's pathological devotion to his boss, and his filthy habit of dispatching a pair of henchmen to kill people, the audience enjoys hissing him.

No Way Out is smashingly stupid, but a lot of people have a hot, jumpy response to the smashingness (and don't seem put off much by the stupidity). They sound excited by the transition from the staidness of the Inaugural Ball to the tigerish friskiness in the limo. They appear grateful for every bit of sex shock they get—mostly a display of thigh—and eager to think of it as something new. (I have heard the girl's instant avidity described as postmodern passion.) And the film extracts some paranoiac flash from the Washington settings and the traces of high-level nastiness: audiences can imagine that it has something to do with the recent investigations, that it gives them a muckraking, inside view of bureaucratic intrigue. (It's an indication of how screwed up the plot is that the C.I.A. men emerge as the good guys.) Finally, the picture, which is told from Costner's point of view, outsmarts itself in a surprise shift that betrays what we've been watching and makes fools of us. It has a logic, if you take the whole movie as a wacko joke on Oliver North as the Manchurian Candidate. But it's a surprise we don't want—a fizzle.

Donaldson has made a box-office wingding out of nothing (nothing but loose ends of plots), and with almost no help from the actors. As an eagerly rising young man, Costner has a pleasant air of not thinking too much of himself, and he gives you the impression that he's doing what's wanted of him. Still, this agile fellow who spends the whole movie in movement is the essence of laid back; he has no inner energy, no kinetic charge. It's Donaldson who provides the film's crude push, but without a richer script he can't provide the humor and the suggestions of meanness and kink that might have given this film-noir material some malevolence, some mystery. (Couldn't Patton have had some attraction to Costner? And why doesn't Costner show any resentment of Hackman? Is he hiding it?) This is a Yuppie thriller: it has no psychological layers. The only image that isn't clean and crisp—the only one that rates a second glance—

comes from the attempt by the Pentagon's computer wizards to produce a photograph of the girl's lover by means of an undeveloped exposed Polaroid; the evolving blur is fascinatingly messy.

■

The title *The Big Easy* is taken from the nickname for New Orleans, and the theme of the movie comes out of the reasons for that name—the patterns of corruption as well as the love of food, of music, of earthly pleasure. Dennis Quaid plays a half-Irish, half-Cajun police lieutenant who is relaxed about petty bribes. Vain and self-satisfied, he accepts free meals and small favors; to him that's part of the flavor of life—it's being friendly, it has nothing to do with crime. Ellen Barkin plays a new assistant district attorney from up North who is assigned to look into corruption in his precinct; she believes in the letter of the law— you can tell that from her drab tailored suits and her asexual prissiness. (Do moviemakers think they're being feminist when they use a heroine as a moral guidance counsellor? This voice-of-conscience role would weigh any actress down.) The lieutenant goes to work on her immediately in a few fairly explicit devilish-charmer-and-nervous-novice scenes, and her inhibitions melt away. The carnal humor of these moments is about the only thing the movie has going for it. But when he is videotaped accepting a bribe she freezes again. After a couple of reels of misunderstandings, he realizes that the police have been involved in a series of drug-related murders, and the two work together to bring the guilty to justice. That should have included the scriptwriters (Daniel Petrie, Jr., and Jack Baran).

Quaid incarnates the pleasure-loving intentions of the film, but the director, Jim McBride, rams him at us as soon as the titles are over. This is the first time I've felt myself pulling back from Quaid's image on the screen; I drew back even further from Barkin. McBride has them playing too broadly, and he has the camera too close in—the performers stick out of the film frame. In other pictures, Quaid and Barkin have had sizzling currents of talent; here they seem to have been told to sizzle, and you watch them trying. Quaid has given himself a breathy, raspy, accented voice that's acting-school goofy—he's got a Cajun cold in the nose. It matches the childlike "Let's pretend" quality of his cockiness. He's still likable, but it's a thin, cartoon performance. And Barkin makes faces at the camera, screwing her features around and twisting her mouth, stretching it across her face. You can't look at her, because she's always looking back in desperation. Most of the rest of the actors—Ned Beatty, Grace Zabriskie, Lisa Jane Persky—also seem impaled by the camera. (So do the apartment interiors.) The picture has an amateurish, fifties-B-movie droopiness. Partly, this is agreeable (especially if you've been watching the hollow dynamics of big-time action films), but the only leading performers who aren't hurt by it are John Goodman, who generally remains in the background of the shots, and the great Charles Ludlam, who thrives on broadness. As a gentleman lawyer of Old Dixie, he rolls his eyes and wraps the picture like a ribbon around his panama hat.

September 7, 1987

TEMPORARY MADNESSES: FORSTER, MAILER, HEPBURN

|||||||||||||||||||||||||||||||||||||||||||||||||||||||||||||||||||||||||||||||||||||||||||||||||||||||||||||||||||||

The previous film produced by Ismail Merchant and directed by James Ivory—a light-comedy adaptation of E. M. Forster's *A Room with a View*—was the exception to their rule of phlegmatic literary knockoffs. Now they're back on track with *Maurice*, also from Forster, which painstakingly reproduces the limp, drawn-out construction of the novel. Forster, who was born in 1879, wrote the book in 1913 and 1914, but it wasn't published until 1971, a year after his death. Set just after the turn of the century and concluding in 1912, it's about a young man's struggle to come to terms with his homosexuality. What makes the novel a museum piece is Forster's determination that his hero, Maurice (pronounced Morris), should not be gifted or especially intelligent, should not be an artist or come from an aristocratic background. He wants Maurice to be an average middle-class Edwardian who lives in the suburbs—a proper hale-and-hearty fellow, narrow-minded and snobbish, like others of his class.

The idea is simple: Forster means to show that homosexuality is natural, by having this ordinary, not particularly sensitive stockbroker discover that he's attracted only to men. And then Forster tries to do something less simple and more romantic: he wants to demonstrate that

359

Maurice's full physical commitment to his homosexual drives is his redemption—that his acceptance of the truth about himself burns away his snobbery and callousness and cruelty, that it turns him into a more perceptive man, a better man. The trap for both the novel and the film is Maurice's blandness. He isn't convincingly homosexual; he wouldn't be convincingly heterosexual, either. He isn't convincingly alive—he's a device that doesn't work. And so the actor who plays him—tall, blond James Wilby—comes across as passive and slow. (You'd think being a gay man was tantamount to being retarded. And the movie treats this as tony.) It isn't until the picture has been on for almost two hours, and Maurice has been through three years of platonic frustration with his upper-class Cambridge friend Clive Durham (Hugh Grant), that he finally has an orgasmic night; it's with Durham's under-gamekeeper, Scudder (Rupert Graves). Then he realizes what he has been missing and what he wants. Once Maurice begins to be decisive, Wilby can come to life as an actor. The role is unformed until this point—we've been watching Maurice's behavior, but we don't know him. Forster was so determined to make this hero the opposite of himself that he failed to think his way inside him, and the Maurice on the screen is uninhabited, a tailor's dummy, until too late.

The novel is about the importance of the flesh, but when Forster gets to the big scenes he doesn't describe anything—he wimps out. And so does the pallid, faithful movie. (Maurice's two nights with Scudder bring a flash of nudity, but the most sensually charged images are the early ones of Durham's and Maurice's platonic roving hands.) Yet, despite James Ivory's fidelity to Forster, we're likely to experience the book and the movie in quite different ways. When you read the novel, you're alone with Forster's befuddled special pleading, and when you see the cloud-borne happy ending coming you take it as a programmatic wish fulfillment. You know that Forster has conned himself into imagining he's thinking daring, fresh thoughts when he has really got lost in a daydream of a homosexual utopia where carnal love is forever. At the movie, we're not let down the way we are by the book; we don't have the expectations of Ivory that we have of Forster. And temporal considerations take over: it's a great relief that Maurice has finally got laid, even if we don't get any sense of his emotions. And it's a relief that Wilby can finally show he's not just a miscast slug.

Forster wanted to rescue homosexuality from its public association with effete weaklings, and in spite of himself he wrote an enervated novel. And here's a movie about a supposedly athletic, sound-of-body stock-

360

broker, a man with real lust in him, who will give up his family, his friends, and his business to go off to make a new life with Scudder. Yet all we see is costumes and set decoration, mansions and grounds. A few of the performers manage to make an impression: Judy Parfitt as Clive Durham's strong-faced mother; Peter Eyre as the vicar—the persevering Mr. Borenius, out to confirm Scudder. But Billie Whitelaw, for all her subtlety as Maurice's mildly foolish mother, is almost buried in the film's slack, novelistic rhythms, along with other acting eminences, such as Denholm Elliott, Ben Kingsley, and Simon Callow, who are not so subtle here. And though Forster made the point that Maurice's arrogance toward his two sisters was part of his priggish conventionality, Helena Michell and Kitty Aldridge, who play them, are treated as part of the furniture. The younger men come through intermittently. Hugh Grant's Durham recalls the young Louis Hayward; Grant has a nifty profile—it suggests a sexy aesthete-rotter. He's amusingly untrustworthy; he makes his villainous role as the quasi-homosexual who sells out to heterosexuality fairly believable. (In the "terminal note" that Forster appended to the book manuscript in 1960, he acknowledged that he might have been unfair to Durham.) As for the gamekeeper—the pagan man-of-the-earth fantasy that D. H. Lawrence was also (in the late twenties) to commit to paper—Rupert Graves, who has a large head and looks rather stocky next to the tall Wilby, doesn't seem to belong to the period, but he brings the role a somewhat redemptive boyishness. (He was the heroine's brother in *A Room with a View*.)

The screenplay, by Kit Hesketh-Harvey and Ivory, follows the book even when this seems a loony waste of screen time, such as when Maurice complains, well into the movie, of the servant Scudder's having refused his tip. If we'd seen Scudder refuse it, maybe we'd understand *why*, even if Maurice didn't. But there's an atrocious bit of invention near the start: Maurice as a boy, on a school excursion to the beach, is getting a graphic (but not at all helpful) lecture on sex, and the schoolmaster draws diagrams in the sand. Ivory brings on a young girl. She looks at the drawings in amazement and is pulled away by an adult, who says, "Come, Victoria." It distorts the meaning of the scene, for the sake of a broad joke that was squeezed dry decades ago. That isn't all that's squeezed dry. Part of what gave boys'-book adventure movies like *Beau Geste* and *The Lives of a Bengal Lancer* and *The Deer Hunter* a romantic charge was their underlying homoeroticism. In this boys'-book movie, the homoeroticism is overt, but it's so suffocatingly discreet that the charge is just about gone. (Classical music in the clinches will do it every time.) Ivory is a stylist in all the subsidiary ways. You feel that the table settings are right—that he would jump if a fork were out of place. And he has a fine, trained eye for light and composition. But when it comes to capturing the feel of repression and of bursting desire he isn't there.

■

Nobody talks about movies and moviemaking more hypnotically than Norman Mailer, but that doesn't seem to do his own movies a lick of good. The new *Tough Guys Don't Dance*, which he adapted from his 1984 novel, is screwed up in a different way from *Wild 90* (1968), *Beyond the Law* (1968), and *Maidstone* (1969–71), all of which he acted in, hosted, and paid off for years. Reaching for raw truth, he didn't prepare scripts for those films; the dialogue was improvised, the acting was "existential," the cinéma-vérité cameraman was left to catch what he could, and the results were ragged. Now Mailer believes that "in a movie the plot is the motor, it is essential." He told *The New York Times*, "It took me two months to write the novel—the screenplay took six months." This murder-mystery movie certainly has a plot: cocaine smuggling, double crosses, five or six murders. And it has a smooth photographic style, and professional actors (Ryan O'Neal, Isabella Rossellini, Lawrence Tierney, Wings Hauser, Debra Sandlund, and John Bedford Lloyd) who deliver scripted lines on sets that have been color-coördinated. But it doesn't have a motor—you don't care who kills whom or why. Even when you see the killings, they have no impact.

When you read Mailer's *An American Dream* or *Why Are We in Vietnam?*, you enter his imagination, and it's like being in some all-encompassing movie. Mailer's pop audacity—his melodramatic streak—can easily make you think he'd be a natural as a moviemaker. And you may think that his sense of dread would be just right for a film noir. But Mailer has already made the movie: he's movie-drunk when he writes a novel; he's not movie-drunk when he makes a movie. And he has no idea how to achieve atmosphere on film. During the opening titles, the cinematographer John Bailey provides melancholy wintry seascapes of Cape Cod, shots of the shoreline with grass and snow, and then views of the pure-white architecture of Provincetown. We seem to be seeing the desolate remnants of a clean, exalted way of life. But when the seedy characters show up and talk, and we're meant to feel the corruption that has seeped into the town—meant to feel that the place is a haunted house—Mailer doesn't make it happen. There's no interaction between the locale and what the actors are doing.

For a real director, shooting a movie is a concentrated, demanding effort—the culmination of months, perhaps years, of preparation. For Mailer, shooting a movie is a vacation; as he put it to *Variety*, "after forty years of writing, you don't feel like coming to the office every day, and making movies satisfies my desire for action." When you saw Mailer's earlier movies, you knew that there was no director on the set, and, different as *Tough Guys* is, there's no director on the set here, either. There's a man trying to turn himself on and expecting moviemaking to do it for him. He may be having a good time, but does he expect us to get off on his taking a vacation? He doesn't seem to grasp that it's his job to build the sequences and shape the performances.

The writer hero (O'Neal) is ravaged from hard living with a rich wife and three years in the pen for dealing drugs, but he can tell his tough old father (Tierney) that in those three years no man used him for a punk. His having remained anally inviolate is the proof of his manhood. Women victimize him, though—at least, the dirty-sex, Pia Zadora blondes (like Sandlund) do. He has a love-hate bond to them. He needs to escape to a true-love earth-mother brunette (Rossellini). This is paltry stuff; it has an eerie, dated quality, like a copy of *Playboy* left out in the sun for fifteen years. The women are subhuman, and most of the actors look stranded—lost and undirected. You can almost see their eyes searching for help. The only performers who don't seem embarrassed by their roles are the stolid, occasionally funny Tierney and big, square-faced Wings Hauser, who, as the rampaging, glittering-eyed chief of police, acts as if he were the monster in a monster movie. In his crude way, Hauser has a clearer idea of what the movie is than anybody else has. Mailer is plumbing the higher depths, and he tries a little of everything: a house with the interiors painted to resemble vaginal walls, a sick-soul-of-America-party orgy, a séance in which a woman envisions herself decapitated, the knifing of a dog, secret burials at sea, confessions, a stroke, a suicide, and a psychic flashback in which the hero can see events at which he was not present. After a while, the movie turns into a burlesque of itself. It has to. It opens with O'Neal delivering the line "I keep saying to myself, 'Death is a celebration.' " Yet the ludicrousness of a nugget like that isn't dull. The tawdriness of Mailer's self-exposure and self-glorification has a low-level fascination.

Writing is hard for Mailer because he goes at it with all he's got;

moviemaking is easy for him because he takes shortcuts. He seems to be trying to put his unconscious on the screen without the mediation of his conscious mind, and the result doesn't have the texture of a fantasy. It's thin—thinner than pulp, lacking the shock and suggestiveness of pulp. Mailer isn't enough of a moviemaker to draw us into the story on a primitive level: we're not caught up in the hero's fear that he may be a murderer, and so we're outside the movie from first to last. What Mailer provides is an intellectual's idea of a pulp thriller. You stare at it knowing it's hopeless yet not really wanting to leave.

■

John Huston, who died on August 28, 1987, was the subject of what is perhaps the best novel about moviemaking ever written, Peter Viertel's *White Hunter, Black Heart* (a Dell Laurel reissue; $4.95). It was published in 1953, when Viertel's emotions about working with Huston on the rewrite of the script for *The African Queen* (1951) were still raw: Huston is its hero and its villain. The portrait of him is marvellously, scathingly full, and convincing. It fits with what we intuit from the movies he made, and it fits with the drawling courtliness he had in his TV appearances, his patriarchal innocence as Noah in *The Bible,* and the curdled face he presented to us in his decaying-old-sinner roles in films such as *Chinatown* and *Winter Kills*. Viertel's account ties it all together, and when you look at Huston in one of his later, gloating roles you can understand Viertel's obsession with him. More wide-ranging than other "Hollywood" novels, *White Hunter, Black Heart* is a running argument between the screenwriter, Pete, and his intimidating boss, the director, John, about art and the movies, passion and responsibility, money and race and destructiveness. It's like *My Dinner with André,* except that it isn't friendly and civilized, and the two men express their polar points of view in the middle of action—it's like *My Dinner with André* crossed with a Hemingway novel.

Katharine Hepburn's just published memoir *The Making of "The African Queen"; or, How I Went to Africa with Bogart, Bacall and Huston and Almost Lost My Mind* (Knopf; $15.95) is conversational and slight. At first, it doesn't seem as if she had anything new to say. In London, where the group (including Viertel and the producer Sam Spiegel) assembles, she's rather put off by Huston's "studied old-Kentucky-colonel charm." She points out that "he put one constantly on the defensive" and that "when Huston is present everyone focuses attention on him, exactly as when there is a small child in the room." And in Africa he's an irritation and a bore: "Oh God, those stories. I don't know how many words came out a minute—but articulation with this genius is a real problem and he's so concentrated that nothing throws him. He doesn't even seem aware of whether anyone is listening." But midway through the book her tone begins to change: "John . . . has read everything under the sun and remembers most of it. And loves to talk and discuss. I like to do this too. The hours passed—delightfully. He tells me the most wonderful long stories." Pretty soon, she notices that "his strong wrists and strong smooth hands are like a young boy's" and—the big thing— "he likes to live." Hepburn prepares us early on by indicating her uncertainty about her relationship with Spencer Tracy: "Did he leave because he was bored or did he leave because he couldn't bear to say goodbye? The eternal question." You know where this memoir is heading when she writes, "John talked. I don't even remember what he talked about but it was magic."

The Making of "The African Queen" is about Hepburn's intense involvement with Huston, and the "and almost lost my mind," in the title, is her pointing up that she knew he was impossible, but was smitten anyway. (He was forty-four and well known to be a charmer monster; she was forty-three). During a break in the filming, Huston decides to go hunting for elephants; this is Hepburn's account of her reaction:

I thought to myself, Well! The probability is that I will never be here again. And rather than loll about the hotel, I think that I would like to go with John. Spiegel nearly had a fit. And quite right he was.

"Katie—setting off with John in a little plane—how can you— *how*? You may be killed. Then what . . . ?"

"Well, John may be killed."

"The hell with John. I can't control John, you know that. But you. . . . You're a reasonable, decent human being."

"Yes, Sam—I have been—and I don't think it pays. I want adventure—I want to hunt elephants with John. Not to kill, just to see."

"Oh my God, Katie. Talk to Bogie. . . ."

Bogie came.

"Katie, what's happened to you? You're a decent human being."

"Not anymore I'm not. If you obey all the rules you miss all the fun. John has fun."

"John," says Bogie. "That son of a bitch has gotten to you."

"He's seeing Africa."

"You're making a picture."

"Yes, I'm making a picture, but I'm seeing life at the same time."

"She's gone," he said to Sam. "Under the spell."

. . . That night I worked on John's clothes. His pants—fly-buttoned—had no buttons. I got some buttons and sewed them on. They had just rotted off in the damp. Next morning we left.

Viertel's novel provides a much fuller account of the elephant hunt. But at the start of the novel he has already been through the seduction Hepburn is experiencing, and her impressionable romanticism is outside his range. Her Yankee reticence is blended with an actress's dizziness. Here's her account of a night when she has been violently sick, and the crew, which has been carousing, tries to serenade her:

But I was past serenading and they finally went to bed. And funny old John. What did he do? He came back to my cabin.

"Just stay asleep, Katie dear. Stay asleep. Asleep—asleep . . ." And he rubbed my back with his smooth, strong hands. And my head and my neck and my hands and my feet. Such a blessing. Took the trouble from me. It is true—the laying on of hands. So quiet—so sweet—soothing. He was gentle. I slept. I don't remember when he stopped. Dear friend.

I don't know that I would read this sort of gush by anyone else. But this is Katharine Hepburn writing about herself and John Huston; it's an icon showing herself in a new light, and it has an element of giddy surprise. So do a couple of the photographs and the captions she has written. On page 104, she sits smiling blissfully, with Huston leaning over her shoulder—his face is ardent, he might be inhaling the perfume of her hair. And the caption is "Oh, John. Isn't he sweet?" On page 122, they're on a bike together, both smiling, and the caption is "On John's bike . . . I've obviously lost my mind." (To know why it was madness, one should read the Viertel book.)

We don't find out what happened—only that, returning to London, "John and I had a paperback, *Miss Hargreaves*, which we were reading.

We read the whole novel on the trip back. Good part for me. We bought it. We never made it."

September 21, 1987

8, 19, 17½

||||||||||||||||||||||||||||||||||||||||||||||||||||||||||||||||||||||||||||||||||||||||||||||||||||||||||||||||||||||||||||||||||||||

It's hard to believe that a great comedy could be made of the blitz, but John Boorman has done it. In his new, autobiographical film, *Hope and Glory*, he has had the inspiration to desentimentalize wartime England and show us the Second World War the way he saw it as an eight-year-old—as a party that kept going day after day, night after night. The war frees the Rohans (based on Boorman's family) from the dismal monotony of their pinched white-collar lives and of their street, with its row of semidetached suburban houses; now they have the excitement of the bomb blasts, the dash to the shelters, the searchlights combing the night skies, the stirring patriotic bilge on the wireless, and the equality that's ushered in with the ration books. Bill Rohan (Sebastian Rice Edwards) diligently collects shrapnel, and, along with the other eight- and nine-year-old boys, pokes through the ruins, smashing whatever's left to smash. Boorman lets his characters say the previously unsayable. Bored with crouching indoors during the nightly raids by the Luftwaffe and listening to the shelling and sirens, the fifteen-year-old Dawn (Sammi Davis), the eldest of the three Rohan children, runs outside for the exhilaration of movement, watches the firefighters at work on a blazing house, and dances in the Rohans' postage-stamp-size front garden. "It's lovely!" she calls to Bill as he hesitates on the porch. Seeing something by the curb, he runs out and picks it up—"Shrapnel! And it's still hot." He tosses it from hand to hand, cooling it. His mother, Grace (Sarah Miles), suddenly laughs at the sight of the burning house down the street, and is shocked at her own reaction. She calls out, "Come in at once, or I wash my hands of you!" And then, as Boorman writes (the script has been published by Faber & Faber): "A shell bursts right overhead and they duck into the open doorway. The four of them are framed there,

367

looking up at the savage sky where the Battle of Britain rages. Bill watches, enraptured."

Boorman's approach makes perfect sense. He doesn't deny the war its terrors: there's an astonishing scene where Grace and the two younger children are heading out to the shelter but don't make it; bright white shellbursts knock them back and fling them about the living room as if they were slow-motion marionettes. Yet he gives everything a comic fillip. Bill and the other schoolkids have to wear gas masks when they go to the school shelter, and the headmaster makes them put their time to use by reciting multiplication tables; exquisitely repulsive sucking-air sounds come out. At one point, when Grace and her kids are at the movies, watching a newsreel of the Battle of Britain, a notice on the screen tells them that there's an air raid and they should take shelter. As Grace leads them up the aisle, Bill says, "Can't we just see the end?" Dawn tells him, "They've got the real thing outside." "It's not the same," he says. And that's true for the movie we're watching: it's the life that goes on outside the theatre, but selected, heightened, polished. And, in the case of *Hope and Glory*, life outside has been given an extra dose of good sense—a jolly luminousness.

The picture recalls what Ingmar Bergman tried to do in *Fanny and Alexander*—to create a whole vision of life out of a man's memories of what, as a child, he perceived about his family. But, rich as Bergman's film is, he got bogged down in Gothic fantasies and Victorian conventionality; he's never at peace with the child's amoral side. Boorman treats the memories more lightheartedly. So his mother didn't love his father and they weren't happy together, but he *survived*. The war came along and shook things up, and if his father (David Hayman), who was like a shrivelled patriotic schoolboy, tried to escape the sense of shame he felt about slipping down from the middle class to the rootless life of the semis, and enlisted, expecting adventures but finding himself put to work as a clerk-typist—well, at least he got to visit his family. And when that semidetached house—emblem of coal pollution and conformity—burned down (in a "normal" fire that couldn't be blamed on the Nazis) nobody missed it. Its destruction provided the excuse for Grace and the children to move into her parents' big, open, ramshackle bungalow on the Thames, where Bill and his six-year-old sister, Sue (Geraldine Muir), could fish and play. And since this was at Shepperton, near the studios that Alexander Korda built, and movie crews frequently worked along the river, Bill could develop the interests that turned him into John Boorman.

The movie is wonderfully free of bellyaching. Grandfather (Ian Bannen) is a gruff, demanding old buzzard who gets drunk at Christmas and subjects the whole clan to his toasts to all the ladies he remembers with lewd satisfaction. But he also instructs Bill in the lore of the river. Now and then, Bill can tease him and get away with it, and when, just hours before the beginning of the fall term, Bill's grim, dreaded school is bombed and burned out, Grandfather laughs like a cartoon anarchist. It's as if his and Bill's dreams had exploded the place. And not theirs alone: arriving for the first day of servitude, the pupils see the bomb debris and riot in the schoolyard. It's a whoop-de-do celebration, because their holidays will be extended; it's also an orgy of hatred for the headmaster, who likes to cane kids, raising welts on their palms. He has told them that discipline wins wars; now the bombs have put a stop to his tyranny. That's the joy of the movie: the war has its horrors, but it also destroys much of what the genteel poor like Grace Rohan have barely been able to acknowledge they wanted destroyed.

Boorman keeps his energy up in all the scenes. He doesn't get so personal he loses control, and he doesn't fall into any of his Jungian pits. The many things that could go wrong didn't; the picture moves along lightly, one incident after another, a collage of memories, dreams, newsreels, old movies, fake old movies. It's like a plainspoken, English variant of the Taviani brothers' *The Night of the Shooting Stars*, which was also the Second World War as seen through the eyes of a child. In that film, the child, grown up, mythicizes her war experiences, converting them into bedtime stories to tell her own child, and Boorman has written that his script began with the stories he told his kids at bedtime. Many of his characters and anecdotes are like archetypes, but they're grounded in definite, "real" characters and situations. They're never forced on us; they simply take hold—maybe because we're always in on the jokes. The picture has a beautiful pop clarity.

Sammi Davis's dimply, pleasure-loving Dawn is always changing her mind. She wants sex but not love and is furious when she falls for a Canadian jokester soldier with dimples of his own (Jean-Marc Barr). Sammi Davis (she was the blond teen-age prostitute in *Mona Lisa*, and she's the blind girl in *A Prayer for the Dying*) makes Dawn's bluntness wittily uncouth; she turns just about every line she has into a kicker. And, as Grace's friend Molly, Susan Wooldridge (she was Daphne Manners in *The Jewel in the Crown*) has moments when she's almost as no-nonsense "common" as Dawn. A few of the characters—such as Molly's husband, Mac (Derrick O'Connor)—don't have any comic turns and so they don't add up to much. And not all the performances are dazzling.

369

(Sarah Miles is actressy without being much of an actress.) But you feel that you're seeing the people with refreshed eyes. Sebastian Rice Edwards' Bill is everything he should be: funny, tough-minded, open-faced. And although the role of Sue takes less doing, Geraldine Muir is a hilarious little trouper. Her misconstruction of what she sees through the keyhole when she watches Dawn and the Canadian and what she sees when she watches Mummy and Daddy is a small classic.

The picture itself is big—a large-scale comic vision, with ninety-foot barrage balloons as part of the party atmosphere. In the opening scenes, kids in a movie theatre are throwing bits of paper at each other, creating a blizzard. Boorman's touch here is so sure it's as if he were handing us popcorn, and saying, "Throw it if you want; just have a good time."

■

Walking down the street at the end of *The Pick-up Artist*, Robert Downey, Jr., and Molly Ringwald match up like Pierrot and Pierrette. Maybe what makes them such a blithe team is that he isn't very tall and there's something buoyant and resilient about him. This little guy has been racing through his days, chasing women compulsively, as if he were under a spell and could never relax. Now he's met this girl, and he's basking in being part of a twosome. Downey's Jack Jericho, a New York schoolteacher, is a happy hedonist, and Ringwald is Randy Jensen, a slender, voluptuous beauty who works as a guide at the Museum of Natural History. But they're also both just kids discovering the pleasures of companionship. The movie is an airy romantic comedy, written and directed by James Toback, in a swing away from the flamboyant pulp pictures he is known for (*Fingers, Exposed*). This time, most of the movie is built on the free-for-all gags that popped out in the margins of his darker fantasies. And Downey, whose soul is floppy-eared, transforms the gags—takes the heat and pressure out of them.

It's a sunny movie, with New York streets full of slim-hipped models and beauty-contest winners. At the start, Jack runs from one to the next, giving them his seductive pitch, asking for their phone numbers, and often getting them. It doesn't bother him when his come-on fails; he enjoys the chase and the conversations, in which he can see himself as a hipster Don Juan. Young men in the audience may spot their own techniques as they watch him rehearsing his routines in the shaving mirror, practicing the sincere look, the even, flattering voice. But when he gives Randy his sales patter she's a shock to him. She's neither encouraging nor rejecting—she's a few leaps ahead of him. This long-legged, nimble-witted redhead, who's nineteen (Ringwald's age), has her own compulsions.

Molly Ringwald has been poised and assured right from her early screen appearances, in *Tempest* and *Spacehunter,* and in *Sixteen Candles* and other John Hughes pictures. But she is more febrile here, and softer, with more womanly undulations. She seems to have acquired lusher, deeper colors. The cinematographer (Gordon Willis) may be partly responsible: in her clinging green dress, she's like Modigliani's lover—too expressive, too unusual to be called a knockout. That's the correct term for the gorgeous babes Jack approaches, such as Mona (Anne Marie Bobby), who tells him she's studying for the priesthood, and Rae (Vanessa Williams), whose dog gives him the brushoff. Ringwald matches Downey in the yearning under both their smiles and in the quick, quiet way they talk. Jack looks as though he could float above anything and never let on if he was in pain, and this weightlessness has its appeal in the middle of the honking city sounds—it makes him seem worthy of this fairy-tale gambling girl, who's determined to pay off the debts of her father (Dennis Hopper), an out-of-it boozer.

The flimsy plot hardly matters, because new, undreamed-of characters keep turning up, and they keep the movie bubbling along. The father is in hock to a graceless, short-fuse racketeer (Harvey Keitel), whose moll, the raucous Lulu, is played in an original, happy-go-lucky style by Victoria Jackson, of *Saturday Night Live.* Bob Gunton, wearing a slithery little mustache, is the second-richest guy in Colombia, who hangs around pining for Randy; Christine Baranski is a live wire Randy meets on the bus to Atlantic City; Mildred Dunnock is Jack's likably dippy grandmother; Robert Towne is Jack's suave principal; Danny Aiello (partly off tone) is Jack's coffee-shop-owner pal; Tony Sirico and the supreme sleazo Joe Spinell are comic-strip hoods; Tom Signorelli is a used-car salesman for the ages; and there are dozens of others. Toback's affection for them is overwhelming; he gets you to share it. Several have worked for him before, and each gets a chance to take a bow.

If the picture is charming or nifty rather than terrific, it's because Toback, who has been doing fine with the scenes—mostly two-character dialogues—that depend on the performers' rhythms (and his snappy lines), holds to that style when the action moves to Atlantic City. He doesn't build up the rush of excitement that's needed when Randy and Jack gamble for huge stakes. When they're inside the casino, we should feel the dislocation of a closed-off night world, and when Jack stands with a container of chips pressed against his chest we need to experience his giddy sense of triumph and recognize it as the flying high that's been part of his crazy sweetness all along. What happens is that the story doesn't peak; a scene where Jack tells off the racketeer is woozily unconvincing; and the ending is earthbound. The film is full of spangly good humor, though. In its own irrepressible way it's sustained. It's not heady enough, not a lift-off, but it's bright and convivial, like the sound of the sixties girl groups on the track. It keeps you laughing.

■

The 1936 comedy *My Man Godfrey* features Mischa Auer as a soulful Russian musician with only one number in his repertoire: "Otchi Tchornyia." Lubitsch's 1940 *The Shop Around the Corner* has a running gag about a couple of dozen musical cigarette boxes that play "Otchi Tchornyia": the shop keeps marking them down, but can't get rid of them. We still aren't rid of that bewhiskered joke of a song: it's back again in Nikita Mikhalkov's *Dark Eyes* (*Otchi Tchornyia*), which opened the New York Film Festival and is now in theatrical release. Shot in Italy and the Soviet Union, *Dark Eyes* amalgamates several short stories by Chekhov, and is the kind of movie that is referred to as a "broad tapestry," or, as *Variety* put it, "a joyful sleighride through the turn of the century." It features obviousness and mugging—each in almost unprecedented amounts. Everything in it is overacted, is too slow and too close. A beaming, twinkling Russian called Pavel (Vsevolod Larionov) is held in full screen so long I still can't get him out of my eyeballs. This hearty fellow shares a carafe of wine, on shipboard, with a foolish-looking Italian, Romano (Marcello Mastroianni), who proceeds to tell him his life story. As a poor student about to begin a career as an architect, he married a choking-rich young woman (Silvana Mangano). Her father died soon after, she became head of the family business interests, and Romano lived in a great villa as a spoiled pet. He took mistresses (Marthe Keller is one of them), became a weak, self-hating buffoon (people snickered at him), and, when he needed to escape, he went off to spas.

This is unfortunate for us, because Mikhalkov, who has stated that *8½* is his favorite movie, and that he has seen it seventeen times, directs the spa scenes like a bumpkin Fellini. And he must believe that it's his job as a Soviet citizen to teach us a thing or two about decadence: every single time he can drag on a worker or a servant, he treats us to a demonstration of how this person is enslaved and humiliated. In all of Europe there doesn't seem to be one bourgeois or aristocrat who isn't callous or one worker who isn't scared and servile. Mikhalkov really comes into his own when he can bring on someone corpulent—a woman singer with the orchestra in the Grand Hotel at the spa, a landlady in the nearby town. He pushes them up against the lens so that their openmouthed, heavily lipsticked pigginess comes through in 3-D; he insists that we laugh at their grossness.

At the spa, Romano meets Anna (Elena Sofonova), Chekhov's woman with the little dog. He is touched by how seriously she takes their brief affair, and when she leaves to go back to her husband he invents a business project—a factory to be built in her town in Russia. At this point, the film turns into a grotesquely tedious satire of bureaucracy in Imperial Russia, as Romano travels to St. Petersburg and goes from ministry to ministry trying to obtain the necessary permit to open his mythical factory in the rural town. Then comes feasting and roistering with villagers in their native costumes. (The peasant merrymaking is a moral lesson to us.) Eventually, he finds Anna; they agree to leave their empty marriages and start a new life together, and he heads back to Italy to tell his wife that he wants his freedom. Many complications later, there's a surprise ending, but it's a surprise only in the sense that you can't quite believe that Mikhalkov and his writing associates would sink so low.

I may not have done justice to the poetic Russian mist near the Volga, in the scene where Romano, eager to regain his manhood, travels by horse-drawn cart to the distant railroad depot. But along with the mist there are bands of gypsies—they sing. And Romano is driven to the depot by an ecological-minded veterinarian, who delivers wholesome speeches. Mikhalkov doesn't spare you much; when he can't think of anything else to do, hats fly off in the wind and are chased. Even in the rare subdued scene, such as Romano's seduction of the shy, unworldly Anna in her quarters near the spa, there are goofs: she touches her finger to her wet eyes and draws a line on the wall, and the line doesn't evaporate. This woman has miraculous powers. Mikhalkov shows her face in closeup during an embrace: a carefully lighted tear forms at the outer corner of her eye, and the silly dab of glycerin won't detach itself. It just rests there, and the director, mesmerized, keeps us staring at it. (It never does fall—he finally gives up and cuts away.)

The Russian scenes are packed with actors who appear to be shoving each other to get in camera range. The women come off much the better: Sofonova, who doesn't have particularly dark eyes but is appealing and resembles the young Shirley MacLaine; and, in the Italian scenes, the imperious, magnificently unflustered Mangano, whose wardrobe speaks well for decadence. (All in all, she may be the greatest clotheshorse in the history of movies.) As for Mastroianni, his makeup is almost alarmingly good. There is a vast difference between his blotchy, sagging face in the shipboard scenes and his smooth skin in the flashbacks to his wasted life. (You can't be certain whether he has been made up to look older or to look younger; probably both.) Mastroianni has been in well over a hundred films; he (deservedly) won the best-actor award at Cannes in 1970 for Ettore Scola's *The Pizza Triangle*. He won again for his performance in this massive hunk of Italo-Russian kitsch. When he's Romano, it's as if he were putting on a classroom exhibition of how to turn yourself into another person—he shows the class every bit of calculation. It's exemplary; it's horrible. (He's like Paul Muni in *Juarez* and *The Life of Emile Zola*.) If I had never seen Mastroianni except in *Dark Eyes*, I wouldn't want to see him again.

October 5, 1987

THE FEMININE MYSTIQUE

*F*atal Attraction is just about the worst dating movie imaginable—a movie almost guaranteed to start sour, unresolvable arguments—but long lines of people curl around the block waiting to see it. At a New York publishing party, a dull but presentable corporate lawyer (Michael Douglas), a settled married man, exchanges glances with a bold-eyed, flirtatious woman (Glenn Close), a book editor. She's wearing a Medusa hairdo—a mess of blond tendrils is brushed high off her forehead and floats around her face. She's made up to get attention, yet she resents it: the lawyer's plump pal (Stuart Pankin) tries a pleasantry on her, and she gives him a drop-dead stare. We see all the warning signals that the

374

lawyer doesn't, and when he runs into her again, on a weekend when his wife and six-year-old daughter are out of town, we sense the hysteria behind her insinuating repartee and the hot looks she fastens on him. She makes all the overtures; he's not particularly eager, but she semi-transforms her frighteningness to sexiness, and he, being frightened, finds it sexy. She makes spending the night together seem casual and grownup—makes him feel he'd be a total wimp to say no—and he goes with her to her loft.

Like a femme fatale in a Cecil B. De Mille picture, she comes from hell: her loft is in the wholesale-meat district, where fires burn in the street. The director, Adrian (*Flashdance*) Lyne, puts on bravura demonstrations of frenetic passion. The two have sex, with her seated on the kitchen sink, and when she reaches for the faucet and splashes her hot face Lyne shoots it as if the water were wildly erotic. After more sex, they go to a Latin club for some (comically) supercharged dancing, then have sex in the elevator to the loft. By morning, the lawyer has had enough, but she pressures him, and he doesn't find it easy to get clear of her. When the weekend is over and he's determined to say goodbye and go back uptown she stops him, temporarily, by slashing her wrists. In the weeks that follow, she hounds him at his office and his home, insisting that he can't use her and then discard her. The picture is a skillfully made version of an old-fashioned cautionary movie: it's a primer on the bad things that can happen if a man cheats on his wife.

Once the woman begins behaving as if she had a right to a share in the lawyer's life, she becomes the dreaded lunatic of horror movies. But with a difference: she parrots the aggressively angry, self-righteous statements that have become commonplaces of feminist fiction, and they're so inappropriate to the circumstances that they're the proof she's loco. They're also Lyne's and the scriptwriter James Dearden's hostile version of feminism. (Dearden's script is an expansion of the forty-two-minute film *Diversion*, which he wrote and directed in England in 1979.) Glenn Close expresses the feelings of many despairing people; she plays the woman as pitiable and deprived and biologically driven. But in the movie's terms this doesn't make the character sympathetic—it makes her more effectively scary, because the story is told from a repelled man's point of view. Lyne and Dearden see her as mouthing a modern career woman's jargon about wanting sex without responsibilities, and then turning into a vengeful hellion, all in the name of love. They see the man as ordinary, sane, hardworking—a man who loves his beautiful homebody wife (Anne Archer) and bright little daughter (Ellen Hamilton Latzen). He's the opposite of a lech; he was a little tickled at being seduced. Yet the woman plays the *Madama Butterfly* music and doesn't regard it ironically; alone in her stark loft, she really sees herself as having been mistreated. When she seeks revenge, she might be taking revenge on all men.

The horror subtext is the lawyer's developing dread of the crazy feminist who attacks his masculine role as protector of his property and his family. It's about men seeing feminists as witches, and, the way the facts are presented here, the woman *is* a witch. She terrorizes the lawyer and explains his fear of her by calling him a faggot. This shrewd film also touches on something deeper than men's fear of feminism: their fear of women, their fear of women's emotions, of women's hanging on to them. *Fatal Attraction* doesn't treat the dreaded passionate woman as a theme; she's merely a monster in a monster flick. It's directed so that by the time she's wielding a knife (from that erotic kitchen) you're ready to shriek at the sight of her. But the undercurrents of sexual antagonism—of a woman's fury at a man who doesn't value her passion, doesn't honor it, and a man's rage at a woman who won't hold to the rules she has agreed to, a man's rage against "female" irrationality—give the movie a controversial, morbid power that it doesn't really earn.

It's made with swank and precision, yet it's gripping in an unpleasant, mechanical way. When we first hear that the little daughter wants a bunny rabbit, an alarm goes off in our heads. And after the lawyer buys the rabbit we wait to see what obscene thing the demon lady will do to it. Educated people may want to read more into *Fatal Attraction*, but basically it's a gross-out slasher movie in a glossy format. (It has special touches, such as a copy of Oliver Sacks' *The Man Who Mistook His Wife for a Hat* next to the bed in the loft.) The violence that breaks loose doesn't have anything to do with the characters who have been set up; it has to do with the formula they're shoved into.

The picture has De Mille's unbeatable box-office combination—an aura of sexiness and a moral message. We know that the lawyer isn't going to chase after the blonde, because Lyne softens Anne Archer's features and sexualizes every detail of the cozy marriage. And the movie is edited so that the audience is breathing right along with the husband as he watches his wife put on her extra-moist lipstick. There are also bits of contrast, like the pal's making fun of himself, or the husband's experiencing a surreal embarrassment, trying to carry the blonde from her sink to her bed and being hobbled by his pants and shorts, which are caught around his ankles. Lyne uses these moments to break into the dreamlike tension of the male erotic reveries of the soft nest at home and of the tempestuous, kinky sex in the loft. The husband loves his wife and prefers her in every way to the interloper, whose rapacity scares him even before she threatens his way of life, even before she sends him porno tapes full of hate. The movie has its sex in the dirty sink, but it's pushing the deeper erotic satisfaction of the warm, sweet life at home. The key to its point of view is that dull, scared everyman husband. The woman was ready to go nuts; if it hadn't been this ordinary guy she tried to destroy, it could have been another. She carries madness, disease, the unknown. This is a horror film based on the sanctity of the family—the dream family. It enforces conventional morality (in the era of AIDS) by piling on paranoiac fear. The family that kills together stays together, and the audience is hyped up to cheer the killing.

■

With *Baby Boom*, the writer-producer Nancy Meyers and the writer-director Charles Shyer prove themselves the monarchs of Yup. This movie is about the feminist as darling, and it rattles along cheerily and empty-headedly. Entrusted with the care of a baby girl, the career woman J.C. (Diane Keaton) loses the single-minded concentration that has made her a Manhattan management-consulting firm's Tiger Lady. Her status diminished, she quits, moves to a farmhouse in Vermont, meets a calm, steadying Gary Cooperish veterinarian helpfully named Cooper (Sam Shepard), and starts a venture that turns her into the biggest employer in town. Soon she's a tycoon, rejecting astronomic offers to sell out. She, her child, her lover, and her business are all booming. Meyers and Shyer aren't moviemakers—they're glorified sitcom writers. They yank laughs by having J.C. (Yale B.A., Harvard M.B.A.) struggle helplessly with the tabs on disposable diapers, and they keep cutting to the child for clever reactions, the way movies used to cut to the family dog.

If there were justice in the world of entertainment, *Baby Boom* would be unwatchable. But Diane Keaton gives a smashing, glamorous performance that rides over many of the inanities. As soon as you see J.C. striding through the corridors of power, her suit cinched in by a broad belt, her body swinging and lurching forward, as if she were diving into the challenges of the day, you know that she finds success sexy. Her having all this drive is played for farce, and Keaton keeps you alert to

377

every shade of pride and panic J.C. feels. J.C. is an ultra-feminine executive, a wide-eyed charmer, with a breathless ditziness that may remind you of Jean Arthur in *The More the Merrier*. She does funny, flighty things, and Keaton shows you the core of confusion that they come out of. She's funniest when J.C. loses control, as in her scene with a Vermont plumber (Britt Leach) who tells her the well has gone dry: she expostulates, then collapses. Keaton is acting in a different range from the frequently inspired work she did in *Shoot the Moon, The Little Drummer Girl, Mrs. Soffel*, and *Crimes of the Heart*. Her J.C. is star acting, but she doesn't treat it as hack work. J.C. gets a kick out of business success; it's a form of conquest, and it satisfies her vanity—it's like being the best student at school. But she also knows that it's time to graduate and find out what else is out there.

■

The director Rob Reiner doesn't have the craft to bring off the kinetic daredeviltry he tries for in *The Princess Bride*, and the movie is ungainly—you can almost see the chalk marks it's not hitting. But it has a loose, likable slobbiness; it suggests a story that's being made up as it goes along. The script, written in 1973 by William Goldman, and based on the 1973 novel that he wrote for his children (one daughter wanted it to be about princesses, the other wanted it to be about brides, hence the title), is set in the late Middle Ages, in the mythical kingdom of Florin. But it's really set in the mythical past as we know it from the swashbuckling movies of the thirties, where people talk in a jumble of accents— the royalty in stage British, the poor people in Americanese, the clowns in vaudeville-Yiddish rhythms. Reiner doesn't make a point of the anachronistic tone; he treats it lackadaisically, as if the characters just happened to be modern people in a fantasy world. Although the material was conceived for Goldman's daughters, it seems to have turned into an affectionate composite parody of what he, as a boy, found exhilarating in adventure movies: the duels, the feats of strength, the rope climbing, the black-masked heroes, the swamps, the dungeons with medieval Rube Goldberg torture machines.

Photographed partly on locations in England and Ireland (Florin Castle is actually Haddon Hall, parts of which date back to the twelfth century), the movie has initial vistas so lovely they seem slightly unreal—

sunnier than life. It begins with blond Buttercup (Robin Wright), said to be the most beautiful woman in the world, and her true love and near-twin, the blond farm boy Westley (Cary Elwes). He goes out to seek his fortune, pledging to return, and is captured by pirates. The handsome, supercilious Crown Prince Humperdinck (Chris Sarandon, a fine, regal villain, wry and mordant) selects her to be his bride, but before the ceremony she is abducted and taken to a ship by a trio of ruffians: Wallace Shawn as the Sicilian mastermind Vizzini, a little guy trying to act tough; and his two hirelings—Mandy Patinkin as the Spanish swordsman Inigo Montoya, and all seven feet five and five hundred and twenty-five pounds of the French-born wrestler André the Giant as the amiable Fezzik. These are the principal players, along with Christopher Guest in one of his peerless specialty acts, with his face clenched, as Humperdinck's helper, the smarmy six-fingered sadist Count Rugen; the English comedian Mel Smith as the Albino; Margery Mason as the ancient woman who boos the royal family; and Billy Crystal and Carol Kane, in makeup that adds centuries to them, as the retired wizard Miracle Max and his nagging crone, Valerie. Offscreen, Crystal has explained that he wanted to "look like a cross between Casey Stengel and Dopey—a very old Dopey—and my grandmother." He *does* look like a very old Dopey, and it's an inspired way to look while doing a Mel Brooks turn. Carol Kane's accent is soul-satisfyingly berserk (like the accent she used when she was partnering Andy Kaufman in *Taxi*); she suggests Madeline Kahn as Mrs. Dopey. The Crystal-Kane scenes are show-biz bliss, and they give the movie a lift that puts it all into perspective. It's shtick softened by childlike infatuation. That's not bad—it's just gentler than what you're used to. (It's only bad when a tired routine from the past—like Peter Cook's clergyman with a speech impediment—is lingered over sentimentally.)

   The Princess Bride gets less lumpy as it moves along, partly because you adjust to André the Giant's smiley, slow-spoken non-acting, and you get used to Patinkin's mock-Spanish accent and can pick up more of what he's saying. Patinkin is always on the verge of showing wit and finesse, but he doesn't get there. (He did in *Yentl*.) Still, his duels, with their simulation of drawing-room badinage, have some of the best gags in the movie—particularly his match with Guest, in which he's wounded and keeps regaining consciousness and saying the same lines over, like a busted phonograph. Reiner doesn't waste his performers—he gives them enough chances to do what they can do. Robin Wright's Buttercup isn't a whole lot of fun (and the camera angles on her aren't always flattering), but her timing is neat when she deliberately tumbles down a hill in pursuit

379

of Westley, who by then is worth pursuing. With his rakish little sliver of a mustache, Cary Elwes is preposterously pretty, like Douglas Fairbanks, Jr., in the thirties, and he has a flair for self-parody. When Westley (a perfect sappy name for a hero) is robbed of his strength and his head flops around on his neck, Elwes is a slapstick version of all the silly-ass Britishers you've ever tittered at. He's funniest when he's playing "mostly dead." He lightens the movie, gives it a featherweight giddiness.

The story is set within a (too hearty and self-satisfied) framing device: Peter Falk, as a grandfather, has brought the heavily illustrated fairy-tale book *The Princess Bride*, which he remembers from his boyhood, to read to his ten-year-old grandson, who's bedridden with flu. The grandfather plunks himself down in a chair facing the boy and starts to read. (At first, the boy, a child of the TV age, is reluctant to listen, but gradually he is caught up in the story, and by the end his bond with the grandfather is strengthened. That's the moral of the movie.) If only it were that easy to read to a child. When you sit in a chair in comfort, the child can't see the pictures (and follow the lines of print). So you prop yourself up on the bed, trying to see the words over and around the child's bobbing head. (You have to turn the pages with the hand wound around his neck.) You also find yourself pepping things up: you transpose archaic or unfamiliar language into modern American, and into whatever innocuous slang phrases come to mind. It might have added to the fun if Falk, with his raucous, streetwise inflections, had been tied in with the characters' vaudeville accents and incongruous remarks. The grandfather could have been the key to the flip-flops in tone.

October 19, 1987

CONS

||||||||||||||||||||||||||||||||||||||||||||||||||||||||||||||||||||||||||||||||||||||||||||||||||||||||||||||||||||||||||||||||||||||

Just about every scene in *Weeds* is at a confusing emotional temperature, and everything seems to happen pell-mell before the audience is prepared for it. But the director, John Hancock, and his wife, Dorothy Tristan, who collaborated with him on the script, have caught the tail of such of a compelling subject that the film holds you anyway. Nick Nolte is Lee, who's in San Quentin for armed robbery and is serving "life without possibility"—that is, without possibility of parole. After flunking two suicide attempts, this despairing convict, who has had only a sixth-grade education, begins to read books from the prison library; he attends a performance of *Waiting for Godot* that is given for the prisoners, and he is deeply moved, as they all are—especially when they hear the line "I can't go on." (*Waiting for Godot* is said to be the prime favorite of prisoners.) And Lee, stirred by a form of expression that is new to him, begins to write plays about imprisonment and then to stage them. He works up a social-protest musical extravaganza about life in the pen which attracts visitors, and his activities win him a champion—a San Francisco theatre reviewer (Rita Taggart)—who eventually persuades the governor to release him. That's the beginning, and you may be afraid you're going to see something unbearably upbeat, but you get a glimpse of how complicated things are when Lee, in the reviewer's bedroom on the day of his release, takes off his shirt and she sees a huge devil's head tattooed on his belly. (She gulps.)

Lee organizes an acting troupe made up of former cons he worked with: a doltish shoplifter called Burt (William Forsythe), who was paroled twice during the time Lee was staging plays; a murderer (Ernie Hudson); an embezzler (Lane Smith); a smart pimp (John Toles-Bey), who taught Lee how to develop the abilities of the convict actors; a flasher (Mark Rolston); and others. But as a writer Lee is something of a faker. And the material that went over big inside doesn't have the same impact outside. Touring in a camper, with no money, the men—Lee included—are torn by impulses to revert to their former crime patterns. The movie is about their efforts to become professional men of the theatre. It's about the ways in which working together changes them and the ways in which it doesn't. (The murderer goes into a drunken rage during a performance, and the crowd perks up—the show has become more dynamic. The flasher, feeling the excitement in the air, can't resist flashing the full auditorium.) It's about how the men react to college-girl groupies, and how they behave during the confrontations with the audience which are held after the play. It's about a performance they give in a prison, where Lee gets so carried away by his ability to arouse the inmates that he starts a riot.

Hancock, who used to be the director of the San Francisco Actors Workshop, did some work with the convict Rick Cluchey and his San Quentin Drama Group (whose late-sixties show *The Cage* toured the United States and Europe). This movie grew out of Hancock's contacts with Cluchey's company and out of his and Tristan's research into other prison theatre groups; it gives the impression that they piled together the stories and anecdotes they liked best, and left the job of unifying them to Nolte. He does it—largely by not overacting. Nolte plays Lee with an incarcerated holdup man's closed expression: there's nothing hopeful in the muscles of his face. Nolte's Lee doesn't pretend to have more feelings than he has. He never comes too close to us; he's a stony, in-articulate man struggling for expression, a man cut off by what twelve years of confinement have done to him, and by his need to control himself. (He thinks only when he's forced to.) Yet his harrowed expression—the caution and fear in his sunken eyes—keeps you watching him. In a scene where he has to summon up all his powers to fight his drive to regress (i.e., to commit an armed robbery), he's like a man fighting back his own animal nature. When we see him dressed up for his New York opening in what he thinks a big-time actor should wear—a white topcoat, like something on a poster of a twenties movie star—he looks ill at ease, drawn, more tense than in his prison uniform. His smiles are gaunt-cheeked and stiff; he doesn't know how to relax.

Weeds is full of surprising effects. I don't think Hancock gets the dramatic value out of most of them—often, they barely sink in. But they're there: Lee's suicidal cry of misery as he flings himself down from the upper tier of the cell block; the way Lee, who has never tried to talk to the other prisoners, eagerly solicits their reactions to his first play; the mixed emotions of the cons who are standing around waiting to au-dition for Lee when Ernie Hudson's tall young murderer decides that it's his turn and sings "The Impossible Dream," a cappella and in tune; after Lee is out, the moment when the paroled pimp tells him that he isn't sure about performing in the show, because he can't stand going back to the joint in his head; the stubborn determination of William Forsythe's Burt the shoplifter to overcome his stagefright; the panic when the men think that the camper is about to be searched and they don't know what to do with their parole-violating weapons; the way a genial Off Broadway actor (Joe Mantegna), who is brought in as a replacement for one of the ex-convict actors, learns to blend in; the inspired stroke of casting that gives Lee a gnomelike mom (Anne Ramsey) whose face—a distorted version of his—suggests the animal he fought back.

The movie encompasses way too much, and it never goes very far into the issues it raises, but the messy collision of energies keeps a viewer feeling alive. Forsythe's Burt is both a comic-strip goof and a believable character; when Lee shouts at him and he holds his ground your sympathies are with Lee, but you feel something like love for Burt. He's magic. Or, to be more precise, Forsythe incarnates the magic of theatre that the convicts are reaching toward.

■

*B*arfly, the director Barbet Schroeder's faithful rendering of a semi-autobiographical script by the sixty-seven-year-old L.A. poet Charles Bukowski, has a howler right smack at its center. Bukowski is writing about himself just after the Second World War, when he was a scrappy young man, in his mid to late twenties—a budding writer who was beginning to be published. But Mickey Rourke, who plays the role, imitates the tortoise movements of the battle-scarred survivor Bukowski, the writer-philosopher, the sage. Looking at the world through puffy, slitted eyes and smiling to himself, Rourke is a facsimile of Bukowski as he is now, and the effect is weirdly romantic. With his face beaten out of shape and his body contorted from broken bones, this wreck of a man—Henry Chinaski, he's called—is always willing to go in the alley behind his East Hollywood hangout, the Golden Horn, and fight his enemy, the powerfully built bartender (Frank Stallone), who kicks him when he's down and leaves him lying there, a lump of bloody garbage. Yet, despite his greasy hair, his split lip, and his skid-row tailoring, beautiful women are drawn to Henry. If he were an energetic young writer, their interest in him might not seem unusual; here, thanks to the howler, it has a comic element, and Rourke responds to them with a bemused, grizzled courtliness. He has a cocky gleam in those barely open eyes. Bukowski (who has said that he doesn't go to bars anymore) loves the movie. Why wouldn't he? He's presented as the eternal rebel boozer, the artist as life spirit.

One day when Henry is refused service in the Golden Horn, he goes down the street to another low dive. That's when he first sees Wanda (Faye Dunaway). After muttering that she looks like "some kind of distressed goddess," he asks the bartender, "How come nobody sits near her?" The bartender answers, "She's crazy." Henry picks up his beer, and as he walks around the bar toward her the camera slowly moves over the faces of the other deadbeats sitting there (among them is Bukowski). Wanda, like Henry, spends her days and nights drinking, but she doesn't write. When Henry isn't in a dive, he's in his flophouse room listening to Mozart on the radio. Wanda's soul is burned out: she doesn't listen to music. But she recognizes Henry as a kindred dedicated drinker and invites him to share her seedy furnished apartment. And Dunaway and Rourke begin to show the facial shine of actors in love. They're a lively bedraggled couple. Wanda has flickerings of real oddity, and Henry talks to her soothingly, in soft, slow rhythms that are like a gentle, honeyed version of W. C. Fields' drawl.

At his most distinctive, Mickey Rourke has a seductive one-to-one manner, wrapped in silence. He sometimes overdoes the sweat and stubble, the bruises and curses, but as the weary I.R.A. soldier in this year's *A Prayer for the Dying* he's isolated in a way that suggests what the life of a terrorist might do to you—the lilt in his muffled speech is painful. And in Schroeder's static barrooms Rourke responds to the possibilities of heroic nonchalance in the role of Henry Chinaski. With his lower lip and his jaw jutting out, his shoulders pushed back, his chest thrust forward, and his arms hanging down, apeman style, as he walks, Rourke comes through with some of his best-humored, subtle clowning. The movie, though, is bilge. ("Henry and Wanda refuse to accept the living death of acquiescence," says Bukowski in his publicity statements. "The film is a focus on their brave madness.") But it's canny bilge, full of the author's self-love, and Rourke seems to revel in that canniness.

He's likable here, and so are the two principal women; he twinkles with amusement at doing Bukowski and they twinkle back. Dunaway plays the destructive Wanda with a minimum of fuss; it's a forthright star turn—she wins your admiration by the simplicity of her effects. She redeems platitudes with a glint of insane conviction; she makes her lines sound right for the character—even lines like "We're all in some kind of hell. And the madhouses are the only places where people *know* they are in hell." And as Tully, the wealthy publisher of a literary magazine, Alice Krige, who wears her lustrous dark hair flowing loose, keeps pushing her hand back through it, in true L.A. nervous-narcissist style. Krige has a touch of Claire Bloom's wit in her acting, and in her beauty. At first, Tully may think Henry is smelly, but after a few drinks . . .

Bukowski's loving view of himself reaches its cartoon apex when Dunaway's Wanda and Krige's Tully fight over their rooster Henry— biting and scratching as they roll on the barroom floor. And, the way the movie is rigged, you know why they go for this bummy little guy: he's the only character with a soul that's intact. His humanity hasn't been corrupted or dried to dust; he isn't afraid of life—he isn't afraid to lose a fight or to hit bottom. This is a mighty simple movie, with its flyblown wisdom spelled out. It doesn't have the vision or the suggestiveness of

Marco Ferreri's 1981 film *Tales of Ordinary Madness*, which was also based on Bukowski's life, and which starred Ben Gazzara as the poet and Ornella Muti as a younger version of the Dunaway character. Gazzara (who gave a marvellous, raspy-voiced performance) played Bukowski as a poseur who was also an artist. Bukowski, in adapting his own material to the screen, seems content to be a poseur. *Barfly* asserts that Henry isn't tempted by security. Offered the guesthouse on Tully's estate, he snubs her; he calls her world "a cage with golden bars." (Of course, she's infatuated with his integrity.) Waking in her bed, he gets up saying, "I belong on the streets. I don't feel right here. It's like I can't *breathe!*" He goes back to his grimy haunts, where—we're supposed to believe—the real people are.

Barfly might be a film about the leader of a religious cult which was made by an altar boy. Schroeder, wanting to please the Master, inadvertently exposes Bukowski's messianic windbag sensibility at its most self-satisfied. You wouldn't guess at Bukowski's talent from this movie. His script is a pastiche of his earlier writing. It's not about finding truth by living among society's rejects—it's about peddling that notion of truth to the well-heeled. (Working-class people aren't likely to be among the buyers; skid row doesn't have the same appeal to them.)

I became impatient with this movie during the scene where the distressed goddess sleeps and Henry writes (on paper torn from a cheap notebook). My reaction was nothing compared with the stupefaction I experienced at Jean-Jacques Beineix's *Betty Blue*: Betty had to go mad and poke her eye out in order for her man to become a writer—she gave up her soul for his art. But what a puny little myth of creation *Barfly* is! So this fellow chose to live like a bum: does that have to be a superior way to live—a spiritual quest? To be blunt about it, a director who stages fights—whether Henry's or the women's—as clumsily as Barbet Schroeder does has to go in for tony quests. But it's surprising that Bukowski couldn't come up with something fresher than a life-affirming hero who (we're actually told) "refuses to join the rat race." There are the obvious Yuppie movies and then there are the ones like *Barfly*, where viewers are guided to thumb their noses at the race to be the fattest rat. This script is a lazy con job. He didn't stay up enough nights.

■

R idley Scott's thriller *Someone to Watch Over Me* is all moods. Prodigious planning and editing have gone into them, along with a lot of smoke, Gothic lighting, and interior decoration. They give the picture a high-class hauntedness. You drift into it. You can even trance out on it, because Scott works like a visual hypnotist: he seduces you by the repetitive monotony of the stimuli. He draws you into a dull, sensual daydreaminess (that TV directors wouldn't dare to attempt—they want you awake for the commercials). But after watching Tom Berenger and Mimi Rogers for a while you look around for the stars. With so much buildup—so much terror-tinged atmosphere—you expect actors with some verve, and you wonder why the script doesn't sneak in a few jokes. (Has a good thriller ever been this solemn? Or this simple?) A Manhattan socialite, Claire (Mimi Rogers), who writes about art and looks expensively asymmetrical, goes to a glamorous disco and wanders down to see her friend the young owner, who's in the basement, where he has a private swimming-pool art gallery. (If you want to know where all this opulence is to be found, the exterior of the disco is the Rex Il Ristorante in the Oviatt, an Art Deco building on South Olive Street in L.A., and the dancing area and the basement were shot on the Queen Mary.) She sees her friend being stabbed to death by a beetle-browed, ferociously evil-looking gangster (Andreas Katsulas), and he catches sight of her and scowls like Dracula. She gets away, but since she's the only witness, the police assign men to guard her. One of them is a cop who has just been promoted to detective (Tom Berenger), a warmhearted, decent, uncultivated fellow who lives in Queens with his smart, happy wife (Lorraine Bracco) and their terrific son. Put in this protective relationship to Claire, he falls for her, and she—less understandably—falls for him. (He must be the first sincere man she's ever met, or, since it's pointed out that he's not superficial or artistic—the same thing here—the first real man.) That's all there is to the movie—that and the moodiness and how Dracula will be prevented from murdering Claire, and how the detective's commitment to the two women will be resolved. Actually, there's no contest, since the wife stands in for the common people who buy movie tickets, and the wealthy dame has her art collection and her refinement. Statues are posted throughout her apartment like sentinels, and she must have rich people's Muzak—classical music pours through her walls.

Berenger gives a perfectly creditable blue-collar, regular-guy performance, but without the vitality and the rough edges that would stir things up. He and his role are so bland that you wonder what Claire is looking forward to when she looks forward to seeing him. He has no conversation—nothing but his soggy solicitude for her. Is it all his brute strength, his courage—and sex? That's an easy out for the scriptwriter (Howard Franklin has the credit); in thirties and forties movies, poor guys won the rich girls' hearts by making them laugh—by knowing how to enjoy life. Berenger's detective isn't gifted in this department; both women seem to need him mostly for protection. Daniel Hugh Kelly brings some kick to the small role of a cop who has split up with his wife; the only performer who really stands out, though, is Lorraine Bracco. Her line readings have a hardheaded urban earthiness. She's saddled with a few big emotional scenes, but when she uses her comedy timing she sparks the movie. It needs her badly, because as an erotic dream this visual spread on the life style of the rich is a bummer. (Not enough irresponsibility.) And you see Ridley Scott red-eyed and anxious hovering over each hypnotic shot. He has put such morbid, finicky care into this silly little story that he's worried the fun out of it.

November 2, 1987

MINDSPEAK

|||||||||||||||||||||||||||||||||||||||||||||||||||||||||||||||||||||||||||||||||||||||||||||||||||||||||||||||||||||||||||||||||||||||||||||||||||||||||||||||

*S*ammy and Rosie Get Laid is an apocalyptic carnival, a celebration of political fireworks—specifically, of race riots in London and other English cities in the Tory eighties. The picture was made by the team responsible for *My Beautiful Laundrette*—the director Stephen Frears, the writer Hanif Kureishi—but this time the writer dominates, and the film is off balance. It's literate to an almost loony degree. Everyone speaks his mind—or Kureishi's mind. The characters rattle off epigrams or semi-philosophical remarks about race and sex and colonialism; they're maddeningly overprecise about their conflicts. Kureishi, who was born in London in 1956, of an English mother and an immigrant Pakistani father, considers himself British, and from the sound of this movie he's British, all right. Nobody ever gropes for a word or stumbles over a phrase; everybody is linguistically confident and ready to go. When the characters are anguished, they just sound more clipped.

387

Most of the picture takes place in a decaying, racially mixed neighborhood, where a black woman, terrified by the police who charge into her kitchen to arrest her son, flings a pan of hot grease at one of them; another panics and shoots her, and the angry young blacks and Pakistanis riot, burning houses and cars, fighting the police with bricks and pieces of pipe. The plump, expensively dressed Rafi (Shashi Kapoor) comes from the airport straight into this uproar. A Pakistani who became a powerful figure in post-colonial Pakistan and was a minister in the repressive, martial-law government, Rafi wound up with a fortune; now he is fleeing threats on his life, and thinks that he can return to the courteous, tolerant, law-abiding England he remembers from thirty years before. He hopes for some human warmth from his son Samir—Sammy (Ayub Khan Din)—who lives in a comfortable middle-class flat in this ghetto, with his wife, Rosie (Frances Barber). And he hopes to reëstablish his relationship with Alice (Claire Bloom), whom he deserted when he went back to his country all those years ago.

Nothing is as Rafi had imagined it would be: the movie is his nightmare experience of the new London. In interviews, Frears uses the term "radical chic" to describe Sammy and Rosie and their friends, who are Third World bohemians. Sammy, a coke-snorting accountant for hip artists, and Rosie, a social worker and Leftist journalist, have an open marriage. They live in the midst of political ferment because of conviction—mostly Rosie's. They live among people whom the system treats as garbage; those are the only ones who mean anything—the garbage heap is where it's at. Sammy, impressed by his wife's wisdom, explains the rioting in the streets to Rafi: "Rosie says these revolts are an affirmation of the human spirit. A kind of justice is being done." This example of Rosie's wisdom is given a twist when Sammy, finding his own car burned out, kicks it and curses, and his father twits him with "An affirmation of the human spirit?" But, in interviews, Kureishi says exactly what Rosie says, and that's what the film—which he calls a declaration of war against Thatcherism—says, too. We are supposed to see the flames as a destructive-creative element. The blacks and Pakistanis, not being allowed to run their own communities, have no way to express their rage and frustration except by throwing bricks and setting fires, even if what they destroy is their own housing. Kureishi wouldn't want us to think he's naïve, though: during the riot, the slumlords (who are eager to clear the area for development and need a police crackdown) pay street kids to keep the vandalism going.

Rafi, Sammy, Rosie, and Alice all represent (and articulate) political positions. So does curly-haired Anna (Wendy Gazelle), an American photographer, who's Sammy's lover, and so do a pair of lesbians—one black, one Pakistani—who hang out at Sammy and Rosie's place. And so does the angelic, light-skinned black Danny (dimply Roland Gift, the lead singer of the British group Fine Young Cannibals), who has an affair with Rosie. Even the ghost of one of Rafi's old political enemies talks up. During all this mindspeak, the director keeps the imagery moving rhythmically. Often it's Godardian, and the compositions are pop and iconic. When Rosie and Danny kiss, their profiles fill the screen. When they have sex, so do Sammy and Anna, and so do Rafi and Alice, and the screen splits horizontally, with the three multiracial couples stretched out on top of each other—a sexual pousse-café. The Godard touches are playful and welcome, and the playfulness of the triple coupling is heightened by a comic effect: it's intercut with the sashaying of four Rastafarians (the Ghetto Lites) who face the camera as they sing a reggae version of the Temptations' "My Girl."

The movie has a documentary manner as stylized as a Hollywood musical, and it's hyperconscious of art, of politics, of itself. It's as if *My Beautiful Laundrette* had been shot on the sets and locations of *Sid and Nancy* and *Absolute Beginners*, with characters from those movies wandering through. At times, it's as if Swinging London had come back as a race riot. Rafi is given Rosie's study for his bedroom; on the wall is a large photograph of Virginia Woolf at her most luminous, and during the rioting the flickering fires in the street are spectral altar lights burning for Woolf. (There's also a postcard of Vanessa Bell on the wall, and you may spot a picture of Jacques Lacan.) Danny's trailer, in a squatters' shantytown, is covered with graffiti in German, French, and English, from the Burial of the Dead section of *The Waste Land*. Just before the start of the riot, a back-yard dog runs in circles, chasing its tail. After a while, you begin to think the picture is that dog.

Shashi Kapoor is marvellous as a man who adapts to whatever happens (or adapts up to a point). Rafi is practical and has a big stash in the bank. A sensualist who sucks on sweets and wants his pleasures, he's much like the slumlord uncle played by Saeed Jaffrey in *Laundrette*. When Rafi undresses to go to bed with Alice, his potbelly enhances him; he earned it—it's his true character. The belly (and the stash) swallowed up the idealistic revolutionary. When Rafi was in the government, he sanctioned the torture of the opposition, and Rosie, who learns about it,

389

gives him no peace. She taunts Sammy by reading him details of his father's crimes; she tries to force Rafi into admissions of guilt. At dinner in a restaurant, she asks loudly, "What does it feel like to maim, to kill, to torture, and what does one do in the evenings?" That's the way she talks. Why is the movie so exasperating? For one thing, its superior tone is intimidatingly, smugly clever, just like Rosie's.

She has created herself—taken a new name to be free of the father who abused her—and she's sexually free, restless, and seductive. At first, you may think she has a wonderful camera face—Frances Barber has suggestions of Nancy Carroll in the early thirties and of Sylvia Sidney and Anna Karina. But the camera dotes on her honeyed gaze, and by the time Rosie surveys the crowd at a party she and Sammy give for Rafi, and narrows her eyes mysteriously—a horny Mona Lisa—you may feel you've had it with her. Barber has described Rosie as the sort of woman she would like to be in an ideal world—no wonder she looks as if she's getting ready to play Joan of Arc. Some of us may take Rosie for one of those people who perpetually seek grounds for indignation. What never comes into focus is that this courageous New Woman, who embodies Kureishi's political-sexual consciousness, humiliates her husband by making advances to other men in his presence, and, taking on the role of judge, torments and destroys Rafi. The film's tone toward her is neutral. Maybe Frears and Kureishi thought that their elliptical, documentary look at things was an objective approach, but all it does is smudge the issues. As Rafi is presented, his political sophistication is more believable than his bad conscience; he's a warm, entertaining scoundrel. Yet his fate is presented unaffectingly. Is the film saying that he brought it on himself by his moral emptiness? You can't tell; the moviemakers seem to think they're just looking at the passing parade.

Most of what *Sammy and Rosie* says about the frustration of the rioters seems to be right and to apply to our cities as well as to English cities, but are the riots the "fine assertions of the human spirit against democratic tyranny" that Kureishi has called them? Or are they more like an angry explosion? This isn't just a quibble, because if the rioting is a fine assertion it's being recommended—or, at the least, thought valuable—while angry explosions are frequently self-destructive. *Sammy and Rosie* appears to be Kureishi's attempt to demonstrate that the artist can be a political force, but the flickering little fires—they go on burning in the windows of dark houses—are mystical, decorative. And when the squatters water their sad-looking cabbage patch, or when the police come with bulldozers to knock down the shantytown, you may think you're watching a TV-news rerun of street theatre in Berkeley in the late sixties. It's all affectless fun.

Kureishi's book, *My Beautiful Laundrette and the Rainbow Sign*—the script and an autobiographical essay about his ambivalence toward the British—takes part of its title from the James Baldwin epigraph ("God gave Noah the rainbow sign, No more water, the fire next time!"). Baldwin is one of Kureishi's masters, and for Kureishi fire is rhetoric and imagery. But is it also fire? There's no emotional force driving this movie. There isn't even much wit in the film's cleverness. It's there in Kapoor's performance, and in the cunning of Claire Bloom's line readings. (She has a genius for bringing the most out of her dialogue, delivering it in a sane, matter-of-fact way even when it's ornate and hectoring. And she makes you laugh in delight at her skill—there's a little witchcraft in it.) But the film suffers from the curse of the British: verbal facility, a terrible empty brilliance. I don't recall ever hearing so many failed epigrams in one movie.

Sammy and Rosie is upsetting, because it has a great central theme (colonialism at home), yet keeps bringing the term "radical chic" to mind. When Seymour Krim first used this term, in his 1962 essay in the *Village Voice*, and, later, when Tom Wolfe used it, it had narrow, derisive—moneyed—overtones. It referred to the fashionable people who took up the cause of the oppressed—people who were susceptible to manipulation by those who made them feel guilty. *Sammy and Rosie* is so deeply unfocussed that it doesn't do much except to demonstrate that by now radical chic, as a set of attitudes, extends almost inevitably to the "oppressed" themselves, when they're hip and educated and angry. Like the guilty rich, these self-designated oppressed identify with victims. And this identification can make them sentimental and ineffective. Radical chic is a huge trap that can gobble up an artist like Hanif Kureishi and turn him into an advocate of affirmative self-destruction. I kept wanting *Sammy and Rosie* to achieve the satiric vision of England that it was reaching for (and that it hit in the "My Girl" sequence), and I kept staring at Rosie, with her knowing half smiles, and finally I was holding my hand to my head.

■

"**T**ell me she couldn't play Charlton Heston's daughter!" the projectionist muttered in my ear as Kelly McGillis pulled her lips back from her teeth in *Made in Heaven* and smiled. It's a slow smile, because granite doesn't move easy. As a pure soul born in Heaven—the sort of lyrical, ethereal girl that Jennifer Jones used to play—she's flagrantly miscast. The idea is that the characters she and Timothy Hutton play have a love literally made in Heaven: he has died while rescuing a drowning family and met her up there. When their souls are returned to earth in newborn babes, they have a spiritual need to find each other, though they don't remember the love they shared. The movie is about finding perfect love, losing it, and stumblingly trying to recover it—in another life. With a theme like this, a picture is bound to attract an audience of hazy heads, no matter how nondescript it is; it could appeal to the romantic haze in all our heads if only it had been worked out more ingeniously—if the scenes took some shape, if they didn't dither and sag. The director, the fanciful Alan Rudolph, generally has a more consistent (and funkier) vision. He is reported to have had differences with the producers; there were three—Raynold Gideon, Bruce A. Evans, and David Blocker—and since Gideon and Evans wrote the script he may not be fully responsible for the film's sponginess. It spans thirty years, in a random sort of way. An example of its plotting: in her new life, McGillis writes a children's book about an imaginary friend, based on her subconscious memories of Hutton; we see him with a copy of the book and wait for the Aha! It never comes.

A batch of smart performers give the picture some flavor around the edges. For the first ten minutes or so, it's a sprightly, eccentric comedy, and Hutton moves along—a small-town boy with a nice, cowlicky quality and gleams of intelligence. He shows an actor's pleasure in the give-and-take with Ann Wedgeworth and James Gammon, as his parents, and with Mare Winningham, who's blissfully piggy as the girlfriend who ditches him when he loses his job. Winningham gives herself a moon face, with blank eyes and doughy cheeks; she's almost something out of *Eraserhead*. The first scenes in Heaven flit by neatly, too: Maureen Stapleton is there, as Hutton's Aunt Lisa—as everybody's dream Aunt Lisa—who welcomes him rather offhandedly, because she has taken up painting and doesn't like her work to be interrupted. Then McGillis appears and guides him around the place (it's actually Charleston, South Carolina, with some special effects), and at the first sound of her heavy voice the whimsy congeals. (Misgivings show on Hutton's face like a shadow.) Eventually, David Rasche turns up, as a fellow who briefly courts McGillis, and his mixture of brashness and polish energizes a few scenes; you think, Who is this guy? And Hutton recuperates whenever he gets someone to act with—notably in his scenes with Amanda Plummer, who's alive and has a no-nonsense charm as a woman who runs a recording studio. The movie touches earth when she's onscreen, and earth is where you want to be.

A number of celebrities show up in bit parts: the singer and songwriter Neil Young as a truck driver, the novelist Tom Robbins as a toymaker, the cartoonist Gary Larson as a guitarist, the rock star Tom Petty as the owner of a roadhouse, the rock star Ric Ocasek, of the Cars, as a mechanic. They don't have any presence, but this movie can use all the quirky drop-ins it can get. It's a romance with a barely audible heartbeat. Ellen Barkin also shows up—uncredited—as the temptress Lucille, a female Lucifer; it's an expendable sequence, a mistake. Debra Winger (who's married to Hutton) appears in disguise in a sizable male role—as Emmett, the fellow who manages things in Heaven. With a red punk hairdo and pasty makeup and a hoarse voice straining for depth, she's almost unrecognizable, except when she smiles. But Hutton clearly has more rapport with this weirdly androgynous Emmett than he has with McGillis.

■

There has probably been no piece of casting this year more ineffably Hollywood than Cher as a busy, weary public defender in Peter Yates's *Suspect*—Cher as a dedicated drudge. Cher being Cher, when she represents a man accused of murder, in a Washington, D.C., courtroom, before a rigid, cold-eyed judge, she wears a black leather jacket, and her long thick hair is loose on her shoulders. She's all wrong for this public defender: her hooded, introspective face doesn't give you enough— she needs a role that lets her use her body. With the camera on her steadily here, you might be watching a still picture. After a while, you get the feeling that if she showed some expression she'd wrinkle, or crack. I heard someone whisper, "She isn't the undead—she's the unold."

It's the movie that's the undead. It's a laboriously set-up thriller: a clerk in the Department of Justice is found with her throat cut, on the bank of the Potomac, and the man put on trial for the slaying is a homeless Vietnam vet (Liam Neeson) who became deaf through the meningitis he contracted in the hospital, and also suffered a traumatic speech loss. His

393

lawyer learns that he's a deaf-mute, then has scenes in which she goes on talking to him and asking him questions. Is there something wrong with her, too? It's impossible to know how we're meant to interpret the lamebrained job she does in court. She'd be lost if one of the jurors—a handsome, semi-cynical young lobbyist (Dennis Quaid) who knows his way around the bureaucracy—didn't do the detective work that helps her out. The screenwriter, Eric Roth, puts a woman lawyer at the center of the movie, as if this were going to be a switch on older courtroom thrillers, and then he provides a man to do the thinking and to rescue her when she gets in trouble. You can't call this feminist backlash, because there's no hostility in it; it doesn't have the nastiness or the kick that hostility would give it. If the moviemakers had just pushed the Quaid character a little further—if he had wanted to help her but wanted to show her up, too—they might have had the hair trigger for a thriller. (And Quaid might have had something to play.) Probably these fellows were just so proud of not having made the woman a bimbo that they didn't notice they'd made her a lummox.

November 16, 1987

THE MANCHURIAN CONFORMIST

||||||||||||||||||||||||||||||||||||||||||||||||||||||||||||||||||||||||||||||||||||||||||||||||||||||||||||||||||||||||||||||||||||||||||

In 1908, the not quite three-year-old Pu Yi was forcibly separated from his mother and set on the Dragon Throne in Peking's Forbidden City. Honored as a god—as the Lord of Ten Thousand Years— he was the titular ruler of a third of the people on earth. Deposed in 1912, by the republican revolution, he was a feudal has-been but didn't know it for several years, because he was allowed to remain in the Forbidden City with his courtiers, chamberlains, and aristocratic ladies, and several hundred eunuchs. He went on playing emperor and presiding over empty ceremonies until 1924, when Nationalist forces evicted him. He was nineteen; he packed up his No. 1 wife (the empress) and his No. 2 wife, his wealth and his entourage, and moved to the coastal city of Tientsin, where he lived the life of a Western-style playboy—he partied.

Then, in the early thirties, he was wooed by the Japanese: accepting their offers, he became the puppet emperor of Japanese-occupied Manchuria, and stayed in office during the Second World War—until the arrival of Soviet paratroopers, in 1945. He spent five years in Soviet custody. When Mao's Communists took power in China and wanted him returned, Stalin sent him home, and for ten years he was "reëducated" in a war-criminals prison. Pardoned in 1959, he worked as an unskilled under-gardener in Peking's Botanical Gardens and then as an archivist until his death, of cancer, in 1967. All that he left behind was an autobiography, and that was written by Communist hacks. It deals with his repentance.

This desperately unlucky man—a cork bobbing on the tides of history—is the subject of Bernardo Bertolucci's *The Last Emperor*. Pu Yi's life story seems made for irony. It could be told so that we'd see his ups and down-down-downs as an extreme example of the crazy bad breaks we all are handed. His life has the pattern for Preston Sturges slapstick—Sturges might see him as a peppy fellow always fighting the storms and getting knocked into the water, the Emperor of China as a poor, sad schmuck. And if Bertolucci wanted to make *The Tragedy of a Ridiculous Man*—which was the title of his last picture—Pu Yi would be the perfect subject. But Bertolucci, and Mark Peploe, who wrote the script with his help, have a different approach. They use three child actors as Pu Yi at three, at ten, and through his wedding, at fifteen, and then John Lone takes over for him at eighteen and plays him to his end, at sixty-two. The movie doesn't have the juicy absurdity that seems to pour right out of the historical story. And it suppresses the drama. But it has a dull fascination.

Bertolucci doesn't intend us to see Pu Yi as the hero or the anti-hero, or even the comic victim, of his life. Rather, he's a man without will or backbone who lives his life as spectacle—who watches his life go by. And since he experiences his life as spectacle we're given only spectacle—a historical pageant without a protagonist. There's an idea here, but it's a dippy idea—it results in a passive movie. There's no toughness in Peploe's writing; the dialogue is waxy. And Bertolucci, given the opportunity to shoot the palaces and courtyards and labyrinthine walled paths of the two-hundred-and-fifty-acre Forbidden City, works so gracefully that the movie is all vistas, all squat façades and heavy silks, reds and brilliant yellows. The chinoiserie is pleasant enough, but Bertolucci's staging, Vittorio Storaro's cinematography, and Ferdinando Scarfiotti's sets aren't in the service of anything in particular, and they make no real mark on you. That's also true of Peter O'Toole's performance as the boy emperor's tutor, a Scotsman, who was reputedly skilled in intrigue but is presented here as no more than a stiff, kindly fellow.

There are tiny set pieces that can get to you. When Pu Yi's wet nurse is taken away, because he's too attached to her, he chases the palanquin carrying her but can't catch up; years later, in Manchuria, his porcelain-doll empress (the gifted Joan Chen) is taken away by the Japanese because they can't control her, and he chases the car and, of course, doesn't catch up. These rhyming incidents of helplessness—of loss—are disturbingly poignant: you feel them like slivers under your skin. And though Pu Yi is a prisoner in the Forbidden City, he's a pampered prisoner, so that when he must leave—when the Nationalist soldiers fall into ranks at the gates and he comes out leading the motorcade, sitting between his two wives—it's like the expulsion from Eden. Images such as that of hundreds of bannermen with coxcomb headgear, or the regiments of eunuchs—who are about to leave the City—standing in formation holding little terra-cotta jars, so that when they are buried they can be buried as whole men, have some staying power. The movie is full of felicities, but the central idea of a man who watches his life go by is only an intellectual conceit. It doesn't make contact with the audience.

Bertolucci's typical men have been passive—the rich or privileged ones especially (Fabrizio in *Before the Revolution*, the Trintignant character in *The Conformist*, the De Niro character in *1900*). Here the whole mood of the film is passive. In a sense, we're being told to watch history acting on people, and the filmmaking itself is not active enough to show us how the people respond. John Lone has the sensuous, modelled features of a matinée idol; he's mysteriously poised and formal—he suggests something between Eastern and Western acting—and there's a tension in his star presence. But the movie, which renounces psychology, gives no weight to Pu Yi's undefined sexuality or to his cruelty; he's written as a figurehead. Lone is gutted as an actor—the conception doesn't allow him to show anything like the fears that Trintignant communicated. All Lone can do with Pu Yi is make him a magnetic figurehead. The child actors who play Pu Yi get a chance to show some spontaneity, and we can smile at how straight they stand in their imperial getups. And we see how the courtiers and the ladies control the growing child by giving him sensual pleasure or withholding it. They're like unscrupulous parents. They're hiding behind columns listening when Pu Yi's tutor is with him. When Pu Yi wants to go off to Oxford, they pick an eligible seventeen-year-old Manchu princess for him, and when she covers the little fifteen-year-old boy's face with lipsticky kisses their hands loosen her clothes so he can get at her.

Lone has to carry the film's dubious message. Bertolucci and Peploe want us to believe that Pu Yi really was reëducated: that he became a model citizen through the ministrations of the governor of the prison, a kindly, shrewd first-generation Communist (Ying Ruocheng), and that in his later years, when he worked as an under-gardener, he experienced freedom for the first time. They want us to believe that his repentance was genuine, and that what some might disparage as Communist brainwashing actually cleaned away his decadence and healed him. They come up with a scene in which Pu Yi, near death, visits the Forbidden City, which is now a tourist attraction, talks to a child there, and, going to his old throne, digs down to find the cricket cage he left there years before, and hands the cage, with its still-living cricket, to the child. The scene would work better if the moviemakers had planted the detail of how long crickets can survive, but it would still have a fuddy-duddy humility about it.

If we're to believe that the reëducation was a success, we have to see it. And Bertolucci and Peploe are too passive to dramatize it. The movie gives us no way to judge whether Pu Yi is pleased merely to have survived, like the caged cricket—survived the revolutions, the prisons, and his own suicide attempts—or has found some deep inner contentment as a Communist citizen. His empress, who has the political instincts he lacks, speaks up freely before she's taken away from him. His No. 2 wife (Wu Jun Mimei) walks out on him in Tientsin, taking nothing—not even an umbrella to ward off the rain. She's soaked but free, like the romantic heroines in movies of long ago. The scene has no substance, yet you know that Bertolucci admires this adventurous woman, while Pu Yi, like the Trintignant and De Niro figures, seems to stand for the part of him that he feels should be expunged—the coddled little boy who grows up wanting to cling, as Pu Yi does, to his mother, his wet nurse, his golden throne, his paradise. The only way I can make sense of this movie is to see it as the reverie of a man who can't justify himself as an artist, who doesn't trust his instincts and keeps leaning on Marxism and other outside forms of discipline, who feels that he needs to be reëducated, changed—that his artistry should be put at the service of ordinary people. He's brainwashing himself in this movie, trying to tell himself that he shouldn't be the star of his life—that he'd be happier as an extra.

Bertolucci is not the kind of moviemaker who can make epics for a huge international audience: he doesn't have the gusto, the animal high spirits, or the low cunning. And, working with Mark Peploe, he can't show us what Pu Yi is missing. Pu Yi is just as passive near the end, when he's a lowly gardener, as he was when he was a weakling playboy—perhaps more so. But now that he's an extra we're supposed to see him as a happy, free man. This makes no sense: Is he never to assert himself? Is happiness supposed to be the acceptance of castration? Pu Yi might as well be given a little terra-cotta jar.

Bertolucci makes pretty pictorial music, but two hours and forty-six minutes is a long time for a movie to dance. Maybe it wouldn't be if his sense of rhythm hadn't become erratic. A scene in which the adolescent Pu Yi plays a game with the eunuchs—he stands on one side of a huge cloth banner, they on the other, and he feels them, trying to guess who is who—has its more explicitly erotic echo when Pu Yi is in bed, under a flesh-toned satin cover, with both his wives, and we watch the rippling movements of cloth. A fire outside darkens the flesh tones—a wonderful idea—but the satin ripples for much too long. The voluptuous lyricism has gone out of Bertolucci's sensual scenes; they've become obvious. And he has taken to redoing his own earlier effects. Parts of the movie suggest that he moved *The Conformist* to Manchuria, but when he stages a lesbian seduction it isn't lush and enticing—it's right out of the Ridiculous Theatrical Company. The seducer, who announces "I'm a spy, and I don't care who knows it," is also an opium addict, a concubine, and a would-be aviatrix who dresses all in leather; she wins the empress by sucking her toes, putting a ring on one of them, and declaring, "Now we're engaged." (The Manchurian scenes are disconcertingly cartoonish, with slimy Japanese on nefarious errands, and the empress stuffing her mouth with flower petals.) The film's most shocking moment comes when Pu Yi, still a boy, is not allowed to go out of the Forbidden City to see his mother, who has killed herself; he takes the pet mouse that he carries in his pocket and smashes it against the City gates. The scene is especially shocking to those who saw *1900* and retain a vivid memory of Donald Sutherland, as the Fascist Attila, smashing a cat. These scraps of Bertolucci's past hint at a problem: he can't get a new vision together, and he's in danger of self-parody.

To enjoy the picture, you have to settle for the set pieces and the many quick, unstressed details, such as a glimpse of women's bound feet, or images such as that of a single huge red star in a detention center, and a single fedora in a crowd of prisoners, on Pu Yi. The Forbidden City itself is visually pleasing but not exactly glorious. Peter O'Toole has

398

said that it wasn't until the movie was actually being shot and he was riding in a golden palanquin, ten feet in the air, that he saw the Imperial Palace as "a sea of yellow triangular and rectangular loops" and realized that the whole Forbidden City was intended to be seen from the height of a palanquin—that it was a maze designed for the eyes of lordlings, not earthlings. I don't understand why the moviemakers didn't get the camera up there. What better way for Bertolucci to show us the true meaning of a life of privilege? Is it possible that Bertolucci (whose movies tell us that he can't tear himself away from that life) didn't want to make the Forbidden City too alluring? It isn't just himself he's trying to reëducate.

■

In *Cry Freedom* the producer-director Richard Attenborough uses his own hero worship didactically. He tells the story of the martyrdom of young Stephen Biko (Denzel Washington) in order to arouse the audience to the tragic injustice of apartheid. Attenborough has the doggedness to do it, but the task also requires great organizing intelligence. That's where *Cry Freedom* falls down.

The movie begins in November, 1975, at dawn in the Crossroads settlement, a large squatter community near Cape Town. Attenborough depends on the usual shorthand to show us how peaceful the squatters are: women preparing breakfast, a black infant at its mother's breast. Suddenly, there's the deafening noise of a large raiding party of police arriving in lorries and Land-Rovers, and, without warning, the officers rush in with dogs and metal-tipped leather whips, beating people, driving them out, and setting fire to their shanties while stunned, injured parents dash about in terror trying to gather their children. Attenborough is not the sort of director to stand back a few feet and let us experience the suffering; he rams it at us. Alone in a shack, a helpless baby in a makeshift crib screams. Will the soldiers let someone come pick it up before it's bulldozed or burned to death? (We don't find out.) On the thin walls that are being destroyed are pictures of Steve Biko; during his college days, he founded the Black Consciousness Movement, and though he is banned, he remains its principal spokesman. While the shacks crumble, one squatter is trying to put Biko's picture back up.

As the movie tells it, Donald Woods (Kevin Kline), the editor of the East London, South Africa, *Daily Dispatch*, accepts an invitation to meet

399

Biko, who isn't allowed to talk to more than one person at a time. Followed by the Security Police who guard him, Biko, who's still in his twenties, takes Woods—forty-one years old and a fifth-generation South African—for his first visit to a black township, and shows him how the blacks live and how they're kept down. As Woods learns, we're supposed to learn, too. Woods has believed that Biko's rejection of white participation in the struggle of the blacks meant that Biko was a black racist, advocating supremacy over whites; he finds out that Biko looks forward to the time when blacks and whites can live together in harmony, and the two men become friends. Soon Woods, in his editorials and front-page headlines, is scrapping with the ruling Afrikaners, and he experiences the methods of the Security Police himself. The movie centers on the education of Donald Woods, but Denzel Washington has a beautiful voice, with drama in it, and he puts so much humor and life into Biko that you don't think much about Woods—especially since Kline, with light-colored hair and specs, seems grayish and undefined. Kline probably intends his performance to be self-effacing—he seems meant to be a white liberal Everyman who goes through a reformation—but he comes across as an unimaginative actor, a void. (Usually we know a character has reformed when he becomes boring; Kevin Kline's Woods has reformed even before *Cry Freedom* begins.) And so when we're less than halfway into the two-hour-and-thirty-seven-minute movie and Biko is badly beaten while in the custody of the Security Police and trucked hundreds of miles over bumpy roads to a police hospital, where he dies, in September, 1977, of brain injuries, and the story shifts to Woods' efforts to get an inquest and then to escape with his wife and five children, taking with him the manuscript of a book he has written about Biko, the picture collapses.

If the audience were made to feel a larger purpose for the escape—if Woods had the spirit to carry on Biko's fight, or even the hope of doing so—maybe the movie wouldn't lose all its steam. But Woods seems like just a fellow carrying a manuscript. And Attenborough and the scriptwriter, John Briley, aren't skillful enough to bring off the suspense scenes. When they start crosscutting from the escape to Woods' flashback memories, and to visions and atrocities, with bursts of choral music, the movie is dumbfounding. Several of these misplaced sequences feature Biko. It looks as if Attenborough staged scenes and then didn't know what to do with them, so he stuck them in by having the escaping Woods think back or forward or sideways. And every time Biko, in his mustache, goatee, and long sideburns, returns and we hear his pungent, rolling cadences our interest quickens; this man with fire in his eyes commands the screen—

Denzel Washington is the star by right of talent. When the movie cuts back to Woods, the family escape story recalls *The Sound of Music*. And we're painfully aware that despite the movie's hopes of raising the white audience's consciousness, we whites are assumed to need a white man to identify with. Attenborough compromises his own hero worship; he betrays Biko by the structure of the film.

The Woods family is finally airborne, flying to safety, early in 1978, and Attenborough crosscuts back to the Soweto massacre of June, 1976, when protesting schoolchildren were slaughtered. The massacre is used to give the movie a grand finale. Do the moviemakers think that if they put it in its chronological sequence—the year before Biko's death—we'd forget it? (This way, it's an event without repercussions.) And Attenborough doesn't trust us to respond sufficiently, so after the police shoot into the crowds of kids and things are almost over we see one little boy fleeing across a dirt lot and a sadistic cop leans out of his car window and deliberately picks him off. Attenborough's crudeness turns tragedy into melodrama.

When he cuts from Soweto back to the little plane carrying the Woods family, you're embarrassed for this catchall movie. What does Soweto have to do with the family's escape? Woods doesn't have to tell the world about Soweto; the world has already known for more than a year. Attenborough doesn't want to burden us with complexities, because—presumably—he wants to inspire us to help end injustice. So blacks don't show rage at whites; they don't even feel it. And Biko is the leader next door—a gentle intellectual prince with answers to everything. (Yet Denzel Washington, in his occasional hesitancies, makes us sense what Biko must be holding back, and that's what makes us identify with Biko. It's the heat behind his cool glibness.) In a basic way, Attenborough treats the audience as children to be lied to, to be patronized. I can't assess whether a picture such as *Cry Freedom* (most of it was shot in Zimbabwe) serves the purposes it's said to be dedicated to—to make audiences press for economic sanctions against South Africa. But I am very leery of a moviemaker for whom reaching the widest audience and serving mankind are the same thing. Sir Dickie makes box-office success seem pure.

November 30, 1987

IRISH VOICES

‖‖

The announcement that John Huston was making a movie of James Joyce's "The Dead" raised the question "Why?" What could images do that Joyce's words hadn't? And wasn't Huston pitting himself against a master who, though he was only twenty-five when he wrote the story, had given it full form? (Or nearly full—Joyce's language gains from being read aloud.) It turns out that those who love the story needn't have worried. Huston directed the movie, at eighty, from a wheelchair, jumping up to look through the camera, with oxygen tubes trailing from his nose to a portable generator; most of the time, he had to watch the actors on a video monitor outside the set and use a microphone to speak to the crew. Yet he went into dramatic areas that he'd never gone into before— funny, warm family scenes that might be thought completely out of his range. He seems to have brought the understanding of Joyce's ribald humor which he gained from his knowledge of *Ulysses* into this earlier work; the minor characters who are shadowy on the page now have a Joycean vividness. Huston has knocked the academicism out of them and developed the undeveloped parts of the story. He's given it a marvellous filigree that enriches the social life. And he's done it all in a mood of tranquil exuberance, as if moviemaking had become natural to him, easier than breathing.

The movie is set on the sixth of January, 1904, the Feast of the Epiphany. The Morkan sisters and their fortyish niece—three spinster musicians and music teachers—are giving their annual dance and supper, in their Dublin town house, and as their relatives and friends arrive the foibles and obsessions of the hostesses and the guests mesh and turn festive. The actors—Irish or of Irish heritage—become the members of a family and a social set who know who's going to get too loud, who's going to get upset about what. They know who's going to make a fool of himself: Freddy Malins (Donal Donnelly)—he drinks. Even before Freddy shows up, the two Misses Morkan—ancient, gray Julia (Cathleen Delany), whose fragile face seems to get skinnier as the night wears on, and hearty Kate (Helena Carroll)—are worried. They're relieved when their favorite nephew, Gabriel Conroy (Donal McCann), arrives, with his wife, Gretta (Anjelica Huston); they can count on Gabriel to keep an eye on Freddy for them. It's the reliable, slightly pompous Gabriel—a college professor and book reviewer—who has an epiphany this night, and we, too, experience it.

During the party, Gabriel tries to entertain Freddy's excruciating old bore of a mother (Marie Kean), a self-satisfied biddy who smiles a sweet social smile at Gabriel but treats her son with contempt. Mrs. Malins wears an evening hat perched on her white ringlets and sits with one hand on her fancy walking stick; she's so old she seems to have the bones of a little bird, yet Freddy looks to her for approval, like a child. When he sees her expression, he's left openmouthed, chagrined, and with a faint—almost imperceptible—stutter. He shrinks. She thinks she would like him to be like Gabriel, but she and Freddy match up beyond one's saddest dreams. She sneers at him for not being the manly son she can be proud of, and turns him into a silly ass. Ever hopeful, he's crushed over and over again, his mustachioed upper lip sinking toward his chin.

Gabriel looks more authoritative than he feels. A stabilizing presence, and the man whose task it is to represent all the guests in a speech thanking the hostesses, he's like an observer at the party, but he's also observing himself, and he's not too pleased with how he handles things—especially his response to a young woman who chides him for spending his summer vacations abroad and for not devoting himself to the study of the Irish language. He would like to be suave with her, but he's so full of doubts about himself that he gets hot under the collar. And Gabriel feels his middle-aged mediocrity when he's speechifying. He plays the man of literary eminence, toasting Aunt Julia and Aunt Kate and their niece, Mary Jane (Ingrid Craigie), after calling them the Three Graces of the Dublin musical world. But when the assembled guests drink to them he sees the ladies' gaiety go beyond gaiety. They can't contain their pleasure at being complimented; Julia's hectic, staring eyes fill with tears, and a high flush appears on her ancient girlish dimples. And he gets a whiff of mortality.

The movie itself is a toast to Irish hospitality and to the spinster sisterhood of music teachers, which has probably never before been saluted with such affection. Starting with the sound of an Irish harp under the opening titles, and with frequent reminders of the importance of the pianists who play for the dancing at the party, the picture is about the music that men and women make, and especially about the music of Irish voices. At supper, the characters go at their pet subjects: opera past and present, and famous tenors, dead and alive. They know each other's positions so well that they taunt each other.

One of the guests—a tenor, Mr. D'Arcy (Frank Patterson)—has declined to sing, but after most of the others have left he succumbs to the pleading of a young lady he has been flirting with, and sings "The Lass of Aughrim." Gretta Conroy, who has been making her farewells and is coming down the stairs to join Gabriel, stands hushed, leaning on the bannister listening. Mr. D'Arcy's voice, resonating in the stairwell, has the special trained purity of great Irish tenors; the whole world seems still while he sings, and for a few seconds after. And Gabriel, seeing his wife deeply affected, is fired with sexual longing for her. He hopes to awaken her passion. But in the carriage she's sad and silent, while he makes clumsy conversation. When they reach the hotel where they are to spend the night, she falls asleep in tears after telling him about her youth in Galway and about a consumptive young boy, Michael Furey, her first love, who sang that song, "The Lass of Aughrim." Michael Furey had left his sickbed to come see her on a rainy night in winter, and died a week later, when he was only seventeen.

In the course of the evening, Gabriel has been evaluating how he's doing, and feeling more and more like a solemn stuffed shirt. Now everything he thought he knew about Gretta and himself has been sent whirling. He feels that his own love for her is a dismal thing compared with the dead boy's, and he gets beyond his own ego—he's moved by the boy's action. He thinks about carnal desire and about "the vast hosts of the dead." He sees Aunt Julia as she had looked a few hours earlier when she danced with him, and imagines that she will be the next to go. And Huston, having intensified our vision of the family life that the final passages of the story come out of, implicitly acknowledges that he can't improve on their music. In the story, these passages are Gabriel's thoughts. Here Huston simply gives over to them, and we hear them spoken by Gabriel, as the snow outside blends the living and the dead. Joyce's language seems to melt into pure emotion, and something in Gabriel melts.

Huston moved to Galway in the early fifties, and it was his home base for roughly twenty years—it's where Anjelica Huston and his son Tony Huston, who wrote the script, grew up. But when he made this movie he shot the Dublin interiors in a warehouse in Valencia, California,

404

and the snow was plastic. Huston wasn't strong enough to travel; he completed the film early in the summer, and died in August, after his eighty-first birthday. The picture he left us is a tribute to Joyce, whose words complete and transcend what we've been watching. But the humor is from the two of them, and from the actors.

The movie is a demonstration of what, in Huston's terms, movies can give you that print can't: primarily, the glory of performers—performers with faces that have been written on by time and skill, performers with voices. It's as if Huston were saying, "Making a movie of a classic isn't anything as simple as just depriving you of the work of your imagination. Your imagination couldn't create these people for you. Only these specific actors could do it." And, of course, they could do it only with Huston guiding their movements and Tony Huston providing their words. And, yes, your imagination is now tied to these actors, but they bring a spontaneity and joy into the movie which you don't experience from reading the story.

It isn't simply that they physically embody the characters; they embody what the movie is saying. When Aunt Julia, once a respected local soprano, is prevailed on to sing, and comes out with "Arrayed for the Bridal," the quaver in her thin voice is theme music. So is her vaguely rattled look. Poor, effusive Freddy tells her that he has never heard her sing so well, then goes even further and tells her he has never heard her sing half so well. That's right out of the story, but it's different when we can see and hear the woman he's praising so idiotically. Cathleen Delany is superb as Julia, whose memory is fading, and who sometimes forgets where she is. There's a moment at the beginning when she's in the receiving line and looks at someone blankly; asked if she doesn't remember the person from last year, she rallies with "Of course, of course." She's leaving this world, but she's still a firm social liar. Donal Donnelly isn't just a great drunk; he knows how to play a drunk sobering up. By the end of the party, Freddy is almost a man of the world. Marie Kean's Mrs. Malins is such a smiley little dragon she makes you laugh; the performance is high clowning. And Helena Carroll's Aunt Kate is wonderfully obstreperous when she berates the pope for turning women (like her sister) out of the choirs and putting in little boys. Ingrid Craigie's Mary Jane, the peacemaker, soothes Aunt Kate's sense of injury (you know it's an oft-indulged sense of injury) and steers people to safe ground; Mary Jane has a softness about her, a loving docility. Dan O'Herlihy is the Protestant Mr. Browne, a florid old gent who is delighted to hear Kate lashing out at the pope; he fancies himself a gallant and jovially

drinks himself to sleep. Huston never before blended his actors so intuitively, so musically.

The change in his work is in our closeness to the people on the screen.
Freddy is such a hopeful fellow, always trying to please, that we can see
ourselves in his worst foolishness. We can see ourselves in Julia and Kate
and in the stiff, self-tormenting Gabriel. And when Anjelica Huston's
Gretta speaks of Michael Furey and says "O, the day I heard that, that
he was dead," we hear the echoes of the pain that she felt all those years
ago. We hear them very clearly, because of the fine, unimpassioned way
that the actress plays Gretta, leaving the tragic notes to Gabriel. Gretta's
is only one of the stories of the dead, but Joyce wrote the work right
after his Nora told him of her early great love, and it's the most roman-
ticized, the most piercing. The stillness in the air during Frank Patterson's singing of the melancholy "Lass" is part of the emotional perfection
of the moment. But the film finds its full meaning in the stillness of Donal
McCann's meticulous tones at the end—in Gabriel's helpless self-awareness.
He mourns because he is revealed to himself as less than he thought he
was. He mourns because he sees that the whole world is in mourning.
And he accepts our common end: the snow falls on everyone.

■

When I began to read Marilynne Robinson's novel *Housekeeping*,
I was elated by the plangent simplicity of the language. It's about two
young girls—Ruth, the narrator, and her younger sister, Lucille—who
live in Fingerbone, a fictional town on a lake in the Rockies, in a crooked,
weather-beaten house hand-built by their long-dead grandfather, a railway worker who made paintings of snowcapped mountains. Their mother
left them there the day she calmly drove off a cliff into the lake; they
were tended to for five years by their grandmother and, after her death,
briefly by two great-aunts, and then, in the fifties, when they're on the
verge of adolescence, Sylvie, their mother's younger sister—an itinerant—arrives to keep house for them. Through the years, the orphans
have been close companions, but their differing attitudes toward Sylvie
cause a permanent rift between them. Sylvie, a nature-loving hobo who
has been riding the rails, working here or there, is also fixated on mountains. Agreeable but abstracted, she's the elusive, poetic center of the
novel. She doesn't care whether the girls go to school or not; she's serenely

happy taking long walks, staring at the railroad bridge over the lake, and filling the house with collections of newspapers, tin cans, and cats. Lucille is shamed by Sylvie's habits, and finds a normal life by moving into the house of her home-economics teacher, while Ruth, devastated by her sister's leaving her, gives up on school and becomes more and more like Sylvie, taking an overnight trip on the lake with her, hopping a freight train. Then the author invokes an antique device: the towns-people begin to worry about Ruth and to question whether Sylvie is a fit guardian, and the two of them find their idyllic existence threatened.

I read eagerly at first, because Robinson's mandarin feminist writing was rapturous, but after a while my enthusiasm shut down, and by the last thirty or forty pages I didn't think the novel was about anything except its own literary sensibility. (When I was finished, the book just about decomposed in my hand; the whole thing is a willed epiphany—a false one.) It does have a wonderful representation of a psychological state: Sylvie seems to spend her life falling into a non-verbal world— staring at nothingness. There's something creepily feminine and familiar about this—it's like depression without depression, a dreamless state of not being bothered by anything. But the novel also has a bag-lady mys-tique—a poetic view of vagrancy, as if it were a painless way for women to see the world. The novel has just about everything imaginable for sensitive women—it's all a rhapsodic dream of women's lives, and men play only a peripheral role in it. (They're the creatures who desert you, whom you can't count on.)

The advertising campaign for the movie version is trying to sell it as a prankish comedy, with the eccentric aunt who appears from nowhere as a demented Mary Poppins. But Bill Forsyth, who wrote the script and directed—it's his first film made entirely outside Scotland—follows the novel in mood and detail. It's a beautiful, accomplished piece of movie-making, except that he can't seem to get a rhythm going. The paperback edition carries a quote from Doris Lessing: "I found myself reading slowly, then more slowly—This is not a novel to be hurried through for every sentence is a delight." I'm afraid that Forsyth, caught up in his admiration of those sentences, never felt free enough to make the material his own and find his own rhythms. The early scenes have some oddity and promise— they seem to be about growing up, albeit in strange circumstances. But by the time the sisters have begun to quarrel, and the principal lectures to them at school, the movie begins to be about not growing up—about going into a state of enchantment—and things slow down. And since watching a movie isn't like reading a book—where you slow down to savor the writing—a slowness that's imposed on you can make you feel sluggish. (This is one movie that might have been helped by stronger music than its string-quartet score—something to pace it.)

Forsyth, who has always worked on material that he conceived (*That Sinking Feeling, Gregory's Girl, Local Hero, Comfort and Joy*), was probably drawn to adapt Robinson's novel because its sensory impact is rather like that of his movies—you feel you're breathing mountain air. And as he himself is given to muted effects and to characters who are part cipher, he may have been entranced by the internalized and estranged nature of Robinson's vision. (It's all subtext.) The fictional Fingerbone, which is based on Robinson's birthplace, Sandpoint, Idaho, was shot in Nelson, British Columbia (the mountain town used in *Roxanne*), which is only ninety miles from Sandpoint. This luminous area is photographed unaffectedly; there's nothing the matter with how the film looks. It's the whole conception that seems to be inside a glass bell. When tall, straight-backed Sylvie (Christine Lahti) and shy Ruth (fifteen-year-old Sara Walker) are in a little rowboat on the lake at night, you may feel you're watching feminized Mark Twain. The book suggests the vision of a sixties flower child who took a doctorate in literature in the seventies but still retained the idea that if you gave up conventional values and material things you could wander the earth and lead a magical life. And so the movie is subtly prejudicial in its attitude toward the townspeople— they are made narrow and uncomprehending—and toward Lucille (twelve-year-old Andrea Burchill): she doesn't move out because she wants to learn something or needs some rootedness and order in her life; she moves out because she wants to be just like the other kids in town. Even though the vagabond Sylvie and her kindred spirit Ruth are kept at an emotional distance, like the figures in a fable, and we're never asked to identify with them, we recognize that they're meant to be in tune with something deep and natural. Sylvie is presented as both a crazy lady and the personification of freedom, with a little earth mother thrown in. (There's enough slippery, fashionable confusion in Robinson's material for viewers to come away from the movie with the idea that Sylvie and Ruth have a gift—a unique spiritual insight. The movie can easily be taken as a haunting account of the freedom of madness versus suffocating conformism. It can be taken as an ode to people who are "different.")

Sylvie is given a minimum of lines, so Christine Lahti's face has to carry the movie. And since Sylvie is always remote and has to wake up out of her basic trance to respond to a situation, Lahti can't call on her full resourcefulness. Gaunt here, and with her curly hair and huge, curlicue dimples, she suggests a pioneer woman who's been bopped on the head. Lahti manages to create a strong presence out of this woman's aimlessness, and she's quite prodigious in staying in character; there's magnetism in the way she moves, and she's airily weird on lines like "I don't know why I stopped reading." But it's not a great role. It's a synthesis of themes from American literature: the nomadic urge that has been passed down from her railroad-man father, the violent doominess in her family (her father's death in a derailment over the lake, her sister's suicide), and so on. The two young-girl actresses are at their best when we see their physical interplay; they aren't particularly expressive, though there's some eloquence in the sight of the older sister hanging her head as she grows tall, like Sylvie. But we don't get close enough to the bond she forms with Sylvie. I guess the real problem is that Ruth may understand her aunt but we don't. When Forsyth places Robinson's ecstatic vision of women and nature and wanderlust in a realistic setting, the result is a kind of clammy, awkward lyricism. Robinson put together a bunch of themes and moods, and, polishing her sentences, she made it all shine. In some awful way, this jewelled, fairy-tale femininity outclasses the movie medium. And you may find yourself fighting back with yawns because it's lifeless.

December 14, 1987

RELIGIOUS EXPERIENCES

||||||||||||||||||||||||||||||||||||||||||||||||||||||||||||||||||||||||||||||||||||||||||||||||||||||||||||||||||||||||||||||||||||||||||||||||||||||||||||||||||||||||||||

Ⅰn the 1935 *Alice Adams*, the affectations of Katharine Hepburn's Alice would make her dislikable if you didn't feel the desperation behind them—if you didn't feel as if you were inside her skin. I was sixteen when the film was first shown, and during the slapstick dinner-party scene, when Alice was undergoing agonies of comic humiliation, I started up the aisle to leave the theatre, and was almost out the doors before I snapped to my senses, and rushed back and sat down. Something similar happened to me a few days ago when I was watching Maggie Smith's performance in *The Lonely Passion of Judith Hearne*: during

Judy's most self-exposing moments, I caught myself trying to escape by glancing down, as if I had urgent business with my notepad. Judy, who lives in Dublin, is all pretension, like Alice. Everybody sees through her, and she knows it, but she can't get rid of her own mealymouthed phoniness: it's ingrained in her. Educated in an exclusive convent school for the daughters of the wealthy, she's a spinster in her late forties or fifties, with nothing but her airs, her polished turns of phrase, and a little jewelry left her by her aunt, along with a moldering gray mink stole. She's impoverished—she doesn't get enough to eat. She keeps up her prim, ladylike manner, though, and when she moves into new lodgings her landlady's brother, James Madden (Bob Hoskins), who has just returned after thirty years in New York City, thinks she must have a bit of money. He asks her out, hoping she'll invest in a business venture he's dreaming up, and she believes herself to be in the midst of a romance.

The movie is about a great deal more than a near-comic misunderstanding. It's about the loneliness that Judy tries to conceal from the people at the rooming house—she pretends she has friends and social commitments. It's about her secret drinking. And it's about the deprivation that she feels every waking minute, and about the Catholicism that has always provided her with ready-made answers to everything. Mortified when she learns that Madden isn't interested in her as a woman, she turns to her priest—gruff, bearded Father Quigley (Alan Devlin)—whose fieriness in the pulpit has impressed her. She confesses her drinking; she explains that she gave her youth to tending her bedridden aunt, and when the aunt died it was too late for her to get an office job—meaning that it was also too late to get a man. She tells Father Quigley of her isolation, and he brushes her off with dogma: if she has faith in God, she can't be lonely. All her life, she has been kept in the position of a child taking the Church fathers' word for everything. Now she demands to be treated as a grownup and given straight answers. She doesn't understand that Father Quigley doesn't have them: he's a company man handing out the company line, and when she isn't content with it he gets testy.

Brian Moore's *The Lonely Passion of Judith Hearne* is perhaps the finest novel ever written about a woman who's a spinster in spite of her sensual nature. It's a beauty of a novel—a work of surpassing empathy—written when Moore was only twenty-seven and, having left Ireland (partly, he has said, because of the religious stranglehold on the country), was living in Canada. The book was published in 1955 and began to be optioned for the stage and the screen almost immediately. José Quintero

410

was among the theatre people; he hoped to do it with Geraldine Page. John Huston optioned it, intending to film it with Katharine Hepburn; Daniel Petrie had Rachel Roberts in mind; Irvin Kershner planned on Deborah Kerr. But nobody had the rights and the financing at the same time until this year. Then George Harrison, whose company, HandMade Films, backed *Mona Lisa* and *A Private Function*, gave the go-ahead to Jack Clayton and Maggie Smith, who worked from Peter Nelson's clear, intelligent adaptation. Clayton is a felicitous choice to direct a character-study movie about a woman's rage against the Church for her wasted life. For one thing, he's Catholic. And Clayton—his first feature was *Room at the Top*, with Simone Signoret, and he made *The Innocents*, with Deborah Kerr, and *The Pumpkin Eater*, with Anne Bancroft—knows how to show women's temperatures and their mind-body interactions.

Maggie Smith lets you read every shade of feeling in Judith Hearne's face. Judy's blue-green eyes are full of misgivings; her thin lips have spokes—nervous pucker lines—and her pinched expression accentuates the long space between nose and mouth. She looks like a gigantic mouse—a mouse who's grown to the height of a giraffe. It's a staggering performance. Maggie Smith becomes the essence of spinster—she makes you feel the ghastliness of knowing you're a figure of fun. When Judith Hearne is at her most proper, she wears a hat flat across her head. (It looks like a poached egg.) Her ludicrous appearance is the image of old-maid torment, and you know you've laughed at women who looked like this—or, at least, you've wanted to. Now you get what it's like to be on the other side of that laugh. Smith makes us understand that when Judy's childish literal-mindedness about religion is shaken, her faith is gone. The Judy who's painfully self-conscious and polite is still a romantic little girl at heart. But when she has some gin in her and she runs down the church aisle and batters on the small gold doors of the tabernacle, demanding that God make his presence known to her—that he open up and take her in with him—her voice is deep and angry. She's suddenly a force of nature, gone crazy-sane.

Hoskins' Madden is a vulgarian who's impressed by Judy's refinement, until he discovers she gives piano lessons—that's the tipoff there's no money there. Madden, who's plump and has a limp, affects sportiness; he's like a little mechanical man when he and Judy go walking and he holds up his arm, crooked at the elbow, for her to hang on to. He has a beady-eyed, out-of-control intensity in the scenes where he lusts after the fresh young slavey Mary (Rudi Davies) who does the dirty work in

411

the rooming house. But Hoskins' acting doesn't have the surprise of Ian McNeice's performance as Madden's nephew Bernard, the landlady's son. A grown man who has already been to university, he looks like a wax angel made of rotten tallow. He's a Dickensian horror, with lewd pink flesh and yellowish hair. (McNeice was Young Wackford Squeers in the 1981 New York *Nicholas Nickleby*.) His belly hangs out of his red silk pajama bottoms, but his mother (Marie Kean) dotes on him and keeps stuffing him; Bernard is writing an epic poem, which he expects will take five more years of being fed and fussed over. It's McNeice's feat that he plays Bernie as a sybaritic slime yet also makes us understand why the sixteen-year-old Mary waits each night for him to sneak up to her bed. Bernie is playful with her—he shows her a good time. (And he's certainly the only one who does.) The picture needs the baroque touch that McNeice provides: Bernie has enough elfish perversity to help offset the shallow, virtuous ending. (Madden is brought back so that Judy can reject him and go forth without illusions.)

The people in this movie are accustomed to the everyday perversity that passes for rectitude: adults tell on each other, like mean-spirited schoolkids. The book is set in Belfast, the movie in Dublin, but it's the same Church, the same infantilization. The devout landladies can't resist the chance to squeal to the mothers of Judy's piano pupils about her drinking. At one point, she goes to give a lesson, and the woman of the house won't let her in—closes the door in her protesting face. Judy goes on talking for a second: she says (to herself), "I used to play in musicales." And there's a cut to Judy at the piano performing for fashionable guests, with Wendy Hiller sitting there as the aunt, regal in her finery. It's a satisfying transition, because we can see that even in Judy's palmier days she was repressed and gawky and not much of a musician. Smith and Wendy Hiller are magnificent together. You feel an ugly, claustrophobic intimacy in the Judy-and-her-aunt relationship: all the love is from Judy's side, and it's self-deception. (She can't admit to herself that her aunt is a tyrant.) Part of what makes the two actresses match up as family is their bond of love and respect for their profession. They both have beautiful restraint. If Wendy Hiller went too far in the aunt's petulant, hysterical scenes, we wouldn't believe that Judy would stay all those years to look after her. And if Maggie Smith went too far in Judy's outbursts at God, we'd stop feeling that we were inside her skin. And the movie would let us off the hook.

∎

412

Empire of the Sun begins majestically and stays strong for perhaps forty-five minutes. It's so gorgeously big you want to laugh in pleasure. Steven Spielberg takes over Shanghai and makes it his city. It's swarming with people, all doing his bidding as the camera moves around the tops of stately buildings to the streets below. And then, first in brief patches and then in longer ones, his directing goes terribly wrong. Working on an enormous scale and with a large theme, he throws himself into bravura passages, lingers over them trying to give them a poetic obsessiveness, and loses his grasp of the narrative. For the sake of emotion— to have something to say, to give the picture some meaning—he pumps it full of false emotion. That's what his poetry is.

At the outbreak of the Second World War, Jim (Christian Bale), an eleven-year-old British boy in Shanghai—a kid who goes to school in a chauffeur-driven Packard—is separated from his parents during the mass exodus when the Japanese Army invades the city, on December 8, 1941. He survives hunger and disease, a detention center, and three years in a prison camp. Evacuated from the camp and forced to march, he's out in the countryside dying of starvation when there's an American airdrop and he gets some cans of Spam and other things to eat. A few days later, he's in a barracks and there's another airdrop—a cannister on a parachute comes crashing through the ramshackle ceiling, and breaks open. It hovers in the air, like a piñata, and the foodstuffs come raining down, along with a shower of glitter. If Spielberg had only stuck with the Spam and forgotten about the pixie dust!

Jim flies model gliders at the beginning, when he still lives in a huge Tudor mansion in the British section of the city, and he reacts with reverence to the Japanese Zeros, the American P-51 Mustang fighters, and all the other warplanes he sees. With that as an excuse, Spielberg glamorizes each flight. A toy glider swerves in the sky for a magical eternity, and an exploding Zero gives off an aureole of sparks. The camp where Jim is imprisoned is adjacent to an airbase, and when he gets close enough to a Japanese plane to caress it choral music soars and he's photographed like a boy who has just found God. This is more than a breach of taste: it's a breach of sanity, and it rattles your confidence in the movie. Presumably, we're seeing all this through the boy's wonder-struck eyes, but it's Spielberg who's saying "Ooh, look!" and showing us a cloying mystical effect. (He tries to give you a miracle every ten minutes.) The scenes about Jim's friendship with a Japanese boy—a smiley teen-age pilot from the airbase—are so full of good will they feel thick, pudgy. And each time we get a demonstration of the gallantry of the flying brotherhood the movie seems to be regressing.

Near the opening, there's a startling effect that feels almost like a throwaway gag: Jim, who's high up in a hotel overlooking the harbor, sees a ship flashing signals and, being a smart kid who knows Morse code, he signals back, and instantly—*bam!*—the hotel is shelled, as if he'd caused it, or even willed it. The scene isn't stressed, but it has a resonance: it speaks to our understanding of the gap between children's play and grownup behavior—the gap that is closed in wartime. Jim is forced to grow up in brutal circumstances. Spielberg tries to use movie magic to transmute these brutal circumstances to beauty—to a myth—and he thinks he can achieve this by putting a veil over events.

He's using an adaptation of J. G. Ballard's autobiographical novel which is credited to Tom Stoppard (it was also worked on by Menno Meyjes), but he doesn't clarify what's going on. A scene in which Basie (John Malkovich), a scavenging American merchant seaman, and his crony Frank (Joe Pantoliano) try to sell Jim to Chinese traders is skipped over fast. And in the prison camp, though you feel something seamy and sadistic in the way Basie—a control freak, a Fagin—teaches Jim the low skills of survival, you can't get a fix on the nastiness. So it's just amorphously nasty. You feel that Mrs. Victor (Miranda Richardson), the aloof, snobbish Englishwoman near whose bunk Jim sleeps, must have something more to her than you're being shown. (In the novel, she treats Jim "like her Number Two Coolie.") Spielberg seems to be making everything nice, and, as with *The Color Purple*, there's something in the source material that's definitely not nice. In its matter-of-fact, boy's-adventure way, the Ballard book tries to get back to the innocent child and how he was warped; Ballard's account recalls the disturbing qualities of *The Painted Bird*. Spielberg's blandness works against the theme. How can he make an epic about the soul-freezing scuzziness of war as experienced by a child if he sweetens things? This is *The Color Yellow*. He treats the hell of the prison camp as if it were the background for a coming-of-age story— as if the rich kid Jim's being on his own and learning to wangle gifts and to steal from the dead made a man of him. You come out saying, "What was that about?"

The boy is a fine performer, directed superlatively—especially in the scene where Jim is chasing after the truck that is leaving the detention center and taking a group of prisoners, including Basie, to a camp. Frantic, babbling like mad, Jim tries to get Basie's attention, but Basie deliberately ignores him and turns on his charm for two littler kids in the truck. It's probably the best dramatic scene in the movie, because it

414

expresses so much of Jim's terror at the thought of losing the only protector he has, and so much of Jim's wartime amorality. (He gets on the truck by claiming he can guide the Japanese driver, who doesn't know the way.) Jim is very appealing when he's hysterically eager to run errands for everybody in the camp in order to survive; we understand his wanting to stay in motion. And we understand Spielberg's madness when he stages the crowds surging through the streets of Shanghai, trying to leave the city by getting to the waterfront or getting to the roads, and caught in human gridlock with tanks bearing down on them. The spectacle is bigger than any damn movie staging you've ever seen—five thousand people, ten thousand, fifteen thousand. Even if it overpowers the story, there's something shamelessly likable about this profligacy: it's a moviemaker's dream. And the imagery makes its own point about the crosscurrents of war.

But often Spielberg doesn't appear to know what effect he's after. When the once rich prisoners on their death march come to a stadium filled with confiscated chandeliers, limousines, grand pianos, paintings, and sculpture, the sheer quantity of the stuff evokes the huge accumulation of objects in boxes and crates in *Citizen Kane,* but what is the image meant to signify—that the rich in Shanghai were too rich and are finding redemption in suffering, or that the Japanese were wasteful to leave these precious objects in the open air, or something else altogether? Perhaps that the old life of privilege is like a dream? What we see is flabby, picturesque surrealism, and when a woman sits down at one of the pianos and we hear what sounds like abandoned-mansion music, people in the theatre whisper that the piano is in tune, and giggle. The audience is trying to fill the vacuum, because scene after scene doesn't go anywhere. When Jim, after being separated from his parents, goes back to the near-deserted house, there's talcum powder on the floor of his mother's room and boot prints, along with a bare footmark and hand prints. Spielberg holds the camera so long on the messy floor that we feel stupid not to understand whether this is a dream-born image of rape and desecration or the sign of something that has actually happened. (To whom?) He luxuriates in images. He holds the camera on Jim, alone in the house doing forbidden things—eating chocolates with liqueur centers, bicycling around on the parquet floors—and then aimlessly circling the grounds. Later, he holds it for a picture-postcard view of Jim saluting the valor of three kamikaze pilots who are about to take off from the airbase. The movie is all "Ooh, look!" It's mindlessly manipulative. To achieve the larger-than-life emotions that Spielberg is after he needs more than the one character—the boy. (The framework is exactly the same as that of the animated film Spielberg produced, *An American Tail*, in which a little boy mouse is separated from his parents, goes through horrifying adventures, and at last is reunited with mama mouse and papa mouse.)

In technical terms, *Empire* is a considerable achievement. Spielberg had permission to shoot in Shanghai for only three weeks, and the settings were matched up and constructed in Spain and in London. But the picture is a combination of craftsmanship and almost unbelievable tastelessness. Every time Spielberg tries to make a humanitarian statement, he falls flat on his face—not just because his statements are so naïve but because they go against the grain of Ballard's material. (The movie actually gives Jim a dawning of moral awareness: he decides he no longer wants Basie for a friend.) Spielberg is stranded with his proud moments. That's where John Williams comes in: his editorializing music swells and swooshes for hours of this movie, trying to make us feel that something religious is going on. It's musical glue poured over candied images.

December 28, 1987

FAKERS

*B*roadcast News has some witty dialogue and it's moderately adult, so I guess we should be grateful. But it lacks any filmmaking excitement, and before it was over I was thinking, Is this all there is to it? The writer-producer-director James L. Brooks (his only previous film was *Terms of Endearment*) puts us inside the world of a network's Washington bureau. He sets up an adversarial relationship between the six-foot-three reddish-blond charmer Tom (William Hurt), a former sportscaster who has an intuitive grasp of how to sell himself to audiences, and dark, broody Aaron (Albert Brooks), a newsman whose brain is a briefing book about the crisis areas that re-ignite. Tom (who's on his way to becoming the network's next anchorman) has to rely on the newsroom team to prepare his copy and coach him, while Aaron—a Renaissance pedant—can do his own writing and thinking yet doesn't know how to

416

present himself. Basically, what the movie is saying is that beautiful, assured people have an edge over the rest of us, no matter how high our I.Q.s are. But, by applying this specifically to the age of television, Jim Brooks uses it as the basis for a satirical critique of what TV is doing to us. On the surface, at least, he's saying that Aaron represents substance and integrity, while handsome, slick Tom—a faker who's essentially an actor-salesman—represents TV's corruption of the news into entertainment. The picture suggests that this view is the lowdown on TV: it satirizes anchorman punditry by showing the rising star as a boob with a smooth, practiced manner. And its thesis may give moviegoers a tingle, because it connects with some of what we see anchormen doing: reading sentences so rhythmically that the meaning is lost, asking questions of the reporters and then not following through even when their answers raise much bigger questions, smiling so falsely that it seems to rot their facial muscles.

This is such a tiny tingle, though. Broadcast news—what's considered newsworthy and why—is what the picture doesn't deal with. It accepts the whole structure of the way the news is packaged, fastening on this one issue, as if everything about the quality of the news depended on whether a Tom reads somebody else's material or writes his own. English television simply calls its anchorpeople "newsreaders"; of course, there's a difference between newsreaders who are honestly treated as that and newsreaders who are presented as thinkers, and the fakery is an insult to the public. But Tom reads the news well; what he does takes skill and concentration. And the fakery he represents is a small insult compared with the systematized way that the evening news skitters across the day's events, giving us headlines, snippets, quick flashes of the world's trouble spots, and assorted horrors and disasters—all of this with almost no interpretation. The heroine of *Broadcast News*, Jane (Holly Hunter), is a producer who's a whizbang at punching up these news segments, and the movie seems to applaud her showmanship.

Jane and Aaron are supposed to be high-principled professionals, as well as close friends who confide in one another. The romantic-comedy dilemma in the film is that Jane finds herself falling in love with Tom, who incarnates everything that she despises. He's the Enemy. Even if you didn't know that Jim Brooks was the co-creator of *The Mary Tyler Moore Show*, you could feel the link between the Mary Richards character in that series and Jane. This new heroine is quicker and more driven and smarter, but she's appealing in much the same way. She's a demon pro who never hesitates, but she agonizes over personal decisions—she doesn't

417

know her own mind. (She interrupts a date with Tom just when things are heating up between them, in order to look in on Aaron.) She's a bit of a mess: when she's alone and can take the time, she has brief nervous breakdowns—crying jags. (And, from the reaction of the audience, young women careerists must love to think of themselves as pros who are adorably screwy kids underneath.) The picture is a sophisticated version of *The Mary Tyler Moore Show*, with Tom as a network version of the poseur Ted Baxter, and Aaron as the reliable Murray. Now they're a romantic triangle, they're dressed up in network garb, and they've got big-time anxieties.

It's entertaining to see a workaday world presented so that it moves and keeps you off balance and looks authentic; this Washington-newsroom world has a hum to it. Jim Brooks (and a lot of other people) must have worked hard to achieve this hum. What limits the interest of the film is that he never questions the routine operations of the newspeople. And so the movie glamorizes a particular version of professionalism—not the glitz that Tom is bringing in but, rather, the professionalism that's being threatened by the present-day cuts in news budgets. (You get the feeling that Jim Brooks thinks the network news of ten years ago was great.)

What I find dispiriting about this film is not just the lightweight conventionality of its satirical approach—it's that, with all the surface authenticity Jim Brooks gives us, he himself represents the corruption of movies into TV. There's not even a try for any style or tension in *Broadcast News*. It's all episodic, like a TV series. When Jane addresses a conference of local news producers and broadcasters and is so tediously moralistic that she empties the hall, the staging is as lax as it often was on *The M.T.M. Show*. And when Jane and Aaron are filming a combat report in Nicaragua, she stops the members of her team who are coaching a Contra on how to put on his new American boots for the camera; she tells him he can do anything he wants, and then accepts it when he does exactly what he had been doing anyway. The directing is so feeble that the joke falls apart, and the feebleness gets you down the way it does when you watch TV. (Something else got me down: the barefaced steal from Budd Schulberg's *What Makes Sammy Run?*, with the sexes reversed, when Tom, making his pitch to Jane, says, "More and more I've been feeling . . . I've been wondering what it would be like to be inside all that energy.")

Even so, this is a more sustained piece of work than *Terms of Endearment* (though it doesn't have that movie's cartoonish highs), and the actors are vivid; they're like pop-up figures in a child's book, as they often are in sitcoms. Joan Cusack, who has dark-red hair that's always mooshed around in different shapes—derangements that suggest what goes on in her head—is an assistant director who's a shameless (and comic) groveller when the high-muck-a-mucks are in the vicinity. She has a slapstick victory scene—hurtling and sliding around the newsroom to get a tape on the air in time. Lois Chiles is right on target as a suave, groomed correspondent. And Jack Nicholson, who's not listed in the opening credits, appears as the big cheese, the New York anchorman who makes millions of dollars a year, surveys the world through mildly curious, jaundiced eyes, and holds his head up high, in full confidence that it's a national treasure. All the actors get chances to shine, because the characters are rumpled and have depths, and are individualized by sudden, tilted bits of dialogue. Yet even their depths are sitcom depths. These pop-up figures are human and complex in sitcom ways.

Albert Brooks is the only one who goes beyond that: he gives the picture its bit of soul. Brooks has made the terrain of the pesky, brilliant schlemiel—the near-genius who doesn't know how to use what he knows—his own. His scene of snookered, man-of-the-world torment—swigging down a vodka and orange juice while singing along in French to Francis Cabrel's "L'Édition Spéciale" and reading a book—is the comic high point of the movie. Luckily, Albert Brooks is tall and trim and has perfectly presentable features, so it's clear that the barriers to Aaron's success are in his psyche—they're in his infatuation with his own knowledge, they're in how he turns pasty and anxious on camera and his curly hair becomes a mop. When he's at his most desperate, he's funniest. Jim Brooks gives Aaron choice opportunities, but also uses him—maybe not intentionally—to give the film a layer of self-pity. Underneath its satire, *Broadcast News* is saying "O to be one of the Gentile beautiful people!"

William Hurt plays dumb and not dumb. He uses his little blue eyes to very cagey effect, and he shows you the ways in which a man who isn't really interested in anything but his own success and his own pleasure—a man who's an ethical idiot—can be smarter than an Aaron. Tom is astute about what works on camera: that's about the only thing he ever studied. But he has something else going for him. Hurt gives him a suggestion of sensitivity: Tom isn't glib like Aaron and Jane—he needs pauses before he speaks, he needs to register things. So at times he seems genuinely attractive.

Everything Holly Hunter does is unexpected. She gets wacky effects from her Georgia twang, and she manages to bring some surprise to every one of her line readings—sometimes just by jumping in so fast that the line explodes. She's amusingly dinky (five feet two)—a cunning, bossy little girl. But I missed the hick charm that she had in *Raising Arizona*. And she doesn't show much emotional range here; the performance seems closed in and tight-faced. I wanted something more expansive, some suggestion of other, grownup possibilities in Jane—a sense of what her compulsiveness about her work is costing her. (Those were only mock crying jags.) As Hunter plays her—which is just how she's written— Jane is funny but a little less than human. She's trivial, and so, in terms of the film's romantic triangle, there isn't a lot at stake. She's also trivial as the pivot for a look at journalistic ethics.

Jim Brooks has made a movie about three people who lose themselves in their profession, and it's all cozy and clean and clever. He plays everything right down the middle. He can't seem to imagine having a conflicted, despairing relationship with your profession. He has no perspective on the disaffected people who work in TV: the ones who become so tired of fighting the constraints of the nightly-news format—tired of fighting to do something besides the attention-grabbing stories that make the network look good—that they give up trying to have an effect on the end result and just do their jobs (or quit). Jim Brooks gives us a newsroom in which people work at peak capacity and believe in the value of what they're contributing to. There are no naysayers in this movie; despite the characters' ambitions and their talents, they're as parochial in outlook as Mary Richards and her pals. Jane and Aaron never ask themselves if maybe Tom isn't the perfect front man for the kind of mechanized news that they are so proud of.

■

*I*ronweed may not be an unparalleled disaster, but it would be sad work to dredge up the parallels. William Kennedy's adaptation of his Albany novel, set in 1938, has no momentum. The picture is sombrely artistic right from its first, bluish-gray pre-dawn frames, with Francis Phelan (Jack Nicholson), the hobo hero, who has been sleeping against a wall in an alley, slowly disentangling himself from the cardboard and newspapers that have been his protection against the cold, getting up, and walking down the street to where some other guys on the bum have got a fire going in a garbage can. The alcoholic Francis, who deserted his wife and children twenty-two years ago, is torn by guilt, and he sees

420

the phantoms of men he has done violence to. And that's it. For the viewer, stunned to find that the director, Hector Babenco, has treated Kennedy's story as a joyless classic, the running time (two hours and twenty-four minutes) is like a death sentence.

Nicholson drops his voice down so heroically low he even has to talk slowly. And Meryl Streep, who is Francis's hobo crony Helen, forces her voice down deep, too. The only moments of reprieve from the reverential slowness come when Streep sings "He's Me Pal" in the all-out, sentimental-Irish manner of a balladeer of a decade or two earlier. It's a spectacular re-creation of the old technique for "selling a song," and Streep's vibrancy lifts the film's energy level. The moviemakers immediately lower it when the song is revealed to be Helen's fantasy. (The "reality" we're given is too bitter, too crude; it would have been far more effective if something of Helen's former skill still came through.) In early glimpses of Tom Waits, as a simpleton standing outside a soup kitchen, he looks right for the period, and he has a soft, childlike expression; soon there's too much dwelling on his otherworldly sweetness, and before he's finished, the camera has given him a phony poetic aura. As the old junk man who briefly employs Francis, Hy Anzell brings the film a change of mood—he's an amorous, pennypinching old buzzard. And, as the sexual provocatrice who seduces the teen-age Francis, Margaret Whitton has no more than the twinkling of an eye in which to do it, but she's a twinkler to cherish—a true madcap.

■

The only fresh element in American movies of the eighties may be what Steve Martin, Bill Murray, Bette Midler, Richard Pryor, Robin Williams, and other comedians have brought to them. They've stirred things up even when they've been in squalid excuses for movies (such as Martin's current hit *Planes, Trains and Automobiles*). The one with the best record is Robin Williams, who made his début in *Popeye*, in 1980, and then appeared in *The World According to Garp, The Survivors, Moscow on the Hudson, The Best of Times*, and *Club Paradise*. He hasn't had many hits, but his films weren't smarmy—not until now. His new picture, *Good Morning, Vietnam*, makes him out to be a vulnerable, compassionate, respectful-of-the Vietnamese, wonderful guy, and the director, Barry Levinson, has a numbing sense of rhythm: he labors the jokes. Williams plays Adrian Cronauer, a disk jockey on Armed Forces Radio who's brought to Saigon in 1965 to improve the morale of the troops during the escalation of the war. Adrian's rock records and line of patter blast everybody awake. The role makes it possible for Williams to do his own manic riffs, but they're chopped short—they don't get a chance to build. And we might as well be listening to a laughtrack: we're told Adrian is funny, instead of being allowed to discover it. The film keeps cutting to soldiers breaking up over his spiel before it's out of his mouth, and the men in the field become passionately enthusiastic about him within two minutes. Throughout the movie, we're alerted to how terrific and how irreverent he is, even though he isn't so terrific and his irreverence sounds tinny. Worse, Levinson goes for heart: we're shown the serious side of what's going on in Vietnam, and that's when you may remember that this is in fact a Disney picture. When Williams is being concerned and thoughtful and arguing with a terrorist, he looks all scrunched up with discomfort, as if he were biting into a lemon, as indeed he is. There is an Adrian Cronauer, and the movie is very loosely based on his exploits, but the way the story line (from the script by Mitch Markowitz) has been directed, it's a clumsier version of the plots of fifties musicals. The priggish officers (played by Bruno Kirby and J. T. Walsh) who give Adrian a bad time, ordering him not to tell his listeners anything about what's really happening in the war, are such dumb meanies you can't even laugh.

Williams' acting is amiable enough. In a subplot, Adrian takes over the teaching of a class in English for adult Vietnamese and turns it into a class in American slang. This device doesn't seem promising, but it provides Williams with some pleasantly relaxed scenes. When he asks the students questions, the straight-faced, skewed answers given by an elderly Vietnamese man (Uikey Kuay) make him laugh with a pleasure that looks utterly spontaneous. But there's more of Williams the hero than of Williams the comic. People who want to see him running wild within a character ought to take a look at Michael Ritchie's 1983 *The Survivors* or Roger Spottiswoode's 1986 *The Best of Times*. (The only good laugh you get from Williams here is from his joke about three up and three down.)

Sanctimoniousness and comedy are a queasy combination. (They may also be the recipe for a hit.) When Adrian, who has become the hero of the troops (though he's only in Saigon for five months), is on the street talking to a truckload of soldiers heading into action, he asks where they're from and ribs them about their sexual innocence, and says things like "I won't forget you," and there's forlorn music on the track. You wonder how the picture can take potshots at Bob Hope and still have Williams do this celebrity-entertainer routine. On Adrian's arrival in Saigon, he's met by a black soldier, Garlick, played by Forest Whitaker, and it's Garlick who laughs hardest at Adrian's jokes all through the movie. But this jovial fellow doesn't have the courage to stand up to the brass and say what he thinks. (Only one man does.) When Adrian is forced out by the prigs, he gives Garlick a final truthtelling tape to put on the air, and Garlick takes the risk of putting it on—he becomes his own man. This movie has had the bad judgment to turn Robin Williams into a role model. *Good Morning, Vietnam* takes a real culture hero and turns him into a false one.

January 11, 1988

LOONY FUGUE

||||||||||||||||||||||||||||||||||||||||||||||||||||||||||||||||||||||||||||||||||||||||||||||||||||||||||||||||||||||||||||||||||||||||||||

Cher is right at home in the screwball ethnic comedy *Moonstruck*. She doesn't stare at the camera and act the goddess. She moves around, she shouts, and when she lets her hair down a huge dark mass of crinkly tendrils floats about her tiny face. (What a prop!) Cher isn't afraid to be a little crazy here, and she's devastatingly funny and sinuous and beautiful. She plays Loretta, a widowed bookkeeper in her late thirties, who lives with her Italian-American family in a big old brownstone in Brooklyn. Doing the levelheaded thing, she accepts the marriage proposal of a timid dullard (Danny Aiello), a bachelor in his forties, and, when he has to fly to Palermo, she does what he asks: she invites his estranged younger brother (Nicolas Cage), a baker, to come to the wedding. Up to that point, you may not be sure how to take the flat-out, slightly zonked dialogue. But when Cher and Nicolas Cage—each with droopy eyelids—start lusting for one another, a fairy-tale full moon lights up the movie. Cage is a wonderful romantic clown: he's slack-jawed and Neanderthal and passionate. He may be the only young actor who can look stupefied while he smolders. And no one can yearn like Cage: his head empties out—there's nothing there but sheep-eyed yearning. *Moon-*

423

struck is an opera buffa in which the arias are the lines the characters deliver, in their harshly musical Brooklyn rhythms. Looking as if he's in a sick trance, the baker tells Loretta he's in love with her; she has just been to bed with him, but when she hears this she slaps him two quick whacks and says, "Snap out of it!" In her dry way, she's more irrational than he is. And when you see that the whole cast of family members are involved in libidinal confusions the operatic structure can make you feel close to deliriously happy.

Working from a script by John Patrick Shanley, the director, Norman Jewison, doesn't go for charm; he goes for dizzy charm. And that's what wins you over. He sets a hyperemotional mood; even the performances of the bit players are heightened. And the musical score, arranged by Dick Hyman, keeps twitting you. It starts, under the titles, with Dean Martin singing "That's Amore," and it reaches a juicy peak with the voices of Renata Tebaldi and Carlo Bergonzi in *La Bohème*. Hyman mixes musical emotion and a teasing parody of musical emotion, and you can't separate them, even when the parody is very broad. That's essentially what Shanley and Jewison are up to: they've blended a slapstick temperament with the pleasures that the synthetic elements in American movies used to give us. And so you get such counterpoint as the baker, whose thought processes are primeval, telling Loretta about the accident that turned him against his brother, and Loretta calmly explaining what happened, in a parody of Freudian explanations that's pure bughouse. And, with David Watkin lighting the scenes and Lou Lombardo (who edited *The Wild Bunch* and *McCabe & Mrs. Miller*) giving them a spin, the picture has a warm, fluky dazzle. Its originality is that the mockery doesn't destroy the overblown romanticism—it intensifies it.

This is ethnic comedy, but it's not noisy or monotonous. Jewison scales down the bullying stage techniques of actors you've been backing away from for years; everything is modulated, so that each voice can be heard. Vincent Gardenia is Loretta's irascible father, whose prosperous plumbing business sustains life in the brownstone. Olympia Dukakis, heavy-lidded, like Cher, and with a similar deadpan matter-of-factness, but with the dry-husk voice of a mummy, is the plumber's worldly-wise wife; she knows he's straying but can't figure out the reason. This woman is of a philosophical bent: she doesn't worry about who—it's the why that plagues her. Louis Guss is her mild brother, who runs a deli with his companionable wife, played by the great, leering Julie Bovasso—she's like a female Bert Lahr. (She also trained the cast in its fugue of contentious Brooklyn accents.) Feodor Chaliapin (the son of the legendary

424

singer-actor) is Loretta's grandfather, who lives in the brownstone with his five dogs—he coaches them (in Italian) to howl at the full moon. John Mahoney is a lonely, lecherous professor of communications at N.Y.U., who dates his impressionable students but has an eye for an older woman, too—he makes overtures to Loretta's mother. Anita Gillette is a fortyish tootsie who has been having a cuddly affair with Loretta's father, and Nada Despotovich is a wistful young girl who works in the bakery and pines for the dopey, tempestuous baker. Most of the characters are gathered at the breakfast table in the closing scenes, when the plot is tied together. And Shanley's theatrical artifice works, partly because he accepts the characters as comic stereotypes—he doesn't try to give them depth—and partly because the actors love their lines, and, as characters, they can flaunt the excessiveness of their emotions. These characters make comedy turns out of everything they do.

Moonstruck is slender, and at times it's a little too proud of its quaintness. When the characters raise their champagne glasses in a toast "To family!" you may dimly recognize that this picture could become a holiday perennial. But you're probably grinning anyway, because the toast has a flipped-out quality. *Moonstruck* isn't heartfelt; it's an honest contrivance—the mockery is a giddy homage to our desire for grand passion. With its own special lushness, it's a rose-tinted black comedy.

■

Woody Allen's *September* fades from mind even before you've seen it. The title, the publicity—it's all pallid and pristine. The movie exists at such a low energy level that it seems to be up to you to project a light onto the screen. A jazz piano is heard—never has jazz sounded more austerely classic—and you watch a roundelay of unrequited love, with two women who are best friends (Mia Farrow and Dianne Wiest) suffering terribly over Sam Waterston, a weakling would-be novelist who writhes with sensitivity. The general anguish spans twenty-four hours at the end of summer, just before September, and the setting is the tasteful yellow-beige interior of the Vermont house that belongs to Lane (Mia Farrow). What are we doing here while the six main characters talk about the storm outside? We're killing time waiting for a revelation. It comes in an effectively staged moment. Lane is a crushed, suicidal mouse, presumably because at fourteen she shot her playgirl mother's brutal lover. The mother (Elaine Stritch), a shallow, vital bulldozer, who is visiting, with her new husband, a physicist (Jack Warden), in tow, has no patience with the daughter's misery over something that happened roughly a quarter of a century earlier, and goads her to the point where the daughter, in front of everyone, blurts out the truth about the shooting. To put it plainly, this movie—which in its refined tone is a generic Chekhov play drained of humor and mixed with Ingmar Bergman's *Autumn Sonata*— draws its only power from the Johnny Stompanato–Lana Turner scandal.

September isn't as self-conscious as Allen's *Interiors*—it's smoother and easier to take. But it's profoundly derivative and second-rate. When Lane lifts up a large bouquet of wilting wildflowers and complains that her mother picked them but didn't bother to put them in water, some part of you refuses to believe that Woody Allen thought this up and that it survived the months of writing and shooting and reshooting and editing. He's a lesson to us all: if you confuse art and gentility, you wind up with symbolic wilted flowers. The only thing that locates Woody Allen in the real world is that he wrote a screenplay about being haunted by the Johnny Stompanato case.

There's an honest dramatic impulse behind that, even if it's shrouded in Chekhov and Bergman. It's also shrouded in Woodiana. The physicist, who, of course, worked at Los Alamos, explains to the novelist, whose book is to be about his history-professor father, who was fired during the McCarthy period, that the nature of the universe is "haphazard, morally neutral, and unimaginably violent." That's the picture's rationale: it's supposed to justify Allen's making morose films in which the actors are either directed to be limp or just naturally get that way. Waterston doesn't give a bad performance—he isn't the disgrace he was in *Interiors*. But the role is effete, and he's played it or its twins so many times you feel effete watching him. (He only comes alive onscreen when he does comedy.) Jack Warden is perfectly pleasant, though he doesn't seem to have any idea why he's here, and Denholm Elliott, as a widower neighbor who's devoted to Lane, doesn't quite seem to have been introduced to the rest of the cast. Farrow does a craftsmanlike job in the kind of role that killed off interest in Liv Ullmann: she's lighter, not so harrowingly wet and sincere. The only moment that's really hers is the revelation, and she makes it work—she makes you feel Lane's unhappiness over the way her mother has ignored her needs. (That's what we react to—not the big secret from the past.) But Dianne Wiest falls into a nasal variant of the whimpering-Ullmann trap, and Allen gives us too many shots of her nervous mannerisms; holding her hand to her head, she shows enough

426

gallant anxiety for three movies. (She also sits straight-backed at the piano playing "What'll I Do?" enough for three movies.) As for Stritch, she's probably giving Allen what he wants: the belting, domineering life-force woman who rides right over weaker people. You get the feeling that she represents everything Allen recoils from, but that he thinks these vital women keep men—other men—from despairing. Still, couldn't the role be played with some shadings?

After you get used to being set-bound, Waterston goes over to the venetian blinds, lifts up a slat, and, peeking through, exclaims, "Look how much it's cleared up!" Where is Woody Allen the satirist while this other Woody Allen—the pompous artist—is shooting this guff? The physicist's summary is supposed to define the human condition. But in what sense can the universe be called haphazard? And of course it's morally neutral. (Can't Allen accept that and move on?) The universe may be unimaginably violent, but not in this movie. Woody Allen is reinventing airless drawing-room drama circa 1923. My favorite example of the higher torment: The unhappily married Wiest, who has been coming on to Waterston, now tells him she loves him but wants him to leave her alone. Her husband is a radiologist, she says, but she never lets him take X-rays of her, "because if he looked inside he'd see things that he wouldn't understand and he'd be terribly hurt." How thin-skinned can you be?

January 25, 1988

TAKE OFF YOUR CLOTHES

||||||||||||||||||||||||||||||||||||||||||||||||||||||||||||||||||||||||||||||||||||||||||||||||||||||||||||||||||||||||||||||||||||||||

Going in to see Philip Kaufman's *The Unbearable Lightness of Being*, I didn't remember anything of the Milan Kundera novel. But as the movie started I knew just what was coming next and I loved seeing it happen—it was like a dream that you long to return to, and lo! there it is. I think I know why the novel, with all its flashing wit, evaporated: the characters were counters to demonstrate a theory that wasn't demonstrated—convincingly, that is—and so neither the characters nor the ideas sank in very deep. The charm (and limitation) of the novel was its

Continental dandyism: Kundera was more cultivated—more elegantly European—than a great writer needs to be. He was too conscious of his themes, his motifs, his paradoxes. He was a rational spokesman for playfulness; there's something the matter with that—it's playfulness as a literary method. (He also sees it as a tradition.) But while watching the movie I began to feel more affection for the novel. Kaufman cuts down on the pastry pensées, and the movie has some of his adventurous spirit. It's a prankish sex comedy that treats modern political events with a delicate—yet almost sly—sense of tragedy. It's touching in sophisticated ways that you don't expect from an American director.

The movie begins in 1968, during the Prague Spring, the culmination of the period of freedom of expression and artistic flowering known as "socialism with a human face," which ended when Soviet tanks rumbled into the city on August 21st. The key word in the title is "lightness." It retains some of its happy, buoyant associations, but it also refers to being cut off from your history, your culture, your memory. To simplify: Unbearable lightness refers to our recognizing that we go through life only once—it's like going onstage unrehearsed. And, more specifically, it's the suspended state of a person in an occupied country—especially if the person, like Tomas (Daniel Day-Lewis), is part of an advanced society under the domination of a backward society. (It's also the floating state of an exile.)

Tomas, a hedonist, a womanizer, and an eminent young brain surgeon, is perhaps at his lightest when he's barred from the practice of medicine and works as a window washer; he enjoys it, and it gives him a chance to practice his specialty, if the woman whose windows he washes invites him in. Tomas, a tall, boyish satyr with thick, curly dark hair that stands up a full three inches, looks at women from under bushy eyebrows and smiles crookedly—seductively. Day-Lewis has acquired a faint Czech accent, and he hits funny, voluptuous low notes when he says abruptly, "Take off your clothes," adding, when persuasion is necessary, "Don't worry—I'm a doctor." (Tomas is an ironic lech.)

He stays clear of love and its entanglements, never spending a whole night with a woman—not even with his longtime sex partner Sabina (Lena Olin), a painter. She's as independent as he is; that's the basis of their friendship. But when Tereza (Juliette Binoche), a childlike barmaid whom he meets when he's sent to perform an operation at a spa in a small town, follows him to Prague and comes to his flat, he takes her in. Tereza knows nothing of his non-involvement policy; she holds tight to his hand while she sleeps, and in spite of himself he loves being bound to her. He admires the pictures she takes; he asks Sabina to help her get a job in photography, and with that help Tereza's work begins to appear in magazines. Tereza and Tomas are married, and he buys her a puppy—they name it Karenin. (She was carrying *Anna Karenina* when they first met.) But his philandering goes on, and she suffers horribly from jealousy—she dreams about having to watch him in bed with Sabina.

Tereza doesn't know real happiness until the arrival of the Soviet tanks. Rushing around taking pictures and pressing rolls of film into the hands of foreign journalists to publish out of the country, she experiences the euphoria of being part of the whole nation in actively hating the Russians. Tomas, meanwhile, dashes around pulling her back from danger, and they join in the anti-Soviet demonstrations. (Through masterly trompe-l'oeil techniques, shots of the actors have been inserted in documentary footage of the crowds defying the soldiers.) When the excitement dies down, Tereza persuades Tomas to accept an offer he has had from a hospital in Geneva, and they join the vast exodus from Czechoslovakia. (Sabina has left ahead of them.) In Geneva, Tereza shows some of her best photographs of the invasion to an illustrated magazine, but the Russian crackdown is already old news to the editors. A woman staff photographer, trying to be helpful, suggests that she try fashion photography, and also offers to introduce her to the editor in charge of the garden section, who might need some photographs of cactuses. When Tereza objects, saying "I'd rather be a waitress, or stay at home," the helpful pinhead says, "But will you be fulfilled sitting at home?"

In the film's centerpiece, Tereza, who has fantasies of accompanying Tomas to his assignations, decides to try her hand at nudes and gets Sabina to pose for her. After Tereza completes the long session, Sabina picks up the camera, says, "Take off your clothes," and, when the half-undressed Tereza tries to hide, chases her with the camera, and another session begins. When it's over, these two women, who represent the poles of Tomas's life—Tereza (weight) lives for him, Sabina (lightness) has to be her own woman—stay stretched out by the fire, quiet, then laughing. The sequence has an erotic formality: it's ridiculously, beautifully resonant—you feel you're watching a classic pas de deux.

At intervals throughout the movie, a scene will have a mysterious seed of comedy. An example: Tomas pauses to watch a group of elderly men in the swimming pool at the spa; they surround a floating chessboard on which two of them are having a match. I can't explain exactly what gives this scene its lovely estrangement, but I know that if Miloš Forman, who was a student of Kundera's at the Prague film school, where Kundera taught literature, had made the movie the scene would be folk humor, and it wouldn't have the slight distancing it has here—the beatitude of the image of the old men at their games, their bodies in the pool seen as in an idyll. (The cinematography is by Sven Nykvist.) Other examples: the scene in bed when Tereza sniffs Tomas's hair and, smelling another woman, whimpers; and the scenes of Sabina in her black net bra and panties, with a black bowler hat on her head—the hat that is the emblem of her sex play. Almost all of Sabina's scenes are tantalizing. Lena Olin (she was the girl in Ingmar Bergman's *After the Rehearsal*) seems to incarnate the many meanings tucked away in the phrase "the unbearable lightness of being"—the freedom and elusive sadness. She's glorious.

And the movie has scenes that may not stir a reaction until a few hours or a few days after you've seen it, when you suddenly remember the deft use of an old movie device (the clinking of glasses on a tray as the first hint of the tanks in the street) or, perhaps, the pinkness of a pet piglet named Mephisto that a smiling, congenial farmer (Pavel Landovsky) carries around on his visit to Prague. (With its long snout and big ears, the pretty little creature suggests a toy elephant.) Or perhaps you think back on Franz (Derek de Lint), the professor whom Sabina takes for a lover in Geneva. His eyes shine with bright-blue virtue; he looks as if he had never known a hangover. He is so straightforward and good that she has to escape him. (His goodness is too heavy for her.) And, late in the film (it runs a short two hours and fifty-three minutes), there's a closeup of Karenin—showing just one blurry eye—that may remind some moviegoers of the shot of the hare in Renoir's *The Rules of the Game*.

But it's the way the variations of jealousy and erotic attraction are played out by the three principal actors—an Englishman, a Swedish woman, and a Frenchwoman, all playing Czechs—that give the movie its wonderfully unresolved texture. The main difference between the movie and the novel is that Day-Lewis is about ten years younger than Kundera's forty-year-old hero, and so the whole spirit of the film has become younger, and less defeated. Phil Kaufman has an exuberant American temperament—he has never let go of the best of the late sixties and early seventies. The sex scenes are rambunctious, with a legs-flying youthfulness. And when Sabina tells Tomas that Franz is the best man she has ever met, only he doesn't like her hat, and she puts it on and she and Tomas whirl in an embrace, the moment has an Ernst Lubitsch giddiness. The material is all there in the book, but Kaufman has instinctively loosened it; if he hadn't, he'd have come out with only a literary adaptation instead of this movie, which is his as much as Kundera's— perhaps more his. (And so it may delight the onetime film-school professor.)

The script, by Jean-Claude Carrière and Kaufman, is possibly too faithful to the book in retaining some gimmickry about the number six. And after Tereza goes back to Prague, to the old flat, and Tomas follows her (and has his passport confiscated), there are a few late plot developments that aren't quite prepared for. (One of them involves Erland Josephson as a barroom janitor who was formerly the Czech ambassador in Vienna.) And I'm not sure that the conception of the gamine Tereza as photographic artist is much more than a literary conceit. But the young Binoche gives the role a sweet gaucheness and then a red-cheeked desperation—the push and pathos of a Clara Bow or a young Susan Hayward. She verges on peasant-madonna darlingness, but that's what the conception requires. Tereza is a waifish little mantrap; she has the appeal of teen-age sexy petiteness. That's what gets to Day-Lewis's Tomas: she has a built-in pornography.

In the novel, the authorial voice leads us along, and the main characters have little depth; only Lena Olin is fully able to compensate for this. But Day-Lewis endows Tomas with a sneaky wit; this lusty Tomas— who *looks* Central European—is a cutup who draws you into his flirtations. Day-Lewis is a vocal trickster, too: he manipulates his Czech accent to throw you curves. A muscular toothpick with a long, skinny face and that cushion of hair, he's playing something new in movie heroes: a harlequin intellectual. And when Tomas is a pleasure seeker without a passport, working on a farm, Tereza, who's backward, like the police state, has him where she wants him. (Janet Malcolm has pointed out that the name Tereza echoes the Czech concentration camp Terezin.) But there's also a strong element of conventionality in Kundera's structure, and you can interpret Tomas's commitment to Tereza as his redemption—his gaining the weight that saves him from the unbearable lightness of being. Kundera—the spokesman for playfulness—is himself divided, a puritan as well as a dandy. (He toys with the idea of life as a concentration camp.) The novel feels the pull of gravity, and this weakens the film's ending. Yet the film's spirit carries through.

Kundera has often spoken of Laurence Sterne, the author of *Tristram Shandy*, as one of his idols. I didn't catch that when I read *Unbearable Lightness*, but there are glimmers of it in Day-Lewis's performance, and

431

in Phil Kaufman's confident waywardness. Kaufman has made movies that should have been hits—the 1978 *Invasion of the Body Snatchers* and, in 1983, *The Right Stuff*. This time, he has made a movie that probably doesn't stand much chance of reaching a wide audience. But it puts him in a different class as an artist. It also puts him and his backer, Saul Zaentz, at the top of the heap for courage.

February 8, 1988

THE LADY FROM THE SEA

Every now and then, I hear from young women who say that they want to write or direct movies but have no interest in car chases, coke busts, or shoot-outs. They want to make movies about personal relations and emotional states. Generally, I encourage them, while acknowledging my dread of the mess of vague, inchoate feelings that could be the result. I caution them that it takes more talent and more tough-mindedness to put a sensibility on the screen than it does to film a gunfight, and, lest they think that their desire is a specifically feminine one, I point out movies such as Kershner's *Loving*, Alan Parker's *Shoot the Moon*, Ichikawa's *The Makioka Sisters*, and Satyajit Ray's *Days and Nights in the Forest* and *The Home and the World*. But young women directors may be drawn to get at emotional states with less plot apparatus—almost nakedly.

Gillian Armstrong reports that when she began work on her new picture, *High Tide*, she pinned a note above her desk: "Blood ties. Water. Running away." That note tells us what the movie is about more truthfully than a plot summary would. Shot from a script by Laura Jones, *High Tide* is a woman's picture in the way that *Stella Dallas* was—it's about the mother-daughter bond. But it's also a woman's picture in a new way: Gillian Armstrong, the Australian who directed *My Brilliant Career* at twenty-seven and then made *Starstruck* and *Mrs. Soffel*, has the technique and the assurance to put a woman's fluid, not fully articulated emotions right onto the screen. And she has an actress—Judy Davis, the

Sybylla of *My Brilliant Career* and the Adela Quested of David Lean's *A Passage to India*—who's a genius at moods.

As Lilli, one of three backup singers for a touring Elvis imitator, Judy Davis is contemptuous of the cruddy act, contemptuous of herself. Too smart for what she's doing, Lilli is a derisive tease—a spoiler. Feeling put down, the dumb-lug Elvis fires her, and she's left alone at the beginning of winter in a ramshackle beach town on the magnificent, windswept coast of New South Wales. There, stuck in the Mermaid Caravan Park while she tries to scrounge up the money to pay for repairs on her car, she encounters her teen-age daughter, Ally (Claudia Karvan).

When Lilli's young surfer husband died, she felt lost; she gave up the baby to her mother-in-law, Bet (Jan Adele), and has been drifting ever since, and getting stinko and passing out. Bet, a singer in talent shows at the local restaurant–night spot, who works at a fish-packing co-op and runs a soft-ice-cream stand, is a rowdy, belligerent woman, and she's devoted to Ally: Bet has taken care of her for thirteen years, but has no idea how unhappy the girl is—the rules Bet lays down to protect the kid cut her off from other kids and make her miserable. Lilli has an immediate rapport with the lonely Ally, even before she knows that Ally is her daughter, and after she knows, she can't take her eyes off the kid. When they're at the public baths at the same time, Lilli stares at Ally's legs under the stall door; Ally is shaving them, and Lilli stands there tranced out, sick with love and longing.

This remote, working-class, tourist-town Australia suggests a corrupted frontier settlement. The view of the cliffs and the sea includes the rusted debris of the caravan dwellers; the Mermaid is like the seedy trailer parks on the outskirts of American towns, but with a more pervasive sense of rootlessness and movement. The men and women, in their faded denims and cheap pastels, blend with the blue of the water. These people survive by changing their occupations with the seasons; they work hard in small businesses that look as if they had been thrown up out of packing crates. You see the crumminess of the town in the big, garish joint where the Elvis act is put on, and where Bet sings. (All the entertainers hit the same high decibel level.) An aging cowboy headliner called Country Joe (Bob Purtell) performs there against a backdrop of a huge bull's skull, and you get a taste of matey entertainment at a smoker, where Lilli earns the money she needs by doing a strip. You also see some less coarse men: Colin Friels as a fisherman who responds to Lilli's wry half smiles and likes her too much to watch her at the smoker, and Mark Hembrow as a garage mechanic who takes a chance on her and lets her have her car. Gillian Armstrong's style is crisp, and the camera whizzes past the scenic wonders, often turning rocks and road lines into abstractions. The superb cinematographer Russell Boyd chose to be his own camera operator this time—so he could have the excitement of giving Armstrong the fast tracking movement she wanted, and she could concentrate on the performances.

Lilli and her young teen-age daughter match up; you feel that they're true kin—they belong with each other. But their scenes together are courtship dances that Lilli keeps pulling back from, terrified of taking on the responsibility of motherhood when she hasn't been able to make it alone. You may intuit that her having abandoned the child who was her only hold on life is the reason she has trashed herself. She doesn't look at her failures that kindly, though. And Bet—piggy-faced and broad in the beam—tells her she's riffraff. At first, Bet seems threatening. It isn't until she has spent a night with Country Joe, and her steady fellow (John Clayton) has used his truck to ram Country Joe's fancy car, that we fully appreciate what a frank, lusty bawd she is. She wins us over when she seeks assurance from Country Joe that he feels the night with her was worth the damage to his car. Bet isn't a monster; she's simply the wrong person to be raising the slender, pensive Ally, whose emotions are hidden away, like her mother's. Even Bet's sensitivities are crude.

Jan Adele makes her film début as the overprotective Bet, but she's a former vaudevillian who has been in show biz since she was three, and has done everything from ballet in tent shows, through singing with bands, to TV comedy. All her experience informs her presence here; it's a real turn, and the fact that she acts in a totally different style from that of Judy Davis (and the fourteen-year-old Claudia Karvan) strengthens the movie. Jan Adele projects to the rafters; she hands you every emotion neatly tagged. She's marvellous at it; she gives you the sense that in this rough country Bet hasn't been exposed to much in the way of amenities, or subtleties, either. The drama is in our feeling that Lilli must not leave her daughter in the embrace of this raucous old trouper. Bet isn't in the spirit of the film.

Lilli is so overcast—so unsure of herself—that we feel a mystery in her, despite her level gaze. Tall, skinny, red-haired Judy Davis was only twenty-three when she played her first leading role onscreen—in *My Brilliant Career*, in 1979. She may never have looked as beautiful as she does here in a motel-room scene with Colin Friels: he's lying on the bed, and she's standing by the window with her wavy hair wet from the shower. She's like a sea goddess. The first time we see her in this movie,

434

she's on the stage in a tawdry mermaid dress of sequins and ruffles. The first time we see Ally, she's in the water, floating in a tidal pool; then she gets on her father's old surfboard—surfing is her refuge from the noisy junkiness of life with Bet. And the sight of the sea is mucked up by what people have done to the coast.

Gillian Armstrong and her scenarist don't connect the dotted lines, and you don't want them to. I expected more to go on between Lilli and the Colin Friels character, maybe because Davis has a special serenity with Friels (he's her husband), but the script doesn't build on this accord. That's a small matter; so is Lilli's unnecessary waffling at the end. The movie's emotional suggestiveness may be off-putting to some people; they may be so trained to expect action that they'll complain that not enough is going on. But a great many young women are likely to feel that this is the movie they've wanted to make. (Some of them have already made pieces of it; the humiliation of the striptease has been the subject of many women film students' shorts.) The acute, well-written script acknowledges the basic ineffableness of some experiences, especially in a self-conscious scene toward the end where Lilli tries to explain to Ally why she deserted her. And it all goes together. It goes with the way Lilli looks when she's about to leave town and abandon her daughter for the second time; paying off the garage mechanic and thanking him, she's white as death. Judy Davis has been compared with Jeanne Moreau, and that's apt, but she's Moreau without the cultural swank, the high-fashion gloss. And there's no movieish gloss here, either. Men don't mistreat Lilli, and she doesn't mistreat them. She just screws herself over, and the film's only question is, Will she stop?

■

Louis Malle's *Au Revoir les Enfants* (or *Goodbye, Children*) is set in Occupied France in 1944, when Malle was an eleven-year-old at a Catholic boys' boarding school near Fontainebleau that sheltered several Jewish boys. The Gestapo learned they were there, and sent the ones they found to Auschwitz, and the headmaster to a work camp. One of the Jewish boys was in Malle's class, but Malle didn't get to know him well and didn't realize that he was Jewish. For the dramatic purposes of the movie, he has conceived a close friendship between his alter ego, the fair-haired Julien Quentin (Gaspard Manesse), and the dark boy who is using the false name Jean Bonnet (Raphaël Fejtö). Malle has every right to fantasize and invent, but I'm puzzled by the kind of fantasizing he does here. The first half of the film is so hushed and enervated that I kept peering into the schoolyard looking for signs of life. It's full of wealthy boys at play; they're even there on stilts, battling and falling down. But their games—which might clue us in to their ruling-class assumptions and their snobbery and the limits of their understanding—are shown at a distance. The camera is so discreet it always seems about ten feet too far away, and the boy who plays Julien is directed so that he never engages us; we can't look into him, or into anyone else.

As the story is presented, Julien, who is quick, grasps almost at once that this new boy, Jean Bonnet, is an impostor, who isn't really Catholic; Julien catches Jean standing by his bed at night, praying silently, with two lighted candles, and Julien rummages in Jean's books and discovers that his real name is the German-sounding Jean Kippelstein. Julien is the only boy in the class who offers Jean friendship; the others play tricks on Jean and gang up on him, because he's different—he's not one of them. Julien, who knows how different Jean actually is, keeps his discovery to himself. He and Jean are the two brightest boys in the class; they both love to read, and they become best friends. This is a rather moist fantasy of Julien's virtue; it's eventually mixed with a fantasy self-accusation of guilt. When the Gestapo chief comes into the classroom asking for Jean Kippelstein, the scared, nervous Julien involuntarily turns and looks at his friend—it's a Judas kiss, but an unintentional one. And Jean exonerates him: when he is packing his gear to go with the Gestapo men, he tells Julien that it didn't matter, that the Nazis would have caught him anyway.

In the finest scene of the movie, Jean shakes hands with the boys near him just before he's taken away; it's a well-brought-up young boy's leave-taking, and nothing has prepared you for it. But throughout Jean is used as an aesthetic object—spiritual, sensitive, foreign. He's often shot in profile, with his lips parted, and in one scene he goes to Mass with the other boys and tilts his face, openmouthed—almost yearning— to receive the holy wafer, which is denied him by the Reverend Father, the headmaster. Is the boy merely seeking acceptance by the other boys— is he just trying to pass as one of them—or is something else implied? The whole movie seems padded and muted; it's designed to make you understand that Julien is stricken by the horror of what happens to his friend. But nothing in it comes into clear focus—not the boys' attitudes, not even the images (and certainly not a lengthy sequence in which the two boys are on a treasure hunt in Fontainebleau Forest).

Malle has said that this is the most personal and important film of his career, and I believe that he thinks that. I also believe that he's wrong. He covered some of the same material in *Murmur of the Heart*, and Francine Racette, who plays Julien's mother, has a facial resemblance to Léa Massari, who was the mother in *Murmur*, but the sensuality and vivacity have been drained out of the character. At the beginning, when Julien's mother kisses him goodbye at the train station in Paris, she doesn't want him to go any more than he wants to leave her; her lipstick mark on his forehead could be an impudent, funny image—it could have associations—if the scene weren't so inert. Later, when she visits Fontainebleau and takes her older son, who's a senior at the school, and Julien and his friend Jean Bonnet out to dinner, and the older boy suggests that the Wehrmacht officers at the next table who reprimanded a loud-mouthed, anti-Semitic militiaman were doing it to impress her, you think, Why? She hasn't been seductive; she hasn't even smiled. Malle keeps the characters straitjacketed. If *Au Revoir* is very personal to him, this may be because as an adult he has felt stricken by the recognition that he wasn't stricken then, and it may involve his feelings of guilt over his own family's safety and prosperity—everything that the film barely touches on.

Malle has said of *Au Revoir*, "I reinvented the past in the pursuit of a haunting and timeless truth." Maybe that's why I felt as if I were watching a faded French classic, something I dimly recalled. I felt that way especially during the near-replay of Malle's *Lacombe, Lucien* in the scenes that involve Joseph (François Négret), a lame orphan boy who works at the school as a kitchen helper and is discharged for some petty black marketeering. It's Joseph, trying to get even with the headmaster for throwing him out and to set himself up with the Gestapo, who is the informer. In pursuit of haunting and timeless truth, Malle has gone back to the anti-Nazi movies of the forties, and polished and formalized the actions until he's turned melodrama into polite reverie.

Yes, it gets to you by the end. How could it not? But you may feel pretty worn down—by how accomplished it is, and by all the aching, tender shots of Jean. He's photographed as if he were a piece of religious art: Christ in his early adolescence. There's something unseemly about the movie's obsession with his exotic beauty—as if the French-German Jews had come from the far side of the moon. And does he have to be so

437

brilliant, and a gifted pianist, and courageous? Would the audience not mourn him if he were just an average schmucky kid with pimples?

February 22, 1988

GOD'S PICKPOCKETS

|||||||||||||||||||||||||||||||||||||||||||||||||||||||||||||||||||||||||||||||||||||||||||||||||||||||||||||||||||||||||||||||||||||||||||||||||||||||||||||

The first half of the two-part documentary *Thy Kingdom Come, Thy Will Be Done* is about the union of Christian fundamentalism and the political right, which was engineered in the past decade by the use of computers, direct mail, and organized phone campaigns. In the introductory moments, the English producer-writer-director Antony Thomas comes on too strong: the clips that he throws at us are almost as overwrought as the scare tactics of the religious right, and so we may pull back. But once Thomas has got hold of the subject he shows great empathy with the people drawn into the movement, and a fine, analytic grasp of how the men with the computer banks manipulate their targets. The "born-again" Christians—many of them probably the country-town and backwoods hippies of the sixties—describe their abuse by parents, their addictions to drugs and alcohol, their misery and feelings of "emptiness." They talk of having wanted God, and we see how the evangelists brought radiance and hope into their lives, and then got them focussed on the dangers of "secular humanism"—abortion, child abuse, prostitution, pornography, homosexuality, the teaching of evolution, the absence of school prayer, and, above all, Communism.

We see Pat Robertson speaking at rallies and on TV, telling frightened people that they're "being hunted down by those who essentially are atheists . . . they hate the Bible." He tells them that the state is attempting to take children away from their parents and is training them in collectivist, humanist philosophy. Other televangelists—Jerry Falwell, Jimmy Swaggart, Jim and Tammy Faye Bakker—are shown ranting at the faithful, pressuring them, while the volunteer telephone troops reach them individually. There's a steady demand for money to support the ministries, to build Christian schools, and, in the case of the Bakkers, to

438

build Heritage USA, the theme park near Charlotte, North Carolina, that suggests an alternative universe—a model pure-minded town with houses and the five-hundred-room Heritage Grand Hotel, and a Main Street that's built under an artificial blue sky.

Working with the cinematographer Curtis Clark and an American crew, Thomas shot the film just before the Bakkers' scandal broke, and so we see the pair in their prime: Jim smiling as he says, "I'm one of the first people that was actually called by God to do television," Tammy Faye pleading for more money, saying they can't meet their payroll, and weeping copiously, and Jim bawling like a kid as he talks about his own dedication to Kevin Whittum—a victim of a bone disease who at eighteen weighs only twenty pounds. Organ music backs up Jim's spiel—"And I said, 'Kevin, I'm gonna build a house for you!' "—and thousand-dollar donations are solicited for Kevin's House. Whittum, who tells Thomas he's under contract to do spots—"usually for advertisements of Kevin's House to make, uh, raise more money"—is seen in one of his TV pitches: "Send in what you can to help them as a ministry. They wouldn't ask if they didn't need it."

Much of the material in this first half is familiar, but you get a full, clear picture of how the exaltation, the healing, and the "miracles" fit together with all the techniques for squeezing money out of the faithful and turning them into right-wing zealots. Religion is only a means for the big-time televangelists. They're engaged in politicking and schlock-empire building. After you've watched people telling you about the terrible pain they were in before they came to Christ, you may breathe in sharply when Tim LaHaye, who runs the Washington-based pressure group the American Coalition for Traditional Values (which then included thirty-three evangelists), talks about using direct mail and religious broadcasting to make "an end run" to reach the American people. Morton Blackwell, who now heads the Leadership Institute, proudly asserts that he started it all about ten years ago when he announced that the conservative Christians were "virgin timber" waiting to be organized politically. He claims that contributions to conservative religious leaders were over a billion dollars in 1986. We see Gary Jarmin, who helped organize Christian Voice, which fights to defeat liberal candidates and officeholders. And, of course, there's Richard Viguerie, the founder of *Conservative Digest*, who has the largest political mailing organization in the country; he's photographed in front of his computer bank on the outskirts of Washington, and he talks about using religious letter campaigns to balance the control of the media by the left. There's a pitilessness about the manipulation this film records. You feel it even in the pipsqueak show-biz sentimentality of the Bakkers, who make themselves adorable. (Their running costs at the time exceeded two million dollars a week.)

Thomas's seriousness—the way he provides a context—deprives you of the satirical wisecracks that come to mind when you catch glimpses of these evangelists on TV. His point of view is that of a Christian who's disturbed by the antics of the clowns—and perhaps crooks—who call themselves Christians. And in the second half, in which he moves on to Dallas and the church that is the "richest and most powerful stronghold" of the religious right, he gets into the subject of how rich Christians keep themselves comfortable in their faith while abandoning the core of Christ's teachings.

Less familiar and less wide-ranging, the second half is much more penetrating than the first. Thomas leads into it with a brief visit to the weekly Bible class held at Mrs. Ruth Hunt's Dallas home, Mt. Vernon. The widow of H. L. Hunt and the stepmother of the silver-monopolizing brothers, Mrs. Hunt is surrounded by expensively accoutred women—a few of them young but most middle-aged and elderly. They have thick, colorful, salon-stiff hair and heavy makeup; there isn't a hint of spontaneity in any of their faces—if you were ever on trial for your life, these are not the faces you'd want to see on the jury. Mrs. Hunt, who's bright-eyed and has an amusingly dippy girlish manner (Lillian Gish could play her), explains to Thomas why every word in the Bible is literally true: it has to be, because if it weren't, everyone would have a different view of what's true in it and what isn't. There's something inspired about the convenience of her way of thinking—she's a token of all the lazyheads we meet.

Mrs. Hunt belongs to the First Baptist Church of Dallas, one of the biggest Protestant congregations in the world. It has twenty-six thousand members, and a vast, palatial church, with its own schools and university in the complex. The dignified, white-haired pastor, Dr. W. A. Criswell— he has been running the church for forty-four years—becomes the film's central character: Thomas tries to understand Criswell's teachings. When Thomas asks him how it is that the American city with the highest percentage of churchgoing Christians should also have the highest crime rate, Criswell blames the crime on the poor blacks and Mexicans who don't go to church. But, according to Thomas, the First Baptist Church devotes less than one-third of one per cent of its income to the needy. Dr. Criswell fought integration, and then, in effect, perpetuated segregation by taking over twenty-six of the city's ethnic churches, which are

440

now run under the aegis of First Baptist. We see a young black minister in one of these churches trying to get his poor parishioners properly riled up about the perils of secular humanism. How does a young man get so far from sense? He was probably trained at the Criswell Center for Biblical Studies—it's right there in the First Baptist complex.

Dr. Criswell explains to Thomas, who expresses concern about his own attachment to worldly goods, that he has the wrong idea of the Gospel. The wealthy, it seems, *can* enter the Kingdom of Heaven. "I tell young men," Criswell says in his orotund voice, " 'Make money. Succeed.' " (Does Thomas really look poleaxed, or is that the viewer's imagination?) Dr. Paige Patterson, the president of the Center, explains to Thomas that without the born-again experience you're doomed to Hell. Even Mother Teresa? asks Thomas. Yes, even Mother Teresa, says the suave, eminent theologian. Thomas talks to a young minister who was booted out of his teaching post at the Center for writing a paper suggesting that the rich had some responsibility to help the poor. What the rich are expected to do is support the Church and right-wing causes and candidates. The poor are kept out of sight.

Do the television evangelists believe what they preach? The question was put to Thomas by an interviewer for the *Chronicle*, when the film opened in San Francisco earlier this year. Thomas answered, "I don't know. . . . All of the evangelists maintained the same persona throughout, except for one . . . Criswell, the person you would probably least expect. . . . In private, he was aware of the discrepancy between his life style and the Scripture—he said he was a prisoner of the culture. He used the illustration that if he wore rags and stood on a street corner no one would listen." Thomas reflects: "The Christian tradition says you do good works on earth, you'll be rewarded in heaven. The born-again fundamentalists say if you give money to the Church, you will get your reward here on earth." The film shows the embattled, paranoid anxieties about the dangers of liberalism which the working-class fundamentalists take on as part of this Gospel of Success, and the complacency it brings to the prosperous. (It's as if God asked, "How can I get these crude, materialistic Americans to believe in me?" and Satan replied, "Why don't you promise them money?")

Thy Kingdom Come, Thy Will Be Done was co-financed by Britain's Central Television and by WGBH (the PBS station in Boston) for the *Frontline* series. It was shown in Britain and elsewhere in Europe, but for reasons that remain cloudy the American showings, which were scheduled for last May, were cancelled. This may or may not have something to do with fear of President Reagan's appointees to the Corporation for Public Broadcasting. Reagan himself appears in the footage—we hear Swaggart and Morton Blackwell celebrating him, and see him with Dr. Criswell—and Thomas states his belief that Reagan's highly public endorsement of the work of the evangelists in 1980, when he was running for President, marked the entry of the movement into the mainstream of American politics. *Thy Kingdom Come* has just opened in New York, and it has been rescheduled for PBS. It's not a great documentary, but it's a very powerful and thoughtful one. And it has a great subject. A lesser director could have killed it, but, the way Thomas handles it, you almost can't help getting involved. He knows how to ask deep-felt, piercing questions without being hostile, and how to keep the footage tense and dramatic.

When you go into the classrooms of the First Baptist's schools and hear a teacher telling the kids that man's time on earth can be measured by genealogy—by adding together the lifespans from Adam through Noah to Abraham—you may bat your eyes in dismay. But when you see the schoolroom rituals the kids are put through—the salutes and recitations—you can't distance yourself so easily. And when you look at the scenes in the charismatics' church—it has eleven thousand members—and see the children kneeling on the floor and raising their arms in feeble supplication, straining to get in the spirit of things, you don't know how to respond. In moments like this, or when we're taken inside Dr. Criswell's Inner City Chapel and see the destitute men sitting on the benches and listening to a minister for hours before they can get the reward of a thin sandwich, and then see and hear the distress of the minister after he locks the men out of the chapel at night, *Thy Kingdom Come* takes us beyond our ability to know how we should feel. It's in the best documentary-film tradition. It's also—particularly in the second half—in an appalled Christian spirit. What comes across is that Antony Thomas is asking himself, "How could Christianity have become so debased, so *mean?*"

■

In *Hairspray*, the spherical Mrs. Edna Turnblad (played by the male actor Divine) and her baby-blimp daughter, Tracy (Ricki Lake), come out of the Hefty Hideaway wearing mother-and-daughter dresses and walk down the street with their bosoms proudly preceding them. It's Baltimore, but they're like floats in the Mardi Gras. Their snazzy new outfits didn't cost them anything: the proprietor of the shop has just asked Tracy to model for him. She's the newest celebrity in town: each day, right after high school, she goes to appear on *The Corny Collins Show*, where she and the other hotshot teen-age dancers do novelties like the Pony and the Roach. It's 1962: Chubby Checker time, "Mashed Potato" time; the kids at the hop do the Madison. Tracy's celebrity status doesn't help her at school, though: the boy seated behind her can't see past her wide, newly "feathered" coiffure, and she's charged with "hairdo violations" and put in a class for slow learners and problem kids. That's where she gets to learn some new dance steps from Seaweed (Clayton Prince), whose mother, Motormouth Maybell (Ruth Brown), is a rhythm-and-blues disk jockey. When Tracy discovers that black kids aren't allowed on *The Corny Collins Show*, she becomes a leader in the fight for integration. The writer-director John Waters treats the message movie as a genre to be parodied, just like the teenpic. Combining the two, he comes up with an entertainingly imbecilic musical comedy—a piece of pop dadaism.

Waters doesn't try to transform the sappy fun of pop into art; he loves it for itself. He's a twenty-year veteran of the midnight-movie circuit; his affection for bad taste is no sham. And he loves narrative: he has half a dozen plots crisscrossing each other. Poor-girl Tracy has a rich-girl rival—slender, blond Amber (Colleen Fitzpatrick), who has been raised to be popular and a star. The two girls are pitted against each other as the top contenders in the Miss Auto Show 1963 contest. To complicate matters, Amber's boyfriend, Link (Michael St. Gerard), a ringer for Elvis, is fed up with her and is drawn to Tracy, white lipstick and all. A blond sweetie with two pert braids and bows, shy-girl Penny (Leslie Ann Powers), whose mother (Jo Ann Havrilla) is a pathological racist, falls for handsome black Seaweed. Corny Collins (Shawn Thompson) wants to integrate his show but can't, because the head of the TV station—WZZT—won't permit it; this rancid boss is also played by Divine. At times, *Hairspray* suggests a home movie made by a gang of celebrities. The many plots involve Debbie Harry and Sonny Bono as Amber's parents, who are monomaniacal about her becoming Miss Auto Show; Jerry Stiller as Tracy's father; Waters himself as a sick psychiatrist; and Ric Ocasek and Pia Zadora as the first of the lank-haired beatniks who are about to displace the ducktail and beehive brigades.

Gaga as all this is, there's some historical basis for it: Baltimore's

443

Buddy Deane Show actually fell apart over the integration issue. But the movie makes no claim to realism—or to absurdism, either. Waters just weaves in and out of his plots, and the girls and boys fuss over their hair. The girls look tiny and doll-like and rather plaintive under their huge, elaborate hairdos. Bitchy Amber, avid for the world's good opinion, is presented as a parent-pecked case, and she's so innocently horrid she's a delight; Penny is a cartoon dream; and Tracy, who has the cherubic face that's often seen on fatties, is a cuddlesome matchup with her lewd mama. It's really Divine's movie: he watches over Tracy and preens like a mother hen. There's a what-the-hell quality to his acting and his funhouse-mirror figure which the film needs; it would be too close to a real teenpic without it. When Divine's Edna Turnblad is onscreen in the sleeveless dresses she's partial to, the movie has something like the lunacy of a W. C. Fields in drag.

March 7, 1988

A SMOOTH SAIL

||||||||||||||||||||||||||||||||||||||||||||||||||||||||||||||||||||||||||||||||||||||||||||||||||||||||||||||||||||||||||||||||||||||||||||

*M*asquerade has a pearly atmosphere of unease. The rich, trustful Olivia Lawrence (Meg Tilly) graduates from Marymount College and returns to the Hamptons, where her mother recently died in an accident; a young hired-hand yachting captain, Tim Whalan (Rob Lowe), who is a practiced seducer, begins to court her. The situation is reminiscent of the courtship of Olivia de Havilland by Montgomery Clift in William Wyler's *The Heiress*, and perhaps the name Olivia is a tribute to that film. Tilly's Olivia isn't considered a dull dowd, like Wyler's heroine; this Olivia is lovely, but she's placid and unaffected—she has no sharp edges. And Rob Lowe's Tim Whalan is a shrewd manipulator, a narcissist who knows how to use his every gift. Lowe certainly isn't the actor that Clift was, but you can see why the director, Bob Swaim, might have wanted him in the role: Lowe brings it his boyish prettiness and sexual ambiguity. Olivia isn't frightened of this honey-mouthed charmer. She confuses his

444

self-absorption with unworldliness: she thinks he's like her, and they have the rapport of two people who love sailing. She has her own sloop, Masquerade, which she inherited, along with eight houses and about two hundred million dollars. (She belongs to the old rich; her money has a patina.)

This is a tranquil, sophisticated thriller: you put it together as it flows past you, and then other pieces fit in when it's over. The script, by Dick Wolf, is crafty and even-toned, and the cinematography, by David Watkin, gives the life of the rich a luxuriance—makes it palpably desirable. The movie was shot in the Hamptons, and the architectural pomposity of the houses recalls the mansions of dullness that Gatsby lusted for, but these romantic undertones are kept down under. The movie has an odd, subterranean pull. Murders take place, but the narrative just keeps unfolding effortlessly, and you're drawn along, wanting to understand the pattern of deceit.

John Glover, who has taken over as the prime rotter of the eighties, is cast as a drunken swine—the last of Olivia's mother's many husbands. A creative comedian, Glover manages to inject some gallows humor into the role: this loathsome stepfather tries to be debonair—it makes him really twisted. Dana Delany makes an effectively quirky impression as his girlfriend, who becomes recklessly suspicious about what's going on. Doug Savant plays the new Hampton Shores police officer; he has known Olivia from childhood and gives indications of having a crush on her. Savant has the kind of young Tab Hunter looks that actors generally can't do much with, but he has an alertness about him—he has learned how to use his eyes and mouth to convey emotions at odds with that all-American-hero face. Rob Lowe hasn't learned how to use anything; his acting is mush. (His bare-chested scenes would be more effective if he wore a mask to blot out his smarminess.) At the beginning, Tim is the captain of one of two sailboats racing for a championship, and the scenes of his crew of young men under pressure have speed and charge. But Lowe's Tim has no instinctive authority, and when he loses the race and hops into bed with the boat owner's wife (Kim Cattrall) it's hardly adultery—it's just snuggling. Lowe brings his role the qualities that would appeal to Olivia, but he automatically lessens what's at stake in the movie.

Nobody is made out to be conventionally likable, except maybe Olivia. You can't be sure about her, because Meg Tilly, who had a modern spark in *Tex*, is still doing the sleepy, lethargic acting that began when she played the space case in *The Big Chill*. She's blandly sincere; maybe that's what Swaim wanted of her, or maybe it's what he had to settle for. She's a little monotonous. (It might have helped if by the end she had come awake.) But at some level her performance works. Olivia has an infinite capacity for love and loyalty, and Tim begins to want to be what she sees in him. So the currents of love and deception run into each other. What makes the movie seductive is its calm surface and conniving, film-noir subtext. It doesn't tell you too much. And almost nothing can be said about what happens in the picture without spoiling it—except that at times it carries suggestions of thrillers such as *Purple Noon* and *Strangers on a Train*. It has a sweet malice.

■

Roman Polanski's *Frantic* begins promisingly—that is, with forebodings. Harrison Ford plays a San Francisco heart surgeon who comes to Paris with his wife (Betty Buckley) to speak at a medical conference; they haven't been there since their honeymoon, twenty years earlier. Polanski is a director with guile and wit, and as they arrive at Le Grand Hôtel and go to their room he builds suspense by having us observe every humdrum detail. (What beast is going to spring at us?) First, the two discover that the wife picked up the wrong suitcase at the airport, and then, while the doctor is in the shower, the wife answers the phone and says something to him that he can't hear; he comes out to find she has disappeared. So there he is, an American who doesn't speak French and doesn't know the city, trying to track down his wife, and being condescended to by the police and by the bureaucrats at the American Embassy. But from there on the episodes might have been picked out of a jar by blindfolded writers. (The script is credited to Polanski and Gérard Brach.) The camera stays on the doctor as he follows clues that take him to shops and streets, to a night club (The Blue Parrot, which was the name of Sydney Greenstreet's café in *Casablanca*), to an apartment occupied by a corpse, to the Paris rooftops, and to another night club (A Touch of Class) and involvement with dope dealers and Arab terrorists and the childlike, amoral tootsie (Emmanuelle Seigner) whose suitcase got mixed up with his wife's.

During all this, the doctor is supposed to be doing dangerous things

446

he has never done before, because of his love for his vanished wife. But what we see is an unhappy, often angry man played by an actor who's concentrating on his role and showing us his fine, strong surgeon's hands. When Ford is Indiana Jones, he's playing on instinct and exhilaration—on all of himself—and we can tune right in to his rascally daring. As the doctor, he's using only the trained-actor part of himself, and it's a joyless, unrevealing performance—he's a lug in a light-gray suit. Since the picture has done nothing to make the wife vivid to us, we don't even share his anxiety about her. All we can think of is the gaping holes in the plot: if the villains lured the wife to the hotel lobby and kidnapped her because they wanted the suitcase, why didn't they tell her to bring it down with her, or just come up and get it? *Frantic* is a misshapen thriller that grinds on without ever being able to compensate for its pathetic plot and its unwritten characters. We seem meant to care about the toots—a painted waif, a child of nature and vice, and all that baloney—but the way she's directed she's too weak a presence to bring it off.

A thriller needs more than an occasional perverse comic undertone; it needs some design, some shapeliness. This picture goes from one location and group of characters to the next, and after a while the episodes become so redundant you may vaguely wonder, Were there only two suitcases?

■

Switching Channels—adapted from *His Girl Friday*, the 1940 film version of the 1928 play *The Front Page*—has lost most of the inspired engineering that gave the material its snap. This new picture is often screechy, but it has its own rambunctious, sloppy humor, and the director, Ted Kotcheff—short as he may be on visual invention—has a sense of tempo. Things don't stall. The milieu has been changed from the original one, of Chicago newspaper reporters in the heyday of tabloid journalism, to present-day Chicago and the newsroom of a cable outfit called Satellite Network News. Burt Reynolds is Sully, the news director; Kathleen Turner is Christy, his ex-wife and star reporter; and Christopher Reeve is Blaine, the New York business tycoon she meets on her vacation, who brings her back to Chicago so she can tell Sully she's quitting the news game to get married. The original political-corruption plot still survives

447

in vestigial form, with Ned Beatty as the shiny-eyed crooked D.A. who means to win the governorship by executing a convicted cop-killer, and Henry Gibson as the gentle little condemned man who's clinging to life. That's the buzz in the air, and the minor players—George Newbern as Sully's assistant, and several fresh performers from Toronto (where most of the film was shot)—contribute to it. The action centers, though, on Sully's sneaky determination to hang on to Christy, and on his efforts to expose the hulking Blaine—a manufacturer of athletic equipment—as the vain twerp he is.

The attempt to update the plot to the age of television seems half-hearted, and even when the scriptwriter, Jonathan Reynolds, comes up with some satire of TV (as in the sequence of cutting from one TV reporter to another and another and another, all delivering the same vacuous account of a jailbreak) Kotcheff fails to point it up. He does better with the spoofy moments featuring a simpering newswoman (Laura Robinson) known as the Twinkie, and the ones featuring the stentorian voice of Christy's male co-anchor. And Kotcheff achieves a bit of comic-strip style in a series of images of the network's viewers as family groups in the clutter of their homes. But the film's chief virtue is that the actors show a gleaming pleasure in their moments of broad farce. (Maybe Kotcheff is a good audience.)

Ned Beatty's first few appearances here are beauties: he's marvellously piggish. And Henry Gibson turns his stare on us and we feel a frazzled, poetic rapport with him; in the night scene after he escapes, when he's confused and running pell-mell in the darkness outside the jail, his arms and legs seem to be flying away from him. Burt Reynolds, who holds the movie together, reins himself in and shows some of the sly grace that made him appealing a decade ago in *Semi-Tough*. He has some nifty gag lines to deliver, and he doesn't milk them—it's almost a modest performance. He looks fit and relaxed; maybe now that he's fifty-two he can depend more on his acting skills and stop pushing his macho image. It may help that next to Christopher Reeve he seems rather small; it's becoming. So is the softness he brings to some of his line readings. When the network owner (Al Waxman) tells him, "Forget the girl; get the story," Reynolds glides into his answer: "The girl *is* the story."

Kathleen Turner is at her most entertaining—and lusty and full-throated—in the beginning, when we see her on the job doing her telecasts, and so overworked she's half hysterical. By the middle, where her scenes are sometimes very close to the ones Rosalind Russell played in *His Girl Friday*, Turner doesn't hit quite the right notes. This may be how Kotcheff directed her; in any case, she's gutsy and funny even when she's off tone. You can see her trying; she's game. Turner and Reynolds don't get verbal rhythms going, the way Rosalind Russell and Cary Grant did, and you don't really feel that they belong together, but then this movie is a burlesque and you hardly think in those terms. Sully's jealousy is simply the motor for the comedy. His rival is younger, rich, and taller; Sully turns all three against him. The joker in the cast is Christopher Reeve, in the Ralph Bellamy role as the square, the outsider who doesn't know how the newspeople feel about their work. Reeve's entire performance is slapstick: he's like Clark Kent sexed up. Blaine is so infatuated with the image of himself as a hip, wired man of the world that he dresses romantically in pale blue and yellow, and has his hair colored Mellow Sun Tone. Reeve sustains this foppish stunt, and his jerky, rattled movements are neatly timed. (He survives even such maladroit cheesiness as the shot of him walking on the street in a loose long jacket while a young woman is heard in voice-over exclaiming "Cute buns!")

Switching Channels has a dumb title (though it's no worse than *His Girl Friday*) and a Michel Legrand score that's just litter on the soundtrack. This is a fairly disreputable movie, but I've seen a lot of reputable ones without anything as purely enjoyable as Ned Beatty mouthing curses while he watches Christy conduct an interview on the box, or as downright silly and good-natured as Reeve crinkling his face in the grin of a goofus.

March 21, 1988

SOFT LIGHT AND HELLFIRE

|||||||||||||||||||||||||||||||||||||||||||||||||||||||||||||||||||||||||||||||||||||||||||||||||||||||||||||||||||||||||||||||||||||||||||||||||||||||||||||||||

Lhe melting beauty of Clare Peploe's *High Season* has a lot to do with a great cinematographer, Chris Menges, and a great setting, a town on the Greek island of Rhodes. There's bliss in the soft light and the acropolis, on its hilltop, and the color of the sea. But the film's seductiveness has even more to do with Peploe's knowing how to frame the shots and then edit them so that the images move just a little faster than

449

you expect. She's always a nuance ahead of you, her wit rippling over the story of the nine principal characters—some of them English, some of them Greek, and one Greek-American. The script, which she wrote with her brother Mark, is a comedy about the type of colonization of undeveloped areas known as tourism: vacationers from prosperous countries taking over the most spectacular scenery at the most desirable times of the year. *High Season* is a high-style, art-house comedy, elegantly calibrated, like the French-Canadian *Decline of the American Empire* but giddier and with more bravura.

Jacqueline Bisset has the pivotal role. She's Katherine, an English photographer who, with her sculptor husband, Patrick (James Fox), came to live in the coastal town long before the tourists discovered it. Their thirteen-year-old daughter, Chloe (Ruby Baker), has grown up here, and even though Katherine and Patrick have separated they have both stayed on, he supporting himself by turning out fashionably modern pieces that she thinks contemptible, and she publishing books of photographs featuring Greek antiquities and peasant life—photographs that he regards as fuddy-duddy endeavors. Her latest book isn't selling, and she's broke. She's going to have to give up her house and leave this island she loves unless she can get a buyer for a vase that was given to her many years earlier by a famous, now elderly art historian, Basil Sharp (Sebastian Shaw), a dear friend who adores her, and who arrives for a visit.

Jacqueline Bisset has generally (and justly) been remarked on more for her lusciousness than for her acting talent, but this is her juiciest performance. Her Katherine is a warm, breathing object of art. Of course, old Sharpie would adore her; the audience does, too—especially when she's in the moonlit water, tipsy, and confused about who the young man is that she's making love with.

Sharpie appears to be in his early seventies, but Sebastian Shaw was born in 1905; he was a handsome leading man in British films of the thirties and forties (more recently, he played the dying Darth Vader in *Return of the Jedi*), and he's still handsome. His face opens to the sunlight and the camera. He's a scenic wonder, like Bisset, and like Irene Papas, who plays Katherine's widowed friend—tough, weather-beaten Penelope. She's as much a part of the magnificence of the island as the honking donkeys. Penelope, who mythologizes everything, talks about her long-dead husband as if he were the Colossus of Rhodes. She regards the tourists as enemies—as an army of occupation, like the Nazis—and she's

450

engaged in a constant battle with her son, Yanni (Paris Tselios), who doesn't mind smiling for the enemies—he wants the prosperity they bring. This is one of those happy occasions when the strong-voiced Papas, who has embodied so many of the tragic heroines of Greek mythology, gets a chance to play comedy, and she exults in it. (Her deeply goofy Penelope is like Katina Paxinou stood on her head.) The whole movie is superbly cast. The wizardly young Kenneth Branagh plays Rick, the practical-minded Englishman who fixes Katherine's toilet so that it finally flushes with a real whoosh—a service that gives her such whole-souled delight that she begins to kiss him passionately. (Rick responds like a Shakespearean fool: he's instantly—ludicrously—smitten.) Meanwhile, Rick's wife, Carol (Lesley Manville), who is a romantic and has just discovered Byron's poetry, keeps herself occupied with the tourist-loving Yanni. The group is completed by Robert Stephens as Konstantinis, an obscenely rich Greek-American, who's eager to buy Katherine's vase but needs Sharpie to declare it a fake, so that he can take it out of the country.

Movies about artists generally turn awed and overadmiring, and when there's talk about art it can be archly inside and gossipy. *High Season* doesn't fall into these standard traps—probably because Katherine and Patrick are mediocre artists. (Each recognizes the other's deficiencies—that's why they can't live together.) But they appreciate beauty; they love the island and respect the Greeks and their customs. Is *High Season* saying that Katherine is spiritually different from the tourists—a flashy breed, who want the undeveloped area to offer them the comforts and entertainments they're used to, and who will inevitably change the way the villagers live? Yes, she's different. The movie centers on her efforts to sell the vase so she can go on living in this place as it is. Patrick puts her down for her conventionality as a photographer, but the movie doesn't. It adores her for the passion of her surrender to the island. (At the same time, the director recognizes that the spoiler tourists help to keep the islanders alive.) *High Season* has a nifty and ingenious plot, but what makes it so satisfying is its empathy with expatriate life. Katherine and Patrick don't have to be great artists to justify living on a Greek island. There's a generosity of spirit in this movie. You feel it in the way each character is treated. And there's enough irony mixed in with the generosity to keep everything buoyant.

This is more than an accomplished first feature; it has some of the yumminess of a picture like *Shampoo*—for example, in the scene where

451

Katherine goes to Patrick's place, wakes him, and asks if he loves her, while ignoring the girl tourist lying next to him. And it has easygoing visual jokes, like the way the camera pans from left to right during the opening titles and then back. (Once the movie gets going it never leaves the island.) And there's a joke about the future being behind you: Katherine's daughter, Chloe, cites an illustration (when you're standing the wrong way on an escalator), and at the end the movie shows Sharpie going backward into the future. Clare Peploe had previously made only the half-hour short *Couples and Robbers*, but she has been talking, working on, and living movies for a couple of decades. She was one of the screenwriters on Antonioni's *Zabriskie Point* (1970), and was one of the writers and an assistant director as well on Bertolucci's *Luna* (1979). She's married to Bertolucci, and her brother Mark, who wrote *The Passenger* for Antonioni and has collaborated with about a dozen directors, also wrote (with Bertolucci) the script of *The Last Emperor*. This début film isn't major or innovative. (And it has rough spots: Patrick's sculpture is perhaps cruddier than necessary, and there's a not too well-informed speech about Communists in the thirties as the only ones who organized against the Nazis.) But it has a lovely equilibrium.

Goats and dogs and donkeys move in and out of the frame. In one scene, Penelope sits under a tree looking at Katherine's book and a goat trots into the background—you want to applaud. That wandering goat represents what Penelope wants to preserve. It's the free spirit of the place. And this first-time director has had the wit to use random donkey honks on the soundtrack as an ancient form of aleatory music.

∎

Set in an Ozark community, *Pass the Ammo* is a piece of rollicky backwoods Americana. This lampoon of television evangelists was shot in Eureka Springs, Arkansas, where the civic auditorium was converted into the studios of the Tower of Bethlehem, a ministry that lays claim to an audience of twenty million people and is systematically bilking them. The story is about a young woman (Linda Kozlowski) from the hill country who's trying to recover fifty thousand dollars that her family was stung for. Her fiancé (Bill Paxton) organizes what's meant to be a small, quiet robbery of the Tower's counting room but finds himself holding the congregation of a couple of thousand people hostage, and on satellite TV. He's an impetuous fellow, and at first he's full of vim—he rather enjoys seeing himself on the box. But the movie doesn't give him any clear negotiating position: he doesn't formulate what he wants for the hostages—he doesn't even tell the TV viewers how the family was bamboozled. The main characters inside and outside the tabernacle seem to be stalled, waiting for what's going to happen next, and you feel that the picture doesn't have a through line. It turns out that it does—that the writers, Neil Cohen and Joel Cohen (not the Coens, and not brothers), have worked a logic into their ruckus. Yet something in the directing, by David Beaird, or perhaps in the editing, gets straggly. *Pass the Ammo* isn't as much of a wingding as *Used Cars* (1980)—it doesn't have the hot-ziggety inventiveness—but it's of that screwball-satire genre. And it has a whole slew of terrifically talented actors—the kind of actors who should (but don't) get the big roles in big pictures.

Tim Curry, with his devil's incisors, is the charismatic Reverend Ray Porter. At the opening of the film, he preaches a television sermon while standing against a nighttime background of the solar system—a special effect provided by the technological freako who runs the control room. Curry floats against the star-studded blackness, the bags under his eyes puffing out and his curly, dimply smile so elfishly dirty that it's as if he were lighted by hellfire. Perhaps the more fertile psychological subject is self-deceiving evangelists, but in farce what's wanted is exaggeration, not psychology—Reverend Ray is a bratty con artist. Boyish, with tousled hair on his forehead, he revels in snookering the public and dallies with the ladies of the choir. (They wear large white wings.) There has never been enough of Tim Curry onscreen, so it's too bad that his role diminishes as *Pass the Ammo* gets under way, but when he's around, you can see why the choirgirls practically cross themselves at the sight of him.

Ray Porter's exhibitionist wife, Darla, who stars in the big musical extravaganzas of the *Tower of Bethlehem Hour*, is played by Annie Potts, who has a figure worth exhibiting. Dressed in tight, spangled satin, she wiggles like the best cootch dancer in Heaven while delivering a sales pitch for expensive Bibles. And when she appears as Delilah, opposite the Sampson of a born-again football player (Brian Thompson), her bare midriff moves spasmodically. The song "Lay Your Money Down for Jesus," performed by baritone twins (John and Paul Cody) in Las Vegas–cowboy outfits, tells us we're hearing Reverend Ray's message, but when we

453

watch Darla writhing through the cloud effects of "You're in Paradise Now" we know that yes she is. She lives in a cloudy world of her own; when she's showing her body, and her eyes promise erotic delights, she's at her most religious.

Anthony Geary is Stonewall, the genius of the control room, who uses the circuitry as if it were part of him. Since Stonewall can control what the outside world sees during the robbery, this quiet pothead with leftover hippie hair is the one who gets the chance to play God. Geary acts the role very close in, with his eyes furtively registering everything. His is the tiniest of comic styles; it's barely visible, yet it makes you laugh. The team of robbers includes the hill-country woman's two hick, ex-con cousins. Glenn Withrow plays the small, perky one, who isn't fazed when the robbery expands to taking thousands of hostages, because it gives him the chance to meet the choirgirls, and this little snookums connects with one of the most sumptuous of the winged angels. The other cousin, played by Dennis Burkley, is a cagey three-hundred-pound giant, who insures himself against future police harassment by singing a tribute to cops and their hard lives—"You're a Policeman." (Darla accompanies him on the organ.) The song goes over the Tower's TV system, and the cops are deeply touched. They're outside, along with irate officials, the National Guard, and crowds of townspeople, and all these groups are so eager to shoot the four invaders who they believe are desecrating the Tower that they're ready to fire indiscriminately. The only person trying to keep order is a smart, hard-bitten Cajun—the local sheriff, played by Leland Crooke. He defies the governor, who was put in office by the high-muck-a-mucks of the ministry. (One mucker, played by Richard Paul, is a ringer for Jerry Falwell.)

You'll probably wish there were more of Ray and Darla snarling at each other, and wish their recriminations had more effect on the TV audience. And you'll probably want the action scenes to have more clarity; the climax—an orgiastic fireworks scene—has us worried for too long about the characters caught in it. But what's there has a klunky freshness; it hasn't been pawed over. The actors don't look rehearsed to death. And, luckily, Bill Paxton has the vitality of a star. He has triumphed in potent, rough-guy parts and, most recently, as the flamboyant wild man in *Near Dark*. Here he's the character who initiates the folly but has a core of sanity. He's clear-faced and white-shirted, like a proper hero, yet he's as spontaneous as ever. This actor knows how to show ardor; he's a real sparkplug.

April 4, 1988

454

BOO!

*B*eetlejuice is a farce about what happens to us after death: it's a bugaboo farce. At the start, the camera seems to be flying over an idyllic New England town, but the town changes into a miniature town on a table, and Adam (Alec Baldwin), the hobbyist who has carved it, takes a spider off a little rooftop. Adam and his wife, Barbara (Geena Davis), are a devoted, though regretfully childless, young couple who have been happy in their cozy old barnlike house—an eccentric pile of angles and peaks—while fending off realtors who want to sell it for them. The two drive into town on an errand, passing through a picture-postcard covered wooden bridge, but on the way back, as they go through the bridge, Barbara swerves to avoid hitting a dog, and the director, Tim Burton, reveals his first great gag: the car hangs over the edge of the quaint red bridge, kept from plunging into the river by the weight of the dog on a loose plank. When the dog gets bored and trots off, the car falls.

The next we see of Adam and Barbara, they're ghosts—tame, sweet, home-loving ghosts, not very different from how they were in life. The movie doesn't really get going until a New York family (who are far more ghoulish) buy the house and start redecorating, turning it into a high-tech space to show off the slinky wife's huge works of sculpture (which are like petrified insects). Miffed, Adam and Barbara want to scare these intruders away, but they're too mild to do the job themselves, so they call upon the services of the rutty little demon Betelgeuse, pronounced Beetlejuice, who is played by Michael Keaton, and who rises from the graveyard in the tabletop town. The movie had perked up when the New Yorkers arrived, because Delia the sculptor, the madwoman who's the new lady of the house, is played by the smudge-faced blond Catherine O'Hara, late of SCTV, and the possessor of the freakiest blue-eyed stare since early Gene Wilder. (She has sexy evil eyes.) Delia is too macabre

455

and uppity to be fazed by ordinary apparitions. Even the decaying Beetle-juice himself—he might be a carnival attraction: This way to the exhumed hipster!—barely distracts her. But Keaton is like an exploding head. He isn't onscreen nearly enough—when he is, he shoots the film sky-high.

This is not the kind of spook show that gives you shivers; it gives you outré shocks. Adam and Barbara are like the juvenile and the ingénue singing their duets in the M-G-M Marx Brothers pictures while we wait for lewd, foxy Groucho to grab the girls' bottoms. Michael Keaton is the Groucho here, but fast and furious, like Robin Williams when he's speeding, or Bill Murray having a conniption fit. And maybe because of the slow start and the teasing visual design—the whole movie seems to take place in a hand-painted nowhere, with the "real" town and the toy town miscegenating—Keaton creates a lust for more hot licks. He appears here with a fringe of filthy hair, greenish rotting teeth—snaggled—and an ensemble of mucky rags. And he keeps varying in size (like the star Betelgeuse). When he's let loose and the transformations start, along with the gravity-defying stunts, I wanted more and more of them. I wanted the overstimulation of prepubescent play—a child's debauch. And that's what Tim Burton, who began in the animation department at Disney, and directed his first movie in 1985 (*Pee-wee's Big Adventure*), offers. He's still in his twenties, and he has a kid's delight in the homegrown surreal. The plot is just a formality. To enjoy the movie, you may have to be prepared to jump back into a jack-in-the-box universe. But it may work even better if it takes you unawares and you start laughing at a visually sophisticated form of the rabid-redneck kids' humor you haven't thought about in years—the kind of humor that features wormy skeletons and shrunken heads. Here the shrunken heads are still attached to full-sized bodies.

The end is subdued. The final scenes have a plot logic that you can't really fault, but logic isn't what you want, and you feel as if the comedy blitz is suddenly over without your having fully grasped that it was ending. The last part isn't very well directed, and neither are the scenes where O'Hara's Delia decides that having a haunted house will bring her some social cachet. Burton may not have found his storytelling skills yet, or his structure, either, but then he may never find them. This movie is something to see, even if it's a blossoming chaos and the jokes sometimes leave you behind. (When Burton picked Robert Goulet and Dick Cavett for small roles, he probably wanted them to make fun of their images, but they don't appear to know how, and the writers—Michael McDowell,

Larry Wilson, and Warren Skaaren—haven't steered them.) Still, the best of W. C. Fields was often half gummed up, and that doesn't seem to matter fifty-five years later. With crazy comedy, you settle for the spurts of inspiration, and *Beetlejuice* has them. When Delia and her New York art-world guests are at the dinner table and, possessed, suddenly rise to sing the calypso banana-boat song "Day-O," it's a mighty moment—a haymaker. And you can't tell why. (If you could, it wouldn't be funny.) The satire of a waiting room in the social-services bureaucracy of the afterlife (which is staffed by suicides) is like great early animation. It features a spectral effect linking cigarettes and death so creepily that the audience sucks in its breath and laughs: when a raspy-voiced social worker, played by Sylvia Sidney, lights up, she exhales smoke through her nose, her mouth, and her slit throat.

The movie, with its toy town, is like Red Grooms' cities: it's an art work that has no depth but jangles with energy. Tim Burton takes stabs into the irrational, the incongruous, the plain nutty. And though a lot of his moves don't connect, enough of them do to make this spotty, dissonant movie a comedy classic. The story is bland—it involves the parental love that Adam and Barbara develop for the sculptor's stepdaughter (Winona Ryder)—but its blandness is edged with near-genius. Michael Keaton has never been so uninhibited a comic; his physical assurance really is demonic. He's a case of the beezie-weezies.

■

Jay McInerney's *Bright Lights, Big City* is a just about perfect pop novel—smart and maudlin and self-centered. You read along quickly, without pausing—without ever needing to think. The book came out in 1984, in paperback—and that was right for it, because the story has no heft, no substance. It's so pop it's almost nothing; it reads like the novelization of a TV movie. You don't read it, exactly—you consume it. The hero—a young writer—is at the center of a coke-spoon variation of your basic misunderstood-adolescent fantasy. He works as a fact checker at a magazine modelled on *The New Yorker* (where McInerney worked for a little under six months in 1980), and he uses dope to block out his misery over his wife's ditching him, which turns out to be delayed mourning for his mother. He spends his nights drinking and snorting with an adver-

457

tising-executive pal until the climactic week when he gets fired, falls apart, meets a wise, thoughtful girl, and rediscovers his values. The fun for readers was in the gossipy glimpses of the workings of *The New Yorker* and in the glamorous sensationalism and heavy spending of the disco-party scene of the early eighties; the book has the appeal of having been written by an insider—who, of course, tells outsiders that the high wild life is joyless. The hero is pure of heart, and once he sees the carelessness and shallowness of the rich he rejects them. What makes the book such a delicious (slim) read is that the fantasy is both utterly shameless and deftly controlled.

The movie version, directed by James Bridges, from a script he devised with McInerney, follows the novel very closely, but something new has entered the equation: Bridges' sense of shame. McInerney took his title from the 1961 Jimmy Reed song that has the refrain "Bright lights, big city/They went to my baby's head." That, essentially, is what the book provided that moviegoers will miss: the kick, the high. Bridges tones down the cute bitchiness that McInerney put into the magazine scenes, and he takes the seductiveness out of the doping and the promiscuity. It's obvious why (drugs and AIDS have created a time warp between the early eighties and the late eighties), but without that sexy glow the movie has no excitement, no vision.

And as storytelling the movie has no peaks. When the hero, who is called Jamie and is played by Michael J. Fox, wangles an invitation to an Oscar de la Renta fashion show where his estranged wife (Phoebe Cates) is modelling, he plows through the crowd next to the runway and tracks her as she struts, yelling her name. We grasp the intended effect, but the garish masochism goes flooey—we don't want to watch it. And when Jamie encounters her later at a party and is so shocked by her casual greeting that he begins to laugh hysterically and then to cough and have a nosebleed, we seem meant to be appalled at her nonchalance. But since we've had only a quick flashback of the two of them as a couple we don't react to it. (To us, her frictionless manner is a relief after all his carrying on.)

Despite this laughing jag, Fox, who's onscreen in every scene, keeps Jamie from being an obnoxious crybaby. Fox has cagey timing that he makes seem natural and easy, and he suggests some interior life. He's a fine actor, but he doesn't bring any spark of personality to the narration he delivers. (The fault may be in the material and in the directing.) John Houseman gives the standout performance, in the small role of the magazine's imposing editor-in-chief, his shoulders slumped in sorrow over the factual errors that Jamie has allowed to creep into the magazine. (The sly Houseman has become a comedian at eighty-five.) Jason Robards manages to make something of his skimpy part. He's a talkative, lonely old swillpot—a onetime writer, now a hanger-on in the fiction department, who guzzles vodka Martinis until his eyes glaze over. When he falls on the office floor, he goes on muttering (about the literary giants he has known) as he passes out. Robards adorns the movie; his performance is a flourish, a plume.

But the film loses its best source of characters when Jamie is fired, and it falls back on cokeheads and family. The result isn't terrible—just terribly dull. The picture has a dated quality, not only because that after-hours disco scene has dried up but because the plot mechanisms click into place without pleasure or surprise: Jamie's delayed grief over his mom (Dianne Wiest, seen in flashbacks) and the explanation that he married hoping to please her; his running away when he sees his younger brother (Charlie Schlatter), who has come to New York looking for him. The more psychology we get, the more conscious we are that the movie has no subject, except the hero's sensitivity (which the dialogue often throws into question). Frances Sternhagen plays the head of the fact-checking department—the woman who dismisses Jamie. Sternhagen makes her clenched and a stickler for company procedures, yet with anxious eyes that show how much she hates having to hurt him. But he regards her as a tyrant who's out to get him, and the picture aims for a laugh by having him say, "It's not my fault she never got married." When the question comes up of whether she uses the ladies' room or the men's, the implication is that if she weren't a butch monster she'd be so charmed by Jamie that she wouldn't mind his goofing off and not showing up for work. Lines like these make you feel how tinny the redemption scenes are. We're put through Dianne Wiest in the agonies of cancer telling her son that the pain is just like what she experienced when he was born— he didn't want to come out. And then we get Jamie leaving his blasé wife and his sleazoid pal (Kiefer Sutherland) at the party and shouting that they'd make a terrific couple. He goes out in the clear dawn air and flashes back to his mother in the kitchen with freshly baked loaves of bread. The banality comes down on you like drizzle.

All through the movie, Jamie identifies with the fetus of a woman in a coma—the "Coma Baby" featured in daily stories in the *New York Post*. Though the mother dies, the baby is delivered. But at the end of the picture when we get the jokey, symbolic headline "COMA BABY LIVES!" we may feel it refers to the audience. (There was an interval with Jamie in the apartment of a friendly co-worker, played by Swoosie Kurtz, telling her about his marriage and how hard it was for him to work on his novel, when I didn't think we'd make it.) It doesn't help that the Donald Fagen score sounds like a filler track put on while the moviemakers were waiting for the real one to be ready. And in key episodes the cinematographer, Gordon Willis, has reverted to his dark period. The atmosphere at the magazine is so sombre you wonder how the checkers can see their reference books.

April 18, 1988

ART TOUR

Colors isn't incendiary in its presentation of L.A.'s two most powerful confederations of drug-trafficking gangs—the Bloods, who wear red, and the Crips, who wear blue. The picture belongs to an honorable tradition of melodramatic muckraking, and it seems to be doing a fine job of embarrassing the L.A. city and county authorities. When one of the gang members says, "We say 'no' to drugs," it's funny—it mocks the empty, P.R. campaign promoted by the Reagan Administration. But *Colors* isn't much of a movie. Right from the beginning, it's deadened by standard cop-movie ploys. The older cop shakes his head over his new young partner's rashness and tries to impart some folk wisdom to him. Pretty soon, the older cop has his partner over to meet his wonderful family. Eventually, the younger cop passes along the "wisdom" he has learned. But before that the moviemakers tell us that the veteran cop is due for retirement, and we groan, knowing that martyrdom is hovering over him—we wait for the inevitable scene in which he'll be killed. (No, I'm not giving the plot away—unless this is the first movie you've ever seen.)

Fuddy-duddy Bob Hodges (Robert Duvall) and young Danny McGavin (Sean Penn), who likes to rough up suspects, are the only characters

460

we get to know. The director, Dennis Hopper, and the cinematographer, Haskell Wexler, try for vividness, with the camera hightailing after the fast-moving kids, and they catch images of the random violence of boys who are high on crack or PCP, carry beepers and thousands of dollars, and have arsenals of assault rifles and submachine guns. But it's an odd thing about this movie: we see dozens of gang members (or bangers) and their young recruits—the peewees—sprinting down alleys and climbing fences whenever the police come in view, and we pick up on their lingo, but we're not brought close enough to the kids themselves to be stirred by the brutal tragedy that we know they represent. TV documentaries and articles in the press have given us the outlines of what's going on, and we expect this movie to give us a feeling for the individuals caught in it. But we never get to tell the kids apart. (Some of them are actual gang members.) Instead, we get these damned quarrelling cops: Danny combing his brush-cut hair—it's like the return of Edd (Kookie) Byrnes—and Bob ashen and fair-minded.

And we get graffiti. Yes, we know by now that graffiti mark the gangs' turfs and serve as warnings to outsiders, and so on. But do the homeboys, or homes, always have to be posed hanging out in front of murals and graffiti-covered walls? *Colors* is like an art tour of ghettos and barrios, of Watts and Venice and downtown L.A. and the San Pedro waterfront. The movie is so art-conscious that when a young kid is caught with his spray can, and Danny cruelly sprays him in the face, the scene takes place against an elegant Christ figure. (Hopper himself played a scapegoat Christ in his 1971 *The Last Movie*, and that's how he casts himself in his famous Hollywood anecdotes—he fought and died for the Method.)

At the start, there's a "drive by" killing: charged up on drugs, a vanload of Crips get even higher by blowing away a Blood. Later—it seems almost unconnected with the shooting—we see the dead boy's funeral service at a storefront Pentecostal church and hear the deep-voiced minister admonishing the mourners against violence and telling them not to be afraid of those who perpetrate violence; his sermon is brought to a shocking halt when Crips drive by and spray the church with bullets. In terms of the underdramatized now-you-see-it-now-you-don't story line, this scene is perhaps too eloquently staged: the viewer has the sense of being in the midst of a major massacre and then is bewildered that there's no loss of life.

Most of the movie seems out of whack in this way: the directing is diversionary, and the events don't link up. The picture leads us to believe

461

that Danny's callousness will cause Bob's death, and then doesn't follow through. It indicates that gang members are out to get Danny, and then doesn't make anything of the black comedy that they're all killed off before they can do it. The best images are the ones that stand alone, without a plot tie-in—the ones that are visual fun, like the jailhouse scene with Bloods and Crips in adjoining holding pens, their colors swaying as the camera moves rhythmically to the rap song on the track, or the arrest of an angel-dusted guy who has a big stuffed rabbit sitting on his shoulders. But the main set pieces—such as the action after the police are tipped off that gang members have unloaded fire extinguishers full of cocaine from a Panamanian freighter, or the fight when Danny chases a murder suspect into a restaurant kitchen and grapples with him by the stove—seem detachable, as if they could be dropped into a TV cop show. That's true of most of the movie: it has no directorial personality, except for its nihilistic existentialism. The picture says that the cops' activities are purposeless and that life doesn't make any sense—the best you can hope for is to die shooting or fornicating. Hopper has some sort of identification with the romantic fatalism of his druggies, but even that isn't very strong. After about five minutes of the movie, I began wishing he were in it instead of directing it.

It would be too much, maybe, to expect Hopper, who's working with a less than inspired script, by Michael Schiffer (from a story plan devised by Schiffer and Richard DiLello), to give us a feel for the way drugs have upped the ante on youth gangs' traditional turf wars and turned the kids sociopathic, or to show us how the gang veterans who have been to prison control the gangs, and how turf becomes sales territory, and—next step—how franchises are set up. But if he's not going to try for that sick, satirical vision of the drug networks spreading across the country, shouldn't he at least do a better job of telling the cops-and-gangs action story?

Dennis Hopper is a culture hero—for making *Easy Rider* (1969), which was the fullest expression onscreen of flower-child confusions, and for being whacked out on drugs and booze and coming back. He was something of a joke in *Apocalypse Now* and *Rumble Fish*, but in *Blue Velvet* he's a master. Even in a vignette role in *Black Widow*, he manages to wear his myth gracefully and use it for an ironic inflection. Here, though, as a director, he isn't inside the material: he doesn't bring us to a fuller consciousness of gang life (or of police life, either). He's a visual aesthete—less a director than an artistic arranger of people in the frame.

If *Colors* were turned into a book of still photographs, it might look charged with graphic energy. As it is, despite its kinetic style it feels slow and long and tame. We're turned into passive voyeurs: we get a look at gang violence without being asked to become emotionally involved. The movie appears to assume that we couldn't get interested in the black and Hispanic characters.

As a Chicana who works at a fast-food stand, Maria Conchita Alonso has a sparky visual introduction: Danny, who's in his car with Bob, looks at her, and the camera gives her the once-over, likes what it sees, and lingers on her devastating eyes, her open smile, her capacity for happiness. But this intro is virtually all the role she has; after that, she dates Danny, is seen visiting with Bob's wife and holding the baby, and so on, until she's repelled by Danny's brutality to her relatives, and her eyes cloud over. Sean Penn tries to suggest the ugliness of machismo—tries to make Danny an ordinary-guy sadist. But the writing doesn't give him the underpinnings he needs, and he seems able to reach into himself only sporadically. As for Duvall, he's turning to stone. He's supposed to be a simple, average cop who's trying to take it easy his last year on the force, but he's more intense than Penn. His concentration is scary: you don't know what it's for. He brings his role presence and technique and an absolute lack of easygoing dailiness. He's a powerful actor and he bores me blind.

■

Animals howl very softly during the opening titles of Dominique Deruddere's *Love Is a Dog from Hell*. The whole film is soft, muted, tactful, and this has a certain piquancy, since it tells the story of Harry Vos, whose love for women is unrequited for all of his short life, and who finds sexual fulfillment only at the end, when he tenderly—almost reverently—caresses a lovely corpse, and mounts her. This Belgian film, which is based on stories by Charles Bukowski, principally "The Copulating Mermaid of Venice, California," isn't like the rowdy Bukowski-derived movies—the wild, lusty 1981 *Tales of Ordinary Madness* and the 1987 *Barfly*—that European directors made in English, with L.A. settings. It's a Flemish-language art film with its own erotic tone—faintly ironic, faintly queasy. That softness gets to you.

463

The three episodes span Harry's life, starting with his sexual awakening. In 1955, the twelve-year-old Harry (Geert Hunaerts) sits in a movie theatre, his eyes glistening with fervor as he watches a gorgeous blond princess in a white gown come running toward the camera, her royal breasts bobbling. After the handsome knight wins her hand, and Harry leaves the theatre, he steals a still of the princess-star from the display case. Back home on his farm, he talks to his amused mother about how his father (who looks like a slug) must have vanquished her other suitors. He has a pal who teaches him a few of the harsher practicalities of sex, but when these two sneak into the house of a bawd who's asleep and his pal urges him to climb onto her he leaps on her too enthusiastically; she screams and, in terror, he screams back. (It's a high comic moment, like the screeching in *The Bride of Frankenstein* and in *E.T.*) Defeated, he watches the pal's demonstration of how to masturbate, and goes home and uses the still of the princess to set him off. The movie doesn't show us any masturbation; the sounds tell us what's going on, and, at climax, the shadow of rain on the window turns into tears that roll down little Harry's face.

In the second episode, in 1962, Harry (Josse De Pauw) is a gangling nineteen and about to graduate from high school. He writes love poetry—especially to his dream-girl classmate, the blond Liza—but for the past two years his face and neck have been covered with acne and boils and pustules. At the graduation ball, the girls recoil from dancing with him, and we empathize with them. Poor Harry—he has the harmless look of the scrawny young Alec Guinness, but it's as if his erotic need had burst out in craters and volcanoes. His skin has turned against him. And as he stands around alone or talking to a pal, we watch the sensual, weaving motions of the vocalist with the band. The American pop tunes ("Love Hurts," "Angel Baby," "I Love How You Love Me") are subdued, but they have a casual, narcissistic zing. The girl singer (Micheline Van Houtem), who wears her hair piled high, off her forehead, has the fresh-faced look of the young Joan Leslie in *High Sierra*—a vacuous, self-absorbed sexiness. And the music, her movements, the cheek-to-cheek couples all seem designed to torture the lovesick Harry, who's dying to dance with Liza. He goes to the men's room and returns with his disgusting sores concealed in a toilet-paper version of a knight's helmet (or the Invisible Man's wrappings). Confidently, he asks Liza to dance; she consents, and they move together in rhythmic surrender to the music. He's fulfilling longings he's had ever since he watched the princess. He returns Liza to her table, tears off the toilet paper, goes out and gets drunk on stolen

464

liquor, and is arrested. This is the best sequence—it has a masochistic potency, and some humor and rage.

Its power may have surprised the young Deruddere, because he'd made the third section first, as a half-hour short, and then (with his co-writer Marc Didden) worked up the two sections of Harry's earlier life in order to make a feature—his first. He didn't shoot the early life until two years after he'd completed the short. This final episode, set in 1976, when Harry is a thirty-three-year-old alcoholic bum, his life destroyed by his failure with women, is a little too shapely—too much the sensitive short story. (It might work better on its own, without the prehistory that explains it so neatly.) It's almost straight Bukowski, but without the grungy harshness that rubs up against some of Bukowski's sentimentality. Josse De Pauw's Harry has horsy teeth now, and a cynical, seedy look—there's a touch of Nicol Williamson about him. After a long night of drinking, he and a pal who's just out of jail have glommed on to a bottle and are ready for anything. Just for the hell of it, they steal a corpse from a van that's taking it from the hospital to the mortuary. When they uncover it and see that it's a warm, resilient young blond woman (the corpse is played by Florence Beliard, who was the movie-star princess), Harry gets his chance to express the passion he still holds inside him. His lovemaking suggests a sacred rite, and his expression changes—he seems exalted.

It may appear a little loony to complain that this necrophiliac sequence is too poetic, but, with Harry reciting marriage vows to the corpse, it's almost as misty and romantic as that princess movie. It glides by in a lyrical trance. You're asked to identify with Harry's pure emotions, though these warm-corpse scenes are just a few tones away from being a parody of an adolescent fantasy. You're also made to think pseudo-deep thoughts about the way living women reject men's sexual needs, particularly if the men aren't conventionally handsome. (Deruddere didn't have to look farther than the cratered face in Bukowski's book-jacket photos to select the disfigurement for Harry.) *Love Is a Dog from Hell*—the European title is *Crazy Love*—makes too many points. But it's a movie for people with a perverse sense of humor or a persistent sexual acne—a low-keyed sexual reverie. At the high-school dance, it's pop music that makes the kids make out. And in having Harry's pals accept him when the girls can't, or won't, the movie touches on sexual mysteries. The high-school pal isn't put off by Harry's boils, and understands Harry's bitterness when he drinks and turns nasty. The high-school girls see that skin and imagine it touching theirs, and it's the essence of all the hairy coarse-

465

ness and threat that boys represent. The girls are dreaming of a Rob Lowe, with skin as smooth as their own.

May 2, 1988

RED ON RED

||||||||||||||||||||||||||||||||||||||||||||||||||||||||||||||||||||||||||||||||||||||||||||||||||||||||||||||||||||||||||||||||||||||||||||||||||||||||

Glamorous, impossibly passionate, hyperbolic romance is integral to the pleasure of the movies, and it seeps into the consciousness of moviegoers the world over. The Spanish writer-director Pedro Almodóvar makes hot comedies in which the characters act out the wildest fantasies they've absorbed, or, like the handsome, wealthy Ángel (Antonio Banderas) in *Matador*, try to act them out, and embarrass themselves. Ángel thinks he loves danger, and he's training to be a bullfighter, but he faints at the sight of blood. When his instructor, a famous retired matador, suggests that he may be homosexual, the virginal Ángel, wearing a red sweater, attempts to rape the matador's enticing young mistress—a fashion model who knows him. (She lives next door.) But Ángel has trouble with the pocketknife he holds at her throat: he gets the corkscrew out instead of the blade. And he can't consummate the rape—he ejaculates prematurely. She slaps him in contempt, and when she's walking off and trips, bruising her cheek, he passes out. Ángel is such a supreme fantasist that he hallucinates and sees what happened in a recent series of murders. Unluckily, he's fantasist enough to think that he committed them. *Matador* is all lush, clownish excess. Everything is eroticized—the colors, the violence. It's all too much—it's sumptuously sick and funny, with hair ornaments used as daggers, tall women in swirling cloaks, and love rites performed on the matador's hot-pink cape spread fanlike on the floor. It's a dizzy bash. It doesn't have the purring wit of Almodóvar's *Law of Desire*, but, then, *Matador* was made earlier.

Almodóvar's movies are opening in this country in something like reverse order. After his 1987 *Law of Desire* we might have expected to see the 1988 *Women on the Verge of a Nervous Breakdown*, which is playing in Spain. Instead, his earlier films are arriving. This gives us a

466

chance to catch up on his development and see the leaps he's been making. Movie-nourished though it is, the 1986 *Matador* has its splendors, but the 1983 convent farce *Dark Habits* gets to be a rather labored series of jokes. Still, Almodóvar already had the disreputable sensuality that links him to early De Palma.

Under the opening titles of *Dark Habits* we see Madrid in the evening, with the headlights of cars on a long, winding thoroughfare, and as we read the titles the night life seems to get going full blast—the traffic grows heavier and the winding street is pure white light. Visually, nothing that follows lives up to the magic vibration of this image, but there's always something frisky to look at. *Dark Habits*—its Spanish name is *Entre Tinieblas*, and the picture is sometimes referred to as *Dark Hideout* or *Sisters of Darkness*—shows us Almodóvar's naughty-Catholic-schoolboy side. (Here, and in his other movies, he uses Catholic fetishism as camp.) In a night club, an entertainer named Yolanda (Cristina S. Pascual), a bottle blonde in tarty, glittering red, is so doped up she can't remember the lyrics of the pop tune she's singing. She has to be prompted, like a schoolchild with stagefright. When two police officers show up backstage to question her about her lover's death, she scrams and—still in her strapless dress—takes refuge with a small, declining order of nuns, the Humble Redeemers.

This convent in the middle of the city specializes in the salvation of murderesses, prostitutes, and junkies, but it has been having a hard time getting recruits. The genteel Mother Superior (Julieta Serrano) is so avid for resident sinners that she'll shoot them up with heroin and supply anything else they want. (She's a junkie herself.) Sister Damned—Carmen Maura, the frustrated cleaning woman in Almodóvar's 1984 *What Have I Done to Deserve This!* and the transsexual heroine of *Law of Desire*—has a husky voice and a big smile. She's the middle figure in a trio of singing nuns, and she looks chaste and demure when she accompanies the songs on her bongo drums; she also beats the drums for her pet tiger, with whom she has conjugal relations. Sister Rat—Chus Lampreave, a regular in Almodóvar's stock company—writes sexy novels based on the lives of the girls who have been in residence. The convent chef, Sister Manure, who was a murderess, drops acid, and Sister Snake designs fancy clothes (her lover, the chaplain, is a devotee of Cecil Beaton's work, especially the costumes for *My Fair Lady*). It all ties together fairly amusingly, but it's not much more than a curiosity—Almodóvar's first film with a real budget. He catches something very appealing, though, in the casual musical numbers: Yolanda and the Mother Superior taking

467

turns singing along to a song on the radio, and the convent party where the three musical nuns serve as backup singers for Yolanda. Carmen Maura at her bongos is a shiny-faced imp, a dadaist clown—which, of course, is what Almodóvar himself is. We're witnessing the director and his star finding each other.

Almodóvar demonstrates his clown side when he turns up in *Matador* as a mad-genius couturier who messes up his curly hair before he appears in public. Supervising the preparations for a fashion show, the couturier orders the model who has been bruised not to conceal it with makeup, and when a model (who has just shot up) pukes on another girl's gown he loves the puke.

Almodóvar's movies are an outburst of a post-Franco hedonistic spirit; in a sense, they're all midnight movies. *Matador*, which opens with horrible, slasher images on a VCR—crimes against women—that the retired, gored bullfighter masturbates to, stuns you for a few seconds before it makes you laugh. *Matador* is a kicky comedy about sex fantasies. It takes off from the lovers killing each other in the operatic climax of *Duel in the Sun*. Two of the characters watch that love-death together, and recognize their fate. (Yes, it's trashy, but brazenly so; this trashiness has its own poetry and bravura.) Sexual pleasure and killing are scrambled in the psyches of the bullfighter (Nacho Martínez), who since being gored can only teach his art, and the woman attorney (Assumpta Serna) who is his greatest fan. She defends the deluded Ángel, after he confesses to the murders he has seen in his visions.

Ángel the clairvoyant sees other people's crimes as his own: there's a surreal dream logic here. And the irrationality feels surprisingly spontaneous. Some of the scenes don't quite spring to life, but the bright, carnal color and Madrid locations carry you along. They suggest a fantasia of passion, and Almodóvar brings it impudence, and an enthusiasm for moviemaking that's contagious. *Matador* is a piece of voluptuous tomfoolery, with poison mushrooms popping out of shallow graves. At the moment of greatest suspense, when the police inspector (Eusebio Poncela), the police psychiatrist (Carmen Maura), Ángel, and the model, whom, it turns out, he'd tried to rape three or four times in the past, are rushing to prevent a double murder, they pause to observe a solar eclipse. (It's like a prank from one of Buñuel's late films.) This gagster director gets the audience heated up and then he cracks a joke. Not everybody can laugh—a lot of taboos are violated. But romantics, who will experience the worst shocks, may love the giddiness of giving in—they'll understand that the director is one of them.

Some of the jokes are old theatrical routines, perfectly timed. Ángel lives with his venomous mother (Julieta Serrano), who belongs to a pious right-wing organization. Almost every time she refers to his dead father, she speaks a blessing—"May he rest in peace"—but she spits out the words like a curse. The visual gags are often just a flash in the sunlight—like the shine of a bullfighting student's tight pants when the police inspector, who has an eye for young men, visits the school. (The timing isn't as deft when the inspector moves on to the bullring where the kids work out, and the camera goes right to their crotches.) The jokes may be as suggestive as the horsetail braid worn by the woman attorney—it swishes from side to side.

Assumpta Serna (she was the tall, loose-limbed beauty in Carlos Saura's 1981 *Sweet Hours*) is playing a culmination of the scarlet-woman tradition of Joan Crawford, Rita Hayworth, Ava Gardner, and Anouk Aimée—all those flaming man-killers with their too vibrant smiles. Assumpta Serna wears the earrings of a magnificent nympho; at one point, she stands posed high up on an iron grillwork bridge, her brilliantly colored silks blowing in the wind, and the friend with me said, "It's James M. Cain on mushrooms." Stretched out on his cape with this powerhouse woman, the gored matador holds a red rose in his teeth and uses it in his lovemaking. Almodóvar takes the two-lovers-destined-for-each-other theme and the two-killers-who-can't-stop-themselves-from-killing theme as far as his imagination will go, and that's pretty far. He reactivates the clichés of film noir and brings them into the land of punk. He finds an obsessive angle on everything, even if it's just the way he points the camera at Assumpta Serna coming down in a wrought-iron elevator. At least he's crazy.

May 16, 1988

ZONE POEM

Seen through the eyes of two angels who hover over the city blocks, Berlin is in tinted black-and-white. The image suggests metal, with a little of the lustre of old coins or tarnished silverware. And as the camera wafts in and out of airplanes, and into rooms high up in apartment buildings, and the angels observe the forlorn, dissociated lives of people who live in reverie, it's as if black-and-white itself had petered out—as if the movie image was exhausted. What you see has a bluish-green softness, and it's clear enough, but it feels at a remove; it's a reminder of an image. *Wings of Desire*—the original title of this Franco-German production is *Der Himmel über Berlin*, which means the heaven, or sky, over Berlin—has the look of a dupe of a dupe. That look is telling you that movies are now ghosts of themselves.

The director, Wim Wenders, who wrote the script with the collaboration of Peter Handke, has a theme: in an approximation of Rilke's words, "Joy has gone astray." We're told that "when the child was a child," stories held together. Now all we have is fragmentation, entropy. And a sad-faced old man called Homer (Curt Bois) wanders through the ruins of the old metropolis trying to keep its story alive; his thoughts trigger flashbacks to Nazi atrocities.

The two angels—Damiel (Bruno Ganz) and Cassiel (Otto Sander)—roam through the bleak concrete buildings of the divided city; its ugliness is almost abstract. Wearing suits and overcoats, the two observers look like civil servants, except for their ponytails. They pick up scraps of stories as they move unseen among desolate individuals, listening to what's in their minds—listening to the questions about existence that these people ask themselves. The angels have a poetic presence: they're antennae for the thoughts of anonymous Berliners who can't speak what they think. (There are no emotional outbursts; the people's interior dialogues are detailed, measured, accurate—as if they could describe something only by its exact dimensions.) The angel Damiel's face is infinitely compassionate, and the angel Cassiel knits his brow in worry; these two are in a muzzy state of empathy for everyone, everything. And they listen with the patience and concern of a seraphic, neutered uncle. Children can see them, and some grownups know when they're around—those who are childlike at heart (moviegoers, perhaps, and Americans), those who aren't split asunder, and still have the ability to feel things directly.

For about forty-five minutes, the mood of the opening shots is sustained. Our overhearing what the angels hear—the thoughts chanted on the track, all in even, quiet tones, as grayed out as the sunless skies—works on us like a tranquillizer. The dim whimsy, the recitations of prose poetry that recall the Beats—it all produces a blissed-out stupor that feels vaguely avant-garde. And this movie, which is dedicated to Ozu, Tarkovsky, and Truffaut, is full of charming (and almost charming) conceits, such as the angels' attentiveness to the murmur of thought in the modern, fluorescent-lighted state library building. (It suggests *Alphaville* with lead weights on the camera.) This is where solitary people—who look as if they were forgotten by the world—come to read and to walk among the books. (These walkers recall the book memorizers in *Fahrenheit 451.*)

The film can hatch conceits in viewers. The angels can make you feel as if you're walking around in the presence of an absent world, in the presence of people you've known. And when you see the angels listening to the people's thoughts you may miss someone to whisper your feelings about the movie to. You have plenty of time for musing while looking at this after-the-apocalypse city, scarred by the Wall—the dividing line of two powers, and the symbol of the divided souls.

Wings of Desire constantly articulates the impossibility of finding any meaning in anything. At the same time, it's a love-story message movie. The angels, in their apartness and in their distress over the spiritual emptiness of the people, are like the cliché kind of intellectuals. Then Damiel, drooping from the sameness of his everlasting rounds and the ennui of seeing in monochromatic tones, eavesdrops on the thoughts of Marion (Solveig Dommartin), a beautiful, lonely French aerialist who's dressed as an angel with feather wings, and performs in a tacky circus. (She recalls Merna Kennedy in Chaplin's *The Circus* and Nastassja Kinski in Coppola's *One from the Heart.*) She goes to a punk-rock club, and Damiel watches her there, dancing by herself, gyrating, her manner zombielike. When he sits among the children who are entranced by her trapeze work, this Chaplinesque girl awakens him to childish joy—of what it's like to believe in the magic of trapeze artists. He feels the stirrings of desire, and he sees her in color. He begins to long for the ordinary pleasures—to hold an apple in his hand, to drink a cup of hot coffee. When he turns in his wings—so to speak—and plunges to earth, he has a new spring in his walk. The film breaks into full color, and he goes to find his aerialist.

He searches the city for her, and she searches, too, for she knows not whom, and they meet in the bar that adjoins the punk club. There, looking right at the camera, Marion speaks to Damiel for the first time, and it's an oration. She goes on and on, declaiming—giving voice to her romantic, enigmatic thoughts in the affectless tone that he found so fetch-

471

ing when he listened to the workings of her mind. (It's as if Merna Kennedy, at the end of the silent *The Circus*, started to speechify.) And she faces the audience and challenges us to take our voyages. *Gott im Himmel!*

A friend of mine says that he loved every second of this movie and he couldn't wait to leave. To put it simply, *Wings of Desire* has a visual fascination but no animating force—that's part of why it's being acclaimed as art. The film's lassitude—the way shots are held for small eternities, and the action seems to begin every three or four minutes—suggests some purpose beyond narrative, suggests that you're experiencing the psychic craving of the Berliners as they drift through their chilly days, searching to be whole again. It's a sluggish, weary-winged fable; it seems to be saying that if you're a grownup living in postwar Germany a reminder of childish joy is the most you can hope for. The halfhearted coming together of Damiel and Marion is a fairy tale that we're not quite meant to believe; the film's tone of high German woe certainly indicates that. Even if Wenders wants to believe it, his moviemaking betrays him: the color sections are tawdry compared with the spooky spirituality of the black-and-white passages. The film's meaning appears to be: We Germans recognize in ourselves a forever-to-be-unfulfilled wish for connectedness.

The only character with any pep is an American, played by Peter Falk, who is starring in a Nazi-period film that's being shot on the site of an actual Second World War bunker. Falk—he's called by his own name—enjoys the pleasures of simple sensory gratifications. With his big noggin and the gruff mischief in the way he plays along with the other characters, he's solidly American. (And he's a relief from Ganz's poignancy; there's so much of it that it gnaws at you.) Falk is the only free agent in the whole movie: when he takes a step, he really wants to go where he's heading. Even when he soliloquizes like the Berliners, his thoughts are practical; they have a funky warmth. (In interviews, Wenders says that Falk wrote this material himself.)

My guess is that the Falk subplot is in the picture mainly because Wenders loves American movies and the people connected with them. But, if I read Wenders right, he's also suggesting (as he has in the past) that movies are the American language, and that American movies (and rock) have colonized the Germans, causing another rift in their consciousness. He's saying, "How lucky the Americans are—they didn't suffer the way we did." He knows he can't make movies that race along, that are all narrative, studded with personalities. He's got his Rilke and that scar of castration, the Wall. The whole movie is saying, "If only I could express myself like a child or an American moviemaker! Then I could unify the divided German soul, or, at least, my own soul."

But, of course, Wenders doesn't get into the spirit of popular art. When he uses a pop form, it's lifeless—a simulation of ascetic high art. Marion is lovely, but on her last night with the circus, when she and one of the roustabouts at the outdoor farewell party sing together, Wenders seems to have just plopped them there. He names the circus for his celebrated cinematographer, Henri Alekan (and includes allusions to Cocteau's 1946 *Beauty and the Beast*, which Alekan shot), yet from the sound of the laughter of the children who are supposed to be showing their joy at the circus they've got infant doses of Weltschmerz. The punk-club scenes are so rhythmless and desolate that they're almost a parody of German anguish. And I have misgivings about Wenders' including actual atrocity pictures; it's as if he wanted to fortify his sense of defeat, his enervation. But then this is a movie with depressive angels—a notion worthy of Tarkovsky (for whom the whole universe was depressive).

Wenders films what makes him feel impotent. Yet he wants to inspire us: when Damiel and Marion embrace, Wenders wants to light a candle in our hearts, or, at least, half a candle. It's this torchbearer Wenders who uses such corny devices as having the children be able to see the angels; he even has a little crippled girl who smiles at Damiel. Sentimentality and meaninglessness: postmodern kitsch. It's enough to make moviegoers feel impotent.

■

George Lucas, who produced *Willow*, says, "It's a pure fantasy film that came out of my psyche." Maybe only a movie mogul can believe that he's the source of the world's treasury of legends and movies. If you took Bible stories and *Peter Pan* and *Robin Hood* and the *Oz* books and the Grimm Brothers' fairy tales and *Gulliver's Travels* and *Lord of the Rings* and *Ran* and *Snow White and the Seven Dwarfs* (and the *Star Wars* trilogy) and put them in a hopper and spun it around until it was a whirring mess of porridge, you'd have the mythical-medieval *Willow*, or something close to it. The evil sorceress Queen Bavmorda (Jean Marsh)

473

is killing all the newborn babies in the Daikini domain, because of a prophecy that an infant born with a special mark will bring about her downfall. The savior baby girl is sneaked away to the forest by a midwife, and after she has been put on a raft of rushes she drifts downriver into the land of a peaceful, elflike people, the Nelwyns. Willow (Warwick Davis), a young Nelwyn farmer, takes her back to Daikini territory and tries to protect her. Eventually, with the help of a Daikini scalawag, the swordsman Madmartigan (Val Kilmer), and a rebel Daikini, Airk (Gavan O'Herlihy), Willow storms the evil queen's black castle. (Queen Bavmorda's armies are led by a Darth Vader–like giant in a death's-head mask, General Kael—an *hommage à moi*.)

There are said to be about four hundred special-effects shots (from Lucas's Industrial Light & Magic), but they're not prepared for dramatically, and there's no feeling of wonder in them. When vicious black boars tear the midwife apart, or when a bunch of little platinum-wigged Tinker Bells flit about, or nine-inch-tall men called Brownies scurry around, or the baby is on a shield that rockets down mountain after mountain, or men and women are transformed into pigs, you feel as if you'd fallen into a pile of mixed metaphors. Disguised in a dress, Madmartigan does a drag act; later, the queen's beautiful warrior daughter (Joanne Whalley) threatens to castrate him; two of the Brownies bustle about like miniature Catskills comics. It's doubtful if any action-adventure director has a strong enough style to give this script (by Bob Dolman, based on Lucas's story) a tone and a shape, and Ron Howard, who's got the job, is lost. When the death's-head general, holding the baby aloft, gallops through the troops on his black horse, slashing right and left, and crying out "No mercy! No mercy!," there isn't any real threat in it. And at the climax, when the baby (crying) is on a high altar, about to be slaughtered, while the evil sorceress queen battles with a good sorceress—it's like *Johnny Guitar*—you're too embarrassed for the moviemakers to feel any suspense.

Ron Howard shows his gentle talent only in his handling of Willow: the three-foot-four-inch Warwick Davis has a sweet-faced humility, which could make parts of the movie appealing to kids. It's always great to see Billy Barty. He plays the High Aldwin of the Nelwyns; i.e., he's Gandalf delivering the message: You have to believe in yourself. The baby (played by Ruth and Kate Greenfield) has endearing little drops of drool hanging from her lip, and the decorative use of chain mail is very chic. But maybe George Lucas should believe less in himself—he keeps trying to come up with an original idea, and he can't. Yet something from his psyche does come through: Lucas, who has undergone a costly divorce, has made a sword-and-sorcery epic in which all the power is in the hands of women.

May 30, 1988

OUTSIDE

||||||||||||||||||||||||||||||||||||||||||||||||||||||||||||||||||||||||||||||||||||||||||||||||||||||||||||||||||||||||||||||||||||||||||||||||||||||||||||||||||||||||||||||||||||||||

Diana Roth (Barbara Hershey) and Gus Roth (Jeroen Krabbé) live in a fine middle-class home in suburban Johannesburg, and they give their thirteen-year-old daughter, Molly (Jodhi May), and her two little sisters a well-ordered, ruling-class life. The polite, well-bred Molly attends a girls' school and takes Spanish-dancing lessons. But Gus is a Communist, and at the beginning of *A World Apart* he flees the country in the middle of the night to escape arrest. The children are told that he's gone away on business. Diana, the editor of a small anti-apartheid newspaper, is straight-backed in the tailored suits she wears to work. She thinks she's protecting the children by not telling them anything; she's a closemouthed woman anyway.

A World Apart, which is set in 1963, is told from Molly's point of view. It's based on a semi-autobiographical script by Shawn Slovo, the daughter of the journalist Ruth First and Joe Slovo, the leader of the banned South African Communist Party, who at that time was also one of the top figures in the African National Congress. Molly's mother, Diana, is an officious, starchy woman who's caught up in subversive activities. This is made pointedly clear early on, when Molly, who has witnessed a bloody hit-and-run accident—a white motorist smashing a black bicyclist—tries to tell her mother what she has seen, and her busy mother doesn't register what the girl is saying, or that she's upset. And when Solomon (Albee Lesotho), a black leader who has been imprisoned, turns up at the Roth home—his sister Elsie (Linda Mvusi) is the maid— Diana greets him with a warmth she never shows her kids. Diana isn't guilty of noblesse oblige. It's that the injustices done to the blacks heat her up—set her on fire. And her activities on their behalf keep her wound tight; they've given her an ulcer. One night, a few seconds before she goes into an illegal meeting she's warned, and she walks away just as the police arrive with straining-at-the-leash German shepherds; she moves quickly—she's not one to lounge around. There's too much to be done.

Diana isn't a bad mother, but the energy and thought that she gives to forbidden activities have drained her of some of her alertness as a mother, and Molly feels shut out. She has to eavesdrop to learn what's going on.

This is the first feature directed by the English documentarian and cinematographer Chris Menges (pronounced men-ghees), who has become well known as the director of photography on such films as *Local Hero*, *The Killing Fields*, *The Mission*, and *High Season*. Menges, who was born in 1940, worked in Johannesburg in 1963, as a cameraman for Granada TV's *World in Action* series, but in *A World Apart* he uses Zimbabwe for South Africa. (That's also where *Cry Freedom* and the TV film *Mandela* were shot.) Most cinematographers who direct fiction films get carried away into pictorialism, but Menges retains the speed and precision of a news cameraman. The movie has a visual snap to it. It's luminous yet very informal. The subversives test themselves against the will of the authorities, and the camera catches the immediacy of their fear, their guesswork.

We see Diana only from the outside, as Molly perceives her or imagines her, but we get a sense of her gallantry and recklessness from some of the things she does—such as giving herself a large interracial birthday celebration, where a black man sings "Let's Twist Again," and Molly and her best friend, Yvonne (Nadine Chalmers), dance along with the mostly black guests, who have to spill out their drinks in a hurry when the police arrive with flashbulb cameras and the inevitable menacing dogs. Confronting them, Diana is flushed and contemptuous; she's rather grand— a bourgeois woman not used to having her guests insulted. Diana's cavalier manner carries her through a nasty scene with the police when she's covering an early-morning work interruption at a power station, but shortly afterward they crack down: she's "detained" for ninety days, and then sentenced to another ninety days. And though the children's grandmother, Mrs. Abrahams (Yvonne Bryceland), comes to help out, and the reliable Elsie is there, Molly's life falls apart. Her schoolmates have been taunting her about her Communist-traitor father, and now that her mother is imprisoned she's no longer welcome at her friend Yvonne's house. Worst of all, she's confused and resentful, because her parents have never discussed their anti-apartheid work in front of her, never explained anything to her—they've treated her like a baby. (And in some ways she *is* one. When the police take Diana away, Molly whimpers, "Mummy, please don't go.")

In her cell, Diana hoists herself up to look out the high, barred window and sees the city traffic outside. And we feel her horror at being trapped. Yet she's ladylike and stiff when she's taken in for interrogation; her thick, curly dark hair is neat, her jaw set, her mouth firmly lipsticked. The daughter is just about the opposite. Molly, as Jodhi May plays her, is undefined in a lovely, almost plain, yet softly glowing way—like the young Peggy Ann Garner in *Jane Eyre* and *A Tree Grows in Brooklyn*. Molly has been raised to respect blacks, and she's sensitive enough to appreciate what she has taken in from her parents. She has an eager mind, and we get glimpses of what she learns, what she thinks. Menges, with his camera, is her co-conspirator: he peeks into things, he's open to moments of revelation. She's his fresh, young pair of eyes, looking at Yvonne's buxom blond mother, who's all kissy-kissy, and seeing that the woman is good-hearted but weak, and afraid of her husband. And the camera records Molly's perceptions of the ugliness of apartheid. She wants to join in the fight against it, yet that fight is also her competitor. In prison or out, her mother is not all there for her. When Molly needs her mom, she bashes her head against a principled person. The theme of the movie is the conflict between fighting injustice and what we owe to our families—or, more poignantly, a young girl's pain at the loss of her mother and father, though she knows the reasons for it.

Jodhi May's performance seems just about faultless—never precocious, never forced. Molly is a kid who's required to grow up fast, and has a rough time of it, but her difficulties never go out of scale. And Barbara Hershey does well by the British–South African accent and gives a creditable, honorable performance. If something is missing from what she does, it may be partly because Menges looks at Diana as if she were a person in a documentary; he seems content with the script's outside view of her. And—what's more central—Hershey's conception is too narrow. Watching Diana is like looking at a series of newspaper shots of Ethel Rosenberg. Molly might think that this public Diana was all there was, but for the movie to have real dramatic power Diana needs to reveal to us what her young daughter can't see. I know I'm asking a lot—a great actress, one who could have helped us find out how Diana's involvement in the struggle became her life, and what she was like before she set her jaw. When Diana, who has been released from prison but is under house arrest, learns that Solomon, the black activist, has been tortured and killed, she boldly appears at his funeral, flanked by her mother and

477

by Molly. No doubt we're supposed to see that she now accepts her daughter as a sentient human being. But we also see that she's willing to return to prison and shatter her family. And we never penetrate the sources of her political flamboyance. A woman who loves humanity so much that she has only a small corner of her heart left for her children has to be something more than rigid and reserved; we never get to her substance.

But the movie itself has substance. At the funeral, the faces of the black mourners—and especially Elsie's grief—are like found art. Here—and elsewhere—Menges achieves the kind of documentary beauty that tricks your subconscious: you feel you're watching the real thing. The cinematographer Haskell Wexler has sometimes done this, but his directors held on to the image—turned it into a still. Menges and his lighting cameraman, Peter Biziou, and his editor, Nicolas Gaster, pass over the images so fleetly that you don't even have time to exclaim or to retain them—all you have is the emotion.

Menges is a wonderful moviemaker, with a deficiency. It isn't a matter of craft; it's that he doesn't trust us. Throughout the movie, the treatment of the whites is balanced: even Diana's interrogator (David Suchet) has conflicting feelings about her and is upset when she's abused. But there's no conflict in the blacks: they're clean and loving. It's the old movie quirk of making it appear that oppression is good for the soul. (What's behind it seems to be the fear that if the oppressed are presented as less than noble the audience will think they're getting what they deserve—will somehow blame them for their oppression.) And at the end Menges violates the mother-daughter story in order to tell us what he's already shown us: that apartheid is obscenely cruel. At the funeral, when the minister makes a defiant speech, and the crowd, including Diana and Molly, raise their fists and chant back and forth *"Amandla! Awethu!"* (Power! Is Ours!), and the police arrive by car and helicopter and start firing tear gas, it makes us feel hollow. We know we're meant to see that the Roths are united with each other and with the blacks. We know we're supposed to be raising our fists with theirs. And the film's radiant intelligence slips away—to be recalled, luckily, when we leave the theatre.

■

*L*ady in White is a ghost movie with an overcomplicated plot, but it has a poetic feeling that makes up for much of the clutter. And its amateurishness often adds to its effectiveness—gives the movie a naïve power. The amateurishness helps you to open your imagination to it. (There's nothing slick to repel you.) The picture was written and directed by Frank LaLoggia, who also composed the score; the location shooting was done in the upstate New York town of Lyons, near Rochester, where LaLoggia was born, and the first two million of the five-million-dollar budget was raised from four thousand investors in the area, many of whom appear in the crowd scenes. The movie is an elaboration of local legends, LaLoggia's childhood memories, and his fantasies of the supernatural. It's a piece of Catholic Americana with a Disney-Spielberg ingenuousness and shafts of horror.

Lukas Haas, the dark-eyed child from *Witness*, is the star. As the nine-year-old Frankie Scarlatti, who dreams of his dead mother, he has a quizzical expression much of the time, and those eyes widen to perfect circles. It all starts on Halloween, 1962, in the fictional town of Willowpoint Falls, when a couple of prankish schoolmates lock Frankie in the school cloakroom and he sees the ghost of a little girl who was murdered by a serial killer. Nothing happens that you haven't seen before, but the boy's rapt belief in his visions lends credibility to the events. In an underdeveloped way, you get a sense that the horrors that beset him relate to his mother's having died—that the story has psychological roots. And there are touches that charm you: the piles of candy corn in the window of the Kandy Kitchen; the pack of dogs that chase after bicyclists but are turned back by a nun's basilisk glare; a jack-o'-lantern left burning in a schoolroom until Frankie blows it out; a scary moment when he's in bed with lighted candles all around, and an ancient madwoman who leans over to kiss him is suddenly yanked away from behind by the killer. And there's endearing, giggly tomfoolery between Frankie and his older brother (Jason Presson). LaLoggia puts on a good show. He has an affection for Maxfield Parrish effects and for such devices as having the little-girl ghost, who's searching for her mother, find her, and then having them both turn into shooting stars flying Heavenward. The editing is patchy, and LaLoggia lingers on actors in a way that exposes their limitations (and his inexperience), but little Lukas Haas has no problem. He loves acting so much that when he's miming spooked terror he's tickled to be doing it. He gives himself the shivers, and probably grins when the director calls for retakes.

June 13, 1988

SUNSHINE

||||||||||||||||||||||||||||||||||||||||||||||||||||||||||||||||||||||||||||||||||||||||||||||||||||||||||||||||||||||||||||

Named for the tobacco, the romantic comedy *Bull Durham* has the kind of dizzying off-center literacy that Preston Sturges' pictures had. It's a satirical celebration of our native jauntiness and wit; it takes us into a subculture that's like a bawdy adjunct of childhood—minor-league baseball. Everybody in it is a comic character, and uses a pop lingo that you tune into without any trouble, though you can't quite believe the turns of phrase you're hearing. You're thrown just enough to do a double take, and recover in time to do another.

As the catcher Crash Davis, who has been playing for twelve years and no longer stands a chance of making it to the majors, Kevin Costner comes through with his first wide-awake, star performance. He keeps you on his side from his very first scene. Crash arrives in Durham, North Carolina, to join the Durham Bulls and gets pretty sore when he's told that he's been brought in to train a wild young rookie pitcher, Ebby (Nuke) LaLoosh (Tim Robbins), who is destined to move up. Crash gets thoroughly disgusted when he sees the woman he's attracted to—the baseball fanatic Annie Savoy (Susan Sarandon)—take this raw kid Nuke on for the season as her lover, the player she'll educate in bed and on the field. Crash is stranded—an old-timer in his early thirties—but there's no pathos in the role. As Costner plays the part, he's hyper-articulate, smart, and cocky. Costner lets you see that Crash is lonely, but he underplays the loneliness; it's just a tone blended in with his other tones. And Annie is no ordinary sports fan. She's a high priestess of baseball who has her own scorecard: "There's never been a ballplayer slept with me who didn't have the best year of his career."

Crash and Annie supply wisecracking wit. Nuke, a six-foot-four-inch pixie with a hopeful, dimpled grin, supplies physical slapstick, twisting himself into curlicues on the field and off. Tim Robbins plays him as an

480

eager young goat, undisciplined, ignorant, and somehow likable—something decent shines through. We follow what happens to each of the three and how they affect each other, and the plot is satisfyingly worked out. But what you keep reacting to is the film's exuberant doodles—its baroque folk humor, and its visual details, like the baseball card that Annie uses as a bookmark. The writer-director Ron Shelton did something similar in his script for Roger Spottiswoode's 1986 film *The Best of Times*, and his dialogue for Spottiswoode's earlier *Under Fire* had real verve. He also worked as second-unit director on both those films, and here, directing his first feature, he's a yarn spinner drawing upon his youth as an infielder in the Baltimore Orioles farm system. He's the director as master of the revels, and he gives the scenes a syncopated yet relaxing texture. It isn't merely that this is a baseball movie without the clichés of baseball movies. (Nothing hinges on a big win or a big loss.) It's a movie that doesn't go at the same tempos as other directors' movies; it has its own nonchalant rhythms, and most of the lines sound as if the wiseacre characters had just flashed on them.

Annie is no little snookums; she's a beautiful, passionate woman with a few years' wear on her. There's no question but that in the movie's terms what she has learned has made her more desirable. And baby-faced Nuke is more than a dumb palooka; Annie is right when she says that he's just inexperienced. Learning has a value in this movie—in both sex and baseball. But learning doesn't cover all contingencies. When Annie and Crash make overtures to each other, they don't always say the right words; somebody gets contentious, tempers flare up. This is a movie in which you can't predict the outcome of a scene. Cool as Crash is, he can be a smart aleck, and he can be ornery or surly. He picks a fight with an umpire in the middle of a game and whips himself up into a goofy frenzy; he goads the guy until he gets thrown off the field. (It's Costner's best scene: he's as berserkly ironic as Jack Nicholson is at some of his peaks.) Trey Wilson (he was the father of the quints in *Raising Arizona*) is the crusty team manager, and Robert Wuhl is the squinty-eyed coach who squirts out floods of tobacco juice. William O'Leary is Jimmy, the virginal locker-room evangelist who holds chapel services each day before batting practice; Jenny Robertson is Millie, the blonde he marries on the mound. And the team is made up of a prime collection of actor-comedians, many of whom spent years in semi-pro and pro baseball; they're like crazed kids. The emblem of their game is Max Patkin, a clown in his late sixties who performs in the stadium, dancing to "Rock

481

Around the Clock," jiggling and flapping like a rooster, and mocking the players. Like all the other clowns here, he's in love with baseball and its myths.

Just about everything here is sunny; the movie warms you. Even the sepia photographs of Willie Mays and Babe Ruth and Fernando Valenzuela that you see under the titles are both rowdy and reverent, and that's the film's tone. Oh, there are small infelicities: Crash's big speech about what he believes in comes out as rehearsed, off-key posturing; and there are little foot-dragging letdowns in the timing. But the music is nifty: it ranges from "Baseball Boogie" and "I Idolize You" to Annie's choice of erotic background music—Piaf's "La Vie en Rose" and "Non, Je Ne Regrette Rien." And Sarandon's Annie is a wonder. She lopes along in her primped-up neo-fifties outfits, and she looks miffed when she has no one to sleep with. She's both a small-town cartoon of sexual magic and the real thing. Sarandon was a gawky beauty when she first appeared onscreen, in 1970, in *Joe*, and she went through years of synthetic, speeded-up line readings before her quick delivery turned into a comedy style, in pictures such as *Atlantic City, Tempest, Compromising Positions*, and *The Witches of Eastwick*. Like Lesley Ann Warren, whom she resembles, she has become a glamorous, ripening presence. When Annie talks about having prayed to "Buddha, Allah, Brahma, Vishnu, Shiva, trees, mushrooms, and Isadora Duncan" before she found her faith in baseball, her huge dark eyes suggest that she has been burning incense for thousands of years.

■

A twelve-year-old boy wishes he were big and is magically given the body of a man in his thirties. *Big*, which stars Tom Hanks, is a formula fantasy movie that has been directed very tactfully, very gently, by Penny Marshall; she sleepwalks you through from start to finish. Hanks gets by with his little-boy act; he doesn't hit any wrong notes, and he doesn't make you want to hide your face. You feel his essential boyishness all the time. Of course, you feel the kid in just about all of Hanks's roles, though generally it's a wise-guy adolescent. I prefer him that way. As a child, he's too predictably "spontaneous." Everything in the movie—it was written by Gary Ross and Anne Spielberg—has a tepid inevitability. The child finds a job with a toy company and is a whopping success, because he understands what kids want. He meets a workaholic executive (Elizabeth Perkins), and this little-boy-in-a-man's-body awakens the child in her. Softened, her neurosis dissolving, she falls in love with him—with his playful, unaggressive niceness. And she initiates him sexually on his thirteenth birthday (not knowing that it's his initiation or that he's thirteen).

Hanks has a neat, flaky moment when the high-powered cutie asks him if he likes her and he rolls his naughty eyes to heaven. He also has a fresh comic scene in a bank when he and his thirteen-year-old perfect pal (Jared Rushton), the only one who knows his secret, confer about how he wants his first paycheck cashed—what denomination bills. The skillful Rushton gives Hanks someone to bounce off in other likable moments. (Alone, Hanks is bland.) Elizabeth Perkins is a slyly sexy comedienne: she lets you read the glints in her eyes and the tiniest tightening of her mouth. (Her double takes are miniatures.) And, as the head of the toy company and a perfect boss, Robert Loggia gives Hanks solid support in a scene at F. A. O. Schwarz where they play a duet ("Heart and Soul") by dancing on a giant piano keyboard, and then get sillier and do chopsticks. But even as you smile you may be groaning inwardly, because *Big* is dedicated to awakening the child in all of us.

Of course, the Hanks character isn't ready to function as an adult; he wants to go back. The movie wants to go back, too. It's nostalgic for childhood, for suburbia, for innocent fun. And it makes people in the audience feel that they're really kids who have got lost in the dirty big world. (It isn't about kids wanting to be big; it's about grownups feeling little.) In its wholesome way, *Big* is selling the slick wonders of immaturity. It turns prepubescence into a dream state.

■

In 1938, when I was a student at Berkeley, I laughed so hard at Harry Ritz playing a hillbilly in *Kentucky Moonshine* that I fell off the theatre seat. (My date said he would take me to anything else but never to another movie. He became a judge.) I think I might have fallen off my seat again at *Big Business* when Bette Midler appeared as a hillbilly girl in a frilly short skirt and petticoats, milking a cow and yodelling, if the damn-fool moviemakers hadn't cut away in the middle of her song. Later in the movie, after Midler has come to New York City, she encounters a steel-drum band near Fifth Avenue and, ecstatic, begins to yodel again. Once more, the moviemakers cut to some stupid story point. Midler is far more free and inspired here than she was in *Outrageous Fortune* or *Ruthless People*. Every time she enters, she blows everything else away. But she has to do it in quick takes.

The movie is an elaboration of the intricate old farce about two sets of identical twins accidentally mismatched at birth; it comes to us from Plautus via *The Comedy of Errors* and from there to the thirties musical *The Boys from Syracuse* and on to the 1970 spoof of swashbucklers, *Start the Revolution Without Me*, with Gene Wilder and Donald Sutherland as mismatched pairs of peasants and aristocrats in eighteenth-century France. This time, it's Midler and Lily Tomlin as Sadie and Rose Ratliff, who live in a backwoods Southern town with one factory, which is about to be shut down by the heartless conglomerate Moramax. The Ratliffs go up north to New York City to protest to Moramax's stockholders and are mistaken for Sadie and Rose Shelton, who control the outfit. The four women and their various courtiers, flunkies, and love objects wind up spending the weekend at the Plaza Hotel. (Actually, it's a more spacious, vacuously glamorized Plaza—most of the interiors were constructed at the Disney Studios, in Burbank.)

The writers (Dori Pierson and Marc Rubel are credited) had a plan: Midler's hick Sadie Ratliff and Tomlin's rich Rose Shelton, who were raised by the wrong parents, feel out of place and fantasize about the life they feel they belong in. Hick Sadie longs to buy expensive clothes and throw money around; rich Rose, a bleeding-heart do-gooder, takes in stray animals and yearns for country living. And the costumer had a smart notion: Midler's two Sadies are drawn to the same styles in clothing, and Tomlin's two Roses are partial to pink. All sorts of good ideas float around in this movie, but the director, Jim Abrahams (he was a member of the trio that directed *Airplane!*, *Top Secret!*, *and Ruthless People*), doesn't have the knack of making the details click into place. Tomlin doesn't thrive. She keeps trying out things that don't add up to much; the effect is a bit dithering. And Abrahams shows no affection for the rural life that Rose Ratliff is trying to protect, or for Tomlin's acting style, which has its roots in that life. You're aware of an awful lot of mistaken-identity plot and aware of how imprecise most of it is. (The big stockholders' meeting is a complete muck-up.) Yet the picture moves along, spattering the air with throwaway gags, and a minute after something misfires you're laughing out loud.

Fred Ward, who plays hick Rose's down-home suitor (and comes on to rich Rose), manages to be both the essence of rube and a forthright, attractive fellow. Serenely unself-conscious, he takes over as the film's hero. And Midler breezes through, kicking one gong after another. Tomlin's two Roses have virtuous impulses, while Midler—as both Sadies—is pure appetite. Sadie Ratliff is the most recognizably human of comic creations—a supplicant abasing herself before the world's goodies. She watches *Dynasty* over and over, and dreams of being Alexis; her eyes dance when she looks in Cartier's windows. Midler, who wrote a children's book about a little girl whose first word is "More!," makes Sadie Ratliff's hankering for luxuries palpable—it's her soul's need. Midler plays this scruffy Sadie as a warmhearted chickabiddy, and she plays rich Sadie as a lusty shrew who has developed a taste for power. (Maybe it's only in a twins story that a performer gets the chance to be both sweetly money-hungry and monstrously money-hungry.)

Midler rescues scenes by using her clothes as props: when Sadie the mogul of Moramax flips up her collar, the gesture bespeaks perfect self-satisfaction. (Chaplin did this sort of thing, and he didn't do it better.) And her snooty asides are terrific: this gorgon keeps her best lines to herself. The film often looks third class, and the plot keeps conking out, but its climax—when the two sets of twins finally confront each other— is a visual brain-twister. (It's derived from *Duck Soup* and goes back to Max Linder, but it has its own kick.) And Midler is a classic figure—a grinning urchin out of *Volpone*. Her appetite is the audience's appetite. It's as if she and we were passing a flask of euphoria back and forth. More!

June 27, 1988

INDEX

André the Giant, 379
Andrews, Lynn C., 21
Angel (Danny Boy) (1982), 166
"Angel Baby," 464
Angel Heart, 286–87
Animal House, see *National Lampoon's Animal House*
Ann-Margret, 75
Anna Karenina, 429
Annie Hall, 113, 115, 235, 314
Antonioni, Michelangelo, 41, 61, 62, 176, 452; dir., *La Notte*, 41, 44, 176; *Zabriskie Point*, 452; *The Passenger*, 452
Antonutti, Omero, 124, 338
Anzell, Hy, 421
Apocalypse Now, 182–83, 252, 305, 462
Apprenticeship of Duddy Kravitz, The, 82–83
Arcand, Denys, 237–40; dir., *The Decline of the American Empire*, 237–40, 450
Arcand, Gabriel, 238
Archer, Anne, 375, 376
Ardolino, Emile, 346–49
Ariane, 33, 35
Armstrong, Bess, 201
Armstrong, Gillian, 432–35; dir., *Mrs. Soffel*, 234, 378, 432; *High Tide*, 432–35; *My Brilliant Career*, 432, 433, 434; *Starstruck*, 432
Arnold, Tichina, 250
Arquette, Rosanna, 14, 39–40, 41, 156–57, 236
"Arrayed for the Bridal," 405
Arrick, Rose, 310
Arthur, Beatrice, 59
Arthur, Jean, 378
Ashby, Hal, 155–57; dir., *Being There*, 9; *8 Million Ways to Die*, 155–57, 180, 251; *Coming Home*, 243; *Shampoo*, 451
Ashcroft, Peggy, 127
Ashman, Howard, 247
Assante, Armand, 101
Astaire, Fred, 138, 141, 312
Asther, Nils, 34
Atlantic City, 482
Attenborough, Richard, 399–401; dir., *Gandhi*, 54; *Cry Freedom*, 399–401, 476
Au Revoir les Enfants (Goodbye, Children), 435–38
Auer, Mischa, 195, 372
Austin, Karen, 57
Auteuil, Daniel, 329
Autumn Sonata, 426
Avery, Margaret, 83

Babenco, Hector, 24–29, 267, 420–21; dir., *Kiss of the Spider Woman*, 24–29, 289; *Pixote*, 25, 267; *Ironweed*, 420–21
Baby Boom, 377–78
Bach, Johann Sebastian, 115
Bach, Steven, 21–24
Back to School, 185–86
Back to the Future, 11–13, 74, 220, 300

Bacon, Francis, 208
Badalamenti, Angelo, 206
Badham, John, 349–51; dir., *American Flyers*, 72, 349; *Saturday Night Fever*, 169, 349; *Stakeout*, 349–51; *Blue Thunder*, 349; *WarGames*, 349; *Short Circuit*, 349; *The Bingo Long Traveling All-Stars and Motor Kings*, 349
Bailey, John, 362
Baker, Ian, 43, 314
Baker, Kathy, 293, 294
Baker, Ruby, 450
Baker's Wife, The, 330
Bakker, Jim, 438
Bakker, Tammy Faye, 438
Balcon, Michael, 119
Baldwin, Alec, 455
Baldwin, James, 390
Bale, Christian, 413
Ballard, Carroll, 240–43; dir., *Nutcracker, The Motion Picture*, 240–43; *The Black Stallion*, 242
Ballard, J. G., 414, 416
Ballhaus, Michael, 40, 226
Bamba, La, 341–43
"Bamba, La" (song), 342
Bancroft, Anne, 300, 411
Band, Richard, 69
Banderas, Antonio, 289, 290, 466
Bank Dick, The, 314
Bankhead, Tallulah, 244
Bannen, Ian, 278, 368–69
Baran, Jack, 358
Baranski, Christine, 173, 371
Barbarosa, 10
Barber, Frances, 388, 390
Barber, Samuel, 251
Barefoot in the Park, 173
Barfly, 383–85
Barker, Patricia, 240
Barkin, Ellen, 222, 358, 393
Barr, Jean-Marc, 369
Barty, Billy, 474
Baryshnikov, Mikhail, 64, 65–67
"Baseball Boogie," 482
Basie, Count, 115
Basinger, Kim, 97, 99, 352
Bass, Ronald, 271, 303
Bates, Kathy, 245
Battle of San Romano, 130
Baum, Thomas, 171, 172
Bay, Frances, 208
Bay of the Angels, 136
Beaird, David, 452–54
Beast with Five Fingers, The, 69
Beaton, Cecil, 467
Beatty, Ned, 359, 448, 449
Beatty, Warren, 63, 235, 310, 311, 348
Beau Geste, 361
Beauty and the Beast, 473
Beauvoir, Simone de, 86
Becker, Desiree, 339
Bedelia, Bonnie, 148, 149–50, 151
Bedroom Window, The, 265–67

Beethoven, Ludwig van, 125
Beetlejuice, 455–57
Before the Revolution, 396
Beineix, Jean-Jacques, 136, 385; dir.,
     Diva, 136; *The Moon in the Gutter*,
     136; *Betty Blue*, 385
Being There, 9
Beliard, Florence, 465
Bell, Tom, 322
Bell, Vanessa, 389
Bellamy, Ralph, 449
Bellocchio, Marco, 290
Belushi, Jim, 177, 178, 181
Benedek, Tom, 5
Benigni, Roberto, 220–21
Bennett, Alan, 295, 297, 298
Benton, Robert, 116, 190, 352–53; dir.,
     Places in the Heart, 50; *Kramer vs.
     Kramer*, 76, 116, 190; *Nadine*, 352–
     53; *The Late Show*, 352
Berenger, Tom, 253, 386, 387
Beresford, Bruce, 233–37; dir., *Tender
     Mercies*, 93; *Crimes of the Heart*,
     233–37, 378
Berger, Helmut, 27
Bergman, Ingmar, 113, 115, 137, 340, 368,
     426, 430; dir., *Fanny and Alexander*,
     113, 368; *The Serpent's Egg*, 137;
     Autumn Sonata, 426; *After the
     Rehearsal*, 430
Bergman, Ingrid, 66, 205
Bergonzi, Carlo, 424
Bergstein, Eleanor, 347, 348
Beri, Shandra, 313, 314
Berkeley, Busby, 250
Berkoff, Steven, 160
Bernhard, Sandra, 41
Bernstein, Carl, 189, 191
Berri, Claude, 329–31; dir., *Jean de
     Florette*, 329–31; *Manon of the
     Spring*, 329
Berridge, Elizabeth, 132
Berryman, Dorothée, 237
Bertolucci, Bernardo, 61, 394–99, 452;
     dir., *The Last Emperor*, 394–99, 452;
     Tragedy of a Ridiculous Man, 395;
     Before the Revolution, 396; *The Con-
     formist*, 396, 398; *1900*, 396, 398;
     Luna, 452
Best of Times, The, 110–13, 188, 300, 421,
     422, 481
Betjeman, John, 296
Betty Blue, 385
Beyond the Law, 362
Beyond the Limit, 167
Bible, The, 364
Bicycle Thief, The, 59
Biehn, Michael, 193
Big, 482–83
Big Bopper, the (J. P. Richardson), 342
Big Business, 483–85
Big Chill, The, 446
Big Clock, The, 356
Big Easy, The, 358–59
Bigagli, Claudio, 123

Bigney, Hugh, 240
Biko, Stephen, 399–401
*Bingo Long Traveling All-Stars and
     Motor Kings, The*, 349
Binoche, Juliette, 428, 431
Birdsall, Jesse, 332
Birthday Party, The, 98
"Birthmark, The," 314
Bishop, Kelly, 346
Bisset, Jacqueline, 450
Bitter Tea of General Yen, The, 34
Biziou, Peter, 478
Black Stallion, The, 242
Black Widow, 270–72, 303, 462
Blackwell, Morton, 439, 442
Blade Runner, 108, 344
Blair, Lionel, 159
Blauner, Peter, 251
Blixen, Karen (Isak Dinesen), 76–80
Blixen-Finecke, Baron Bror von, 77, 78,
     79–80
Block, Lawrence, 155
Blocker, David, 392
Blondell, Joan, 228
Blood Simple, 292
Bloody Kids (TV), 120
Bloom, Claire, 384, 388, 391
Bloom, Verna, 39
Blow Monkeys, the, 349
Blow Out, 320
Blue Thunder, 349
Blue Velvet, 202–209, 306, 307, 462
Blumenfeld, Alan, 282
Boam, Jeffrey, 336
Bobby, Anne Marie, 371
Body, The, 197
Body Double, 228
Body Heat, 272
Bogart, Humphrey, 136, 137, 365–66
Bohème, La, 424
Bois, Curt, 470
Bonet, Lisa, 287
Bonham Carter, Helena, 126
Bonheur, Le, 152
Bonnaire, Sandrine, 151, 152
Bonnard, Pierre, 331
Bono, Sonny, 443
Boorman, Charley, 18, 19
Boorman, John, 18–21, 367–70; dir., *The
     Emerald Forest*, 18–21; *Excalibur*,
     18; *Hope and Glory*, 367–70
Boothe, Powers, 18, 20
Border, The, 182
Botsford, Sara, 173
Boucher, François, 68
Boudu Saved from Drowning, 103
Bounty, The, 54, 121
Bovasso, Julie, 154, 424
Bow, Clara, 431
Bowens, Malick, 77, 80
Bowie, David, 159, 160
Boyar, Sully, 172
Boyd, Guy, 74–75
Boyd, Russell, 434
Boyle, Richard, 180, 182

490

Conde, Eduardo, 19
Conformist, The, 396, 398
Connery, Sean, 162, 319
Conservative Digest, 439
Considine, John, 137
Cooder, Ry, 142
Cook, Peter, 379
Cooke, Alistair, 190
Cooke, Sam, 50, 337
Coolidge, Martha, 132; dir., *Valley Girl,*
    132, 134
Cooper, Gary, 16, 377
Coppola, Francis, 61, 136, 219–21, 303–
    306, 471; dir., *The Cotton Club,* 65,
    220; *Rumble Fish,* 136, 220, 462;
    Apocalypse Now, 182–83, 252, 305,
    462; *Peggy Sue Got Married,* 219–21,
    305; *One from the Heart,* 220, 471;
    The Outsiders, 220, 317, 348; *Gardens
    of Stone,* 303–306; *The Rain People,*
    303; *The Godfather,* 303, 304; *The
    Godfather, Part II,* 303, 304
"Copulating Mermaid of Venice, Califor-
    nia, The," 463
Coquelin, 312
Corbin, Barry, 200
Corman, Roger, 232, 247; dir., *The Little
    Shop of Horrors* (1960), 247
Corporation for Public Broadcasting, 442
Costa-Gavras, 54; dir., *Z,* 54; *State of
    Siege,* 182; *Missing,* 182
Costner, Kevin, 14, 318, 356, 357, 480, 481
Cotten, Joseph, 263
Cotton, Oliver, 73
Cotton Club, The, 65, 220
Couples and Robbers, 452
Cousin, Cousine, 195
Cowper, Nicola, 53, 54
Cox, Alan, 100
Cox, E'lon, 145
Cox, Sura, 98
Coyote, Peter, 56, 57, 273–74
Craigie, Ingrid, 403, 405
Crampton, Barbara, 68
Craven, Matt, 282
Crawford, Joan, 27, 469
Crawford, Martha, 98
Crazy Love, see *Love Is a Dog from Hell*
Crenna, Richard, 348
Cresson, James, 245
Crimes of the Heart, 233–37, 378
Cristofer, Michael, 324
Criswell, Dr. W. A., 440–41, 442
Cronauer, Adrian, 422–23
Cronenberg, David, 209–12; dir., *The Fly*
    (1986), 209–12; *The Brood,* 210
Cronenweth, Jordan, 220, 305
Cronyn, Hume, 5, 6
Crooke, Leland, 454
Crosby, Bing, 187
Crossroads, 142–44
Cruise, Tom, 168, 223, 224, 225, 226, 265
Cruz, Celia, 232
Cry Freedom, 399–401, 476
Cryer, Jon, 133, 134

Crystal, Billy, 379
Cummings, Robert, 265
Curry, Tim, 453
Curzi, Pierre, 238
Cusack, Joan, 419
Cyn, Mme., *see* Payne, Cynthia
Cyrano de Bergerac, 312, 313
Czerniakow, Adam, 85

Dafoe, Willem, 253
Daily, Elizabeth, 58
Daley, Robert, 34
Dance, Charles, 42, 338
Dance with a Stranger, 29–31, 45, 283
D'Angelo, Beverly, 51
Dangerfield, Rodney, 185–86, 280
Daniels, Jeff, 54–55, 190, 228, 230, 277
Danner, Blythe, 258, 259
Danny Boy, see *Angel*
Danson, Ted, 150
Dante, 129, 139
Dante, Joe, 336–38; dir., *Gremlins,* 101;
    Innerspace, 336–38
Dark Eyes (Otchi Tchornyia), 372–74
Dark Habits (Entre Tinieblas), 467–68
Dark Hideout, see *Dark Habits*
Darling, 45
Daudet, Alphonse, 330
Davi, Robert, 170
Davies, Ray, 159
Davies, Rudy, 411
Davis, Geena, 209, 212, 455
Davis, Judy, 432–33, 434–35
Davis, Miles, 294
Davis, Sammi, 367, 369
Davis, Warwick, 474
Day Lewis, C., 119
Day-Lewis, Daniel, 118, 119, 121, 128,
    428, 430, 431
"Day-O," 457
Days and Nights in the Forest, 432
Days of Heaven, 98
"Dead, The" (story), 402, 404, 406
Dead, The, 402–406
Deakins, Roger, 279
de Almeida, Joaquim, 338
Dean, James, 316
DeAngelis, Gina, 277
Dearden, James, 375
Death of a Salesman, 200, 351
Death Wish, 344
de Casabianca, Camile, 256
Decline of the American Empire, The,
    237–40, 450
DeClue, Denise, 177
"Deep in the Heart of Texas," 59
Deer Hunter, The, 23, 32, 33, 35, 361
Defense of the Realm, 278–79
de Havilland, Olivia, 444
Delaney, Shelagh, 30
Delany, Cathleen, 403, 405
Delany, Dana, 445
De Laurentiis, Dino, 33
Delerue, Georges, 251
de Lint, Derek, 430

492

493

495

496